P9-DFX-086

Taming *the* Flame

Taming *the* Flame

Secrets for Hot-and-Quick Grilling and Low-and-Slow BBQ

Elizabeth Karmel

Photographs by Christopher Hirsheimer

Wiley Publishing, Inc.

For general information about our other products and services, please contact our Customer Care Department within the United States at (800) 762-2974, outside the United States at (317) 572-3993 or fax (317) 572-4002.

Wiley also publishes its books in a variety of electronic formats. Some content that appears in print may not be available in electronic books. For more information about Wiley products, visit our web site at www.wiley.com.

Library of Congress Cataloging-in-Publication Data:

Karmel, Elizabeth.
   Taming the flame: secrets for hot-and-quick grilling and low-and-slow BBQ / by Elizabeth Karmel.
      p. cm.
   Includes index.
   ISBN 0-7645-6882-5 (cloth : alk. paper)
   1. Barbecue cookery. I. Title.
   TX840.B3K37 2005
   641.5'784--dc22

                              2005004687

Printed in the United States of America
10 9 8 7 6 5 4 3 2

For my grandmother, Mary Bennett Odom, who cooked
because that was what women did, and she did it exceptionally well.
She gave me the pleasure of her food and the cultural history
that went along with it, so that I could create my own way without
losing my heritage.

For my sweet nephews, August and Alexander,
who ignite the flames in my heart.

Table of Contents

Introduction

This book is my love letter to barbecue and grilling. Growing up in North Carolina, I was raised on the original barbecue—pulled pork. So I knew I had a fine appreciation for barbecue, but it would never have occurred to me that anyone, much less me, would make it in her own backyard—or balcony. You see, in North Carolina, you cook out steaks, burgers, shrimp, and fish, but you always buy barbecue from a barbecue pit, joint, or restaurant. I grew up 40 miles from the famed Lexington barbecue, and many of the originators moved to my hometown as they grew successful. So I could have barbecue any time I pleased, until I moved away from North Carolina. That is when, out of a sense of loss and desperation, I taught myself how to make North Carolina pulled pork with pretty good results. Serendipitously, around that same time, I got a job with a client who would fan these barbecue fires—literally and figuratively!

I was already intrigued by the flame, but I fell head-over-heels in love with outdoor cooking when the makers of Weber grills became my client. It's hard to believe today, but in 1992, when I started to promote Weber grills, there were very few barbecue and grilling books to use as references. I set about teaching myself how to grill and barbecue anything I could. Everything I grilled tasted great! Buoyed by my success, I tried more, and with every new item that I grilled, I became more and more attached to my outdoor grill, using my oven only to bake and my stove only to boil water.

Along the way, I also started hanging out on the barbecue circuit as a sponsor representative and evolved into a judge and, finally, into a member of two competition teams. (I am currently a member of the Memphis in May team, *Swine and Dine*, and you can get a taste of pork heaven by making their super-secret Cooks' Ribs on pages 252–253.) One thing that I noticed was that more times than not, I was the only "girl at the grill"—not necessarily a bad thing; I got a lot of atten-

tion, but this didn't make sense to me. We live in a country where 95 percent of the cooking is done by women. So why weren't they using the grill? When I cooked on the grill, I got way more raves for much simpler food, there were very few dishes to wash, and the food was intrinsically healthy. It was a win-win way of preparing food. I decided that I was going to lead the charge to get women to embrace the outdoor grill and to make grilling and barbecuing everyday cooking techniques.

I had to wait a few years until America traded in charcoal grills for user-friendly gas grills and realized that there was nothing to lose in the taste category. I chose gas as my preferred grill. The first time I made pulled pork on it, a houseful of male barbecue aficionados couldn't tell the difference and couldn't stop talking about how it was the best pulled pork they'd ever eaten! I figured with the proliferation of well-made gas grills, the rest of America would join me.

And America has followed gas grills all the way. Today more than 70 percent of Americans cook on gas, according to the Barbecue and Hearth Industry Association. That statistic is amazing since just a few years ago, most people were die-hard charcoal grillers. But the convenience, ease, and consistent heat that gas grills offer won everyone over. When I knew that outdoor cooking was as easy as flipping a switch for most people, I started my campaign to get women in the backyard by creating Girls at the Grill® and GirlsattheGrill.com in 2001.

Interestingly enough, more women are taking over the tongs; and, even better, grilling is America's favorite way to prepare food. That means everyone is doing it—and if the statistics are right, they are doing it together! I have a large number of male followers on my web site (they unabashedly belong to my Ladybug Club), which was my hope all along. As the sole woman out there who has devoted herself to grilling and barbecue, I felt it was my duty to bring other women into the fold, but I've always enjoyed the company of men and didn't want to exclude them from my take on outdoor cooking—even if it used to be their domain. They might even learn a thing or two from someone who approaches grilling without all that macho testosterone-charged stuff and makes great tasting grilled food and mouthwatering barbecue. And that's just what you will be able to do once you read, learn from, and cook outdoors with this book.

Most days you can find me on my loft balcony in downtown Chicago, dressed in jeans, my signature flame clogs, maybe a baseball hat (de rigueur in the barbecue circuit), and sunglasses. My balcony holds two well-used gas grills that are the equipment in my daily laboratory. When that isn't enough, I travel a few miles to my dear friend Gretchen Belmonti's suburban backyard. Gretchen is the other "girl at the grill" and she (and her husband, Jeff) have very generously let me park a mind-boggling barbecuer's dozen of grills (that's thirteen more grills for those who are counting) at their house. It is there the fabulous Primo Grill (Japanese Kamado) resides and where we made beer-can turkey for the first time.

My fifteen-year (and growing strong) love affair with outdoor cooking makes me feel like the luckiest girl in the world. It is the most generous and congenial of the cooking arts, as everyone has a favorite story to tell or a prize-winning recipe to share. This book celebrates many of my fabulous fiery experiences on the barbecue trail as well as the close friendships that are sparked by a love of live-fire cooking—grilling or barbecue.

I can't think of a better way to spend all day every day.

Fire away!

Elizabeth

P.S. Outdoor cooking is casual and fun, not stuffy or pretentious, and that is how I wrote this book, casually, with a lot of colloquialisms and humor, and also real-world tips and suggestions. Think of it as a grill friend in the backyard with you, guiding you along. If your questions aren't answered by the book, feel free to e-mail me at elizabeth@GirlsattheGrill.com and check out tamingtheflame.com.

||||| have been perfecting outdoor cooking for nearly two decades. Back at the beginning, there weren't many books for me to refer to, so I rolled up my sleeves, went outside, and figured things out by trial and error. When I wasn't in the backyard, I was hanging around the barbecue circuit, picking up tips from the salty characters who have been barbecuing since they were knee-high to a grasshopper. This was an advantage for me because, instead of learning from a book and perpetuating the misinformation that gives people so many problems, I created my own road map to get superior grilling results more quickly and efficiently.

In this section, I share my barbecue and grilling secrets to save you all that trial and error and to help demystify outdoor cooking for you. If you think grilling is difficult or have had bad experiences, just put all that behind you. Some of my techniques and ideas may seem different than what you have heard or read; but I promise you, they work. Once you have the basic techniques down, you'll have the tools to grill for any meal, any night of the week.

Most people don't realize that the essence of grilling and barbecuing is learning to control (tame) the fire, heat, and flame. The fire is the large entity of heat, the heat is how hot the fire is, and the flame is the occasional flare-up. That is why I call this book: *Taming the Flame*; by controlling the heat, you can use it to the best advantage to cook great-tasting food. Once you learn how to control the heat and which cooking method to use (Direct or Indirect Heat), you can make great food with as little as my grilling trilogy of olive oil, kosher salt, and freshly ground pepper to flavor the food. (I also offer hundreds of other recipes in this book, because all that variety makes grilling fun!)

Grilling Versus Barbecuing

There are many people in the barbecue world who feel that there is an important distinction between the terms *grilling* and *barbecuing*. *Grilling* refers to the quick cooking of foods—less than 20 minutes—over high, hot heat (in short, the Direct Method of cooking). *Barbecuing*, on the other hand, refers to the slow cooking of large and tough cuts of meat with indirect (and lower) heat (i.e., the Indirect Method). Most important, true barbecue is flavored with hardwood smoke. Technically and historically speaking, there is merit in this distinction—especially as it relates to regional variations in outdoor cooking. For example, in most of the South, the term *barbecue* does not refer to a hamburger or steak grilled in the backyard but to large cuts of meat (primarily pork) that have been slow cooked over low heat and flavored by wood smoke.

While the distinction may seem to be relatively unimportant, for some people the difference between grilling and barbecuing can become a very significant point of contention. For example, my buddies on the barbecue circuit cringe when anyone talks about their boneless, skinless barbecued chicken recipe that takes 15 minutes to make. To them, it isn't barbecue unless it takes at least 90 minutes to cook and the barbecue sauce only accents the meat and is not the reason for calling it barbecue.

In the interest of being open minded and to acknowledge that many use these terms interchangeably, I too will use them loosely—even though I am North Carolina born and bred and a card-carrying member of the authentic Barbecue (with a capital "B") Brigade. The one exception will be in the chapter on authentic barbecue, where nothing is quickly grilled. Throughout the book, I will use the more clear-cut terms "Direct Method" or "Indirect Method" to refer to the quicker and slower cooking processes.

Choosing a Grill

Gas or Charcoal?

The first decision you need to make is what kind of grill to use. The grill you buy is basically a lifestyle choice; both charcoal and gas grills produce great food. (Some of us who are grill obsessed avoid making a choice and use both!)

To help you decide which type of grill is most suited to your lifestyle, review the following characteristics of each type of grill to figure out which fits your needs. If the grill fits—cook on it!

CHARCOAL GRILLS: PROS & CONS
- Portable, easy to move
- Costs less initially but charcoal has to be purchased for each cookout
- Requires building, starting, and maintaining the fire
- Requires disposing of ashes and cleaning the grill

If you like the hands-on experience of building a fire, want to take your grill with you, want to spend less money up front, and you can wait 30 minutes for the coals to be ready, charcoal is for you.

GAS GRILLS: PROS & CONS
- Not portable but wheels, if provided, allow mobility
- Costs more initially but is inexpensive to maintain
- Easy to light and to control cooking temperature (little fire maintenance needed)
- Preheats and is ready to cook in 10 to 15 minutes
- Easy to operate and clean

If you like being able to push a button and be ready to grill in minutes, then gas is for you.

Shopping for a Grill

So, you've decided to buy your first charcoal or gas grill or perhaps a new grill. You should approach this purchase as you would any other major appliance. First, determine your needs and your budget. Then do the research. If you buy a high quality grill, you won't have to replace it for a long time. When you look at grills, feel free to "kick the tires" a bit before purchasing to get a feel for the quality of the grill and to see what it would be like to use it. Before making your decision, consider the following questions and guidelines:

GAS AND CHARCOAL
- How much will you use the grill? Are you or will you be a daily griller, weekly, monthly, or a special-occasion griller? If you grill more than once a week, look for grills with heavy-duty enameled, stainless steel or cast-iron cooking grates and a larger cooking surface.
- How safe is the grill? Will it roll or topple over in a strong wind? Is the cart factory-welded? If you are looking at gas grills, is the propane tank a safe distance from the igniter and burners? Go ahead and move the grill around to determine if you are comfortable with it. If you still have safety questions, ask a salesperson at the store or the manufacturer via its customer service hotline or web site.
- Is there a lid on the grill? If you want to use the grill for indirect cooking—from beer-can chicken to baked potatoes to authentic-style barbecue—you must buy a grill with a lid.
- Does the grill come with accessories that you will use? A side burner looks great on the showroom floor, but if you don't already have a need for it, chances are you'll end up wishing you had an extra work surface instead of a side burner. Also beware of too many shelves on a gas grill surface; some shelves cannot be removed and thus all the food has to be under four inches or so thick, meaning no grilled turkey, whole chicken, squash,

GAS GRILLS ARE HOT

The popularity of grilling has surged dramatically in the last five to ten years—largely because of the rise of gas grills. Industry stats put gas grill ownership in the United States at about 70 percent. That means most of the grilled food that we are eating is cooked on gas, not the traditional charcoal. The availability of good gas grills has made backyard cooking more accessible to more people. No longer is fire building, fire tending, or getting your hands messy a necessary part of the equation. Women are joining the grilling ranks because of gas grills as well as many men who prefer this easier method of outdoor cooking.

Some people would argue that there is a difference in taste when you compare basic gas grill versus charcoal cooking. I disagree. I've conducted dozens of taste tests and no one ever guesses which one is which. Most people choose the food cooked on gas as the better tasting but assume that it was cooked on charcoal. So it's really a perception that charcoal grilling is better.

The real grill flavor comes from the fat and juices dripping from the food onto the heat source. The juices hit the heat element and instantly vaporize, creating the smoke that flavors the food. The food absorbs this smoke, giving it that distinctive "grilled" flavor.

There is one big exception in the taste debate and that is when you grill using wood chips. Wood chips—or even woody herbs like rosemary—really do add flavor; this technique is commonly referred to as smoking. See pages 13–15 for more on smoking.

remember, you should be assembling, not building. Or better yet, buy a grill from a retailer who will assemble it and deliver it to your door.

- What is the warranty? For how long is the grill covered? When does the manufacturer recommend replacing the grill? What parts are covered or not covered in that limited lifetime warranty? A well-made grill should last years, even decades, before it needs to be replaced; but you should expect that any parts that a manufacturer doesn't cover will have to be replaced.
- Is there a drip pan? Make sure that your grill has a drip pan (or ash catcher for charcoal), and that it is safely contained. The pan collects the fat and juices that drip away during the cooking process, as well as the occasional piece of food that falls through the cooking grates. Believe it or not, there are some expensive gas grills that don't have drip pans. Their suggestion is to use an empty soup can for a drip pan. Because most people forget to do this, it means that the fat drips out of the grill into a puddle on your patio.

CHARCOAL

- What are the options for a charcoal grill? There are fewer choices and a broader range of prices. Most people start out with a standard 22½-inch Weber kettle grill. Once you have mastered the kettle, and if price is no object, look into the Japanese Kamado-style grills, Weber's 36-inch Ranch Kettle, Hasty Bake, or a custom-made "rig." See Sources (pages 343–345).

GAS

- How large a gas grill do you need? For almost everyone, a standard-size grill with a main cooking area of about two feet with three burners will suffice. Many people say they don't need such a large grill, because they aren't sure how they are going to use the grill besides that day's hamburger, etc. But make sure that you don't use size as the

roasts, and other large foods. A glass window will blacken very quickly with use and may break. If the accessory looks nifty, ask yourself the simple question: Will I use it, or is it just a gimmick?

- Are there a lot of parts to assemble? Look for a grill with factory-welded parts and few bolts, screws, and sections to put together. Assembling the grill should be an easy procedure—and excuse to buy a grill that won't go the distance. The grill always looks bigger in the store before you fill it with food. You wouldn't choose a toaster oven over a standard-size oven, just because you thought an oven looked too big. Think about your grill purchase in the same way.

- How many BTUs (British thermal units) do you need? This is the way the grilling industry measures heat output for gas grills. Many retailers promote their grills based on the number of BTUs. Remember this rule of thumb: A gas grill needs 35,000 BTUs to reach a grilling temperature of 550°F. The more BTUs, the more heat. But, remember, there is almost no food that you would ever want to cook at a temperature higher than 550°F. Too many BTUs can cause damage to your burner system and reduce the life of the grill.
- Does the manufacturer's packaging indicate that the grill is designed for both direct and indirect heat? (Charcoal grills are configured for direct and indirect heat by where you position the charcoal.) Outdoor cooking is only versatile if you can set your grill up for both indirect and direct heat. And this doesn't just mean turning a burner off. You want the heat to be even and consistent (no cold spots), and that will only happen if the burner or cooking system is specifically engineered to be equally efficient with direct and indirect heat.
- How many gas burners are there? If you are going to cook foods by indirect heat (and once you get into grilling, you will definitely want to), you need to make sure that you can control the heat for multiple settings. This means you need a minimum of two burners so that heat is circulated evenly around the circumference of the cooking box. Three or more individually controlled burners are even better. If in doubt, call the manufacturer before purchasing your grill.

Picking Favorites

Many people ask me which is the best grill and why. You should buy the best grill that your budget can handle. The better the grill, the more you will use it,

and it will pay for itself. And, if price is not an issue, it doesn't mean that you should buy the most expensive grill on the market; go out and look, and make sure it will both look good and cook well—and in the style you like. For example, some of the really expensive stainless steel "super grills" have so many BTUs and cook at such a high temperature that you can't do any slow cooking on them at all. They are basically expensive steak broilers!

That said, I do have a few favorites. I've been using my Weber grill for years, and it has stood up to a lot of grilling challenges. Here are a few lesser-known grills I like. You can get more information on them in Sources (pages 343–345).

Primo Oval: This charcoal grill is patterned after the Japanese Kamado. Similar in style to the Big Green Egg, the Primo Oval is almost the same size as a gas grill and offers about 30 percent more cooking space than the traditional egg-shaped cooker. Made from a high-tech ceramic material, the Primo ceramic grill and smoker seals in the heat and keeps air out. It does not lose heat like a metal smoker or grill—even in windy winter months—and the heat can be regulated with the vents much more accurately than with metal grills. The grill is so well insulated that natural lump charcoal lasts about five times longer than in a traditional charcoal grill.

Hasty-Bake Legacy: The Legacy model is the original Hasty-Bake design and a charcoal grill that is loved by die-hard charcoal fans. It is rectangular and as large as a gas grill. I have highlighted this grill for its adjustable fire box, which is a coveted feature among charcoal cooks. The fire box is adjusted with a crank handle that raises or lowers the fire depending on the style of cooking, raised for searing (Direct Cooking), and lowered for slow-cooking (Indirect Cooking), etc.

Coleman: This well known product company makes good-looking, very sturdy, competitively priced gas grills. It is difficult to recommend a specific model, because they change the models and the features every year. I tested a grill that came with a professional deep fryer instead of a side burner. How brilliant to take the smell of deep frying outside! I loved the whole unit, but then it was discontinued. See if they have a model you like.

Dynasty: This is one of the "super grills" with super powerful BTUs and all of the bells and whistles that you would expect from the makers of Jade Ranges—

the folks that outfit the kitchens of Ruth's Chris Steak Houses. They are introducing a side burner that sears food just like a restaurant salamander (high-heat broiler) and is worth looking into, especially for people who like black and blue steaks (seared on the outside, cool—rare—on the inside).

The Broilmaster "Super P" Series: This gas grill has a brilliant stainless steel smoker shutter system. When I first tested it, I couldn't believe that no one had developed an indirect cooking system like this before. The smoker shutter looks like a window shutter and

can be pushed shut from a lever on the outside of the grill. This cuts off direct heat from the burners. There are no burners to turn off, and

you don't need to be careful about where to position the food. The bow tie–shaped burner is also bottom-ported, meaning the burners are only open to the bottom, thus reducing flare-ups.

Preparing and Maintaining the Grill

Seasoning the Grill

You've just bought a shiny new grill, and you can't wait to host a cookout. But before you grill those steaks, burgers, and vegetables, take some of that shine away by seasoning the grill. Seasoning takes the "newness" out of the grill, depositing flavor particles on the grill surfaces, which will help flavor your food, and provide a protective—think: nonstick—coating to the grill grate. Grills are like cast-iron skillets, they get better the more you use them.

When food cooks on the grill, the fats and juices are vaporized by the heating element and create the smoke that flavors the food. The smoke accumulates on the inside of the grill's cooking box. The more you use your grill, the better the food will taste, the more defined the sear marks will be, and the easier the food will come off without sticking.

After years of experimenting with seasoning methods, my favorite way to season the grill is to fill the cooking grate with raw, fatty sausages and cook them over medium-low heat until very brown. The low temperature will control the flare-ups and slowly render the fat so the maximum seasoning is deposited onto the grill. I prefer to cook them until they turn to weightless cinders, but you can of course take them off much sooner and eat them. To season by cooking sausage only until done, you will need three sausage cookouts to get the same level of seasoning. (See discussion on sausage, page 137.) You can also season your grill by cooking a large pork shoulder or other fatty piece of meat or poultry over low direct heat for a minimum of four hours.

The smoke that is created by the fats and juices vaporizing provides a nice start to seasoning your new grill.

This seasoning should be done every spring if you don't use your grill year-round.

Cleaning the Grill

You don't need to scrub your grill like you would a roasting pan. The more you use your grill, the better the food will taste; all those cookouts season the grill. If you wash it off every time, you'll lose the seasoning. Once a year, clean the inside with warm soapy water. Never use harsh cleaners or anything abrasive. Make sure you rinse the grill well and let it preheat with all burners on high for 30 minutes to burn off any residue.

NOTE: Although the grates are dishwasher safe, I never put them in a dishwasher, because you'll take all the "good stuff" off.

CLEANING THE GRATES

Clean cooking grates are essential to great grilled food and will help prevent flare-ups and food from sticking. Always brush hot cooking grates, after preheating and after cooking. It is very simple but, like flossing your teeth, requires the discipline to do it regularly and thoroughly. You will need a special grill brush for this job. I recommend a long-handled brass-bristle brush. Do not buy a brush with stainless steel or plastic bristles. The steel is too hard and can damage porcelain-enamel finishes on the cooking grates. Plastic isn't stiff enough and even heat-resistant plastic will melt over time at high temperatures. The brushes will need to be replaced one or two times a year, depending on how much you use your grill. The heating process loosens the baked-on food and sterilizes the cooking box at

the same time. Be sure to brush hard, bearing down in the same direction as the grates.

TIP: If you find yourself without a grill brush, don't blow off the cleaning step. In a pinch, crumple a sheet of heavy-duty aluminum foil until it is the size of a navel orange and pick it up between

PEELING PAINT IN THE BBQ?

The number one concern that people have after using their grill for a year or two is that they think that black paint is peeling from the inside of the lid. With most grills—at least all that I know of—this is not the case. What is happening is that all that great seasoning that you've been giving the grill has resulted in a buildup of blackened residue. Eventually that residue will dry out and peel off. A little elbow grease, warm soapy water (for that once-a-year cleaning), and a nylon scrubber will get rid of the remaining black chips. Follow the basic cleaning instructions at left and you should rarely have too much buildup.

locking chef tongs. The tongs will act as the handle. Holding onto the ball of foil, brush away!

TIP: Some people recommend oiling the grates before grilling. I am not one of those folks. My mantra is "oil the food, not the grates." I am emphatic about oiling the food, not the cooking grates. And here's why: If you oil the hot cooking grates (remember, you always preheat the grill) the oil will instantly start to "cook," smoke, and most likely flare-up. By the time most people put the food on the grill, the oil on the grates has completely "cooked" and become tacky, making the food stick even more. Think about the sticky bottom of skillets that haven't been cleaned properly— that is the build-up of cooked-on grease, the same as on a grill.

RAPID-FIRE GRILL-CARE CHECKLIST

Follow these tips and grill cleaning will never be a big job:

- ✓ Preheat every time you use the grill.
- ✓ After removing the food from the cooking grate, allow food to burn off the grate for 10 minutes.
- ✓ After each use, use a brass-bristle grill brush or crumpled aluminum foil to loosen and clean residue off the cooking grate.
- ✓ Remove accumulated ashes from charcoal grills frequently.

- ✓ Replace exterior drip pan once a month or as needed, and clean the area under the cooking grates at least twice a year to remove any ashes or food that has fallen through the grates. Failure to do this can result in a grill fire.
- ✓ Clean once a year with warm soapy water and a sponge but no harsh abrasives.

Choosing the Grilling Method: Direct, Indirect, or Combo

To prepare the fire on the grill, you need to know which cooking method you will use. Here are the basics of the three types of grill-cooking:

Direct Grilling means that the food is set directly over the heat source.

Indirect Grilling means that the heat is on either side of the food, and the burners are turned off under the food or the charcoal briquettes are banked on either side.

Remember this general rule of thumb:

- If the food takes less than 20 minutes to cook, use the Direct Method.
- If the food takes more than 20 minutes to cook, use the Indirect Method.

Combo Grilling means that you sear the food over Direct Heat (perhaps to sear a roast) before moving it to Indirect Heat to finish the cooking process.

Once you've mastered cooking by Direct and Indirect Heat, you are ready for the Combo Method—searing the food over direct heat then finishing (cooking) over indirect heat. This technique works well for everything from chops and steaks to whole tenderloins and even slices of hard squash and potatoes. It is a time-honored and well-respected method and as well the outdoor grill version of the way most restaurant chefs cook almost everything—searing on the stove and finishing the dish in the oven. For details of cooking food by these methods, see Cooking on the Grill, pages 10–16.

Lighting the Fire

First, you must learn how to "build" the fire. When you learn the proper technique, it will be as natural as turning on your stove—and with a gas grill, it really is that simple! It will take a few minutes to learn how to turn a gas grill on, control the temperature, and set it up for the two main cooking methods, direct and indirect. With a charcoal grill, it will take about 30 minutes to master these same principles—exactly the amount of time it takes to get the briquettes in perfect gray-ash grilling condition. Once you learn how, you'll never struggle with lighting a fire again.

CHARCOAL GRILLS

Starting a charcoal grill concerns and confuses many people. Here is a step-by-step guide to the charcoal process:

1. Remove the lid and open all air vents.
2. Place a charcoal grate, mound about 50 briquettes into a pyramid-shaped pile and light. Or pile the charcoal into a high-capacity chimney starter (preferred method). Place either non-toxic fire starters or crumpled newspaper under chimney starter and light with a long kitchen match or a long butane lighter.
3. Briquettes are ready to cook over when they are covered with a white-gray ash (usually 20 to 30 minutes). Arrange them according to the cooking method (Direct or Indirect) you are going to use.
4. For smoke flavor, consider adding hardwood chips or chunks (soaked in water for at least 30 minutes

and drained) or mois-
tened fresh herbs such as
rosemary, thyme, or lavender. Place the wet wood
or herbs directly on the
white-gray briquettes just
before you begin cooking.

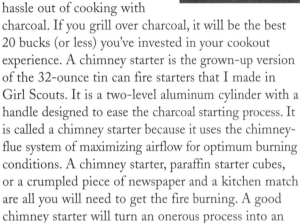

Chimney Starters

Chimney starters take the
hassle out of cooking with
charcoal. If you grill over charcoal, it will be the best
20 bucks (or less) you've invested in your cookout
experience. A chimney starter is the grown-up version
of the 32-ounce tin can fire starters that I made in
Girl Scouts. It is a two-level aluminum cylinder with a
handle designed to ease the charcoal starting process. It
is called a chimney starter because it uses the chimney-
flue system of maximizing airflow for optimum burning
conditions. A chimney starter, paraffin starter cubes,
or a crumpled piece of newspaper and a kitchen match
are all you will need to get the fire burning. A good
chimney starter will turn an onerous process into an
easy one. Look for a chimney starter with:

- A heat-resistant handle
- High capacity—can hold enough charcoal for one
  cookout, about 50 briquettes
- Heavy-duty metal construction

My favorite chimney starter is made by Weber-Stephen
Products Co. It holds twice as much charcoal as most
other models and has a second handle to help you
steady the weight of the unit as you pour the red-hot
briquettes from the chimney starter into the grill.

Chimney Starter Steps

1. Pour 50 to 60 briquettes into the top of a high-
   capacity chimney starter.
2. Place a ball of crumpled newspaper or a fire starter
   in the center of the charcoal grate or in a disposable aluminum drip pan set on top of concrete.
3. Light the newspaper or fire starter.
4. Set the chimney on top of the flame.

LIGHTER FLUID: FOUL FUEL

*Before you light the fire, there are a few things that
you need to know about fueling your charcoal fire. I
do not recommend using lighter fluid or lighter fluid–
impregnated briquettes. They can give your food that
distinctive "lighter fluid" taste, especially if you don't
wait until all the briquettes are covered with a white-
gray ash. I can't think of a worse fate for a piece of
chicken or that really expensive beef tenderloin that
you sunk a Benjamin into. And yet, because many
people have grown up using lighter fluid, they associate
the lighter fluid taste with grilled food.*

*You may need to retrain your palate, as did my child-
hood friend Michael Krusch. Many years ago, I helped
Michael buy a new grill. At the time, he lived on the
thirtieth floor of a high-rise in the middle of Chicago's
Gold Coast. After the grill was delivered and seasoned,
we went to the grocery store to buy chicken pieces and
all kinds of vegetables to grill. Michael was thoroughly
enjoying his grill lesson and, proud as a peacock,
couldn't wait to eat the food he made, golden-brown
crispy chicken, tender, caramelized veggies—all prepared using the Grilling Trilogy (olive oil, kosher salt,
and pepper, see pages 19–20)—until he took his first
bite. He was crestfallen. His grilled food didn't have
that lighter fluid taste, and that is what he had grown
up thinking grilled food should taste like. But his
palate quickly adjusted, and if you have had a similar
experience to his, your palate can adjust too.*

5. Let the starter sit for 25 to 30 minutes, or until
   briquettes are covered with a white-gray ash.

Preparing a Charcoal Grill for Direct Cooking

When you prepare the grill, light 50 to 60 charcoal briquettes in either a chimney starter or in a pyramid-shaped mound on the bottom grate, known as the charcoal grate. Once the briquettes are covered with a white-gray ash, spread them in a single layer over the charcoal grate. Double-check that the air vents are open on both the top and bottom of the grill, and put the lid on for five minutes to preheat the grill and sterilize the cooking grates (the contained high heat sterilizes the grill). Cook the food following your recipe instructions.

I almost always cook with the lid closed over the grill. Uncovered grilling takes longer and often requires more fuel than covered grilling.

Preparing a Charcoal Grill for Indirect Cooking

When you prepare the grill, light 50 to 60 charcoal briquettes in either a chimney starter or in a pyramid-shaped mound on the bottom grate, known as the charcoal grate. Once the briquettes are covered in a white-gray ash, you are ready to prepare the grill for the Indirect Method. Pour or rake half of the briquettes to each side of the charcoal grate on the lower section of the grill, clearing a space in the center. Place a disposable aluminum drip pan in between the two piles of gray-ashed briquettes. The drip pan will catch fats and juices as the food cooks. Add soaked wood chips if desired and replace the cooking grate. Put the lid on the grill and preheat for five minutes. Place the food in the center of the cooking grate over the drip pan and proceed with your recipe. Always cook with the lid on the grill.

The secret to Indirect Cooking with charcoal is to add briquettes to the fire as needed to maintain the cooking temperature (add about 10 briquettes per side every hour or so—or when the temperature inside the grill gets below 300°F). Charcoal briquettes can be added to the fire by dropping additional unlit briquettes through the opening by the handles on each side of the cooking grate. However, I find that it is more efficient to light briquettes in a chimney starter set in a heavy-duty disposable aluminum pan 20 minutes

before you need to add them. This way, the new briquettes are already at their prime temperature and covered with a white-gray ash when you add them. Add the hot briquettes to the charcoal grate by carefully pouring them out of the chimney or by using a pair of tongs to add them one by one.

GAS GRILLS

Although gas grills are less intimidating than charcoal grills, starting the fire concerns and confuses many people. Here is a step-by-step guide to the process:

1. Open the lid. Check that all burner control knobs are turned off and that your liquid propane (LP) tank is not empty.
2. Turn the LP gas tank on.
3. Light the grill according to the manufacturer's directions, using either the igniter or a match, if necessary. Generally, when lighting a gas grill, only one burner should be turned on for ignition. Then simply push the ignition switch one or two times and the burner will light. Turn the remaining burners on high, and they will ignite.
4. Close the lid and preheat with all the burners on high until the thermometer reaches the maximum heat—more than 500°F. This will take 10 to 15 minutes. Before cooking, adjust the burner controls and lower the heat as your recipe directs.
5. For smoke flavor, place water-soaked wood chips in the smoker box if your grill has one or place soaked chips in a small disposable foil pan in the upper left hand corner of the grill directly on the heat source (heat tents, flavorizer bars, ceramic briquettes, or lava rock). This must be done during the preheating stage when all the burners are turned to high. (See discussion on smoking, pages 13–15.)

Preparing a Gas Grill for Direct Cooking

Once the grill is preheated, reduce the heat by turning all the burners to medium—this should result in a temperature between 425°F and 500°F. Place the food directly on clean cooking grates and grill as your recipe instructs—it's that easy.

GRILL THERMOMETERS

Almost all grills, gas and charcoal, come with a built-in thermometer that reads the internal temperature of the grill. These thermometers are helpful but not always completely accurate. They tend to gauge the temperature that surrounds the probe. If your gas grill has a thermometer inset on the side of the grill, directly over a burner, the registered temperature might be slightly off. The best position for the thermometer is in the middle of the grill. If your grill doesn't have a thermometer, purchase an oven thermometer at a housewares store (OXO makes a very good one) and place it in the center of your grill. You will have to lift the lid to check the temperature, so close it quickly afterward to avoid losing heat.

Preparing a Gas Grill for Indirect Cooking

Setting a gas grill for Indirect Cooking is just as simple as turning it on. Once the grill has been preheated with all burners on high, simply turn off the burner that is directly underneath the food and reduce the heat of the other burners to medium or medium-low. If your grill has two burners, chances are that the burners are on the perimeter of the grill and the center of the cooking grate is already set up for indirect cooking. A three- or four-burner grill is the easiest to set—turn the middle burner or burners off and reduce the heat on the outside burners. Because there are many different models of gas grills, it is always best to refer to the manufacturer's instructions. Most new gas grills are designed to be used for both Direct and Indirect Cooking. If you are in the market for a new grill, make sure it can be set for Indirect Cooking.

Cooking on the Grill

Direct Grilling 101

Direct Grilling is cooking food directly over the heat, either grayashed charcoal briquettes or gas burners.

For a charcoal grill that means that you will have a single layer of white-gray briquettes on the charcoal grate.

For a gas grill that means that all burners should be turned on to medium or medium-high, depending on your grill. Most food only needs to be turned once, halfway through the cooking time.

Always use longer heat-resistant mitts and long-handled, locking chef tongs to move the food. The chef tongs, instead of traditional grilling tongs, allow you the best dexterity; and both tongs and mitt will prevent burning.

Once you place the food on the grill, cover the grill with the lid. This helps to keep in heat, which speeds cooking time and cuts down on flare-ups. It also keeps the heat consistent and shields the food from dust, wind, and rain.

DIRECT GRILLING GUIDELINES,
BY FOOD CATEGORY
Beef, Lamb, and Other Red Meat

Steaks, chops, and burgers are most frequently cooked by the Direct Method. However, you should not try to cook very thick steaks using the Direct Method—the outsides of the steak will be burned long before the centers are done.

Because of the danger of food-borne illness from ground meat, the United States Department of Agriculture (USDA) now recommends that all burgers be cooked completely through—i.e., until they are well done and no longer pink. While you are obviously free to follow this recommendation as you see fit, I recommend following USDA recommendations, or grinding your own meat at home using a KitchenAid meat grinder attachment for your standing mixer, or having a reliable butcher grind meat for you.

Pork and Veal

As with beef and lamb, the Direct Method can be used to cook thinner pork and veal chops and small cuts such as pork tenderloins. Veal can be safely cooked rare, but most people prefer it cooked to medium.

The pork chop of today is not your mother's pork chop. Hog farmers are bringing a much leaner, and cleaner, animal to market. The National Pork Producers

Grilling is much more of an art than a science, and with that you must remember that there are no absolutes. The variables of food, ambient temperature, wind, fuel, grill temperature, etc., change from cookout to cookout. That is what makes it so much fun and what I love most about it. Since every time is a little different, every cookout is an adventure and never gets boring or routine. I like to say that being a good outdoor cook is 80 percent the will to grill and 20 percent skill. Every recipe, instruction, and tip in this book is a guideline to help you have a successful experience. But you will also need to become intimately acquainted with your grill and learn its nuances so you can orchestrate great meals together. I know that sounds a little silly, but it is true. Ask any great griller or barbecuer what divides the proverbial men from the boys in outdoor cooking and they will all agree it's "feeling the love!" that makes the difference between acceptable and mind-blowingly great food.

The best thing about outdoor cooking is that it is almost impossible to ruin the food, and, with time, everyone can master this sport. Unlike baking, grilling is very forgiving. The only thing that will ruin your food is burning it—undercooked food can always go back on the grill for a few minutes. And slow-cooked foods, aka barbecue, are almost impossible to overcook. So if you have patience and time, you are already on your way to being an expert outdoor cook.

All of the recipes in this book call for a specific grilling method and the general temperature of the heat. To give you an idea of what temperature I have in mind when I call for high, medium, and low, I've put together the fol-

lowing chart for Indirect Grilling. Direct Grilling temperatures will be slightly higher since all of the burners are turned on. (Note: These are my definitions as there are no industry standards that I know of.)

The temperature correlations between low, medium, and high are based on preheating your gas grill for 10 minutes with all burners turned to high. These temperatures are the same for charcoal briquettes that have burned down and are covered with a white-gray ash (after 25 to 30 minutes).

High	425°F–500°F
Medium-High	375°F–425°F
Medium	325°F–375°F
Medium-Low	300°F–325°F
Low	275°F–300°F

Council recommends cooking pork to medium (160°F). A combination of both Direct and Indirect Grilling is the best way to cook thicker chops, and this is the way that I usually cook smaller pieces of meat.

Poultry

You must cook chicken and turkey all the way through. This is especially true as salmonella becomes more pervasive in the poultry industry. Almost all poultry can be successfully cooked using the Indirect Method. The only cuts of poultry that are easier to cook using the Direct Method are boneless skinless chicken breast halves, small pounded chicken or turkey breasts, chicken tenderloins (i.e., paillards), satays, and small chicken or turkey on kabobs. Duck breasts can

also be cooked using the Direct Method and do not need to be cooked until well done, according to the Duckling Council. However, I prefer my duck cooked to a high temperature because I find it more flavorful and tender.

Fish and Shellfish

Seafood tends to be more delicate than meat or poultry and should be treated carefully. That said, "steaks" of the sea such as firm pieces of tuna, shark, or swordfish, as well as shellfish such as shrimp, oysters, clams, and mussels, are best cooked on medium-high Direct Heat. Delicate fish fillets, while small, are usually best cooked using indirect heat, as they can burn easily and are difficult to turn. The best tip for cooking fish is to lightly coat the exterior with olive oil and turn only once halfway through the cooking time. Fish steaks should not break apart unless they are turned too soon. Mollusks in the shell should be cooked until they open and do not need to be turned at all.

Vegetables and Fruit

Americans are crazy about grilled vegetables. Potatoes and corn are still popular but so are fennel, asparagus, even Brussel sprouts! Before grilling, vegetables should be lightly coated with olive oil to help prevent sticking and to prevent sliced vegetables from drying out. Vegetables such as asparagus, bell peppers, sliced squash, zucchini, sliced sweet potatoes, eggplant, green onions, onion slices, and large mushrooms such as portobello are best grilled using the Direct Method. Sliced fruit should be cooked on a very clean cooking grate over medium-low Direct Heat.

Indirect Grilling 101, aka Barbecuing, Grill-Roasting, and Grill-Baking

The Indirect Method is typically used for large cuts of meat or large whole vegetables that require more than 20 minutes to cook through. When cooking with the Indirect Method—especially when preparing traditional American barbecue—think low and slow: low heat, slow cooking. The heat should be significantly lower than it is when using the Direct Method—somewhere between 325°F and 375°F—or even lower in some cases. This low heat will enable the food to cook gently and develop flavor from the fat that renders out while it cooks. The natural fat bastes the meat, resulting in tender meat and a deeply caramelized crust. When cooking large cuts of meat, fish, or poultry by the Indirect Method, you don't need to turn the food at all.

Indirect Heat is the method used for barbecuing; cooking ribs, brisket, pork shoulder, or any other large piece of meat slowly over a low heat using wood to flavor the food. Grill-roasting is cooking food like chicken, prime rib, or a large whole fish over a higher indirect heat without any wood smoke. Grill-baking refers to baking cornbread or other items like the

SEARING

Searing food seals in juices and gives food those beautiful, telltale grilling marks. The best way to sear is to place oiled, salted food directly on preheated cooking grates for two minutes on each side. Closing the lid during this process will keep the grates hot and allow for a better sear on the other side of the food. Searing quickly brings out the deep caramelization that makes grilled food taste so much better.

The Role of Caramelization in Grilling: Have you ever noticed that a grilled meal gets twice the raves of a nongrilled meal? I watched this happen over and over again and decided I would investigate why. The reason is that grilled food becomes caramelized. That means that the cooking process concentrates the natural sugars (all food contains some natural sugar) and the high heat browns, or caramelizes, those sugars.

Take this simple asparagus test at your next cookout: Boil or steam asparagus in salted water until bright green and set aside. Next, grill asparagus by brushing it lightly with olive oil and seasoning it with kosher salt. Grill the spears for about 10 minutes, turning until brown on all sides.

When the asparagus are done, take the taste test. Close your eyes and eat a spear of steamed asparagus, sip water, and then eat a grilled piece of asparagus. 99.9 percent of the time—it's no contest—the grilled entry wins the taste test. The reason: The grilled asparagus is caramelized, sweet, toasty, and intensely flavorful.

Tri-Berry Crisp with Pecan Topping (page 332) over Indirect Heat without wood smoke. These three types of outdoor cooking are essentially the same technique. The only difference is the type of food you are cooking, the use of wood, and the temperature.

Barbecuing: My barbecuing temperature is generally between 300°F and 325°F, notably higher than that of many of my barbecue buddies. Most of the circuit guys cook at temperatures as low as 210°F. I prefer not to use a temperature that low with the average backyard grill. These guys have completely different equipment than the rest of us backyard barbecuers. See the Low-and-Slow Barbecue chapter (pages 241–258). I've found that a higher temperature results in better barbecue, because you are assured that all of the fat renders out; the meat becomes meltingly tender; and it doesn't take as long to achieve comparable results. And, for me, it's all about the taste; the process is only what takes me there.

Grill-Roast: Grill-roasting temperatures can be as low as 350°F and as high as 400°F. Beer-can chicken is perfect grill-roasted at 350°F, whereas a whole prime rib needs the higher temperature of 400°F.

Grill-Bake: The grill-baking temperature is generally 350°F, but for foods like cornbread, it is as high as 400°F.

Always use long, heat-resistant mitts and long-handled, locking chef tongs to move the food. The chef tongs, instead of traditional "grilling" tongs, allow you the most dexterity, and both tongs and mitt will prevent burning.

Once you place the food on the grill, cover the grill with the lid. This helps to keep heat in, which speeds cooking time and cuts down on flare-ups. It also keeps the heat consistent and shields the food from dust, wind, and rain.

INDIRECT GRILLING GUIDELINES BY FOOD CATEGORY
Beef, Lamb, and other Red Meat
Prime rib, whole bone-in leg of lamb, beef brisket, and other large cuts are perfect for the Indirect Method. Bear in mind that, unless you first sear the exterior of the meat, the food will not have a dark sear, or grill marks, when finished. When cooking beef brisket or other tough cuts of meat, plan on three to seven hours (depending on the size of the meat) of slow cooking to break down the fibers and produce a tender dish.

Pork and Veal
Because of the low fat content in pork and veal—pork is now as lean as chicken—the Indirect Method is in most cases the best way to grill because it cooks the food more slowly and will never scorch it like direct heat. In the case of most chops, I call for the Combo Method (combination of Direct and Indirect, see page 7), which will reduce the amount of time the food spends over a direct flame. In addition to large roasts, ribs (like all barbecue) should only be cooked using the Indirect Method—again, allowing at least 90 minutes to break down the fibers and make the ribs tender.

Poultry
This is a big problem area for backyard cooks. Here is a big insider's tip: Chicken pieces, whole poultry (chicken, turkey, and duck), half chickens, or turkey breasts should always be cooked indirectly—unless they are boneless and skinless. Bone-in chicken pieces look like they would take less than 20 minutes to cook, so most people grill chicken directly and end up with a burned or raw mess (see Poultry, pages 31–35). The secret is that bone-in chicken pieces take between 40 and 60 minutes to cook, depending on size, and whole birds take about 1½ hours. As with all poultry preparations, it is essential that indirectly cooked poultry reaches an internal temperature of at least 180°F in the thigh and 170°F in the breast.

Seafood
The Indirect Method is the right choice for most whole fish, large fish fillets, and large shellfish, such as lobsters and crabs.

Vegetables and Fruit
Firm whole vegetables like potatoes, carrots, large squash, heads of garlic, artichokes, corn in the husk, and other root vegetables are best cooked by the Indirect Method, as are whole fruits like apples and pears and vegetable side dishes such as gratins, casseroles (like baked beans), and other long-cooking foods.

Smoking: Using Wood Chips to Flavor the Food
I love the taste of smoke-kissed barbecued meat and fish—even vegetables. But it is a personal preference and not to everyone's liking. If you are someone who

prefers smoked turkey to roasted and craves the flavor of applewood-smoked bacon or hickory-scented pulled pork, this section is for you.

SMOKING WITH CHARCOAL GRILLS

Using wood chips on a charcoal grill is much simpler than a gas grill. There is no special equipment necessary; all you do is soak the chips and put a handful directly on top of the white-gray ashed briquettes. The charcoal grill will be set up for indirect cooking with two equal piles of ashed briquettes on each side, separated by a drip pan. If you want just a hint of smoke, only use one handful of chips. If you want a more pronounced smoke flavor, add a handful or two more, but be careful. Too much smoke will turn the meat acrid, and your food will taste more like ashes than smoke.

NOTE: There is a barbecue contingent that believes that smoke dehydrates the cooking chamber and steals moisture from the meat. To prevent any loss of moisture, I usually add some liquid in a drip pan to both charcoal and gas grills. After all, it can't hurt, and we all know that steam does tenderize and cook food.

SMOKING WITH GAS GRILLS

Using wood chips in a gas grill is very easy but takes a little planning. If your grill has a smoker attachment,

follow the manufacturer's instructions and fill it with wood chips that have been soaked in water or other nonflammable liquid for 30 minutes. If you don't have a smoker box, follow these simple instructions: Fill a small disposable aluminum pan with soaked wood chips, remove the cooking grate, and place the pan in the upper left corner of the grill, or at the spot where all the burners come together. The pan of wood chips will be resting directly on the ceramic briquettes, flavor bars, or lava rocks (built into the grill over the burners).

Preheat the grill with all the burners on high until smoke begins to appear around the edges of the grill.

At this time, set the grill for Indirect Cooking (turn the burners that will be directly under the food off) and turn the other burners down to medium-low heat. Immediately place the food in the center of the cooking grate, and close the lid of the grill to retain the heat and the smoke. You won't need to add more chips, as one panful is enough to impart a nice smoky flavor to the food.

NOTE: With gas grills, it is essential that you add the soaked wood chips in a gas grill during the preheat stage. Once you set the burners for indirect heat, there won't be enough heat to smolder the chips. Also, if you don't soak the chips, they will ignite and burn, not smoke.

CHIPS OR CHUNKS

Wood is sold in either chips or chunks, and I have used both with success. However, I've found that chips are usually more effective when smoking in a gas grill, and they need less time to soak so they won't burn. They also take less time to smolder and start smoking. If using chunks, remember to use just a few—it's easy to overdo the smoke with larger pieces of wood.

BULLET SMOKER

A water smoker, or bullet smoker as they are sometimes called, is the preferred piece of cooking equipment at the American Royal Barbecue Contest in Kansas City. Many of the teams have their "bullets" lined up like soldiers to cook the quantity of ribs and chicken and brisket and mutton and vegetables they need to enter the contest and feed the crowd. The familiar bullet-shaped black cylinder is also uniquely suited to the size and shape of a turkey and makes the best smoked turkey I've ever eaten.

Smokers are available for charcoal, gas, and electric grills. They work on the principle of consistent, low, indirect heat to cook the meat. Although bullet smokers are fun to cook on, you do not have to have one to smoke or barbecue ribs. For most of us, it is a secondary piece of grilling equipment. As previously noted, any grill with a lid and the capacity to cook indirectly can be used to smoke ribs or other meats.

STOVETOP SMOKER

I mention the Cameron Stovetop Smoker throughout the book, and I recommend it to everyone who loves to smoke food. It is the simplest way I know to infuse small and delicate foods with wood smoke without using a water smoker or a big barbecue rig. I use it to smoke fish, vegetables, even salt, butter, and cheese. It is composed of four pieces and uses wood (chip) dust that looks like sawdust. The stainless steel body of the smoker looks like a lasagna or roasting pan. Inside this pan is a flat stainless liner (they call it a drip pan) that covers the wood dust. A cooking grate fits on top of the liner and a stainless top slides over the food to hold in the smoke. The smoker is placed on a burner on the stovetop or on your grill's side burner, and the heat is turned to high. The wood dust begins to smoke and the food is cooked by both heat and steam, resulting in very smoky, moist, and succulent meat, fish, vegetables, or anything else you can think of to smoke. See Sources (pages 343–345) for more information.

Dealing with Flare-Ups

The quickest way to extinguish flare-ups is to put the lid on the grill. The lid will reduce the amount of oxygen that feeds the fire—thus limiting or snuffing out the flare-ups.

Don't be tempted to use a water bottle to extinguish flare-up flames. When the water hits the hot cooking grates and the flames, it can splatter, causing burns, or crack the porcelain-enamel finish on the grill.

Is it Done Yet? Testing for Doneness

In addition to lighting the grill, telling when the food is "done," much less perfectly prepared, makes many of us otherwise confident hostesses quiver in our proverbial boots. Do not worry; arm yourself with two inexpensive tools: a timer and an instant-read thermometer.

Set the timer for the number of minutes that you think the food will need before turning, etc. Base this estimate on the recipe or your past experience. There are many kinds of timers—manual, digital, even the

TIME WHAT YOU COOK

Getting all of the food prepared and ready to serve at the same time is like being the conductor of an orchestra. You are orchestrating your meal to get it to the table in time to eat it all together. My best tip for this is to design your menu to include both recipes that can be done in advance and recipes that need last-minute attention. Read your recipe and count backward for the time needed, including extras—such as time for the meat to rest. Plot out, even on paper if necessary, what needs to go on the grill when or whether foods can be cooked at the same time. This will help make the cooking go more smoothly.

one on your stove will do. I don't have a favorite but make sure that the alarm stays on until you turn it off and check the food.

Use your instant-read thermometer to check the internal temperature to see if your timing is correct. My favorite instant-read thermometer model is made by OXO and has a large face and USDA guidelines for the most popular foods printed on both the face and the case. Until you grill a cut of meat enough times to really know by sensory cues when it is done, an instant-read thermometer is crucial equipment.

To guide you in determining when food is done, at the end of all the Grilling 101 sections in this book you'll find charts featuring USDA end temperatures, plus basic grilling and resting times. The USDA recommends that all ground meat, including hamburger, veal, pork, poultry, and lamb, be cooked until no longer pink. If you have questions, consult the USDA Meat and Poultry Hotline at 1-800-535-4555 or the USDA web site at www.usda.gov. Keep in mind that they are a safety guideline; but there are exceptions to the rules, and you will create your own based on your experience cooking with your grill and your food preferences.

Remember, grilling is much more of an art than a science, and cooking times will vary slightly based on many factors, including wind, thickness of food, starting temperature of food (refrigerator cold vs. room-temperature warm), proper preheating of the grill, cooking temperature, and your preference for doneness.

LET FOOD REST

If you already cook meat or poultry, you are familiar with the instruction to let meat "rest." Besides seasoning the food with the Grilling Trilogy (pages 19–20) and grilling it properly, letting the cooked food rest is the key to juicy, perfectly cooked meat. The resting process allows the juices to relax and redistribute themselves throughout the meat. When any protein is exposed to high heat, the juices are forced toward the outside of the food. When you remove the food from the heat, the food relaxes and the juices are distributed evenly throughout the food. I prefer to let my meat "rest" uncovered, because the covering causes the food to steam and can make the golden brown crust or skin soggy.

I also deviate somewhat from the USDA guidelines (as do many restaurant chefs) by taking meat off the grill before it reaches the USDA recommended temperature. I prefer to eat my beef and lamb rare, and I always let the meat rest the maximum amount of time. The meat continues to cook during the resting process, resulting in an increase of 5 to 10 degrees. I know this will happen, so I always take any meat that I want to eat rare off the grill 5 to 10 degrees before it reaches its end temperature for rare. A good rule of thumb is that meat will always rise 5 degrees. If you find that it is overdone after it rests, take it off 10 degrees sooner the next time, and so on.

The one caveat here is poultry. Because of the well-known dangers of eating undercooked poultry, I make sure to cook it all the way to the recommended end temperature on the grill. But you don't want to overcook it, so be sure to use an instant-read thermometer.

GRILLED-OVERS

Every time you cook out, think about what you can grill that will make your meals easier and tastier in the days to come. I call this food that is grilled, then chilled (in your refrigerator or freezer) and served at another meal "grilled-overs." It might be a roast that is served in slices the day you grill it and made into a scrumptious "grilled-over" sandwich the next day, or it may be adding a few extra peppers, heads of garlic, or other items to the grill while it is hot so you have grilled ingredients to toss into dips, pasta or salads later in the week. (Note: Fish and shellfish do not make good grilled-overs.) With a little forethought, grilled-overs can replace leftovers in your house for good. The chart below lists a few basic food safety guidelines developed by the USDA that I've adapted. Use it to time how far in advance you can make your grilled-overs.

Grilling Safety

You now have all the basic guidelines for great grilling. By following a few simple precautions, you can ensure that all of your barbecues are as fun and safe as the food is delicious.

Fire Safety Tips

- Never place the grill close to a combustible material. The outside of the grill can radiate a lot of heat, and accidental ignition could result if placed too close to wood, paper, or other flammable material.
- Do not set a chimney starter on the grass or near any combustible material (leaves, twigs, etc.). Even green grass will burn, and you'll be left with a burned-out patch of grass on your lawn.
- Make sure that your grill is of sturdy construction and doesn't wobble or lean to one side and the gas connection is secure and free of rust.
- If there is a flare-up, close the lid to reduce the oxygen reaching the fire.

Storage **Chart** *for* **Leftovers** *(Grilled-Overs)*

PREPARED FOOD ITEM	REFRIGERATED	FROZEN
Cooked meat or poultry	3 to 4 days	3 to 6 months
Potato salad, grilled vegetables	3 to 5 days	Does not freeze well
Grilled meat and vegetable salads	3 to 4 days	Does not freeze well

- When you're done grilling, place the lid on the charcoal grill and close all vents. Turn a gas grill off at the burners and the source.
- Know where your fire extinguisher is and have it handy in case of a mishap.
- In case of a fire, turn off the grill, cut gas off at the source, and close the lid until the fire is extinguished. In the case of small grease fires, suffocate flames with baking soda or kosher salt, not water.
- Do not use a spray water bottle to extinguish flare-ups. The water can turn into steam, causing burns and cracking the porcelian-enamel finish of your grill.

Grill Safety Tips

- Gas or charcoals grills should never be used indoors; they are outdoor cooking appliances.
- All manufacturers of charcoal and gas grills have specific instruction manuals and warnings for proper use. Follow the instructions and pay attention to the warnings.
- Tie up anything loose: long hair, long flowing sleeves, long necklaces, and bracelets.
- Dress for the weather. Once you've mastered outdoor cooking, you'll be using your grill come rain, sleet, snow, or shine. Make sure you dress for the elements.

- Do not lean over the grill when igniting.
- When lighting a gas grill, the lid should always be open.
- Keep children and pets a safe distance from a hot grill.
- Use high heat–resistant barbecue mitts or gloves and long-handled tools.

Food Safety Tips

Food safety concerns are just as important as fire safety. Follow these few tips to keep your meals safe.

- Wash your hands thoroughly with hot, soapy water before starting any meal preparation and after handling fresh meat, fish, and poultry.
- Do not defrost meat, fish, or poultry at room temperature or on a countertop. Defrost in the refrigerator.
- Avoid cross-contamination by using two sets of tongs and platters, one for raw food and one for cooked food.
- If a sauce will be brushed on raw meat during grilling, divide the sauce, reserving part for brushing and part for serving at the table; or bring a basting sauce to a full rolling boil before serving.
- Wash all platters and cooking utensils with hot or warm soapy water.

RAPID-FIRE CHECKLIST FOR PERFECT GRILLING

✓ Use the direct and indirect rules of thumb: Direct Method (takes less than 20 minutes to cook); Indirect Method (takes more than 20 minutes to cook).

✓ Preheat the grill or let the charcoal burn until covered with a white-gray ash.

✓ Keep the lid closed while cooking.

✓ Oil the food, not the cooking grates.

✓ Use more salt that you think you need to bring out the natural flavors of the food.

✓ Leave the food alone! Only turn once halfway through the cooking time.

✓ Use an instant-read meat thermometer to test for doneness.

✓ Let all meat rest a minimim of 5 minutes before carving.

Flavoring *the* Fire

here are several ways to ensure great flavor in your grilled foods: by using high-quality ingredients, appropriate flavorings at the right stages of the grilling process, and, if you like, adding wood to the fire for that great smoky taste.

The simplest and most satisfying flavorings are salt, pepper, olive oil.

The Grilling Trilogy

The story of the holy trilogy of grilling (or Grilling Trilogy for short) is a simple one. Years ago, I developed this technique (of using salt, pepper, and oil to flavor grilled foods) to use in my grill training for chefs and food writers. I wanted to showcase the inherent flavors of grilled food without masking them with rubs, marinades, or sauces so I focused on teaching the techniques of grilling without the flourishes of other flavors. I firmly believe that a little bit of oil is essential to great grilled food, so I added olive oil. I still wanted the food to taste good and knew that salt was essential to the taste and caramelization process, so I added salt. Finally, I added salt's companion pepper to add a subtle dimension to the food. That was the genesis of the holy trilogy of grilling.

What I discovered was that, assuming you buy the best-quality raw ingredients and use the Grilling Trilogy principles, everything that you grill will be guest-ready and delicious. In most cases—in life and cooking—less is more, and the Grilling Trilogy is the epitome of that! I promise, if you employ the Grilling Trilogy, your grilled food will make you the reigning king or queen of your grilling kingdom!

Don't worry about the oil and don't eliminate it. It is truly essential, and you don't need to use very much. Coat all the outside surfaces with a thin layer of olive oil. (I prefer olive oil, but you can use any other kind of oil except butter; don't use butter because it burns easily.) Grilling is intrinsically a low fat and healthful technique because you aren't frying or sautéing in loads of oil or butter. If you don't oil the food, it will dry out and become tasteless.

Salt is important to taste, because it draws out natural sugars and juices, promotes caramelization, and thus enhances the flavor. Salt really does make a difference. It is a natural mineral and, used in moderation, I think it is the most important seasoning. There are a few things to keep in mind when cooking with salt. Season food with salt just before it goes on the grill, otherwise it will draw the juices to the surface of the meat as it sits. You want the juices to stay inside the meat so it is tender and juicy when you serve it. And, a dry surface always results in better sear marks and a more caramelized exterior. Start with a little salt and add a little at a time; there is a fine line between just right and too much—it's easier to add than take away.

Last, but not least, pepper. Pepper is best freshly ground from a pepper mill or spice grinder every time you use it. The flavor from pepper is propelled by the oils in the peppercorns. These oils dry up very quickly, which is why preground pepper has much less taste than freshly ground pepper.

TIP: Before putting the peppercorns in your pepper mill, put them in a dry sauté pan, stir occasionally, and heat gently just until a wisp of smoke is present and you can smell the pepper—about 3 minutes. Let the pepper cool before grinding. This is how you roast a spice to bring out the maximum flavor. You can do this with all whole spices before grinding them, and they will all taste fresher and deeper in flavor.

When you've mastered pepper, move up to my new favorite spice, grains of paradise, which are a cousin to pepper. They are from West Africa and reminiscent of

I love salt and all the different kinds of salt that are available to us today. Use kosher or sea salt for the Grilling Trilogy and everyday cooking. Splurge and buy fleur de sel (flower of salt—hand—raked once a year in France) for your table. The natural minerals and the shape of the fleur de sel crystals add a mild, distinctive flavor and texture to salads, meat, and vegetable dishes. But don't stop there; try the pink salt from Hawaii, black salt from India, gray salt from Brittany, chunky Sicilian sea salt, the pale pink salt from the Himalayas, and any other salt you can find. E-mail me with your favorite salts or if you find an interesting one that I might not have tried. I'd love to hear from other salt lovers at elizabeth@GirlsattheGrill.com

Table salt (granular salt) is produced by a vacuum-pan evaporation process that produces dense, bouncy, crystals of sodium chloride that are packaged with additives to keep them from clumping.

Iodized salt is table salt to which sodium or potassium iodine has been added to reduce the incidence of goiter, which is caused by iodine deficiency. It is especially important for people who do not eat seafood. However, goiter is no longer an issue in this country.

Kosher salt is coarser than table salt and contains no additives. It is produced by one of several methods that produce larger, lighter, flakier granules. Chefs often choose to use kosher salt because it sticks to the surface of foods better than the small, bouncy granules of table or iodized salt and has a purer flavor.

Sea salt usually has large granules produced by surface evaporation. Its crystals can be a variety of different colors depending upon the additional minerals present. Sea salts, including fleur de sel, are said to have more flavor and the flavor varies from one to another. (There have been many articles recently disputing this claim; still, I believe different sea salts have different flavor nuances. Regardless, they are fun to work with and add tremendous pleasure to my and many others' food experience).

pepper, coriander, and cardamom. I am hooked! Since I can't say it better than Amanda Hesser of the *New York Times*, here is what she wrote, "I put a few [grains of paradise] between my teeth and crunched. They cracked like coriander, releasing a billowing aroma, and then a slowly intensifying heat, like pepper at the back of my mouth. The taste changes in a second. The heat lingered. But the spice flavor was pleasantly tempered, ripe with flavors reminiscent of jasmine, hazelnut, butter, and citrus, and with the kind of oiliness you get from nuts. They were entirely different from black peppercorns and in my mind, incomparably better."

Throughout the book, I call for freshly ground grains of paradise when the recipe calls for a more refined pepper seasoning, but if you don't like the spice or can't find it, you can substitute freshly ground pepper. (See Sources, pages 343–345.)

Seasoning the Food

Season to taste, adjust seasonings, salt and pepper to taste. These phrases are used over and over again on cooking shows, in magazines, and in cookbooks, and specifically in this cookbook. What do these statements really mean to the home cook?

The more you cook and grill, the better you will be at adjusting the level of salt and pepper to suit your palate. Because taste is objective, I have opted in almost every recipe to list salt, pepper, and olive oil (the Grilling Trilogy) without specific amounts. The reason is that the size of food is variable, as everyone who grocery shops knows—every chicken breast, steak, piece of fruit or vegetable, etc., is slightly different in shape and size. The most important thing to focus on is to make sure that all the surfaces of the food are lightly coated—lightly being the operative word—with olive oil and that a light (again, light is very important) sprinkle of kosher or sea salt is evenly distributed over the entire piece of food on both sides.

For seasoning novices, I recommend measuring out one-quarter teaspoon of salt, putting it in the palm of your hand and sprinkling it over the food one pinch at a time. You can always add more salt, but it is impossible to fix food that is oversalted. As you salt the food, hold your hand as high over the food as possible when you are distributing the seasoning. The salt will be more evenly distributed and you'll reduce the possibility of having it all land on one section of the food. This sprinkling technique can be applied to pepper or any dry spice rubs as well as salt.

Once you follow these basic seasoning guidelines a few times, and taste your food, you'll know whether or not you need a lighter or heavier hand with the salt and pepper, and you'll become adept at seasoning to taste.

Here are a few things to remember:

- Many ingredients are naturally salty. If a recipe, sauce, or marinade calls for capers, anchovies, mayonnaise, salty cheese, soy sauce, etc., the recipe will get its saltiness from those ingredients and will need less, or sometimes, no added salt.
- Taste at every stage of the recipe (except when raw, for poultry, meat, and fish). The only way you will learn to season properly is to taste, taste, and taste—at every step—before you can adjust the salt, pepper, and other spices. Don't take a written recipe as the final word (except for baking); use it as your guideline to make the dish, adjusting flavoring as your palate deems necessary.
- It's better to undersalt slightly and serve prepared food with fleur de sel or a nice, coarse sea salt at the table. This allows people to finish seasoning their food tailored to their individual palates.

Big, Bold Flavor Enhancers

Crowd-pleasing barbecue is truly a work of art, combining sweet, sour, spicy, and smoky flavors. You'll be learning more about slow-cooked ribs and barbecue in later chapters. Once you've mastered barbecued foods using bottled sauces, try adding flavors with rubs, marinade mops, homemade barbecue sauces, fresh herbs, salsas, and wood chips.

COOKING WITH SALT

To maximize the flavor benefits from salting, it is important to choose the right salt for the job from the many choices available. I recommend seasoning uncooked food for the grill with kosher salt because it has an irregular surface that sticks to the food better than table salt. I recommend seasoning cooked food with a sprinkle of fleur de sel or coarse sea salt to add both the final salt note and a nice crunchy texture.

Everyday: Morton kosher salt. The grains are flakier and harder and aren't absorbed as readily as Diamond Crystal kosher salt, and, therefore, you are less likely to oversalt. If you already use Diamond Crystal, continue to do so for everyday cooking, just make sure you have a light hand. Diamond gives the appearance of being saltier than Morton kosher salt because it is denser, and you actually get more salt in a teaspoon of Diamond Crystal than you do Morton.

Light Crusting: Toss with Morton kosher salt just before grilling. Diamond Crystal melts too fast and you risk oversalted food.

Heavy Crusting: Coat with coarse sea salt such as the red label La Baleine brand or with pink Hawaiian sea salt. This salt has the texture of small pebbles and will not melt completely during the cooking process, making it ideal for adding seasoning and texture and acting sometimes as a bed on which to cook the food (for dried tomatoes, oysters, duck breast, etc.).

Baking: The fine-grain blue label La Baleine sea salt is not iodized and is fine enough to dissolve quickly and distribute through any batter evenly.

Finishing: This is my favorite stage. I use fleur de sel to finish most of my dishes because I am addicted to the crunchy texture and the subtle salty notes. This is also a great time to use the other sea salts, such as the gros (large) sel from France, Malton from Ireland, Grosso (coarse) sea salt from Sicily, gray sea salt (sel de mer) from France, and any other rough, naturally harvested sea salt from around the world.

Marinades

Most of us are familiar with marinades. They are a great way to flavor meat, and ribs are no exception. Rib marinades at their simplest have one acidic ingredient and usually a base ingredient of vegetable or olive oil. Good acidic choices include cider vinegar, lemon juice, pineapple juice, wine, beer, orange juice, and lime juice. Common flavoring elements include grated or minced fresh ginger, garlic, onion, hot sauce, ketchup, soy sauce, spices, Worcestershire sauce, and Asian chili sauce. Be careful when adding sugars in a marinade because they burn quickly and it's similar to putting barbecue sauce on at the beginning of the cooking time. By the time the meat is cooked, the outside will be burned. When marinating, I recommend a relatively short soak for most foods. Much more than an hour or two in the marinade can overtenderize and result in a mushy texture.

Brines

Brining has become very popular in recent years, especially for lean cuts of meat like pork loin, chops, and country-style ribs, as well as chicken and turkey. In the brining process, the meat absorbs a portion of the seasoned salt and sugar solution, making the meat juicier and more flavorful. A brine technically only has to be a strong salt solution, but the sugar balances the salt and promotes browning. I call for kosher salt in my brines, but you can substitute table or sea salt— just use half as much. A simple brine formula is one cup of kosher salt and one-half cup of sugar to one gallon of water. (See also Basic Brine, page 83.)

While other meats may brine for a long time, because the bone to meat ratio is so small, soak ribs for 15 to 30 minutes, no more.

Spice and Barbecue Rubs

A spice or barbecue rub is a mixture of spices that is sprinkled or lightly "rubbed"—thus the derivation of the term—onto the ribs prior to cooking. Think of a rub as a dry marinade. Rubs add flavor and can help form a crispy crust on the ribs. The best way to use a

rub is to put it on the meat about 20 minutes before you plan to cook it. This helps the spices to penetrate and season the meat.

Some people like to "rub" the ribs and other food that is going to be barbecued the night before. If you do this, make sure the rub mixture doesn't have any salt in it or it will dehydrate the ribs. "Rub" your food the right way by holding your hand at least a foot above the food and sprinkling back and forth over the food. The height and the back and forth motion help the rub to be evenly distributed. Then gently pat the rub into the food.

Never rub hard into the food, or you will damage the fibers and texture of the food and run the risk of overseasoning it.

Many varieties of premixed rubs are available commercially, but they are also easy to make at home. Common ingredients include salt (sea salt or kosher salt is best), white or brown sugar, black, red, and white peppers, paprika (sweet and smoky), granulated garlic and onion powders, dry mustard, cumin, fennel, parsley, thyme, and oregano. This list is by no means exhaustive. Let your culinary inner child go free and mix and match to your palate's delight. (See the rubs chart on page 279.)

Mops

A mop is a thin basting sauce that is "mopped" or brushed on the ribs (or other barbecue) during cooking. It can be a leftover marinade, although most barbecuers like to mix a special mop for the cooking process. Typical mops are mostly beer, water, apple cider, or some other neutral-flavored liquid. To this base, add whatever spices and seasoning you like, but be careful with the salt, as it is very easy to oversalt. To use a mop, check on the ribs periodically as they cook, about every 20 minutes. Baste the ribs with the mopping sauce and close the lid. If using wood chips, let the ribs cook unchecked for at least 30 minutes before adding the first mop.

Barbecue Sauces

For many people, barbecue sauce is the heart and soul of the barbecue flavor. The most popular types of barbecue sauces are sweet, red, tomato-based sauces, although there are some other varieties available. Vinegar sauces have made North Carolina famous, and yellow mustard-based sauces are popular in some parts of South Carolina and Georgia. There is even a mayonnaise-based sauce from Alabama. But typical sauces start with a base of either ketchup, American chili sauce, tomatoes, or tomato sauce and are heavily flavored with onions, garlic, and other aromatic vegetables like bell peppers or celery that have been cooked down and pureed into the liquid. The key ingredient is actually Worcestershire, as the tangy tamarind flavor in that sauce is what most of us associate with barbecue sauce. Other common ingredients include hot pepper sauce, cider vinegar, red wine vinegar, whiskey, honey, molasses or brown sugar, coffee, soy sauce, dried fruits, juices, herbs, and spices.

Remember, don't apply your barbecue sauce until the last 15 minutes of cooking time. This way, your food will be done inside and the sauce will coat it with a nice warm glaze. If you put the sauce on earlier, it may burn.

NOTE: Quick-cooking foods, such as boneless skinless chicken breasts, which take less than 20 minutes to cook, should be sauced during the final 5 minutes of the grilling time.

Fresh Herbs

Fresh herbs can add both subtle and intense flavors to grilled foods. Herbs can be used effectively as skewers for kabobs, such as shrimp on rosemary branches, or can be tied together and placed on the heat source similar to wood chips. Food can also be cooked on a bed of herbs that have been placed directly on the cooking grate. This technique is especially good for very delicate foods.

Salsas, Relishes, and Chutneys

To complement the flavor of simple grilled foods, fresh salsas, relishes, and chutneys to save alongside are gaining popularity. For example, a fresh fruit or vegetable salsa that combines sweet, sour, and spicy flavors that are roughly chopped and mixed together is a perfect balance to smoky grilled fish. The tangy vinegary relishes and sweeter chutneys are also complementary flavors for sharp, smoky barbecued foods.

Wood Chips and Chunks

The real secret of a traditional barbecue is in the slow, smoky cooking of the meat, and the best way to get that smokiness is to add wood chips or chunks to your fire. There is a tremendous variety of wood types available for adding smoke to your barbecue. Some of the most popular include hickory, mesquite, oak, apple, alder, and grapevines. To use, soak the chips or chunks in water for 30 minutes before you put them on the white-gray ash of briquettes or in a smoker box in your gas grill. See pages 13–15 for more on smoking.

PAIRING WOOD FOR SMOKING AND FOOD

The predominant flavor of all smoking wood chips or chunks, is smoke, but there are subtle nuances to the different wood varieties. Pairing wood flavors with food to be cooked is a little like matching food and wine, but, whatever type of wood you have will work. And like wine, it is fun to experiment with the different options, including cedar planks.

Alder: This wood has a mild taste. Ideal for use with vegetables or fish, such as salmon.

Apple: This wood has a unique slightly fruity flavor. It is my favorite wood to use to smoke a turkey. It is also great with fresh ham, pork chops, sweet sausages, Cornish hens, and salmon.

Cherry: This wood is similar to applewood, but with a slight tart aftertaste. Ideal for use with lamb, pheasant, duck, venison, and steak.

Maple: This wood has a hint of sweetness to it. Ideal for use with turkey, ham, tenderloins of beef and pork, poultry, and most root vegetables.

Hickory: This wood has a strong, bacon-like flavor. It is ideal for use with ribs, pork shoulder, Boston butt, and other traditional barbecued foods. It is also superb with fresh trout.

Oak: Some say this is a mellow version of mesquite. It is good for steaks, duck, pork, game birds and hamburgers. Post oak is the wood used for tradition Hill Country (Texas) brisket.

Mesquite: This wood has a Southwest tang, leaving a slight burning sensation and a bit of an aftertaste. It is very popular in restaurants and used with pork, spare ribs, steak, and most red meats. It is also available in mesquite hardwood charcoal, which is less intense than the wood.

Sweet Birch: This wood leaves a sweet delicate taste on the palate. Ideal for use with chicken, swordfish, tuna, salmon, lamb, pork, and all vegetables—especially onions, shallots, and garlic.

Pecan: This wood has a nutty mellow flavor. It is used with pork, chicken, duck, and most wild fowl.

Grapevines: This wood has a mellow flavor—it is typically used in regions that grow grapes for wine. Particularly good on simple dishes such as grilled beef, vegetables, fish, or poultry.

Sassafras: This wood has a spicy sweeter smoke. It is an esoteric wood, not commonly used, but gaining popularity and good with fish and poultry.

TIP: Almost any wood except pine can be used for smoking. Fruit and nut tree woods are particularly good. If I haven't mentioned the wood that you'd like to use, think about what foods the fruit tastes best with—that is generally a good sign that the smoke will pair nicely with the food.

Tools *of the* Trade

I am a tough customer, always looking for the best ingredient, cooking gadget, or appliance for a specific job or recipe, but I am also often disappointed. That is why when I find a tool or ingredient that works really well, I spread the word. This is also why I started my own line of grill tools (GrillMat and Super Silicone Angled BBQ Basting Brush) and ceramic serving pieces (Grill Friends). I design items that are both functional and fun to look at.

In the food publishing business, it is hotly debated whether or not to include brand names. After years of being politically correct and nonpartisan, I have decided if the brand affects the outcome of the recipe or the enjoyment and ease of cooking, then specifying the brand is as essential as listing the ingredient. For that reason, I am specific about the tools and ingredients that really do make a difference for me. If you have a favorite that differs from mine, by all means, keep using your favorite; but if you don't, give my recommendation a try—you may find your new favorite tool or ingredient.

I've organized this section into lists of Must Have, Need to Have, Nice to Have, and Extra Nice to Have items. Use the key at right to guide you through my lists and realize that, like everything in life, these lists are not the law, just a guideline that will help you build your outdoor cooking toolbox and pantry. Start out with just the basics that will get you out there and grilling. As you grill more often, you'll find yourself adding the nice and extra nice gadgets because it makes the process a little easier and more efficient, and the food tastier.

Key

Must Have: Everything you need to follow the 101 recipes.

Need to Have: Add a few things and your grilling experience gets easier.

Nice to Have: You are a committed griller and you "need" all the right tools.

Extra Nice to Have: You are the master of your grilling universe.

Dry Goods Pantry

Must Have
- Olive Oil
- Kosher Salt, preferably Morton
- Freshly Ground Pepper

Need to Have
- Tabasco or other hot pepper sauce
- Brown Sugar
- Honey
- Bourbon
- Ketchup
- Soy Sauce, preferably low-sodium
- Apple Cider Vinegar
- Dried Red Chile Flakes
- Real Mayonnaise, preferably Hellman's
- Strong Dijon Mustard, such as Amora or Maille
- Barbecue Sauce
- Fresh Lemons
- Beer in a can

Nice to Have

- Thai Garlic–Chili Sauce (often called *sriracha*)
- Fine-Grain Sea Salt, such as the one in the blue container from La Baleine
- Fresh Limes
- Smoked Chipotle Chile Powder
- Smoked Hot Spanish Paprika
- Smoked Sweet Spanish Paprika

- Authentic Barbecue Rub, such as WHAM from John Willingham in Memphis, TN, or Magic Dust from Mike Mills in Murphysboro, IL (Sources, pages 343–345)
- Sugar in the Raw—a larger and darker crystal than white granulated sugar; it has a more complex flavor and is good for toppings and rustic presentations
- Toasted Sesame Oil

Extra Nice to Have

- Fleur de Sel
- Pink Hawaiian Sea Salt
- Extra-Virgin Olive Oil
- White Truffle Oil
- Nut Oils

Spice Pantry

Need to Have

- White Sugar
- New Mexico Chile Powder
- Cumin Seeds
- Rosemary
- Dry Mustard
- Garlic Powder
- Cinnamon

Nice to Have

- Ancho Chile Powder
- White Peppercorns
- Cayenne Pepper
- Celery Salt
- Dehydrated Garlic
- Thyme
- Oregano
- Tarragon
- Herbes de Provence
- Sage

Extra Nice to Have

- Szechuan Peppercorns, if you can find them—importation has recently been restricted
- Grains of Paradise
- Fennel Seed
- Cardamom
- Chinese Five-Spice Powder (make your own, page 99)
- Cloves
- Mace
- Star Anise
- Dried Lavender Flowers

Grilling Toolbox

Must Have

- Silicone or Natural-Bristle Basting Brush
- Two pairs of OXO Long-Handled Locking Chef Tongs (one for raw food, one for cooked food); I prefer the 12-inch tongs

- Brass-Bristle Cleaning Brush—stainless steel bristles can damage porcelain-enamel cooking grates
- Instant-Read Thermometer

CHOOSING YOUR TONGS

After the grill, I think the right tongs are the most important piece of equipment that you need for great grilling. Traditionally, the tongs that are sold for grilling are large, awkward, and not at all precise. They might look impressive, but they give even master grillers two "left" hands. It is very difficult to turn the food on the grill with these tongs. That is why I strongly recommend investing in long-handled, locking chef tongs. They are under $10 and readily available (OXO makes a great pair in three different lengths—choose the medium or long for the grill). These tongs will make turning food on the grill a breeze instead of a chore.

TIP: Use two pairs of tongs; one to handle raw food and one to handle cooked food. This will prevent cross-contamination.

Need to Have

- Heavy-Duty Oven Mitt
- Long-Handled Spatula
- Resealable Plastic Bags for marinating or oiling food
- High-Capacity Chimney Starter—I think Weber makes the best one
- Fire Starters and long wooden kitchen matches
- Bottle Opener, preferably church-key style
- Small Aluminum Drip Pans for smoking

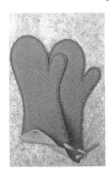 

Nice to Have

- Heat-Resistant Silicone Basting Brush—try the Precision Grill
- Tools Super Silicone Angled BBQ Basting Brush (Sources, pages 343–345)
- Rib Rack or a V-Rack Roast Holder, because it is one piece of equipment that works for two different purposes—ribs or roasts and poultry.
- Tray to carry all of your grilling supplies—I use a restaurant-style half sheet pan.

- Lodge Logic Barbecue Grill Grate—made by the manufacturers of Lodge cast-iron skillets
- Extra Tank of Propane or Extra Bag of Charcoal
- Smoker Box for gas grills
- Wood Chips, especially hickory, apple, oak, and mesquite

Extra Nice to Have

- Pizza Peel
- Vertical Turkey Roaster from www.GrillFriends.com— I call this a "turkey sitter" and use it to make beer-can turkey because the wide bottom of the ceramic cup keeps the turkey stable.
- Cameron Stovetop Smoker
- Instant Marinater from Vacu Vin or Reveo— vacuum pressure forces the flavors in marinades into the fibers of the food

- Outdoor Grill Light
- Instant-Read Thermometer with remote monitor—reads the internal temperature without lifting the lid
- Cedar Planks—buy packaged planks at gourmet stores or have your hardware store cut an untreated cedar 2 x 4 into 14-inch pieces for grilling salmon and other foods

Kitchen Equipment

Must Have

- Measuring Spoons and Cups

- Set of Graduated Mixing Bowls, preferably stainless steel
- Basic Steel-Shanked Knife Set (chef, paring, and bread knives plus a sharpening steel)
- Two Heavy-Duty Wood Cutting Boards—one for raw and one for cooked foods
- Wood Mixing Spoon
- Nonreactive Bowl
- Silicone or Rubber Spatulas (large and small)
- Absorbent Kitchen Towels

DOUBLE-SKEWER IT, AKA THE LADDER METHOD

Skewering makes cooking shrimp, vegetables, chunks of meat, and other small items very simple. It eliminates the need to place each small piece of food on the grill and turn it just minutes later. That isn't such an issue with larger pieces of food or even jumbo or large shrimp, but it is with medium-sized shrimp, cherry tomatoes, okra, etc. How many times have you threaded food down the middle, only to have it twirl around and around the skewer? My solution is to double-skewer it. I like to use inexpensive bamboo skewers that I've soaked in water for about 30 minutes. This step is necessary or your skewers

will burn. If I were getting ready to make a shrimp kabob, I would do the following: For each kabob, lay out two skewers and thread the shrimp through both ends instead of the middle. The skewers end up looking like shrimp ladders (thus my nickname for the method) and hold the shrimp so they cook evenly on both sides. Now all you have to do is place the shrimp on the cooking grate and turn once halfway through the cooking time. (Note: You can only skewer shrimp that has been peeled.)

Need to Have

- OXO Vegetable Peeler
- Two Whisks, large and small
- Box Grater
- Bamboo Skewers, 10- or 12-inch lengths
- Timer

Nice to Have

- Heat-Resistant Kitchen Scissors
  - SuperGrater—a ceramic dish with a continuous rough surface that facilitates grating garlic and ginger (Sources, pages 343–345)
  - Microplane Grater—a carpenter's rasp that is the perfect tool for grating hard cheeses and nutmeg and zesting citrus
- Restaurant-Quality Sheet Pans—these multipurpose aluminum pans look like jelly roll pans and are great for taking all your ingredients to the grill and cooking. They are used for almost everything in commercial kitchens. The half sheet pan is the size of a home oven and the quarter sheet pan is half that and great for small jobs.
- Two to four Melamine Plastic Platters—for taking food to and from the grill (one for raw food, one for cooked food)

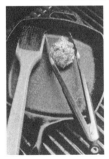

  - Small Bowls or soufflé cups for small amounts of ingredients
  - Lodge Logic Cast-Iron Skillet or Petite Braiser (All Clad) for cornbread and other casserole dishes
  - Funnel
  - Plastic Cutting Sheets (Flexible Cutting Boards)

Extra Nice to Have

  - Dutch Oven, preferably Staub or Le Creuset
  - Lodge Logic Wedgie Pan for cornbread or muffins
  - Silicone Baking Mat, preferably Silpat
  - Silicone Bakeware, preferably Lékué
  - Immersion Blenders, large and small

- Poultry Shears
- Tomato Knife
- Whetstone for knife sharpening
- Meat Carving Set

The Barbecue Bar

Not essential to a grilled meal, but it makes it much more fun!

Must Have

- Beer
- Red Wine
- White Wine
- Sparkling Water

Need to Have

- Bourbon
- Vodka
- Gin
- Rum
- Homemade Lemonade
- Iced Tea
- Soft Drinks

Nice to Have

- Rum, preferably Mount Gay, because it tastes different from all other rums
- Scotch
- Rosé Wine
- Tequila, preferably Blue Agave
- Kahlua or Bailey's
- Simple Syrup (page 316)

Extra Nice to Have

- Microbrew Beers
- Reserve Wines
- Liqueurs

Poultry

Poultry 101

Rapid-Fire Checklist

✓ Preheat grill
✓ Trim poultry of excess fat
✓ Brush poultry all over with olive oil; season with kosher salt and pepper, if desired
✓ Place poultry on cooking grate and cover grill
✓ Grill all pieces except boneless skinless breasts using Indirect Heat
✓ Wait until the final 5 to 15 minutes of grilling time to brush with any sweet barbecue sauce
✓ Test for doneness with an instant-read thermometer: It should be 180°F in the thickest part of thigh
✓ Let all poultry rest a minimum of 5 minutes before eating (whole turkeys should rest 20 minutes)

Tools of the Trade

• 12-inch locking chef tongs
• Instant-read thermometer
• Silicone or natural-bristle brush
• Heavy-duty oven mitt

Common Problems

• Using the wrong cooking method
• Burned on the outside, raw on the inside
• Dry, overcooked poultry
• Flare-ups
• Cross-contamination of cooking and serving utensils (see page 33)

Barbecued chicken is as all-American as baseball and apple pie. However, it is the food that gives backyard cooks the most trouble. It seems as if it would be easy to grill; but it often doesn't turn out the way the cook and the guests envisioned it. So what does a backyard cook need to know? First, start with the most basic seasoning: olive oil, kosher salt, and pepper (aka the Grilling Trilogy, page 19). Second, have patience.

On the Fire: Direct or Indirect Heat

A boneless skinless chicken breast takes just a few (five to seven) minutes on both sides over Direct Heat; but any piece of chicken with a bone in it (bone-in pieces) or a whole chicken will take longer. Anything that takes longer than 20 minutes to cook uses the Indirect Method. I sometimes refer to this method as grill-roasting, because you are essentially roasting a large piece of food on the grill. The Indirect Method is the most versatile, as it is how you "barbecue," "grill-roast," and "grill-bake." With Indirect Heat, the inside of the chicken will be done and still juicy at the same time as the outside turns a golden brown and the skin gets crispy. The added bonus is that you don't need to turn the chicken. Place the pieces bone-side down in the center of the cooking grate, and let the grill do the rest. This is what I call "walk-away" chicken because you put it on the grill and do other things while it cooks.

This technique is basically the same for all whole poultry; but, remember, the larger the bird, the longer it will take to cook. Fattier birds like duck and goose need to be grill-roasted in a pan on almost every grill to prevent grease flare-ups. There are a few grills with advanced drip pan systems that can handle the excess drippings. But I love catching them in a foil pan because then I can use the drippings for sautéing and other recipes. Indirect Heat also reduces the incidence of flare-ups since there is no direct flame under the chicken. The juices and fats that are naturally rendered create a little smoke to flavor the food and then run into the drip pan system of the grill.

Testing for Doneness

Bone-in chicken pieces will take between 30 minutes for legs and 60 minutes for a large leg quarter or half a chicken over indirect heat. Depending on size, boneless chicken breasts should be done in 15 minutes over Direct Heat, and a whole chicken usually takes between $1\frac{1}{4}$ and $1\frac{1}{2}$ hours to cook (Indirect Method). Because the timing depends on a set of variables including weight and size of poultry, heat of the grill, and weather (wind slows down the cooking time), I recommend using an instant-read thermometer. A thermometer will take the guesswork out of testing for doneness. Refer to the chart on page 35 for chicken or poultry end temperatures. For example, chicken is done when it registers 170°F in the breast and 180°F in the thigh. However, since the heat varies from grill to grill, start checking for doneness ten minutes before a recipe says it should be done.

Give Your Bird a Rest

Ever since my years working with the Butterball Turkey Talk Line, I have been a big believer in letting meat rest before carving or cutting into it. I watched as an army of turkeys were carved too hot, too cold, and just right in the Turkey University test kitchens. The turkeys that were carved after resting 20 minutes were just right—tender, juicy, and still warm. Here's what happens: As the bird cooks and comes to the right temperature (180°F in the thigh) all the juices are propelled toward the exterior of the bird. When the meat is taken off the fire, it "rests" as it cools,

and the meat fibers reabsorb the juices, making each piece juicy. If you don't wait, you'll have all those juices pooling around your plate or carving board, and the meat will be dry.

What Is Cross-Contamination?

You should be careful not to cross-contaminate your food no matter what you are preparing, but it is especially important with poultry because about 25 percent of both free-range and conventionally raised chickens test positive for salmonella bacteria. The good news is that cooking to the correct end temperature kills the bacteria. Cooked chicken rarely infects us with salmonella poisoning. What causes the problem is cross-contamination.

Simply put, cross-contamination means mixing raw juices with cooked food or contaminating cooked food with the juices from raw foods. For example, this can happen when you take a platter of chicken to the grill, cook the chicken, then put the cooked chicken on that same platter. Although it may seem convenient to use one dish, don't risk cross-contamination and mix the cooked with the raw. Another way that the raw juices get into other foods is when rinsing the chicken. Water and raw juices often splatter, and if you have other ingredients for the meal, such as salad fixings on the counter, you run the risk of contaminating them. For this reason, I never wash poultry, or other meats or fish, I will be grilling. The heat of the grill will cook and "clean" the food. If you are used to washing poultry, just be careful not to splash and spray the juices around your kitchen.

You can prevent cross-contamination by using two separate platters or washing your prep platter immediately with hot water and soap. I have a set of four melamine (heavy-duty plastic) platters that I use to transport food to and from the grill. They were very inexpensive (under $5 each), and are lightweight, virtually indestructible, and go right into the dishwasher after each use. If you want to be extra careful, you can wipe your counters, platters, etc., with a diluted bleach solution (one part bleach to ten parts water).

Bone-In Chicken Pieces 101

I recommend grilling chicken pieces over indirect heat so that they are cooked on the inside and golden brown on the outside at the same time. Cooking over direct heat can result in a raw interior and a burned exterior—especially if you put the barbecue sauce on too soon.

Makes 4 servings

Grilling Method: Indirect/Medium Heat

> 4 **Chicken breasts or thighs, bone-in, or other chicken pieces**
> **Olive oil**
> **Kosher salt**
> **Freshly ground pepper**

1. Build a charcoal fire or preheat a gas grill. Remove and discard any excess fat from the chicken. Pat it dry with paper towels. Brush lightly with oil. Season with salt and pepper. Place the chicken, bone-side down, in the center of the cooking grate over indirect medium heat.
2. Cover and grill until the breast meat near the bone registers 170°F and the thigh meat registers 180°F, 35 to 45 minutes, depending on size. You do not need to turn the chicken pieces. If you don't have a thermometer, cook it until the meat is no longer pink and the juices run clear. If preparing barbecued chicken, season with your favorite barbecue rub and brush the sauce on the chicken during the last 15 minutes of cooking time to prevent burning.
3. Remove and let the chicken rest for 10 minutes before serving.

Boneless Skinless Chicken Breasts 101

The size of chicken breasts varies widely. Small chicken breasts will take six to eight minutes total. The larger and thicker the breasts, the longer they will take to cook—up to 20 minutes total cooking time.

Makes 4 servings

Grilling Method: Direct/Medium Heat

> 4 **Boneless skinless chicken breast halves**
> **Olive oil**
> **Kosher salt**
> **Freshly ground pepper**

1. Build a charcoal fire or preheat a gas grill. Pat the chicken dry with paper towels. Brush with oil and season with salt and pepper. Place the chicken in the center of the cooking grate over direct medium heat. Cover and grill for about 15 minutes or until the meat is no longer pink and the juices run clear. Turn the chicken only once during cooking time.
2. If using barbecue sauce, brush on the chicken during the last 5 minutes of cooking time to prevent burning. Remove and let the chicken rest for 5 minutes before serving.

Whole Turkey on the Grill 101

Once you grill your first turkey, you'll never want to prepare it any other way. The convection action of the grill cooks the turkey faster than a conventional oven and browns the skin picture-perfect! The turkey takes on a slightly smoky grilled flavor, and it is a cinch to smoke with wood chips if you prefer a more intense turkey. The grill will give the turkey that distinctive pride-of-barbecuers' pink smoke ring next to the skin—so don't think the turkey is undercooked if you see a smoke ring, just congratulate yourself for a job expertly done! This method works well with a whole breast of turkey, too.

Makes 12 to 15 servings

Cooking Method: Indirect/Medium Heat

> 1 **whole turkey, 14 to 16 pounds, thawed**
> **Olive oil**
> **Kosher salt**
> **Freshly ground pepper**

1. Build a charcoal fire or preheat a gas grill. Remove the neck and giblets; reserve them for other uses or throw them away. Remove and discard any excess fat. If desired, rinse the bird and pat it dry with paper towels. Twist the wing tips under the back—this is called "wings akimbo."
2. Brush the turkey with oil and lightly sprinkle with salt and pepper.
3. Place the turkey breast-side up on the cooking grate on a charcoal grill or on a roasting rack in a

Approximate **POULTRY** *Cooking Times* **(°F)**

TYPE OF POULTRY	WEIGHT	GRILLING METHOD	GRILLING TIME	INTERNAL TEMP.	REST TIME
Chicken breast halves, boneless skinless	4 ounces	Direct Medium	6 to 8 minutes/side	170°	5 minutes
Chicken breast halves, bone-in	6 to 8 ounces	Indirect Medium	20 to 30 minutes	180°	5 minutes
Chicken drumsticks	4 ounces	Indirect Medium	16 to 24 minutes	180°	5 minutes
Chicken legs or thighs	4 to 8 ounces	Indirect Medium	20 to 30 minutes	180°	5 minutes
Chicken wings or drumettes	2 to 3 ounces (each)	Indirect Medium	16 to 24 minutes	180°	5 minutes
Chicken, whole fryer	3 to 4 pounds	Indirect Medium	60 to 75 minutes	180°	10 minutes
Cornish hen, whole	18 to 24 ounces	Indirect Medium	45 to 55 minutes	180°	10 minutes
Duck breast	6 ounces	Indirect Medium	20 to 40 minutes	180°	5 minutes
Duck, whole	4 to 5 pounds	Indirect Medium	1½ to 2 hours	180°	10 minutes
Hen, whole roasting	5 to 7 pounds	Indirect Medium	18 to 25 minutes/pound	170°	10 minutes
Turkey cutlets	4 to 6 ounces	Direct Medium	6 to 8 minutes/side	180°	5 minutes
Turkey drumsticks	1 to 1½ pounds	Indirect Medium	60 to 90 minutes	180°	10 minutes
Turkey roast	5 to 7 pounds	Indirect Medium	18 to 20 minutes/pound	170°	20 minutes
Turkey tenderloins	6 to 12 ounces	Indirect Medium	20 minutes	170°	5 minutes
Turkey wings	12 ounces	Indirect Medium	45 to 60 minutes	180°	5 minutes
Turkey, whole	12 pounds	Indirect Medium	2 to 2½ hours	180°	20 minutes

All internal temperatures are based on USDA recommended values, using an instant-read thermometer.
Times and temperatures in the chart are guidelines. Specific recipes may call for variations.

disposable foil roasting pan on a gas grill. The grill should be set for indirect medium heat. There's no need to baste it; the thin coating of oil will promote browning and keep the juices inside the bird.

4. Cover and cook 11 to 13 minutes per pound or until an instant-read thermometer inserted in the thickest part of the thigh (not touching the bone) registers 180°F and the juices run clear. Transfer the turkey to a platter and let it rest for 20 minutes before carving.

TIP: Charcoal grillers will have to add about 12 briquettes to each side every hour; gas grillers don't need to do any tending; but about 30 minutes before the bird is done, remove the foil roasting pan and place the bird directly on the center of the cooking grate. This allows the bottom of the bird to brown. Use the drippings in the foil pan to make gravy. Make sure to bring the drippings to a boil before mixing them in with the rest of the gravy ingredients.

Tequila Sunrise Chicken

I never soak my food in anything I would not drink. Well, there is nothing like a tequila sunrise to make you smile, giggle, or fall down laughing—and this tequila sunrise marinade makes chicken sing with flavor, which is my way of saying that this is a very happy, snappy recipe. Make an extra pitcher of sunrises for yourself—just be careful to make sure only the chicken gets sauced!

Makes 4 to 6 servings

Grilling Method: Indirect/Medium Heat
Special Equipment: Vacu Vin Instant Marinater

- 2   whole chickens, 3 to 4 pounds each
- 3   bunches green onions, trimmed
- 1½ cups fresh orange juice
- 1   cup tequila
- ½   cup grenadine
- 1   small white onion, roughly chopped
- 8   cloves garlic, roughly chopped
- 1   teaspoon kosher salt
      Freshly ground pepper
      Olive oil
      Lime wedges

1. Use a large knife or poultry shears to split each chicken down the middle into 2 halves. Pat the chickens dry with paper towels. Place the chickens and green onions in a large bowl or 2 large resealable plastic bags.
2. Whisk together the orange juice, tequila, grenadine, onion, garlic, salt, and pepper to taste in a medium bowl. Pour the marinade over the chickens and onions and turn several times to coat. Cover the container and refrigerate at least 4 hours (or, preferably, overnight), turning the chickens several times. Alternatively, use the Instant Marinater and marinate for 30 minutes.
3. Build a charcoal fire or preheat a gas grill. Remove the chickens and green onions from the marinade and discard it. Lightly brush the chickens and green onions with oil and season with salt. Place them on the cooking grate, skin-side up over indirect medium heat. Cover and grill for 30 to 45 minutes or until the chickens register 180°F in the thickest part of the thighs and the juices run clear. Remove the chickens from the grill and let them rest for 10 minutes.

4. While the chickens rest, grill the green onions over direct medium-heat for 6 to 8 minutes, turning occasionally until browned in spots and wilted.
5. Serve the chicken hot, garnished with grilled green onions and lime wedges.

TIP: You can also use a rib rack or roast holder to hold the half chickens upright during grilling.

Buffalo-Style Chicken Wings

This is the easiest chicken wing recipe you're bound to encounter, especially since the wings don't need to be marinated. All the flavor and the traditional sweet heat are added to the wings once they've crisped up on the grill. In memory of my favorite Buffalo, New York native, Harold Herman, I call for serving them with Buffalo's favorite sides—blue cheese dip and celery sticks—but they are equally good on their own.

Makes 6 to 10 servings

Grilling Method: Combo/Medium Heat

- 4 to 5 pounds chicken wings or drummettes (24 pieces)
      Olive oil
      Kosher salt
      Freshly ground pepper
- 1   6-ounce bottle Louisiana hot sauce
- 2   tablespoons butter,
- 1   tablespoon honey
      Blue Cheese Lovers' Blue Cheese Dip (page 294)
- 6   celery stalks, cut into sticks

1. Build a charcoal fire or preheat a gas grill. Pat the chicken pieces dry with paper towels. Coat them all over with olive oil and season with salt and pepper. Place the wings in the center of the cooking grate over indirect medium heat, cover, and grill for 20 to 25 minutes, turning once halfway through the cooking time.
2. Meanwhile, combine the hot sauce, butter, and honey in a small, heavy-bottomed saucepan. Bring to a gentle boil, whisking occasionally, and reduce the heat to low. Season to taste with salt and pepper. Divide the sauce, taking about ⅓ to the grill

to brush on the wings, keeping the rest warm. Turn the wings over and grill for the final 10 minutes and remove them from the grill.

3. Switch to medium direct heat. Pour the remaining sauce over the wings and toss to coat them evenly. Take the coated wings back to the grill and place them on the cooking grate. Cover and grill 4 to 5 minutes on each side or until very brown and caramelized. Remove from the grill onto a clean platter.

4. Serve hot, with the blue cheese dip and celery stalks on the side.

Chipotle Chicken Thighs

Two years ago, I had the opportunity to travel the Isthmus region of Oaxaca, Mexico, with Suzanna Trilling, Mexican cooking expert and host of the television cooking show Seasons of My Heart. *The highlight of the trip was attending a vela or festival (called* Vela de la Virgen de la Candelaria) *where the women (including yours truly) dressed in hand-embroidered velvet costumes with lots of gold jewelry. The price of admission was a case of Coronitas (pony-size Corona beers—so small you finish them off before they have a chance to get warm) per person. To go with the beer, the local ladies also offered bowl after bowl of homemade food. A spicy and piquant chipotle chicken dish was made by many of the women, each adding her own special touch to the basic recipe. Be sure to serve this chicken with a wedge of lime and an ice cold Corona.*

Makes 4 servings

Grilling Method: Indirect/Medium Heat

- 1   white onion, chopped
- 1   bunch fresh cilantro, chopped
- 1   7-ounce can chipotles in adobo
- 2   limes, 1 juiced and 1 quartered
     Kosher salt
- 2 to 3 cups mayonnaise
- 8   chicken thighs or 2 chickens, cut into pieces

1. In a blender, mix the onion, cilantro, chipotles with adobo sauce, and lime juice. Add a pinch of salt. Remove to a large nonreactive bowl. Fold in 2 cups of mayonnaise. Taste and adjust the seasonings. If it is too hot, add more mayonnaise. Add the chicken pieces, cover, and refrigerate for 2 to 4 hours, turning occasionally.

2. When ready to cook, build a charcoal fire or preheat a gas grill. Place the chicken, bone-side down, in the center of the cooking grate over indirect medium heat.

3. Cover and grill-roast until the breast meat near the bone registers 170°F and the thigh meat registers 180°F, about 45 minutes. You do not need to turn the chicken pieces. If you don't have a thermometer, cook until the chicken is no longer pink and the juices run clear. Remove the chicken from the grill using tongs and a spatula to preserve the crust on the top of the thighs. Let the chicken sit for 10 minutes before serving.

TIP: I created this recipe to capture the essence of the food that I ate and cooked during my two-week culinary exploration of Oaxaca. Although it seems that mayonnaise is an inauthentic ingredient for Mexican cooking, in fact, it is purchased there in large quantities in local warehouse stores and used for cooking everything—even in the most remote villages. The truth is that mayonnaise is really just a great way to lubricate and flavor meat or fish. My mayo-based wet rub can be used equally well on thick fish steaks or large whole fish such as snapper.

Chicken Paillard with Greek Farmer's Salad and Tzatziki

Sometimes cooking is as therapeutic as it is nourishing. And making a paillard is the ultimate in stress relief since you pound the meat until it is uniformly thin. The fresh lemon and oregano rub infuses the thin pieces of chicken, making them sparkle with flavor. Served on top of a Greek farmer's salad (horatiki) and dressed with the pungent garlic-cucumber-yogurt sauce called tzatziki, it's a dish that's hard to beat. The chicken is also good served on top of the salad with a spicy oregano vinaigrette.

Makes 4 servings

Grilling Method: Direct/Medium Heat
Special Equipment: Meat pounder or rolling pin

4   boneless skinless chicken breast halves
    Olive oil

Lemon-Oregano Wet Rub
2   large cloves garlic, minced
3   lemons, 2 zested and 1 cut in wedges
1   teaspoon coarse sea salt or kosher salt
$1/4$ teaspoon water

2   teaspoons dried oregano
$1/2$ teaspoon freshly ground pepper
2   tablespoons chopped fresh parsley
    Lemon zest for garnishing, optional
    Yogurt-Cucumber Sauce (at right)
    Greek Farmer's Salad (at right)

1. Build a charcoal fire or preheat a gas grill. Rinse and dry each chicken breast, remove the tenderloins if they're still attached, and save them for another use. Brush the chicken lightly with oil on both sides (this will make the pounding easier). Place each chicken breast between 2 pieces of parchment or waxed paper about 8 x 8 inches. Using a meat pounder (or rolling pin), flatten each breast to about an even $1/4$-inch thickness. Set aside.

2. Make the rub: Mix the garlic, lemon zest, salt, and water in a mortar or a shallow bowl. Grind with the pestle or the back of a fork. Add the oregano and pepper and grind again to mix. Divide the mixture into 4 equal portions.

3. Brush each chicken paillard with olive oil on both sides.

4. With clean hands, rub each piece with $1/4$ of the wet rub on both sides, making sure to coat evenly. (The rub is very flavorful and will be too strong if left in clumps on the pieces of chicken.)

5. Using tongs, place the paillards on the cooking grate over direct medium heat, cover, and grill for about 6 minutes, turning once halfway through the cooking time. When the chicken is marked and cooked through, remove it from the grill.

6. Immediately squirt 1 to 2 lemon wedges over each piece of chicken, and let it sit for 2 to 3 minutes. Garnish with the parsley and strips of lemon zest, if desired. Serve with Yogurt-Cucumber Sauce and Greek Farmer's Salad.

Yogurt-Cucumber Sauce (Tzatziki)
Makes 2 cups

2   cups nonfat plain yogurt
$1/2$ medium seedless cucumber, peeled and diced
3   cloves garlic, crushed
1   tablespoon olive oil
$1/2$ teaspoon fresh lemon juice
    Kosher salt
    Freshly ground pepper

1. Put the yogurt in a strainer, and set over a large bowl. Allow it to drain overnight in the refrigerator. Discard the liquid.

2. Wipe out the bowl, then put the yogurt into it. Add the cucumber, garlic, olive oil, lemon juice, and salt and pepper to taste. Mix well. Refrigerate before serving.

TIP: Make the tzatziki up to 3 days in advance. The flavors intensify and actually taste better once they've had a chance to meld.

TIP: The older the garlic, the stronger it tastes. If your garlic is a little past its prime but hasn't started sprouting yet, you can still use it, just reduce the quantity by half if you don't like a strong garlic flavor. Likewise, if you love the taste of garlic and your garlic is extremely fresh and firm, increase the amount of garlic for a more pronounced flavor.

Greek Farmer's Salad
Makes 4 to 6 servings

4   medium fully ripe tomatoes, cut into wedges
1   medium (seedless) cucumber, peeled and cut into $1/2$-inch chunks
1   small red onion, cut in half and sliced into semicircles
20   oil cured black olives, more or less to taste
    Kosher salt
    Freshly ground pepper
1   teaspoon dried oregano
2   ounces feta cheese, cut into 8 slices (optional)

1. Put the tomato wedges, cucumber chunks, sliced onions, and olives into a large bowl. Mix well and season with salt, pepper, and dried oregano.
2. Serve with chicken paillard and tzatziki immediately. If using the optional feta cheese, serve authentic Greek style with the cheese laid on top in thick slices (do not crumble or mix into salad).

Rose's Tandoori Chicken

Rose Levy Beranbaum, an acclaimed master baker, also loves to grill. She adapted this recipe from one she brought back more than 30 years ago from a trip to India. In attempting to duplicate the special, intense flavor of a clay tandoori oven, she found that grilling the chicken was the only method that worked. Rose says that the fantastic flavor comes from marinating the chicken for three days. I find that overnight works just as well. Rose adds the traditional red food coloring to her chicken, but I omit it, preferring the orange red color of the turmeric. Feel free to add about a teaspoon of the coloring to the marinade, if you like. Serve this spicy, flavorful recipe with cool cucumber raita or the Crunchy Cucumber Salad on page 303.

Makes 6 servings

Grilling Method: Indirect/Medium Heat

2	whole chickens, 2 to 3½ pounds each, cut into pieces
1½	tablespoons coarse sea salt
¼	cup fresh lemon juice
¼	cup fresh lime juice
1	cup plain yogurt
4	medium cloves garlic, quartered
1	tablespoon cayenne pepper
2	teaspoons peeled fresh ginger, minced
1	teaspoon cumin seeds
1	teaspoon ground coriander
½	teaspoon turmeric
½	teaspoon freshly ground pepper
¼	teaspoon ground cinnamon
	Large pinch ground cloves
1	large sweet onion, preferably Vidalia or Bermuda
1	tablespoon vegetable oil
	Fresh cilantro sprigs
	Lemon and lime wedges

1. Pat the chicken dry with paper towels. If separating the chicken into pieces yourself, cut the chicken with kitchen scissors at all the joints and cut the breast and back section in half. Remove as much skin as possible.
2. Put the chicken in a large nonreactive bowl or a resealable plastic bag. Sprinkle with the salt; add the lemon and lime juices and toss to coat well. Set it aside for 30 minutes while mixing the rest of the marinade.
3. Put the yogurt, garlic, cayenne, ginger, cumin, coriander, turmeric, pepper, cinnamon, and cloves in a food processor or blender and blend on high speed until well mixed, about 20 seconds. Pour the mixture over the chicken, mixing to coat the pieces on all sides. Cover tightly and refrigerate for 24 hours or as long as 3 days. Turn the chicken pieces occasionally during this time so that all the pieces are coated evenly with the marinade.
4. Remove the chicken from the marinade and discard the marinade.
5. When ready to cook, build a charcoal fire or preheat a gas grill. Place the chicken pieces bone-side down on the cooking grate over indirect, medium heat. Cover and grill 30 to 45 minutes or until the juices run clear. The white meat will finish first and register 170°F on an instant-read thermometer; dark meat should read 180°F. Smaller pieces will also take less time than larger pieces of chicken. Remove each piece when it is done.
6. While the chicken is cooking, heat a large, heavy cast-iron pan over high heat until very hot. Cut the onion in half lengthwise and then slice each half lengthwise into thin slices.
7. Add the oil to the pan; tilt the pan to coat it evenly, and add the onions. Season with salt. Cook on high heat, stirring constantly, for 3 to 5 minutes, or until browned but still crisp. Remove at once and drain on paper towels.
8. Place the chicken on a large serving plate. Let it rest for 10 minutes before serving. Garnish with the onions, cilantro, and lemon and lime wedges. Serve hot or at room temperature.

Classic Grilled Chicken Caesar Salad

More people download this recipe from my Girls at the Grill web site than any other, proving that sometimes it doesn't pay to reinvent the wheel. If you want to put a spin on the classic, add slivers of sun-dried tomatoes and Niçoise olives when you toss the lettuce in the dressing, or try the shrimp variation.

Makes 4 servings

Grilling Method: Direct/Medium Heat

    1   large head romaine lettuce
    3 to 5 cloves garlic, minced
    1   tablespoon strong Dijon mustard
    1 to 2 anchovies or 2 teaspoons anchovy paste
        Sea salt
        Freshly ground pepper
    1   lemon, juiced
    2   teaspoons Worcestershire sauce
    ½ to ⅔ cup olive oil
    2   boneless skinless chicken breast halves, about
            8 ounces each
        Olive oil
    ½   cup grated Parmigiano-Reggiano cheese
    1   cup croutons, preferably homemade

1. Build a charcoal fire or preheat a gas grill.
2. Wash and dry the romaine leaves, and cut them into 1-inch pieces. Set aside.
3. Mix the garlic, mustard, anchovies, 1 teaspoon salt, and 1 teaspoon pepper into a paste in a small bowl. Add the lemon juice and Worcestershire; mix well. Slowly whisk in the oil until smooth and creamy. Season to taste. Set aside.
4. Brush the chicken with oil, and season with salt and pepper. Place it on the cooking grate over direct medium heat, cover, and grill for 15 to 20 minutes, or until completely cooked through. Remove the chicken and let it cool. When cool, slice it into strips and set aside.
5. To assemble the salad, put the lettuce in a large bowl and toss it with enough dressing and cheese to coat the leaves. Top it with chicken strips, croutons, and an additional sprinkling of parmesan cheese. Serve immediately.

Caesar Salad with Jumbo Shrimp: Omit the chicken in step 4. Instead, brush 1 pound jumbo shrimp with oil, and season with salt and pepper. Grill over direct, medium-high heat, turning once halfway through the cooking time, for 5 to 8 minutes, or until completely cooked through. Let the shrimp cool. Complete the recipe as in step 5, topping the salad with the shrimp.

Chinese Five-Spice Chicken Salad with Purple Grapes

If you're tired of deli chicken salad but still love the ease of pulling a meal together out of what's in the fridge, try this refined version of the American standard. You can buy Chinese five-spice powder at most grocery stores; a shake or two of it will transport ho-hum into humdinger! The sweet-savory spice combination of the five spices (cinnamon, clove, fennel, star anise, and Szechuan peppercorns) complements the smoky grilled chicken and enhances the cool tang of the grapes. Serve the salad in a small lettuce leaf with Garlic Melba Toast, and you'll be the hit of your book or cooking club. This salad is even better after sitting in the fridge for a day, making it a great choice for a do-ahead party or picnic.

Makes 4 to 6 servings

Grilling Method: Direct/Medium Heat

    4   boneless skinless chicken breast halves
        Olive oil
        Kosher salt
        Freshly ground pepper
    ½   cup mayonnaise, or more to taste
    1   scant tablespoon Chinese Five-Spice Powder
            (page 99)
    1   cup halved purple or red grapes
    2   sticks celery, minced
    1   head Boston or butter lettuce
    ¼   cup toasted slivered almonds
    16 to 24 pieces Garlic Melba Toast (page 41)
            or store-bought melba toast

1. Build a charcoal fire or preheat a gas grill. Rinse the chicken and pat it dry with paper towels. Brush

with olive oil and season with salt and pepper. Place the chicken in the center of the cooking grate over direct, medium heat, cover, and grill for about 15 minutes or until the meat is no longer pink and the juices run clear. Turn the chicken only once during cooking time.

2. Let the chicken cool. Meanwhile, mix the mayonnaise and five-spice powder in a large bowl.
3. Chop the cooled chicken into ½-inch cubes and add them to the bowl with the dressing. Mix well, adding more mayonnaise, if necessary. Add the grapes and celery and mix again. Add salt and pepper to taste and adjust the seasonings. Refrigerate for at least 4 hours or preferably overnight to let the flavors develop.
4. When ready to serve, place a scoop of salad on the inside of a lettuce leaf and sprinkle with the almonds. Serve with Garlic Melba Toast.

Garlic Melba Toast
Makes 20 pieces

4   cloves garlic, grated
½   cup olive oil
1   loaf French bread, cut into ¼-inch slices

Preheat the oven to 250°F. Mix the garlic and olive oil in a small bowl. Place the bread rounds on a cookie sheet and brush the tops with the garlic oil. Bake for 1 to 2 hours or until completely crisp and golden. Serve warm or let cool, then store in an airtight container for up to 2 weeks.

Sliced Chicken with Five-Sprout Salad

I have long been a fan of French chef Alain Ducasse. During a recent trip to Paris, I ate at one of his newer and more modern restaurants SPOON (Food and Wine). I had a salad composed entirely of different bean sprouts. It was crunchy and refreshing. Here, I've adapted his idea, adding thin slices of grilled chicken to turn the salad into a main dish.

Makes 4 servings

5   cups assorted fresh bean sprouts, such as alfalfa, clover, mustard, radish, sunflower, lentil, mung
⅓   cup fresh lemon juice
1   tablespoon heavy whipping cream
1   lemon, zested
⅔   cup extra-virgin olive oil, preferably French Sea salt
2   freshly grilled boneless skinless chicken breast halves (page 34)
    Grains of paradise or freshly ground white pepper (optional)

1. Mix the sprouts together in a large bowl; set aside.
2. Whisk together the lemon juice and cream in a medium bowl. Add the zest, then slowly whisk in the olive oil until the dressing is emulsified (well combined). Season to taste with salt.
3. Slice the warm chicken breasts very thinly and toss in a medium bowl with half the dressing. Let sit for 5 minutes.
4. Meanwhile, toss the sprouts with 2 tablespoons of the dressing—just to moisten them; too much dressing will cause them to become soggy. Divide among 4 plates. Top with the chicken and a grind of grains of paradise, if using. Serve immediately.

TIP: If you can't find all five varieties of sprouts, use what you can find to equal five cups. Sprouts are located in the produce section of the grocery store. More varieties can be found at natural (health) food stores, or you can grow your own very easily.

Thai Chicken Salad

I have been a Fine Cooking *magazine groupie for a very long time. An issue a few summers ago particularly intrigued me and I wanted to cook everything from it. I didn't make it through the whole issue, but I discovered a few new favorites. This sweet-savory dish is based on Su-Mei Yu's recipe for a chicken-apple salad from that issue. It has a great mix of crunchy raw and softer cooked ingredients, bursts of tangy sweet, sour, and citrus notes, and hot undertones that you would expect from an Asian-flavored salad. I make it most often with leftover beer-can chicken. The charred poblano chiles give the salad its smoky quality.*

Makes 4 to 6 servings

Dressing

- ½ cup Sweet and Sour Sauce (below)
- ¼ cup fresh lime juice
- 3 tablespoons Thai fish sauce

Salad

- 1 orange
- 2 cups shredded chicken breast (page 34) or leftover beer-can chicken (page 47)
- 1 Granny Smith apple, unpeeled, cored, quartered, and thinly sliced,
- 1 cup halved red or white seedless grapes
- 1 bunch of arugula, torn into bite-size pieces
- 1 shallot, thinly sliced crosswise
- 1 poblano or jalapeño chile, charred until soft, peeled, and diced (page 210)
- 1 tablespoon fresh lemon juice

- ¼ cup unsalted, dry-roasted peanuts, coarsely chopped
- ¼ cup fresh mint leaves, crushed and slightly torn

1. Make the dressing: In a small bowl, combine the Sweet and Sour Sauce, lime juice, and fish sauce; set aside.

2. Make the salad: With a paring knife, peel the orange down to the flesh and remove any excess pith from the surface. Working over a large bowl, carve out the segments by cutting along the dividing membranes of the fruit toward the center, letting the segments fall into a large bowl. Discard the membrane and peel. This is also referred to as "supremed" oranges.

3. Add the chicken, apple, grapes, arugula, shallot, chile, and lemon juice and toss. Add the dressing, gently tossing again to mix thoroughly. Transfer to a shallow bowl or platter. Sprinkle with the peanuts and mint, and serve.

Sweet and Sour Sauce

Makes about ½ cup

- 1 tablespoon red chile flakes
- ¼ cup plus 2 tablespoons rice vinegar
- ¾ cup sugar
- ½ teaspoon kosher salt
- 7 cloves garlic, minced

In a dry saucepan, toast the chile flakes over high heat until fragrant, about 2 minutes. Add the rice vinegar, sugar, and salt and continue to cook, stirring over medium-low heat until the ingredients are dissolved. Stir in the garlic, remove the sauce from the heat, and cool to room temperature.

TIP: Fish sauce is a staple in the Southeast Asian pantry. It is made by fermenting small, whole fish (usually anchovies) in brine (a saltwater solution), drawing off the liquid, and steeping the liquid in the sun before it is bottled. Thailand and Vietnam are the two main producers. Thai fish sauce is known as *nam pla*, and Vietnamese fish sauce is known as *nuoc mam*. Either work well in recipes and keep indefinitely in the refrigerator. You can buy fish sauce from Asian markets, specialty stores, and on the Internet.

Chicken Tortilla Soup

Chicago chef Rick Bayless grew up in an Oklahoma barbecue restaurant family, so it's not much of a stretch for him to blend his famed authentic Mexican flavors with modern America's infatuation with grilling. There are so many of Rick's recipes that I love to make at home, but Sopa de Tortilla is my favorite. Here I've added grilled chicken to his excellent recipe for this traditional tortilla soup, from his book Mexico: One Plate at a Time. *The addition of the shredded grilled chicken turns this appetizer soup into a one-dish meal. Besides grilling the chicken, I follow his recipe until I serve it, when I put all the accompaniments in separate bowls so my guests can add in as much or as little of the goodies as they want.*

Makes 4 to 6 servings

- 6 corn tortillas
  Peanut or vegetable oil
- 4 cloves garlic, peeled and left whole
- 1 small white onion, sliced
- 2 dried pasilla chilies or 1 dried ancho, stemmed, seeded, and torn into several flat pieces
- 1 15-ounce can good-quality whole tomatoes in juice, drained
- 6 cups good chicken broth, store-bought or homemade
- 1 large sprig epazote, optional (look in Mexican or ethnic markets)
  Kosher salt

4 boneless skinless chicken breast halves, grilled and shredded (page 34) or leftover beer-can chicken (page 47)

2 ounces Mexican queso fresco or other crumbly fresh cheese, such as salted, pressed farmer's cheese or feta, cubed

1/2 cup grated Chihuahua or Monterey Jack cheese

1 large ripe avocado, peeled, pitted, and cut into 1/2-inch cubes

1 large lime, cut into wedges

1. Cut the tortillas in half, then cut them crosswise into 1/2-inch strips. In a medium-large (4-quart) saucepan, heat 1/2 inch of oil over medium heat until it reaches 350°F on a frying or candy thermometer. Add half of the tortilla strips. Stir them around in the oil constantly until they are golden brown and crispy. With a slotted spoon, scoop them out and drain on paper towels. Repeat with the remaining tortillas and set aside until ready to use.

2. Pour off all but a thin coating of oil from the saucepan and return to the heat. Add the garlic and onion to the pan and cook, stirring regularly, until golden, about 7 minutes. Use the slotted spoon to scoop out the garlic and onion, pressing them against the side of the pan to leave behind as much oil as possible, and transfer them to a blender or food processor.

3. Add the chile pieces to the hot pan. Turn quickly as they fry, toast, and release their aroma—about 30 seconds in all. Too much frying and toasting will make them bitter. Remove and drain them on paper towels. Set the pan aside.

4. Add the tomatoes to the blender containing the garlic and onion and process to a smooth puree.

5. Set the saucepan over medium-high heat. When hot, add the puree and stir constantly until it has thickened to the consistency of tomato paste, about 10 minutes. Add the broth and epazote, if using, and bring to a boil, then partially cover and gently simmer over medium to medium-low heat for 30 minutes. Taste and season with salt—you will probably need about 1/2 teaspoon, depending on the saltiness of your chicken broth.

6. Divide the shredded chicken among 4 soup bowls. Ladle a portion of the broth into each bowl, top with a portion of the tortilla strips, and crumble on a little toasted chile. Put the remaining tortilla strips, both cheeses, avocado, and lime wedges on

small plates. Serve the soup with these so everyone can add as much of the garnishes as they like.

TIP: If you don't want to fry the tortilla strips, substitute ready-made unsalted tortilla chips.

Rubbed and Sauced Barbecued Half Chickens

Even if barbecued chicken is not "authentic barbecue," I'd bet that 90 percent of the barbecue sauce sold in stores is used for slathering onto chicken—even if cooked in an oven. Because I have a fondness for the real thing, I make my own rub and my own sauce. Both keep well and yield enough for at least two cookouts—so it's easy to make when you have the time, and it's nice to have on hand for when you don't.

Makes 6 to 8 servings

Grilling Method: Indirect/Medium Heat
Special Equipment: Rib rack

2 whole chickens, 3 1/2 to 4 pounds each
  Olive oil
  Kosher salt and freshly ground pepper or Classic Barbecue Rub (page 44)
  Sassy Brown Sugar and Bourbon Barbecue Sauce (page 44) or your favorite barbecue sauce

1. Build a charcoal fire or preheat a gas grill. Using poultry shears or a chef's knife, split the chickens down the breastbone to cut them in half.

2. Brush lightly with olive oil on all surfaces and sprinkle with salt and pepper or Classic Barbecue Rub. Set aside. Using a slotted rib rack, place the 4 chicken halves vertically, skin-side facing out, in each of the 4 slots. (The chickens in the holder will resemble slices of toast in a toast rack.)

3. Place the rack in the center of the cooking grate over indirect medium heat Cover and grill for about 1 hour, or until the chicken registers 180°F in the thickest part of the thigh. After 30 minutes, check the internal temperature with an instant-read thermometer. Brush liberally with barbecue sauce during the final 15 to 20 minutes. (If the chicken is sauced too early, it will burn on the outside before the interior meat is cooked through.) Remove the chicken to a platter and let it rest for 5 minutes before serving.

Classic Barbecue Rub
Makes about 1½ cups

3	tablespoons sugar
2	tablespoons smoked paprika
2	tablespoons kosher salt
2	tablespoons packed brown sugar
1	tablespoon ground cumin
1	tablespoon freshly ground pepper
1	tablespoon onion powder
1	tablespoon garlic powder
1	tablespoon celery salt
2	teaspoons chili powder
1	teaspoon dried oregano
½	teaspoon cayenne pepper

In a medium bowl, combine all the ingredients; mix well. For a smoother rub, process the ingredients in a spice grinder until well combined and all the pieces are uniform (the rub will be become a very fine powder and tan in color). It is important to grind the spices if adding the rub to any home-made barbecue sauce. (The rub can be stored in an airtight container for up to 6 months.)

Sassy Brown Sugar and Bourbon Barbecue Sauce
Makes 4 cups

1	28-ounce can crushed tomatoes
1	cup packed brown sugar
½	cup bourbon
½	cup ketchup
¼	cup Heinz Chili Sauce
¼	cup apple cider vinegar
¼	cup Worcestershire sauce
2	tablespoons red wine vinegar
2	tablespoons molasses
2	teaspoons Classic Barbecue Rub (above)
	Kosher salt
	Freshly ground pepper
1	tablespoon unsweetened cocoa

1. In a large saucepan, combine the tomatoes, sugar, bourbon, ketchup, chili sauce, cider vinegar, Worcestershire sauce, wine vinegar, and molasses, stirring after each ingredient to combine.

2. Add the Classic Barbecue Rub and simmer over low heat until the flavors have blended and the sauce has thickened somewhat, about 30 minutes.

3. Let the sauce cool for about 10 minutes or until it is warm but no longer boiling hot. Puree it using an immersion or traditional blender. Taste and adjust the seasonings with about ½ tea-spoon salt and pepper. (Remember, the chicken will have plenty of spice rub on it, so don't over-season the sauce.) Add the cocoa powder and mix well to combine. Let sit for 5 minutes and stir again to make sure the cocoa powder is well distributed. Let cool and pour into a clean glass jar for storing. The sauce can be made in advance and kept for 2 weeks in the refrigerator.

Rosemary Chicken and Red Potatoes

Rosemary is a comforting herb that complements almost every meat and root vegetable and just about everyone likes the flavor. This recipe works well with pork or beef, but chicken is my personal favorite. Put the potatoes on the warming rack of your grill while the chicken is cooking and they'll be done when the chicken is done. All you need to add is a simple salad and a soft red wine for a feel-good, satisfying meal.

Makes 4 servings

Grilling Method: Indirect/Medium Heat

1	whole chicken, 4 to 5 pounds
	Olive oil
	Kosher salt
2	teaspoons dried rosemary
	Freshly ground pepper
4	lemons, cut in half
8	ounces pearl onions, peeled

12 to 24 new potatoes (about 3 per person), depending on size, washed

¼	cup olive oil
1	tablespoon dried rosemary
1	tablespoon kosher salt

1. Build a charcoal fire or preheat a gas grill. Remove and discard the neck, giblets, and any excess fat from the chicken. If desired, rinse the chicken, and pat it dry with paper towels. Brush the skin all over with olive oil. Season liberally with salt and the rosemary. Season the inside of the cavity with salt and pepper add the cut lemons and pearl onions.

2. Place the chicken on the cooking grate, breast-side up, over indirect medium heat. Cover and grill until the juices run clear and an instant-read thermometer reads 170°F in the breast and 180°F in the thickest part of the thigh, $1\frac{1}{4}$ to $1\frac{1}{2}$ hours.

3. About 45 minutes before the chicken is done, make the potatoes: Put the potatoes in a metal bowl. Pour the oil over them and toss to coat. Sprinkle with the rosemary and salt and toss again to coat evenly.

4. Place the potatoes in the center of the cooking grate or on the warming rack over indirect medium heat and roast the potatoes for 30 to 40 minutes or until tender. The potatoes are done when the skin puffs slightly and the potatoes are very soft in the center, about 40 minutes for an average red potato. The bigger the potato, the longer it will take to cook and vice versa with smaller potatoes.

5. Transfer the chicken to a platter, and allow it to rest for about 10 minutes before carving. Serve warm with pearl onions and red potatoes.

"French Chicken" with Dijon Mustard and Scallions

When I was growing up, my mother subscribed to Julia Child's television cooking show through our local PBS station. The station sent the recipes in advance and my mother cooked along with Julia, watching from a tiny black and white TV in the kitchen. On the nights that my mother followed along with Julia or had a dinner party, I got to taste food that my grandmother never even thought of cooking. This is what created my culinary schizophrenia—I love down-home Southern cooking and traditional French cuisine equally. My favorite main dish was what we referred to as "French chicken." It may not be exactly as Julia envisioned, but it certainly brought her spirit into our home and influenced my culinary life. And, unbeknownst to both my mother and Julia Child, it works

even better on the grill. The grill facilitates the browning and crisping of the skin and the mustard glaze, making this one chicken that you have to eat skin and all!

Makes 4 to 6 servings

Grilling Method: Indirect/Medium Heat

2   small chickens, about $2\frac{1}{2}$ pounds each, preferably Amish or organic
    Olive oil
    Kosher salt
    Grains of paradise or freshly ground pepper
$\frac{1}{3}$ cup strong Dijon mustard
2   tablespoons white wine
$\frac{1}{4}$ cup olive oil
3   tablespoons unsalted butter, melted
3   green onions, chopped
1   teaspoon dried thyme
    Pinch cayenne pepper
1   cup panko or fresh white bread crumbs
2 to 3 tomatoes, cut in half

1. Pat the chicken dry with paper towels. Using poultry shears or a very sharp knife, cut on each side of the backbone and remove it. Turn the chicken breast-side up and break the breastbone by striking it sharply with a blunt object. Open 2 sides of the chicken as if you were opening a book, and lay it flat. Tuck the wing tips under the upper wings and brush all over with olive oil. Season the chicken with salt and grains of paradise.

2. Build a charcoal fire or preheat a gas grill. Place the chickens in the center of the grill skin-side up over indirect medium heat and cover. Meanwhile, whisk the mustard and wine together. Slowly drizzle the oil and butter into the mixture to blend. Add the onions, thyme, and cayenne and mix to combine.

3. After 20 minutes, turn the chickens over and spread some of the mustard sauce on the bone sides of the chickens. Grill for 10 more minutes. Turn the chickens back over breast-side up and spread more mustard sauce (reserving a little bit) on the skin; grill for 5 more minutes.

4. Sprinkle the breast side of the chickens with most of the bread crumbs. Continue grilling for 10 to 15 more minutes or until the juices run clear and the thigh registers 180°F. Make sure you do not touch the bone when testing with the thermometer.

5. Transfer the chicken to a platter and let it rest while the tomatoes cook, about 10 minutes. Meanwhile, spread each tomato half with the reserved mustard sauce and sprinkle with the remaining bread crumbs. Place on the warming rack of the grill or on the cooking grate. Grill for 10 minutes or until the tops are crunchy and the tomatoes are warmed through. Serve hot with the chicken.

Roast Chicken with 40 Cloves of Garlic and Shallots

This recipe is one of my winter comfort foods. I've added shallots to the classic recipe made with garlic to make the chicken even more fragrant and delicious. The beauty of this recipe is that the garlic and shallots cook in the flavorful chicken fat that is rendered out as the chicken roasts. I like making it with a whole chicken and two extra leg quarters (thigh and leg together). Once the garlic and shallots are roasted, you can remove the chicken from the roast holder and put it on the cooking grate for added brownness.

Makes 4 to 6 servings

Grilling Method: Indirect/High Heat
Special Equipment: V-rack roast holder; disposable aluminum roasting pan

1   whole chicken, 4 to 5 pounds, preferably
        Amish or organic
2   leg quarters
        Olive oil
        Kosher salt
2   heads garlic, separated but not peeled
10 medium shallots, unpeeled
        Grains of paradise or freshly ground pepper

1. Pat the chicken dry with paper towels. Brush all over with olive oil and sprinkle with salt. Place all the chicken in the center of the V-rack, put the rack in the roasting pan, and set aside.
2. Build a charcoal fire or preheat a gas grill. Meanwhile, put the garlic and shallots in a bowl and drizzle with oil. Toss to coat. Season with salt; toss again. Scatter the garlic and shallots around the bottom of the roasting pan.

3. Place the roasting pan in the center of the cooking grate over indirect high heat, cover, and grill-roast for 1 to 1½ hours or until the skin is crisp and brown and an instant-read thermometer registers 180°F in the thickest part of the thigh, making sure not to touch the bone.
4. Stir the garlic and shallots occasionally to baste them in the chicken juices and to prevent burning. The shallots and garlic may be roasted before the chicken is done; they'll be browned and soft. Remove them from the roasting pan and replace the chicken on the cooking grate without the roasting pan. Remove any excess drippings from the pan and keep the shallots and garlic warm until ready to serve.
5. When the chicken is done, remove it from the grill and let it sit for 10 minutes before carving. Season with grains of paradise or pepper. Place it on a platter with the 4 leg quarters intact and slices of white meat surrounded by the roasted shallots and garlic. To eat, slip the garlic and shallots out of the skins and spread them on the meat.

"Kosher" Chicken

Kosher chicken delivers the juiciest chicken with the best-tasting skin you have ever eaten. The salting process makes the bird retain water (aka precious juices), which isn't something that I aspire to do, but it works miracles with chicken and turkey and pork, too. And, you can "kosher" a chicken at home. I think of koshering as a dry brine. You simply bury the meat in kosher salt, and let it sit for at least an hour and up to four hours. All you need is a chicken, a container large enough to hold it, and a box of kosher salt. My friend and fellow griller Jamie Purviance swears it makes a roast chicken surpassed by none—and I agree! You can do this with bone-in chicken parts, but don't try it with boneless skinless chicken breasts. And don't worry, you brush all the excess salt off before oiling and grilling, so it is not oversalted—just perfectly seasoned.

Makes 2 to 4 servings

1   whole roasting chicken, 4 to 5 pounds,
        preferably Amish or organic
1   3-pound box kosher salt
        Olive oil

1. Pat the chicken dry with paper towels.
2. Put the chicken in a nonreactive container deep enough to cover it and cover all parts with salt, making sure some salt goes into the cavity. Cover and refrigerate for 1 to 4 hours.
3. Build a charcoal fire or preheat a gas grill. Take the chicken out of the container and brush off the salt with a dry brush or a paper towel. Brush all over with olive oil.
4. Grill-roast following the directions for the desired recipe. (Do not add any more salt to the chicken.) It will be perfectly seasoned, and the skin will be unbelievably crisp. Serve hot.

TIP: Amish chickens are raised by Amish farmers across the United States. They are fed all-natural food with no growth hormones and no preservatives. The chickens are not force fed and grow at their own pace, keeping them tender and lean. Amish chickens are raised in open, spacious chicken houses with access to plenty of fresh air and water. This allows them to be delivered to your store firm and white, not yellow. True Amish chickens are marketed regionally, distributed locally, and never trucked across country—making them fresher than national brands. They are more expensive, but I think they are well worth it.

The Original Beer-Can Chicken

I first discovered this method for cooking chicken—literally grilling a chicken set over a beer can—at the Memphis in May Barbecue competition in the early 1990s. I was so amazed that I couldn't stop talking about it. I'm not taking credit for the beer-can chicken craze, but I taught it to many distinguished culinary writers and chefs. It's a technique that is easy to love, and now more and more people are roasting a chicken perched on top of a beer can. To make your chicken doubly great, try koshering your chicken before setting it on a beer can. (See "Kosher" Chicken, pages 46-47.)

Makes 4 servings

Grilling Method: Indirect/Medium Heat

1   **whole roasting chicken, 4 to 5 pounds, preferably Amish or organic**
    Olive oil
3   **tablespoons dry spice rub, divided, or Classic Barbecue Rub (page 44)**
1   **12-ounce can domestic beer, such as Budweiser**

1. Remove the neck and giblets, and rinse the chicken inside and out if desired; pat it dry with paper towels. Coat the chicken lightly with oil and season with 2 tablespoons of the dry rub. Set aside.
2. Build a charcoal fire or preheat a gas grill. Open the beer can, pour out about ¼ cup of the beer, and make an extra hole in the top of the can with a church-key can opener. Sprinkle the remaining tablespoon of the dry rub inside the beer can. Place the beer can in the center of the cooking grate over indirect medium heat and sit the chicken on top of the beer can. The chicken will appear to be sitting on the grate.
3. Cover and cook the chicken for 1 to 1½ hours or until the internal temperature registers 165°F in the breast area and 180°F in the thigh. Remove it carefully to a platter, holding the can with tongs. Let it rest for 10 minutes before carving.

NOTE: When removing the chicken from the grate, be careful not to spill the contents of the beer can, as it will be very hot.

TIP: If you prefer a more classic roasted chicken flavor, omit the dry rub and use only kosher salt and black pepper.

Beer-Can Turkey

If you thought beer-can chicken was amazing, just imagine what beer-can turkey is like. I recommend using a large vertical roaster (aka turkey sitter) instead of a beer can because it offers better stability and is safer. You can purchase a turkey sitter from www.GrillFriends.com, just type in "vertical roaster" in the search engine. If you are in a pinch and promise to be careful, you can also use a 32-ounce beer can. For optimal results, I suggest brining it before roasting it beer-can style.

Makes 10 servings

Grilling Method: Indirect/Medium Heat
Special Equipment: Large vertical roaster (turkey sitter) or 32-ounce beer can such as Fosters

1	whole turkey, about 14 to 16 pounds, thawed and preferably brined (see page 22)
	Olive oil
3	tablespoons dry spice rub, divided, or Classic Barbecue Rub (page 44)
2	12-ounce cans beer (only necessary if using the "turkey sitter")

1. Remove the neck and giblets and pat the turkey dry with paper towels. Coat it lightly with oil and season with 2 tablespoons of the dry rub. Set aside. (If you prefer a more classic roasted turkey flavor, omit the dry rub and use only kosher salt and black pepper.)

2. Build a charcoal fire or preheat a gas grill. Open the beers and pour them into the vertical roaster until it is two-thirds full. Sprinkle the remaining tablespoon of the dry rub inside the roaster. Place the roaster in the center of the cooking grate over indirect medium heat and "sit" the turkey on top of it. The drumsticks should be resting on the cooking grate and the turkey will look like it is sitting on the grate.

3. Cover and grill-roast the turkey for 3 to 3½ hours or until the internal temperature registers 165°F in the breast area and 180°F in the thigh. Remove it from the grill and let it rest for 20 minutes before carving. If your turkey is done well before you want to serve your meal, tent it with foil and leave it on the sitter off the heat. The heat of the beer will keep the turkey piping hot for up to 1 hour, and by that time all the juices will be completely reabsorbed.

TIP: To remove the turkey, slide a pizza peel or a flat cookie sheet under the vertical roaster and balance the turkey with an oven mitt.

Orange-Brined, Maple-Glazed Turkey

Sweet maple syrup combined with sharp citrus and vanilla bourbon notes glazes the turkey skin to an ebony sheen and flavors the drippings for extra-rich and delicious gravy. My friends Timmy Warmath and Ned Walley like this American-flavored turkey so much that they packed the recipe in their luggage when they moved to London, where they grill Thanksgiving turkey every year for a lucky group of ex-pats. The brining helps ensure that the turkey stays extra juicy during the roasting process. Remember to glaze only during the final 30 minutes of the cooking time to prevent burning.

Makes 12 to 15 servings

Grilling Method: Indirect/Medium Heat

Orange Brine

6	cups water
2	cups kosher salt or 1 cup iodized table salt
1	cup sugar
2	oranges, quartered
1	tablespoon whole cloves
3	bay leaves
2	teaspoons whole peppercorns
1	whole turkey, 12 to 14 pounds, thawed
1	tablespoon olive oil or vegetable oil

Maple Glaze

½	cup pure maple syrup
1	small orange, juiced
1	tablespoon bourbon

1. Make the orange brine: In a large saucepan over high heat, bring the water, salt, and sugar to a boil, stirring to dissolve the sugar and salt. Cool to room temperature.

2. In a new or clean 3-gallon plastic bucket or other food-safe container large enough to hold the turkey, combine 1 gallon water, the oranges, cloves,

CARVING TURKEY

Follow the technique I learned from my friend Jeff Belmonti, who worked in a butcher shop when he was in high school and now applies his well-honed butcher skills in turkey carving. His approach is easier and smarter than the traditional method; it keeps the turkey juicier (because the pieces are smaller and denser), avoids shredding the meat, and the turkey looks better when presented.

To carve the turkey: Instead of cutting large slices from the breast lengthwise, remove the whole breast from the bone and cut across it to make crescent shaped chunks. Put it back on the platter as the whole breast and then cut off and add the drumsticks, thighs, and wings.

bay leaves, and peppercorns. Add the sugar-salt solution and stir.

3. Remove the neck and giblets from the turkey; reserve for other uses or discard. Remove and discard any excess fat. Rinse the turkey inside and out and pat it dry with paper towels.

4. Submerge the turkey in the brine. If necessary, add more water to cover the turkey and top it with a weight to make sure it is completely covered with the liquid. Refrigerate for 8 to 12 hours.

5. Make the maple glaze: In a small bowl, mix all the ingredients; cover and store in the refrigerator until about 20 minutes before you're ready to use it.

6. When ready to cook, build a charcoal fire or preheat a gas grill.

7. Remove the turkey from the brine and pat it dry. Brush all over with a thin coating of olive oil, but no salt and pepper, as the brine takes care of the seasoning.

8. Place the turkey breast-side up in the center of the cooking grate of a charcoal grill or in a turkey roasting pan on a flat roasting rack on a gas grill over indirect medium heat. Cover and cook 11 to 13 minutes per pound. About 30 minutes before you expect the turkey to be done, brush the glaze all over the turkey.

9. The turkey is done when an instant-read thermometer inserted in the thickest part of the thigh (not touching the bone) registers 180°F and the juices run clear. Transfer the turkey to a platter and let it stand for 20 minutes before carving.

TIP: To get drippings for gravy, place the turkey in a foil roasting pan when using a gas grill. About 30 minutes before the bird is done, remove the foil pan and place the bird in the center of the cooking grate. This allows the bottom of the bird to get brown and allows you to make gravy from the drippings that have accumulated in the pan. (There won't be any drippings that you can use if you put the turkey on the cooking grates of a charcoal grill.)

Wild Rice–Stuffed Cornish Game Hens

Cornish hens look like miniature chickens and make an impressive presentation. Here they are stuffed with a mixture of wild rice, pecans, dried cherries, and shallots and then grill-roasted to a golden brown. When I'm feeling a little flush or particularly civilized, I add chestnuts to the mix. When you are ready to dine, each person is served his or her own whole game hen. All you need is a bed of sautéed spinach or green beans to complete the plate. It's a little old-fashioned and makes me think of my parent's dinner parties, but that doesn't mean it should be reserved for nostalgic evenings. Make it tonight, and it might just become your new family favorite.

Makes 4 servings

Grilling Method: Indirect/Medium Heat

4   whole Cornish game hens, thawed
    Olive oil
    Kosher salt
3   cups cooked 100 percent wild rice (about ²/₃ cup dry wild rice
½   cup dried cherries
½   cup toasted pecans, chopped
¼   cup dry sherry
1   medium shallot, finely chopped
1   stick celery, finely chopped
1 to 2 tablespoons unsalted butter
    Freshly ground pepper
    Solid wooden toothpicks, soaked in water for 30 minutes

1. Clean the game hens, removing any giblets and drying the birds inside and out with paper towels. Brush all over with oil, and season with salt. Refrigerate, covered, while preparing the wild rice stuffing.
2. Prepare the wild rice according to the package directions. Do not overcook. When the rice is just cooked, add the cherries, pecans, sherry, shallot, celery, and butter. Taste and adjust the seasonings with salt and pepper, remembering that the wild rice mixture will be enriched by the game hen juices as it cooks. Let the rice mixture cool.
3. Build a charcoal fire or preheat a gas grill. Using a long-handled spoon, stuff each game hen with wild rice stuffing. Close the skin by threading a toothpick through the skin. Place the stuffed hens on the cooking grate over indirect medium heat, cover, and grill for 1 to 1½ hours, or until an instant-read thermometer reads 180°F in the thickest part of the thigh, not touching any bone.
4. Remove from the grill and let the hens sit for 10 minutes before serving. Serve hot.

Salt-Cured Duck Breast with Fig Jam

One recent fall I was in the heart of Provence in Arles, France, with my mother. We shopped the weekly market until all the vendors had packed up and then, famished, went looking for a place to have lunch. We stumbled on a charming local restaurant with gorgeous tablecloths and no tourists. La Mule Blanche was a family affair where the wife sat in front of the restaurant with a cash box and the husband tended the bar. I almost never order duck in restaurants, preferring to grill it myself, but I figured that since I was in France, it would probably be okay. Well, it was scrumptious and memorable. This recipe is my recreation of that wonderful lunch. I added the fig jam because the sweetness perfectly complements the rich flavors of salt and rendered duck fat.

Makes 4 servings

Grilling Method: Indirect/Medium Heat

4   skin-on boneless duck breasts
2   cups very coarse sea salt (not kosher)
1   cup packed dark brown sugar
1   tablespoon coarsely ground pepper
¼   cup best-quality fig jam, preferably with whole figs or large pieces of fig
    Juice of half a lemon (about 4 teaspoons)

1. Pat the duck dry with paper towels. Score the skin by making diagonal cuts (about 5) across each breast, taking care not to cut completely through the skin. For fancier scoring, repeat the cuts in the opposite direction, so that it creates a diamond pattern. Put the breasts in a square, 8-inch disposable aluminum container. It should be deep enough to hold all 4 breasts with space in-between. Set aside. Mix the salt, sugar, and pepper and pour it over the duck. Cover and refrigerate for 4 hours or overnight.
2. When ready to cook, build a charcoal fire or preheat a gas grill. Remove the duck breasts from the pan and shake off the excess salt. Place the duck fat-side up in the center of the cooking grate over indirect medium heat, cover, and grill-roast for about 40 minutes. Turn duck over on the skin side and continue grilling until the skin is crispy and the meat is tender, about 5 to 10 more minutes. (If the skin is not crisp, move duck to an area of direct heat, skin-side down for 3 to 4 minutes to caramelize the skin.) When the skin is caramelized, return to an area of indirect heat and turn over to glaze.
3. When the duck is almost done, mix the jam with the lemon juice and brush it generously onto the skin of the duck breasts. Grill for 5 more minutes or until the fig glaze is set. Remove from the grill and let the breasts rest for 5 minutes before serving.

TIP: Contrary to popular duck cookery methods, I cook the duck breasts slowly, until they are cooked through, because I find them to be more tender and flavorful this way. If you like duck breasts served rare, alter the timing accordingly.

Crispy Duck Stuffed with Apples, Oranges, and Onions

If I had to choose just one food to grill (such torture!), it would have to be duck. In fact, I hardly ever eat it unless I grill it—that's how particular I've gotten. The reason is simple. Most chefs serve duck rare, and I don't like duck rare. In my opinion, the meat hasn't had long enough to cook to become tender and the fat hasn't had time to slowly render out, flavoring the meat and crisping the skin. I roast a whole duck until it is almost falling apart and everyone who tastes it is transfixed.

Makes 4 to 6 servings

Grilling Method: Indirect/Medium Heat
Special Equipment: V-rack roast holder

2   crisp, tart apples, such as Granny Smith, unpeeled
2   yellow onions
1   navel orange
1   whole duck, 4 to 5 pounds
1   tablespoon kosher salt

1. Cut the apples, onions, and orange into quarters. Remove the seeds from the apples and set fruit aside. Discard the giblets and organ meats from the duck. Rinse the duck with cold water and pat it dry with paper towels. Trim all loose fat from the inner cavity. You can do this step up to 24 hours in advance, storing the duck uncovered in the refrigerator. This will dry out the skin and result in crispier skin on the grilled duck.

2. Build a charcoal fire or preheat a gas grill. Just before cooking, stuff the cavity with the apples, orange, and onions. Sprinkle the duck liberally with salt and pierce the skin with a fork or paring knife in several places under the wings.

3. Place the duck, breast-side up, in a roast holder (which is placed in a drip pan for a gas grill) in the center of the cooking grate over indirect medium heat. Cover and cook 1½ to 2 hours, piercing the underside of the duck every 30 minutes to remove excess fat. When the duck juices run clear and the internal temperature is 170°F to 180°F on an instant-read thermometer, remove the duck from the grill and let it rest for 15 minutes.

4. Serve the duck warm, with the apples, orange, and onions, if desired.

Duckling with Sweet Dried Plum Glaze

Prunes are really just dried plums (and now they are officially called dried plums). Imagine the tart sweetness of plums matched with the richness of grill-roasted duck. It's delicious. I also add rum, marmalade, and lime juice to recapture the flavors of a tamarind jam glaze that I made after buying Tamarind jam in the Bahamas. If you are traveling to the Bahamas be sure to pick up a jar and use it in this recipe, omitting the dried plums.

Makes 2 to 4 servings

Grilling Method: Indirect/Medium Heat
Special Equipment: V-rack roast holder, disposable aluminum pan

1   whole duck, 4½ to 5 pounds, thawed
    Kosher salt
    Freshly ground pepper

Sweet Dried Plum Glaze
1   cup dried plums (prunes)
¼   cup apple cider vinegar
¼   cup packed brown sugar
¼   cup dark rum
3   tablespoons marmalade
1   lime, juiced
     Tabasco sauce

1. Remove any lumps of fat from the duck and sprinkle it inside and outside with salt and pepper. Place the duck on a roasting V-rack set on a disposable drip pan. Cut slits under the wings of the duck to allow the fat to render. Refrigerate,

uncovered, for up to 24 hours to dry the skin and facilitate crisping.

2. Build a charcoal fire or preheat a gas grill. Meanwhile, make the glaze: Combine the dried plums, vinegar, and sugar in a heavy saucepan and boil until reduced by half. Add the rum and marmalade. Simmer the sauce, uncovered, until thick and syrupy, about 10 minutes. Add the lime juice, salt and Tabasco to taste. Puree and set aside.

3. Place the duck in the center of the cooking grate over indirect medium heat, cover, and grill-roast for 1 hour. After the first hour, baste the duck generously with the glaze every 15 minutes for another 30 to 45 minutes, or until the glaze is golden and the duck is completely cooked through. It will read between 180°F and 200°F on a meat thermometer. Let the duck rest for 15 minutes before carving. Serve hot.

Big Bob Gibson–Style White Barbecue Sauce

Many years ago, a friend from Birmingham, Alabama, introduced me to her local white barbecue sauce. Like the mustard sauce of South Carolina, this is a sauce that hasn't traveled far—but it should. The sauce is used mostly for chicken, and I've been told that after the chickens are barbecued, they are dunked into a very large pot of Big Bob Gibson's signature white sauce. I created this version based on a bottle that was given to me; but if you go to Alabama, you should definitely pick up a souvenir of the original and have lunch or dinner at Big Bob Gibson's award-winning barbecue restaurant.

Makes 2 cups

1 cup mayonnaise
1 cup apple cider vinegar
1 lemon, juiced
1½ tablespoons freshly ground pepper
1 tablespoon sugar
½ teaspoon salt or more to taste
½ teaspoon cayenne pepper

Whisk all the ingredients together in a medium nonreactive bowl. Pour into a glass or plastic bottle. Refrigerate until ready to use, or for up to 2 weeks.

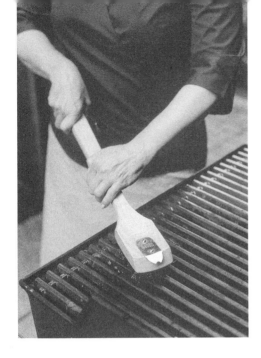

Beef

Steak 101

While there are many ways to grill beef, steak is by far the most popular and easiest cut to cook. Here's what you need to know.

Rapid-Fire Checklist

✓ Preheat grill
✓ Brush steak all over with olive oil
✓ Season with kosher salt and pepper, if desired
✓ Reduce heat to medium, choose the right cooking method
✓ Place steak on cooking grate and cover
✓ Turn once halfway through cooking time, if cooking by the Direct Method
✓ Remove steak from grill
✓ Let meat rest 5 to 20 minutes, depending on size

Tools of the Trade

• 12-inch locking chef tongs
• Instant-read thermometer
• Silicone or natural-bristle brush
• Heavy-duty oven mitt

Common Problems

• Underseasoned meat
• Overcooked meat
  ▪ steaks are too thin
  ▪ cooked too long
• Not letting meat rest

Statistically, steak is the number one favorite food to grill, hands down—for male or female, young or old. If you eat meat, you love a grilled steak. So why do outdoor cooks have such a hard time grilling this backyard classic? Maybe because we want the steak to have a crust and taste like those served at Ruth's Chris Steak House or Peter Luger's in Brooklyn. Well, those guys have two things we don't. First, they have experience; they cook steaks all day every day; they can tell whether the steak is rare or medium—and what it tastes like—just by looking at it; and they have a piece of restaurant equipment called a salamander. The salamander broils at close range (about an inch away) at a temperature of 1,800°F. A few years ago, I was on a steak mission and visited Peter Luger's to see if I could learn the secret. I was told by one of the grill cooks, who asked to remain anonymous, that the secret to their crust was that they "slathered cold butter on an almost-done steak and put it under the salamander to bubble and broil until a crust (of blackened butter and protein) was formed." I can't tell you how many times and with how many variations I tried to do this on the grill. I finally concluded that it can't be done without a salamander—I should have taken the guy's word for it!

However, I did perfect my steak-grilling skills and often use a seasoned butter to add that little extra flavor and give my steaks a steakhouse presentation. The other trick that anyone can do at home is to take the meat off the grill and to let it rest five minutes before cutting into it. The rest time allows the meat to reabsorb its natural juices, resulting in a juicier steak.

Cuts of Beef

Fresh beef has cream-colored fat and bright red meat. The USDA grades meat according to the amount of marbling that is in the meat itself. The grades are Prime, Choice, and Select. Prime beef is the most marbled, the most expensive, and the hardest to find because it is sold mostly to restaurants. Choice and Select are sold in every grocery store and meat market. Choice is the most common and a better grade of beef than Select. My advice is to buy Prime if you can find it, and don't be afraid of the extra fat; it melts and cooks out during the grilling process, basting the meat, keeping it moist and flavorful in the process. When you can't find Prime, buy your meat from the best butcher your town has and choose Choice over Select, if possible. Below are details of the basic and most popular cuts of steak (and other parts of the cow).

THE LOIN SECTION
The most tender and expensive cuts.

New York Strip or New York Steak: This flavorful and fairly expensive cut comes from the most tender part of the cow, the top loin section. It is known by more than 15 names. Among them are the Kansas City strip, strip sirloin steak, and the hotel steak. A boneless top loin steak is also sold as a shell steak. Think of the New York strip as a porterhouse or T-bone that has been stripped of the tenderloin portion.

T-Bone: This American favorite comes from the sirloin section of the loin (near the rump). It is named for its distinguishing T-shaped bone. It is similar to a porterhouse except that it doesn't have as much tenderloin in it.

Porterhouse: Steakhouses in our country have perpetuated the porterhouse as the king of steaks. And it is the best choice for two people who want to share a steak but have different tastes. The porterhouse has parts of two muscles separated by the bone; the flavorful top loin, where the New York strip comes from, and the soft buttery tenderloin.

Sirloin: The sirloin is near the rump so the meat is a little tougher (chewier) than cuts from the loin (New York strip) or the rib (rib-eye). There are several different sirloin cuts, named for the shape of the hip bone that is left in them when cut (pin bone, flat bone, round bone, wedge bone). There is a boneless sirloin steak that is referred to as a rump steak or a Boston butt steak.

Tenderloin: The loin yields the most tender and expensive cuts of beef. The priciest and choicest part is the tenderloin, which is so tender that is it soft and extremely lean. Cuts from the loin require very little to make them taste great. Steak aficionados consider it sacrilege to grill tenderloin beyond medium-rare.

Filet Mignon: Individual steaks cut from the whole tenderloin; most butchers refer to all the pieces cut from the tenderloin as filet mignon, but technically only the cuts at the small end of the tenderloin are filet mignon.

Veal Chop: Basically the real version of beef steak, it comes from the loin or rib section of a young cow. It is preferable to purchase veal chops with the bone in. Veal is leaner and more delicate than beef.

RIB
Tender, well marbled, juicy, and flavorful.

Rib-Eye: The rib-eye steak is cut from a rib-eye roast and is also known as Delmonico. It comes from the rib end of the same muscle that gives us the top loin and sirloin cuts. The rib-eye is juicy and tender and very well marbled. The name is attributed to the eye-shaped pocket of fat that runs all the way through the rib roast. Because of the high concentration of fat (read: flavor), many people prefer a rib-eye over all other steaks. The whole roast can be grill-roasted as a boneless version of a rib roast or cut into steaks and quickly grilled. Most of these steaks are boneless, but you can ask your butcher to leave the bone in. Niman Ranch sells a bone-in rib-eye under the name Cowboy Steak, and if you can get it for the rib-eye recipe on page 66, I highly recommend it.

BREAST AND FLANK
Extremely flavorful, grainy or tougher texture, less expensive.

Flank Steak: A lean, flat cut that is extremely flavorful and fairly tender. The first London Broil recipes in the 1930s called for cooking a flank steak. Overcooking will make it tough, so grill to medium-rare, let it rest at least five minutes, and slice thinly against the grain at a 45-degree angle.

London Broil: Contrary to popular opinion, London broil refers to a cooking method and is not a cut of meat. Most London broil recipes marinate and grill either a flank steak or a top round steak to medium-rare and cut it across the grain.

Skirt Steak: The skirt steak comes from the breast and flank of the cow. This is the same section that brisket and short ribs come from. It is a also known as a Philadelphia steak and is mostly used for fajita meat. It looks like a thick-grained flank steak and is well marbled, making it a very juicy steak. Like a flank steak, take care not to overcook it, and slice it against the grain for the most tender strips.

Hanger Steak: This cut comes from the part that hangs (thus the name) between the last rib and the loin. It is often ground into hamburger, or the butcher takes it home because it makes a first-rate steak.

CHUCK
Flavorful and economical but tougher and fattier; most of these cuts are best cooked by braising or a combination of searing and braising, such as the Pot Roast with Red Zinfandel and Extra Veggies on page 76.

Flat Iron: Also known as the top blade steak, a petit steak, or a top chuck steak. This cut is tender enough to grill and is very flavorful and economical. It may have a little gristle attached; as long as you don't mind cutting around it, it is a great choice. Like the skirt and the flank steaks, it can be marinated and used for fajita meat as well.

Veal Scaloppine: Veal leg cutlets, pounded thinly, are usually sold as scaloppine. However, any boneless piece of veal can be pounded thinly and used.

Size Matters: Thick Steak Rules
It goes without saying that the thicker the steak, the longer it will take to cook. A standard 1-inch-thick steak will take an average of 5 minutes per side for medium rare. Less time if you like it rare and longer if you like it cooked more. Because I think that a 1¼-inch steak is best suited to grilling, that is the size that I call for in the recipes. If you choose a smaller steak, reduce the cooking time. Remember, the fun of grilling is that it is much more an art than an exact science and the variables of heat, size of food, etc., all affect the time it takes to cook. Experience is the only thing that will make you a master griller, and then you will have created your own timetable for perfectly grilled steak.

Searing Secret
Everytime I teach a class on grilling steaks or even a whole tenderloin, my students look at me with saucer-wide eyes as I wrap the fresh beef mummy-style in paper towels and let it sit for 5 to 10 minutes. But there's a reason: What I'm doing with the towels is removing the excess moisture from the surface of the meat, the surface will sear more easily, resulting in great grill marks.

On the Fire: Direct, Indirect, or Combo
I usually grill really thick steaks because I prefer a deeply caramelized exterior and a rare center, and this

is much easier to accomplish with a thicker steak. The best method in this case is a combination of the Direct and Indirect Methods (the Combo Method). This way of grilling steaks borrows a page from all the top restaurant chefs who sear their meat and then finish it in the oven. You can replicate this technique perfectly on the grill by searing the steaks on both sides, directly over the heat, and then moving the steak to the cooler, Indirect Heat to finish the cooking.

If your steak is 1-inch thick or less, grill it directly over the heat for about 5 minutes per side, depending on how rare you like your meat (see Testing for Doneness below). The smaller the steak, the less time it will need to rest, but always let it rest at least 5 minutes to reabsorb all the natural juices. And, unless you are making crosshatch marks, turn the steak only once halfway through the total cooking time.

Crosshatch Marks

Steaks look steakhouse perfect with crosshatch marks, and they are easier to achieve than they look. Just before turning the steaks, rotate them ¼ turn to the right and grill for about 2 minutes. If cooking by the Combo Method, sear for 2 minutes, rotate ¼ turn for another 2 minutes, turn over and repeat, then move to indirect heat to finish cooking. To make sure you don't have 3 sets of marks, carefully place your steaks in the same position or turn them ¼ turn when you move them to Indirect Heat, then the marks will be seared in during the final cooking time.

Testing for Doneness: A-OK Technique

If you read a lot of cookbooks or watch a lot of cooking shows, you've probably seen someone make a fist to show you how to test the doneness of meat with your finger. When I was first taught this trick, I understood where we were going, but I thought it was too difficult to get other people to see the point. So I took the same principle and created my "A-OK" tip.

GETTING THAT STEAKHOUSE CRUST

There are a lot of spice rub products on the market that promise to give a grilled steak that steakhouse crust, but I have never had any luck with them. I've found that the best way to mimic that steakhouse crust at home is to follow these steps.

1. While the steak is grilling, move your oven rack to the highest position and preheat your broiler and a broiler pan to as high a temperature as it will go.

2. Remove the steak from the grill a few minutes before you think it is done. Spread a layer of (1 to 2 tablespoons) soft but not melted butter on the top of the steak.

3. Place the steak under the broiler for about 2 minutes or until the butter broils and almost burns.

4. Remove the steak, let it sit for about 1 minute, turn over, and butter and broil the other side of the steak. Remove from the oven, turn off the broiler, and let the steak rest at least 5 minutes. Serve hot.

I only recommend this with a steak that is 1½ to 2 inches thick, otherwise, it is almost impossible not to overcook. You can also broil only one side, just make sure you plate the steak with the broiled side facing up, so guests don't know you didn't do both sides!

NOTE: Use very good oven mitts, as the oven will be very hot. You have to broil the butter and remove the steak from the oven very fast to accomplish the crust without burning the steak.

1. Everyone knows the OK sign, where thumb and forefinger make a circle. Start there, make an OK sign with the right hand, then hold it.

2. Feel the meaty part of the palm just under the thumb with your other forefinger—that is the equivalent of raw meat.

3. Next, move your right index finger to the thumb and feel with the other forefinger how the palm has gotten a little tighter—that is equivalent of rare meat.

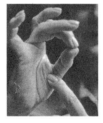

4. Next, move your right ring finger to the thumb and feel how the palm tightens again—that is the equivalent of medium meat.

5. Finally, move your right pinkie finger to the thumb and touch the palm under the thumb again; it should be really tight by this time and that is what well-done meat feels like when you poke it with your finger.

This test takes a while to master. While you are still getting the hang of it, make the OK sign that is the temperature you like your steaks. For example, I like mine rare, so I'd put my index finger on the thumb to check on the feel of the steak when it is rare. Now, alternate between poking your palm and poking the meat until you memorize how the tension feels on the meat. But the proof is in the eating. Take your steak off the grill, let it rest, and cut into it—were you right?

NOTE: All end temperatures cited in the book are USDA recommended, but if you like meat rarer, take it off the heat sooner.

Let the Beef Take a Break

Don't touch steaks, once cooked, for 5 minutes and you will be rewarded. For most steaks this is enough time to let all the juices re-distribute and this alone will result in a juicier more tender steak. (Refer to chart at right for larger pieces of meat.) Here's the short version of the science behind letting your meat rest: As the meat cooks and comes to temperature, especially over a high heat, all the juices are propelled toward the exterior. When the meat is taken off the fire, it relaxes as it cools and the meat fibers reabsorb the juices, making each piece juicy. If you don't wait before you cut in, you'll have all those juices pooling around your plate or carving board and your beef will be dry and gray instead of rosy.

Approximate **BEEF** *Cooking Times* (°F)

TYPE OF BEEF	THICKNESS OR WEIGHT	DEGREE OF DONENESS	GRILLING METHOD	GRILLING TIME	INTERNAL TEMP.	REST TIME
Beef kabobs	1 to 1½ pounds	Medium	Direct Medium	6 to 7 minutes/side	160°	5 minutes
Brisket	3 to 4 pounds	Medium	Indirect Medium	2 to 3 hours	160°	15 minutes
Rib roast, bone-in (2 ribs)	4 to 6 pounds	Medium-rare Medium Well done	Indirect Medium	23 to 25 minutes/pound 27 to 30 minutes/pound 32 to 34 minutes/pound	145° 160° 170°	15 minutes 15 minutes 15 minutes
Rib roast, boneless, rolled	4 to 6 pounds	Medium-rare Medium Well done	Indirect Medium	28 to 32 minutes/pound 32 to 38 minutes/pound 37 to 42 minutes/pound	145° 160° 170°	15 minutes 15 minutes 15 minutes
Round or rump roast	2½ to 4 pounds	Medium-rare Medium	Indirect Medium	30 to 35 minutes/pound 35 to 40 minutes/pound	145° 160°	10 to 15 minutes 10 to 15 minutes
Short ribs	4 inches long and 2 inches thick	Well done	Indirect Medium	6 to 7 minutes/side, then braised	170°	5 to 10 minutes
Steaks, boneless: New York strip, filet mignon	¾ inch thick	Medium-rare Medium	Direct Combo Medium	4 to 5 minutes/side 6 to 7 minutes/side	145° 160°	5 minutes 5 minutes
Steaks, bone-in: rib-eye, porterhouse, T-bone, tenderloin	¾ to 2 inches thick	Medium-rare	Direct, Indirect, or Combo Medium	4 to 5 minutes/side for ¾ inches; 18 to 25 minutes for 2 inches	145°	5 to 10 minutes
Steaks, other: flank, flat iron, skirt, (London broil), tri-tip	1½ to 2 pounds	Medium-rare	Direct or Combo Medium	4 to 6 minutes/side	145°	5 to 10 minutes
Tenderloin, whole	4 to 6 pounds	Medium-rare	Combo Medium	45 to 60 minutes	145°	10 to 15 minutes
Tenderloin, half	2 to 3 pounds	Medium		35 to 45 minutes	160°	10 minutes
Veal chops	1½ to 2 inches thick	Medium-rare	Combo Medium	18 to 25 minutes	145°	5 to 10 minutes
Veal cutlets	½ inch thick	Medium	Direct Medium	2 to 3 minutes/side	160°	5 minutes

All internal temperatures are based on USDA recommended values, using an instant-read thermometer.
Times and temperatures in the chart are guidelines. Specific recipes may call for variations.

Steak 101

Most people think steak should be cooked over direct high heat but that often results in overcooked burned steaks. In this foolproof steak recipe, I grill the steaks over an indirect heat. This virtually prevents flare-ups and burned steaks. Just make sure you preheat the grill with all burners on high so the cooking grates are hot enough to sear the meat as soon as you put it on the grill. Once you get the hang of it, try searing over direct heat and then finishing the steak over indirect heat. This combo method is my favorite way to grill steaks and the most common way that restaurant chefs prepare steaks.

Makes 4 servings

Grilling Method: Indirect/Medium

4	New York strip steaks or other favorite steak, about 1½ inches thick and ¾ pound each
	Olive oil
	Kosher salt
	Freshly ground pepper, to taste
2	tablespoons softened unsalted butter, optional
	Chopped fresh parsley, optional

1. Allow meat to come to room temperature 20 to 30 minutes before grilling.
2. Build a charcoal fire or preheat a gas grill.
3. Just before grilling, brush both sides of the steaks with oil and season with the salt and pepper.
4. Place the steaks on the cooking grate over indirect medium heat, cover, and cook for about 5 minutes or until well marked. Turn the steaks over and continue cooking for 7 to 10 more minutes for medium-rare. Use the A-OK test (see page 57) or an instant-read thermometer to determine if the steaks are done to your liking. They will also continue to cook a little as they rest.
5. Remove the steaks from the grill to a platter or to dinner plates and allow them to rest at least 5 minutes but no longer than 10 minutes before serving. Top the steaks with ½ tablespoon of butter and a sprinkle of parsley, if desired.

Classic Steakhouse New York Strip

This is a classic restaurant steak preparation. I call for New York strips because that is my favorite cut of steak, but this recipe will work well with any cut. I am one of those people who likes a flavorful steak with a little "chew," and a New York strip is a little chewier than a tenderloin or a rib-eye. This rub-enhanced steak is the "kicked-up" version of a basic grilled steak. When you make the rub, consider doubling or tripling it. It is a great flavor addition for any cut of beef and keeps for months in an airtight container. That way, this recipe is reduced to: oil, sprinkle, and grill! A big bonus when you're short on time.

Makes 4 servings

Grilling Method: Direct/Medium-High Heat

Steakhouse Rub

1	tablespoon whole black peppercorns, toasted
¼	teaspoon dried rosemary
1	tablespoon kosher salt or coarse sea salt
1	teaspoon dry mustard
½	teaspoon granulated garlic
4	New York strip steaks, about 1¼ inches thick and ¾ pound each
	Olive oil

1. Coarsely grind the peppercorns in a spice (coffee) grinder. Add the rosemary, and grind again. Put the pepper and rosemary mixture in a bowl and mix in the salt, mustard, and garlic. Set aside.
2. Build a charcoal fire or preheat a gas grill.
3. Pat the meat dry with paper towels and allow it to come to room temperature about 20 to 30 minutes before grilling.
4. Brush lightly with olive oil. Sprinkle the steakhouse rub evenly and lightly on both sides of the steak.
5. Place the meat on the cooking grate over direct high heat. Cover and grill 10 to 12 minutes, turning once halfway through the cooking time for medium-rare. Use the A-OK method (see page 57) or an instant-read thermometer to make sure the steak is done to your liking.

6. Remove the meat from the grill and place it on a clean platter. Let the steaks rest for 5 minutes before serving.

NOTE: Too much rub will overseason the meat.

Steakhouse-Style Cookout with à la Carte Sauces

I love hosting dinner parties because everyone always has more fun at someone's home than at a restaurant. This recipe celebrates the restaurant renaissance of steaks being served tableside with luxurious toppings or sauces. Try this build-your-own steak buffet by offering at least three of the options at your next party, and I promise you will be the talk of the town! Most of the toppings and sauces can be prepared in advance and brought to room temperature just before serving. Give everyone a plate with a steak and let them loose to customize their own meal. (And if these aren't enough options, try the Chimichurri Sauce on page 71, or any of the barbecue sauces in this book.)

Makes 4 servings

Grilling Method: Indirect/Medium Heat

4   New York strip steaks, about 1½ inches thick and ¾ pound each
    Olive oil
1   teaspoon kosher salt
1   teaspoon whole black peppercorns, coarsely ground

1. Build a charcoal fire or preheat a gas grill. Pat the meat dry with paper towels and allow it to come to room temperature about 20 to 30 minutes before grilling.
2. Just before grilling, brush both sides of the steaks with oil. Mix the salt and pepper together, and season the meat on both sides with the mixture.
3. Place the steaks on the cooking grate over indirect medium heat, cover, and grill for about 5 minutes. Turn the steaks and continue cooking for 7 to 10 more minutes for medium-rare. Remove the

steaks from the grill and place them on a clean platter. Allow the steaks to rest at least 5 minutes but no longer than 10 minutes before serving them with a variety of sauces.

TIP: Store sauces in glass mason jars. The glass won't react or absorb the flavors, they are easy to wash, and they fit easily in the refrigerator. Best yet, they are much better looking than those plastic containers we all use, and you can even serve from them!

Blue Cheese Vinaigrette
Makes 1 cup

⅓   cup white wine vinegar
1   teaspoon heavy whipping cream, at room temperature
⅔   cup olive oil or canola oil
¼   cup crumbled blue cheese
    Fine-grain sea salt
    Freshly ground pepper, optional

1. Whisk the vinegar and cream in a medium bowl. Slowly add the oil a little at a time, whisking until well incorporated (emulsified). Continue until all the oil is used.
2. Stir in the blue cheese and mix well. Season to taste with salt and pepper, if desired. This can be made up to 2 days in advance and stored in a glass jar in the refrigerator. Shake before serving.

EXPERT STEAK GRILLING

All the steak recipes in this book have been written with the simplest method in mind. However, the more you grill steaks, the more it's likely that you will gravitate to the Combo Method, which I think results in the best texture and flavor. See On the Fire, page 56.

Anchovy-Caper Sauce

The anchovies and capers should provide enough salt; but if you want to add more, season to taste with a fine grain sea salt.

Makes 1 cup

6 anchovy fillets, drained and finely minced
4 cloves garlic, finely minced
1 tablespoon capers, drained and coarsely chopped
⅔ cup extra-virgin olive oil
   Fine-grain sea salt, to taste (optional)

Combine the anchovies, garlic, and capers in a small bowl or a food processor. Slowly whisk in the olive oil or add it with the machine running. This can be made up to 2 days in advance and stored in a glass jar in the refrigerator. Shake before serving.

Saffron Aioli

Makes 2½ cups

6 large cloves garlic, roughly chopped (about ¼ cup)
1 large lemon, zested and juiced
¼ teaspoon saffron threads, crumbled and dissolved in a little lemon juice
1 heaping tablespoon Dijon mustard
1 whole egg
1 egg yolk
½ cups vegetable oil, plus a little extra if needed
1 cup best-quality extra-virgin olive oil
½ teaspoon kosher salt

1. In a food processor fitted with the steel blade, combine the garlic, lemon juice, and saffron and pulse until the garlic is pureed and the saffron is dissolved (about 15 seconds). Add the mustard and pulse again until combined.

Add the egg, egg yolk, and lemon zest and process for 10 seconds (if you are concerned about the raw eggs, use pasteurized eggs). Very slowly add the oil in a trickle, as the machine is running, until the sauce is thick and well combined (emulsified). As the aioli becomes thicker, the machine sounds more like a purr than a whirr, and you will know it is done. If you like a thicker texture, add a little more oil; if you like your sauce thinner, stop at the 2½ cups.

2. Add the salt and process until well combined. Taste and refrigerate until needed. This can be made up to 2 weeks in advance and stored in a glass jar in the refrigerator.

TIP: If you don't like saffron, omit it and you'll have classic Provençal aioli (garlic mayonnaise).

Mixed Herb Butter

Makes ½ cup

½ cup (1 stick) unsalted butter, softened
2 teaspoons minced fresh parsley
2 teaspoons granulated garlic
2 teaspoons mixed dried herbs such as tarragon, basil, rosemary, thyme etc.
   Fine-grain sea salt
   Freshly ground pepper

1. Combine the butter, parsley, garlic, and dried herbs in a small bowl. Mix together, mashing with the back of a fork to make sure all the ingredients are incorporated. Season to taste with salt and pepper, and mix well.
2. Meanwhile, cut a piece of plastic wrap about 6 inches long and spread it out flat. Spoon the soft butter mixture onto the plastic wrap and wrap it around the butter. Roll to make into a smooth log. Twist the ends to close them and refrigerate it at least 2 hours and up to 2 weeks, until ready to serve.

Dijon Mustard Butter
Makes ¾ cup

½ cup (1 stick) unsalted butter, softened
⅓ cup strong Dijon mustard
2 teaspoons Worcestershire sauce
Fine-grain sea salt
Freshly ground pepper

1. Combine the butter, mustard, and Worcestershire sauce in a small bowl. Mix together, mashing with the back of a fork to make sure all the ingredients are incorporated. Season to taste with salt and pepper, and mix well. Take care not to oversalt, the mustard and the Worcestershire will supply the salt notes.
2. Meanwhile, cut a piece of plastic wrap about 6 inches long and spread it out flat. Spoon the soft butter mixture onto the plastic wrap and wrap it around the butter. Roll to make into a smooth log. Twist the ends to close them and refrigerate it at least 2 hours and up to 2 weeks, until ready to serve.

Blue Cheese and Pecan Butter
Makes 1 cup

½ cup (1 stick) unsalted butter, softened
⅓ cup Gorgonzola or Roquefort cheese, softened
2 tablespoons finely chopped pecans
Freshly ground pepper, optional

1. Combine the butter, cheese, and pecans in a small bowl. Mix together, mashing with the back of a fork to make sure all the ingredients are incorporated. Season to taste with pepper if desired and mix well.
2. Meanwhile, cut a piece of plastic wrap about 6 inches long and spread it out flat. Spoon the soft butter mixture onto the plastic wrap and

wrap it around the butter. Roll to make into a smooth log. Twist the ends to close them and refrigerate it at least 2 hours and up to 2 weeks, until ready to serve.

Grilled Bacon and Onions
This classic accompaniment to grilled calf's liver is even better with steaks.

Makes 4 to 6 servings

1 pound best-quality, lean, thick-cut bacon, divided
2 large sweet onions, thinly sliced in rings
Kosher salt
1 spring fresh thyme

1. Build a charcoal fire or preheat a gas grill. Separate the slices of bacon. Chop 2 slices of bacon, put them in a large sauté pan over medium heat, and cook slowly to render all the fat and crisp the bacon; make sure not to burn it. When the bacon is browned, transfer it to paper towels to drain.
2. Add the onions and a sprinkle of salt to the pan and cook, stirring occasionally, until all of the onions are golden brown, about 15 minutes. Add the thyme, then take the pan off the heat.
3. Meanwhile, grill the remaining slices of bacon by placing them strip by strip across the cooking grates over direct low heat. Grill for 5 minutes on each side. When golden crisp, remove the bacon from the grill and put it on a clean platter lined with paper towels.
4. Crumble half of the grilled bacon and add it and the reserved fried bacon to the onions. Gently reheat the mixture. When warm, put it on a platter garnished with the remaining grilled strips of bacon. Store covered in the refrigerator for 1 day and reheat gently before serving.

Sautéed Mushrooms with Truffle Oil
Makes 4 to 6 servings

- 2 tablespoons unsalted butter
- 1 tablespoon olive oil
  Kosher salt
- 1 pound mushrooms, cleaned and sliced
- 2 to 3 teaspoons white or black truffle oil
- 1 tablespoon minced fresh parsley

1. Heat the butter and oil in a large sauté pan. Add about 1 teaspoon salt and the mushrooms. Turn the heat to high and sauté, stirring frequently to prevent burning. Continue cooking until the mushrooms are well browned and the liquid has evaporated. Turn off the heat.
2. Drizzle the mushrooms with the truffle oil and sprinkle with the parsley. Mix well and taste to adjust the seasonings. Serve warm. Store covered in the refrigerator for 1 day and reheat gently before serving. If making in advance and reheating, add all ingredients except the parsley.

Tuscan Steak with White Anchovy and Truffle Butter

This preparation of steak is the traditional bistecca alla Fiorentina *for which Tuscany is so famous. One of the main reasons that such a simple preparation tastes so great—besides the fact that you are in Italy, drinking red wine and eating great food—is that the Chianini beef they raise and serve is exceptional. With such great raw ingredients, you don't need a lot of flavor enhancers. I prefer a porterhouse, but any steak will work as long as it is about two inches thick. In this recipe, white anchovies and a hint of truffles flavor a compound butter that dresses up the basic Tuscan-style steak.*

Makes 4 servings

Grilling Method: Direct/Medium Heat

- 2 T-bone or porterhouse steaks, about 2 inches thick and 1½ to 2 pounds each
- 2 tablespoons extra-virgin olive oil, preferably Tuscan
  Freshly ground pepper
  Kosher or sea salt
  White Anchovy and Truffle Butter (below)

1. Pat the steaks dry with paper towels. Place the steaks on a platter and brush them generously on both sides with the olive oil. Let stand at room temperature for 45 minutes to 1 hour.
2. Build a charcoal fire or preheat a gas grill.
3. Season steaks on both sides with salt and pepper just before grilling.
4. Place the steaks in the center of the cooking grate over direct medium heat. Cover and grill for about 10 minutes per side for rare (the Tuscan preference) or longer to desired doneness.
5. Let the steak rest for 5 to 10 minutes, and then carve it away from the bone into individual portions. Serve hot, topped with a shaving of the White Anchovy and Truffle Butter. (To "shave" butter: Use a vegetable peeler to cut across the length of the cold log of butter.)

White Anchovy and Truffle Butter
This recipe makes more than you'll need for four people, but it keeps for weeks in the refrigerator and is terrific in scrambled eggs on Sunday morning.

Makes 1 cup

- 2 white or regular anchovies in oil
- 1 to 2 teaspoons white truffle oil
- 1 cup (2 sticks) unsalted butter, softened
  Sea salt
- 2 teaspoons minced fresh parsley

1. In a shallow, nonreactive bowl, mash the anchovies with the back of a fork until they resemble a paste. Add 1 teaspoon of the truffle oil and mix with the fork. Work this paste into the butter. Taste and adjust the amount of truffle oil to suit your taste. The butter should be salted enough by the anchovies. If not, add sea salt or another mashed anchovy to the butter until it tastes right. Add the minced parsley.

2. Meanwhile, cut a piece of plastic wrap about 6 inches long and spread it out flat. Spoon the soft butter mixture onto the plastic wrap and wrap it around the butter. Roll to make into a smooth log. Twist the ends to close them and refrigerate it at least 2 hours and up to 2 weeks, until ready to serve.

3. Cut into coin-size pieces or shave with a vegetable peeler directly onto hot or warm food to season.

Rock-Star Skirt Steak with Jicama–Orange Salad

Kirsten West was born in Bavaria, but her heart is Mexican through and through. Skirt steak with Jicama–Orange Salad was her most requested dish during her 15 years as a caterer and personal chef in Los Angeles. Her high-profile clientele included Mick Jagger and other well-traveled palates. The richness of the grilled skirt steak is balanced by the refreshing and crunchy salad and the very tangy fuschia-colored pickled onions for a meal that spells S-A-T-I-S-F-A-C-T-I-O-N.

Makes 4 to 6 servings

Grilling Method: Direct/Medium-High Heat

Pickled Red Onions
1   large red onion, sliced in rings about ¹⁄₈ inch thick
¹⁄₄   teaspoon cumin seeds
¹⁄₄   cup apple cider vinegar
2   limes, juiced
2   cloves garlic, cut in half
¹⁄₄   teaspoon kosher salt

Jicama–Orange Salad
1¹⁄₂ to 2 pound jicama (the size of a small grapefruit)
3   navel oranges
2   limes, juiced
3 to 4 sprigs fresh cilantro
    Cayenne pepper, optional
2   skirt steaks, about 1 pound each
    Kosher salt
    Olive oil

1. Make the onions: Put the onion rings in a heavy-bottomed saucepan. Cover with salted water and bring to a boil for 1 minute. Immediately remove the parboiled onions from the heat and drain the water from the saucepan.

2. Coarsely grind the cumin in a mortar or spice grinder. Add it to the saucepan along with the remaining ingredients. Pour in enough water to just cover the onions, bring to a boil over medium heat, and boil for 3 minutes, until the onions are crisp-tender. Remove from the heat and pour into a small nonreactive bowl. Let stand for 3 hours to allow the flavors to combine. Drain the liquid off and use the onions immediately or refrigerate for up to 2 weeks.

3. Meanwhile make the salad: Peel the jicama with a very sharp vegetable peeler or a knife. (The skin is too thick for a standard potato peeler.) To do this, you cut off a slice on the top and bottom with a knife, set it cut-side down on your cutting board, and cut of the rest of the peel like you would cut off the peel of an orange. Using the tip of your knife works best.

4. Cut the peeled jicama into ¹⁄₄- to ¹⁄₂-inch slices, and then cut them into sticks like french fries. If the jicama is very wide, cut the sticks in half.

5. Peel the oranges in the same manner as the jicama. Next, hold each peeled orange in a cupped hand over a bowl to catch the juices. Cut each orange section from between the membranes and transfer them to a plate. When you have removed all of the sections from each orange, give the left-over membranes a squeeze with your hand to collect as much of the juices as possible.

6. Arrange the jicama and orange wedges on a platter or on individual plates, pour the orange and lime juices over them, garnish with the cilantro leaves, lime wedges, and sprinkle with cayenne, if desired.

7. Build a charcoal fire or preheat a gas grill. Pat the steaks dry with paper towels. Brush them with olive oil

8. Sprinkle the steaks on one side with kosher salt, just before placing that side on the grill over direct medium-high heat. Cover and grill for 8 to 10 minutes for medium-rare, turning once halfway through the cooking time. Before turning the meat over, sprinkle the top side with the salt. (Salting each side just before it will be directly in contact with the grill is Kirsten's secret to success; but you can salt both sides before cooking, if you prefer.)

9. Remove the steaks from the grill and place them on a clean platter. Let the meat rest for 5 minutes before slicing it into serving pieces or strips. Serve it with the jicama-orange salad and the pickled onions.

TIP: When selecting a jicama, it should be firm and its skin should be without blemishes and look shiny— very similar to the skin of fresh ginger. A good jicama should be juicy and very crunchy when you bite into a piece of it; if it is dry or soft and mealy with brown spots, discard it.

Three Chile–Rubbed Rib-Eye with Guacamole and Mashed Black Beans

One of my favorite dishes at Frontera Grill in Chicago is carne asada. *This Mexican steak cookout is served with guacamole, mashed black beans, and fried plantains. I've taken it one step further and created a three-chile rub for the rib-eye. The heat of the rub is perfectly balanced by the rich cooling guacamole. Don't be tempted to use store-bought guacamole; try the quick and easy recipe from scratch—it's worth it.*

Makes 4 to 6 servings

Grilling Method: Direct/Medium Heat

Rib-Eye Rub

1 tablespoon New Mexican (or any other) chile powder

1 tablespoon chipotle chili powder or 1 additional tablespoon New Mexican chili powder

1 tablespoon sugar

$\frac{1}{2}$ tablespoon smoked paprika

$\frac{1}{2}$ tablespoon white pepper

1 teaspoon freshly ground pepper

4 prime cut bone-in rib-eye steaks, about $1\frac{1}{2}$ inches thick and 1 pound each, such as Niman Ranch Cowboy Steaks (Sources, pages 343–345)
Kosher salt
1-2-3 Tomatillo Salsa Guacamole (below)
Mashed Black Beans (page 67)

1. Make the rub: In a medium bowl, combine the chile powders, sugar, paprika, and peppers.

2. Pat the meat dry with paper towels. Generously coat the meat with the rub mixture. Cover the steaks with waxed paper or plastic wrap, and let them sit at room temperature for 30 minutes.

3. Build a charcoal fire or preheat a gas grill.

4. Season the steaks just before cooking by sprinkling each side with a generous pinch of salt.

5. Place the steaks on the cooking grate over direct medium heat. Cover and grill the steaks 5 to 6 minutes and turn over. Continue cooking for 6 to 7 more minutes for medium-rare. Remove from the grill, and let the steaks rest for 5 minutes before serving. Slice and serve with the guacamole and black beans.

1-2-3 Tomatillo Salsa Guacamole

I first made this recipe for a very large event at The Culinary Institute of America Worlds of Flavor conference. Daunted by the task of making guacamole for 500, my friends at Frontera Foods suggested that I try their easy recipe, made with tomatilla salsa. Well, it was so good that it was the hit of the event, and I couldn't stop eating it myself! Since I tried this recipe, I've never made guacamole any other way.

Makes 2 cups

3 ripe Hass avocados
1 cup store-bought tomatillo salsa, preferably Frontera Foods brand
¼ cup chopped fresh cilantro
Kosher salt

Cut the avocados in half, scoop the soft flesh into a bowl, and mash it. Stir in the tomatillo salsa. Stir in the cilantro; season to taste with salt. Refrigerate in an airtight container for up to 5 hours. Serve immediately.

Mashed Black Beans
Makes 4 to 6 servings

Olive oil
1 small white onion, chopped
4 cloves garlic, finely chopped
1 teaspoon ground cumin
2 15-ounce cans black beans, drained and rinsed
½ cup Mexican or domestic beer
1 lime, zested and juiced
Kosher salt
Freshly ground pepper
⅛ to ¼ cup chopped fresh cilantro
2 tablespoons sour cream, optional

1. Heat about 2 tablespoons of oil in a large, heavy saucepan over medium-high heat. Add the onion, garlic, and cumin. Sauté until the onions begin to brown, about 10 minutes.
2. Add the beans and beer to the sautéed vegetables and cook for 10 minutes, stirring occasionally. Coarsely mash the beans with the back of a spoon. Bring to a low boil and continue boiling, stirring frequently, until the mixture thickens, about 10 minutes. Remove from heat. Season to taste with the lime juice, salt, and pepper. Transfer the mixture to a bowl. Sprinkle with the lime zest, cilantro, and a dollop of sour cream, if desired. Serve immediately.

Flat-Iron Steak with Pernod Butter and Grilled Frites

My brother-in-law Karl is a steak frites aficionado. Together we've conducted serious (albeit pleasurable) research to find a cut of beef that is most similar to the steak used in France for this very simple and satisfying entrée. I recently discovered a new cut called the flat iron. The flat iron is a thin and flat steak (thus part of the name) that has a rich succulent flavor. It was introduced to the market under this name a few years ago, but it was previously sold as a petit steak or a top blade steak. I love grilling it because it cooks fast. With the addition of a compound butter spiked with Pernod, a little Dijon mustard, parsley, and some frites, it's like having a Paris bistro in your own backyard.

Makes 4 servings

Grilling Method: Direct/Medium High Heat

Pernod Butter
½ cup (1 stick) unsalted butter, softened
1 small shallot, minced
3 sprigs fresh tarragon, chopped or ½ teaspoon dried tarragon
2 teaspoons Pernod or Ricard (pastis)
Fine-grain sea salt
White pepper

4 flat-iron steaks or other favorite steaks, about 1 inch thick and ¾ pound each
Olive oil
Kosher salt
Freshly ground pepper, optional
Chopped fresh parsley

1. Make the Pernod butter: Put the butter, shallot, and tarragon in a small bowl. Mix together, mashing with the back of a fork to make sure all the ingredients are incorporated. Add the Pernod and mix again. When the texture is smooth, season to taste with salt and pepper and set aside.

2. Meanwhile, cut a piece of plastic wrap about 6 inches long and spread it out flat. Spoon the soft butter mixture onto the plastic wrap and wrap it around the butter. Roll to make into a smooth log. Twist the ends to close them and refrigerate it for at least 2 hours and up to 2 weeks, until ready to serve.

3. Pat the steaks dry with paper towels.

4. Lightly brush both sides of the steaks with olive oil and season with the salt and pepper, pressing the spices lightly into the meat. Allow to stand at room temperature for 10 minutes before grilling.

5. Build a charcoal fire or preheat a gas grill.

6. Place the steaks on the cooking grate over direct medium-high heat for 8 to 10 minutes or until medium-rare, turning once halfway through grilling time. Use the A-OK method or an instant-read thermometer to make sure the meat is done to your liking.

7. Remove the steaks from the grill and place them on a clean platter. Allow them to rest for 5 minutes. Cut the cold Pernod butter into 4 generous slices. Serve the steaks warm with the butter on top and grilled frites on the side. For a restaurant touch, garnish with chopped parsley, if desired.

Grilled Frites with Dijon Mustard
Makes 4 servings

Grilling Method: Direct/Medium-Low Heat

3 large baking potatoes, scrubbed
   Olive oil
   Fine-grain sea salt
   Freshly ground pepper
   Strong Dijon mustard, such as Amora or
     Maille

1. Build a charcoal fire or preheat a gas grill.

2. Leaving the skins on, cut the potatoes to resemble thick-cut french fries (about ½ inch thick). Soak them in a large bowl of ice water for 15 minutes. Drain the potatoes and pat them dry with paper towels. Put them in a resealable plastic bag and drizzle with just enough oil to coat all surfaces of the potatoes.

Seal the bag and massage the contents to ensure even coating. Transfer the potatoes from the bag to a large bowl and sprinkle with salt and pepper.

3. Place the fries across the cooking grates so they won't fall through. Cover and grill over direct medium-low heat for 12 to 16 minutes, turning occasionally to mark both sides. When done, you should have grill marks on all sides of the potatoes, and they should be tender on the inside. If the potatoes are marked before they are tender, move them to the warming rack or another place of indirect heat to finish cooking without burning. Serve immediately with strong Dijon mustard as a dipping sauce.

TIP: The flat-iron steak is cut from the chuck. Its official name is "shoulder top blade steak." It is cut in a way that eliminates the connective tissue that normally runs through the center; each half resembles a flank steak in shape. These pieces are then cut crosswise into individual steaks.

Gaucho Jack's Legendary Argentinean Steak

My culinary compatriot Bob Blumer comes by his sense of food adventure honestly. His great-uncle was a gaucho in Argentina and passed his recipe for South American beef on to Bob's father, Jack Blumer. Jack told me the story of his family's gaucho steak sauce, which he used to manufacture and sell in Canada and the United States. The gauchos herded cattle across the country, and would kill one of the steers every few days to cook and eat. To flavor the meat, they would baste it with a simple sauce as the meat cooked over an open fire. The basic ingredients were easy to carry in their pocket: cayenne pepper and salt. Just before cooking, they would mix the spices with water, and presto—great Argentinean grilled beef. There is something about basting the meat with this simple sauce, letting it evaporate over and over again while the meat is grilling, that really does make the beef taste different than a simple sprinkle of salt and pepper!

Makes 4 to 6 servings

Grilling Method: Direct/Medium Heat

Gaucho Jack's Argentinean Pepper Sauce
  1   tablespoon cayenne pepper
  1   tablespoons kosher salt
  1   cup hot water
  3   pound sirloin steak or roast, 1½ inches thick
      Olive oil
  2   French baguettes, sliced into ¼-inch-thick slices

1. Build a charcoal fire or preheat a gas grill.
2. Dissolve the cayenne pepper and salt in the hot water. Transfer to a squeeze container. You will only use about ¼ cup for the recipe. Store the remaining sauce in the refrigerator for up to a month, making sure the nozzle is covered.
3. Pat the steak dry with paper towels and brush it lightly with oil.
4. Place the steak on the cooking grates over direct medium heat, cover, and sear 2 to 3 minutes on both sides. Continue grilling and baste with the sauce every couple of minutes. Continue this process until the steak is of the desired doneness, about 15 minutes for the outside pieces to be medium-rare.
5. Remove the steak from the grill and slice long strips from the ends of the steak.
6. Instruct guests to pick up a steak slice from the cutting board with their fingers, place it on a slice of baguette, and enjoy.
7. Return the remaining undercooked steak to the grill, baste, and grill until more of the steak is cooked. Remove and repeat the slicing and serving procedure until all of the steak is consumed.

TIP: For best results, buy a three-pound steak or sirloin roast from the butcher. The meat will cook at different rates—with the ends cooking first. You can slice and cover the meat as it finishes cooking to serve it all together when it is all done, or prepare and eat it the way the gauchos did—carve and serve the meat as it finishes, serving it to guests with slices of baguette all the while. It's less formal but more fun.

Beer-Soaked Filet Mignon Stuffed with Gorgonzola

Every May for the past 13 years, my buddy Lynne Wilkinson and I have barbecued together at the famous Memphis in May World Championship Barbecue Contest, aka the Mardi Gras of the Barbecue World. Whenever we are together we can't stop eating, drinking, laughing, and sometimes even dancing. But before the barbecue, we start the weekend off with her Memphis-style beer-soaked ("when you go to the fridge to get a beer, get one for the steaks as well; open your beer, take a sip, open another can and pour it on the steaks"), Gorgonzola-stuffed, bacon-wrapped filets. Talk about gilding the lily! But hey, we only live once, and it is mighty tasty.

Makes 4 servings

Grilling Method: Direct/Medium Heat

  4   filet mignons, about 2 inches thick and
      ½ pound each
  1   12-ounce bottle domestic beer of your choice
  8   small chunks of Gorgonzola cheese, about
      8 teaspoons
  4   slices bacon
      Solid wooden toothpicks, soaked in water for
      30 minutes
      Olive oil
      Kosher salt
      Freshly ground pepper

1. Put the filets in the bottom of an airtight container and pour the beer over them. Cover and place in the refrigerator. Marinate for 1 hour, turning once.
2. Build a charcoal fire or preheat a gas grill. Remove the filets from the beer. Insert a grapefruit spoon or paring knife in the side of each filet to make an incision halfway into the filet. With a spoon, take 2 chunks of the Gorgonzola and stuff the cheese into each incision. Wrap a piece of bacon around the side of each filet, covering the edges and the holes that the cheese went into. Secure the ends of the bacon with a wet toothpick. Brush the filets lightly with olive oil and season with salt and, if desired, pepper.

3. Place the filets on the grill over direct medium heat, cover, and cook for 9 to 12 minutes, turning occasionally to mark all sides and make the bacon crisp. The filets will be medium-rare and the cheese will be melted inside. Use the A-OK method or an instant-read thermometer to make sure the meat is cooked as you like.

4. Remove the meat from the grill and place it on a clean platter. Let the filets rest for 5 minutes before serving.

Guinness-Marinated Flank Steak Sandwich with Grilled Onions and Boursin

During a trip to the Ballymaloe Cookery School in County Cork, Ireland—and more than a few hours logged in the local pub—I developed a definite fondness for Guinness. When I returned to the States, I started cooking everything from gingerbread to flank steak with the sudsy brown nectar. This recipe makes a great sandwich for any sports occasion. I usually serve it warm, but it is also perfect packed in a picnic and eaten at room temperature.

Makes 4 servings

Grilling Method: Direct/Medium Heat
Special Equipment: Vacu Vin Instant Marinater

2	pounds flank steak or top round steak, sometimes called London broil, at least 1 inch thick
1	14.9-ounce bottle Guinness beer
2	large red onions, cut into $\frac{1}{2}$-inch slices
8	bamboo skewers, soaked in water for 30 minutes
	Olive oil
	Kosher salt
	Freshly ground pepper
1	5.2-ounce container Boursin cheese, frozen
8	slices thick sourdough or country bread, optional

1. Pat the steak dry with paper towels. Put it in a nonreactive container with a tight seal or the Vacu Vin Instant Marinater. Pour the Guinness over the steak and set aside.

2. Peel the onions and cut them into slices $\frac{1}{2}$- to $\frac{3}{4}$-inch thick. Put the onion slices on top of the steak. Cover the container and marinate in the refrigerator for 1 to 2 hours or 30 minutes in the instant marinater.

3. Build a charcoal fire or preheat a gas grill. When ready to grill, remove the meat and onions from the marinade and pat them dry. Thread the center of each onion slice with a bamboo skewer (they will resemble onion lollipops). Brush the steak and onions with a thin coating of oil and season with salt and pepper.

4. Place the steak and onions on the cooking grate over direct medium heat, cover, and sear. Cook for 6 to 8 minutes, then turn the steak and onions with a pair of tongs and sear the second side. Continue grilling another 6 to 8 minutes. Use the A-OK method or an instant-read thermometer to determine if the meat is done to your liking. The steak and onions will take about the same amount of time to grill.

5. Remove the steak and onions from the grill and place them on a clean platter to rest for 5 minutes. While the meat is resting, shave a thin layer of Boursin on the top of the meat and the tops of the onions. (The steak and onions can be served at this point as a main course instead of as a sandwich.)

6. If serving as sandwiches, spread 1 side of the bread slices with olive oil and grill 1 to 2 minutes or until toasty and marked. Remove the bread from the grill and spread the untoasted sides with Boursin cheese.

7. Put 2 onion slices each on 4 pieces of bread and set aside. Slice the steak in long thin slices about $\frac{1}{4}$ inch thick. Place the slices of meat on top of

the onions and top each with another piece of bread. Push down to compact the sandwiches a little before cutting them in half. Serve while still warm or wrap and refrigerate until ready to eat.

TIP: To get just the right amount of cheese, freeze the Boursin for at least 1 hour to make it easier to shave onto the top of the meat and onion. When the cheese is soft, it is easy to use too much.

Cumin-Rubbed Flank Steak with Chimichurri Sauce

This simple cumin, garlic, and smoked paprika rub and the chimichurri sauce elevate the humble flank steak into a signa-ture dish. Chimichurri sauce originates from South America and tastes like a garlic-rich parsley pesto. This recipe can be served on small slices of baguette for a substantial cocktail party appetizer, on hearty whole-grain bread for a Dagwood sandwich, or sliced and drizzled with the chimichurri sauce and served with roasted new potatoes for a main course.

Makes 8 to 10 appetizer or 4 main course servings

Grilling Method: Direct/Medium Heat

Cumin Rub
- 1   teaspoon granulated garlic
- $^1/_2$ teaspoon smoked paprika
- $^1/_2$ teaspoon cumin seeds

- 1   flank steak, about $^3/_4$ inch thick and $1^1/_2$ to 2 pounds each
  Olive oil
  Kosher salt

Chimichurri Sauce
- 2   cups loosely packed chopped fresh curly parsley, about one bunch
- $^3/_4$ cup olive oil
- 3 to 5 cloves garlic
- 3   tablespoons sherry wine vinegar or red wine vinegar
- 3   tablespoons fresh lemon juice
- 2   tablespoons minced shallot or onion
- 1   teaspoon kosher salt
- $^1/_2$ teaspoon freshly ground pepper
- $^1/_2$ teaspoon red chile flakes
- 1   baguette, sliced thinly (about $^1/_2$ inch wide)
  Fleur de sel

1. In a small bowl, mix the rub ingredients until well combined. Set aside.
2. Pat the steak dry with paper towels. Trim it of any surface fat. Brush it lightly with olive oil. Press the rub into both sides of the steak.
3. Build a charcoal fire or preheat a gas grill.
4. Meanwhile, make the Chimichurri Sauce: Put all the ingredients in a blender or food processor and pulse until well chopped but not pureed.
5. Just before grilling, season the steak with salt. Place the meat on the cooking grate over direct medium heat, cover, and sear. Cook for 4 to 6 minutes. Turn the steak with a pair of tongs and sear the second side. Continue grilling 3 to 5 more min-utes for medium-rare. Use the A-OK method or an instant-read thermometer to test the meat.
6. Remove the steak from the grill and put it on a clean platter to rest for 5 to 10 minutes before carving. While the meat rests, spread the baguette slices with Chimichurri Sauce and set aside.
7. Cut the steak across the grain into thin diagonal slices. Place a slice on each piece of bread spread with the Chimichurri Sauce and sprinkle with a pinch of fleur de sel. Serve hot or warm.

Rockin' Rolled Stuffed Flank Steak

I love to make meats that can be stuffed with all sorts of savory ingredients, then rolled up and grilled. This recipe for butterflied, stuffed flank steak is based loosely on the South American **matambre** *but with more vegetables than the traditional recipe. This is one of the most versatile dishes that I make. I love it cut into pinwheel slices and served at room temperature as an appetizer or hot off the grill as a main course with Chimichurri Sauce (page 71) on the side. If you prefer, ask your butcher to butterfly the steak for you.*

Makes 6 servings

Grilling Method: Combo/Medium Heat
Special Equipment: Kitchen twine, soaked in water for 30 minutes

Marinade
¼ **cup red wine vinegar or sherry vinegar**
¼ **cup olive oil**
3 **cloves garlic, minced**
  Kosher salt
  Freshly ground pepper
1½ to 2 **pounds flank steak**

Matambre Stuffing
8 **ounces Swiss or provolone cheese, thinly sliced**
8 **ounces prosciutto or cooked country ham, thinly sliced**
8 **large spinach leaves, washed and stemmed**
8 **spears asparagus, raw or grilled (see pages 204–205)**
½ **cup oil-packed sun-dried tomatoes**
½ **cup chopped fresh basil**
2 **tablespoons minced garlic**
½ **cup freshly grated parmesan cheese**
  Olive oil

1. Make the marinade: Combine the vinegar, oil, garlic, and salt and pepper to taste in a large, nonreactive bowl. Set aside.
2. Cut the steak by slicing through it horizontally, leaving the meat attached at one end. Open it like a book, laying it cut-side up. Season the cut side with salt and pepper.
3. Make the stuffing: Layer the slices of cheese and prosciutto over the cut side of the steak. Lay the spinach, asparagus, and tomatoes over the slices. In a bowl, combine the basil, garlic, parmesan, and enough olive oil to make a paste. Spread the mixture over the cheese filling, then starting at a short end, roll the steak up tightly like a cigar.
4. Secure the roll in several places with kitchen twine. Brush the outside all over with the marinade and let it soak in the extra marinade, covered or in the instant marinater for 30 minutes. While the meat is marinating, build a charcoal fire or preheat a gas grill.
5. Sear the rolled and stuffed steak on all sides over direct medium heat for 10 minutes. Move it into the center of the grill over indirect heat. Cook for 10 to 15 more minutes, until the meat is rare to medium-rare. Remove the meat from the grill, place it on a clean platter, cover loosely with foil, and let it rest for 10 to 15 minutes. Cut the meat into ½-inch-thick slices. Serve hot or at room temperature.

TIP: Flank steak should be served medium rare and cut across the grain for maximum tenderness.

All-American Steak Salad

The all-American meal is a steak and a salad. Here, I combine the two for a light and tasty version of a backyard classic. Instead of using the predictable romaine or iceberg lettuce, mesclun greens mixed with basil and crunchy Belgian endive provide the base. Prep this recipe in advance so grilling the steak is the only thing left to do before serving.

Makes 4 to 6 servings

Grilling Method: Combo/High Heat

2 **heads Belgian endive, washed and cut into thin strips (julienned)**
4 **cups mesclun greens, washed and dried**
1 **bunch fresh basil, leaves only**
2 **stalks hearts of palm, canned or jarred**

Dressing

¾ cup olive oil
6 cloves garlic, peeled and cut in half
1 teaspoon red chile flakes
¼ cup red wine vinegar
1 teaspoon Worcestershire sauce
  Kosher salt
  Freshly ground pepper

Rub

1 teaspoon dry mustard
1 teaspoon granulated garlic
1 teaspoon cumin seed

1 small tri-tip or sirloin roast, about 1½ pounds
  Olive oil
  Kosher salt

1. Mix the endive, greens, and basil in a large bowl; set aside. Cut the hearts of palm into ¼-inch slices and set aside.

2. Make the dressing: Add the garlic to the oil in a small pan. Over low heat, bring the oil to a simmer; it should be warm but not hot enough to cook anything. Turn off the heat and add the red chile flakes; stir to combine. Let the mixture sit for at least an hour to infuse the seasonings into the oil.

3. When ready to cook, build a charcoal fire or preheat a gas grill.

4. Make the rub: Combine the spices in a spice (or coffee) grinder and grind to a powder.

5. Pat the meat dry with paper towels and brush it with olive oil. Sprinkle it with the spice rub and season with salt. Place the meat on the cooking grate over direct high heat, cover, and sear for 2 to 3 minutes on each side. Move the steak to indirect high heat and cook for 10 to 15 more minutes or until it reaches medium-rare.

6. Remove the steak from the grill and place it on a cutting board. Let it sit for 10 minutes before carving it into thin slices.

7. While the steak is resting, remove the garlic cloves from the oil with a slotted spoon. Make the dressing by whisking together the oil and vinegar in a small bowl; add the Worcestershire and season to taste with salt and pepper.

8. Add dressing to greens; toss to combine. Divide the greens among plates. Top each plate with warm beef. Garnish with the hearts of palm; season with salt and pepper. Serve immediately.

Pink Salt–Crusted Beef Tenderloin with Tarragon Butter

I love salt. It adds so much to food. Not only does it bring out the best in the taste of food, but all the new types of salts that are available add their own special nuances. I know there are scientists who say salt is salt, but I think they are full of salt! Using the Hawaiian pink sea salt to crust a whole tenderloin is very different from using kosher, sea, or iodized salt. Because the pink salt is larger and denser, it melts very slowly. And because it melts so slowly, you do not risk oversalting your meat when you use it to crust the tenderloin. If you can't find the pink sea salt, use the coarsest sea salt you can find.

Makes 6 servings

Grilling Method: Combo/ Medium High Heat

Tarragon Butter

½ cup (1 stick) unsalted butter, softened
4 teaspoons minced fresh parsley
2 teaspoons granulated garlic
2 teaspoons dried tarragon

1 beef tenderloin, about 4 pounds
¼ cup coarse pink Hawaiian or white sea salt
2 tablespoons olive oil

1. Make the tarragon butter: Combine the butter, parsley, garlic, and tarragon in a medium bowl. Mix together, mashing with the back of a fork to make sure all the ingredients are incorporated. Meanwhile, cut a piece of plastic wrap about 6 inches long and spread it out flat. Spoon the soft butter mixture onto the plastic wrap and wrap it around the butter. Roll to make into a smooth log. Twist the ends to close them and refrigerate it at least 2 hours and up to 2 weeks, until ready to serve.

2. Build a charcoal fire or preheat a gas grill.

3. Remove meat from refrigerator 20 to 30 minutes before cooking to let it come to room temperature. Pat it dry with paper towels.
4. Meanwhile, mix the salt and oil together to form a paste, rub the tenderloin evenly with the mixture, and grill it immediately. Place the tenderloin on the cooking grate over direct medium high heat, and sear for 2 to 3 minutes on each side. After all the sides are seared, move the tenderloin to indirect medium heat, cover, and finish cooking, about 30 more minutes or until an instant-read thermometer reads 135°F for medium-rare. Remove it from the grill, place it on a clean platter, and let it rest for 15 to 20 minutes.
5. Brush off any excess salt. Slice the tenderloin into $\frac{1}{2}$-inch thick slices and serve them with small coin-size pieces of Tarragon Butter.

Beef Tenderloin Kabobs with Bacon, Shallots, and Mushrooms

I came up with this recipe one night when a few friends popped in unexpectedly. It was a gorgeous fall night, and we decided grilling out would be much more fun than going out. Since I only had two filets and four mouths to feed, I cut the filets into chunks and threaded them onto skewers with bacon. I did the same thing with the mushrooms and roasted the shallots until they started oozing that yummy caramelized onion sugar. The trick here is to precook the bacon for a few minutes to get the fat rendering and then assemble the skewers. The bacon is mostly for seasoning and flavoring the filet and mushrooms, but why waste good bacon? Serve it with the rest of kabob ingredients.

Makes 4 servings

Grilling Method: Direct/Medium Heat

  8 **shallots**
      Fleur de sel or coarse sea salt
  2 **filet mignons, about $\frac{1}{2}$ pound each**
 18 **whole white mushrooms, cleaned and stemmed**
      Olive oil
  8 **slices center-cut bacon**
  8 **long bamboo skewers, soaked in water for 30 minutes**

1. Build a charcoal fire or preheat a gas grill.
2. Keeping the shallots in their skins, place them on the warming rack of the grill to roast slowly while you prepare the kabobs. Turn, if necessary, to insure even cooking. The shallots will take 30 to 45 minutes to caramelize and get soft. Remove them when they are tender, and when they are cool enough to touch, peel the skins, place them in a bowl, and sprinkle them with fleur de sel or coarse sea salt.
3. Meanwhile, cut each filet lengthwise into thirds, turn them 45 degrees and cut the slices again into thirds (like a tic-tac-toe board); you should have 9 pieces.
4. Brush the cleaned mushrooms with oil and put them on a plate. Meanwhile, precook the bacon in the microwave or frying pan for 3 to 5 minutes or until it is soft and translucent.
5. Lay the filet pieces on a clean work surface as follows: 6 pieces of meat alternating with 6 mushrooms. Take a slice of bacon and interweave it on the work surface under the meat then around and above the mushrooms until you get to the last piece of mushroom. (The bacon will be threaded between the mushrooms and meat and will resemble "ribbon" candy.) Using 2 skewers for each kabob, push them parallel through each line of filet, mushrooms, and bacon, forming what looks like a ladder (see page 28).
6. Grill the kabobs over direct medium heat for about 5 to 7 minutes per side or until the bacon is crispy and the meat and mushrooms are marked, tender, and cooked. Remove from the grill and place on a clean platter. Let the kabobs rest for 5 minutes. Serve hot with the grill-roasted shallots.

Charred Carpaccio with Capers and Fleur de Sel

Have you ever wished you could make that delicious restaurant carpaccio at home? Well, you can. It is easy and fun to make. One large piece of filet mignon will feed four people—so it is impressive and economical! My version has a charred crust, which gives the carpaccio a nice presentation on the plate and has the added benefit of searing away any surface bacteria for those who are nervous about eating raw beef. So don a chef's hat, pick up a rolling pin, and serve carpaccio at home tonight.

Grilling Method: Direct/High Heat
Special Equipment: 24 to 32 pieces of parchment paper cut into 6 x 6-inch pieces, rolling pin

- 1 filet mignon, about 2 inches thick and ¾ pounds
  Best quality extra-virgin olive oil
  Kosher salt
  Capers
  Fleur de sel or coarse sea salt

1. Build a charcoal fire or preheat a gas grill. Just before grilling, pat the filet dry with paper towels. Brush it lightly with olive oil and sprinkle with salt.
2. Place the cold filet on the cooking grate over direct high heat. Sear the meat about 1 minute per side or until browned and marked, but make sure not to cook more than ⅛ inch of the surface. Remove it from the grill, place on a clean platter, and let cool. Cover the filet tightly and refrigerate it for 4 hours or overnight.
3. When ready to serve, cut the filet very thinly into ⅛-inch slices vertically so the charred crust is on the top and bottom of the slice and the meat is raw inside. You should end up with 12 to 16 slices from your 2-inch piece of filet mignon.
4. Place the slices of meat between 2 pieces of parchment and roll them out with a rolling pin until they are almost as thin as a piece of paper. Refrigerate, covered by the parchment, for up to 1 day. Peel the paper off just before serving and place 3 or 4 slices on a plate with the edges overlapping slightly. Finish with a sprinkling of olive oil, capers, and fleur de sel. Serve chilled.

Christmas Prime Rib with Decadent Horseradish Cream

Ever since I convinced my mother to buy a gas grill, this recipe has become our traditional Christmas dinner. Make sure to order an untrimmed rib roast from your butcher with the fat and the rib bones still intact. They may fight you on this, but let them know that you know what you are asking for! The fat will baste the meat and keep it juicy during the long cooking time and the rib bones will act as a natural roast holder. Serve the rare prime rib with the rich and spicy horseradish cream and a side of sizzling Yorkshire pudding.

Makes 10 servings

Grilling Method: Indirect/Medium Heat

- 2 tablespoons black peppercorns
- 2 tablespoons dried rosemary
- 2 tablespoons kosher salt
- 2 tablespoons sweet paprika
- 2 tablespoons smoked paprika
- 1 7-rib prime rib roast, 16 to 18 pounds, untrimmed
- 1 small head garlic, peeled and cut into slivers
- 6 to 8 woody sprigs fresh rosemary
  Decadent Horseradish Cream (below)

1. Build a charcoal fire or preheat a gas grill.
2. Combine the peppercorns, dried rosemary, salt, and paprika in a small bowl, and then grind them in a spice (or coffee) grinder until finely blended; set aside.
3. Using a paring knife, cut a series of slits at least 2 inches apart into the roast. Insert garlic slivers into half the holes and the leaves from 1 sprig of rosemary into the others. Rub roast with the rub.
4. Place the roast fat-side up on a bed of the remaining rosemary in the center of the cooking grate over indirect medium heat. Cover and grill for 3½ to 4½ hours for medium-rare (11 to 13 minutes per pound), or until an instant-read thermometer reaches 135°F.
5. Transfer the roast to a platter and cover loosely with foil to rest for 20 minutes. The meat will continue to cook and will gain 10 degrees to a perfect medium-rare temperature of 145°F. Serve hot, with the Decadent Horseradish Cream.

Decadent Horseradish Cream
Makes 2 cups

- 1 pint heavy whipping cream
- 1 to 2 tablespoons refrigerated prepared white horseradish (not horseradish cream)
  Fine-grain sea salt

While the roast rests, pour the cream into a clean stainless steel bowl. Using an electric beater, whip it on high until the cream forms soft peaks. Add the horseradish to taste and adjust, adding more if you like it stronger. Season with sea salt. Serve immediately.

Pot Roast with Red Zinfandel and Extra Veggies

Pot roast on the grill? It may seem counter-intuitive, but the high heat searing of the meat works much better than traditional pan browning. This method delivers a richly caramelized crust, and the grill marks stay on the meat through the long braising process to give the pot roast eye appeal as well as taste appeal! I used to find myself fishing around for the last carrot or onion, so I added extra veggies here to make sure there would always be enough to go around.

Makes 6 servings

Grilling Method: Combo/Medium Heat
Special Equipment: Extra-large, heavy Dutch oven, preferably cast iron

3	tablespoons olive oil
4	large onions, sliced
1	tablespoon packed brown sugar
2	tablespoons all-purpose flour
1	$14^{1}/_{2}$-ounce can low-sodium vegetable or beef broth
2	cups red Zinfandel wine, plus more if needed
$4^{1}/_{2}$ to 5	pounds beef rump roast or boneless short ribs
	Kosher salt
	Freshly ground pepper
1	pound carrots, peeled and cut into 4-inch pieces
3 to 6	parsnips, peeled and cut into 2-inch pieces
1	pound Baby Bella or cremini mushrooms, wiped clean, stems trimmed
8	red potatoes, cut in half
12	small shallots, peeled
24	cloves garlic, peeled (about 2 small heads)

1. Heat the olive oil over medium heat in an extra large, heavy Dutch oven or large roasting pan with a lid. Sauté the onions in the oil until very soft and beginning to caramelize, 15 to 20 minutes. Stir in the sugar and flour and cook, stirring, for 2 minutes. Slowly pour in the stock and 2 cups of the wine, stirring until smooth and slightly thickened, 3 to 4 minutes. Remove from heat.

2. Meanwhile, build a charcoal fire or preheat a gas grill.

3. Lightly coat the meat with olive oil, and season generously with salt and pepper. Place it on the cooking grate over direct medium heat and cover. Sear the meat on all sides, 3 to 4 minutes per side. After searing, place the roast in the Dutch oven (with the onions, stock, and wine) and cover.

4. Place the covered pot on the cooking grate over indirect medium heat. Cover and cook for 1 hour. Turn the meat occasionally to prevent overbrowning and add more wine, if all the liquid has evaporated.

5. After the first hour, add the vegetables, garlic, and another cup of wine, cover the pot again, and continue cooking over indirect heat for 2 to $2^{1}/_{2}$ hours, or until the meat and vegetables are tender. If all the vegetables won't fit in the pot with the meat, put them on the warming rack to roast and add to the meat and other veggies when serving. If roasting the vegetables on the grill, they will take less than an hour. Either remove when done and keep warm or put on the grill an hour before the pot roast is done.

6. Let the roast rest for 20 minutes after taking it off the grill. Slice the pot roast and serve it with plenty of the vegetables and sauce. This pot roast is even better the next day.

TIP: If you are searching for the perfect cut of meat for your winter pot roast, try short ribs, and it will bring back your mother's pot roast memories—if your mother made pot roast. If you have a good butcher, ask for boneless short ribs, and you won't have to pick out the bones. *NOTE:* On a gas grill, try to maintain a temperature of 350°F. On a charcoal grill add 10 to 12 coals on each side every hour to maintain the heat.

New World Veal Scaloppini

No matter how old world the idea of veal scaloppini is, it hits the spot. The grill makes it easier and tastier to prepare at home by eliminating the need to flour and panfry the thin pieces of veal. The contrast of the grilled veal with the silky white wine and mushroom sauce updates this Italian–American classic for today's new world. This is a dish that you will want to cook all in one trip to the grill. Because the veal is cut so thinly, it will cook more quickly than you can say scaloppini!

Makes 4 servings

Olive oil
1   large shallot, chopped
2   cloves garlic, grated
1   pound mushrooms, cleaned and sliced
1 to 2 cups white wine
1   15½-ounce can Italian-style chopped tomatoes
4   veal cutlets, about ¼ inch thick and ½ pound each
Kosher salt
Freshly ground white pepper or grains of paradise
Finely chopped fresh parsley or chives

1. Build a charcoal fire or preheat a gas grill.
2. Heat about 2 tablespoons of olive oil in a deep-sided sauté pan. Add a pinch of salt, the shallots, and garlic, and cook over medium heat for 2 to 3 minutes or until the shallots are translucent. Add the mushrooms and sauté on high heat until brown. Remove the mushrooms from the pan.
3. Pour the wine 1 cup at a time into the hot pan. Stir with a wooden spoon to mix in all the browned bits that were left in the pan. Add the tomatoes, and let them cook down until slightly thickened. Return the mushrooms to the pan and cook for 5 minutes more. Taste and adjust the seasonings and wine if necessary. The mushroom sauce should be chunky but have enough liquid to spoon over the veal when the sauce is done. Turn off the heat and cover the pan.
4. Brush the veal with olive oil and season it with salt. Place the veal on the cooking grate over direct medium heat. Cover and cook for about 4 minutes, turning once halfway through the cooking time. This is enough time to mark and cook the veal.
5. Remove the cutlets from the grill and place them on a clean platter for 2 to 3 minutes. While the meat rests, gently reheat the sauce and spoon it onto individual plates. Place the grilled veal on top. Season with white pepper or grains of paradise and garnish with chopped parsley or chives. Serve immediately.

Double-Cut Veal Chops with Lemon and Garlic Butter

When I first moved to Chicago, my Uncle Bobby introduced me to all kinds of food that I couldn't find in my hometown of Greensboro, NC. One of his favorite haunts was an old-world Italian restaurant that he and my father frequented as young men. The restaurant specialized in Al Capone stories and triple-cut veal chops sizzling with lemon and garlic. The dish wasn't on the menu, but if you were an insider, you could order it when you made your dinner reservation. Now that you have the recipe, you are "made in the shade," as the old-timers liked to say.

Makes 4 servings

Grilling Method: Combo/Medium-High Heat

4   double-cut veal chops, about 2 inches thick and 1 to 1½ pounds each
Olive oil
Kosher salt
Freshly ground pepper

Lemon and Garlic Butter
4   tablespoons (½ stick) unsalted butter, melted
5   cloves garlic, minced
2   sprigs fresh oregano
2   lemons, cut in quarters
Fleur de sel, optional

1. Build a charcoal fire or preheat a gas grill. Pat the chops dry with paper towels.

2. Just before grilling, brush them all over with olive oil. Season with salt and pepper. Place the chops on the cooking grate, over direct medium-high heat to sear, about 3 to 4 minutes on each side. To make a crosshatch pattern, rotate each chop $1/4$ turn to the right after 2 minutes, and sear for 2 minutes more. Turn over and repeat on the other sides. Once the chops are seared on the other side, turn the burners directly under the chops off or move the chops to an area of indirect heat. Cover and continue cooking for 10 to 15 more minutes or until they are medium-rare on the inside. Use the A-OK method or an instant-read thermometer to make sure the meat is done as you like.

3. Meanwhile, in a small saucepan, combine the butter, garlic, and oregano and let steep for 10 minutes on very low heat to extract the flavors from the herbs. Remove from the heat and set aside.

4. When the chops are done, remove them from the grill and place them on a clean platter. Squirt each chop on both sides with fresh lemon juice and brush with the garlic butter. Let them rest for 5 minutes. Just before serving, brush more of the garlic butter on top, sprinkle with fleur de sel, if using, and serve hot, with a quartered lemon.

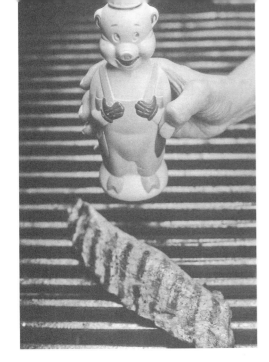

Pork

Pork 101

Rapid-Fire Checklist
- ✓ Preheat grill to High
- ✓ Brush pork all over with olive oil, season with kosher salt and pepper, if desired
- ✓ Reduce heat to medium, choose the right cooking method
- ✓ Place pork on cooking grate and cover
- ✓ Turn once halfway through cooking time, if cooking by the Direct Method
- ✓ Remove pork from grill
- ✓ Let meat rest 5 to 20 minutes, depending on size

Tools of the Trade
- 12-inch locking chef tongs
- Instant-read thermometer
- Silicone or natural-bristle brush
- Heavy-duty oven mitt

Common Problems
- Underseasoned meat
- Overcooked meat
- Mistaking a pink smoke ring for undercooked pork
- Using premarinated products

I think that pork is the most versatile food, both to eat and to grill. Almost every part of a pig is transformed into cuts that are tailor-made for outdoor cooking, from sausages to ham, tenderloins, and chops. Of course, the most revered of all pork preparations is barbecued pork shoulder, but that's for low and slow cooking (see Low-and-Slow Barbecue, pages 241–258). This chapter focuses on grilling pork over both direct and indirect heat with contemporary flavors. The main difference between grilled pork and barbecued pork is the use of wood smoke. With a little practice and a few tips, you'll see the merits of grilled pork as much as barbecued pig!

Pork is one of the best protein choices we have. Pigs have been bred to be as lean as chickens, which is good for our health, and it is readily available. However, the new leanness contributes to problems people have with grilling pork. Natural fat both delivers a better flavor and protects the delicate meat from overcooking. The reduction of natural fat, aka leaner meat, makes it harder to cook; but that doesn't mean that today's pork is not worth cooking. You just have to be choosier about the pork you buy. Look for pork that still has a little fat running through the meat and is a brownish pink in color (not bright white). There are several brands of pork, such as Niman Ranch and Pipestone, that market pork from small farmers who practice old-fashioned farming and the proof is in the (taste of the) pig! Their products may be a little more expensive, but they're worth it.

Cuts of Pork
Pigs today are raised to be much leaner than they were years ago, and are reported to have 35 percent to

50 percent less fat. And, despite the ad campaign ("the other white meat"), pork is considered to be red meat. Chicken and fish are the only true white meats. The pig is split into four main primal cuts before being processed into case-ready products:

SHOULDER

The shoulder is one of the most flavorful and economical cuts. It is the primal cut that includes the front leg and the section at the top of the leg. It contains more fat than the other cuts of pork, which make it tender and flavorful and particularly good for grill-roasting. The boneless Boston Butt comes from the blade (butt end) of the shoulder, and the picnic roast or ham comes from the arm end. Kabob cubes and ground pork often come from the shoulder. Blade shoulder roasts are considered a better cut than the picnic shoulder and are generally leaner and more expensive.

LOIN

The loin is located on either side of the backbone, from the shoulder to the hind leg. It is the leanest, largest, most tender, and most expensive cut of the pig. These are the cuts of meat that are most troublesome to grillers and home cooks because they are so lean and will dry out when overcooked. The loin is made up of the rib or blade end, the center, and the sirloin.

Rib End: This section of the loin is the closest to the shoulder. Cuts from this end are fattier than the center and sirloin sections and are particularly suited to grilling. They include chops (boneless and bone-in) back ribs and country-style ribs.

Center Cut: This is the middle section of the loin. Cuts from this section are the most tender, lean, and expensive. They include the center loin roast, crown roast, tenderloin, center-cut chops, loin chops, back ribs, and Canadian-style bacon. The narrow boneless tenderloin muscle can be cut into smaller pieces that are sold as "cutlets," "medallions," and "scallops."

Sirloin: This is the section of the loin that is closest to the rump of the pig. These cuts have more bone than any other section of the tenderloin. Familiar cuts include the sirloin roast, tenderloin, sirloin chops, steaks, and sirloin cutlets.

LEG/HAM

Just as you would think, the leg is made up of the rump and hind leg. The meat is lean and flavorful but less tender than the loin section. Most cuts can be purchased bone-in or boneless and can be found fresh. This is where the coveted fresh ham comes from. However, most of the cuts from this section are cured and smoked. The leg is subdivided into two sections, the butt half (or end) and the shank half (or end).

Butt End: This half of the leg is located on the upper part of the leg near the rump. It is meatier than the shank but difficult to carve because of the location of the bone. This section is cut and sold as fresh ham roasts, ham, ham steaks, and center ham slices. If cured and smoked, hams are ready to eat when purchased. Ham steaks and center ham slices are usually cured and smoked before being cut into thick slabs that are delicious grilled just long enough to mark and warm through.

Shank End: This bottom half of the leg includes the shank bone. It is a bonier cut, but it is easier to carve than the butt end. Just like the butt end, the shank is cut into fresh ham roasts, ham, ham steaks, and shanks (ham hocks).

SIDE/BELLY

Directly beneath the loin, on the lower half of the pig, is the side/belly. The cuts from this section are wonderfully flavorful, because they contain more fat than the other parts of the pig. The side is divided into the side rib and the side pork.

The side rib contains the spareribs, which have at least 11 bones. St. Louis–style are spareribs with the brisket bone removed.

The side pork is the section of the side and belly that is left after the spareribs have been removed. This is where the oft revered bacon, side meat (pork), and salt pork come from. Bacon is both cured and smoked, side meat is neither cured nor smoked, and salt pork is cured but not smoked before being sold. The trendy "pork belly" is actually good old-fashioned, Southern side meat (pork) and has been cooked in the rural South forever.

On the Fire: Direct or Indirect Heat

The safest way to decide between the Direct and Indirect cooking methods is to use this rule of thumb: 20 minutes or less, Direct Heat; more than 20 minutes, Indirect Heat. However, pork is one of the best meats to grill using a combination of the two cooking methods, or the Combo Method as I call it. The Direct Heat gives an instant sear to the meat, promoting caramelization and sealing in the juices. Once it is seared, you move the meat to Indirect Heat to finish the cooking with a gentle lower heat. This assures that the outside doesn't overcook before the interior is done. Once you get used to it, you'll see that using this method actually guarantees success, time after time.

To Turn or Not to Turn

I usually base whether or not to turn the meat on another rule of thumb: If it takes more than 20 minutes to cook (for which you would use indirect heat), you don't need to turn it unless you want the aesthetic of grill marks. Tenderloin, chops, and pork loin always look more appetizing with those tell-tale grill marks, so those should be turned and cooked by the Combo Method. Larger roasts don't need to be turned. For recipes that take 20 minutes or less to cook, turn the meat only once, halfway through cooking time.

Crosshatch Marks

Pork chops look picture perfect with crosshatch marks, and they are easier to achieve than they look. Just before turning the chops, rotate them one-quarter turn to the right and leave for about two minutes. If cooking by the Combo Method, sear for two minutes, rotate one-quarter turn for another two minutes, turn over and repeat, then move to Indirect Heat to finish cooking. To make sure you don't have three sets of marks, carefully place your chops in the same position

or turn them one-quarter turn when you move them to indirect heat and the marks will appear during the final cooking time.

Testing for Doneness

Since 1970, trichinosis has been virtually extinct, yet the majority of home cooks still overcook pork until it is leathery and devoid of flavor. Combine this overcooking with the new super-lean pork and you've got a much-maligned meat. The USDA and the Pork Council assure us that trichinosis is not an issue, and the correct end temperature is 155°F, which means that the center of the cut will still be juicy and a little pink. So buy fresh pork, and don't be tempted to overcook it. Use the doneness chart on page 85 and an instant-read thermometer to guide you. If you are still leery, limit your porcine grilling to slow-cooked barbecue, which cooks to an end temperature of at least 190°F while the inherent fat flavors the meat and keeps it moist.

Smoke Ring, or "My Pig's Pink!"

The pink ring around the outside of a cut of pork is an outdoor cook's pride and joy. It is called the smoke ring. The smoke ring is a natural chemical reaction between the meat and the smoke and does not mean that the pork is undercooked. On the contrary, it is the ultimate goal. Interestingly enough, you can get this same pink ring by cooking meat in a gas oven. Whole poultry and large pieces of beef, such as brisket, also get a smoke ring around the perimeter of the meat if cooked long enough.

Brining

A brine at its essence is a very simple salt and sugar solution that is used in much the same way as a marinade. Once you have the right proportions of sugar and salt, you can add aromatics and other flavoring agents; but it is the sugar and salt that does the trick.

Brining has become very popular lately for turkeys (to make them juicier and perfectly seasoned; see page 48), but it isn't just for Thanksgiving. Brining benefits pork even more than turkey. In fact, it can be your secret grilling weapon.

Basic Brine

 8   **quarts water, divided**
 1   **cup kosher salt**
 1   **cup sugar or sweetener (honey, maple syrup, brown sugar)**

1. Boil 2 quarts of the water, and add the sugar and salt, stirring until completely dissolved. Add the rest of the water (or ice to speed the process) and let it come to room temperature before submerging the meat or poultry. Add extra water if necessary to cover meat. (Do not put raw meat in a hot brine.)
2. Cover and refrigerate for up to 24 hours—the larger the piece of meat, the longer it might need to soak. Tenderloin or chops only need 30 to 60 minutes.

NOTE: Don't season brined meats with salt; the brining takes care of the seasoning. Pat dry, brush with oil, and grill—it's that simple!

Premarinated Products

In general, I am not a fan of premarinated products sold in plastic packages. They are often too salty, have too many preservatives, and tend to result in meat that, when cooked, is mushy, discolored, and artificial tasting. Food manufacturers are trying to offer consumers covenenience by making the cuts ready for cooking. But, I think you are much better off buying raw meat and following the Grilling Trilogy (pages 19–20)—a little olive oil, kosher salt, and freshly ground pepper. It will take about the same amount of time as opening the premarinated package, and your pork will taste so much better.

NOTE: I am not referring to the prepared meat that butchers provide these days in the fresh meat case. The rubbed and stuffed roasts and kabobs are great if prepared that day. The difference is that the prepped meats from your butcher are freshly prepared and have not been sitting for days in acidic marinating liquids or artificial flavoring agents that make the texture of the meat mushy and give it an off flavor.

Pork Chop 101

Makes 4 servings

Grilling Method: Direct/Medium Heat

 4 bone-in single-cut pork chops, about 1 inch
     thick and ¾ pound each
     Olive oil
     Kosher salt
     Freshly ground pepper

1. Build a charcoal fire or preheat a gas grill. Pat the pork chops dry with paper towels. Brush lightly on all sides with olive oil and season with salt and, if desired, pepper.
2. Place the chops on the cooking grate, cover, and grill over direct medium heat for 6 to 8 minutes. Turn and continue grilling for another 8 minutes, or until well marked and the meat registers 160°F in the center of the chop on an instant-read thermometer. Transfer the chops to a clean platter and let them rest for 5 minutes. Serve hot.

TIP: It is difficult to use a meat thermometer on a single-cut pork chop, so I recommend using my A-OK technique (see page 57) to check doneness. Take the chop off when it feels medium or you feel a good bit of firm resistance when you touch the center of the chop with your finger.

Boneless Pork Chop 101

Boneless pork chops will take a little less time to cook than chops with the bone.

Makes 4 servings

Grilling Method: Direct/Medium Heat

 4 boneless pork chops, about 1 inch thick and
     ½ pound each
     Olive oil
     Kosher salt
     Freshly ground pepper

1. Build a charcoal fire or preheat a gas grill. Pat the pork chops dry with paper towels. Brush lightly on all sides with olive oil and season with salt and pepper.

2. Place the chops on the cooking grate, cover, and grill over direct medium heat for 5 to 6 minutes. Turn and continue grilling for another 6 to 7 minutes, until they are cooked to medium, using the A-OK method (see page 57). Transfer the chops to a clean platter and let them rest for 5 minutes. Serve hot.

Pork Tenderloin 101

Makes 4 servings

Grilling Method: Combo/Medium Heat

 2 pork tenderloins, about 1 pound each
     Olive oil
     Kosher salt
     Freshly cracked pepper or your favorite
       barbecue rub, such as Classic Barbecue Rub
       (page 44)

1. Build a charcoal fire or preheat a gas grill. Brush the tenderloins with olive oil and season with salt and pepper or a rub to taste.
2. Place the tenderloins on the cooking grate over direct medium heat to sear. Cover and grill 2 to 3 minutes per side. Once seared, move to the center of the cooking grate and cook over indirect heat for 12 to 15 minutes, turning once halfway through cooking time to ensure even cooking. If using an instant-read thermometer, the meat should register 160°F.
3. Transfer the tenderloins to a clean platter. Let the meat rest for 5 minutes. Slice the tenderloins into ½-inch slices. Serve hot.

Pork Loin Roast 101

Makes 6 to 8 servings

Grilling Method: Indirect/Medium Heat

 1 pork loin roast, about 3 pounds
     Olive oil
     Kosher salt
     Freshly ground pepper

1. Build a charcoal fire or preheat a gas grill. Pat the pork dry with paper towels. Brush lightly on

Approximate **PORK** *Cooking Times* (°F)

TYPE OF PORK	THICKNESS OR WEIGHT	DEGREE OF DONENESS	GRILLING METHOD	GRILLING TIME	INTERNAL TEMP.	REST TIME
Boston Butt	4 pounds	Well done	Indirect Medium	1½ to 2 hours	180°	10 minutes
Chops, bone-in: rib, loin, shoulder	1 inch thick	Medium	Direct Medium	10 to 20 minutes	160°	5 minutes
Chops, boneless: rib, loin, shoulder	1 inch thick	Medium	Direct Medium	10 to 15 minutes	160°	5 minutes
Ham steaks	1 pound	N/A	Direct Medium	8 to 10 minutes	N/A	2 to 5 minutes
Ham, fresh (leg of pork)	12 to 17 pounds	Medium	Indirect Medium	4 to 6 hours	160°	20 minutes
Loin roasts: blade, sirloin, center rib	3 to 5 pounds	Medium	Indirect Medium	1 to 1½ hours	160°	10 minutes
Pork belly	About 6 x 2 inches	Well done	Indirect Medium	1 to 1½ hours	180°	5 minutes
Rib crown roast	4 to 6 pounds	Medium	Indirect Medium	1½ to 2 hours	160°	15 minutes
Ribs: country-style, baby back, spareribs	3 to 4 pounds	Medium	Indirect Medium	1½ to 2 hours	160°	5 minutes
Tenderloin, whole	¾ to 1 pound	Medium	Combo Medium	15 to 20 minutes	160°	5 minutes

All internal temperatures are based on USDA recommended values, using an instant-read thermometer.
Times and temperatures in the chart are guidelines. Specific recipes may call for variations.

all sides with olive oil and season with salt and pepper.

2. Place the roast in the center of the cooking grate, cover, and grill-roast over indirect medium heat for 45 to 60 minutes, or until an instant-read thermometer registers 160°F. (There is no need to turn the roast during the grilling time.)

3. Transfer the roast to a clean platter and let the meat rest for 10 minutes before carving into thin slices. Serve hot.

Chop-Chop Pork Chop with Sage Butter

This is one of my favorite recipes to make in the fall. The thought of grilled pork, a touch of butter, and the unmistakable flavor of sage puts me in a "sweater weather" mood and makes me want to go apple picking. Although this recipe is super simple, the flavors are sophisticated and contemporary. The boneless pork chops take less time to cook (chop-chop!) and are as lean as a chicken breast, so don't eliminate the colorful Sage Butter—it's what takes the recipe from simple to sublime! If you've gone apple picking (at an orchard or your local market), make either the Grilled Apple Slices (page 100) or the more traditional homemade applesauce (see at right).

Makes 4 servings

Grilling Method: Direct/Medium Heat

Sage Butter
$^{1}\!/_{2}$	cup (1 stick) unsalted butter, softened
1	tablespoon dried cranberries, chopped
2	teaspoons Calvados, optional
1	teaspoon granulated garlic
1	teaspoon dried sage
$^{1}\!/_{2}$	lemon, zested
	Pinch sea salt

4	boneless center-cut pork chops, about 1 inch thick and $^{1}\!/_{2}$ pound each
	Olive oil
	Kosher salt
	Freshly ground pepper
	Tart Homemade Applesauce (at right)

1. At least 3 hours in advance, make the Sage Butter: Combine the butter, cranberries, Calvados, garlic, sage, and lemon zest in a medium bowl. Mix, mashing with the back of a fork to make sure all the ingredients are incorporated. Season to taste with salt, and mix well. Meanwhile, cut a piece of plastic wrap about 6 inches long and spread it out flat. Spoon the soft butter mixture onto the plastic wrap and wrap it around the butter. Roll to make into a smooth log. Twist the ends to close them and refrigerate it at least 2 hours and up to 2 weeks, until ready to serve.

2. When ready to cook the chops, build a charcoal fire or preheat a gas grill. Cut four $^{1}\!/_{2}$-inch slices of butter off of the Sage Butter log (you will have some left over); set aside.

3. Pat the chops dry with paper towels. Brush with a thin coating of olive oil and season with salt and, if desired, pepper.

4. Place the chops on the cooking grate over direct medium heat, cover, and grill 5 to 6 minutes on each side. The chops will be done when they feel firm to the touch. (Use the A-OK method, page 57.)

5. Transfer the chops to a clean platter and immediately top each with a piece of sage butter. Let the chops rest for 5 minutes before serving with Tart Homemade Applesauce (below) or Grilled Apple Slices (page 100).

Tart Homemade Applesauce

Makes about 4 cups

10	fresh-picked apples, or half Granny Smith, half Macintosh
1	lemon, juiced
1	teaspoon ground cinnamon
1	tablespoon liqueur, such as Calvados or Grand Marnier, optional
	Kosher salt
2	tablespoons sugar, optional

1. Peel and quarter the apples, removing the core and seeds. Transfer them to a large bowl. Add the lemon juice and toss the apples to coat them.

2. Transfer the apples to a heavy-bottomed, 4-quart saucepan. Cook, covered, over medium heat for 20 minutes, stirring occasionally to help the apples soften and cook down. Add the cinnamon and liqueur, if using. Stir and add a pinch of salt. Taste, and add the sugar if it is too tart. Stir to mix. Simmer, covered, until the apples are the consistency that you like, usually about 15 more minutes.

3. Serve hot or at room temperature. Refrigerate leftovers, covered in the refrigerator, for up to 3 days.

Chop-Chop Pork Chop with Sage Butter
(page 86)

Grilled Vegetable Antipasto Platter
(page 216)

Three Chile–Rubbed Rib-Eye
(page 66)

The Original Beer-Can Chicken
(page 47)

Butterflied Leg of Lamb 101, Stuffed
(page 108)

Bubba's Bunch Barbecued Baby Back Ribs
(page 266)

Bahamian-Style Whole Grilled Red Snapper
(page 170)

Grilled Shrimp and Grits
(page 183)

Jack and Coke–Soaked Pork Chops

Usually I drink my bourbon neat and eat my pork pulled, but in this recipe, I make an exception and put my sippin' whiskey where my pork is! You can't believe how delicious this unlikely marinade is. The sweet Coke syrup and the vanilla notes of the spirits are a perfect match. They deepen the flavor of the pork without making it too sweet. Since it's a sin to waste good whiskey, I boil and reduce the marinade (instead of discarding it) while the pork grills and use it to glaze the finished chops. Choose double-cut chops that take a little longer to cook or a boneless pork loin for best results.

Makes 4 servings

Grilling Method: Indirect/Medium Heat
Special Equipment: Vacu Vin Instant Marinater, optional

- 4   double-cut pork chops, about 2 inches thick and 1 pound each
- 1   12-ounce can Coke or other cola
- ½   cup Tennessee whiskey, preferably Jack Daniel's, or bourbon
       Olive oil
       Kosher salt
       Freshly ground pepper

1. Pat the chops dry with paper towels. Set aside.
2. Pour the Coke and whiskey into a container with a lid or into the bottom of a Vacu Vin marinater. Stir to mix. Put the pork chops in the marinade and turn each chop over to wet all surfaces with the marinade. Put on the lid and marinate in the refrigerator for 1 hour or 30 minutes in the marinater.
3. When ready to grill, build a charcoal fire or preheat a gas grill. Meanwhile, remove the chops from the marinade, drain to remove excess, then brush them lightly with olive oil. Season with salt and, if desired, pepper. Set aside.
4. Put the reserved marinade in a small saucepan and bring to a boil over high heat. Lower the heat and simmer for about 5 minutes, or until the marinade is reduced by about half.
5. Place the chops on the cooking grate over indirect medium heat, cover, and grill for 10 to 15 minutes. Turn the chops over and brush with the reduced marinade glaze. Continue grilling for about 15 more minutes, or until an instant-read thermometer placed in the thickest part of the chop registers 160°F.
6. Transfer the chops to a clean platter and let the meat rest for 5 minutes before serving. Serve extra glaze on the side if desired.

NOTE: I use the indirect method for this recipe because the marinade is very sweet. When using any sweet marinade or sauce, grilling by the indirect method will reduce flare-ups and prevent the pork from burning on the outside before the inside is cooked through.

Crusty Double-Cut Pork Chops with Grilled Oranges

These double-cut pork chops are coated with a sweet and salty rub and then cooked slowly over indirect heat until the outsides of the chops are deeply caramelized and crusty. That sounds good enough for me, but the real taste trick is in grilling cut oranges flesh-side down directly over the heat, then squirting the hot smoky orange juice on the pork chops just before serving.

Makes 4 servings

Grilling Method: Indirect/Medium Heat

Chop Rub
- ½   cup packed dark brown sugar
- 1   tablespoon kosher salt
- 1   tablespoon sugar
- ½   tablespoon smoked or sweet paprika
- ½   tablespoon coarsely ground pepper

- 4   double-cut pork chops, about 2 inches thick and 1 pound each
       Olive oil
- 2   juice oranges, cut in half

1. Make the chop rub: Mix all the ingredients together in a small bowl and stir until well combined. Store in an airtight container until ready to use.

2. Build a charcoal fire or preheat a gas grill. Pat the chops dry with paper towels. Brush lightly all over with oil. Set aside on a clean platter or tray. Using your hands or a spice bottle, sprinkle the meat all over with the chop rub. Pat gently into the meat to form a crust, but do not rub hard.

3. Put the chops back on the platter and let them sit for 5 minutes. When ready to grill, place the chops in the center of the cooking grate over indirect medium heat and cover. Grill for 15 minutes before turning. Turn and cook 10 to 15 more minutes, or until an instant-read thermometer registers 160°F. The outside of each chop should be crusty and the inside juicy and just a little pink.

4. Transfer the chops to a clean platter and let them rest for 5 to 10 minutes.

5. While the pork chops rest, put the orange halves on the cooking grate cut-side down, over direct–medium-high heat (increase the heat if need be) for 5 minutes, or until the flesh is marked and the oranges are warmed through.

6. Remove the oranges from the grill and squeeze the juice from half of an orange over each chop. Or, for a more dramatic presentation, serve a chop and an orange half together and let everyone squeeze their own juice over their meat. Serve hot.

This Ain't Your Mother's Pork Chop

This is definitely not your mother's pork chop, but one bite and you'll wish you had been eating it all your life! Although this recipe uses a marinade, rub, and glaze, all of the ingredients are pantry items and take just a few minutes to gather together. The aromatic rub is known as Chinese five-spice powder—its predominantly sweet-spicy notes come from cinnamon, clove, fennel, and star anise. If you can't find it already mixed in the spice section of your grocery, use the recipe on page 99 and make enough to keep on hand. You'll find yourself using it for everything from meat, fish, and poultry to apple pies!

Makes 6 servings

Grilling Method: Direct/Medium Heat
Special Equipment: Vacu Vin Instant Marinater

6 large center-cut pork chops, about 1 inch thick and $^1/_2$ pound each
$^1/_3$ cup olive oil
$^1/_2$ cup fresh orange juice
3 tablespoons Chinese five-spice powder
Kosher salt
Freshly ground pepper

Marmalade-Rum Glaze
$^1/_4$ cup orange marmalade
$^1/_4$ cup dark rum

1. Several hours before cooking, pat the chops dry with paper towels. Place the pork chops in a nonreactive dish or marinater and pour the orange juice and olive oil over them. Marinate, covered, in the refrigerator for several hours, turning occasionally, or 30 minutes in the marinater.

2. Just before cooking, build a charcoal fire or preheat a gas grill. Remove the chops from the dish; discard the marinade. Rub the chops with the five-spice powder, sprinkle with salt and pepper, and set aside.

3. Meanwhile, make the glaze: Mix the marmalade and rum in a small bowl until it is smooth.

4. Place the pork chops on the cooking grate over direct medium heat. Cover and grill for 5 to 6 minutes per side, or until they feel firm to the touch (see the A-OK method, page 57). The outside of each chop should be crusty and the inside juicy and just a little pink.

5. Brush the chops with the glaze and continue grilling for 2 to 3 minutes, or until glaze is set. Remove from grill, let rest 5 minutes, and serve.

TIP: If the marmalade is too cold to mix well, microwave it in a glass bowl for 10 seconds until it is warmed through.

TIP: This recipe works equally well with pork tenderloin. Follow the directions above but increase cooking time to 18 to 20 minutes, turning once halfway through grilling.

Open-Faced Croque Monsieur

This simple knife and fork sandwich is the French version of a grilled ham and cheese. Most of the time, it is made with a creamy white sauce called béchamel and soft white bread, resulting in a soggy sandwich with the cheese melted on the outside. My grilled version is assembled on slices of hearty brown country loaf. If you can get the Poilâne bread (look in specialty stores or go to www.zingermans.com), it is worth the splurge! Otherwise, any good, fresh, crusty, artisanal bread will work. I also substitute a mixture of mayonnaise and Dijon mustard for the white sauce. Since the cheese needs to melt at the same time as the bottom of the bread browns, I grill this sandwich on indirect low heat. Be patient; you will be rewarded.

Makes 4 servings

Grilling Method: Indirect/Low Heat

- ¼ cup mayonnaise, preferably Hellmann's
- 1 tablespoon strong Dijon mustard
- 4 large (about 6 inches long) center slices country bread, 1 inch thick, 4 slices Poilâne bread, or a good artisanal bread (If your bread is smaller, make 8 slices)
- 8 thin slices French ham or best-quality sliced ham
- 8 long slices Gruyère cheese (enough to cover ham with 2 layers cheese)
  Freshly ground pepper

1. Build a charcoal fire or preheat a gas grill on medium heat. This will insure the cooking grates are not too hot and won't burn the bread. Once the grill is preheated, set the burners to low indirect heat.
2. Begin assembling the open-face sandwiches: Mix the mayonnaise and mustard in a small bowl. Spread a generous layer on 1 side of each piece of bread. Add the ham and then the cheese on top of the mustard-mayo spread.
3. Carefully place the sandwiches on the cooking grate over indirect low heat, at least 2 inches apart. Cover and grill for 10 to 15 minutes, or until the cheese bubbles. If you are concerned about burning the bread, you can place the sandwiches on a cookie sheet and put the cookie sheet on the grill until the bread is toasty and the cheese melts.
4. Serve immediately topped with freshly ground pepper.

Pressed Cuban Sandwich with Caramelized Garlic Butter

Knowing my predilection for a great Cuban sandwich, my friend Richard Ruben introduced me to Chelsea Havana in New York City. One day, I went alone and sat at the bar watching the sandwich guy grill sandwich after sandwich. That's when it hit me—I should make my favorite sandwich on the grill! It's also a great way to serve leftover slow-roasted pork or slices of pork loin. I use a cast-iron skillet to press the sandwich, but you could also use a brick wrapped in foil.

Makes 4 to 6 servings

Grilling Method: Indirect/Medium Heat
Special Equipment: Cast-iron skillet, bacon press, or foil-wrapped bricks

Caramelized Garlic Butter

- 1 head garlic, roasted (see page 207)
- ¾ cup (1½ sticks) unsalted butter, softened

- 1 loaf soft French bread (about 24 inches long), cut into 6-inch pieces and sliced in half
  Dill pickle slices
- 1 pound Pork Loin Roast 101 (pages 84–85), thinly sliced
- 1 pound best-quality sliced ham
- 8 ounces sliced Swiss cheese

1. Build a charcoal fire or preheat a gas grill on medium heat. This will insure the cooking grates are not too hot and won't burn the bread.
2. Meanwhile, make the garlic butter: Remove the garlic from the skins and mix it with the butter, until the garlic is completely incorporated. Cover and keep at room temperature.

3. Spread both sides of the bread with the caramelized garlic butter.

4. Layer the sandwich ingredients on each piece of the buttered bread in the following order: pickles, pork, ham, and cheese. (Be generous with the fillings, it will make a better sandwich, and you can always save half.) Place the top bread half on each of your 4 sandwiches. Press down evenly to compress the sandwiches.

5. Place the sandwiches on the cooking grate over indirect medium heat. Put the skillet or brick on the sandwiches (in batches if necessary) to press them down. Cover and grill for 5 minutes, then remove the weight, turn over the sandwiches, and replace the weight. In about 5 more minutes, when the cheese has melted and the bread is toasted, the sandwiches are done. Transfer the sandwiches to a platter, slice in half diagonally, and serve immediately.

Barbecued Pork Belly

Praise the god of bacon! Pork belly—an old farmhouse standby—has come back into vogue. When not being traded on the floor of the commodities exchange, pork belly is simply a slab of uncured bacon. Some chefs braise the fatty piece of meat. I say let them have the braise, which makes the pork belly flabby and soft. Barbecuing is the answer—it renders out the fat, resulting in tender, flavorful meat and a burnished crust that has the most glorious, almost mahogany, color. It is decadent, delicious, and extremely rich, so eat it in small pieces with a simple grilled fish like sturgeon or on a bed of frisée lettuce with a tangy vinaigrette.

Makes 4 servings

Grilling Method: Indirect/Medium Heat

1 piece fresh pork belly, about 6 x 2 inches
 Kosher salt
 Freshly ground pepper

1. Build a charcoal fire or preheat a gas grill. Pat the pork dry with paper towels. Season with a generous sprinkle of salt and pepper.

2. Place the pork in the center of the cooking grate over indirect medium heat, cover, and grill-roast

for 1 to 1½ hours, or until the fat has rendered out, the top is crisp, the color is a burnished red brown, and the meat is tender when poked with a fork.

3. Transfer the pork belly to a carving board and let it rest for 5 minutes. Cut into 1-inch chunks and serve hot.

Mexican Pork Tortillas

During a recent trip to Texas to "study" the state's indigenous barbecue, I stumbled on a number of Mexican barbecue joints. They were actually more like counters in the back of grocery stores that served tortillas and daily specials like posole—that fabulous soup of broth, pork, and hominy. I fell in love with these simple pork tortillas that reminded me of North Carolina pulled pork but with Mexican accompaniments. The fat in the avocado tempers the heat in the chipotle barbecue sauce, and the crunchy onions and cilantro take the place of coleslaw. This recipe is easy to make in advance, reheating the pork and slicing the vegetables before serving.

Makes 4 to 8 servings

Grilling Method: Combo/Medium Heat

1 small Boston Butt (or boneless shoulder roast), about 4 pounds
 Olive oil
 Kosher salt
8 corn tortillas
1 medium white onion, thinly sliced
½ cup Mexican-style barbecue sauce, preferably flavored with chipotle chilies
2 ripe avocados, pitted, peeled, thinly sliced
8 sprigs fresh cilantro

1. Build a charcoal fire or preheat a gas grill. Pat the pork dry with paper towels. Lightly oil the pork, and season it with salt.

2. Place the pork on the cooking grate over direct medium heat, and sear it on all sides. Move the pork to indirect heat. Cover and grill until the pork registers about 180°F on an instant-read thermometer, 1½ to 2 hours. Remove the pork from the grill, and let it rest for 10 minutes.

3. Put the tortillas in damp paper towels and microwave on high for 30 to 45 seconds to warm or place them on the grill over indirect heat to warm. Carve the pork on the diagonal into very thin slices, or shred it into bite-size pieces.

4. Serve the pork hot in warm tortillas topped with onions, avocado, a drizzle of the barbecue sauce, and a sprig of cilantro. Season lightly with salt, if desired.

TIP: If you can't find a good store brand of barbecue sauce, follow the directions for Lexington-Style Vinegar Sauce (page 249), substituting a small can of chipotle peppers in adobo sauce for all the pepper ingredients. Puree in a blender and use to moisten the meat.

Duck Bacon–Wrapped Pork Tenderloin

I keep this recipe in my culinary pocket at all times because it is the simplest way to make a to-die-for dinner without a complicated or time-consuming marinade or sauce. I like to use the excellent duck bacon that is distributed by D'Artagnan, but a good-quality center-cut pork bacon can be substituted. A trick for this recipe is to let the bacon come to room temperature so it sticks to itself as you wrap the tenderloin. Because you want the bacon to cook slowly and become crisp, you cook the tenderloin indirectly over medium heat and turn it halfway through the cooking time.

Makes 4 servings

Grilling Method: Indirect/Medium Heat

2 pork tenderloins, about 1 pound each
8 ounces D'Artagnan duck bacon or pork bacon
   Solid wooden toothpicks, soaked in water for 30 minutes
   Fleur de sel or coarse sea salt

1. Build a charcoal fire or preheat a gas grill. Pat the tenderloins dry with paper towels. Beginning at one end of each tenderloin, wrap the bacon around it (mummy style), overlapping the ends of the bacon with each new piece. Secure wherever

necessary with toothpicks. The bacon provides both fat and seasoning, so no other preparation is necessary.

2. Place the tenderloins on the cooking grate over indirect medium heat, toothpick-side down. Cover and grill for 20 to 25 minutes, turning them once halfway through the cooking time, or until the bacon is crisp and the pork registers 160°F on an instant-read thermometer.

3. Transfer the tenderloins to a carving board and let them rest for 5 minutes. Cut the tenderloins in half—one half per serving—and serve hot, with a sprinkle of fleur de sel or coarse sea salt.

Pork Tenderloin with Truffled White Bean Puree

It is amazing how a little drizzle of truffle oil turns your basic pork and beans into fancy food. This recipe is great for adding a little luxury to your grilling repertoire. The white beans soak overnight to quicken the cooking time, and the puree can be made up to three days in advance. If you have any leftover puree, use it to make the Truffled White Bean and Caramelized Onion Toasts (page 296).

Makes 4 servings

Grilling Method: Direct/Medium Heat

White Bean Puree
2 cups dried white beans, such as Great Northern, soaked overnight
3 cloves garlic, cut in half
1 sprig fresh rosemary
   Best-quality Italian olive oil, such as Monini or Lucini
   Kosher salt
   Truffle oil
   White pepper

2 pork tenderloins, about 1 pound each
   Olive oil
4 fresh rosemary sprigs, for garnish
   Fleur de sel or coarse sea salt

1. Make the puree: Drain the beans, put them in a large saucepan, and cover with fresh water. Add the garlic and rosemary. Bring to a boil, reduce the heat, and simmer until the beans are very tender and almost falling apart, about 30 to 45 minutes. Reserve ½ cup of the beans and about ½ cup of the bean water. Remove the rosemary sprig.

2. Using an immersion blender, puree the garlic and beans in the pot. Add about 2 tablespoons of olive oil, a little at a time as you blend, until you a reach a creamy consistency. Add a couple tablespoons of the bean water to thin out the consistency, if necessary. Season with salt and puree again.

3. Mix in truffle oil a few drops at a time, and taste occasionally until you get a dominant, but not overwhelming, truffle flavor. (Since truffle oils differ in strength, you must do this by taste rather than by measurement.)

4. Add the reserved beans and mix with a fork, leaving some lumps and larger pieces of beans for texture. Taste and adjust the seasonings with salt and white pepper. The puree can be made up to 1 week in advance, but must be refrigerated and brought back to room temperature before using.

5. Build a charcoal fire or preheat a gas grill. Pat the tenderloins dry with paper towels. Brush all over with olive oil and season with salt.

6. Place the tenderloins on the cooking grate over direct medium heat, cover, and grill for 15 minutes, turning once halfway through the cooking time, until an instant-read thermometer registers 160°F.

7. Transfer the tenderloins to a carving board and let the meat rest for 5 minutes. Put the bean puree on a serving platter.

8. Cut the meat on the bias into ½-inch slices, and place the slices on top of the bean puree. Sprinkle with fleur de sel or other sea salt. Drizzle with olive oil and top with a sprig of rosemary. Serve hot.

Pork Paillard with Orange Marmalade Vinaigrette and Grilled Scallions

This is a recipe that will put a spring in your step and a jig in your pig! It is especially good to make toward the end of winter when you crave lighter, greener days. I am usually not a fan of sweet and meat, but the bitter undertones of the vinegar and the orange peel in the marmalade balance the flavors and complement both the pork and the scallions. The meat and onions are simply grilled with olive oil, salt, and pepper and dressed with the vinaigrette as soon as they come off the grill. Serve with buttered new potatoes and an arugula salad.

Makes 4 servings

Grilling Method: Direct/Medium Heat
Special Equipment: Meat pounder or rolling pin

2 boneless pork chops, about ½ pound each, cut in half horizontally (to make four ½-inch boneless chops),
2 bunches scallions (green onions)
Olive oil
Kosher salt
Freshly ground pepper

Orange Marmalade Vinaigrette
⅓ cup fresh orange juice (about 1 orange)
2 teaspoons apple cider vinegar
2 teaspoons heavy whipping cream, at room temperature
2 tablespoons orange marmalade
⅔ cup olive oil
⅓ cup canola oil
Sea salt
Freshly ground pepper

1. Build a charcoal fire or preheat a gas grill. Brush each piece of meat on both sides with a little olive oil (this will help make the pounding process smoother). Place each piece between 2 sheets of parchment or waxed paper large enough to cover meat with a 3-inch border around all sides (about 8 x 8 inches). Pound or roll out each piece of pork with a rolling pin until it is about ¼ inch thick all over. Lay each piece of pork on a clean piece of waxed paper or clean platter.

2. Trim the tops and roots of the scallions, leaving the root intact. Brush all over with olive oil and season with salt and pepper, if desired. Place the pork and onions on the cooking grate over direct medium heat. Cover and grill both for 3 to 4 minutes on each side. They should be finished at the same time. The pork will be well marked and cooked until firm to the touch. The onions will be wilted and have caramelized spots on the exterior.

3. While the pork and onions cook, make the Vinaigrette: Whisk the juice, vinegar, and cream in a medium bowl. Add the marmalade and whisk again. Slowly add the oil a little at a time, whisking until well incorporated (emulsified). Season to taste with salt and pepper.
4. When the pork and onions are done, transfer them to a platter to rest for a few minutes.
5. While the pork and onions are still hot, drizzle with the Vinaigrette and serve immediately.

Smoky Pork Tenderloin Tacos

This recipe delivers Mexican barbecue flavor in record time. The smoky three-chile rub flavors the meat, which is quickly seared over direct heat before grilling over a gentler indirect heat. The key to this recipe is to dry the meat of all its surface moisture and rub the dry meat with the spice rub. Add oil and salt just before grilling and let the meat rest for five minutes before serving with cilantro, salsa, and avocados.

Makes 4 to 6 servings

Grilling Method: Combo/Medium Heat

    Rib-Eye Rub (page 66)
2   pork tenderloins, about 1 pound each
    Kosher salt
8 to 12 fresh corn tortillas
2   ripe avocados, pitted and thinly sliced
1   cup favorite salsa
8   sprigs fresh cilantro, finely chopped

1. Build a charcoal fire or preheat a gas grill. Pat the tenderloins dry with paper towels. Put the meat into the bowl, rolling it in the Rib-Eye Rub mixture, and patting the rub onto the meat, so it is evenly coated. Cover the meat with waxed paper or plastic wrap and let sit at room temperature for 10 minutes.
2. Season the meat with salt. Place the meat on the cooking grate over direct medium heat. Sear the meat on both sides, 2 to 3 minutes per side, until it is marked on all sides.
3. After searing, move the tenderloins to indirect medium heat. Cover and cook for 12 to 15 more minutes, or until an instant-read thermometer registers 160°F.

4. Transfer the meat to a carving board and let it rest for 5 to 10 minutes.
5. Warm the tortillas: Loosely wrap them in damp paper towels and microwave on high for 30 to 45 seconds or place them on the grill over indirect heat.
6. Slice the tenderloins into very thin pieces and serve hot with the warm tortillas, avocados, salsa, and cilantro in separate bowls so all guests can make their own tacos.

Honey-Marinated Sesame Pork Kabobs

This simple honey, water, and rice wine vinegar marinade will make pork lovers everywhere swoon with delight. The marinade sweetens the pork chunks and enables the sesame seeds to stick, forming a crust that will get toasty and crunchy. This recipe makes a great appetizer or main course. For best results, cut kabob pieces from the tenderloin or a loin roast and marinate the chunks.

Makes 4 servings

Grilling Method: Indirect/Medium Heat
Special Equipment: Vacu Vin Instant Marinater, optional

2   pork tenderloins, about 1 pound each
    Kosher salt
1   cup honey
½   cup water
½   cup unsweetened rice wine vinegar
¼   cup toasted sesame oil
2   teaspoons garlic-chili sauce (often called *sriracha*)
    12 bamboo skewers, soaked in water for 30 minutes
¼   cup sesame seeds
    Gingered Honey Sauce (page 102)

1. Pat the tenderloins dry with paper towels. Cut them into 1-inch chunks and season lightly with salt. Set aside while making the marinade.
2. Whisk together the honey, water, vinegar, sesame oil, and chili sauce. Put it in a container with a lid or in the bottom of the instant marinater. Add the pork and mix lightly to make sure that all the meat is exposed to the liquid. Put on the lid and refrigerate for 1 hour or for 30 minutes in the marinater.

3. Just before grilling, build a charcoal fire or preheat a gas grill. Remove the pork from the marinade and discard it. Thread the pork chunks onto skewers, using the ladder technique (see page 28) to secure the pieces.

4. Lay the sesame seeds flat on a piece of waxed paper and press both sides of the kabobs onto the seeds to coat the meat.

5. Place the kabobs on the cooking grate over indirect medium heat so the seeds do not burn before the meat cooks. Cover and grill for 8 to 10 minutes, turning once halfway through the grilling time, until the meat is firm to the touch.

6. Transfer the kabobs to a platter and let them rest for 5 minutes. Serve hot with Gingered Honey Sauce.

Apple Cider–Brined Pork Loin with Root Vegetable Puree

The inspiration for this recipe is a dish that I had at Tuscana Saporita, the Italian cooking school owned and run by the late Anne Bianchi and her cousin Sandra Lotti. It was part of a perfect week of cooking, touring, drinking wine, and talking into the early morning hours. By the last meal, we had made all the pasta we could eat, so a very simple pork roast took its place. The pork dinner was the best culinary memory of the week. When I got back to Chicago, I added a very American brine and turned the roasted vegetables into a heady puree rich with roasted garlic, olive oil, and balsamic vinegar.

Makes 6 to 8 servings

Grilling Method: Indirect/Medium Heat
Special Equipment: V-rack roast holder

Apple Cider Brine
- 4 cups apple cider
- 1/3 cup kosher salt
- 1/3 cup sugar
- 2 bay leaves, crumbled
- 1 teaspoon black peppercorns
- 1 teaspoon whole cloves
- 2 cups cold water

- 1 pork loin, about 3 pounds
- 4 medium onions, peeled
- 6 large carrots, trimmed
- 3 stalks celery, trimmed
- 1 head garlic, wrapped in foil
  Olive oil
  Kosher salt
  Freshly ground pepper
- 1/4 to 1/2 cup balsamic vinegar

1. Make the brine: Combine the cider, salt, sugar, bay leaves, peppercorns, and cloves in a large stockpot. Bring to a boil over medium-high heat and cook for about 3 minutes, stirring occasionally, until the sugar and salt dissolve. Remove from the heat, add the water (or 2 to 3 cups ice cubes to cool to room temperature faster).

2. Put the pork loin in a nonreactive pan or resealable plastic bag and cover it with the cooled brine. Cover or tightly close the bag and refrigerate for 6 to 12 hours. If you are using an extra-large resealable bag, rotate the pork a few times to make sure all of the meat gets brined. Before roasting, remove the pork and pat it dry with paper towels.

3. Build a charcoal fire or preheat a gas grill. Put the vegetables in a roasting pan. Drizzle them with the oil, then toss the vegetables until they are evenly coated.

4. Just before grilling, lightly brush the pork with olive oil. Place the pork on a V-rack roast holder and place the rack into the roasting pan with the vegetables. Place the foil-wrapped garlic on the warming rack to roast.

5. Put the pan of pork and vegetables over indirect medium heat for 1 hour, covered, or until an instant-read thermometer placed in the center of the roast registers 160°F.

6. Transfer the pork to a carving board. Let the meat rest for 10 minutes.

7. Meanwhile, put the vegetables and any pan juices in a food processor, squeezing the garlic cloves from the skins, add 1/4 cup balsamic vinegar and 2 tablespoons of olive oil and puree. Taste and add more vinegar or oil, or both, as needed to thin out the puree. Adjust the seasonings again, to taste.

8. Cut the pork into thin slices on the diagonal. Transfer the slices to a platter and coat them with the puree. Serve hot.

Spicy Pork Roast with Pickled Peaches

This is a recipe that you have to plan, but it's special and worth the effort. The peaches are pickled in a spicy sweet and hot liquid and set aside to rest for a day in the refrigerator. The peaches are drained, and the spiced peach juice becomes the marinade for the roast. When the roast is resting, you can gently sear the peach halves before serving them or serve them cold as a contrast to the hot roasted pork. Either way, it is a study in perfect porcine pleasure!

Makes 8 servings

Grilling Method: Indirect/Medium Heat
Special Equipment: Vacu Vin Instant Marinater, optional

Pickled Peaches
 1   cup sugar
 $^1/_2$ cup white vinegar
 $^1/_2$ cup water
 1   tablespoon chopped crystallized ginger
 10   whole cloves
 1   cinnamon stick
 8   firm, ripe peaches, peeled, cut in half, and pitted

 1   pork loin roast, about 3 pounds
     Pickled peach liquid
     Olive oil
     Kosher salt
     Freshly ground pepper

1. Make the Pickled Peaches: Combine all the ingredients, except the peaches, in a large saucepan over medium heat and bring to a boil. Reduce to a simmer and add the peach halves. Bring back to a low boil, then reduce the heat slightly. Cook the peaches for 10 minutes, stirring occasionally to make sure all the peaches are submerged in the liquid. Remove from the heat and refrigerate for at least 1 day.

2. Transfer the peaches with a slotted spoon to a clean container and reserve the juice for the pork marinade.
3. Build a charcoal fire or preheat a gas grill.
4. Pat the pork dry with paper towels. Put the pork in a container with a lid or in the bottom of an instant marinater and add the reserved peach liquid. Seal the container and marinate in the refrigerator for 30 minutes. After marinating, discard the marinade. Shake any excess liquid off the roast, brush it with olive oil, and season with salt.
5. Place the pork on the cooking grate over indirect medium heat, cover, and grill-roast for about 60 minutes or until an instant-read thermometer registers 160°F.
6. Transfer the roast to a carving board. Season with pepper, if desired, and let the meat rest for 10 minutes. Carve on the diagonal into thin slices and serve with the peaches.

Country Ham Steak with Buttered Grits and Cheddar Biscuits

Just add black-eyed peas and greens, and you've got the world's best New Year's Day supper. Because the meal is so simple, it is essential that you use the best possible ingredients—no substitutions allowed. Coarse stone-ground grits, real butter, homemade biscuits, and a thick center-cut ham steak will give soul to anyone who takes a bite— guaranteed!

Makes 6 servings

Grilling Method: Direct/Medium Heat

Grits
 $2^1/_2$ cups water
 1   cup coarse stone-ground grits, such as Anson Mills
 2   tablespoons unsalted butter
     Kosher salt
     Freshly ground pepper

Biscuits

- 2 cups all-purpose flour, plus more for rolling
- 2 teaspoons sugar
- 2 teaspoons baking powder
- 1/2 teaspoon sea salt
- 3/4 cup grated sharp white cheddar cheese
- 1 tablespoon minced fresh chives
- 1 1/2 cups heavy whipping cream, plus more for brushing tops

- 2 bone-in center-cut ham steaks, 1 inch thick
  Olive or peanut oil

1. Preheat the oven to 450°F.
2. Make the grits: Boil the water in a medium sauce-pan. Add the grits, stirring to separate. Cover, lower the heat, and simmer for 15 minutes. Uncover and stir for 5 minutes. Cover again and simmer for 10 more minutes, then uncover and stir. Taste the grits to see if they are at the desired texture. Grits are done when they are smooth and creamy and there's still a little texture or bite to them, like al dente pasta. If the grits are too watery, simmer, uncovered, until any excess water has evaporated. If they are too stiff, add a little milk or water to thin out the texture. When done, remove the grits from the heat, stir in the butter, and season with salt and pepper to taste. Cover and keep warm.
3. Meanwhile, build a charcoal fire or preheat a gas grill. While the grits simmer, make the biscuits: Combine the flour, sugar, baking powder, and salt in a large bowl and whisk until completely incorporated. Add the cheese and chives and stir with a fork until well mixed. Add about 1 cup of the cream and stir with a fork until the dough comes together. If the dough is still very dry, add the rest of the cream. If it is coming together, add half the remaining cream (1/4 cup) and stir with a fork—you don't want the dough to be too wet.
4. When the dough forms a ball, turn it out onto a floured surface and knead until smooth. Roll out with a rolling pin until the dough is 3/4 inch thick all the way around. Cut with a floured biscuit cutter and place on an ungreased cookie sheet. (You can reroll the scraps or bake them in irregular shapes for a snack or for your pet.) You should have 12 biscuits. Brush the tops with cream and bake for 12 to 15 minutes, or until the tops are

browned. Transfer the biscuits to a cooling rack. Let them rest for a few minutes, then transfer them to a basket or bowl and cover lightly with a kitchen towel to keep warm.

5. While the biscuits are baking, brush the ham steaks with oil. (Do not season them with salt or pepper since the ham is already highly seasoned.)
6. Place the steaks on the cooking grate over direct medium heat, cover, and grill for 8 to 10 minutes, turning once halfway through the grilling time.
7. Transfer the ham steaks to a clean platter and cut them in thirds. Serve each person a piece of ham steak, a generous portion of grits, and 2 biscuits.

TIP: To time the meal components, start with the grits, then preheat the grill and prepare the biscuits. When the biscuits are in the oven, it will be time to grill the ham.

Grandmother Odom's Fresh Ham with Cloves and Brown Sugar

My grandmother died in 1979, long before my sisters and I knew that we'd want to know how to make this recipe one day. Like many women of her generation, she cooked by rote, instinct, or memory. Thus went her fresh ham with mustard glaze. Grandmother Odom always made the ham on a spring Sunday. Early in the morning she would put the bright yellow mustard-glazed fresh ham in the oven and let it cook for hours until the glaze had baked into the meat and turned the darkest shade of brown. It's no surprise that the outside "burnt ends" were my favorite, since they were the most flavorful. The grill is perfectly suited to this recipe as the convection-like heat roasts the ham to a beautiful burnished brown all the way around without having to turn it.

Makes 12 to 14 servings

Grilling Method: Indirect/Medium Heat
Special Equipment: V-rack roast holder, optional

- 1 fresh ham (bone-in leg of pork), 12 to 17 pounds
- 1/4 cup whole cloves
- 1/2 cup packed dark brown sugar
- 1 1/2 tablespoons kosher salt
- 9 ounce jar yellow (ballpark) mustard

1. Build a charcoal fire or preheat a gas grill. Pat the ham dry with paper towels. If not already done, use a sharp boning or paring knife to remove the skin, but leave the layer of fat just beneath the skin. Score the fat by making diagonal cuts from right to left and again across the original cuts to create a diamond pattern. Put a whole clove in the center of each of these diamonds.

2. Mix the sugar and salt in a small bowl. Rub the mixture all over the exterior of the ham. Using a flexible spatula, spread a thick layer of the mustard all over the ham.

3. Place the ham in the center of the cooking grate—either directly on the grates or in a V-rack roast holder—over indirect medium heat. Cover and grill-roast the ham for 4 to 6 hours, or until an instant-read thermometer inserted in the thickest part registers 180°F (about 20 minutes per pound). The outside should be darkly caramelized and the inside should be meltingly tender and come away from the bone very easily.

4. Transfer the ham to a clean platter. Let it rest for 20 minutes before carving. Serve hot or cold. Leftovers make a great Cuban sandwich (pages 89–90).

TIP: To simplify the ham preparation, have the butcher remove the skin from the ham but leave the layer of fat (fat cap) beneath it.

TIP: Dr. Seuss wasn't too far off with his famous Green Eggs and Ham story. A fresh, uncured, unsmoked ham is referred to in the pork trade as a "green" ham.

Slow-Roasted Fresh Ham with Spicy Bourbon and Brown Sugar Glaze

This is the epitome of slow food, Southern style. And since the most important ingredients are a top-quality fresh ham and time, make sure you have both before starting this recipe. I've included an optional Spicy Bourbon and Brown Sugar Glaze for those days when company is coming. The real jewels are the slow-roasted meat that falls from the bone and the crispy-brown skin or cracklings. The cracklings

are a delicacy in the South, where whole hogs are frequently slow-roasted this same way. If you use the glaze, serve the tender meat with a side of Drunken Fruit (page 99).

Makes 12 to 14 servings

Grilling Method: Indirect/Medium Heat

1   **fresh ham (bone-in leg of pork), 12 to 17 pounds**
     Kosher salt
     Freshly ground pepper
     Olive oil
     Spicy Bourbon and Brown Sugar Glaze
       (below), optional

1. Build a charcoal fire or preheat a gas grill. Pat the ham dry with paper towels. Score the fat by making diagonal cuts from right to left and again across the original cuts to create a diamond pattern. Rub the ham all over with salt and season gently with pepper. Brush a thin coat of olive oil over the meat.

2. Using 2 pairs of tongs, place the ham in the center of the cooking grate over indirect medium heat, cover, and grill-roast for 4 to 6 hours, or until an instant-read thermometer inserted in the thickest part registers 180°F (about 20 minutes per pound). There is no need to turn the pork or baste it while it roasts slowly. If using the Glaze, brush it on during the final 30 minutes of grilling time.

3. Transfer the ham to a clean platter, and let it rest for 20 minutes before carving. Serve hot.

TIP: The ham (leg of pork) can be purchased two ways, with the fat cap exposed, meaning that the skin has been removed, and with the skin on (the natural fat under the skin is intact). As long as there is enough fat left on the roast to keep the ham self-basting during the grill-roast process, either cut is fine. When the skin is left on and scored, you will get cracklings. If you score the fat cap, it will still baste the meat beautifully, but there will not be any cracklings.

Spicy Bourbon and Brown Sugar Glaze
If using the glaze, make it after the roast has been placed on the grill.

Makes 2 cups

1 cup bourbon
1 cup packed brown sugar
1 teaspoon whole cloves
1 teaspoon ground ginger
$1/2$ teaspoon red chile flakes
$1/2$ teaspoon ground cinnamon
$1/4$ cup ($1/2$ stick) cold unsalted butter, cut into
    4 pieces
1 teaspoon sea salt

1. In a small, heavy-bottomed saucepan, heat the bourbon and sugar slowly over medium low heat, stirring occasionally, until the sugar is completely dissolved. Add the cloves, ginger, red chile flakes, and cinnamon; stir to combine. Simmer for 5 minutes to reduce slightly.

2. Whisking continually, add the butter, 1 piece at a time, to thicken the sauce. Add another piece of butter only after the previous piece has been fully incorporated. The glaze should foam slightly when it is done and all the butter has been incorporated.

3. Taste the glaze, add the salt, taste again, and adjust the seasonings. Take off the heat until ready to use. The glaze can be made up to 1 week in advance and stored covered in the refrigerator.

East Meets Midwest Hoisin-Glazed Country-Style Ribs

I love the flavor of the plummy sweet Chinese hoisin sauce when it slowly cooks and caramelizes. This recipe is dynamite on country-style ribs because the meat to bone ratio is much higher than on traditional spareribs, and you get more meat to balance the sweetness of the sauce. Country-style ribs are really like baby pork chops. If you can't find them in your supermarket, you can make this recipe with pork tenderloin as well. Just be sure to purchase authentic hoisin sauce at an Asian grocery instead of the Chinese-American variety that has loads more sugar.

Makes 4 servings

Grilling Method: Indirect/Medium-Low Heat

4 pounds country-style ribs (see Tip below)
3 teaspoons kosher salt, divided
4 teaspoons Chinese five-spice powder
    (store-bought or homemade, page 99)
2 tablespoons untoasted sesame oil
1 cup hoisin sauce
2 tablespoons molasses or cane syrup
2 tablespoons apricot jam with chunks
4 teaspoons garlic-chili sauce (often called
    sriracha) or more to taste
1 knob fresh ginger (1 to 2 inches), peeled and grated
1 small bunch fresh chives, minced

1. Build a charcoal fire or preheat a gas grill. Pat the ribs dry with paper towels. Combine 2 teaspoons of the salt and 3 teaspoons of the five-spice powder in a small bowl, and then rub the mixture all over the ribs. Brush with sesame oil.

2. Place the ribs on the cooking grate over indirect medium-low heat, cover, and grill for 30 minutes. Turn the ribs over and grill for another 30 minutes.

3. Meanwhile, whisk together the hoisin sauce, molasses, jam, garlic-chili sauce, ginger, and sesame oil. Taste and add the remaining 1 teaspoon of five-spice powder and 1 teaspoon of salt if you think the sauce needs it. (Every brand of hoisin sauce varies in spice and salt content, and it is easier to add than subtract seasonings.) Cover the sauce and set it aside until ready to use.

4. After 1 hour of cooking, brush the sauce on the ribs and continue grilling 45 minutes more, or until the sauce is caramelized and slightly shiny. If you like a lot of sauce, turn after 20 minutes and brush the other side with sauce and cook for another 25 minutes.

5. Transfer the meat to a clean platter and let rest for 5 minutes. Garnish with the chives and serve hot.

TIP: Country-style ribs come from the pork loin rib ends. They are cut from the "prime rib" of the pork loin and are rich and meaty. They look more like chops than traditional pork ribs.

Chinese Five-Spice Powder

If you can't find Chinese five-spice powder in your local grocery, here is a simple recipe for making your own. This spice mixture is very easy to make in any quantity, as you use equal amounts of each ingredient.

Makes 5 tablespoons

1 tablespoon ground cinnamon
1 tablespoon ground cloves
1 tablespoon ground toasted fennel seeds
1 tablespoon ground star anise
1 tablespoon ground toasted Szechuan or black peppercorns

Mix all the spices together in a small bowl until well combined. Keep in an airtight container for up to 6 months.

Crown Roast of Pork Stuffed with Drunken Fruit

This is the recipe of my June Cleaver dreams! I love the retro feel of serving a crown rack that is grill-roasted. Instead of making a hole in the meat and stuffing it—as many housewives did in the fifties—I've made this dish simple and elegant by filling the inside of the crown with a rich concoction of dried fruit, brandy, and spices. Have your butcher trim and tie the roast so it is circular and resembles a crown and if he has some of those wonderful paper hats, be sure to get them for the table presentation!

Makes 6 to 8 servings

Grilling Method: Indirect/Medium Heat

1 crown roast of pork, 8 to 10 pounds, trimmed and tied together
   Kosher salt
1 orange, zested
1 lemon, zested
   Olive oil
   Grains of paradise or freshly ground pepper

Drunken Fruit

14 ounces whole dried apricots
12 ounces pitted dried plums (prunes)
12 ounces dried cherries
12 ounces dried Mission figs
1½ cups brandy or cognac
1 lemon, zested and juiced
2 tablespoons sugar or more to taste
5 cardamom pods
1 vanilla bean, slit down the middle with a sharp knife
1 teaspoon sea salt
½ teaspoon ground ginger
½ cup hazelnuts, toasted

1. Build a charcoal fire or preheat a gas grill. Pat the crown roast dry with paper towels.

2. Mix about 1 tablespoon of salt with the citrus zests in a small bowl and rub the mixture onto the meat. Brush all over with olive oil.

3. Holding the roast with both hands, place it on the cooking grate, bone-side–up, over indirect medium heat. Cover and grill-roast for 2 to 3 hours (15 to 20 minutes per pound). There is no need to turn or baste the roast as it cooks.

4. While the roast cooks, make the Drunken Fruit: Add all the ingredients except the hazelnuts to a large, heavy-bottomed saucepan. Bring the liquid to a boil over medium-high heat. Reduce the heat to low and simmer, covered, for 1 to 2 hours, or until the fruit is soft and has absorbed a lot of the cooking liquid. If you need more liquid, add a little water. Stir the fruit occasionally while it cooks. Remove the vanilla bean and scrape out the seeds. (Discard the bean or reserve it for other uses.) Add the vanilla seeds to the fruit and stir to distribute. Taste and adjust the seasonings if necessary. Stir in the hazelnuts. Cover and keep warm.

5. When the roast is done, transfer it to a carving board, season with freshly ground grains of paradise or pepper and let the meat rest for 15 minutes. When ready to serve, place the crown (with paper hats, if using) on a serving platter and fill the

cavity with Drunken Fruit. At the table, cut into chops by following the outside bones with the edge of a carving or chef's knife.

6. Serve hot with a generous spoonful of fruit.

TIP: The crown roast is traditionally made from 2 center-cut racks of ribs, which are bent to form a circle and then tied together with the bones facing out. The racks are tied together with string to hold their shape and the bones are frenched at the top so that at least 1 inch of bone is exposed. The frenching of the bones looks nice and makes the roast easier to cut. You can also use a rack of pork (a center-cut loin roast with the bones frenched) for this recipe. Both of these cuts are considered expensive cuts of pork.

TIP: Drunken Fruit can be served with other dishes— it's fabulous served over vanilla ice cream for dessert.

Grilled Apple Slices

Simple slices of caramelized apples dress up basic grilled pork and add a tart, slightly sweet flavor to the smoky grilled pork. Add a green vegetable and you've got dinner.

Makes 4 servings

Grilling Method: Direct/Medium-Low Heat

2 tart apples, such as Granny Smith or Pink Lady
   Neutral vegetable or nut oil, such as canola, peanut, or walnut
   Sprinkle of sugar or cinnamon-sugar, optional

1. Build a charcoal fire or preheat a gas grill. Wash and dry the apples. Cut them in half crosswise. Using a small spoon or melon baller, scoop out the hard core and seeds. Cut the apples in $\frac{1}{2}$-inch slices so each slice has a circular hole in the middle where you removed the core (because of the center holes, the slices will resemble donuts).

2. Brush the apples with oil and sprinkle with sugar, if using. Place the slices on the cooking grate over direct medium-low heat, cover, and grill for 2 to

4 minutes on each side, or until well marked and warmed through. Remove from the grill and serve warm.

NOTE: Be sure to slice the apples at least $\frac{1}{2}$ inch thick and coat them with oil, or they may fall apart and stick to the cooking grate.

The Dragon's Blueberry Barbecue Sauce

Crescent Dragonwagon—known as Dragon to her close friends—is both a prolific writer and a prodigious cook. She had her first fifteen minutes of fame when she was chosen by former president Bill Clinton to cater one of his first inaugural brunches. Of all of her recipes, this delicious and different blueberry barbecue sauce recipe is my favorite. I love the sweet and tangy, many-spiced sauce that uses blueberries instead of tomatoes as the base.

Makes about 4 cups

2   quarts fresh or frozen blueberries (if using frozen berries, thaw, but reserve the juices)
$1\frac{1}{2}$ cups finely chopped celery
$1\frac{1}{2}$ cups finely chopped onions
$1\frac{1}{2}$ cups finely chopped green bell pepper
1   carrot, minced
1   clove garlic, minced
1   cup apple cider vinegar, or more to taste
$\frac{1}{2}$ cup honey, or more to taste
2   tablespoons molasses
2   tablespoons ketchup
1   tablespoon paprika
$1\frac{1}{2}$ teaspoons coarse sea salt
1   teaspoon freshly ground pepper
1   teaspoon ground cinnamon
$\frac{1}{2}$ teaspoon dry mustard
$\frac{1}{2}$ teaspoon ground ginger
$\frac{1}{4}$ teaspoon ground nutmeg
$\frac{1}{4}$ teaspoon celery seed
$\frac{1}{4}$ teaspoon cayenne pepper, or more to taste
$\frac{1}{8}$ teaspoon ground cloves

1. Puree the blueberries and any juices in a blender or food processor.
2. Combine the blueberry puree, vegetables, vinegar, honey, molasses, ketchup, and spices in a large, heavy, nonreactive saucepan. Gently simmer over medium heat until the vegetables are soft and the sauce is thick and flavorful, 15 to 20 minutes.
3. Return the sauce to the blender and puree until smooth. The sauce should be thick but pourable; if it's too thick, add a little water. Taste and adjust the seasonings, if necessary. The sauce will keep, covered in the refrigerator, for 2 weeks.

Off-the-Eaten-Path Barbecue Sauce

My friend Richard Ruben is an inventive and inspiring cooking teacher. He calls this recipe Spicy Barbecue Sauce. But I prefer my name because Richard's signature sauce calls for a few unusual and off-the-eaten-path ingredients, including cardamom pods, Indonesian ketjap manis *and my favorite—pomegranate juice. Whatever you call it, it is good eatin' and tailor-made for pork.*

Makes 2½ cups

1½ cups ketchup
½ cup *ketjap manis*
1 small onion, diced
¼ cup tomato paste
¼ cup honey
¼ cup pomegranate syrup
2 canned chipotle chiles in adobo sauce
3 cloves garlic, chopped
2 tablespoons apple cider vinegar
2 teaspoons kosher salt
5 black cardamom pods
½ teaspoon freshly ground pepper

1. Combine all the ingredients in a 4-quart saucepan and bring to a boil. Lower the heat and simmer for 20 minutes, until thickened and the onions are cooked and soft.
2. Pour the sauce through a strainer into a bowl. Discard the cardamom pods and diced onion.
3. Blend until smooth by using either an immersion blender in the bowl, or by putting the strained ingredients in a blender or food processor. This sauce will keep, covered in the refrigerator, for 2 weeks.

TIP: Indonesian *ketjap manis* (also spelled *kecap manis*) is a dark brown, syrupy-thick, sweet soy sauce flavored with palm sugar, star anise, and garlic. It is pronounced like the American ketchup, but it doesn't taste anything like it.

Gingered Honey Sauce

Makes ½ cup

1 cup apricot nectar
½ cup honey
1 knob fresh ginger (2 to 3 inches), peeled
    and grated
1 teaspoon dry jerk seasoning
1 teaspoon cornstarch mixed with 1 tablespoon
    water, optional (see Tip)

Pour the apricot nectar and honey into a small saucepan. Add the ginger and whisk to mix well. Bring to a boil and simmer until it is reduced by about one-third. Add the jerk seasoning and taste. Adjust the seasonings. Remove from the heat and let cool. Serve warm or at room temperature. If making in advance, refrigerate until using, then reheat slightly.

TIP: For a thicker sauce, add the cornstarch paste and bring the sauce to a boil over medium-high heat. Continue cooking, stirring, until the sauce thickens.

Lamb

Lamb 101

Rapid-Fire Checklist

✓ Preheat grill
✓ Brush lamb all over with olive oil
✓ Season with kosher salt and pepper, if desired
✓ Reduce heat to medium, choose the right cooking method
✓ Place lamb on cooking grate and cover
✓ Turn once halfway through cooking time if cooking by the Direct Method
✓ Remove lamb from grill
✓ Let meat rest 5 to 20 minutes, depending on size

Tools of the Trade

• 12-inch locking chef tongs
• Instant-read thermometer
• Silicone or natural-bristle brush
• Heavy-duty oven mitt

Common Problem

• Overcooked meat

Not too long ago, I was in Provence during "lamb season." It seemed that every restaurant I went to was featuring a lamb dish. I ate lamb for days and never got tired of it, even though it was all prepared exactly the same way—grilled or high-heat roasted and served rare. As this trip included pilgrimages to some of the world's highest gastronomic temples, it proved to me that, in the case of lamb, there is no need to reinvent the proverbial—or provincial—wheel. When you are grilling any cut of lamb except lamb shanks, which braise much better than they grill—high, dry heat and an end temperature no higher than medium will result in a sweet succulent dish. Some people think they don't like lamb because they don't like the smell of lamb fat cooking, but that is just another good reason to cook lamb outdoors. I also find that lamb turns from sweet to slightly more gamey in flavor the longer it cooks. For best results, I recommend lamb loin chops, a loin roast, a frenched rack of lamb (which can be cut into chops), and a leg of lamb, butterflied or bone in.

Cuts of Lamb

CHOPS

Lamb chops come from both the loin (loin chops) and the rib (rack of lamb and rib chops) sections of the lamb. The loin chops are cut from the loin roast. They are the most expensive and the most tender of the chops and can be identified by the T-bone. They are sometimes referred to as lamb T-bone chops. The rib chop is second only to the loin chop in tenderness and flavor. It is slightly fattier and thus more flavorful than the loin chop. Other chops come from the leg (sirloin) chop and the shoulder (blade) chop.

RIB RACK OF LAMB

Rack of lamb is actually a whole rib roast; it has seven or eight ribs and comes from the rib section. It may be grilled as a roast or cut into chops with either a single bone or double bones. I prefer cutting a rack into double-boned portions, because it is easier to keep the interior meat medium-rare and get a nice seared and caramelized exterior. Grilled chops served as cocktail or finger food should always be single boned.

Frenched Rack of Lamb: The term "frenched," or French style, means that the ends of the exposed bones of the rack have been cleaned; all the meat and fat have been stripped off, and the bones are dry. This is a traditional technique that is done for aesthetic value but can also be useful too. The cleaned bones on frenched lamb chops make them easy to serve at cocktail parties and wedding receptions, as the bone makes a handy holder for the chop—nature's finger food! (Check out Lamb Chopsickles, page 109).

LEG OF LAMB

Although a lamb has four legs, only the two hind legs are used in the cut commonly referred to as leg of lamb. It is a large, lean, and tender cut and can be grilled whole or divided into smaller pieces. The whole bone-in leg generally weighs from five to nine pounds and may be American style (no shank bone) or French style (with a shank bone). A whole leg that has been boned, rolled, and tied (referred to as BRT in the meat biz) makes a compact roast that is easy to grill and can be stuffed, or butterflied and stuffed before cooking.

Butterflied Leg of Lamb: Butterflying simply refers to taking the bone out of the leg of lamb and flattening it. When the meat is laid out flat, it somewhat resembles a butterfly and thus the name.

Kabobs: Choose cubes of meat that are free of fat, gristle, connective tissue, and bone. You can buy the meat precubed or cut your own. I prefer to buy a boned leg of lamb and cut my own meat because I know it is pristinely fresh and I can cut the cubes in the size that I need. (Kabob meat can also come from the shoulder, which is more flavorful but requires longer cooking in a braise or stew after grilling, as in the Coconut Lamb Curry, pages 112–113.)

TENDERLOIN

This cut from the loin muscle is very tender and very small; it serves one person and is perfect for quick grilling.

MEDALLIONS OR NOISETTES

These are crosswise slices of the boneless loin. They are very small, tender, and perfect for grilling. They can be used interchangeably with the tenderloin.

Single, Double, Triple

Are we talking shots? No. (Not in this chapter anyway.) Single, double, or triple refers to the number of bones you have in a single lamb rib chop. You can buy these to order from your butcher, but I like to buy the frenched rack and cut them myself. That way, I am assured of the freshest possible meat, and it's cheaper. In most restaurants, a triple, or "three bones," is considered a portion if cooking whole; if cutting into chops, the double, or two-bone, chop is classic. Count on serving two double chops or four bones per person. Single-bone lamb chops are usually reserved for cocktail food; they are easier to eat and take very little time to cook.

On the Fire: Direct or Indirect Heat

- Single and double chops: Direct
- Triple chops, roasts, leg of lamb: Indirect
- Butterflied leg of lamb, full rack of lamb: Combo

To Turn or Not to Turn

I usually base whether or not to turn the meat on a rule of thumb: If it takes more than 20 minutes to cook (Indirect Heat), you don't need to turn it unless you want the aesthetic of grill marks. Butterflied leg of lamb, the rack, and chops always look more appetizing with those tell-tale grill marks and should be cooked using the Combo Method.

Testing for Doneness

Don't overcook the lamb. Be sure to use an instant-read thermometer for just about every cut of meat over three pounds or longer than four inches. The exceptions are tenderloin and single and double chops—these are easier to "eyeball" than test with a thermometer. The meat is generally done when browned on both sides and firm to the touch. The bone also recedes slightly from the meat. Lamb is medium-rare at 145°F, which means that the center of the cut will still be juicy and a rosy red.

Grilled Lamb Chops 101

The only variable in this basic recipe is the thickness of the chops. The thicker the chop, the longer it will take to cook. The cooking time will vary slightly based on how hot the grill is, but use this basic rule: Calculate four to five minutes for every one-half inch of thickness for medium-rare. For example, a one-inch chop will take eight to ten minutes total cooking time. Brush each chop with olive oil, season with salt and pepper, and turn only once halfway through the relatively short cooking time. Even two-inch chops should take less than 20 minutes over direct heat to be cooked to medium-rare perfection.

Makes 2 to 4 servings

Grilling Method: Direct/Medium Heat
Special Equipment: Sharp 10-inch chef's knife

1   rack of lamb (8 bones), frenched (bones trimmed), about 1½ pounds, or 4 lamb loin chops, about ⅓ pound each
    Olive oil
    Kosher salt
    Freshly ground pepper, optional

1. Build a charcoal fire or preheat a gas grill. Pat the lamb dry with paper towels. Place the rack on a secure wooden cutting board and cut through the lamb every 2 bones, using the bones as a guideline. You will have 4 chops with 2 bones each, about 1½ inches thick.
2. Brush all over with olive oil and season with salt and pepper to taste, if desired. Place the chops on the cooking grate over direct medium heat, cover, and grill for 6 to 7 minutes per side for medium-rare (145°F). Cook them longer if you prefer your meat more fully cooked. Test the internal temperature by inserting an instant-read thermometer in the center of the thickest part of the meat, being careful not to hit the bone.
3. Remove the lamb from the grill and place it on a clean platter. Let the chops rest for 5 minutes before serving. Season with additional salt and pepper, if desired, and serve.

NOTE: Make sure that the cutting board is stable and unmoving before cutting on it. Wet a paper towel, wring it out, and lay it flat on the counter. Place the cutting board on top and push away from you. It should not move easily. Now you are ready to wield that knife.

Rack of Lamb 101

I think that a whole rack of lamb is one of the most elegant main courses around. It used to be that this dish was reserved for restaurants or the occasional home meal because it was so hard to find a rack of lamb. Now, the wide distribution of tender Australian and New Zealand lamb makes it much easier to serve at home, and for a fraction of the restaurant price. One rack, preferably frenched, will serve two adults handsomely.

Makes 2 to 4 servings

Grilling Method: Direct/Medium Heat

1   rack of lamb (8 bones), frenched (bones trimmed), about 1½ pounds
    Olive oil
    Kosher salt
    Freshly ground pepper

1. Build a charcoal fire or preheat a gas grill. Pat the lamb dry with paper towels. Brush all over with olive oil and season with salt and, if desired, pepper.
2. Place the rack in the center of the cooking grate, bone-side down, over direct medium heat. Cover and grill for 45 to 55 minutes or until the lamb is browned on the outside and medium-rare (140°F) on the inside. Test the internal temperature by inserting an instant-read thermometer in the center of the thickest part of the meat, being careful not to hit the bone.
3. Remove the rack from the grill onto a clean platter and let the lamb rest for 10 minutes before slicing and serving. You can cut the rack in half and serve a 4-bone mini-roast or cut it into 4 pieces, carving every 2 bones.

TIP: The grill-roasting time will change based on the weight of the rack of lamb. A small Australian rack of lamb weighs about 1½ pounds and will be cooked to a perfect medium rare in 45 to 55 minutes. A larger American rack of lamb can weigh up to 3 pounds and will take about 1½ hours.

Approximate **LAMB** *Cooking Times* (°F)

TYPE OF LAMB	THICKNESS OR WEIGHT	DEGREE OF DONENESS	GRILLING METHOD	GRILLING TIME	INTERNAL TEMP.	REST TIME
Chop, loin	1½ inches thick	Medium-rare	Direct Medium	12 to 14 minutes	145°F	5 minutes
Chop, rib	1 inch thick	Medium-rare	Direct Medium	8 to 12 minutes	145°F	5 minutes
Chop, shoulder	1 inch thick	Medium-rare	Direct Medium	12 to 14 minutes	145°F	5 minutes
Chop, sirloin	1 inch thick	Medium-rare	Direct Medium	12 to 14 minutes	145°F	5 minutes
Cubes for kabobs	1½ to 2 inches thick	Medium-rare	Direct Medium	8 to 12 minutes	145°F	5 minutes
Leg of lamb, bone in	5 to 7 pounds	Medium-rare	Indirect Medium	1½ to 2 hours	145°F	15 to 20 minutes
Leg of lamb, boneless, stuffed	3 to 4 pounds	Medium-rare	Indirect Medium	45 to 60 minutes	145°F	10 minutes
Leg of lamb, butterflied	3 to 4 pounds	Medium-rare	Direct Medium or Combo	16 to 20 minutes	145°F	10 minutes
Rack of lamb	1½ pounds	Medium-rare	Indirect Medium or Combo	45 to 55 minutes	145°F	10 minutes
Shoulder, boneless	3½ to 5 pounds	Well done	Indirect Medium	1 to 2 hours	180°F	10 minutes

All internal temperatures are based on USDA recommended values, using an instant-read thermometer.
Times and temperatures in the chart are guidelines. Specific recipes may call for variations.

Butterflied Leg of Lamb 101, Unstuffed

There are two ways to prepare leg of lamb: whole and butterflied. For years, I chose the former, preferring the rich flavor of a slowly grill-roasted piece of meat. But then my grill friend John Mose convinced me of the wonders of a boneless (butterflied) leg of lamb. The boned meat takes a lot less time to cook since it is so thin; and it is so versatile—perfect for wet or dry rubs, marinades, and stuffing. I also like it grilled quickly with the Grilling Trilogy (see pages 19–20) of olive oil, salt, and pepper, so the natural flavor of the lamb and the smoky goodness of the grill really shine through. This way of grilling works best with a boneless butterflied leg of lamb that is roughly the same thickness throughout.

Makes 6 to 8 servings

Grilling Method: Direct/Medium Heat

1 leg of lamb, 3 to 4 pounds, butterflied
Olive oil
Kosher salt
Freshly ground pepper

1. Build a charcoal fire or preheat a gas grill. Pat the lamb dry with paper towels. Brush it all over with olive oil. Season with salt and, if desired, pepper.
2. Place the lamb on the cooking grate over direct medium heat, laying it out as flat as possible. Cover and grill for 8 to 10 minutes per side for medium-rare. The time will vary based on the thickness of the lamb. Use long-handled tongs to turn the lamb over. Remove the lamb from the grill and place it on a clean platter. Let it rest for 5 minutes before carving and serving.

Butterflied Leg of Lamb 101, Stuffed

Once you have boned and flattened the leg of lamb, you can stuff it with all kinds of seasonings that make it even more delicious. Guests get a kick out of the surprise in the center of the roast, and the extra ingredients add a touch of luxury to a simple grilled meat. Stuffed lamb also makes great sandwiches the next day. Below are two basic fillings. Once you've mastered these, try the Butterflied Lamb with Garlic, Lemon, Spinach, and Feta Cheese (page 116) or any of your own favorite combinations.

Makes 6 to 8 servings

Grilling Method: Indirect/Medium Heat

1   leg of lamb, 3 to 4 pounds, butterflied
     Olive oil
     Kosher salt
     Freshly ground pepper
½ to 1 cup stuffing, such as pesto or tapenade
     Solid wooden toothpicks, soaked in water for
     30 minutes

1. Build a charcoal fire or preheat a gas grill. Pat the lamb dry with paper towels. Brush it all over with olive oil. Season with salt and, if desired, pepper. Spread one side with pesto or another stuffing.
2. Beginning with the smallest end, begin rolling the meat with your fingers until you come to the end. Secure it with wet toothpicks or trussing pins. Place the rolled meat, toothpick-side down, on

PRESERVED LEMONS

This Mediterranean condiment is tailor-made for lamb (fish and chicken, too). To make preserved lemons, cut 10 lemons as thinly as possible—a mandoline works very well for this job. Mix equal parts of sugar and kosher salt (about 1 cup each). Line the bottom of a resealable plastic container with lemons, sprinkle the lemons with the sugar-salt mixture, and repeat the layers until all the lemons are covered. Let the mixture sit in the refrigerator for 24 hours. The preserved lemons keep indefinitely and get better as they age, covered in the refrigerator. Cook with the preserved lemons or serve them as a garnish or condiment.

the cooking grate over indirect medium heat, cover, and grill for 15 minutes. Turn over and continue grilling for 20 to 25 more minutes or until the meat is cooked to the desired doneness. Use an instant-read thermometer to gauge doneness: Rare is 135°F.
3. Remove the lamb from the grill to a clean platter, and let it rest for 10 minutes. Slice it vertically (like a roast) and serve immediately. Can be served the next day in sandwiches or gently reheated.

Whole Bone-In Leg of Lamb 101

Like any roast, a whole bone-in leg of lamb is one of the easiest pieces of meat to grill. Because it grill-roasts over indirect heat for a long period of time, the meat will naturally caramelize and brown on the outside without any need for turning. The only thing this recipe needs is adequate time, great raw ingredients, and the Grilling Trilogy (see pages 19–20).

Makes 6 to 8 servings

Grilling Method: Indirect/Medium Heat
Special Equipment: V-rack roast holder, optional

1   bone-in leg of lamb, 5 to 7 pounds
     Olive oil
     Kosher salt
     Freshly ground pepper

1. Build a charcoal fire or preheat a gas grill. Pat the lamb dry with paper towels. Brush it all over with olive oil. Season with salt and, if desired, pepper.
2. Place the lamb, fat-side up, on the cooking grate or in a V-rack set in a disposable aluminum pan over indirect medium heat. Cover and grill-roast for 1½ to 2 hours or until the lamb registers 140°F in the thickest part of the leg. When inserting the instant-read thermometer, make sure you do not hit the bone or it will not give you an accurate reading. There is no need to turn the lamb.
3. Remove the lamb to a clean platter, and let it rest for 15 to 20 minutes before carving and serving.

Variation: Make random slits in the meat every couple of inches and insert half a peeled garlic clove in each before brushing with oil and seasoning with salt and pepper.

Lamb Chopsickles

You may have enjoyed these finger-licking lamb chops at a wedding or a special event where guests gobble up the lamb chops with one hand while balancing a champagne flute with the other. Although I love the taste of these simple single-bone chopsickles, I much prefer eating them at a backyard cookout than a formal soiree. Because, just like ribs, I think that meat eaten right off the bone lends itself to a more down-home atmosphere. Serve the chops sizzling hot off the grill with a refreshing squeeze of lemon juice and plenty of napkins.

Makes 4 to 6 servings

Grilling Method: Direct/Medium Heat
Special Equipment: Vacu-Vin Instant Marinater, optional

$^2/_3$	cup extra-virgin olive oil
8	cloves garlic, minced or pureed
2	teaspoons capers, minced
2	lemons, zested and cut into wedges
16	single-bone lamb chops, cut from 2 frenched racks of lamb
	Kosher salt
	Freshly ground pepper
	Fleur de sel
	Lemon wedges

1. In a small bowl, mix the olive oil, garlic, capers, and zest and set aside.
2. Pat the chops dry with paper towels. Place the lamb chops in a single layer in a shallow, nonreactive dish or the instant marinater. Pour the olive oil mixture over the chops and turn the chops to make sure they are evenly coated. Cover and marinate in the refrigerator—turning the chops over once halfway through—for 1 to 4 hours. If using the instant marinater, you will only need to marinate for 30 minutes.
3. Just before grilling, build a charcoal fire or preheat a gas grill. Season the chops with salt and pepper. Place the chops on the cooking grate over direct medium heat, cover, and cook 3 to 4 minutes per side for medium-rare. Serve the chops literally hot off the grill. Before passing them to your guests, squeeze a lemon wedge over the chops and sprinkle with fleur de sel. Serve with lemon wedges.

TIP: Each lamb chop should have three- to four-inch long "frenched" bones attached to the medallion of meat. Since these chops are to be served as finger food, the bones serve as the handle that your guests hold while eating.

Herbes de Provence–Crusted Lamb Chops

This is the classic marrying of garlic, herbes de Provence, and tender lamb. If you only add one lamb recipe to your backyard grilling repertoire, make it this one. I've borrowed the technique of rubbing the exposed meat with garlic before coating it with the herbes de Provence from cookbook author Mark Bittman. Rubbing the meat lightly flavors it, so if you prefer your lamb with a strong garlic flavor, mince the garlic and mix it with the herbs instead of rubbing the meat with the garlic cloves. Serve this with Sparkling Roasted New Potatoes (pages 210–211), but keep in mind that the potatoes will take longer to cook than the lamb chops, so start them 40 minutes before you want to eat.

Makes 4 servings

Grilling Method: Direct/Medium Heat

1	rack of lamb (8 bones), about $1^1/_2$ pounds
	Kosher salt
4	large cloves garlic, cut in half
3	tablespoons Dijon mustard
1	tablespoon herbes de Provence
	Freshly ground pepper, optional
$^1/_4$	cup chopped fresh parsley
	Fleur de sel, optional

1. Build a charcoal fire or preheat a gas grill.
2. Pat the lamb dry with paper towels. Cut the rack into 4 double-chop portions and spread them out on a sheet of waxed paper. Sprinkle both sides with salt. Using half a clove per side, rub the garlic all over to "scent" the meat. Discard the garlic cloves and set the meat aside.
3. In a small bowl, mix the mustard and herbs and the pepper, if using. Spread the mustard-herb mixture over both sides of the lamb chops.
4. Place the lamb in the center of the cooking grate over direct medium heat, bone-side down. Cover and grill 8 to 10 minutes without turning. During the last 2 to 3 minutes of cooking time, sear both sides of the lamb over the heat to add grill marks.
5. Remove the lamb to a clean platter, and let it sit for 5 minutes before serving on a bed of parsley with the bones interlocking. Sprinkle with fleur de sel, if using.

NOTE: The bones make their own "rack," holding the chops away from the cooking grates.

Lamb Tenderloins with Hazelnut Butter

A few years ago, I noticed that my grocery store started carrying lamb tenderloins, so I bought one to experiment with. As I was walking home, I began to imagine the sweet rare "noisettes" of lamb that I was about to grill. Noisette is French for hazelnut and also the term for small tender round pieces of meat. The dual meaning of noisette inspired this very simple and delicious recipe. If you can't find lamb tenderloins or lamb noisettes, substitute lamb chops or thin slices of leg of lamb and follow the relevant 101 recipes at the beginning of this chapter.

Makes 4 servings

Grilling Method: Direct/Medium-High Heat

4   lamb tenderloins, or medallions, about
      ¼ pound each
      Olive oil
      Kosher salt
½   cup (1 stick) unsalted butter
½   cup whole hazelnuts or filberts, shelled
2   sprigs fresh thyme, leaves only
1   orange, zested
      Fine-grain sea salt
      Grains of paradise or white pepper

1. Build a charcoal fire or preheat a gas grill.
2. Pat the lamb dry with paper towels. Place the tenderloins in a small glass dish or plate. Drizzle them liberally with olive oil and season with salt. Cover and set aside.
3. Put the butter in a cold pan and melt it slowly over medium heat. Add 1 tablespoon of olive oil and stir in the hazelnuts. Continue to cook slowly until the hazelnuts are brown, about 15 minutes. Remove from the heat.
4. Place the lamb on the cooking grate over direct medium-high heat, cover, and grill 6 to 8 minutes total, turning to sear all sides. It will cook very quickly, so be careful not to overcook. I generally set a timer so I don't get distracted and leave it on the grill too long. The meat will be marked by the grill, reduced in size, and firm to the touch.
5. Remove the lamb from the grill to a clean platter and let it rest while you finish the sauce.
6. Slowly reheat the butter and hazelnuts, and add the orange zest and thyme. Stir to mix well. Season with sea salt and freshly ground grains of paradise, if using, or white pepper and stir again. Taste and adjust the seasonings if necessary. Make sure that the butter does not burn, but keep it warm on the stovetop (over the lowest flame possible), while you slice the meat.
7. Slice each tenderloin on the bias and put the slices on a dinner plate. Drizzle each plate with ¼ of the sauce and nuts. Serve immediately.

Patio Daddy-O Shish Kabobs

In the fifties, shish kabobs were a favorite for entertaining around the barbecue. These popular skewers of meat and vegetables are said to be Turkish in origin, but many of us associate them with Greek cuisine. The classic shish kabob is still the preferred version of this famous food on a stick: peppers, tomatoes, white onions, button mushrooms, and chunks of lean meat. I love the flavor combination but find the tradition of threading all the foods together impractical since the ingredients take different amounts of time to cook. In my recipe, I assemble the skewers by the type of food so you can remove each from the grill when it is perfectly done.

Makes 6 servings

Grilling Method: Direct/Medium Heat
Special Equipment: Vacu Vin Instant Marinater, optional

1   orange, zested and juiced
1   lemon, zested and juiced
¼   cup olive oil
3   cloves garlic, minced
1   tablespoon coarsely chopped fresh rosemary or
      2 teaspoons dried rosemary
3   pounds boneless lamb (from leg or shoulder),
      cut into 2-inch chunks
28   bamboo skewers, soaked in water for 30 minutes
1   large red onion, cut into 1½-inch wedges
2   yellow bell peppers, cut into 3-inch squares
8   ounces medium mushrooms, stems trimmed
6   ripe Roma tomatoes, cut in half
      Sea salt
      Freshly ground pepper

1. In a medium bowl, whisk together the juices, zests, olive oil, garlic, and rosemary. Arrange the lamb chunks in a single layer in a glass dish and pour the marinade over it or use a Vacu Vin Instant Marinater. Cover and refrigerate for 1 to 2 hours (30 minutes in the marinater), stirring every now and again to coat the lamb evenly.

2. When ready to cook, build a charcoal fire or preheat a gas grill.

3. To assemble the kabobs, put the vegetables on a cutting board with the skewers nearby. Drain the meat from the marinade (discard marinade). Thread the meat onto 2 skewers, so they resemble a ladder. Leave room in between the meat so the pieces cook evenly. You should have about 4 kabobs.

4. Repeat the skewering process with the onion, peppers, mushrooms, and tomatoes, using 2 bamboo skewers for each kabob. Brush all the kabobs with oil and season with salt and pepper.

5. Place the kabobs in the center of the cooking grate over direct medium heat, turning to sear all sides. Cook to the desired degree of doneness, 8 to 10 minutes for the lamb to reach medium-rare. The meat and vegetables will take different amounts of time to cook. The tomatoes will be done first, the mushrooms next and then the meat, onions and peppers.

6. As the skewers are done, remove them from the grill. Place them on a clean platter. Let the meat rest for 5 minutes while you unskewer the vegetables. Serve the shish kabobs surrounded by the grilled veggies.

Lamb Kabobs with Lavender Honey and Mashed Sunchokes

In the Alpilles mountains of France, animals graze on garlicky grass and wild lavender. In the process, the lamb is naturally flavored and only needs a little salt to finish off the seasoning. Although the lamb isn't exported to the United States, you can have the same taste sensation by making these kabobs. Ask your butcher for meaty chunks from the leg or the shoulder and marinate it in rosé wine

SUNCHOKES OR JERUSALEM ARTICHOKES

This root vegetable is native to America and marketed under both names. The tubers resemble small, nubby potatoes with a thin skin that must be peeled before eating. They are available year-round, but they are "in season" and at their best from late fall through early spring. The vegetable has no literal connection to either Jerusalem or artichokes (although I personally think the flavor is similar to that of artichokes). The plant is part of the sunflower family, which is where "sun" choke comes from. They can be eaten either cooked or raw. Important fact: The sunchoke has almost as much iron as meat but no fat.

and raspberry vinegar before grilling. The sunchokes are grill-roasted and then mashed with lots of green olive oil and a touch of the lavender honey.

Makes 6 servings

Grilling Method: Direct/Medium Heat
Special Equipment: Vacu Vin Instant Marinater, optional

3	pounds boneless lamb (from leg or shoulder), cut into 2-inch chunks
2	cups rosé wine, plus 1 tablespoon for glaze
1/2	cup raspberry vinegar, plus 1 tablespoon for glaze
2	teaspoons (untreated) lavender flowers, plus a pinch for glaze
	Best-quality extra-virgin olive oil
3/4	cup lavender honey, divided
	Sea salt
	Pinch herbes de Provence
12	bamboo skewers, soaked in water for 30 minutes

Mashed Sunchokes

3	pounds sunchokes or Jerusalem artichokes, peeled and soaked in enough water to cover mixed with the juice of 1 lemon
1/2	cup best-quality olive oil, preferably French
1	tablespoon lavender honey or more to taste
	Fine-grain sea salt
	Grains of paradise or freshly ground pepper

1. Pat the lamb dry with paper towels. Cover and set aside while you make the marinade.

2. In a large bowl, whisk together the wine, vinegar, lavender, olive oil, and ¼ cup of honey. Add a pinch of salt and herbes de Provence. Put the marinade in a nonreactive container with a lid or in the Vacu Vin Instant Marinater. Add the lamb, toss with the marinade to coat, and cover the bowl. Refrigerate for 1 to 2 hours. If using the Vacu Vin Instant Marinater, you can reduce the marinating time to 30 minutes.

3. Meanwhile, make a lavender honey glaze by mixing the remaining ½ cup honey with about 1 tablespoon wine and 1 tablespoon vinegar in a medium bowl. Stir to combine, and add a pinch of lavender and salt. If the honey is still too thick to brush onto the meat easily, add a little more vinegar. Cover and set aside.

4. About 1 hour before you want to eat, build a charcoal fire or preheat a gas grill.

5. Make the Mashed Sunchokes: Drain the sunchokes and toss them with olive oil and salt. Place them on the warming rack of the grill or on the cooking grate over indirect medium heat. Turn occasionally to grill them evenly, until tender when tested with a fork, about 40 minutes.

6. Preheat the oven to the lowest setting. Remove the sunchokes from the grill and transfer them to a large ovenproof bowl. While still hot, mash them with enough olive oil to give them a roughly mashed texture. Add about 1 tablespoon honey and, using a large fork, mix well to blend. Taste and season as necessary with salt and grains of paradise or pepper. Cover with foil and keep warm in the oven while you grill the kabobs.

7. Drain the meat and discard the marinade. Using 2 skewers for each kabob, divide the meat evenly into 6 portions and thread the meat onto the skewers so they look like ladders (see page 28). Brush the kabobs with olive oil and season with salt.

8. Place the kabobs on the cooking grate over direct medium heat, cover, and grill for about 10 minutes, turning once halfway through the cooking time for medium-rare meat. Remove the kabobs from the grill. Transfer them to a clean platter and immediately brush them with honey glaze. Let the kabobs rest for 5 minutes before serving them hot with the mashed sunchokes.

Coconut Lamb Curry

I hesitate to call this recipe lamb curry since it is so far removed from an authentic lamb curry, but I love the combination of the smoky caramelized meat and chunks of potatoes with the rich spicy curry sauce. You can make this dish in advance and reheat it just before serving. The baby peas add a little extra color, texture, and sweet flavor. Serve with fragrant jasmine rice and loads of Indian condiments— my favorite is a cilantro-mint relish.

Makes 6 to 8 servings

Grilling Method: Direct/Medium Heat

2	pounds boneless lamb (from leg or shoulder), cut into 1-inch chunks
12	red-skinned or Yukon Gold potatoes, quartered
	Olive oil
	Kosher salt
	Freshly ground pepper
	Bamboo skewers, soaked in water for 30 minutes
1	red onion, thinly sliced
2	tablespoons clarified butter or *ghee* (see Tip, page 113)
2 to 3	tablespoons curry powder
1	cup chicken stock or broth
1	14-ounce can coconut milk
2	teaspoons Thai fish sauce
1	cup frozen green peas
4	cups cooked jasmine or basmati rice
2	sprigs fresh cilantro or parsley, chopped

1. Build a charcoal fire or preheat a gas grill.
2. Pat the lamb dry with paper towels. Coat the lamb and potatoes with olive oil and season with salt and pepper, if desired. Thread the lamb chunks onto skewers, using 2 on each side of the food to resemble ladders (see page 28). Repeat the process with the chunks of potatoes. Place the lamb and potatoes on the cooking grate over direct medium heat. Cover and grill 10 to 15 minutes, turning occasionally to brown all sides. Remove the kabobs from the grill. Transfer to a clean platter. Cover with foil and set aside.
3. Pour about 2 tablespoons of olive oil in a sauté pan. Add a pinch of salt and heat over medium heat until the oil ripples. Add the onions and cook until they are soft and browned (caramelized), stirring occasionally, for 10 to 15 minutes.
4. Meanwhile, in a small bowl, mix the curry powder with the clarified butter and add to the onions to distribute. Add the stock and stir again until the curry powder is completely dissolved. Add the coconut milk and fish sauce and stir until mixed. Add the lamb and potatoes.
5. Simmer for 30 minutes, covered, or until the lamb is completely tender. Remove the cover, then taste and adjust the seasonings. Cook uncovered for another 15 minutes. Add the peas and cook for a final 10 minutes, or until the peas are tender but still bright green in color. Serve with jasmine rice and a sprinkle of chopped cilantro.

TIP: To clarify butter, melt it over medium-low heat, then let it sit until the white milk solids come to the top. This happens quickly in the refrigerator (or the freezer if you are short on time). Remove and discard the cloudy top with a spoon and you will be left with a clear yellow oil that is called clarified butter in Western cuisine and *ghee* in Indian cuisine. If you make a large quantity, it keeps indefinitely when covered in the refrigerator.

Lamb Satay with Smoked-Paprika Butter Sauce

This pounded-out lamb dish is marinated in garlic and lemon, then grilled quickly over direct heat. Buy a butter- flied leg of lamb and ask your butcher to cut it into thin strips. These strips are easy to flatten between two pieces of strong plastic wrap or parchment paper, giving them the shape of the classic Asian satay. But that is where the Asian influence ends. The seared meat is served with a smoked- paprika butter sauce, making it much more west than east! Thread the marinated lamb onto skewers before grilling. The skewers will serve double duty, as each satay can be dipped into the smoked butter sauce and eaten straight from the stick. The skewers make a great appetizer.

Makes 6 to 8 servings

Grilling Method: Direct/Medium Heat
Special Equipment: Meat pounder or rolling pin

1 pound butterflied leg of lamb or sirloin, cut into strips about $\frac{1}{2}$ inch wide
Olive oil
Kosher salt
Bamboo skewers, soaked in water for 30 minutes
1 cup (2 sticks) unsalted butter
2 tablespoons hot smoked (Spanish) paprika
Sea salt
Chopped fresh parsley

1. Build a charcoal fire or preheat a gas grill.
2. Pat the lamb dry with paper towels. Pound out the strips of lamb between 2 pieces of parchment or plastic wrap until they are $\frac{1}{2}$ inch thick and no more than 3 inches wide. Brush all over with olive oil and thread the meat onto bamboo skewers, as if you were sewing; think of the meat as the fabric and the skewer as the needle. (Because the meat is so thin you need to thread the skewer in and out of the meat, from one end to the other.)

3. Season the satays with salt. Place the skewers on the cooking grate over direct medium heat, cover, and grill for 3 to 4 minutes on each side or until well marked and cooked through to medium.

4. Meanwhile, put the butter in a small saucepan. Melt it over medium heat, add the paprika and turn off the heat. Taste and adjust the seasoning with salt and more paprika, if desired; set aside and keep warm over a very low heat. Stir again just before serving.

5. Remove the lamb satays from the grill and place them on a clean platter. Sprinkle them with chopped parsley and serve immediately with the paprika butter sauce.

Navy Bob's Leg of Lamb

This is the grilling specialty of my Navy Seal friend, "Sideshow" Bob. Like a good Navy boy, he wanted me to know that he originally got the recipe out of Playboy magazine. Apparently some men really do get it for the articles— or recipes! This garlicky roasted lamb is so good that he isn't allowed to serve anything else when his family comes to visit. In fact, his parents have been known to pack a leg of lamb in their suitcases, just to make sure he grills it. This recipe is pungent with garlic, and I really like it that way; but if you prefer a lighter garlic flavor, feel free to reduce it to suit your taste. Add your favorite seasonal vegetables along with or instead of the potatoes, tomatoes, and carrots.

Makes 6 to 8 servings

Grilling Method: Indirect/Medium-High Heat
Special Equipment: V-rack roast holder and roasting pan

Sauce
- ¼ cup best-quality olive oil
- ¼ cup soy sauce
- 6 cloves garlic, chopped
- 2 teaspoons kosher salt
- 2 teaspoons freshly ground pepper
- 2 teaspoons ground ginger
- 2 teaspoons dried thyme
- 2 teaspoons dried sage
- 2 teaspoons dried marjoram
- 2 bay leaves, crushed

- 1 bone-in leg of lamb, 6 to 7 pounds, trimmed of excess fat
- 6 cloves garlic, slivered
- 6 medium yellow onions, cut into quarters
- 8 plum tomatoes
- 8 small Yukon Gold potatoes
- 8 carrots, quartered

1. Make the sauce: In a medium bowl, mix the olive oil, soy sauce, chopped garlic, salt, pepper, ginger, thyme, sage, marjoram, and bay leaves until well combined. Set aside.

2. Build a charcoal fire or preheat a gas grill.

3. Pat the lamb dry with paper towels and then pierce it all over with a paring knife. Insert slivers of garlic into the holes. Place the lamb in a V-rack and set into a large roasting pan. Pour the sauce evenly over the lamb. Surround the lamb with the onions, tomatoes, potatoes, and carrots.

4. Place the lamb in the center of the cooking grate over indirect medium-high heat. Cover and grill-roast for 20 minutes. Reduce the heat to medium and grill for 1½ to 2½ more hours, depending on the size of the leg, or until an instant-read thermometer registers 140°F (medium-rare).

5. Remove the lamb to a clean platter, and let it rest for 15 to 20 minutes. Transfer it to a carving board to slice and serve with the roasted vegetables and sauce.

Red Wine–Marinated Leg of Lamb with Roasted Cipollini Onions

I usually don't see much of a reason to marinate foods overnight, especially since too much acid in the marinade can ruin the texture of the meat, turning it into mush. But with a hearty bone-in leg of lamb, soaking it in a red wine marinade overnight perfumes the meat and deepens the flavor. It also tints the meat a very pleasing light pink color. I marinate the cipollini onions with the lamb for the same reason. While the lamb cooks, reduce the marinade with a cup of balsamic vinegar until thickened to make a gravy that bursts with flavor!

Makes 6 servings

Grilling Method: Indirect/Medium Heat

 1 bone-in leg of lamb, 6 to 7 pounds, excess
    fat trimmed
 6 cloves garlic, minced or pureed
    Olive oil
 2 tablespoons dried thyme
 1 bottle red wine, such as Pinot Noir, Shiraz,
    or Beaujolais
 ½ cup whole-grain mustard
 3 tablespoons coarsely cracked pepper,
    toasted
16 cipollini onions, unpeeled
    Kosher salt

1. Pat the lamb dry with paper towels. The day
   before you are going to grill the lamb, combine
   the garlic, 3 tablespoons of olive oil, and the
   thyme. Rub the lamb all over with this mixture.
   In a large glass or nonreactive container, combine
   the wine, mustard, and pepper until all the ingredients are equally distributed. Add the lamb and
   onions and marinate, covered in the refrigerator
   overnight, turning occasionally to submerge all
   surfaces with the marinade.
2. About 20 minutes before you are ready to cook,
   build a charcoal fire or preheat a gas grill.
3. Remove the lamb and onions from the marinade
   discard marinade and pat them dry. Brush them
   with olive oil and season with salt. Place the lamb
   in the center of the cooking grate over indirect
   medium heat. Cover and grill for 1½ to 2 hours,
   until an instant-read thermometer registers 140°F
   (medium-rare) in the roast's thickest part. During
   the final 40 minutes of the lamb's cooking time,
   put the onions on the cooking grate or warming
   rack over indirect heat and roast them until soft
   and the sugars are oozing out of the skin, about
   40 minutes.
4. Remove the lamb and onions from the grill, tent
   loosely with foil, and let rest for 15 minutes before
   carving and serving.

Fresh Herb and Panko–Crusted Rack of Lamb

Fresh herbs and Dijon mustard are combined to make a wet rub that flavors the lamb and turns into a yummy crust as the whole rack grill-roasts. I've replaced the traditional bread crumbs with Japanese panko crumbs because they stay crunchy and brown more easily. If you are feeling particu-larly indulgent, drizzle the panko crumbs with butter before patting them on the lamb.

Makes 4 servings

Grilling Method: Indirect/Medium Heat

 1 rack of lamb (8 bones), about 1½ pounds,
    frenched (bones trimmed)
    Olive oil
 3 tablespoons Dijon mustard
 ½ cup chopped fresh herbs, such as parsley, mint,
    basil, and lemon thyme
 ½ cup panko or other dry bread crumbs
    Kosher salt
    Freshly ground pepper
 2 tablespoons unsalted butter, softened
 2 cloves garlic, minced or pureed

1. Build a charcoal fire or preheat a gas grill.
2. Pat the lamb dry with paper towels. Trim any
   excess fat from the roast with a sharp knife. This
   will probably not be necessary as today's meat
   department generally sells racks of lamb trimmed
   and frenched. Brush the lamb all over with olive
   oil and spread the mustard over the lamb. Place
   the lamb, rib-side up, on a tray or a piece of
   waxed paper.
3. In a small bowl, combine the panko, herbs, and
   salt and pepper to taste. Stir in the butter and garlic. Pat the mixture on the meaty side of the roast.
4. Place the lamb in the center of the cooking grate
   over indirect medium heat. Cover and grill-roast
   for 45 to 55 minutes, or until an instant-read
   thermometer inserted in the center of the rib roast
   reads 140°F (medium-rare).
5. Let the rack stand off the heat for 15 minutes
   before carving into individual portions.

Butterflied Lamb with Garlic, Lemon, Spinach, and Feta Cheese

Opa! This stuffed, boned, rolled, and tied leg of lamb is a meal-in-one. The spinach filling is redolent of quintessential Greek flavors and makes a pretty plate when paired with saffron rice or mashed Yukon Gold potatoes. It tastes of spring and is perfect as the centerpiece of an Easter dinner. Make it even more festive by hiding a row of peeled hard-cooked eggs in the center so every slice of the stuffed roast reveals a bright circle of Easter egg.

Makes 8 to 10 servings

Grilling Method: Indirect/Medium Heat

1	leg of lamb, 5 to 6 pounds, boned and butterflied
12	cloves garlic, cut into slivers
1	tablespoon fresh oregano or 1 teaspoon dried oregano
	Sea salt
	Freshly ground pepper
	Olive oil
2	shallots, chopped
2	9-ounce packages frozen chopped spinach, thawed
8	ounces feta cheese, crumbled
1	lemon, zested and juiced
	Solid wooden toothpicks or butcher's twine, soaked in water for 30 minutes
³/₄	cup white wine

1. Pat the lamb dry with paper towels. Early in the day, place the lamb in a large nonreactive dish. Using a small paring knife, cut several ¹/₂-inch deep slits across the surface of the meat on both sides and insert a garlic sliver into each. (If there are already slits in the meat from the butchering process, stuff those holes before cutting new ones.) Rub the oregano evenly over the meat on each side. Season with salt and pepper.

2. Preheat a heavy-bottomed sauté pan with about 1 tablespoon of olive oil and a pinch of salt. When the oil is hot, but not smoking, add the shallots and sauté for 5 to 7 minutes, or until beginning to brown. Remove from the heat to a medium bowl, and set aside. Squeeze all the excess water out of the spinach, then mix it with the shallots. Add the feta and zest. Mix until well combined. Spread the spinach mixture evenly over the meat and, using your hands, roll up the lamb. Fasten the ends with toothpicks or secure with twine.

3. Whisk together the wine, ¹/₂ cup of oil, and the lemon juice and pour it over the meat. Marinate the lamb, covered in the refrigerator, turning it 3 or 4 times, for at least 6 and up to 12 hours.

4. About 20 minutes before you are ready to grill, build a charcoal fire or preheat a gas grill.

5. Remove the meat from the marinade, letting any excess drip back into the pan. Discard marinade. Place the lamb in the center of the cooking grate, toothpick-side down, over indirect medium heat. Cover and grill for 45 to 55 minutes or until an instant-read thermometer inserted in the center reads 140°F (medium-rare). Let the lamb rest for 15 to 20 minutes, then carve it into thin slices and serve warm.

Burgers and Ground Meat

Hamburgers 101

Rapid-Fire Checklist

✓ Preheat grill
✓ Brush burgers all over with olive oil
✓ Reduce heat to medium, choose the right cooking method
✓ Place burgers on cooking grate and cover
✓ Turn once halfway through cooking time to mark both sides
✓ Remove burgers from grill
✓ Let burgers rest 3 to 5 minutes
✓ Serve immediately

Tools of the Trade

• 12-inch locking chef tongs
• Instant-read thermometer
• Silicone or natural-bristle brush
• Heavy-duty oven mitt
• Large flat spatula

Common Problems

• Overworked meat
• "Swollen belly" syndrome
• Meat sticking to the grill or falling apart
• Dry, tasteless meat
• Flare-ups

When I was growing up, homemade hamburgers tasted so different from those at the drive-through down the street that I hated the ones my mom made. I fed them to my dog and prayed we'd never have them again. I couldn't understand why my father was eating seconds. I had what I now call my "homemade syndrome"—it happened a lot in my family. I preferred store-bought to homemade because it was different, seemed more sophisticated, and my friends were eating store-bought. Thank goodness I saw the light as I got older and wiser. Not only do I understand why my father had a second burger, but now I eat burgers almost only at home.

A good hamburger requires as much finesse as any other grilled recipe and can be one of the best tasting and most economical foods to grill. And you can experiment with lots of ground meats—don't limit yourself to beef. A combination of ground veal, pork, and beef makes a great Italian meatball, so why not an Italian hamburger? Substitute lamb for the beef and you've got a Greek burger worthy of the gods. Ground turkey is a tasty substitute for any ground meat, but I especially like it paired with its traditional holiday side for a Turkey Burger with Cranberry Sauce (pages 130–131). My good friend John Lineweaver likes to grill ground meat so much that he has declared every

Sunday night "burger night" at his house. I've included his favorite burger recipe on page 122. I also love to stuff vegetables with a mixture of ground meat, herbs, and cheese; that's not really a classic burger, but I think of it as a burger without the bun!

Choosing the Meat

Choosing meat for burgers is the most important part of the process. When I was growing up, my mother bought ground (beef) sirloin (from the rump end of the loin), and so that is what I did as an adult. But then I did some sleuthing. The most important thing about a grilled burger is the beef flavor, and the best tasting ground meat comes from the chuck portion of the cow. Chuck has a higher fat content than sirloin, and the fat gives it more flavor. Most of the time I mix chuck and sirloin, finding it to be the perfect balance of fat and lean.

Be sure to experiment with other kinds of ground meat, including turkey, pork, and lamb. If your butcher doesn't have any meat already ground, it is very simple for him to grind it to order or for you to take it home and grind it yourself using a stand mixer and the meat grinder attachment.

Mixing the Meat

Don't overmix. The more you mix and knead ground meat, the tougher the meat fibers become; and when they cook, they get even tougher. You should mix everything together loosely and make the patties quickly by literally "patting" the meat together. They may not look perfect; but don't worry, they'll taste good.

Swollen Belly Syndrome

As you may know, we eat with our eyes before our tastebuds even touch the food. That is why presentation is so important to the dining experience—even at home. And I know there are a few million people who would heartily protest a burger that looks like a hockey puck with a swollen belly.

So what's the trick? Make a small depression in the middle of the uncooked burger. After you gently make your patties, place your thumb in the middle of each patty and press down to make a thumbprint. This indentation will prevent the burgers from swelling up and rounding out while cooking. Here's why: As the patties cook, the individual fibers in the meat expand. If the patties are even and flat, there is nowhere to expand except up, thus resulting in the "swollen belly." If you have a well or thumbprint in the raw meat, the expanding fibers will fill that well and make a finished flat and even burger.

Ground Meat Food Safety

Ever since the much publicized incidence of e. coli from a fast-food chain, we've become a country with ground-meat concerns.

Food-borne bacteria live on the outside of raw meat. They cannot penetrate the interior of the meat because the inside is sterile until it has been cut or ground. When meat is seared and cooked, it kills all the surface bacteria, thus making it perfectly safe to eat a steak or chop at a rare temperature as long as the outside has been brought up to the right temperature. Ground meat has to be cooked all the way through to kill the surface bacteria because, in the act of grinding, the surface bacteria has been mixed through the entire piece of meat.

On the Fire: Direct or Indirect Heat

You can certainly grill hamburgers over Indirect Heat. Indirect Heat will assure that the inside is cooked all the way through and the outside is browned. However, Direct Heat will give your burger a slightly darker crust, which I prefer. Set your grill on medium or medium-low heat depending on how hot your grill runs.

Preventing Broken or Dry Burgers

- To avoid burgers that break or fall apart, turn them only once, about halfway through the cooking time.
- Don't press the burgers with a spatula. You will press all the delicious juices out of them, which contributes to dry burgers.

Controlling Flare-Ups

Flare-ups can sometimes be a problem, especially when you are grilling a lot of burgers at the same time. Do two things: Make sure you have a clean cooking grate with no residue from previous cookouts and move burgers to a low Direct Heat or a medium Indirect Heat. Either cooking method works well. If a flare-up occurs when cooking with low Direct Heat, control it by keeping the lid of the grill closed during the cooking process. Indirect Heat will virtually guarantee no flare-ups, but it will take longer to mark and cook the burgers. I always start out on medium Direct Heat and change the grilling method only if I have problems.

If you do get a flare-up, never use water to extinguish it. Simply close the lid, which will reduce the oxygen and eliminate the flare-up naturally. For really bad flare-ups, see Sausage 101 (page 139).

Testing for Doneness

Fully cooked hamburgers are done when they are browned on the outside and firm. Generally, any ground meat will shrink about 30 percent. I recommend using the A-OK method (see page 57) to test for doneness, as it is difficult to test with an instant-read thermometer. If you choose to use the thermometer, you will need to insert it horizontally into the middle of the burger to make sure it is cooked all the way through. If you can't imagine liking a well-done burger, suggested by the USDA, and you aren't sure of the meat source, I suggest you grind your own meat at home from a whole muscle. KitchenAid makes an attachment for their stand mixer that is easy to use.

Approximate GROUND MEAT Cooking Times (°F)

TYPE OF GROUND MEAT	WEIGHT	DEGREE OF DONENESS	GRILLING METHOD	GRILLING TIME	INTERNAL TEMP.	REST TIME
Ground beef	5 to 8 ounces	Well done	Direct Medium	8 to 10 minutes	160°	3 to 5 minutes
Ground chicken	5 to 8 ounces	Well done	Direct Medium	8 to 10 minutes	165°	3 to 5 minutes
Ground lamb	5 to 8 ounces	Well done	Direct Medium	8 to 10 minutes	160°	3 to 5 minutes
Ground pork	5 to 8 ounces	Well done	Direct Medium	8 to 10 minutes	160°	3 to 5 minutes
Ground sausage meat other than poultry	5 to 8 ounces	Well done	Direct Medium	8 to 10 minutes	160°	3 to 5 minutes
Ground sausage poultry	5 to 8 ounces	Well done	Direct Medium	8 to 10 minutes	165°	3 to 5 minutes
Ground turkey	5 to 8 ounces	Well done	Direct Medium	8 to 10 minutes	165°	3 to 5 minutes
Ground veal	5 to 8 ounces	Well done	Direct Medium	8 to 10 minutes	160°	3 to 5 minutes

All internal temperatures are based on USDA recommended values, using an instant-read thermometer.
Times and temperatures in the chart are guidelines. Specific recipes may call for variations.

Burgers 101

Makes 6 servings

Grilling Method: Direct/Medium Heat

2 **pounds ground chuck or other meat**
 Olive oil
 Kosher salt
 Freshly ground pepper

1. Build a charcoal fire or preheat a gas grill.
2. Being careful not to overwork the meat, season it with salt and pepper, and mix just until combined. Gently shape the meat into 6 burgers of equal size and thickness (about ¾ inch thick). Make an imprint in the center of each patty with your thumb. Spread the top and bottom of each patty with a thin layer of olive oil.
3. Place the burgers on the cooking grate over direct medium heat, cover, and grill for 4 minutes. Turn and continue grilling until the meat is cooked through and no longer pink, 4 to 6 more minutes. Let rest 3 to 5 minutes and serve.

TIP: If you like rare burgers, try the ice cube burger trick—placing an ice cube in the center of the burger, which melts slowly as the burger cooks and keeps the meat rare and juicy on the inside while the outside develops a crisp coating. Assemble the patties just before you grill them or the ice cube will melt. Enclose an ice cube within each patty. Depress the meat on the top of the patty and grill as usual. The USDA recommends that all ground meat should be cooked until no longer pink, but if you grind your own meat or trust your butcher, cooking burgers until rare should be OK.

Classic Backyard Burgers

I am one of those basic burger gals. Although I like changing my toppings as my mood dictates, I mostly crave a traditional flavor profile that I remember from my childhood. When I was a teenager, my best friends—known collectively as the Luasions—ate as many meals as we could at our neighborhood grill. Most days, we ordered these simple hamburgers. All they did was shape the patty, add a little salt and pepper, and fry them in butter, which gave the burgers the most divine crust! It is still the best hamburger that I have ever eaten. It hinges on two things: the best-quality ground chuck and mixing the meat only until it is combined. Overmixing the meat toughens the fibers.

Makes 6 servings

Grilling Method: Direct/Medium Heat

2 **pounds ground chuck**
 Kosher salt
 Freshly ground pepper
4 **tablespoons (½ stick) unsalted butter, softened**
6 **slices cheddar or Swiss cheese**
6 **sesame seed buns**
6 **slices Vidalia or other sweet onion, optional**
6 **crisp lettuce leaves, optional**
6 **slices ripe tomato, optional**

1. Build a charcoal fire or preheat a gas grill.
2. Being careful not to overwork the meat, season it with salt and pepper and mix just until combined. Gently shape the meat into 6 burgers of equal size and thickness (about ¾ inch thick). Make an imprint in the center of each patty with your thumb. Spread the top of each patty with a thin layer of soft butter.
3. Place the unbuttered side on the cooking grate over direct medium heat, cover, and grill for 4 minutes. Turn and spread the cooked side with a thin layer of butter. Continue grilling until the meat is no longer pink, 4 to 6 more minutes. If making cheeseburgers, top each burger with a slice of cheese after you turn it.
4. Meanwhile, butter both sides of the buns and grill them over direct medium heat until lightly toasted, 1 to 2 minutes.
5. Serve on the buttered rolls with a lettuce leaf, a slice of raw onion, and a slice of tomato. Serve with traditional condiments on the side.

John's "Burger Night" Burgers

John Lineweaver and I grew up together in Greensboro and then both left for the big city, he to pursue advertising and I—marketing and public relations. John is the most creative person I know, and the look and feel of this book and all my ventures is courtesy of his design brain. About eight years ago, he started his own firm, and we began to work together on grill-related projects. In the process, a grillmeister was born. As soon as John got a grill, he started Sunday Burger Night at his house, and I just love the concept! You have a meal to look forward to all week, and you have a great meal to start the week off with. When he doesn't make his basic burger, he mixes it up with his mother Ann's burger variation. Try them both.

Makes 6 servings

Grilling Method: Direct/Medium Heat

2	pounds ground sirloin
2	cloves garlic, minced
	Kosher salt
	Freshly ground pepper
	Olive oil
6	slices cheddar cheese
6	kaiser rolls
6	slices Vidalia or other sweet onion, optional
6	crisp lettuce leaves, optional
6	slices ripe tomato, optional

1. Build a charcoal fire or preheat a gas grill.
2. Being careful not to overwork the meat, season it with garlic, salt, and pepper and mix just until combined. Gently shape the meat into 6 burgers of equal size and thickness (about ¾ inch thick). Make an imprint in the center of each patty with your thumb. Spread the top and bottom of each patty with a thin layer of olive oil.
3. Place the burgers on the cooking grate over direct medium heat, cover, and grill for 4 minutes. Turn and continue grilling until the meat is cooked through and no longer pink, 4 to 6 more minutes. If making cheeseburgers, top each burger with a slice of cheese after you turn it.
4. Meanwhile, brush both sides of the rolls lightly with olive oil and grill them over direct medium heat until lightly toasted, 1 to 2 minutes.
5. Serve on the rolls with a lettuce leaf, a slice of raw onion, and a slice of tomato. Serve with traditional condiments on the side.

Ann's Variation: Mix the meat as directed but make 8 patties; they will be much flatter than the traditional hamburger. Grate sharp cheddar cheese (1 cup total for 4 hamburgers) and white onion into the center of 4 of the patties, put another patty on top and pinch the sides to close. Wrap each of the burgers with 1 piece of bacon and secure it with a toothpick—it will look like a ribbon over the center of the burger. Brush the burgers with olive oil and grill for 5 to 6 minutes per side or until the bacon is crisp, the meat is cooked through, and the cheese inside is melted.

Build-Your-Own Burger Bar

The real stars in this recipe are the breads, cheeses, and toppings for the burger bar. When Gretchen Belmonti and her husband Jeff traded in their charming coach house in downtown Chicago for a spacious suburban house, they hosted one last bash. I helped Gretchen with the grilling, and we came up with a "build-your-own" burger bar. What could be more fun than getting to choose among every possible burger topping? It's also much easier for the cook or host than having to top and plate individual burgers—especially if you have a large crowd. It was such a hit that we had to grill up a fourth round of burgers (the "in case of emergency burgers"). I recommend this recipe to anyone having a drop-by cookout when your guests will be coming and going throughout the party.

Grilling Method: Direct/Medium Heat

For every 6 people (see Table below)
1   pound ground sirloin
1   pound ground chuck
1   tablespoon Worcestershire sauce
1   teaspoon Coleman's dry mustard
     Kosher salt
     Freshly ground black pepper
     Olive oil
     Softened butter

Rolls

Kaiser	Onion
Hamburger	Rye bread
Seeded	Bagels

Toppings

Sliced Swiss cheese	Pickle relish
Sliced cheddar cheese	Dill pickles
Sliced provolone cheese	Bread and butter pickles
Blue cheese sliced from a wedge	Pickled tomatoes
Sautéed onions	Hot and sweet pickled peppers
Sautéed mushrooms	Ketchup
Cooked bacon	Mayonnaise
Fire-roasted peppers	Yellow mustard
Sliced onions	Dijon mustard
Lettuce	Course-grain mustard
Sliced tomatoes	Hoisin sauce
Sprouts	Barbecue sauce
Sliced Granny Smith apples	Steak sauce

1. Build a charcoal fire or preheat a gas grill.
2. Being careful not to overwork the meat, season it with the Worcestershire sauce, dry mustard, salt, and pepper, and mix just until combined. Gently shape the meat into 6 burgers of equal size and thickness (about $3/4$ inch thick). Make an imprint in the center of each patty with your thumb. Spread the top and bottom of each patty with a thin layer of olive oil. Sprinkle salt on the tops.
3. Place the burgers on the cooking grate over direct medium heat, cover, and grill for 4 minutes. Turn and continue grilling until the meat is cooked through and no longer pink, 4 to 6 more minutes. If making cheeseburgers, top each burger with the guest's choice of cheese after you turn it.
4. Meanwhile, butter both sides of the rolls or bread and grill them over direct medium heat until lightly toasted, 1 to 2 minutes.
5. Serve buffet style, and let your guests build their own burgers.

HOW MUCH MEAT?

If you are making this for a crowd, you will need to multiply the amount of meat you need by the number of guests expected. Plan to use $1/3$ pound of meat per person; it makes it very easy to multiply or subtract the necessary quantities, as you can see in the chart below.

Number of Guests	Pounds of Meat
3	1
6	2
12	4
18	6
24	8

Better Butter Burgers with Bacon

Don't be put off by the title of this luxurious recipe; if it was on a menu at a three-star restaurant, it would be all the rage. The butter adds flavor and keeps the meat juicy, just like the fancy restaurant burgers that are stuffed with foie gras, but at a much more reasonable price. Serve these definitely fancy burgers at your next dinner party and watch your guests sigh with pleasure.

Makes 6 servings

Grilling Method: Direct/Medium Heat

	Mixed Herb Butter (page 62)
1	pound ground sirloin
1	pound ground chuck
	Olive oil
	Kosher salt
6	slices Gruyère cheese
12	slices bacon, cooked
6	kaiser rolls
	Mayonnaise, optional
	Dijon mustard, optional

1. Remove the butter from the refrigerator just before making the burgers and cut it into 6 pieces. Set aside.
2. Build a charcoal fire or preheat a gas grill.
3. Being careful not to overwork the meat, season it with salt and pepper and mix just until combined. Gently shape the meat into 6 burgers of equal size and thickness (about ¾ inch thick). Gently shape each burger around 1 piece of the Herb Butter, making sure that it is securely in the middle of the meat. Make an imprint in the center of each patty with your thumb. Spread the top and bottom of each patty with a thin layer of olive oil.
4. Place the burgers on the cooking grate over direct medium heat, cover, and grill for 4 minutes. Turn and continue grilling until the meat is cooked through and no longer pink, 4 to 6 more minutes.

Top each burger with cheese and cooked bacon after you turn it.
5. Meanwhile, wrap buns in aluminum foil and place on the grill over indirect medium heat for 3 to 5 minutes or until warmed through.
6. Serve the burgers on the warm rolls with mayonnaise and mustard, if desired.

Mini Cocktail Burgers

These burgers are the homemade version of a "slider"—they slide right down, easy as you please! Since they are minis, presentation is key. That means buying the best looking soft party rolls you can find to serve them on. I also like to pat out the meat on a jelly roll pan and cut it into small pieces to fit the rectangular rolls. But the real secret is the onion-poppy seed condiment that is baked into the buns before adding the burgers. This concoction was created in memory of my late great friend Alex Gant, who celebrated all things civilized and loved this onion–poppy seed spread on her ham biscuits.

Makes 12 appetizer servings

Grilling Method: Direct/Medium Heat

1	pound ground sirloin
1	pound ground chuck
	Kosher salt
	Freshly ground pepper
	Olive oil
½	cup (1 stick) unsalted butter, softened
2	medium shallots, finely chopped
3	tablespoons poppy seeds
1	tablespoon Worcestershire sauce
1	tablespoon Dijon mustard
½	teaspoon dehydrated onion or onion powder
1	package 12 soft white party rolls (Pepperidge Farm or another brand that comes in a foil tray)

1. Being careful not to overwork the meat, season it with salt and pepper, mix just until combined, and set aside. Oil a small jelly roll pan and pat the

meat inside the pan until it fills the pan evenly. Brush oil on top of the meat to cover all areas. Cut the meat into rectangles slightly larger than the size of the rolls. Make an imprint in the center of each patty with your thumb. Remove the patties from the pan (you may need to use a flexible silicone spatula to ease the meat out of the pan), smooth the sides of each patty, and refrigerate them, covered, until ready to grill.

2. Build a charcoal fire or preheat a gas grill.

3. Meanwhile, in a medium bowl, mix the butter, shallots, poppy seeds, Worcestershire, mustard, and dehydrated onion. Season the mixture with salt and pepper.

4. Cut the rolls in half horizontally and spread both the inside tops and bottoms with the poppy seed mixture. Put the rolls back together, return them to the original foil pan, and cover with foil.

5. Just before grilling the burgers, heat the rolls in the oven at 375°F or on the grill for 10 minutes.

6. Place the burgers on the cooking grate over direct medium heat, cover, and grill for 2 to 3 minutes. Turn and continue grilling until the meat is no longer pink, 2 to 3 more minutes.

7. Remove the foil from the rolls, remove the top layer of rolls, and place the burgers on the bottom, about 3 on each row. Replace the top and cut the whole thing into individual cocktail burgers by following the lines of the burgers, not the rolls. Serve warm.

Bistro Burgers

What's in a name? Well, if you ask me... everything! For me, this recipe title conjures up visions of a warm, bustling French bistro—my favorite kind of place to frequent. I see pomme frites dipped into pungent Dijon mustard and a big juicy hamburger glazed with melted Brie and fringed with glistening caramelized onions—are you hungry yet? Make these patties thicker than most and serve them on crusty French country bread or brioche buns.

Makes 6 servings

Grilling Method: Direct/Medium Heat

  Olive oil
  Kosher salt
2 yellow onions, thinly sliced
2 pounds ground sirloin
  Freshly ground black pepper
12 ounces Brie cheese, sliced into strips
6 brioche buns, country bread, or baguettes, cut in half
  Dijon mustard

1. Build a charcoal fire or preheat a gas grill.

2. Meanwhile, heat about $1/4$ cup of olive oil in a large, heavy-bottomed skillet, add a generous pinch of salt, stir, and add the onions. Stir the onions until they are coated with the hot oil. Let them sit over medium-high heat for 3 to 5 minutes, stirring occasionally. The onions should not stick to the bottom of the pan, but if they do, add a very small amount of water (or wine) and stir to loosen the onions. The liquid should evaporate very quickly. Continue cooking until the onions are caramelized and golden brown, about 10 minutes. Set aside.

3. Being careful not to overwork the meat, season it with salt and pepper and mix just until combined. Gently shape the meat into 6 burgers of equal size and thickness (about $3/4$ inch thick). Make an imprint in the center of each patty with your thumb. Spread the top and bottom of each patty with a thin layer of olive oil.

4. Place the burgers on the cooking grate over direct medium heat, cover, and grill for 4 minutes. Turn and continue grilling until the meat is cooked through and no longer pink, 4 to 6 minutes. Top each burger with some Brie after you turn it.

5. Meanwhile, wrap the buns in aluminum foil and place on grill over indirect medium heat for 3 to 5 minutes or until warm, if desired.

6. Place each burger on a roll with caramelized onions and serve it with Dijon mustard.

Country Club Bacon Cheeseburgers

A variation of this burger is served at country clubs coast to coast. The meat is an equal mixture of chuck and sirloin, enhanced by Worcestershire and dry mustard—making the burgers taste meatier. The simplicity of pure beef, cheese, and bacon is what makes this mouthwatering burger a backyard staple—what's not to like?

Makes 6 servings

Grilling Method: Direct/Medium Heat

1	pound ground sirloin
1	pound ground chuck
1	tablespoon Worcestershire sauce
1	teaspoon Coleman's dry mustard
	Kosher salt
	Freshly ground pepper
	Olive oil
6	slices cheddar or Swiss cheese
6	kaiser rolls
4	tablespoons (½ stick) unsalted butter, softened
6	slices cooked bacon
6	crisp lettuce leaves, optional
6	slices raw onion, optional
6	slices ripe tomato, optional

1. Build a charcoal fire or preheat a gas grill.
2. Being careful not to overwork the meat, season it with the Worcestershire sauce, dry mustard, salt, and pepper and mix just until combined. Gently shape the meat into 6 burgers of equal size and thickness (about ¾ inch thick). Make an imprint in the center of each patty with your thumb. Spread the top and bottom of each patty with a thin layer of olive oil.
3. Place the burgers on the cooking grate over direct medium heat, cover, and grill for 4 minutes. Turn and continue grilling until the meat is cooked through and no longer pink, 4 to 6 more minutes. Top each burger with a slice of cheese after you turn it.
4. Meanwhile, butter both sides of the rolls and grill them over direct medium heat until lightly toasted, 1 to 2 minutes.
5. Top burgers with a slice of bacon. Serve immediately on the buttered rolls with a lettuce leaf, a slice of raw onion, a slice of tomato, and traditional condiments on the side.

Philly-Style Cheese Steak Burgers

My assistant and good friend, Kirsten Newman Teissier, hails from Philly and I created this recipe to satisfy her hometown cravings. When we first met, I had yet to enjoy the pleasure of tasting an authentic Philly cheese steak. One bite of the legendary cheese steak and I was hooked on the flavor but found the shaved meat a little dry. I made the sandwich with ground meat, and this burger was born. To me, it is every bit as delicious as the original; even better, it passes Kirsten's tough standards. Shape the patties like logs so they fit in the Italian rolls more easily.

Makes 6 servings

Grilling Method: Direct/Medium Heat

1	pound ground sirloin
1	pound ground chuck
	Kosher salt
	Freshly ground pepper
2	large white onions, finely chopped
	Olive oil
6	slices provolone cheese
6	Italian or small French rolls, about 6 inches long
	Sweet green pickled peppers, sliced in rings
	Hot red pickled peppers, sliced in rings
	Ketchup, optional

1. Build a charcoal fire or preheat a gas grill.
2. Being careful not to overwork the meat, season it with salt and pepper and mix just until combined. Gently shape the meat into 6 log-shaped burgers

of equal size and thickness. Cover and refrigerate until ready to grill.

3. Meanwhile, in a heavy-bottomed pan, sauté the onions in about 2 tablespoons of olive oil over medium heat for about 10 minutes or until soft and lightly browned. Keep warm until ready to make the burgers.

4. Just before grilling, brush the burgers all over with oil and place them on the cooking grate over direct medium heat. Cover and grill for 4 minutes. Turn and continue grilling until the meat is cooked through and no longer pink, 4 to 6 more minutes. Top each burger with a slice of cheese after you turn it.

5. Meanwhile slice a thin piece of bread off the top of each roll. Hollow out the roll (like hollowing out a baked stuffed potato) so it will be able to hold the burger and all the toppings without spilling out.

6. To assemble the sandwiches, place each burger in the bottom of a hollowed-out roll, top with onions and slices of hot and sweet peppers. Add ketchup, if desired. Replace the top piece of bread and serve warm.

Cheddar-Stuffed, Pepper-Crusted Burgers

The colorful orange cheddar cheese and the black coarsely ground pepper remind me of Halloween so I usually make these in the fall. But they are good any time of the year—especially for pepper lovers. The patties are formed around a cube of cheddar cheese and the sides are rolled in pepper. Rimming the sides accomplishes two things: First, the pepper on the sides doesn't come into direct contact with the heat and won't burn and turn bitter, and, second, the rim of pepper adds a nice bite, which is tempered by the rest of the relatively unseasoned meat and the melted cheddar cheese center. For an even cheesier burger, top with more cheddar cheese a few minutes before the burger is taken off the grill.

Makes 6 servings

Grilling Method: Direct/Medium

1 pound ground sirloin
1 pound ground chuck
1 tablespoon Worcestershire sauce
1 teaspoon Coleman's dry mustard
   Kosher salt
1/4 cup coarsely ground pepper
6 2-inch cubes sharp cheddar cheese
   Softened butter
6 hamburger buns
6 slices cheddar, optional
6 crisp lettuce leaves, optional
6 slices ripe tomato, optional

1. Being careful not to overwork the meat, season it with the Worcestershire sauce, dry mustard, and salt and mix just until combined. Portion the meat into 6 equal pieces and gently shape each portion in a patty around 1 cube of cheese. Set aside. Brush the patties all over with olive oil. Make an imprint in the center of each patty with your thumb.

2. Meanwhile, put the pepper on a shallow plate and roll the rim of each burger in the pepper until it is coated in a "stripe" of pepper. (The burgers can be made up to this point 1 day earlier and kept refrigerated.)

3. Build a charcoal fire or preheat a gas grill. Place the burgers on the cooking grate over direct medium heat, cover, and grill for 4 minutes. Turn and continue grilling until the meat is cooked through and no longer pink, 4 to 6 more minutes. If using additional cheese, top each burger with cheese after you turn it.

4. Meanwhile, butter both sides of the buns and grill them over direct medium heat until lightly toasted, 1 to 2 minutes.

5. Serve the burgers immediately on the buttered rolls with a lettuce leaf and a slice of tomato, if desired. Serve with traditional condiments on the side.

Pimento Cheese Burgers

William McKinney is a Southern Foodways Alliance buddy who is one of the few who straddles both North and South Carolina with gentle diplomacy. He grew up in Columbia, SC, and went to school in Chapel Hill, NC. While he was at UNC, he founded the Carolina Barbecue Club, which has earned accolades and been featured on national television and radio. One day, while we were discussing the finer points of barbecue, he mentioned the little known Pimento Cheese Burger. This burger is served all over Columbia, SC, but has yet to get national exposure—until now! It may sound a little strange, but the proof is in the tasting and it tastes great!

Makes 6 servings

Grilling Method: Direct/Medium Heat

2 pounds ground sirloin
  Kosher salt
  Freshly ground pepper
  Olive oil
½ cup homemade Easy Pimento Cheese (below), or more to taste
6 hamburger buns

1. Build a charcoal fire or preheat a gas grill.
2. Being careful not to overwork the meat, season it with salt and pepper and mix just until combined. Gently shape the meat into 6 burgers of equal size and thickness (about ¾ inch thick). Brush the patties all over with olive oil. Make an imprint in the center of each patty with your thumb.
3. Place the burgers on the cooking grate over direct medium heat, cover, and grill for 4 minutes. Turn and continue grilling until the meat is cooked through and no longer pink, 4 to 6 more minutes.
4. Remove the burgers from the grill and top with a generous spoonful of Easy Pimento Cheese. Put the burgers on buns and serve.

Easy Pimento Cheese

This recipe can be doubled or tripled for a crowd. It is also good with crackers, on its own, in a sandwich, stuffed in celery, or with corn chips! It is important not to buy pregrated cheese, which has been treated with additives to prevent clumping.

Makes about 1 cup

1 shallot, grated
8 ounces sharp cheddar cheese, grated
½ cup mayonnaise, or more to taste, preferably Hellmann's
¼ cup diced pimentos, plus some liquid, preferably Dromedary
  Freshly ground pepper

1. In a medium bowl, mix the shallot and cheese. Add the mayonnaise and stir with a large fork just until it holds together. Add the pimentos and some of their liquid. Mix to distribute. Add more mayonnaise or pimentos, if needed to achieve the right consistency and flavor. Season with pepper to taste. (The cheese and mayonnaise should be salty enough so you won't need to add any salt.)
2. Refrigerate, lightly covered, until ready to use. Keeps for 1 week in the refrigerator.

Hail Caesar! Salad Burgers

Caesar salad lovers and low-carb dieters rejoice! This burger incorporates the classic salad seasonings in the meat of the burger. Grilled and served between two pieces of romaine lettuce, it is your steak and salad rolled into one mighty tasty burger.

Makes 6 servings

Grilling Method: Direct/Medium Heat

2 pounds ground sirloin
½ cup grated parmesan cheese
3 cloves garlic, minced
2 tablespoons Dijon mustard, plus more for garnish
1 tablespoon lemon zest
1 tablespoon Worcestershire sauce
2 teaspoons capers, drained
2 teaspoons anchovy paste
  Kosher or sea salt
  Freshly ground pepper
  Olive oil
6 to 12 thin slices parmesan cheese
12 large romaine lettuce leaves, washed and dried
  Mayonnaise, optional

1. Build a charcoal fire or preheat a gas grill.
2. Combine the sirloin, grated cheese, garlic, mustard, lemon zest, Worcestershire, capers, and anchovy paste in a large bowl. Using your hands, or a large fork, quickly blend everything together until evenly incorporated. Season lightly with salt and pepper. Shape the mixture into 6 burgers of equal size and thickness (about ¾ inch thick). Make an imprint in the center of each burger with your thumb. Brush the top and bottom of each patty with a thin layer of olive oil.
3. Place the burgers on the cooking grate over direct medium heat, cover, and grill for 4 minutes. Turn and continue grilling until the meat is cooked through and no longer pink, 4 to 6 more minutes.
4. Remove the burgers from the grill and immediately top them with thin slices of parmesan. Let them rest for 3 to 5 minutes.
5. Place each patty between 2 pieces of romaine lettuce and serve with mayonnaise and Dijon mustard, if desired.

French Onion Dip Burgers

When I was in college, I had a friend who ate potato chips and French onion dip for many of her meals because they tasted so good. Well, this burger really tastes that good! The soup seasoning packet serves two purposes in this recipe: First, it is mixed in with the meat to season it, and then it is mixed with sour cream to make the "dip" that tops the grilled burger. Serve any leftover dip with potato chips and think of your college days.

Makes 6 servings

Grilling Method: Direct/Medium Heat

2   pounds ground chuck
1   1.3-ounce package onion soup mix
    Kosher salt
    Freshly ground pepper
1   pint sour cream
3   dashes Tabasco, or more to taste
6   hamburger buns

1. Being careful not to overwork the meat, mix it with half of the package of onion soup mix just until combined. Gently shape the meat into

6 burgers of equal size and thickness (about ¾ inch thick). Make an imprint in the center of each patty with your thumb and season the outsides with salt and pepper. Brush patties all over with olive oil. Cover and refrigerate for 1 hour to allow the flavors to develop.
2. Meanwhile, in a small bowl, mix the rest of the onion soup mix with the sour cream and Tabasco. Cover and refrigerate for 1 hour or up to 24 hours.
3. Just before grilling, build a charcoal fire or preheat a gas grill. Place the burgers on the cooking grate over direct medium heat, cover, and grill for 4 minutes. Turn and continue grilling until the meat is cooked through and no longer pink, 4 to 6 more minutes.
4. Remove the burgers from the grill, place them on the bottom buns, and top with a dollop of French onion dip. Cover with the top buns and serve immediately.

Sweet Italian Sausage Burgers

This is not your basic hamburger made with beef and topped with Italian seasonings. It is made from sweet Italian sausage. If you can't find the bulk sausage at an Italian grocery store or butcher, buy linked sausages and remove them from their casings to get the ground meat for this recipe. The sausage patties are seared over direct heat and then moved to indirect heat to make sure that the meat is cooked all the way through. Top with sautéed sliced mushrooms and provolone cheese, and serve on an Italian roll sprinkled with olive oil and vinegar.

Makes 6 servings

Grilling Method: Combo/Medium Heat

1   pound sweet Italian sausage
1   pound hot Italian sausage
    Olive oil
1   pound mushrooms, trimmed and sliced
6   slices fresh mozzarella or provolone cheese, plus more to taste
6   Italian rolls or focaccia bread
    Tuscan Red Sauce (page 132), optional

1. Being careful not to overwork the meat, mix the sweet and hot sausages. Gently shape the meat into 6 burgers of equal size and thickness (about ¾ inch thick). Make an imprint in the center of each patty with your thumb. Brush the top and bottom of each patty with a thin layer of olive oil. Cover and refrigerate until ready to grill.
2. Build a charcoal fire or preheat a gas grill. In a heavy-bottomed pan over medium heat, add about 2 tablespoons of oil and a pinch of salt. When the oil is hot, add the mushrooms and sauté, uncovered, until browned and soft, about 10 minutes. Turn off the heat and set aside.
3. When ready to grill, place the burgers on the cooking grate over direct medium heat and grill for 4 minutes. Turn and continue grilling over indirect medium heat until the meat is cooked through and no longer pink, about 12 more minutes. Top each burger with a slice of cheese after you turn it.
4. Serve the burgers on an Italian roll or focaccia bread topped with the mushrooms, optional red sauce, and more cheese, if desired.

Turkey Burgers with Cranberry Sauce

Eat this burger because it tastes good, not because you think it is "good" for you. Unless you buy all white meat turkey, chances are that the ground turkey has both the dark meat and the skin ground up in it. This is what makes it taste so good, but it also means that it is no longer fat free. Remember, fat is what carries the flavor to our palates, and life is too short to eat tasteless food! I've matched the burger with the classic accompaniment of cranberry sauce mixed with walnuts and cream cheese—try it and you'll see it is a burger worthy of a new post-Thanksgiving tradition!

Makes 6 servings

Grilling Method: Direct/Medium Heat

2 pounds ground turkey, lean but not all white meat
1 red onion, finely chopped
⅛ cup chopped fresh parsley
1 teaspoon dried sage
  Olive oil
  Kosher salt
  Freshly ground pepper
8 ounces cream cheese, softened
½ cup toasted walnuts, roughly chopped
6 thick slices raisin bread or buns, such as semolina-raisin buns
1 cup Cranberry Sauce with Port Wine (page 131), chilled
6 Boston lettuce leaves, optional

1. Being careful not to overwork the meat, season it with the onion, parsley, and sage and mix just until combined. Add a drizzle of olive oil if the meat and seasonings are too dry. Season with salt and pepper. Gently shape the meat into 6 burgers of equal size and thickness (about ¾ inch thick). Make an imprint in the center of each patty with your thumb. Spread the top and bottom of each patty with a thin layer of olive oil and refrigerate, covered, until ready to grill.
2. Build a charcoal fire or preheat a gas grill. Meanwhile, mix the cream cheese and walnuts; cover and set aside. (If you haven't already made the cranberry sauce, do so and rapidly chill it in a large bowl of ice.)
3. Place the burgers on the cooking grate over direct medium heat, cover, and grill for 4 minutes. Turn and continue grilling until the meat is cooked through and no longer pink, about 10 more minutes.
4. To assemble the burgers, spread both pieces of bread with a thin layer of walnut cream cheese. Add a burger and spread it with a generous amount of Cranberry Sauce with Port Wine. Top with lettuce, if desired and serve warm.

Cranberry Sauce with Port Wine

Makes 2 cups

1	12-ounce package fresh cranberries
¾	cup sugar
½	cup water
½	cup port wine
¼	cup fresh orange juice
	Kosher salt
1	orange, zested

1. Rinse the cranberries, discarding any overripe berries. Set aside.
2. Mix the sugar, water, wine, and juice in a saucepan over medium heat, and stir until the sugar is dissolved. Add a pinch of salt and stir. Add the cranberries and bring to a boil. Reduce the heat and simmer for 20 minutes, stirring occasionally.
3. Add the zest, remove from the heat, and let cool completely. Refrigerate the sauce and serve it cold or at room temperature. It is best made the day (or days) before and keeps, covered in the refrigerator, for a week.

Yellowfin Tuna Burgers with Ginger and Wasabi Mayonnaise

I started traveling to New York for business about the same time Union Square Café opened. Their lunchtime tuna burger was one of my culinary epiphanies. I began obsessing about this burger made of the scraps of the tuna fillet served on the dinner menu—or at least this is what I was told by the bartender, who kept me company on my solitary trips to get my tuna burger fix. I finally decided that I had to try it at home. This is not their recipe, but it is based on my memory of their dish. I strongly suggest grinding or chopping the tuna yourself. If you own a KitchenAid mixer, the meat grinder accessory works beautifully, for this recipe.

Makes 4 servings

Grilling Method: Direct/Medium Heat
Special Equipment: KitchenAid stand mixer and meat grinder attachment, wide metal spatula, tongs

1½	pounds yellowfin tuna steaks, cold
1	tablespoon toasted sesame oil
	Kosher salt
	Olive oil
2	teaspoons wasabi powder
1	teaspoon water
¼	cup mayonnaise, preferably Hellmann's
4	potato rolls or brioche buns
	Pickled ginger (from an Asian market or specialty aisle)
	Plum sauce, optional

1. Chill the meat grinder attachment for at least 1 hour. When chilled, grind the tuna steaks to a texture similar to ground beef. Alternatively, you can have the tuna ground for you at a full-service grocery store or your local fishmongers.
2. Being careful not to overwork the meat, mix the tuna with the sesame oil and season it lightly with salt. Gently shape the meat into 4 burgers of equal size and thickness (about ¾ inch thick). Make an imprint in the center of each patty with your thumb. Refrigerate for at least 30 minutes. (This will help keep the burgers from falling apart on the grill.)
3. Build a charcoal fire or preheat a gas grill. Meanwhile, in a small bowl, mix the wasabi powder and water together to form a paste, then mix that into the mayonnaise; set aside.
4. Brush the burgers all over with olive oil and place them on the cooking grate over direct medium heat. Cover and grill for 7 minutes. Turn carefully using both a wide metal spatula (for leverage) and a pair of tongs. Continue grilling 4 to 7 more minutes, until burgers are firm to the touch and well marked.
5. Serve the burgers on buns with wasabi mayonnaise, pickled ginger, and plum sauce, if desired.

Little Italy Meatballs with Tuscan Red Sauce

These meatballs reign supreme, with three kinds of ground meat and Romano cheese to give them flavor. Unlike panfrying or deep frying, grilling the meatballs lets the excess fat slowly drip out, leaving the flavor but losing the fat. I also like the crunchy texture of the outside and the grill marks, which tell me that it tastes great even before I bite into one. These meatballs can be made in advance and reheated in the homemade sauce before being served with pasta or ladled into an Italian roll for a meatball hero (sandwich).

Makes about 20 meatballs

Grilling Method: Direct/Medium Heat

1	large sweet onion, roughly chopped
1/4	cup chicken broth
	Olive oil
6	medium cloves garlic, cut in half
1/4	cup chopped fresh parsley
2	teaspoons kosher salt
1	teaspoon red chile flakes
1/2	pound ground chuck
1	pound ground pork
1/2	pound ground veal or sirloin
2	eggs, whisked together
1	cup grated Romano cheese
1/2	cup grated Parmigiano-Reggiano cheese
1/4 to 1/2	cup fresh bread crumbs
	Tuscan Red Sauce (at right)

1. In a blender or food processor fitted with a steel blade, combine the onion, chicken broth, 1/4 cup of olive oil, the garlic, parsley, salt, and chile flakes. Pulse to mix and set aside.
2. Build a charcoal fire or preheat a gas grill. Mix all three meats until just blended together. Add the onion-parsley mixture and fold it into the meat. Make a well in the center, add the eggs and cheeses, and mix well. Add enough bread crumbs to make the mixture just hold together. Coat your hands with a bit of olive oil and roll the meat mixture into 2-inch balls (about the size of golf balls).
3. Place the meatballs carefully (they will be soft) on the cooking grate over direct medium heat, cover, and grill for 3 to 4 minutes per side until well marked and almost cooked through. Put the meatballs in a pot of Tuscan Red Sauce or favorite tomato sauce and simmer over low heat for 1 hour before serving.

Variation: This recipe can also be fitted into a greased loaf pan and prepared as a meatloaf.

Tuscan Red Sauce
Makes about 4 cups

Special Equipment: Food mill

4	pounds plum tomatoes
4	cloves garlic, roughly chopped
2	sprigs fresh sage (about 5 leaves)
2	teaspoons kosher salt
	Best-quality extra-virgin olive oil

1. Place a 4- or 5-quart saucepan on the stove. Break each tomato open by squeezing it gently (to avoid splattering) in your fist over the saucepan. Once each tomato is cracked, put it in the saucepan. Add the garlic, sage, and salt and cover.
2. Cook over medium heat for 45 to 60 minutes, stirring occasionally. The tomatoes will break down and liquefy as they cook. When the tomatoes are thick and saucy, remove the pan from the heat. Let cool to room temperature.
3. Process through a food mill or strainer and adjust the seasonings. Whisk in a little extra-virgin olive oil to taste, if desired.

Spinach and Veal–Stuffed Peppers

When I moved to Chicago, I met a lot of people who grew up on stuffed cabbage and stuffed peppers—foods I had never tasted, much less made myself. I love the idea of stuffing vegetables and serving a meal that is self-contained. I created this recipe in honor of my Hungarian friend Marian and her mother Maria. When making something similar for a dinner party, they made a vegetarian version for a guest and we all fell in love with it. My version is by no means a traditional recipe, but it reminds me of that night. I added veal to the mixture because I like the body that the meat gives the filling, and I wanted the lighter, more delicate flavor that veal provides. You could add another cup of chopped sautéed mushrooms in place of the veal to make this a vegetarian meal. Make this decidedly nontraditional mixture in advance so all the flavors marry well.

Makes 6 to 8 servings

Grilling Method: Direct/Medium Heat

4	yellow bell peppers
4	red bell peppers
2	9-ounce packages frozen chopped spinach, thawed
	Olive oil
1	large shallot, finely chopped
	Kosher salt
1	pound ground veal
	Grains of paradise or freshly ground pepper
¼	cup heavy whipping cream
2	tablespoons cognac or brandy
1	cup crumbled feta cheese
1	lemon, zested
1	cup sautéed chopped mushrooms, optional
	Tuscan Red Sauce (page 132), optional

1. Slice off and reserve the pepper tops. Trim the membranes, remove the seeds from the peppers, and set aside. Squeeze out the spinach to remove all the excess liquid. Set aside.
2. In a heavy-bottomed skillet or sauté pan, cook the shallots in olive oil over medium heat, add a pinch of salt, and cook until translucent, about 10 minutes. Add the veal and sauté until no longer pink. Season with grains of paradise or pepper. Add the spinach and stir to mix with the onions and veal. Add the cream and cook 1 to 2 more minutes. Add the cognac and continue cooking and stirring for an additional 1 to 2 minutes, until well combined.
3. Take the pan off the heat and let cool until the mixture is just warm. Add the feta cheese, lemon zest, and mushrooms, if using. Taste and adjust the seasonings. Stir well and set aside.
4. When the mixture is cool, stuff it lightly into the peppers and replace their tops. Build a charcoal fire or preheat a gas grill. Cover the bottoms of the peppers with aluminum foil, folding and crinkling the foil to make a flat surface for the peppers to sit on. (Alternatively, you can put the peppers in a square aluminum pan and put that on the grill.)
5. Put the peppers on the cooking grate over direct medium heat, cover, and grill for 25 to 30 minutes or until the peppers are tender and the stuffing is steaming. Serve hot off the grill with the Tuscan Red Sauce, if desired.

Big Lou's Grilled Meatloaf Sandwiches

My father's nickname is Big Lou, and even his grandsons call him Big Lou—a name he much prefers to "grandfather." When we were kids, my mother would make meatloaf just so he could have a meatloaf sandwich the next day. I have to admit that it wasn't my favorite dinner, but once I grew up and my palate matured, I saw the appeal of the meatloaf sandwich. I've taken it one step further from linoleum-topped kitchen tables by grilling the cold slices of meatloaf quickly on each side so they are warm on the outside but still pleasantly cool on the inside. If you want a sandwich just like Big Lou's, serve it on fresh rye bread with lots of ketchup! The meatloaf will serve four for dinner the first night and make four sandwiches the next day—or make it just for the sandwiches.

Makes 8 servings

Grilling Method: Direct/Medium Heat

1	pound ground beef or veal
½	pound ground lean pork
2	cups fresh bread crumbs
1½	cups milk
¼	cup minced onion
1	egg, beaten
2	teaspoons salt
¼	teaspoon freshly ground pepper
¼	teaspoon dry mustard
⅛	teaspoon dried sage
	Ketchup
	Olive oil
8	slices fresh soft rye bread

1. Preheat the oven to 350°F. Mix the beef, pork, bread crumbs, milk, onion, egg, salt, pepper, mustard, and sage together in a large bowl.
2. Pack into a greased 9 x 5 x 3–inch loaf pan and "ice" the top with 3 tablespoons of ketchup.
3. Bake for 1½ hours, or until the loaf is browned and has pulled away from the sides of the pan. Remove the meatloaf from oven and spread more ketchup over top. Serve or refrigerate overnight for sandwiches.
4. To prepare meatloaf sandwiches, build a charcoal fire or preheat a gas grill. Cut 1-inch slices from the cold meatloaf. Brush each slice generously with olive oil. Place the slices on the cooking grate over direct medium heat, cover, and grill 2 to 3 minutes on each side or until well marked. Serve on rye bread, with ketchup.

A CULINARY CLASSIC

The original Betty Crocker's Picture Cookbook *is my culinary bible because that is what I learned to cook from. Before the publisher reissued the classic cookbook, I spent five years tracking down rare original copies for my mother (to replace her loose-paged, sauce-stained, much-loved copy), my sisters, and me. This meatloaf recipe is from the 1950 edition. I highly recommend buying the reprinted edition of the original; there isn't a lemon in the whole book.*

TOP IT OFF

The following are ideas for varying the classic burger that don't warrant an entire recipe, but were too much fun to pass up. Let me know if you have a favorite burger combination that I've omitted, and I'll post it on my web site, www.GirlsattheGrill.com.

1. Barbecue Burger: Favorite barbecue sauce, Monterey Jack cheese

2. Big Apple Burger: Blue cheese and thin slices of Granny Smith apples

3. Pizza Burger: Pepperoni, mozzarella, pizza sauce

4. Patty Melt Burger: Swiss cheese, rye bread, sautéed onions

5. Mexican Burger: Guacamole, cilantro, bean dip, raw white onion

6. Greek Burger: Feta cheese, kalamata olives, tomatoes, tzatziki

7. Frito Burger: Mix 1 cup of crushed Fritos per pound of ground meat, top with lettuce, mustard, and mayo

8. Chili Cheeseburger: Chili without beans, grated cheddar cheese, scallions, sour cream

9. Asian Burger: Hoisin sauce, peanut butter, bean sprouts

10. Windy City Burger: Green pickle relish, chopped onions, mustard, ketchup, mayo, tomatoes

Sausages

Sausage **101**

Rapid-Fire Checklist

✓ Preheat grill
✓ Reduce heat to medium, choose the right cooking method
✓ Place sausage on cooking grate and cover
✓ Turn sausage occasionally through cooking time to mark all sides
✓ Remove sausage from grill
✓ Let sausage rest 3 to 5 minutes

Tools of the Trade

- 12-inch locking chef tongs
- Silicone or natural-bristle brush
- Heavy-duty oven mitt

Common Problems

- Undercooked sausages
- Overcooked sausages
- Splitting
- Flare-ups
- Soaking brats before grilling

When I was 18, I took an "if it's Tuesday, it must be Belgium"–style trip to Europe with my best friend.

This wasn't intended to be a glamorous gastronomic exploration.

So it is surprising that one of my biggest food epiphanies happened on this trip. Four weeks into the six-week tour, we wound up in Zermatt, Switzerland. After being dumped at the foot of the hill by the train and struggling to carry our luggage, I was awestruck to see the most romantic hotel that I have (to this date) ever seen. It was like the set of a romance novel, complete with animal pelts for blankets and an 8-inch solid wooden door carved with cavorting nymphs. When I looked out the window onto the courtyard of the hotel, I saw a robust man dressed in lederhosen—named George, I later found out—dancing around an open grill, turning the plumpest sausages I had ever seen.

Not only did George attract my attention, but the smell of the grilling sausages against the crisp mountain air made me run downstairs. On closer inspection, each sausage was beautifully burnished and on the verge of bursting its skin. Flushed from the fire and the beer, George looked like he was having more fun than anyone I had ever seen. He handed me a steaming sausage on a hard roll and a cold beer, and in that moment, I fell in love with the grill—and sausages.

Seasoning the Grill with Sausage

Sausage is the perfect choice for new grills and new grillers. Keep in mind that the more you use your grill, the better your food will taste. This will happen slowly over time, regardless of what you cook on it. But if you want to jump-start the process, grill up a whole mess of sausage. The fat in the sausage will render out and season your grill as it cooks, and besides—nothing could be easier or tastier!

Fill your cooking grate with uncooked (raw) sausage and grill over direct low heat until the sausages have rendered all their fat and are golden brown. If you are more interested in seasoning the grill than eating the product of this cookout, let the sausages cook down until they are black embers, brush off the residue with a brass-bristle brush, and reheat the grill. Now you are ready to start grilling.

Cooking Sausage

Sausage is the perfect choice for new grillers because it is virtually impossible to overcook raw sausage or undercook the fully cooked variety that just needs to be marked and warmed through And there is no preparation. All of the flavor is inside the casing. You don't even have to coat the sausages with olive oil, although they will sometimes stick—and burst—if you try to cook them over heat that is too high. To prevent this, prick sausages with toothpick or a sharp fork and cook on consistent medium heat.

Place the sausages on the cooking grate separated by about two inches—so the sausages can "breathe"—and turn them occasionally to brown on all sides. On a preheated grill, raw sausage takes 20 to 25 minutes to cook and precooked or fully cooked sausage takes 5 to 7 minutes to brown and heat through.

Types of Sausage

There is great debate among sausage aficionados as to how to classify a sausage. Many like to categorize sausage by meat or by the added ingredients and spices. The simplest and most important thing to know about sausage is whether it is precooked. In the English-speaking world, there are five basic types of sausage.

Cooked Sausages are made with fresh meats and then fully cooked. They are safe to eat as is but are best kept in the refrigerator and grilled or reheated before eating. Almost all packages state that the sausages are fully cooked and many are also smoked for flavor.

Cooked Smoked Sausages are cooked and then smoked, or smoke-cooked. They are eaten hot or cold but need to be refrigerated. These are the most popular for grilling. Examples include all hot dogs, wieners, and many varieties of Polish kielbasa, bologna, bratwurst, and knockwurst.

Fresh (Raw) Sausages are made from meats that have not been previously cured or cooked. They must be refrigerated and thoroughly cooked before eating. Examples include Southern bulk-style sausage meat (not in a casing), sweet or hot Italian pork sausage, fresh beef, bockwurst, Mexican chorizo (usually sold as bulk sausage), and some bratwurst. You can tell just by looking at the sausage if it is raw. The casing is clear and the ground meat and spices are easily identifiable.

Fresh (Raw) Smoked Sausages are fresh sausages that are smoked. They should be refrigerated and cooked thoroughly before eating. Examples include some styles of bratwurst, Polish kielbasa, and other more exotic and hard to find sausages such as mettwurst.

Dry Sausages are fresh sausages that are dried and safe to eat straight from the package. They do not typically need refrigeration until the packaging is opened and keep almost indefinitely in the refrigerator. They are generally eaten cold and will keep for a long time. Examples include pepperoni, linguica, and Hungarian and Spanish chorizo.

Raw Versus Fully Cooked Sausage

Sausage comes in a multitude of flavors and just about any type of meat. Flavored chicken sausage, for example, has become very popular. Sausages come in two forms, fully cooked and raw. You can easily tell the difference just by looking at the sausage—one looks raw, translucent, and slightly limp and the other looks plump and fully cooked, with a dark, tight skin (like hot dogs). But check the package wording or ask your butcher if you

BEER BATH: BEFORE OR AFTER GRILLING?

In the Midwest, grilling and soaking sausages in beer is a bonafide hobby! And everyone who knows sausages will tell you that the secret to perfect brats is soaking them in beer. Here's the skinny: Grill the sausages, then put them in the beer bath. Most people do it the other way around (precooking the sausages), but my way is tastier because by grilling the sausages first, the natural fats and juices flavor the meat as the meat cooks and the fats drip out. Since they are fully cooked when you put them in the beer, they can absorb some of the flavor of the beer, making them tastier and juicier. If you put them in the beer first then boil them, you are boiling all the fat and the flavor away before you put them on the grill; then they dry out even more on the grill because all the natural fats that act as a lubricant for the sausage are gone.

aren't sure. It is very important to grill raw sausages slowly over relatively low heat so they are fully cooked inside at the same time that they are deeply browned and caramelized on the outside. This makes Indirect medium Heat a foolproof way to grill raw sausages. This is not the case with the fully cooked variety. Those are done as soon as they are marked and warmed through.

But even with fully cooked sausage, you do not want to use a high heat or they will crack open and break apart. In fact, the reason that the English and Irish refer to sausages as "bangers," is that they are so often poorly prepared that they "bang" open!

Be careful not to confuse a pink smoke ring with undercooked ground meat. The smoke ring is always near the surface of the meat and undercooked meat is usually in the middle of the sausage or patty. A pink smoke ring is a reaction between the chemical properties in smoke and protein as it cooks. This is common in most grilled foods and a source of pride for all barbecuers. The smoke ring is a good thing!

On the Fire: Direct or Indirect Heat

Fully Cooked Sausages: Direct/Medium Low Heat
Raw Sausages: Indirect/Medium Heat

Controlling Small Flare-Ups

Flare-ups are only really a problem with raw sausages. The best way to control flare-ups is to cook raw sausages over a Direct low Heat or an Indirect medium Heat. The low Direct Heat may trigger the occasional flare-up, which can be controlled by keeping the lid of the grill closed during the cooking process. Indirect Heat will virtually guarantee no flare-ups, but it will take longer to mark the sausages. I generally use a Direct low Heat for fully cooked sausages and an Indirect medium Heat for raw ones.

If you do get a flare-up, never use water to extinguish it, simply close the lid, which will reduce the oxygen and eliminate the flare-up naturally.

Controlling Really Bad Flare-Ups

There may be a time when you will forget to clean out the food you've lost through the cooking grates into your grill or your drip pan. Then the slightest bit of grease, from grilling sausages for example, will create an inferno. In this case, follow these simple instructions:

1. Turn off burners immediately
2. Pour kosher salt directly on the flames (another good reason to keep that big blue box around)
3. Let the grill cool down
4. Remove debris and salt from the drip pan and cooking box
5. Preheat the grill and start over

Ground Meat Food Safety

Ever since the incidence of e. coli from a fast-food restaurant, we've become a country with ground-meat concerns. Sausage is made from ground meat, thus it is important to cook sausage completely.

Food-borne bacteria live on the outside of raw unground meat. They cannot penetrate the interior of the cut of meat. The inside is sterile until it has been cut or ground. When meat is seared and cooked on the surface, it kills all the surface bacteria, making it perfectly safe to eat a steak or chop rare. Ground meat has to be cooked all the way through to kill the surface bacteria because in the act of grinding, the surface bacteria have been mixed through the entire piece of meat.

Testing for Doneness

Fully cooked sausages are done when they are browned on the outside and warmed through. You can tell when this has happened because of the grill marks and, generally, the sausage will plump up and increase in size. For raw sausage, the meat will shrink about 30 percent and become very round, the juices in the case will bubble, and the outside will be marked and browned.

Hot Dogs and Sausage 101

The key to making sausages, including hot dogs, that are darkly caramelized on the outside and done on the inside is controlling the heat. The best sausages are cooked on a much lower heat than you would think. Keeping the heat consistent at a medium-low heat will also prevent the skin from splitting, which spills the precious juices (aka flavor) and can cause flare-ups.

Fully Cooked

Makes 4 servings

Grilling Method: Direct/Medium Low Heat

4   fully cooked hot dogs or sausages
4   hot dog buns or rolls

1. Build a charcoal fire or preheat a gas grill.
2. Place the sausages on the cooking grate over direct medium low heat, cover, and grill, turning occasionally, for 5 to 7 minutes or until browned, plump, and warmed through.
3. Remove the sausages from the grill, let them sit for about 3 minutes, and then serve on buns with traditional condiments, if desired.

Uncooked

Makes 4 servings

Grilling Method: Indirect/Medium Heat

4   uncooked sausages, such as **Polish, Italian, chicken,** or **bratwurst**
4   hot dog buns or rolls

1. Build a charcoal fire or preheat a gas grill.
2. Place the sausages on the cooking grate over indirect medium heat, cover, and grill, turning occasionally, for 20 to 25 minutes or until browned, plump, completely cooked through, and sizzling. If there is any question whether or not they are completely cooked through, leave them on the grill another 5 to 10 minutes. If you are using indirect heat, as instructed, they won't burn or overcook.
3. Remove the sausages from the grill, let them sit for about 3 minutes, and then serve on buns with traditional condiments, if desired.

George's Heavenly Grilled Sausages

Serve these basic sausages on a crusty bun with lots of brown, German mustard, like my friend George from Zermatt, and you'll be transported to sausage heaven! Serve with steins of iced cold beer.

Makes 4 servings

Grilling Method: Indirect/Medium Heat

4   uncooked sausages, such as bratwurst or Italian
4   hard rolls
    Spicy brown German mustard, optional

1. Build a charcoal fire or preheat a gas grill to high.
2. Place the sausages on the cooking grate over indirect medium heat, cover, and grill, turning occasionally, for 20 to 25 minutes or until browned, plump, and sizzling.
3. Remove the sausages from the grill, let them sit for about 3 minutes, and then serve on buns with brown mustard.

Chicago Cheddar Dawgs

A few years ago, a very famous hot dog chain from New York tried to set roots in Chicago. They built a two-story restaurant in the fancy part of town and set about selling dogs. Well, apparently no one was interested, so they had a dog-off with my then favorite hot dog stand, Gold Coast Dogs. Much to the chagrin of many New Yorkers, the Chicago dog won! I guess the dog business is a tough one with so many people grilling their own at home, because Nathan's—that famous chain—quickly shuttered its doors and sadly, a few years later, so did Gold Coast Dogs. But you can now make this cheddar cheese dog at home and remember the day!

Makes 4 servings

Grilling Method: Direct/Medium-Low Heat

4   fully cooked all-beef franks, preferably Vienna
1   container Merkt's cheddar cheese spread (looks like port wine cheese without the wine)

4   poppy seed hot dog rolls
    Yellow mustard
    Sweet (neon green) pickle relish
    Chopped white onion
    Fresh tomato slices
    Dill pickle spears
    Pickled peppers (pepperoncini)
    Dash of celery salt

1. Build a charcoal fire or preheat a gas grill.
2. Place the hot dogs on the cooking grate over direct medium-low heat, cover, and grill for 6 to 8 minutes, turning occasionally, until brown and warmed through.
3. Remove the hot dogs from the grill and, while still very hot, spread them with a generous amount of cheddar spread. Serve on the rolls, Chicago style, with a choice of any of the other ingredients as condiments.

Bacon and Cheddar Knockwurst Wrap-Arounds

When I was a kid, the hot dogs in our house were knockwurst. These plump all-beef alternatives to hot dogs were a treat anytime but especially in the fall after playing in— instead of raking—the leaves all day! My mother would split them down the middle, stuff the centers with cheddar cheese, and wrap them with bacon before broiling until the cheese bubbled and the bacon was crisp. They are even better now, grilled, so the top and the bottom get deliciously brown and crunchy! Try these with all sorts of sausages and cheese for a change of flavor.

Makes 4 servings

Grilling Method: Indirect/Medium Heat

4   knockwursts, such as Boar's Head
4   ounces cheddar cheese, cut into strips
8   slices center-cut bacon
    Solid wooden toothpicks, soaked in water for 30 minutes
4   poppy seed buns, optional

1. Build a charcoal fire or preheat a gas grill.
2. Using a sharp paring knife, make a $\frac{1}{2}$-inch slit down the middle of each sausage, leaving a $\frac{1}{2}$-inch margin on each end so it will stay together. Stuff each slit with cheese and wrap with bacon. Secure the bacon with toothpicks as necessary.
3. Place the wrap-arounds on the cooking grate, cheese-side up, over indirect medium heat. Cover and grill for 20 to 25 minutes or until the bacon is crisp and the cheese is melted. Serve on buns, if desired, or with a knife and fork.

Polish Sausage Kabobs with Grilled Red Peppers and Onions

Chicago has the largest Polish population of any city outside of Poland, so we Chicagoans are lucky to have a large selection of sausage from which to choose. This recipe is inspired by my Polish friend, Sylvia, who eats grilled kielbasa and onions on rough pieces of country bread as a breakfast sandwich. The bacon may seem like it is gilding the lily, but it really flavors the red onion and red pepper as it grills. If you can't find Polish sausage, substitute best-quality knockwurst or an all-beef frank. Serve as an appetizer or entrée (or for breakfast).

Makes 6 servings

Grilling Method: Direct/Medium-Low Heat

6	fully cooked Polish or kielbasa sausages, cut into 1-inch pieces
12	wooden or bamboo skewers, soaked in water for 30 minutes
1	large red onion, sliced into 12 wedges
1	large red pepper, sliced into 12 strips
12	pieces center-cut bacon
	Red chile flakes
6	slices rustic bread, 1 inch thick
	Olive oil

1. Build a charcoal fire or preheat a gas grill.
2. Using 2 skewers, thread a piece of sausage, then onion, then pepper, evenly on both skewers at the same time (as if you were creating a ladder, see page 28). Add a slice of bacon and thread it between the sausage, pepper and onion. Repeat 3 times per set of skewers. (You will end up with 6 kabobs, each held together with 2 skewers.)
3. Sprinkle the kabobs lightly with chile flakes and place them on the cooking grate over direct medium-low heat. Cover and grill 6 to 8 minutes per side, turning once halfway through the cooking time.
4. Meanwhile, brush both sides of the bread with olive oil. Place the bread slices on the cooking grate over direct heat for 1 to 2 minutes per side to toast.
5. When the bacon is crispy and the vegetables are charred on the outside, remove the kabobs from the grill and serve immediately with the grilled bread.

TIP: You may find only large horseshoe-shaped cooked Polish or kielbasa sausages in the packaged deli department. In this case, buy two packages, not six.

NOTE: If your grill is prone to flare-ups, use indirect medium heat.

Smoked Sausages with Apple-Fennel "Sauerkraut"

Fully cooked smoked sausage makes this crowd pleaser a snap to grill up and serve. The mock sauerkraut is made in advance, so all you have to do is grill the sausages to warm and brown them—you can even use vegan sausages to tasty effect. The dressed-up sauerkraut substitutes grated apple and fennel for the traditional cabbage. The result is a fresher, sweeter alternative to ballpark sauerkraut. This recipe transforms the same-ol' grilled sausage to a much asked for "secret" grill recipe.

Makes 8 servings

Grilling Method: Direct/Medium-Low Heat

Apple-Fennel "Sauerkraut"

- 1 large fennel bulb
- 1 tablespoon olive oil
- 1 large Vidalia onion, chopped
  Kosher salt
- 5 Granny Smith apples, grated
- ½ lemon, juiced
- 1½ tablespoons unsalted butter
- ½ cup hard cider or apple juice
- 2 teaspoons caraway seeds
  Freshly ground pepper

- 8 fully cooked smoked sausages
- 2 tablespoons unsalted butter, melted
- 8 poppy seed hot dog buns or French rolls
  Spicy brown or Dijon mustard

1. Clean and cut the fennel bulb in long strips (julienne) and trim the tops. Reserve the furry leafy part that resembles dill and chop it finely for later use. Heat the oil in a heavy-bottomed saucepan over medium heat, and add the onion and several pinches of salt. Cook until the onion begins to brown, add the strips of fennel, stir, and cook covered for about 5 minutes, or until the fennel begins to wilt. Reduce the heat to medium-low.
2. Build a charcoal fire or preheat a gas grill.
3. Meanwhile, mix the grated apple with the lemon juice and add it to the pan. Cover and cook, stirring occasionally, for 15 minutes. Add the butter, mixing well. Add the cider, reserved fennel tops, and caraway seeds. Cook for an additional 5 minutes, uncovered or until the mixture is soft and cooked down. It will look like sauerkraut. Season to taste with salt and pepper.
4. Remove from the heat and set aside to allow the flavors to mingle. The sauerkraut can be made up to 2 days in advance and kept covered in the refrigerator until ready to use. Just before serving, rewarm the sauerkraut.
5. Place the sausages on the cooking grate over direct medium-low heat, cover, and grill for 6 to 8 minutes, turning occasionally to mark all sides of the sausage. Meanwhile, split the buns and brush a little butter on the insides. Toast until lightly browned by placing them cut-side down on the cooking grate over direct heat for 1 to 2 minutes or until marked.
6. When ready to serve, place 1 sausage and a generous amount of the sauerkraut on each bun and serve with mustard on the side.

NOTE: The medium grate attachment of a food processor makes short work of grating the apples and gives them the look of traditional sauerkraut. You don't even need to peel the apples; just make sure they are washed well and cored.

Hot and Sweet Italian Sausages with Savory Sicilian Caponata

When I lived in New Orleans, I spent a lot of time with a Sicilian-American family who made their own Italian sausage. Often they would start family outings with some of their sausage, grilled, and caponata—a thick, slightly tart eggplant and tomato relish. It was an unbeatable combination! In my recipe, you don't have to make your own sausage, but seek out the best fresh Italian sausage in your area and buy equal amounts of hot and sweet. This hearty recipe can be served as either an appetizer or a main course. Be sure to serve your guests a sampling of both the sausages.

Makes 4 to 8 servings

Grilling Method: Combo/Medium Heat

Savory Sicilian Caponata

- 2 large eggplants, cut in half lengthwise
- 1 large zucchini, cut in half lengthwise
  Olive oil
  Kosher salt
- 2 sweet onions, sliced
- 2 sticks celery, chopped
- 10 plum tomatoes, peeled, seeded, and diced or 3 cups canned diced Italian tomatoes
- ½ cup small green olives, such as picholine
- 3 tablespoons red wine vinegar or balsamic vinegar
- 1 tablespoon capers
  Pinch red chile flakes, optional

1   bunch fresh basil, cut into chiffonade (thin strips) or chopped just before using
4   uncooked hot (spicy) Italian sausages
4   uncooked sweet Italian sausages
    Solid wooden toothpicks

1. Build a charcoal fire or preheat a gas grill.
2. Make the caponata: Cut the eggplant and zucchini halves into strips about ½ inch thick. You should have 16 to 20 eggplant strips and 12 to 16 zucchini strips, depending on the thickness of the vegetables. Brush them all over with oil and sprinkle with kosher salt.
3. Place the eggplant and zucchini on the cooking grate over direct medium heat, cover, and grill for 3 to 4 minutes per side or until tender and well marked. Remove the vegetables from the grill and put them on a clean platter. Set aside to cool.
4. Meanwhile, heat enough olive oil to coat the bottom of a deep sauté pan and add the onions and celery. Sprinkle with salt and cook until golden brown. Add the tomatoes, olives, vinegar, capers, and chile flakes, if using. Simmer for 15 minutes.
5. While the tomato mixture is cooking, dice the grilled eggplant and zucchini. Add the grilled vegetables to the tomatoes and simmer uncovered for another 10 to 15 minutes or until slightly thickened. Taste and adjust the seasonings, adding more vinegar and salt if necessary. Remove from the heat and stir in the basil. Serve warm or cold.
6. The caponata can be made up to 5 days in advance and refrigerated in an airtight container. Stir before serving with the hot grilled sausage.
7. Meanwhile, place the sausages on the cooking grate over indirect medium heat, cover, and grill for 20 to 25 minutes, turning occasionally until completely browned and cooked through. Remove them from the grill to a clean platter and let them rest for 5 minutes.
8. Cut the sausages into 2-inch pieces and spear each one with a toothpick. Serve the caponata in a bowl alongside the sausage.

TIP: If you prefer a sweeter version of caponata, add a tablespoon or so of both raisins and toasted pine nuts.

Sweet Pork Sausages in a Dijon–White Wine Sauce

This recipe is adapted from my friend, Sarah Leah Chase. Sarah was my first serious food friend and it has been my pleasure to both work and play with her during the 17 years of our friendship. Sarah has one of the best palates I know and creates luxurious recipes that go all out! Many of my family's favorite recipes originally came from Sarah, as did this simple but very special sausage dish made in the vigneronne *style—cooked with wine or grapes. The contrast of the cool green grapes served with the intense mustard–Chardonnay sauce and grilled Italian sausage proves that it only takes a few extra steps to make a meal go from fair to fabulous! The original recipe appeared in Sarah's cookbook* Peddling through Burgundy. *Serve with crusty bread to mop up the sauce.*

Makes 4 main course or 8 appetizer servings

Grilling Method: Indirect/Medium Low Heat

8   uncooked sausages (about 1½ pounds), such as sweet Italian
2   tablespoons unsalted butter
3   shallots, minced
1½ cups dry white Burgundy or Chardonnay wine
2 to 3 tablespoons imported Dijon mustard, such as Amora
1   cup seedless green grapes, halved
    Sea or coarse salt
    Freshly ground pepper
3   tablespoons minced fresh parsley

1. Build a charcoal fire or preheat a gas grill. Place the sausages directly on the cooking grate over indirect medium heat. Cover and grill, turning occasionally to brown on all sides, 12 to 15 minutes. Remove to a clean platter.
3. Meanwhile, preheat the oven or grill to 425°F (medium to high). Generously butter a shallow 2-quart gratin dish. Sprinkle the shallots over the bottom and arrange the grilled sausages on top. Pour the wine over all.
4. Place the gratin dish in the oven or in the center of the cooking grate on your grill. Bake the sausages

(covered if on the grill), turning them occasionally so that they cook evenly. This usually takes 35 to 40 minutes, during which about half the wine will evaporate.

5. Remove the cooked sausages from the gratin dish and cover to keep warm.

6. Place the gratin dish on top of a burner over medium-low heat. Swirl in the mustard—2 tablespoons for a milder sauce and 3 for a pronounced mustard flavor. Add the grapes and continue to cook until they are heated through. Season the sauce with salt and pepper. Place the sausages back in the gratin dish; sprinkle with the minced parsley. Serve immediately.

Sausages with Bitter Broccoli Rabe

Sweet Italian sausage, smoky from the grill, pairs equally well with either bitter broccoli rabe or silky escarole, which is mostly used for soup. When I am in the mood for a simple, tasty, and healthy meal, I choose one of the greens, sauté them quickly—so they are still bright green—with lots of garlic and good olive oil and serve them with piping hot grilled Italian sausage. Be sure to make extra because the "grilled-overs" are just as good gently warmed and tossed with pasta the next day.

Makes 4 main course or 8 appetizer servings

Grilling Method: Indirect/Medium Heat

  8 uncooked sweet Italian sausages
     Olive oil
  6 cloves garlic, grated
  2 small green pepperoncini peppers (Italian pickled peppers), optional
     Pinch red chile flakes
  4 pounds broccoli rabe or escarole, cleaned and trimmed
     Sea salt
½ lemon, cut into wedges

1. Build a charcoal fire or preheat a gas grill.
2. Place the sausages on the cooking grate over indirect medium heat, cover, and grill, turning occasionally, for 20 to 25 minutes or until they are well marked and cooked all the way through.

3. Meanwhile, on the stovetop, heat the olive oil and garlic in a large sauté pan over medium heat. Add the pepperoncini, if using. Add the chile flakes and stir well. Add the greens and sauté for 5 minutes, stirring constantly. Cover and cook for 5 to 10 more minutes, stirring occasionally. You want the greens to be wilted and tender but still a little crisp. Taste and adjust the seasoning.

4. Add the grilled sausage to the pan, cover, and cook 3 to 5 minutes. Remove the cover and sauté for another 3 to 5 minutes to reduce the pan juices. Season with sea salt and lemon and serve immediately.

Chorizo, Chihuahua Cheese, and Roasted Poblano Quesadillas

Jennifer Fite is one of those refreshing friends who is naturally dramatic and full of life. Needless to say, she is loads of fun to spend time with. As the director of the Frontera Institute in Chicago, she is very busy, so a lot of our meals together are spent at the restaurant that spawned the institute. My favorite time to meet Jen is for breakfast, when we splurge and start with a bowl of decadent but oh-so-worth-it Chili Con Queso, which we spoon into fragrant corn tortillas. This easy quesadilla recipe takes the best flavors of that dish, adds grilled chorizo (spicy Mexican sausage) and grills up a dish that no one can resist.

Makes 5 servings

Grilling Method: Direct/Medium Heat

½ pound bulk uncooked Mexican chorizo or 1 piece Spanish chorizo
  2 generous cups shredded Chihuahua (Mexican) or fontina cheese
  3 green onions, trimmed and minced
  1 teaspoon granulated garlic
     Freshly ground pepper
10 corn tortillas, preferably 6-inch
  2 poblano peppers, fire-roasted and cut into strips (see page 210)
     Olive oil
½ cup sour cream, optional
  1 small bunch fresh chives, chopped, optional

1. Build a charcoal fire or preheat a gas grill.
2. Crumble and fry Mexican chorizo in a skillet and drain very well on paper towels or grill and slice the Spanish chorizo.
3. Place the cheese, onions, and garlic in a medium bowl. Mash them together with a fork until thoroughly blended. Season to taste with pepper.
4. Lay 5 tortillas out on large work surface and spread each with a generous layer of the cheese mixture. Add a layer of chorizo and strips of peppers. Top with the remaining tortillas, pressing gently to make the 2 sides stick together.
5. Brush both sides lightly with olive oil and place them on the cooking grate over direct medium heat. Cover and grill each side until lightly browned, about 2 minutes per side. Cut each quesadilla into 8 wedges and garnish with a dollop of sour cream and a sprinkle of chopped chives, if desired. Serve immediately.

Sheboygan Brat Fry

The first time I visited Sheboygan, WI, I asked everyone I saw where I could get a good brat (pronounced "braht"). The locals all looked at me like I was from a different world—which I clearly was, especially when I kept telling them that I wanted a grilled bratwurst not a fried one! For some reason, the traditional bratwurst cookouts are called "frys," even though there is no hot oil deep frying involved. As I was soon to learn, the best brats in Sheboygan are not at restaurants but made by natives for community fund-raisers and Green Bay Packer football games. Even though I prefer grilling then simmering the brats in beer, this recipe is the classic (simmering then grilling) way they do it in Sheboygan the brat capital of the world.

Makes 4 main course or 8 appetizer servings

Grilling Method: Direct/Medium-Low Heat
Special Equipment: 5- to 8-quart stockpot

8   uncooked pork bratwursts
1   large white or yellow onion, divided
4 to 6 cans beer, such as Old Milwaukee
4   tablespoons ($\frac{1}{2}$ stick) unsalted butter
2   cloves garlic, chopped or smashed
    Pinch red chile flakes
8   hoagie or French rolls (hot dog buns are too small)
1   cup sauerkraut, warmed, preferably jarred not canned
    Brown mustard
    Prepared horseradish

1. Place the brats in the bottom of the stockpot. Cut the onion in half. Cut $\frac{1}{2}$ into half-moon slices, chop the other half (for topping the cooked brats), and set aside. Add the half-moon slices of onions to the brats; add the beer, butter, and garlic. Make sure the brats are completely submerged in the beer; this will determine how much of the beer to use. Add a pinch of chile flakes. On the side burner of your grill or on the stove, bring the pot to a boil and then reduce the heat to a gentle simmer. Cook for 1 hour.
2. Meanwhile, build a charcoal fire or preheat a gas grill.
3. Remove the brats from the simmering liquid and put them on the cooking grate over direct medium low heat, cover, and grill, turning occasionally until they are a deep brown all over. Return the brats to the stockpot and bring it back to a gentle boil. Immediately reduce the heat to very low and simmer for 20 minutes. The brats are now ready to serve directly from the stockpot. Do not let them sit out or they will get dry.
4. Spread mustard on 1 side of the buns and horseradish on the other. Place the brats in the buns. Cover with sauerkraut and sprinkle with the reserved chopped onions. Serve with good beer and German potato salad.

Fish

Fish 101

Rapid-Fire Checklist

✓ Thaw fish, if necessary
✓ Preheat grill
✓ Brush fish all over with olive oil
✓ Season fish with kosher salt and pepper, if desired
✓ Reduce heat to medium, choose the right cooking method
✓ Place fish on extra-clean cooking grate and cover
✓ Turn once halfway through cooking time, not before or it will stick
✓ Remove fish from grill
✓ Let rest 3 to 5 minutes, then serve

Tools of the Trade

• 12-inch locking chef tongs
• Silicone or natural-bristle brush
• Heavy-duty oven mitt
• Long flat spatula with a thin wide edge
• GrillMat

Common Problems

• Fish sticking to the grates
• Fish falling through the grates
• Not knowing when fish is done
• Overcooked fish

Most Americans only eat fresh seafood at restaurants and don't cook it themselves. The reason this surprises me is that I love to grill fish. In fact, if I lived closer to the ocean (instead of the middle of the Midwest), I probably wouldn't grill anything else! Good fish is so flavorful on its own that it rarely needs anything besides a little olive oil, a sprinkling of kosher salt, and the heat of the grill to flavor it perfectly—and it generally takes less than 20 minutes to cook even a large piece of fish. That is a winning combination: easy, tasty, and fast.

Research points to two main reasons that prevent Americans from cooking fish at home: We don't like the smell, and we don't know how to cook it. To help, home cooks combat their fish fears, I've developed techniques that make grilling fish foolproof and fun. And the first thing that you need to know is that the grill is the way to get all of us to the seafood counter more often.

Let's start with the number one complaint—the smell. There are two simple steps to prevent this. One: Make sure the fish you are buying doesn't have an odor before leaving the store. If the fish is fresh, it should only smell sweet and slightly salty like the water it swam in. If it smells bad, don't buy it. Two: If you don't want the smell of cooking fish in your house, take it outside and grill it.

Tips on Buying Fish

Find a fishmonger you like and develop a relationship with him or her. This is a pretty good way to ensure that all the fish you get is the pick of the catch. The fishmonger will be able to suggest new fish to try and will also be more willing to help with special requests, for example sushi-grade tuna or whole blocks of frozen shrimp or scallops. After you've found a fish department or store that you like, keep the following in mind:

- Buy fresh fish the day you plan to grill it or, at least, within 24 hours.
- Ask to smell fish before buying it.
- Thaw frozen fish the day you plan to grill it.
- Only buy packaged fish if it is frozen.
- When buying a whole fish, make sure the skin is shiny and the eye is clear, not cloudy.

Fillets: The best fillets for grilling are dense and at least one-half inch thick. This includes snapper, catfish, cod, halibut, and salmon. Other more delicate fillets, such as sole, tilapia, trout and skate, are well-suited to the GrillMat (see page 150) but are difficult to grill without another grilling surface to protect them from being scorched and falling apart.

Steaks: These are the most popular fish cuts for grilling. They should be close to one inch thick and be very firm. Sometimes a bone (as in salmon steaks) holds the steaks together. If you are buying one piece of fish and cutting it into steaks at home, ask for the center cut of the loin. This is especially important with tuna. Popular fish steaks include swordfish, tuna, steak, mahi mahi, and halibut.

Whole Fish: If you can find whole fish in the store, consider buying it this way. Whole fish is actually the easiest form of fish to grill, has a more intense flavor (but never fishy) because the bones and skin add to the flavor while cooking, and offers an inherently dramatic presentation. Even though it requires the simplest

preparation, it is the one that intimidates most grillers. Choose whole fish that are between one and three pounds and have your fish guy clean and dress the fish for you. That way, when you get home, all you need to do is oil and season it, and you are ready to grill. Rainbow trout, red and yellow snapper, and grouper are among my favorite whole fish. With whole fish, you also have another way to test freshness. If the eye of the fish is clear, then it is optimally fresh; if the eye is cloudy, it is not as fresh. Don't behead your fish until after you grill it. It adds a lot of flavor and after cooking, the head will also be much easier to remove, as will the bones.

Preventing Fish from Sticking and Falling Through the Grates

Besides the smell, the other issue that grillers of all levels have is that the fish sticks to the grate, breaks apart, and falls through. Here's my big secret: Just leave the fish alone. When you put raw fish (and most proteins) on the hot cooking grate, it does stick—at first—but if you wait until that side is cooked to turn it, it will release itself. Breaking and falling through the grates happens when you try to force the fish to turn too soon. The force of the spatula or tongs causes the delicate fish to break into pieces and fall apart instead of turning easily like it will if you wait patiently. The way to cook foolproof fish is make sure the grill is preheated and the grates are clean. Brush both sides of the fish lightly with oil, season it, and put it on the grill—turning only once halfway through the cooking time. The fish shouldn't stick or fall through the grates. Lift it gently at first; if it sticks a little on the edges, gently separate the fish from the grates with the edge of a flat metal spatula.

I buy fish fillets with skin on one side and don't turn the fish during cooking. The skin provides a natural barrier to the grill's direct heat so that the fish gets a delicate grilled flavor. If you prefer having grill marks on both sides, you can, of course, flip the fish fillet as you would a fish steak—halfway through the cooking time—but this also gives the fish a much more intense flavor, which to my palate, tastes scorched.

If you still need a little help, try my GrillMat. It is a heat-resistant silicone cooking mat (a nonstick version of a sheet of foil) with holes that prevent fish from sticking and from falling through the grates. It lays directly on the cooking grate (over Indirect Heat) and is perforated to let the excess juices drip away from the fish. You place the fish directly on the mat. The best news is that nothing will stick to it, it is dishwasher safe, and rolls up—taking up very little space when it's not in use. Because of the way the heat is transferred through the silicone, you don't need to turn the fish. I recently grilled skate wing on the GrillMat and served it with a garlic parsley butter—it was so moist and flavorful, I'll never sauté skate again!

On the Fire: Direct or Indirect Heat

The rule of thumb for grilling is: If it takes longer than 20 minutes to cook, use the Indirect Method. This means that all fish steaks should be cooked over Direct Heat and fillets over 8 ounces should be cooked over indirect heat. Use the Direct Method for small (less than 1 pound) whole fish. Larger whole fish should be grilled by the Indirect Method, and they do not need to be turned. Because fish is so delicate, I recommend that beginner fish cooks grill all fish over indirect medium heat. Most recipes—and all the recipes in this book—will tell you which grilling method to use.

Foil Tools

Foil is a griller's best friend—at least one of them! And I recommend spending the extra money and buying the thicker, heavy-duty aluminum foil for the simple reasons that it is stronger, doesn't tear as easily, and can hold the weight of the food you are putting in it. Foil can be used to make fish grilling trays and grilling packets (hobo packs) and as a grate cleaner.

FOIL TRAY

This works best for large fillets, especially salmon. Make the tray by cutting two pieces of heavy-duty foil about four inches longer and wider than the fish. Put the foil sheets on top of each other and crimp the sides to make a frame for the fish. You want the sides to be at least one inch high. The advantage of making a tray like this is that you can "poach" the fish with a flavorful marinade or liquid (because the fish sits in the liquid, which is gently absorbed during cooking, adding flavor and moisture) and grill it at the same time. (The tray will hold both the fish and about $1/2$ cup of liquid.) It is guaranteed not to stick and you can easily lift the fish off the grill with the foil tray. But beware, the tray may be flimsy and will contain hot liquid and hot fish. Use an extra-wide spatula or a pizza peel to help take it off the grill and place the foil "tray" on a platter to take inside.

FOIL WRAP

This is the simplest form of a hobo pack. Fish can be wrapped in foil and grilled. The fish will cook in its own juices and have the texture and taste of steamed fish. This method is good for people who don't want the smoky grilled flavor to overpower a delicate fish.

HOBO PACK

Along with s'mores, this foil packet technique is the quintessential camping food memory. Tear off two sheets of heavy-duty aluminum foil that are twice as big as the food you want to cook. Lay one sheet out flat and put the food (ideally a combination of protein, vegetables, and grain) in the middle. Bring the sides up and wrap tightly on all sides—like you are wrapping a gift. Put the first foil package in the center of the second foil sheet and repeat the process. The second foil sheet will reduce leakage and keep any juices from escaping the packet. This technique works for lots of food but is especially good for delicate pieces of fish.

IN-A-PINCH GRATE CLEANER

When cooking fish, it is extremely important that the cooking grate is extra clean to help prevent sticking. Foil is not only good to cook with, but is a great pinch hitter for a grill brush. Crumple up one piece of heavy-duty foil. Place the ball of foil at the end of your locking chef tongs and clean away. It is almost as good as a grill brush. It is good for one use; if you want to be super-ecological, you can even clean with the used foil from your cookout rather than tearing off a new sheet.

FOIL FOIBLES

There are a couple of things that you should never do with foil—for reasons of safety. Never line the entire cooking grate with foil and never line the bottom of your grill with foil. If you line the grill or cooking grate (to try to keep it clean), you run the risk of trapping the grease and juices that are rendered off all food. If the foil tears or if any juices drip when you remove the foil, you run the risk of a huge flare-up or fire.

Remember, you want to season both the inside of the grill and your cooking grate—most likely the dirtier it looks, the more seasoned it is, and the better your food tastes. The one caveat is that you must keep the cooking grate clean (scraped off) at all times. A clean cooking grate is essential to grilling fish.

Fish Skin Trick

If you like puzzles, then this fish technique is for you. It works especially well for fish fillets with thick skins, like salmon. Buy a center-cut piece of fillet and have your fishmonger carefully trim the skin of the fillet off the flesh, keeping it in one piece (alternately, you can do this yourself if you have a really sharp knife). When you are ready to grill, cut the fish fillet into four equal portions and put it back together (like a puzzle) directly on the skin. Brush with oil, season according to the recipe, and put the fillet pieces back on the grill on top of the skin on the cooking grate over Indirect medium Heat. Don't turn the fish; when it is done, slide the spatula between the skin and the flesh of the fish and remove the fish to a platter. If you consider crispy fish skin a delicacy, leave it on the grill for a few more minutes, switching to medium-low direct heat, and it will caramelize and crisp up deliciously; otherwise you can discard the skin.

Flavor Wraps

Instead of wrapping fish in foil, which essentially steams the fish, try using flavor enhancing wraps— to help prevent sticking and enhance the presentation. This is my favorite way to prepare whole fish, but you certainly could do this with any piece of fish.

This is a cooking technique that looks complicated and sophisticated but is actually easy to execute. My two favorite ingredients for wrapping whole fish are center-cut (meatier) bacon and its Italian cousin, pancetta. After that, I like to use brined grape leaves for a Greek flair, whole lettuce leaves, thinly sliced potatoes, fresh fig and banana leaves, and green corn husks. This trick should always be "performed" over Indirect Heat.

Bed of Herbs or Citrus

Infuse fish with nuances of herbs or citrus (orange, lemon, lime, or grapefruit) by making a bed of one or the other or both, laying them across the direction of the cooking grates so they don't fall through.

Place the fish directly on the sliced citrus or tangle of herbs. You will not need to turn the fish halfway through the cooking time. This trick can is best suited to medium-low Direct Heat or medium Indirect Heat—you don't want to burn the herbs or citrus.

Testing For Doneness

In terms of grilling, fish is usually done when it is opaque in color and releases easily from the cooking grate.

The denser the fish, the longer it will take to cook. But even dense fish will cook in less time than most cuts of poultry and meat. Refer to the times in your recipe or use the chart on page 154–155 as a general guideline. Some fish folks use the rule of thumb that you cook fish 10 minutes for every inch of thickness, but I've found that the guideline only works with fish steaks, since fillets can be ½ to 1 inch thick but easily weigh 2 pounds and take about 45 minutes to cook.

Remember that all grills vary slightly in the way that they cook and the charts are only a guide. You are safer using visual clues to tell when fish is done. For example, all cuts of salmon have fat and protein that runs between layers of the flesh. This is what creates the white stripes on raw salmon. These white stripes darken and turn opaque as the fish cooks, a sign that the fish is done. You can also take a fork and look into the center of the fish to make sure it is cooked through to your liking. I try not to use this method because I don't like to serve fish that has been broken or cut, but it is foolproof. If you haven't cooked fish much, you can use the "flaking with a fork" method, then save the test piece for your own plate.

A Note on Doneness

If you like fish cooked through, follow the above instructions and it will taste just fine. These days though, most restaurant chefs prefer to cook fish only to medium doneness; it is still a little rare (translucent) in the center. I actually prefer my fish cooked this way because it is moister and more flavorful. I also like the texture better. If you know you are buying quality fish and are grilling fillets, steaks, or whole fish, there isn't a food safety issue in leaving the center a bit rare.

Keep in mind that while fish should be eaten hot, all protein should rest before being served, so the moisture settles again into the food from the surface, where it is pushed when subjected to heat. Fish should rest 3 to 5 minutes usually—longer if the fish is very thick— before serving.

FISH FLAVORING OPTIONS

Pancetta, Bacon, or Prosciutto: Wrap seasoned, oiled fish loosely with thinly sliced and unrolled pancetta, bacon, or prosciutto, leaving the head and tail exposed. Turn the fish once halfway through the cooking time to brown both sides of the meat.

Brined Grape Leaves: Wrap seasoned, oiled fish with brine-packed California or Greek grape leaves. Drape 1 leaf loosely over the other to enclose the fish, leaving the head and tail exposed. No need to turn fish.

Romaine Lettuce Leaves: Wrap seasoned, oiled fish between 2 large leaves of romaine lettuce. Tie together with kitchen twine that has been soaked in water for 30 minutes. No need to turn fish.

Bed of Herbs: Place seasoned, oiled fish on a bed of rosemary, thyme, or any woody fresh herb soaked in water for 10 minutes. No need to turn fish.

Bed of Citrus: Place seasoned, oiled fish on a bed of ½-inch slices of lemons, limes, oranges, or grapefruits. No need to turn fish.

Seafood Steaks 101

This is the basic recipe for seafood steaks, using the Grilling Trilogy (see pages 19–20). Once you've mastered this technique, start adding your own seasonings. Serve with fresh salsa, pesto, or lemon wedges, if desired.

Makes 4 servings

Grilling Method: Direct/Medium Heat

> 4   fish steaks, such as yellowfin tuna, halibut, swordfish, salmon, or sea bass, about 1 inch thick
>   Olive oil
>   Kosher salt
>   Freshly ground pepper

1. Build a charcoal fire or preheat a gas grill.
2. Brush the steaks on both sides with oil. Season to taste with salt and pepper.
3. Place on the center of the cooking grate over direct medium heat. Cover and grill, turning once halfway through cooking time, until the fish is opaque but still moist in the center, about 10 minutes. Serve immediately.

Whole Fish 101

If you've never worked with whole fish, start with the simplest method, then move on to some of the flavor enhancers.

Makes 4 to 6 servings

Grilling Method: Indirect/Medium Heat

> 4   whole fish, such as trout, snapper, whitefish, about 1 pound each, cleaned
>   Kosher salt
>   Freshly ground pepper
> 1   cup fresh herbs, such as thyme, tarragon, marjoram, optional
>   Olive oil

1. Build a charcoal fire or preheat a gas grill.
2. Rinse the fish and pat it dry. Season the inside and outside with salt and pepper. Lightly oil the inside cavity and both sides of the fish. Place fresh herbs inside the cavity, if desired. Wrap the fish (see Sidebar at left), if desired.
3. Set the fish in the center of the cooking grate over indirect medium heat. Cover and cook until opaque but still moist in the thickest part, 15 to 20 minutes, without turning. If you are only grilling 1 fish, it will take only 10 to 15 minutes. Remove the fish from the grill.
4. Slide the fish onto a platter. Peel off the top layer of skin, if desired. Let rest for 3 to 5 minutes. To serve, slide a wide metal spatula inside the cavity of the fish between the flesh and bones, and lift off each portion.

Approximate **FISH** Cooking Times

TYPE OF FISH	THICKNESS OR WEIGHT	GRILLING METHOD	GRILLING TIME	REST TIME
Arctic Char	½ to 1 inch thick	Direct Medium	5 to 10 minutes	3 minutes
Bluefish	1 pound 2 to 2½ pounds 3 pounds	Indirect Medium	15 to 20 minutes 20 to 30 minutes 30 to 45 minutes	5 minutes
Catfish	½ to 1 inch thick	Direct Medium	5 to 10 minutes	3 minutes
Cod	½ to 1 inch thick	Direct Medium	5 to 10 minutes	3 minutes
Flounder	1 pound 2 to 2½ pounds 3 pounds	Indirect Medium	15 to 20 minutes 20 to 30 minutes 30 to 45 minutes	5 minutes
Grouper	½ to 1 inch thick	Direct Medium	5 to 10 minutes	3 minutes
Haddock	½ to 1 inch thick	Direct Medium	5 to 10 minutes	3 minutes
Halibut	½ to 1 inch thick	Direct Medium	5 to 10 minutes	3 minutes
Mahi Mahi	1 to 1¼ inches thick	Direct Medium	10 to 12 minutes	5 minutes
Monkfish	1 pound 2 to 2½ pounds 3 pounds	Indirect Medium	15 to 20 minutes 20 to 30 minutes 30 to 45 minutes	5 minutes
Ocean Perch	1 pound 2 to 2½ pounds 3 pounds	Indirect Medium	15 to 20 minutes 20 to 30 minutes 30 to 45 minutes	5 minutes
Orange Roughy	½ to 1 inch thick	Indirect Medium	5 to 10 minutes	3 minutes
Pike	½ to 1 inch thick	Direct Medium	5 to 10 minutes	3 minutes
Pollack	½ to 1 inch thick	Direct Medium	5 to 10 minutes	3 minutes
Pompano	½ to 1 inch thick	Direct Medium	5 to 10 minutes	3 minutes
Red Snapper	1 pound 2 to 2½ pounds 3 pounds	Indirect Medium	15 to 20 minutes 20 to 30 minutes 30 to 45 minutes	5 minutes
Rockfish	1 pound 2 to 2½ pounds 3 pounds	Indirect Medium	15 to 20 minutes 20 to 30 minutes 30 to 45 minutes	5 minutes
Salmon	1 pound 2 to 2½ pounds 3 pounds	Indirect Medium	15 to 20 minutes 20 to 30 minutes 30 to 45 minutes	5 minutes

TYPE OF FISH	THICKNESS OR WEIGHT	GRILLING METHOD	GRILLING TIME	REST TIME
Sea Bass, domestic or Chilean	1 to 1¼ inches thick	Direct Medium	10 to 12 minutes	5 minutes
Sea Trout	1 pound 2 to 2½ pounds 3 pounds	Indirect Medium	15 to 20 minutes 20 to 30 minutes 30 to 45 minutes	5 minutes
Sole	4 to 8 ounces 1 pound 2 to 2½ pounds 3 pounds	Indirect Medium	5 to 7 minutes 15 to 20 minutes 20 to 30 minutes 30 to 45 minutes	5 minutes
Swordfish	1 to 1¼ inches thick	Direct Medium	10 to 12 minutes	5 minutes
Tilapia	½ inch thick	Indirect Medium	5 to 10 minutes	3 minutes
Tuna	1 to 1¼ inches thick	Direct Medium	10 to 12 minutes	5 minutes
Whitefish	½ to 1 inch thick	Indirect Medium	5 to 10 minutes	3 minutes

The USDA recommends cooking fin fish until it is opaque and flakes easily with a fork. The grilling times are based on the author's experience and fish industry standards. Times in the chart are guidelines. Specific recipes may call for variations.

Whole Fish in Foil 101

This is a simple way to cook fish healthfully and keep it moist. Sealing it in the foil helps it steam in its own juices, while the seasonings enhance the flavor.

Makes 4 to 6 servings

Grilling Method: Indirect/Medium Heat
Special Equipment: Heavy-duty aluminum foil

 4   whole fish, such as trout, striped bass, pompano, snapper, about 1 pound each, cleaned
 1   cup fresh herbs, such as thyme, tarragon, marjoram
 1   tablespoon olive oil
     Kosher salt
     Freshly ground pepper

1. Build a charcoal fire or preheat a gas grill.
2. Rinse the fish and pat it dry. Season the inside and outside with salt and pepper. Lightly oil the inside cavity and both sides of the fish. Place fresh herbs inside the cavity. Place each fish in the center of a square of heavy-duty aluminum foil. Fold ½ of the foil square over the fish to meet the other half, then crimp all edges to seal.
3. Set the foil packets in the center of the cooking grate over indirect medium heat. Cover and cook until opaque but still moist in the thickest part, 10 to 15 minutes.
4. Carefully unwrap 1 packet to test the fish for doneness. Rewrap it to seal and continue cooking if necessary.
5. Let the fish rest for 3 to 5 minutes. Unwrap each fish and slide it onto a platter. Peel off the top layer of skin, if desired. To serve, slide a wide metal spatula inside the cavity of the fish between the flesh and bones, and lift off each portion.

Skin-On Fillet 101

Try the fish skin trick on page 151, to ensure that the fish doesn't stick and comes off the grill easily.

Makes 4 to 6 servings

Grilling Method: Indirect/Medium Heat

1   skin-on fillet, such as salmon, trout, or snapper, about 2 pounds, about 1 inch thick
    Olive oil
    Kosher salt
    Freshly ground pepper

1. Build a charcoal fire or preheat a gas grill.
2. Rinse the fish and pat it dry. Brush all over with olive oil. Season to taste with salt and pepper.
3. Lay the fish, skin-side down, on the cooking grate over indirect medium heat. Cover and cook until the fish is opaque but still moist, 15 to 25 minutes. Do not turn the fish during the cooking time.
4. Supporting the fish with a wide metal spatula, transfer it to a platter by sliding the spatula between the skin and the flesh. Leave the skin on the grill to crisp up or remove and discard it. Serve the fish immediately.

GRILLED LEMONS FOR FISH

These grilled lemons are unbelievably simple and sophisticated. They dress up a meal like a good string of pearls dress up a basic black dress.

Cut the lemons in half or quarters. Put them cut-side down on the cooking grate over direct medium-low heat, cover, and grill until marked or warmed through, about 5 minutes. To intensify the caramelization, sprinkle the cut sides with a pinch of white sugar and let them sit for 5 minutes before grilling. Serve grilled lemons with Whole Fish 101 (page 153) or substitute them for fresh lemon wedges in any recipe.

Grilled Fish with a Ginger-Soy-Citrus Marinade

This marinade is good on almost any fish and takes just a few seconds to whisk together. I created it one night when I was testing the Vacu Vin Instant Marinater. The marinater literally forced the flavor into the fish in only five minutes and the lemon zest tasted fresh, sparkling, and bright—as if I just zested it—even after grilling for 20 minutes. The marinater is one of the few pieces of special equipment that I recommend, but if you don't have one, you'll still get great flavor if you marinate the old-fashioned way—in a covered, nonreactive bowl in the fridge.

Makes 4 servings

Grilling Method: Indirect/Medium Heat
Special Equipment: Vacu Vin Instant Marinater, optional

¼   cup olive oil
¼   cup toasted sesame oil
3 to 5   cloves garlic, grated, or more to taste
1   1-inch knob fresh ginger, grated, or more to taste
2   tablespoons rice vinegar (not sweetened)
2   tablespoons low-sodium soy sauce (such as Kikkoman)
1   tablespoon Thai chili-garlic sauce (*sriracha*)
1   lemon, zested and cut into wedges
    Kosher salt
4   fresh fish fillets, about 1¼ pounds total, such as wild salmon, mahi-mahi, pompano, shark

1. Combine the olive oil, sesame oil, garlic, ginger, rice vinegar, soy sauce, chili-garlic sauce, zest, and a pinch of salt. Mix well. Add the fish to the marinade, making sure all surfaces are coated. Cover and marinate for 5 to 30 minutes in the instant marinater and in the refrigerator up to 1 hour in a nonreactive bowl. Turn occasionally to coat all sides.
2. Build a charcoal fire or preheat a gas grill.
3. Remove the fish from the marinade and gently shake off excess. Put the fish on the cooking grate, skin-side down, over indirect medium heat. Grill for about 15 to 20 minutes without turning, or until done but pink in the center. Do not overcook.

4. Sliding the spatula between the bottom of the fish and the skin, remove the fish and place it on a platter. While the fish rests, increase the heat to high to crisp up the skin (it only takes about 2 minutes). Remove the skin from the grill and serve it with the moist fish. Garnish with lemon wedges, if desired.

TIP: Chili-garlic sauce, or *sriracha*, is that delicious pungent sauce in the clear bottle or jar with a kelly-green plastic top and a picture of a rooster. It is easily found in Asian grocery stores or on the Internet. If you don't have it, don't substitute American (Heinz) chili sauce, which will ruin the flavor profile; just omit that ingredient or add a few dashes of Tabasco. However, I strongly urge you to add this sauce to your pantry— it lasts forever (it's pretty strong so you only use a little at a time) and is a great ingredient to have on hand.

TIP: There are two options that deliver the best grated ginger and garlic for a marinade. One is the Microplane kitchen tool and the other is the SuperGrater ceramic grater. Both these tools revolutionize all grating tasks, from cheese to ginger, garlic, nutmeg, and chocolate. They are a must-have for any home cook who likes to make short work of grating. The SuperGrater is particularly suited to garlic and ginger, and the Microplane works best for hard cheese and nutmeg.

Halibut with Heirloom Tomato Salsa

My absolute favorite food in the world—besides anything grilled—is a garden-fresh heirloom tomato. I often make up a mixed plate of all different varieties, sizes, and shapes, drizzle it with a strong green extra-virgin olive oil and a dusting of fleur de sel. But on the other occasions when I want to combine the smoky flavor of grilling with the sweet, tart flavor of the tomatoes, I make this very simple heirloom tomato salsa and serve it with grilled halibut. This halibut is equally at home in winter served with room-temperature Grilled Ratatouille (pages 216–217). If they aren't available, heirloom tomatoes can be replaced with any home-grown, farm-fresh tomato.

Makes 4 servings

Grilling Method: Direct/Medium Heat

 4 large heirloom tomatoes (mixed selection), such as Green Zebra, Rainbow, Red Ruby, Black, Brandywine
 2 shallots finely chopped
 ¼ cup chopped fresh herbs, such as parsley, mint, lemon thyme, basil, plus sprigs for garnish
 3 large cloves garlic, minced or grated
 1 fresh jalapeño chile, stemmed, deseeded, and minced
 1 lime, juiced
   Kosher salt
 4 fresh halibut steaks, about 6 ounces each, ¾ inch thick
   Olive oil
   Freshly ground pepper or grains of paradise

1. Build a charcoal fire or preheat a gas grill.
2. Wash and chop the tomatoes into coarse chunks, reserving all juices. Put the tomatoes and juices into a large glass bowl. Add the shallot, herbs, garlic, and jalapeño; mix gently until the ingredients are well combined. Add the lime juice a little at a time, tasting and adding until you think the balance of the tomato juice with the lime is right. (It should taste more like tomatoes than lime.) Season with salt, stir, and set aside covered, at room temperature, until ready to serve. (Do not make this too far in advance or you will lose the flavors of the freshly cut tomatoes.)
3. While the salsa flavors meld, brush the fish all over with a thin layer of oil and season with salt and pepper. Place the fish on the cooking grate over direct medium heat. Cover and grill for 8 to 10 minutes, turning once halfway through the cooking time. Cooking time may be longer, depending on the size of the fish.
4. Remove the fish from the grill and place 1 steak in the center of each plate. When done, let the fish rest for 3 to 5 minutes. Top with salsa and a sprig of fresh herbs to garnish. Serve additional salsa on the side. Refrigerate any leftover salsa and serve the next day with chips.

Lettuce Wrap Your Fish

Bob Blumer, aka The Surreal Gourmet, is both creative and logical. He won't use any tool or ingredient unless he thinks it is essential to the recipe—one of the reasons we bonded so quickly. I think that philosophy is what motivated him to come up with this very simple and foolproof way to grill fish, which I use with all kinds of fish fillets and seasonings. It is particularly useful for Dover sole, which is too delicate to grill any other way. For the sole, I use butter, white wine, and a touch of fleur de sel for a classic preparation. But here, I am including Bob's original recipe for salmon flavored with dill and capers.

Makes 4 servings

Grilling Method: Direct/Medium-Low Heat

- 8 large romaine lettuce leaves
  Olive oil
- 4 salmon or other fish fillets, such as Dover sole, about 6 ounces each, 1 inch thick
  Kosher salt
  Freshly ground pepper
- 2 lemons, 1 juiced and 1 thinly sliced
- 1 tablespoon capers in brine
- 4 sprigs fresh dill
- 4 3-foot pieces kitchen twine, soaked in water for 30 minutes

1. Build a charcoal fire or preheat a gas grill.
2. Pat the fish dry with paper towels. Rinse the romaine leaves in water, but do not dry. Rub 1 teaspoon of oil over the inside (concave side) of each of the lettuce leaves. Place each fillet in the center of 1 leaf (concave side up). Season lightly with salt and pepper.
3. Pour 1 teaspoon of oil and the juice of ½ lemon over each piece of fish, trapping the juices in the leaf. Top with capers, dill, and 1 lemon slice. Place a second leaf over each piece of salmon, fold the ends of the bottom leaf up to keep the juices trapped, and wrap the wet kitchen twine around the leaves to seal the package. Tie the twine in a knot.
4. Place the fish on the cooking grate over direct medium-low heat, cover, and grill for 5 minutes. Turn the packages over and grill for another 5 minutes. Cooking time will vary according to the thickness of the fillets.
5. When done, let the fish rest for 3 to 5 minutes. Cut the string and remove the top leaves. (Although you may want to leave the string on for presentation value.) Serve immediately.

Hobo Pack of Arctic Char, Spinach, and Couscous

This recipe is a riff on the meal-in-one pouches that I made as a Girl Scout. If you were a Girl or Boy Scout for even one camping trip, I'm sure you made something like this as well, so it hits all those nostalgia buttons but with grown-up flavor! I always loved the concept, but I never liked the ingredients that went into most of those recipes. So now I make all kinds of "gourmet packs" like the one here that cooks the fish, couscous, and vegetables together for a color-ful, delicious, and balanced meal in one. Try substituting precooked wild rice for the couscous for a heartier cold-weather entree. The best part is that you can assemble the packs early in the day, stick them in the fridge, and all you have to do when your family comes home or your guests arrive is take them to the grill, cook, and serve—talk about easy!

Makes 4 servings

Grilling Method: Indirect/Medium Heat
Special Equipment: Heavy-duty aluminum foil

- 1 cup uncooked couscous
- ⅓ cup cashews, toasted
- 3 green onions, chopped
- 1 tablespoon grated orange zest

Cooking Marinade
- ½ cup fresh orange juice
- ⅓ cup dry sherry
- 2½ tablespoons low-sodium soy sauce
- 2½ tablespoons sweetened rice wine vinegar (mirin)
- 1½ tablespoons grated fresh ginger
- 1 tablespoon toasted sesame oil
  Olive oil

- 4 cups baby spinach
- 4 boneless skinless arctic char fillets, 6 ounces each
- 2 leeks, trimmed, washed, and cut into 2-inch julienne strips
- 2 carrots, peeled and cut into 2-inch julienne strips

1. Build a charcoal fire or preheat a gas grill.
2. In a small bowl, combine the couscous, cashews, onions, and orange zest. Set aside.
3. To make the marinade, whisk all the ingredients together in a measuring cup or other container with a pour spout. Set aside.
4. Tear off 4 large (about 24-inch) pieces of heavy-duty aluminum foil; fold each in half to form a rectangle and brush lightly with oil. Place ¼ of the couscous mixture in the center of each rectangle. Top with 1 cup of baby spinach, add one fish fillet to each portion, and then scatter the remaining vegetables equally over the fish. Begin folding the edges of the foil up and inward to make a packet around the contents—as if you were wrapping a package.
5. Rewhisk the marinade and pour about ¼ cup over the vegetables and fish in each packet. Seal the foil by continuing to roll the edges tightly inward into the center to completely enclose the fish.
6. Place the packets on the cooking grate over indirect medium heat. Cover and grill without turning, 25 to 30 minutes, or until the vegetables are crisp-tender and the fish is just opaque in the center. Let them rest for 3 minutes, then cut a hole in the top of the foil, and place the packets on serving plates.

Limey Grouper Sandwich with Jerk Mayo

I first ate a version of this grilled grouper sandwich many years ago in Morehead City, NC, with my childhood best friend, Ann Rucker. The young chef of a local restaurant had just come back from Jamaica and was "hot" on everything jerked. We had just finished our freshman year in college, and it sounded like just the thing for two new "sophisticates" to munch on while listening to reggae and drinking Red Stripes. Authentic jerk flavoring is a wet paste based on the scotch bonnet chile. My dry rub has a lot of ingredients, but it is a simpler version of the classic, made with dried spices and red chile flakes.

Makes 4 to 6 servings

Grilling Method: Indirect/Medium Heat

2 pounds grouper or catfish fillets
4 limes, juiced
½ cup dark rum
Olive oil

Dry Jerk Seasoning
1 tablespoon dried parsley
1 tablespoon dried onion flakes or powder
2 teaspoons ground thyme
2 teaspoons brown sugar
2 teaspoons dehydrated garlic
2 teaspoons cayenne pepper
1½ teaspoons kosher salt
1 teaspoon ground allspice
1 teaspoon red chile flakes
1 teaspoon freshly grated nutmeg
¼ teaspoon ground cinnamon
¼ teaspoon freshly ground pepper
¼ teaspoon ground star anise

½ cup mayonnaise
1 lime, juiced
4 to 6 white buns or rolls
1 ripe tomato, sliced
Boston lettuce leaves

1. Pat the fish fillets dry with paper towels. Transfer them to a nonreactive container and cover with lime juice and rum while preparing the jerk seasoning. Marinate, covered, in the refrigerator for no more than 15 minutes.
2. Meanwhile, make the dry jerk seasoning: Mix all the ingredients together in a small bowl. Set aside.
3. Remove fish from the marinade and discard the marinade. Sprinkle the fish with the dry jerk rub on both sides. Cover and let the fish sit in the refrigerator for another hour.
4. Mix the mayonnaise, lime juice, and 1 tablespoon of the dry jerk seasoning in a small bowl until smooth and well combined.
5. Build a charcoal fire or preheat a gas grill.
6. Remove from the refrigerator just before grilling, and brush the fish with olive oil.
7. Place the fish on the cooking grate over direct medium heat, cover, and grill 3 to 4 minutes on each side.
8. Letting the fish rest, toast or warm the buns, spread them with jerk mayo, top with lettuce and tomato, and add a hot fish fillet. Enjoy immediately.

Slow-Roasted Monkfish Wrapped in Serrano Ham

This recipe combines the poor man's lobster (monkfish) with the rich man's ham! I love ham from any country, and my newest favorite comes from Spain. Serrano ham is dry-cured ham and looks and tastes like a cross between Italian prosciutto and Southern country ham. If you can't find it in your local market, consider buying it online at www.tienda.com, where you'll find all manner of great food products from Spain, including the smoked paprika that I use in dozens of recipes.

Makes 4 servings

Grilling Method: Indirect/Medium-Low Heat

4	monkfish fillets, about 6 ounces each
½	cup olive oil
	Kosher salt
	Freshly ground pepper
1	roasted yellow bell pepper (see page 210), cut into strips
8	slices Serrano ham, room temperature
	Solid wooden toothpicks, soaked in water for 30 minutes

1. Build a charcoal fire or preheat a gas grill.
2. Pat the fish dry with paper towels. Place the fillets on a plate and pour the olive oil over them. Turn occasionally, and let sit for 15 minutes. Shake the excess oil off, and season the fish lightly with salt and pepper. Top each piece of fish with strips of roasted yellow peppers and wrap each fillet with 2 slices of ham, securing it with toothpicks if necessary.
3. Place the fish in the center of the cooking grate over indirect medium-low heat, cover, and grill for 20 to 25 minutes, turning once halfway through the cooking time. You may need both a wide metal spatula on one side of the fish and tongs on the other to turn the fish.
4. Remove the fish from the grill, let it rest for 2 to 3 minutes, and serve immediately.

Classic Nantucket-Style Grilled Fish Steaks

The first time my Nantucket Island friends Nigel Dyche and Sarah Chase made this for me, I was incredulous at how fabulous it was, yet so simple. The fish tastes of the sea and the smoke from the grill with no extraneous flavors to mask the ocean-fresh steaks. The mayonnaise coats the thick pieces of fish, keeping them moist inside and promoting a golden caramelized color on the outside. Nantucket Islanders use this recipe mostly for swordfish, and it is one of their favorite summer meals, especially when paired with thick slices of ruby-red garden tomatoes.

Makes 4 servings

Grilling Method: Direct/Medium Heat

4	seafood steaks, such as yellowfin tuna, halibut, swordfish, or sea bass, about 10 ounces each, 1 inch thick
½	cup mayonnaise
	Kosher salt
	Freshly ground pepper
	Lemon wedges, optional

1. Build a charcoal fire or preheat a gas grill.
2. Coat the steaks on both sides with mayonnaise. Season to taste with salt and pepper.
3. Place the fish on the cooking grate over direct medium heat. Cover and cook, turning once halfway through the cooking time, until the fish is opaque but still moist in the center, about 10 minutes.
4. When done, let the fish rest for 3 to 5 minutes. Serve with additional salt, pepper, and lemon wedges, if desired.

Tuna Niçoise Salad with Lemon-Thyme Vinaigrette

This is a perfect ladies' lunch or light supper recipe. Everything but grilling the tuna steaks is done in advance, which makes it easy for "us hostesses" both to enjoy the gathering and to turn out great food. This recipe can be easily stretched in case you have an extra friend or two drop by. For a contemporary twist, substitute grilled asparagus spears for the green beans.

Makes 4 servings

Grilling Method: Direct/Medium Heat

Lemon-Thyme Vinaigrette
1/3	cup white wine vinegar
1	heaping teaspoon Dijon mustard
1	teaspoon minced fresh thyme
1/2	lemon, zested
	Pinch kosher salt
	Freshly ground pepper
2/3	cup extra-virgin olive oil
8	cooked small new potatoes, at room temperature
2	hard-boiled eggs
12	cherry tomatoes, cut in half
2	tuna steaks, 12 ounces each, 1 inch thick
	Olive oil
	Kosher salt
4	cups mesclun salad greens
8	ounces French green beans, blanched and chilled
1/4	cup Niçoise or kalamata olives
2	teaspoons capers

1. Build a charcoal fire or preheat a gas grill.
2. Make the vinaigrette: In a small bowl, whisk together the vinegar, mustard, thyme, lemon zest, and salt and pepper to taste. Slowly whisk in the olive oil, making sure it is well blended before adding more oil. Set aside.
3. Cut the potatoes in half or quarters, depending on size; cut the eggs in quarters and the cherry tomatoes in half. Set aside.
4. Meanwhile, prepare the tuna steaks by coating them with olive oil and sprinkling with kosher salt. Place the steaks on the cooking grate over direct medium heat, cover, and grill 3 to 5 minutes

each side, until the tuna is medium but still pink in the center. Remove the fish from the grill and let it sit for 5 minutes.
5. While the tuna is resting, assemble the salad by dividing the greens between 4 dinner plates or bowls. Add 4 pieces of potato (2 whole per salad), 2 wedges of hard-boiled egg, 6 tomato halves, 1/4 of the green beans, and 1/4 of the olives. Set aside.
6. Slice the tuna into long strips approximately 1/4 inch thick. Place equal amounts on top of each salad. Sprinkle each plate evenly with capers and drizzle with the vinaigrette. Season to taste with salt and pepper. Serve immediately.

Gingered Tuna Fillets with Wasabi-Soy Dipping Sauce

Next to anything grilled, one of my favorite styles of food is sushi—and tuna is my favorite sushi fish. An evening eating the world's best sushi at Kuni's in Evanston, IL, inspired me to create this recipe. At Kuni's the tuna is so fresh that it glistens like polished pink tourmalines. I prefer this recipe cooked "black and blue"—seared on the outside and cool on the inside. For this preparation, you must purchase sushi-grade fish and cook it the day you buy it.

Makes 4 servings

Grilling Method: Direct/High Heat

1	tablespoon dark brown sugar
2	cloves garlic, minced or pureed
1	teaspoon ground ginger
1	teaspoon kosher salt
4	sushi-grade tuna, such as toro or yellowtail fillets (cut from center piece of tuna), 2 inches thick
	Olive Oil
	Freshly ground pepper

Dipping Sauce
½ cup low-sodium soy sauce
1 orange, zested and juiced
1 tablespoon wasabi powder mixed with a teaspoon of water
1 tablespoon grated fresh ginger

1. Build a charcoal fire or preheat a gas grill.
2. In a small bowl, combine the sugar, garlic, ginger, and salt to make a rub. Coat the fish with olive oil, and rub it liberally with the spice mixture. Let sit for 10 minutes.
3. Place the fish on the cooking grate over direct medium heat, cover, and grill for 5 to 10 minutes, about 3 minutes on each side. If the tuna pieces are shaped more like a cube, sear on all the sides that are exposed. Remove the fish when it is seared on the outside and still a bit cool in the center. Cook longer if you prefer it more fully cooked.
4. While the fish is cooking, make the dipping sauce: Combine all the ingredients in a small bowl and mix well.
5. Remove the fish from the grill, and let it rest for 3 to 5 minutes. Serve with the sauce.

Seared Tuna with Coconut-Peanut Sauce

The idea for this recipe came to me one night while I was eating sushi across from a friend eating a peanut-flavored satay dish. I spontaneously dipped my piece of tuna into his sauce and instantly, a new flavor combination was born. The next day, I bought the best piece of center-cut tuna I could find and made a peanut sauce. I seared the tuna but left it rare inside and served it with this sauce, made all the richer by the addition of coconut milk. The toothsome sauce has notes of sweet, salt, and hot, and the crunchy natural peanut butter loads it up with both flavor and texture. This recipe is also good with the tuna cut into cubes and served on a platter as an appetizer—dipping sauce on the side!

Makes 4 servings

Grilling Method: Direct/High Heat

Peanut Sauce
1 13 to 14-ounce can unsweetened coconut milk, light or full fat
¼ cup natural peanut butter, preferably crunchy
½ cup roasted unsalted peanuts, chopped
1 tablespoon garlic-chili paste (such as *sriracha*), or more to taste
2 teaspoons Thai fish sauce
2 teaspoons unsweetened rice wine or malt vinegar
½ lemon, juiced
4 sushi-grade tuna steaks, 8 ounces each, at least 1½ inches thick
2 teaspoons toasted sesame oil
1 tablespoon olive oil
Kosher salt

1. Build a charcoal fire or preheat a gas grill.
2. Make the peanut sauce: Put the coconut milk, peanut butter, half of the peanuts, the chili paste, fish sauce, and vinegar in a blender. Process to combine. Pour the sauce into a small saucepan. Simmer for 10 minutes and taste. Add the lemon juice and adjust seasonings as needed. Set aside to cool. If the ingredients separate, put them back into the blender or use an immersion blender to re-emulsify.
3. Pat the tuna dry with paper towels. Combine the sesame and olive oils and brush them on all surfaces of the tuna steaks; season with salt. Sear the steaks on clean cooking grates over direct high heat, covered, for about 3 minutes on each side. The tuna will be rare in the center. If you want to cook the tuna all the way through, reduce the heat to medium and grill for 6 minutes on each side.
4. Remove the tuna from the grill, and let it rest 3 to 5 minutes before cutting into thick slices. Drizzle the tuna with peanut sauce and serve immediately.

Pomegranate-Glazed Swordfish with Grilled Radicchio

I've loved pomegranates ever since I was a child. My mother was a painter and frequently used them in her still-life portraits. When the painting was done, we would crack open the fruit and eat the gemlike seeds one by one. They are exotic, pretty enough to paint, and, as it turns out, contain one of the most powerful antioxidants known to humans.

Now you can find pure pomegranate juice in most every grocery store (POM Wonderful is one brand). It sure beats peeling and squeezing hundreds of seeds to make this glaze. The glaze is not only beautiful, but its sweet-tart taste is a perfect counterpoint to the meaty swordfish, the slightly bitter watercress, and the smoky grilled radicchio.

Makes 4 servings

Grilling Method: Direct/Medium Heat

1	cup pomegranate juice
½	cup apple juice
1	tablespoon cornstarch
1	lemon, zested
4	swordfish steaks, 10 ounces each, about 1 inch thick
1	large head round radicchio or 2 small, cleaned
	Olive oil
	Kosher salt
	Freshly ground pepper
1	bunch watercress, cleaned

1. Pour both juices into a small, heavy-bottomed saucepan. Simmer over low heat until the liquid is reduced by half and thickened, about 10 minutes. Whisk in the cornstarch, and bring the mixture to a boil. Simmer for about 2 minutes or until thickened. Add the zest, and take off the heat to cool to room temperature.
2. Cut the cleaned radicchio in half, or in quarters if it is large enough, leaving the core intact. This will allow you to grill it without losing the leaves. Brush the swordfish and radicchio with olive oil and season with salt and pepper, set aside.
3. Place the swordfish and radicchio in the center of the cooking grate over direct medium heat, cover, and grill 4 to 5 minutes. Turn the fish over and brush it with some of the glaze, cover the grill, and continue cooking for another 4 to 5 minutes, or until the fish is opaque and flakes. The radicchio will take about the same amount of time, depending on the size. Watch it closely, because you want grill marks and slight charring on all the visible surfaces and the leaves wilted.
4. Remove the fish and radicchio from the grill. Let the fish rest for 3 to 5 minutes. Arrange the watercress on plates and serve the fish on top with a wedge of radicchio on the side. Drizzle the fish and radicchio with the remaining pomegranate glaze.

Nantucket Swordfish with Browned Butter and Sautéed Pecans

In 1983, I packed up my duffel bag and headed off to Nantucket to work—and play—for the summer. Little did I know that it would be a great culinary experience as well. In addition to scalloping with a fifth-generation fisherman, I ate out at all the great restaurants—most now defunct. At every dinner, it seemed that at least half the table would order swordfish with béarnaise sauce. When I started grilling, I remembered that dish and decided that I liked the richness of the sauce but that it needed some crunch.

The browned butter is easy enough for anyone with patience to make, and the pecans sauté and lightly brown as the butter slowly turns color. It not only looks good on a plate, but the flavor combination is in perfect harmony. The sauce can be made in advance and gently reheated just before serving. This recipe would also be good with any firm white fish such as tilapia, halibut, or sturgeon.

Makes 4 servings

Grilling Method: Direct/Medium Heat

½ cup (1 stick) unsalted butter
1 cup pecan pieces
   Fine-grain sea salt
   White pepper
4 center-cut swordfish steaks, 10 to 12 ounces
      each, about 1 inch thick
   Olive oil

1. Build a charcoal fire or preheat a gas grill.
2. Put the butter in a cold sauté pan. On medium-
   low heat, slowly melt the butter. Add the pecans
   and let them brown and toast as the butter
   slowly browns. Season lightly with salt and white
   pepper. You will need to watch the pan closely
   as the butter can burn very quickly. When the
   butter reaches a dark caramel color, remove it
   from the heat, cover, and set aside. Either keep
   it warm or gently reheat before topping the fish.
3. Brush the fish steaks on both sides with oil.
   Season with salt and pepper. Place them on the
   cooking grate over direct medium heat, cover, and
   grill about 5 minutes on each side, until the fish is
   opaque and releases easily from the grill.
4. Place the fish on a clean platter. Let the fish rest
   for 3 to 5 minutes. Top with the brown butter and
   pecans. Serve immediately.

Sesame-Miso Cod

*Mark Bittman, writer of the New York Times recipe column
"The Minimalist," has the unique ability to distill complicated restaurant flavors into just a few steps. Many years
ago, I fell in love with a miso-flavored fish dish at a fancy
restaurant in the Napa Valley. I am thrilled that Mark created this version for the home cook, so I can get my fish-miso
fix without the bother of a train, plane, and automobile! The
original recipe was written for the broiler, but I've adapted
it for the grill. The sauce works beautifully on other fish
such as halibut, as well as on green vegetables—especially
green beans, spinach, and asparagus.*

Makes 4 servings

Grilling Method: Indirect/Medium Heat

¼ cup sesame seeds
¼ cup miso, preferably red
1 tablespoon sugar
1 tablespoon mirin
1 tablespoon soy sauce, plus more to taste
1½ to 2 pounds cod fillets, of equal thickness
   Extra-virgin olive oil
   Pinch cayenne pepper
   Kosher salt

1. Build a charcoal fire or preheat a gas grill.
2. In a small dry skillet over medium heat, toast the
   sesame seeds, shaking the pan until they color
   slightly. Grind to a powder in a spice or coffee
   grinder or use a mortar and pestle.
3. Use a whisk to combine the powdered seeds
   with the miso, sugar, mirin, and soy sauce. If
   the mixture is more like a paste than a sauce,
   thin it with 3 tablespoons of water or a combination of water, mirin, and soy sauce. Taste and
   adjust seasonings. (The sauce may be covered
   and refrigerated for up to 2 days. Stir before
   serving.)
4. Brush the fish with a small amount of oil and
   sprinkle with cayenne and a small amount of
   salt—the sauce adds a salt note to the dish, so
   you need to be careful of overseasoning. Place
   the fish on the cooking grate over indirect medium heat. (This recipe would would work well
   with the GrillMat, see page 150.) Cover and
   grill for 10 to 12 minutes, turning once halfway
   through the cooking time. If desired, spread some
   of the sesame-miso sauce on top of the cooked
   side of the fish after turning so it can bake into
   the fish.
5. The fish is done when the point of a thin-bladed
   knife inserted into the thickest part meets a little
   resistance. Remove from the grill and place on a
   clean platter. Let the fish rest for 3 to 5 minutes.
   Serve with the sesame-miso sauce on top.

Cedar-Planked Salmon

Legend has it that the Pacific Northwest Indians would stand a large plank of cedar upright next to a campfire and pin a whole salmon to it. The radiant heat from the fire would make the cedar smoke and the fish cook, scenting the salmon with the cedar smoke. Using a cedar plank over indirect heat on a grill results in moist fish that is almost impossible to overcook. The cedar smoke is enough flavor for some, but I think a light brush of a sweet tomato-based barbecue sauce is even better! And don't stop at salmon; cedar planks work well for other types of fish, as well as pork and chicken.

Makes 4 servings

Grilling Method: Indirect/Medium Heat

1   9 x 15–inch untreated cedar plank, soaked in
     water for at least 1 hour
1   wild salmon fillet, 1½ pounds, about 10
     inches long
    Olive oil
1   lemon, cut in thin slices
    Kosher salt
    Freshly ground pepper
    Favorite barbecue sauce, optional

1. Build a charcoal fire or preheat a gas grill.
2. Remove the plank from the water, and place the fillet skin-side down on the wood. Brush the fish with olive oil, cover the top with lemon slices, and season with salt and pepper.
3. Place the planked salmon in the center of the cooking grate over indirect medium heat. Cover and grill for 15 to 20 minutes, or until the salmon is pink in the center and flakes easily with a fork. Brush with sauce, if using during the final minutes of grilling time.
4. Let the salmon rest a few minutes, then serve it directly from the plank.

TIP: You can purchase fancy packaged planks at gourmet cooking stores or rough it and have a lumberyard cut the planks for you. They are exactly the same, just make sure you use untreated cedar wood.

TIP: Ask your fishmonger to stock wild salmon. It may be a little more expensive, but it is worth every penny because the flavor and the texture are barely a cousin to the more common farm-raised variety.

PLANK SALMON VARIATIONS

Cool as Cucumber: Serve with Yogurt-Cucumber Sauce (page 38) or a refreshing cucumber salad.

Just Dilly: Serve with dill, capers, lemon, and sour cream or crème fraîche.

Barbecued: Ten minutes before removing from the grill, brush with a thin coat of your favorite barbecue sauce.

Smoked Butter Sauce: Melt together 1 stick unsalted butter, 1 tablespoon smoked hot paprika, and a pinch of salt. Whisk together and brush onto the fish during the final 10 minutes of cooking.

Citrus Maple Glaze: Mix ½ cup maple syrup with the juices of 1 orange and 1 lime. Add a pinch of salt and brush a thin coat onto the fish during the final 10 minutes of cooking.

Salmon BLTs with Herbed Mayonnaise

This sandwich is best served in the summer, when fresh tomatoes abound and you are looking for a new way to use them. The freshness of wild salmon pairs perfectly with the smoky bacon, acidic tomatoes, crunchy lettuce, and cool herbed mayo. If you want to take this sandwich one step further, leave the salmon skin on the grill until it gets crisp and substitute it for the bacon. I guarantee this will be one recipe you'll make again and again. In a pinch, you can flavor Hellmann's mayonnaise (my favorite brand) with the garlic and herbs or, better yet, make the homemade mayo in advance—it will keep refrigerated for a week and is good for anything that calls for plain mayo.

Makes 4 servings

Grilling Method: Indirect/Medium Heat

- 4 wild salmon fillets, about 6 ounces each, 1 inch thick
  Olive oil
  Kosher salt
  Freshly ground pepper
- 8 slices bread from a rustic oval loaf, grilled on 1 side only
- ½ cup Herbed Mayonnaise (below)
- 12 slices (about 8 ounces) best-quality bacon, cooked and drained
- 2 tomatoes, cut in slices
- 4 to 8 crisp leaves romaine, cleaned and dried

1. Build a charcoal fire or preheat a gas grill.
2. Pat the salmon fillets dry with paper towels, brush them lightly with oil and season with salt and pepper.
3. Place the salmon, skin-side down, on the cooking grate over indirect medium heat, cover, and grill for 10 to 12 minutes. When the salmon begins to bubble at the skin, take a flat spatula and, turning it upside down, separate the flesh of the fish from the skin. Leave the skin to continue cooking. Remove from grill and transfer to a clean platter, letting it rest for a few minutes.
4. Spread the ungrilled side of each slice of bread with Herbed Mayonnaise. Place a piece of salmon on each slice of bread. Top with the bacon (or crispy salmon skin). Layer with the tomato and lettuce. Put the tops of the sandwiches in place. With a long, sharp knife, cut the sandwiches in half and serve immediately.

Herbed Mayonnaise
Makes 2 cups

- 1 large egg, at room temperature
- 1 large egg yolk, at room temperature
- 3 tablespoons fresh lemon juice, divided
- 2 tablespoons minced fresh chives, basil, and tarragon
- 1 tablespoon strong Dijon mustard
- ½ lemon zested
  Fine-grain sea salt
  Freshly ground pepper
- 1 cup olive oil
- ½ cup light olive oil or untoasted walnut oil

1. In a food processor fitted with a steel blade, combine the egg, egg yolk, and 1 tablespoon of the lemon juice. Pulse to mix.
2. Add the herbs, mustard, zest, a pinch of salt and pepper, and process until fairly smooth. With the motor running, slowly add the oils through the feed tube of the food processor. The mayonnaise will begin to thicken; watch closely and add the oil until it is the right consistency.
3. Taste the mayonnaise and adjust the seasonings, adding more lemon juice (the mayonnaise should be tart), herbs, salt, and pepper to suit your taste. Transfer to a storage container with an airtight lid. Cover and refrigerate for at least 2 hours to develop the flavors before using. The mayonnaise can be prepared up to 3 days in advance and will keep for 1 week in the refrigerator.

Salmon Pastrami with Red Cabbage and Apple Slaw

Who hasn't packed a pound or two of pastrami in their luggage—or at least wanted to after a trip to one of New York's legendary Jewish delis? I know I have! Here is a pastrami you can have anywhere. The classic spices from cured beef pastrami are rubbed into a fillet of salmon for a lip-smacking dinner that's every bit as good as its deli cousin. Don't rub the salmon too far in advance or the salt and sugar will make the salmon weep; a crust will form more easily on a relatively dry surface. Serve the salmon "pastrami" with Red Cabbage and Apple Slaw and best-quality rye bread.

Makes 4 servings

Grilling Method: Indirect/Medium Heat

Pastrami Rub
1 tablespoon dark brown sugar
2 teaspoons kosher salt
2 teaspoons ground ginger
2 teaspoons coriander seeds
1 teaspoon black peppercorns
1 teaspoon granulated garlic
1/2 teaspoon ground allspice
1 center-cut salmon fillet, about 2 pounds
Olive oil
Red Cabbage and Apple Slaw (at right)
8 slices rye bread

1. Build a charcoal fire or preheat a gas grill.
2. Make the pastrami rub: Combine all the ingredients in a spice grinder (coffee grinder) and process until the spices are medium fine. Set aside.
3. Pat the salmon dry with paper towels. Brush it lightly on all sides with olive oil. Sprinkle it with the Pastrami Rub and press gently so that the spices adhere. Place the salmon on a platter lined with paper towels, and let it sit uncovered in the refrigerator to "cure" for 15 minutes.
4. Place the fillet, skin-side down, in the center of the cooking grate over indirect medium heat, cover, and grill for 20 to 25 minutes or until the fish turns opaque. There is no need to turn during grilling.
5. Remove the fish from the grill, and let rest for 3 to 5 minutes. Serve with the Red Cabbage and Apple Slaw and rye bread.

TIP: Granulated garlic is pure dehydrated garlic. If you can't find it in your area, substitute 2 cloves of minced garlic. Do not use garlic salt, which adds a salt note, and if you are using garlic powder, use 1/4 teaspoon instead of the full teaspoon. Online source: www. thespicestore.com.

Red Cabbage and Apple Slaw
1/2 head red cabbage
2 Granny Smith apples, grated
1/4 cup toasted walnut halves
Kosher salt
Freshly ground pepper
1/2 cup fresh orange juice
1 tablespoon malt vinegar
1/2 teaspoon caraway seeds
2 tablespoons light sour cream

1. Slice or chop the cabbage in the food processor or by hand. Put it in a large nonreactive bowl. Add the apples and walnuts.
2. Make the dressing: Stir the ingredients in a small bowl to mix well and add to the slaw mixture. Season to taste with salt and pepper. The slaw is best refrigerated for 3 hours or overnight before serving. It can be made up to 1 day in advance.

Beer-Brined Smoked Catfish

I created this recipe in honor of a barbecue fest that I hosted for John T. Edge in Oxford, MS. John T. is the director of the Southern Foodways Alliance and the arbiter of all matters of good and bad taste, Southern style. He introduced me to the world's best fried catfish at Lynne Hewitt's Taylor Grocery, so I decided to introduce him to barbecued catfish. The smoked catfish is great on its own but even better when made into the decadent smoked catfish pâté.

Makes 4 to 6 servings

Grilling Method: Indirect/Medium-Low Heat
Special Equipment: Cameron Stovetop Smoker

NOTE: This recipe is written for the Cameron Stovetop Smoker, which provides great flavor quickly. It can also be adapted to a gas or charcoal grill.

Brine

- **4** cups hot water
- **1** cup kosher salt
- **½** cup packed brown sugar
- **3½** ounce cans beer
- **1** tablespoon coarse ground pepper
- **6** bay leaves, crumbled
- **4** catfish fillets, about 12 ounces each
  Olive oil
- **2** tablespoons Cameron wood chips

1. Make the brine: In a large container, dissolve the salt and sugar in the hot water. Add the beer, pepper, and bay leaves. Whisk well to remove any carbonation. Add about 4 cups of ice to reduce the temperature of the brine. Put the fillets into the cool brine, adding cold water if more liquid is necessary to cover all the fillets. Brine the fish for 4 hours or overnight in the refrigerator. Remove the fish from the brine, rinse in cold water, and air dry for 10 minutes before smoking.
2. Prepare the stovetop smoker with wood chips.
3. When ready to smoke, brush the fish lightly with oil, but do not season with any salt or pepper—the brine provides the seasoning, and the smoke intensifies the salt note.
4. Smoke the fish in the stovetop smoker on the stove over a burner set on high or direct high heat on a grill. Smoke for 20 to 30 minutes. The fish will be opaque, firm, and a dark caramel color. Alternatively, if not using the stovetop smoker, place the fish in the center of the cooking grate over indirect medium-low heat, and smoke for 1 hour, or until the fish is cooked through, firm, opaque, and slightly colored from the smoke. Serve the catfish at room temperature or make it into Smoked Catfish Pâté (at right).

Smoked Catfish Pâté

This spread, or pâté, is so good, I know you won't be able to stop at just one bite! Serve on homemade melba toast (page 41) or simple water crackers. Bluefish and trout are both good substitutes for the catfish.

- **4** Beer-Brined Smoked Catfish Fillets (page 167)
- **8** ounces cream cheese, at room temperature
- **½ to ¾** cup sour cream
- **2** large shallots, minced
- **2** tablespoons capers in liquid (not in salt)
- **2** teaspoons caper juice
- **¼** teaspoon granulated garlic
- **5** shakes of Tabasco
- **6** grinds fresh ground pepper, or more to taste

1. While the catfish is still warm, break the fillets into pieces, removing any bones. Add the cream cheese and mix well. Add ½ cup of the sour cream and mix well. Add the shallots, capers, caper juice, garlic, and Tabasco. Taste for seasoning. Add more sour cream at this point if the pâté is a little dry or tastes a little salty. Adjust the Tabasco and add pepper to taste.
2. Refrigerate the pâté at least 3 hours or preferably overnight. Taste once more before serving and adjust the seasonings if necessary. Serve on the cold side of room temperature on homemade melba toast or your favorite crackers. Top with a dollop of sour cream, if desired.

NOTE: Do not add any salt to this dish because the brine and the smoke "salts" the fish before it is mixed into the pâté.

Hickory-Smoked Bacon-Wrapped Rainbow Trout

My cousin Ben lives in Cashiers, NC, on a beautiful piece of land nestled between mountains that look like a movie set, complete with a trout stream. During a recent family gathering, the young cousins fished and I grilled. The trout was so fresh, I should have slapped it. Instead, I opted to season it simply with olive oil and salt before wrapping it in thick hickory-smoked bacon. The bacon adds flavor, bastes the trout while it grills, and prevents any sticking. Keeping the head and tail on the fish while it grills results in better flavor and helps keep the fish intact during the cooking time. Serve this with a favorite vegetable or Crunchy Cucumber Salad (page 303).

Makes 4 servings

Grilling Method: Indirect/Medium Heat

4   **whole trout, about 1 pound each, cleaned but with head and tail on**
     Olive Oil
     Kosher salt
12 **slices (about 8 ounces) hickory-smoked bacon, at room temperature**

1. Pat the trout dry with paper towels. Brush them inside and out with olive oil and season with salt. Starting with the head, just beneath the eye, begin to wrap the bacon around the circumference of the fish, slightly overlapping so you do not see any of the fish skin. Each fish will take about 3 pieces of bacon to wrap. Stop wrapping when you get to the last inch of the tail. Put the fish on a clean platter. This step can be done up to 1 day in advance. Cover the fish tightly and refrigerate it until ready to grill.
2. Build a charcoal fire or preheat a gas grill.
3. Place the fish in the center of the cooking grate over indirect medium heat, cover, and grill for 10 minutes. Turn the fish over and continue to cook for 5 to 10 minutes more or until it flakes and is cooked through.
4. Let rest for 3 to 5 minutes, then serve hot.

TIP: Sunburst Trout Farms is a family-owned farm, nestled into the great Smoky Mountains in western North Carolina. Its trout are pristine and taste of mountain spring water and sunshine. Look for Sunburst Trout in your local market; you'll know its their trout by the distinctive red color of the flesh—it almost looks like salmon.

THE STOVETOP SMOKER

I am crazy about the stove-top smoker and it is responsible for expanding my grilling horizons. I've long been a gas griller, and I work hard to duplicate authentic wood-fire flavors in new and more convenient ways. I even barbecue on a gas grill, and if you didn't know it, you couldn't tell by the taste. I've fooled my share of Barbecue Grand Champions! Rick Smilow, president of the Institute of Culinary Education (ICE) in New York City (where I am a guest instructor) gave me the push to develop an indoor grilling technique. When I started Girls at the Grill in 2002, he invited me to teach grilling and authentic Southern barbecue to his smoke-starved Manhattan students. At first I was unsure that I could teach a class that I could hang my barbecue hat on since ICE does not have outdoor space. But then I met Chris and Ann Malone, U.S. distributors of the Cameron Stovetop Smoker. Chris sent a smoker to me, I tested it with fish, and I was hooked. I could now teach and cook authentic-tasting Southern barbecue indoors. Between the smoker, convection ovens, and a grill with a domed lid, I can successfully grill indoors. And although I much prefer cooking outdoors, it is a great alternative for people who don't have outdoor space—especially for smoking fish and vegetables.

Smoked Trout with Apple Relish and Trout Caviar

This is the one recipe that can be done inside on the stovetop as easily as outside on the grill. The trout is delicate and doesn't take very long to cook, so the Cameron Smoker is a great tool for this recipe. It is compact and gives the fish a very pronounced smoke flavor in a short period of time. The trout is then topped with a cool raw apple and purple grape relish, a dab of crème fraîche and plump orbs of trout caviar. It is equally good served hot or at room temperature.

Makes 4 servings

Grilling Method: Indirect/Medium-Low Heat
Special Equipment: Cameron Stovetop Smoker

	Cameron apple wood chips,
4	boneless trout fillets, 8 ounces each
1/2	cup seedless purple or red grapes, washed and cut in half
2	Granny Smith apples, peeled and chopped
1	lemon, juiced
1	small shallot, diced
1/2	teaspoon dried ground ginger
1	tablespoon dark brown sugar
	Pinch cinnamon
	Pinch ground cloves
	Fine-grain sea salt
1/4	cup crème fraîche or sour cream
	1-ounce jar golden trout (or salmon) caviar

1. Follow the instructions on the stovetop smoker: Place the wood chips in the center of the smoker. Cover the metal drip pan. Insert the cooking grate and place the trout fillets on the grate. Slide the cover on the smoker until it is sealed. Either smoke on the stovetop by placing the burner in the center of the stove or directly on the burner of a gas grill or gray-ashed charcoal briquettes. Watch the smoker: From the time you first see a thin wisp of smoke, it will take about 15 minutes to smoke the trout from that point. (See Sidebar, page 169.) If you are smoking more than 4 fillets, it will take longer.

2. Using mitts on both hands, remove the smoker and slowly slide the lid to one side. If the fish is slightly colored and opaque, it is done. Put the cover back on and let the fish come to room temperature.

3. Meanwhile, make the relish by combining the grapes and apples with the lemon juice. Mix the ginger, shallot, sugar, cinnamon, cloves, and a pinch of salt. Sprinkle over the fruit and toss well to combine. Let sit for 10 minutes, stirring occasionally.

4. When ready to serve, place a smoked fillet on a plate, and top with a generous spoon of apple relish so that it spills over the sides. Add a dollop of crème fraîche or sour cream and finish with a small spoon of golden trout caviar. Serve immediately.

Bahamian-Style Whole Grilled Red Snapper

In the mid 1990s, I traveled to Nassau, Bahamas, more than a dozen times in less than a year. On my first trip, I fell hook, line, and sinker for their simple and flavorful seafood preparations. During subsequent trips, I would make a beeline for Arawak Cay for conch salad (Bahamian Seafood Salad, page 186) and at night, I would celebrate at The Poop Deck. My menu of choice was fried grouper fingers and the whole fish of the day—which always tasted of sunshine and salt water.

Be sure that when the fishmonger scales and cleans your fish, he keeps the head and tail intact.

Makes 4 servings

Grilling Method: Indirect/Medium Heat

1	teaspoon red chile flakes
1/4	cup olive oil, plus more if necessary
1	whole red snapper, about 2 1/2 pounds, scaled and cleaned
	Kosher salt
	Freshly ground pepper
2	cloves garlic, thinly sliced
2	lemons, sliced in rounds
1	bunch fresh chives or green onions

Solid wooden toothpicks, soaked in water for
    30 minutes
6   green onions, julienned in 2-inch lengths
1   lemon, cut into wedges

1. Build a charcoal fire or preheat a gas grill.
2. Put the chile flakes and oil in a small cold saucepan. Slowly heat the oil until the chile flakes begin to change color. Turn off the heat and let the oil cool to room temperature. Set aside until ready to grill.
3. With a sharp knife, cut 2 to 3 diagonal slashes on both sides of the fish. This will hold the garlic and lemons and help to evenly cook the fish. Place the slices of garlic and lemon in each of the diagonal cuts. Put the garlic in first and then the lemon slices, letting some of the lemon "peek" out from the slit.
4. Brush the insides and outsides of the fish with a small amount of the chile oil and sprinkle with a little salt and pepper. Stuff the cavity with chives, and close with a toothpick or trussing pin.
5. Carefully place the fish in the center of the cooking grate over indirect medium heat. Cover and grill for about 30 minutes There is no need to turn the fish.
6. When done, let the fish rest for 3 to 5 minutes. Garnish with plenty of green onions and lemon wedges.

TIP: If using green onions instead of chives, cut them into very thin, 2-inch long strips (julienne) before stuffing the fish. "Julienne" is a cooking term that means to cut food into very thin strips. Round vegetables are squared off, cut into slices, stacked on top of each other and cut again into long pieces that resemble matchsticks.

Whole Fish with Thai Flavors

A few years ago, my friend Bob Blumer convinced me to go with him on a bike tour of Thailand—from Chang Rai to Chang Mai. This wasn't a tour for wimps or those seeking white tablecloth restaurants! During the 10-day trip, we averaged 100 kilometers a day and at night we ate the most amazing food at backroad huts, where often we were the only people there—certainly the only foreigners. As often as we could, we would order fish grilled whole over a wood fire and seasoned with garlic and chilies. In the cool night air, the steaming fish and ice cold Singha beer made 100 kilometers on a bike seem like a small price to pay for the meal.

Makes 4 to 6 servings

Grilling Method: Indirect/Medium Heat

1 or 2 cleaned whole fish, such as grouper, sea bass, snapper, or catfish, 3½ to 4 pound total
    Olive or peanut oil
1   small (1 to 2 inch) knob fresh ginger, grated
3   cloves garlic, grated
2   teaspoons garlic-chili paste (such as *sriracha*)
1   lime, juiced
2   teaspoons fish sauce
1   teaspoon toasted sesame oil
2   limes, sliced in rounds, divided
    Solid wooden toothpicks, soaked in water for
    30 minutes

1. Build a charcoal fire or preheat a gas grill.
2. Brush the fish all over with oil and set aside.
3. Meanwhile, make the marinade, which will resemble more of a paste than a traditional marinade. Mix the ginger, garlic, chili paste, lime juice, fish sauce, and sesame oil in a small bowl. Taste and adjust the seasonings as necessary. If it needs more salt, add a few more drops of fish sauce, which provides the salty notes in this recipe.
4. Spread the paste generously and evenly inside the fish and add half of the lime slices. Secure the fish with a wet toothpick threaded through the cut in the stomach. This will prevent the limes and seasonings from spilling out.
5. Place the fish on the cooking grate over indirect medium heat, cover, and grill 30 to 35 minutes of total cooking time.
6. When the fish is done and opaque in the thickest part, remove it from the grill. Let the fish rest for 3 to 5 minutes. Serve hot, with the remaining slices of lime.

The Grand Aioli

The Grand Aioli is traditionally served in Provence for lunch on meatless Fridays. And though it is not served in many restaurants anymore, Le Bistro du Paradou in Maussane des Alpilles serves a sumptuous version of this regional dish. Whatever the history, this dish of cod and vegetables is a great excuse to eat aioli—that pungent rich mayonnaise flavored with garlic and good first-press olive oil. My grilled version is made even more flavorful—and more balanced— by grilling the fish and vegetables. If you are familiar with the dish, you will notice that I've made the traditional escargot (snails) optional. "Sans escargot" is in honor of my friend Wycke Baker who ate one escargot too many at the bistro, and neither one of us has been able to eat them since—but feel free to add them if you'd like.

Makes 4 to 6 servings

Grilling Method: Indirect/Medium Heat

Aioli

1	large lemon, zested and juiced (about 3 tablespoons)
6	large cloves garlic, roughly chopped
1	heaping tablespoon Dijon mustard
1	whole egg
1	egg yolk
1¹⁄₂	cups vegetable oil, plus a little extra if needed
1	cup best-quality extra-virgin olive oil
¹⁄₂	teaspoon kosher salt
2	pounds cod fillets of equal thickness
	Olive oil
	Kosher salt
6	eggs, hard-boiled, peeled, and halved
8	ounces carrots, peeled
8	ounces cauliflower florets
8	ounces green beans
8	ounces potatoes, cleaned
24	snails, cleaned and cooked, optional

1. Make the aioli: In a food processor fitted with the steel blade, combine the lemon juice and garlic, and pulse until the garlic is pureed (about 15 seconds). Add the mustard and pulse again until combined. Add the egg, egg yolk, and lemon zest and process for 10 seconds (if you are concerned about the raw eggs, use pasteurized eggs). Very slowly add the oil in a trickle through the feed tube of the food processor until the sauce is thick and well combined (emulsified). As the aioli becomes thicker, the machine sounds more like a purr than a whirr and you know it is done. If you like a thicker texture, add a little more oil, and if you like your sauce thinner, stop at the 2¹⁄₂ cups of oil. Add the salt and process until well combined. Even if the aioli seems like it needs a little salt, resist the urge to add more because the seasoned fish and veggies will more than compensate. Set aside.

2. Build a charcoal fire or preheat a gas grill.

3. Slice the cod into 6 equal pieces. Brush all over with oil and season with salt.

4. Meanwhile, cut the carrots into 3-inch pieces and put them in a resealable plastic bag. Add the green beans. Drizzle them with enough oil to coat the vegetables. Seal the bag and toss the veggies until all surfaces are coated with oil. Sprinkle with salt. Repeat the process with the cauliflower and potatoes.

5. When ready to cook, remove the vegetables from the bag and place the carrots, potatoes, and cauliflower on the warming rack of the grill, away from the direct heat. Leave the green beans in the bag. Turn the vegetables occasionally and grill-roast for 30 minutes before putting the fish and green beans on the grill.

6. When the other vegetables are almost done, place the fish and green beans on the cooking grate over indirect medium heat, cover, and grill for about 5 minutes per side or until well marked and cooked through. This recipe works well with the GrillMat (see page 150). If using the mat, it is not necessary to turn the fish.

7. Remove the vegetables and fish to a clean platter. Let the fish rest for 3 to 5 minutes. If serving snails, add the snails to the platter. Serve individual dipping bowls of the aioli and pass the platter.

TIP: You may have some leftover aioli, but once you've tasted it, you'll want to slather it on everything from grilled asparagus to a ham sandwich. It will keep for 2 weeks refrigerated.

Shrimp and Other Shellfish

Shrimp 101

Shrimp is by far the most popular shellfish, so here are the basics for cooking it, with notes on other shellfish, too.

Rapid-Fire Checklist

✓ Thaw shrimp, if necessary
✓ Preheat grill to High
✓ Toss shrimp with olive oil, as needed
✓ Season shrimp with kosher salt and pepper, if desired
✓ Reduce heat to medium
✓ Place shrimp on cooking grate over Direct Heat
✓ Remove shrimp from grill with tongs
✓ Let rest briefly then serve immediately

Tools of the Trade

• 12-inch locking chef tongs
• Heavy-duty oven mitt
• Stainless steel bowl
• Silicone or natural-bristle brush

Common Problems

• Cooking peeled shrimp
• Shrimp falling through the grates
• Overcooked shrimp

Growing up in North Carolina, it was impossible not to love shrimp. We ate it all year round, in everything from classic shrimp cocktail to shrimp and grits. But my favorite way of preparing shrimp was and is, grilling it. Shrimp is not only one of the easiest foods to grill, it is as versatile as food gets and adapts to almost any seasoning. It shines in dishes with flavors from around the globe and fits in easily as an appetizer or main course. But the most important reason to choose shrimp is that practically everyone loves it.

As opposed to boiling shrimp, which removes and dilutes its flavor, grilling intensifies it in part due to the caramelization process and because you don't add liquid or fats that can leach some of the flavor away. I'm confident that if you conduct a side-by-side taste comparison, you'll never want to boil shrimp again! I also recommend grilling it in the shell to protect the delicate flesh and because it adds a lot of flavor.

Buying Shrimp

Most of the shrimp that is beautifully displayed at the fish counter has been conveniently thawed for you. But here is the rub: you don't know how and you don't know for how long it has been thawed—so it's better to thaw it yourself. Frozen shrimp comes two ways: frozen in a solid block of ice and IQF (individually quick frozen). Either works well.

The best shrimp are flash-frozen in blocks of water like giant ice cubes within hours of being pulled from the net. This is the best way to preserve the flavor and the texture of the shrimp—it seals the shrimp and prevents it from getting freezer burn. The solid block comes in five-pound increments. If you can buy these blocks, this will be your best store-bought option. Most of the time, these blocks of frozen shrimp are in the back, behind the counter. This is usually how it is delivered to the store and then thawed before selling it to you. If it isn't possible to buy the "ice cube" shrimp or five pounds is too much shrimp for one cookout—you never want to thaw and refreeze it—you should opt for the IQF shrimp. I prefer to buy frozen raw unpeeled shrimp and thaw it just before grilling. The IQF shrimp are just as fresh but not protected from freezer burn like the ice-cube shrimp, so check for excessive ice crystals. The IQF shrimp are sold in bags by the pound and take less than 10 minutes to thaw. You can buy them in the peel, peeled without tails, and peeled with tails on. (Do not buy frozen cooked shrimp for grilling.)

The Bigger the Better

When you choose shrimp to grill, the bigger, the better, I say. My preference is for the large or jumbo shrimp. Without getting too technical, the industry classifies shrimp by the number that make up a pound. This obviously varies by the size (thus the weight) of the shrimp.

So now you know how to answer when the person behind the counter says, "Do you want 11 to 15 counts?" This refers to "jumbo" shrimp. The small shrimp are not really suitable for grilling, because they might fall through the cooking grates and will be done almost as soon as you put them on the grill—risking almost unpreventable overcooking.

SHRIMP PER POUND	SHRIMP SIZE
10 shrimp or less	Colossal
11 to 15	Jumbo
16 to 20	Extra-large
21 to 30	Large
31 to 35	Medium
36 to 45	Small
About 100	Miniature

To maximize the flavor and protect the delicate shrimp meat, I grill most of my shrimp in the shell, even if I peel it before using it in a recipe like the Shrimp Margaritas with Avocados and Garden Tomatoes (page 185). The only exception to my rule is when I want to infuse the shrimp with a richly flavored marinade. Then I remove the shells for maximum flavor absorption. I do just that for the Firecracker Shrimp with Hot Pepper Jelly Glaze (page 181).

Make Your Own Easy-Peel Shrimp

This shrimp, often labeled E-Z Peel, has the shell split down the middle of the back to make it much easier to work with. You get the bonus of the extra flavor that cooking in the shells brings and the ease of peeling to finish your recipe or eat on the spot.

I like making my own easy-peel shrimp, because the full shell protects the shrimp until after it is thawed. With a pair of kitchen shears or even regular (sharp) scissors, hold the thawed shrimp between your thumb and forefinger at the top of the shrimp (head off) and simply insert the scissors under the shell to snip down the spine, stopping at the tail. This separates the shell into easy-to-remove sections.

But be forewarned, the easier the shrimp are to peel, the more your guests will eat! Plan accordingly. The one caveat for easy-peel shrimp is that it doesn't work well when you are crusting the shrimp with a strong flavor, like salt. The slit down the center will allow too much of the seasoning to penetrate the shrimp. Salt crusting, like in the Salt-Crusted Shrimp with Potent Lemon-Garlic Sauce (page 182), is best prepared with whole unpeeled shrimp.

Thawing Shrimp (and Other Shellfish)

The best way to thaw frozen shrimp and other shell-fish is to place it in a colander under cold running water. This is essential to preserving the texture of the shrimp and takes the shortest amount of time. Thaw just before cooking for the best results. Once you've thawed the shrimp, keep it in the refrigerator until the very minute you are cooking it and, if marinating, do that in the refrigerator as well. Shrimp deteriorates very quickly if not properly handled, which is why I recommend you thaw it at home.

To Devein or Not to Devein; That Is the Question

A lot of the shrimp that you buy has already been deveined, either deliberately or because the vein often comes out naturally if the heads are cut off within a few hours of catching. The sand vein is harmless but it is sometimes unsightly and a bit gritty. Does it affect flavor? No, it is the gross-out factor! When cooking whole shrimp (head on), there is nothing you can do, but any other time, it is very easy to devein before cooking by following the instructions below. You can buy a shrimp deveiner in stores, but a pair of kitchen shears is faster and easier.

To remove the vein running along the spine, follow the easy-peel shrimp trick above to split the shell, then with scissors or a toothpick, pick up the vein in the middle and pull it out. If you are preparing shrimp that will be grilled without the shell, follow the steps for easy-peel shrimp, then remove the out-side shell. Your shrimp are now ready to be grilled.

Oil Shrimp Before Grilling

Whether you are cooking shrimp in the shell or out of the shell, it is essential that you coat the shrimp with a little olive or vegetable oil. The oil will prevent shrimp from sticking—especially peeled shrimp—and will seal in the natural juices, keeping the shrimp moist and tender.

Double-Skewer It, aka Ladder Method

Skewering makes cooking peeled shrimp very simple. It eliminates the need to place each shrimp on the grill and turn it just minutes later. That isn't such an issue with larger or jumbo shrimp, but it is with medium-sized shrimp. How many times have you threaded a shrimp down the middle, only to have it twirl around and around on the skewer? My solution is to double-skewer it. I use inexpensive bamboo skewers that I've soaked in water for about 30 minutes. This step is necessary or your skewers will burn. For each shrimp kabob, lay out two skewers and thread the shrimp through both ends instead of the middle. The skewers end up looking like ladders (my nickname for the method) and hold the shrimp so they cook evenly on both sides. Now all you have to do is place the shrimp on the cooking grate and turn once halfway through the cooking time.

NOTE: You can't skewer shrimp in the shells; the skewers won't penetrate easily enough to make it worth the effort.

On the Fire: Direct Heat

Hot and fast is the only way to cook shrimp and other shellfish, with the exception of a really large lobster. Grilling is an ideal way to cook shrimp, because shrimp needs quick high heat to keep it tender and flavorful. Always grill shrimp on Direct Heat over medium-high heat. That means that the shrimp is placed directly over the heat source on either a gas or a charcoal grill. This way of grilling is referred to as the Direct Method. The grill must already be hot before you start cooking the shrimp. So, it is imperative that before grilling you preheat a gas grill to 550°F or wait until the briquettes are covered with a white-gray ash if cooking over charcoal.

Cooking Shrimp

Overcooking, unfortunately, is very easy with shrimp, so stay close by once you've put them on the grill and keep these pointers in mind:

Shrimp are usually done in 3 to 6 minutes, depending on size. During grilling, the shrimp liquids become milky in color and the flesh opaque with the tell-tale sign of pink accents. And here's a surefire test: Peel one shrimp. If it is grilled properly, the shell will come off neatly and cleanly. Take the rest off the grill immediately.

If cooking in the shell, the shell will stick to the meat if it is overcooked.

Testing for Doneness

Shellfish gives us the most natural doneness clues of any food out there. Shrimp is done when it turns pink and opaque, and that only takes a few minutes on each side. Also, it should be very easy to peel. If you have trouble peeling shrimp after it has been cooked—meaning the shell sticks to the meat—it is overcooked.

Live mollusks like mussels, clams, oysters, etc., are done when the shells open up. Any that do not open during cooking should be discarded, as this indicates that they died before cooking.

Approximate SHELLFISH Cooking Times

TYPE OF SHELLFISH	GRILLING METHOD	GRILLING TIME	NOTE	REST TIME
Clams	Direct Medium-High	8 to 10 minutes	Discard any that do not open	N/A
Lobster, whole (1½ pounds)	Direct Medium	8 to 12 minutes		2 minutes
Lobster, large tail	Direct Medium-High	10 to 14 minutes		2 minutes
Lobster, small tail	Direct Medium-High	6 to 8 minutes		2 minutes
Mussels	Direct Medium-High	5 to 7 minutes	Discard any that do not open	N/A
Oysters	Direct Medium-High	4 to 6 minutes	Discard any that do not open	N/A
Prawns	Direct Medium-High	5 to 7 minutes		2 minutes
Scallops	Direct Medium-High	2 to 5 minutes		N/A
Shrimp in the Shell (jumbo or large)	Direct Medium-High	3 to 6 minutes		N/A
Peeled Shrimp, tail on (jumbo or large)	Direct Medium	2 to 4 minutes		N/A
Squid	Direct Medium	8 to 10 minutes		N/A

The USDA recommends cooking shellfish until the flesh becomes opaque and firm and mollusks until the shells open. The grilling times are based on the author's experience and U.S. Fisheries recommended values.

Shrimp and Scallops 101

Both shrimp and scallops are cooked in a very short time, so be sure to have everything you need at your fingertips before putting them on the grill.

I prefer mixing the two shellfish, but you can use all shrimp or all scallops, just double the amount of each. If you decide to use peeled shrimp, keep a close watch; they cook more quickly than those with the shells. Use sea scallops; bay scallops can only be grilled skewered or in foil packages. If you want to use these shellfish in a seafood salad or a cold shrimp cocktail preparation, chill them in the refrigerator before using.

Makes 4 servings

Grilling Method: Direct/Medium-High Heat

1   pound unshelled jumbo shrimp
1   pound large sea scallops, such as Alaskan
    Olive oil
    Kosher salt
    Freshly ground pepper, optional

1. Build a charcoal fire or preheat a gas grill. If frozen, thaw shrimp in cold running water just before cooking.
2. Rinse and dry the shrimp and scallops. Toss them in a little olive oil to coat all surfaces. Season with salt and pepper, if desired.
3. Using long-handled tongs, place the shrimp and scallops across the cooking grate to prevent them from falling through. Cover and grill over direct medium-high heat for 1½ to 5 minutes on each side, depending on size. The shrimp is done when it curves and becomes pink. The scallops are done when they are firm and opaque. Take care not to overcook, or they will be rubbery.
4. Remove the shellfish from the grill and put it on a clean platter. Let rest for a few minutes, then serve immediately, or let cool briefly before using them in another preparation.

Mollusks in the Shell 101

Shellfish is the general category for aquatic animals that have a shell. They are technically either mollusks (mussels, clams, oysters, snails, squid) or crustaceans (crabs, shrimp, prawns, lobster). It is best to buy shelled mollusks alive (ask the fishmonger if you're not sure). Some varieties, including oysters, are available out of the shell; but to grill or smoke them, you will need to have at least the bottom shell to hold the oyster during the cooking process. For best results, all shellfish should be cooked within 24 hours of being purchased.

Makes 4 servings

Grilling Method: Direct/Medium-High Heat

24   fresh oysters, clams, or mussels, in the shell
     Seasoning, as desired
½   cup barbecue sauce or clarified butter, warmed, optional (page 205)

1. Build a charcoal fire or preheat a gas grill.
2. Scrub the mollusks with a stiff brush under cool running water. Place the mollusks on the cooking grate over direct medium-high heat, cupped-side down. Cover and grill until the shells pop open (4 to 6 minutes); there is no need to turn mollusks.
3. Remove each shell from the grill when it opens, protecting your hands with tongs or hot pads. Discard any mollusks that have not opened.
4. Season to taste, and drizzle with sauce or butter, if desired.

Lobster 101

If you love lobster but are squeamish about handling them, check out the sidebar for tips to reduce the hassle. I personally don't prepare the lobsters with a knife or an ice pick, but if you are accustomed to this technique, feel free to continue to do so. I'm not really squeamish, but that is one thing that I just can't do, which is exactly how I devised the other tricks—necessity being the mother of invention!

Makes 4 servings

Grilling Method: Direct/Medium Heat
Special Equipment: Lobster crackers, lobster picks

4   whole lobsters, about 1½ pounds each
    Olive oil
    Melted butter, optional

1. Build a charcoal fire or preheat a gas grill.
2. Cut off the rubber bands that are holding the lobster claws together. Brush olive oil on both sides of the lobster.

PREPARING LOBSTER FOR THE GRILL

Almost everyone I know loves to eat lobster. It's mostly associated with something you eat only in restaurants for simple reasons: People either don't want the hassle of dealing with a live lobster or are too squeamish to even consider it!

For those with live lobster phobias, buy frozen lobster tails and thaw them in cold running water just before grilling. Lobster tails are just as easy to grill as shrimp and the payoff is huge, because everyone is always impressed and psyched to eat lobster. On the technical side, the high heat of the grill intensifies and concentrates the sweet, slightly salty flavors of the meat, allowing lobster to hold its own against more flavorful seasonings. Here are a few tricks that I use to minimize the task of handling live lobsters.

Presteaming: Number one, if you live in an area where lobster is indigenous, see if you can have your fishmonger steam the fresh lobster for only 10 minutes (half the recommended cooking time) before you buy them. Make sure you tell him not to crack the claws or the precious juices will leak out when you finish the lobster on the grill. You might also be able to have this done at a good fish store that sells live lobsters. Be fearless when you ask for the steaming, because your fish guy doesn't get asked this very often. But it does happen; I often do this, particularly if I'm in Maine during the summer.

Freezing Briefly: If you have live lobsters, about 20 minutes before you want to grill them, clear a large space in your freezer, then move the lobsters from the refrigerator to the freezer for 20 minutes. This will put the lobsters in a deep sleep or stun them, and then they don't move around when they are placed on the grill.

Keeping the Tail Straight: I personally don't mind a slight curve in my lobster's tail when cooked, especially since that (and the bright red color) is a clue that the lobster is done. However, if you want to keep the lobster tail straight while it is grilling, thread a metal or bamboo skewer through the tail before grilling (if you're not squeamish). This will keep the tail straight while it cooks.

Microwaving: I recently picked up this tip from Roger Berkowitz' cookbook, *The New Legal Sea Foods Cookbook.* It is the perfect alternative to having your fishmonger precook a fresh lobster before grilling. You will, however, still need to freeze the lobster for 20 minutes before cooking.

Microwaving is an ideal way to prepare lobster for the grill, especially if you are cooking only one or two—or want lobster meat for a cold dish. Stick the lobster in the freezer for 20 minutes before cooking, place each lobster in a microwavable resealable plastic bag or on a glass plate. Remove the rubber bands from the claws. Add two tablespoons of water to the bag or the plate and place it in the microwave.

Turn the microwave on to the highest setting. A one-pound chicken lobster will steam in six to seven minutes. Add one minute for each additional quarter pound. Let the lobster cool in the microwave for 10 minutes and then follow your chosen recipe instructions.

NOTE: Chicken lobsters are only available in the summer—they are smaller, about one pound each, and have softer shells than the lobsters available in the winter.

3. Place the lobsters, bottom-side down, on the cooking grate over direct medium heat. Cover and grill 6 to 8 minutes or until the shells are red. Turn over and finish grilling 2 to 4 more minutes.

4. Remove the lobsters, and using kitchen scissors or shears, cut the soft inside membrane on the bottom of the tail and crack the shells of the claws. Serve the lobsters with metal lobster crackers and picks and warm butter, if desired, or pick the meat from the shells and reserve for lobster rolls, salads, etc.

Rosemary-Skewered Jumbo Shrimp

Once you've mastered the art of grilling with bamboo skewers, you are ready to try any woody herb as a skewer. Shrimp or scallops work best threaded onto sprigs of rosemary. I've added a little lemon to the basic trilogy of olive oil, salt, and pepper, but you can grill these up with any citrus—even grapefruit! The fragrant rosemary delicately scents the food as it cooks and makes a stunning presentation. If you can't find long rosemary sprigs, you can skewer one shrimp in the center of each smaller sprig of rosemary.

Makes 6 servings

Grilling Method: Direct/Medium Heat

1	tablespoon olive oil
$^1/_2$	lemon, zested (try a Microplane grater)
24	jumbo shrimp, about $1^1/_2$ pounds, peeled and deveined
4	fresh rosemary sprigs, 8 to 10 inches long
	Kosher salt
	Freshly ground pepper
	Lemon wedges

1. Build a charcoal fire or preheat a gas grill. Mix the olive oil and lemon zest together.
2. To skewer 6 shrimp on each rosemary sprig, place the shrimp in a row on a board and, holding them down with 1 hand, push the rosemary branch through the shrimp, allowing the rosemary branch to stick out on both ends. If this is too difficult to do, make a hole with a metal or bamboo skewer, remove and use this track as a guideline for the rosemary.
3. Brush the shrimp with the lemon oil and season with salt and pepper. Place the skewers on the cooking grate over direct medium heat, cover, and cook for 3 to 4 minutes on each side. Let rest for a few minutes. Serve on the rosemary skewers.

NOTE: Because I don't want the rosemary to burn, I grill these shrimp on a slighter lower heat than usual.

Barefoot Shrimp

When my sisters and I were kids, we loved walking barefoot at the beach, dancing on the hot sand so our toes wouldn't burn. Often my family would walk to the end of the dock and buy head-on shrimp from a fisherman bringing in his daily catch. We'd take them home, grill 'em, and spill 'em on newspapers to peel and eat—dipping into either melted butter or a spicy horseradish cocktail sauce. Serve this recipe barefoot with frosty bottles of beer or the Sweet Southern Iced Tea (page 316).

Makes 4 to 6 servings

Grilling Method: Direct/Medium-High Heat

Spicy Horseradish Cocktail Sauce

2	cups ketchup
2	small lemons, zested and juiced
$^1/_4$	heaping cup prepared white horseradish (or more to taste)
8	shakes of Tabasco, or more to taste
$^1/_2$	teaspoon sea salt
	Freshly ground pepper, optional
30	unshelled jumbo shrimp, about 2 pounds
	Olive oil
2	tablespoons Old Bay Seasoning (not liquid)
$^1/_2$	cup (1 stick) salted butter, melted, optional

1. Build a charcoal fire or preheat a gas grill.
2. Make the cocktail sauce: In a nonreactive bowl, mix the ketchup, lemon juice, zest, horseradish, Tabasco, and salt until well combined. Add pepper, if desired. Taste and adjust the seasonings. If you like a lot of horseradish, add more. Set aside. The sauce can be made and refrigerated in a sealed container up to 1 week in advance.
3. If frozen, thaw shrimp in cold running water. Just before cooking, toss shrimp in the oil to coat, and sprinkle with the Old Bay Seasoning, coating all shrimp evenly. This step can be done very easily in a resealable plastic bag.
4. Place the shrimp on the cooking grate over direct medium-high heat, cover, and cook for 6 to 8 minutes, turning once halfway through the cooking time. The shrimp are done when

curled, its shells are bright pink, or the meat is white.

5. Remove the shrimp from the grill, place it in a pile on newspapers, and let rest for a few minutes. Peel and eat the shrimp—still hot off the grill—with the horseradish cocktail sauce, melted butter, and lots of paper towels.

TIP: Try grilling whole shrimp for maximum flavor. When the heads are left on, all of the natural fats and juices flavor the shrimp as it cooks. Once cooked, the heads are easy to remove, or leave them on for a dramatic presentation.

Firecracker Shrimp with Hot Pepper Jelly Glaze

These shrimp explode with flavor. The marinade sings with pungent ginger and chile-rich notes tempered by the sweet rice wine called mirin. Do not substitute fresh for the dried ginger in the marinade because it will overly tenderize the delicate shrimp, resulting in a tough and chewy texture. These skewers are full of sweet heat and make an impressive presentation, especially when served stuck into a wedge of fresh watermelon. Bring it out and watch the fireworks go off in your guests' eyes.

Makes 4 to 6 servings

Grilling Method: Direct/Medium-Low Heat

24 jumbo shrimp, about 1½ pounds, peeled, tails on
12 bamboo skewers, soaked in water for 30 minutes
¼   cup mirin (sweetened rice wine)
2   tablespoons toasted sesame oil
1   tablespoon low-sodium soy sauce
2   teaspoons ground ginger
2½ teaspoons unsweetened rice vinegar
2   heaping tablespoons hot pepper jelly
2   teaspoons sesame seeds, toasted

1. Build a charcoal fire or preheat a gas grill. If frozen, thaw shrimp in cold running water just before cooking.

2. In a nonreactive bowl, combine mirin, sesame oil, soy sauce, ginger, and 2 teaspoons of the vinegar. Set aside.

3. Heat the hot pepper jelly and the remaining ½ teaspoon vinegar in a small saucepan until warm and liquid, stirring occasionally. Keep warm over a very low heat until ready to use.

4. Meanwhile, prepare the shrimp. Place the shrimp in a resealable plastic bag and pour the mirin marinade over them. Seal the bag and massage to coat each shrimp evenly. Place the bag in the refrigerator for 30 minutes.

5. Make sure the grilling grate is very clean. Skewer the shrimp by inserting bamboo skewers on either side of shrimp so that the shrimp resemble the rungs of a ladder (see page 176). You will end up with a total of 6 skewers with 4 shrimp on each skewer; make sure there is room between each shrimp.

6. Make sure the grill is only at medium-low heat, or the sugar in the marinade will burn and blacken before the shrimp are cooked. If your grill is too hot, lower the burners of a gas grill and lift the lid of both gas and charcoal grills until the cooking grate has cooled off.

7. When the grill is the right temperature, place the skewers on the cooking grate over direct medium-low heat for 4 to 5 minutes. Turn the shrimp over (since the marinade contains sugar, you may need to use a spatula to pry the edges of the shrimp as you turn the skewers with tongs). Once all the skewers are turned, lightly coat the cooked side of the shrimp with the pepper jelly glaze using a long-handled basting brush. Cook for an additional 4 to 5 minutes or until the shrimp are cooked through.

8. Remove from the grill and sprinkle with the sesame seeds. Let rest for a few minutes. Serve hot.

TIP: Freeze extra soaked bamboo skewers in foil or a resealable plastic bag so they'll be ready at a moment's notice.

Salt-Crusted Shrimp with Potent Lemon-Garlic Sauce

This is my signature shrimp preparation, and I grill it almost every time I entertain. The salt on the shells stays on your fingers as you peel the shrimp, seasoning the shrimp as you dip into the potent lemon-garlic sauce. My favorite way to serve it is outdoors next to the grill, where the whole party feels like they are "in" on the backyard action. If you are not already great friends, you will be once you share this finger-lickin' good eatin' experience.

Makes 4 servings

Grilling Method: Direct/Medium-High Heat

Dipping Sauce

½	cup best-quality extra-virgin olive oil, plus extra as needed
2	lemons, juiced
½	lemon, zested
2	cloves garlic, grated
4	stems fresh oregano, leaves only
	Freshly ground pepper
16	unshelled jumbo or colossal shrimp, 1 to 1½ pounds, or frozen black tiger shrimp (Do not use Easy-Peel shrimp)
3	tablespoons olive oil
¼	cup Morton kosher salt or other coarse sea salt

1. Make the dipping sauce: Whisk together the oil, lemon juice, and lemon zest. Stir in the garlic. Add the oregano leaves. Let the mixture sit for at least 20 minutes to marry the flavors—or make it up to 12 hours in advance and refrigerate. Set aside.
2. Build a charcoal fire or preheat a gas grill.
3. If frozen, thaw shrimp in cold running water just before cooking. Place the shrimp in a large bowl and toss them with some olive oil to coat lightly all over. Just before putting them on the grill, sprinkle the salt evenly over the shrimp and toss well to make sure each shrimp is thoroughly coated in a crust of salt. (Do not use fine-grain kosher salt, such as Diamond Crystal brand, as it melts too quickly.)

4. Place the shrimp in the center of the cooking grate over direct medium-high heat, cover, and grill 3 to 4 minutes per side or until the shrimp is pink and the flesh opaque (white). Serve immediately with the dipping sauce.

TIP: It is important that you use the largest shrimp you can buy. The larger shrimp will be more tender and large enough to benefit from this crusting technique. With smaller shrimp, you run the risk of disturbing the balance between salt and shrimp meat. Likewise, do not use Easy-Peel shrimp for this recipe as the slit down the center will absorb too much salt.

SHRIMP PARTY

This is my favorite party "ice breaker" appetizer. I place the oil-tossed shrimp in a bowl on a tray with a small bowl of the kosher salt, my tongs, lots of napkins, a platter, and the prepared dipping sauce. Once everyone is armed with a cocktail, we hit the deck to start the party. While we are talking, I toss the shrimp in the salt, grill them, and place them on the platter. Then the fun begins: Everyone takes a shrimp, peels it, and dips it in the sauce for a fun, casual, and interactive happy hour. Alternatively, you can arrange four shrimp on each serving plate and accompany with a small ramekin of the dipping sauce, but I think serving them hot-off-the-grill is so much more fun!

Shrimp Scampi with Artichokes and Black Olives

I love Chicago-style shrimp scampi. In most restaurants, the shrimp are battered and deep fried, only to become soggy once they are simmered with the other ingredients. In my version, the butterflied shrimp are quickly grilled before they're simmered in a casserole of braised artichokes, black olives, and garlic. The beauty of this recipe is that it can be made in advance—unlike most shrimp preparations—which makes it a great appetizer or entrée. If it is served as an entrée, all you need to make is white rice or pasta to fill out the meal.

Grilling Method: Direct/Medium Heat

24   jumbo butterflied shrimp, about 2 pounds, peeled, tail on
     Olive oil
     Kosher salt
12   artichoke hearts, fresh or frozen
 4   cloves garlic, minced or grated
 1   lemon, zested and juiced
$\frac{1}{2}$ cup white wine
 1   tablespoon red wine vinegar
$\frac{1}{4}$ cup whole pitted black olives
 1   tablespoon chopped fresh oregano
     White pepper

1. Build a charcoal fire or preheat a gas grill.
2. If it hasn't already been done, butterfly the shrimp by cutting vertically through the middle of the back of each shrimp with a sharp paring knife, stopping just before the tail. Toss the shrimp with oil and season with salt.
3. Place the shrimp on the cooking grate over direct medium heat, cover, and grill for 2 minutes per side. You will be reheating the shrimp with braised artichokes, so you don't want to overcook them. Transfer the shrimp to a clean platter and let them cool.
4. Meanwhile, preheat the oven to 450°F to braise the artichokes. If the artichokes are frozen, thaw them under cold running water.
5. In a large sauté pan, pour in enough olive oil to coat the bottom. Add the garlic and turn the heat to medium-low. Slowly heat the oil and garlic. As soon as the garlic begins to change color, add $\frac{1}{4}$ cup more olive oil, the lemon juice, lemon zest, wine, and vinegar. Add the artichokes and cover. Bring the pan to a boil and simmer for 10 minutes. Stir the artichokes and add the olives and shrimp. Transfer to 1 large or 4 individual oven-safe casseroles.
6. Place the scampi in the oven and bake for 5 to 10 minutes or until the artichokes are tender, slightly brown, and the liquid has reduced. (Individual casseroles will take less time.) Season the scampi with the fresh oregano and a grind of white pepper, if desired. Let rest for a few minutes. Serve immediately.

Grilled Shrimp and Grits

Anyone who cooks and is from the Carolinas believes that shrimp and grits is his or her legacy. Not surprisingly, the dish's origin has led to a "friendly" controversy. I am on the side that credits the late Bill Neal, chef and owner of 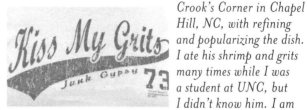 *Crook's Corner in Chapel Hill, NC, with refining and popularizing the dish. I ate his shrimp and grits many times while I was a student at UNC, but I didn't know him. I am fortunate, however, to know one of his protégés, John Currence. John is one of my favorite people and the most generous—and modest—food friend that I have. Like Bill Neal, his restaurants are destination points and beacons of contemporary Southern cuisine, especially Central Grocery in Oxford, MS. John learned shrimp and grits at the hand of the master and shared it with me. Since every cook has to leave his mark, John tweaked Bill's recipe and now I've tweaked his—grilling instead of sautéing the shrimp.*

Makes 4 servings

Grilling Method: Direct/Medium Heat

 2   pounds jumbo shrimp, peeled and deveined
$2\frac{1}{2}$ cups water
 1   cup stone-ground grits, such as Anson Mills
$\frac{3}{4}$ cup grated sharp white cheddar cheese
$\frac{1}{2}$ cup grated parmesan cheese
$\frac{1}{2}$ cup half-and-half
 2   tablespoons butter, optional
     Pinch freshly grated nutmeg
     Kosher salt
     Cayenne pepper
     Tabasco
 8   slices center-cut bacon, cut in $\frac{1}{2}$-inch pieces
     Peanut oil
 1   pound white mushrooms, sliced
 1   bunch green onions (white and some of the green), chopped
 2   cloves garlic, grated
$\frac{1}{2}$ lemon, juiced
 1   tablespoon chopped fresh parsley

1. About an hour before you want to eat, make the grits by boiling the water in a large saucepan or the top of a double boiler (the double boiler insures against scorching). Slowly add the grits by sifting them through 1 hand while whisking with the other. Cover the pan and simmer on low heat for 30 to 40 minutes. Stir occasionally to prevent scorching. Add the cheeses, half-and-half, and butter and stir well. Continue cooking if the grits are not yet tender or watery. When they are "just right," season the grits to taste with nutmeg, salt, pepper, and Tabasco. Set aside, but keep warm.

2. Meanwhile, cook the bacon in a large sauté pan until crisp. Remove the bacon to a plate covered with paper towels and drain the excess grease from the pan.

3. Add 1 to 2 tablespoons of peanut oil to the pan. Sauté the mushrooms over medium heat until caramelized, about 10 minutes. Add half of the onions and continue to sauté 2 to 3 more minutes or just until they are wilted but still crisp. Remove the pan from the heat and stir in the garlic, lemon juice, and reserved bacon. Cover and set aside while you grill the shrimp.

4. Build a charcoal fire or preheat a gas grill.

5. If frozen, thaw shrimp in cold running water just before cooking. Pat the shrimp dry with paper towels. Toss them with oil and season lightly with salt. Place the shrimp on the cooking grate over direct medium heat, cover, and grill 2 to 3 minutes on each side or until the shrimp are pink and slightly curled (smaller shrimp take less time to cook).

6. Remove the shrimp from the grill to a clean platter and add them to the bacon-mushroom mixture. Stir and reheat on medium-low heat until very hot, about 5 minutes. Stir the grits if necessary. Taste both dishes and adjust the seasonings if necessary, being careful not to oversalt.

7. Divide the grits equally among 4 plates, top with equal portions of the shrimp, and sprinkle with the parsley and the remaining green onions. Let rest for a few minutes. Serve hot.

Shrimp Salad with Old Bay Mayonnaise

When I was growing up, my best friend's family had a house in Morehead City, NC, near where shrimping was the main industry. Because of this, shrimp were both plentiful and economical, and they wound up in every possible dish, including salad. Shrimp salad is an easy lunch or dinner entrée that is infinitely improved by grilling the shrimp. Adding Old Bay Seasoning to the mayo is the "secret" of many a shore cook and really makes a difference in the way the salad tastes. To gussy up the presentation, serve the salad in a hollowed out home-grown tomato instead of a lettuce leaf.

Makes 4 to 6 servings

2 pounds large shrimp, grilled (page 178) and chopped into 1/2-inch pieces
1/2 to 1 cup mayonnaise, preferably Hellmann's
1 tablespoon Old Bay Seasoning
1 large shallot, minced
6 ribs celery, chopped
4 to 6 large, ripe but firm, tomatoes, tops removed and hollowed out
Freshly ground pepper

1. In a large nonreactive or glass bowl, mix the chopped grilled shrimp with the mayonnaise until well combined. Sprinkle in the Old Bay Seasoning and mix thoroughly. Add the shallots and celery. Gently fold the ingredients together until well mixed. Taste and adjust the seasonings. You probably will not need to add salt.

2. Cover the bowl tightly, and refrigerate for 2 to 3 hours or overnight. Spoon the salad into hollowed-out tomatoes or a lettuce leaf and top with freshly ground pepper.

Shrimp-Stuffed Avocados with Dijon Mayonnaise

When I lived in Paris, I ate "Avocat de Crevettes" at least once a week at the well-known Brasserie Lipp. My variation on a theme calls for grilled shrimp that is peeled and chilled. Just before serving, the shrimp are stuffed into a ripe avocado half and topped with a dollop of homemade Dijon mayonnaise. You can make your own mayonnaise or add a good strong Dijon mustard to best-quality store-bought mayonnaise. Try this recipe for your next baby or wedding shower or as an appetizer. Serve with a glass of Sauvignon Blanc or another crisp white wine.

Makes 4 servings

- 4   small, ripe, Hass avocados
- 1   lemon, cut into wedges
- 1   pound large shrimp in the shell, grilled (page 178), peeled, and chilled
- ½   cup homemade or Hellmann's mayonnaise
- 1 to 2 tablespoons strong Dijon mustard
       Pinch granulated garlic
       Sea salt or fleur de sel
       Grains of paradise, optional

1. Slice the avocados in half and remove the seeds. Sprinkle them with lemon juice to prevent the avocados from discoloring. Stuff each half evenly with chilled shrimp and set aside.
2. Meanwhile, mix the mayonnaise and mustard until smooth and creamy. Season with granulated garlic and blend again.
3. Place a dollop of the Dijon mayonnaise on the shrimp. Sprinkle with the fleur de sel and freshly ground grains of paradise, if using. Serve immediately.

Shrimp Margaritas with Avocados and Garden Tomatoes

This recipe is one that I never get tired of making or eating and neither do my guests. The beauty of this dish is that it is loaded with flavor, impressive to serve, and has to be made in advance, making it a great choice for a low-maintenance dinner party. Mix the avocado and tomatoes just before serving to layer the flavors and keep all the ingredients fresh and chunky. For a festive appetizer, serve this in a margarita glass rimmed with a mixture of kosher salt, lime zest, and smoked paprika. Splurge and sprinkle with fleur de sel before serving.

Makes 4 to 6 servings

Grilling Method: Direct/Medium-High Heat

- 1   pound unshelled large shrimp,
- 2   tablespoons olive oil
- ¼   cup tequila, preferably 100 percent Blue Agave
- ¼   cup fresh lime juice
- ¼   cup fresh orange juice
- 2   tablespoons ketchup
- 2   tablespoons green Tabasco, or other jalapeño hot sauce
- 1   bunch green onions, green tops only, finely chopped
       Kosher salt (omit if serving with fleur de sel)
       Freshly ground pepper
- 2   cups diced ripe heirloom or garden tomatoes, drained
- 2   large ripe avocados, diced
- 1   small white onion, chopped
       Lime wedges, optional
- 18   Saltine crackers (or more)
       Fleur de sel or coarse sea salt, optional

1. Build a charcoal fire or preheat a gas grill.
2. If frozen, thaw shrimp in cold running water just before cooking. Place the shrimp in a nonreactive bowl. Mix them with olive oil until well coated.
3. Place the shrimp on the cooking grate over direct medium-high heat, cover, and grill until pink and almost cooked through, 4 to 6 minutes, turning them once halfway through the cooking time. Let the shrimp cool completely.
4. Meanwhile, whisk together the tequila, citrus juices, ketchup, and Tabasco. Peel and cut the shrimp into large pieces (about ½ inch) and toss them with the tequila mixture. Cover and chill in the refrigerator for 15 minutes. Add the green onion tops and return to the refrigerator for 1 hour.
5. Just before serving, season the mixture with salt and pepper to taste. (Omit this step if serving with fleur de sel.) Gently fold in the tomatoes and avocados, mixing well. Using a slotted spoon, portion into individual serving bowls or margarita glasses. Garnish with a sprinkling of white onion and a wedge of lime. If you haven't already salted the mixture, sprinkle each serving with fleur de sel. Serve immediately with Saltine crackers.

Bahamian Seafood Salad

When I was on the island of Nassau, in the Bahamas, I absolutely fell in love with fresh conch salad—preferring to eat it at the dusty stalls of Arawak Cay rather than a restaurant. I was a frequent visitor to this locals' hang-out and couldn't get enough of the slightly chewy, sweet conch that tasted of fresh salt water doused with citrus and hot peppers. I soon chose my favorite conch vendor and memorized his technique. Unfortunately, it is impossible to get fresh conch anywhere in this country, except possibly Miami, so I've come up with a version that is just as light and refreshing and substitutes shrimp and scallops for the conch. If you ever have a chance to visit Arawak Cay, you'll be amazed at the swash-buckling knife skills of the conch vendors as well as the addictive conch salad.

Makes 4 to 6 servings

Grilling Method: Direct/Medium-High Heat

1	pound scallops, chopped into ½-inch pieces
2	pounds shrimp in the shell, grilled (page 178), peeled, and chopped into ½-inch pieces
1	cup fresh lime juice, divided
½	cup fresh orange juice
	Kosher salt
1	stick celery, finely chopped
½	white onion, diced
2	green tomatoes, diced
1	very ripe red tomato, diced
	Minced bird pepper or other chile to taste

1. Build a charcoal fire or preheat a gas grill.
2. Mix the scallops with ½ cup of the lime juice and set them aside. (If using small bay scallops, you will not need to chop them before marinating them in lime juice.) Cover and refrigerate for 30 minutes, stirring occasionally. The acid in the lime juice will "cook" the scallops, just like ceviche.
3. Remove the scallops from the refrigerator and drain to remove excess liquid. Put them in a non-reactive bowl and add the shrimp. Mix well with your hands or a wooden spoon. (In the Bahamas, the vendors use their hands on a wooden cutting board, scooping and mixing each ingredient as it is added.)
4. Mix the remaining lime juice and the orange juice; add a little at a time to the seafood until it is lightly dressed with juice. Season with salt. Add the celery, onion, and tomatoes, mixing gently after each addition. Taste for salt and citrus, adjusting if necessary. Add chile pepper to your taste. It should have a nice bit of heat but not so hot as to lose the nuances of the dish.
5. Serve the salad in a small glass bowl or martini glass. It can be refrigerated for up to 1 day.

Orange and Green Mango Salad with Spot Prawns

One of my fondest food memories of Thailand is the sweet, salty, spicy, and refreshing green mango and papaya salads that I ate daily. These salads were made at tiny roadside stands with no separate kitchen. Every day, I had a front-row seat to watch the cooks—often a husband and wife team. This version combines both ripe and unripe mangos, and is topped with grilled Alaskan spot prawns for a change, but large tiger shrimp work just as well. The sweet and soft ripe mango counterbalances the tart and crunchy green mangos for a salad that rivals those found "in country." If you can't find green mangos or green papayas, you can use grated Granny Smith apples or jicama instead.

Makes 4 to 6 servings

Grilling Method: Direct/Medium-High Heat

16	unshelled Alaskan spot prawns or extra-large tiger shrimp, about 2 pounds
2	limes, juiced
2	teaspoons cumin seeds, toasted
2	teaspoons sesame oil
1	lime, zested
½	teaspoon red chile flakes

Green Mango Salad

1 ripe mango, diced
2 green (unripe) mangoes or papayas, peeled and julienned
4 green onions, chopped
$\frac{1}{2}$ cup fresh mint leaves, chopped
$\frac{1}{4}$ cup fresh cilantro, chopped
4 limes, juiced
2 tablespoons light brown sugar
1 teaspoon garlic-chili sauce (*sriracha*) or 1 red chile, chopped
1 to 2 teaspoons fish sauce or sea salt

1. Build a charcoal fire or preheat a gas grill.
2. Cut each prawn or shrimp in half along the spine so the meat is exposed and the shell is still on.
3. Combine the lime juice , cumin seeds, sesame oil, zest, and chile flakes, and brush all over the flesh sides of the prawns. Set aside for 5 minutes.
4. Place the prawns on the cooking grate, shell-side down, over direct medium-high heat. Cover and grill for 5 to 7 minutes or until the prawns are cooked through (opaque). Do not turn them over. Remove the prawns from the grill and set aside.
5. Make the salad: In a medium bowl, mix the mangoes together and set aside. In another bowl, combine the onions, mint, cilantro, lime juice, sugar, and chili sauce. Season with fish sauce or sea salt to taste. Toss the mangoes with the dressing.
6. Divide the salad among individual serving plates and top with the warm, grilled prawns. Serve immediately.

Grill-"Fried" Green Tomatoes with Shrimp Remoulade

When I lived in New Orleans, I was addicted to Uglesich's restaurant. Once you get past the neighborhood and the restaurant façade, it is the most beautiful place—at least as far as the food was concerned. They offer the same traditional raw oysters, po' boys, fried green tomatoes, remoulade, etc., that dozens of other restaurants offer, but everything they do, they do better. I hear that the Uglesiches are getting ready to retire; that will certainly end an era in New Orleans. In the meantime, try this grilled recipe that was inspired by many a meal spent at the restaurant.

Makes 4 servings

Grilling Method: Direct/Medium Heat

Remoulade Sauce

1 cup mayonnaise
2 tablespoons Creole mustard or other coarse-grain mustard
2 tablespoons ketchup
1 rib celery, finely chopped
3 tablespoons finely chopped green onions
2 tablespoons finely chopped fresh parsley
2 cloves garlic, grated
1 teaspoon smoked sweet paprika
1 teaspoon Louisiana hot sauce
Kosher salt
Freshly ground pepper

Shrimp

$1\frac{1}{2}$ pounds jumbo shrimp, peeled
Olive oil
Kosher salt
Freshly ground pepper
Grilled Green Tomatoes (page 214)

1. Build a charcoal fire or preheat a gas grill.
2. Early in the day, make the sauce and the shrimp.
3. Make the sauce: Combine the mayonnaise with the mustard and ketchup and mix well. Add the celery, green onions, parsley, garlic, paprika, and hot sauce. Mix thoroughly. Season to taste with salt and pepper. Put the sauce in an airtight container in the refrigerator to chill completely until ready to use. You will have leftover sauce, but it will keep covered in the refrigerator for 2 weeks and is a great condiment for almost anything grilled. Or substitute it for mayonnaise to make shrimp—or even tuna—salad.

4. Make the shrimp: Pat the shrimp dry with paper towels and toss with olive oil to coat thinly. Season with salt and pepper.

5. Place the shrimp on the cooking grate over direct medium heat, cover, and grill 2 to 3 minutes or until they curl and begin to turn pink. Turn the shrimp over and grill on the other side for another 1 to 2 minutes. Remove the shrimp from the grill into a clean bowl. Add about ½ cup of the Remoulade Sauce and toss to coat, adding more sauce if necessary. Cover and store in the refrigerator for at least 2 hours.

6. Build a charcoal fire or preheat a gas grill when ready to finish the dish. Make the Grilled Green Tomatoes. While the Tomatoes are still warm, divide them among 4 plates, top with the chilled shrimp remoulade, and serve immediately.

Bacon-Wrapped Sea Scallops

When I was a guest chef at the James Beard Foundation House, I started the meal with these crispy bacon-wrapped scallops, and they were eaten in a flash! Since there are so few ingredients, it is essential to use the absolute best quality bacon and scallops. I recommend Niman Ranch or another specialty bacon and large Alaskan sea scallops. A bigger scallop is better since it won't overcook during the time it takes to cook the bacon.

Makes 8 to 10 servings

Grilling Method: Direct/Medium-Low Heat

1   pound sea scallops, preferably Alaskan
8   ounces center-cut bacon, such as Niman Ranch
     Solid wooden toothpicks, soaked in water for
        30 minutes

1. Build a charcoal fire or preheat a gas grill.
2. Pat the scallops dry with paper towels. Cut the bacon in half width-wise and wrap ½ piece around each scallop, securing with a wooden toothpick. Cover and let the bacon come to room temperature before grilling.
3. Place the scallops on the cooking grate over direct medium-low heat, cover, and grill until the bacon is crisp, about 5 minutes on each side. If you have

trouble getting the bacon crispy by the time the scallops are done, you can precook the bacon in a microwave on high for 30 seconds before wrapping the scallops.

4. Remove from the grill, let rest a few minutes then serve immediately.

NOTE: If you are like me, you think bacon makes everything taste better. Granted, it is great on its own, but I think it is even better as a flavor enhancer. If you are ready to expand your bacon horizons, check out The Bacon of the Month Club and the artisanal bacons available from www.thegratefulpalate.com.

Cake and Steak

This is a perfect Saturday night meal and a riff on classic surf and turf. The cake is a crab cake that is grilled instead of sautéed and the steak is a six-ounce filet. Contrary to what you might think, the crab cake doesn't fall apart during the grilling process because it is held together by egg whites. If for some reason your cakes aren't holding together, add another egg white to the mixture. The texture should be similar to burgers. The bread crumbs add stability to the cakes and give a nice crunchy texture to the smooth crab filling, which has much less bread filling than traditional crab cakes.

Makes 4 servings

Grilling Method: Direct/Medium Heat

Cake
⅓ to ½ cup mayonnaise, preferably Hellmann's
2   tablespoons roasted red bell pepper (page 210)
        or chopped fresh chives
2   egg whites, beaten
1   lemon, juiced
1   tablespoon Dijon mustard
3 to 5 dashes Tabasco, or more to taste
1   pound canned pasteurized crabmeat, such as
        Phillip's
½   cup panko (Japanese bread crumbs), or more
        to taste
     Olive oil
     Kosher salt
1   cup fresh bread crumbs
2   tablespoons unsalted butter, melted

Steak

4   **filet mignons, 6 ounces each**
     Olive oil
     Kosher salt
     Freshly ground pepper
½   **tablespoon unsalted butter, optional**
     Chopped fresh parsley, optional

1. Make the cake: Combine ⅓ cup of mayonnaise (you can add more if you need it after you've added the crabmeat and panko crumbs), the bell pepper or chives, egg whites, lemon juice, mustard, and Tabasco. Mix until well incorporated. Fold in the crabmeat and panko crumbs until the mixture is stiff enough to make into patties.

2. Form the mixture into 4 patties of equal size and brush them on top and bottom with olive oil. Put the patties on a platter and cover with plastic wrap. Refrigerate for 1 hour to set them so they don't fall apart during grilling.

3. About 20 minutes before you are ready to grill, allow the filets to come to room temperature.

4. Build a charcoal fire or preheat a gas grill. Just before grilling, brush both sides of the steaks with oil and season with salt and pepper.

5. Place the steaks on the cooking grate over direct medium-high heat and cover, and grill them for about 5 minutes. Turn the steaks over and continue cooking for about 5 more minutes for medium-rare (or longer to taste). Remove the steaks from the grill and allow them to rest for 5 minutes before serving.

6. While the steaks are cooking, mix the bread crumbs and melted butter in a small bowl. Divide the bread crumbs in 4 portions and pat the crab cakes on the top and bottom with the buttered bread crumbs, like icing. The cakes will look slightly crusty and rustic.

7. While the steaks are cooking or just after you remove them, carefully place the crab cakes on the cooking grate over direct medium heat. Cover and grill for 5 minutes without turning or moving the cakes. Turn the cakes over gently with both a spatula and a pair of tongs and cook for 5 more minutes, until marked and warmed through. (If you are not comfortable grilling the cakes, sauté them in 2 tablespoons of melted butter in a preheated skillet.)

8. Remove the cakes from the grill. Top the steaks with the butter and parsley, if desired. Serve the cakes and steaks hot.

Smoked Gazpacho with Lump Crabmeat

I first had a taste of smoked gazpacho when my barbecue buddy Steven Raichlen made it for me in the middle of a Chicago winter. And even though outside it was well below zero, the gazpacho sparkled with summertime flavor. Since then, I have made the recipe my own, adding more of some vegetables and fewer of others until I have what I consider one of the best recipes to come off the grill. I often leave the soup thick and serve it as fire-roasted salsa or a sauce for fish, but in this recipe, I thin it out with a mixture of rosé wine and Clamato juice and garnish it with lump crabmeat.

Makes 4 servings

Grilling Method: Indirect/Medium Heat
Special Equipment: Cameron Stovetop Smoker, optional

8   **large ripe tomatoes, halved**
1   **yellow or red bell pepper, cored**
2   **seedless cucumbers, peeled and halved**
2   **sweet onions, such as Vidalia, peeled**
2   **bunches green onions, trimmed**
1   **head roasted garlic (page 207)**
1   **cup Clamato juice**
¼   **cup rosé wine, optional**
¼   **cup olive oil, or more to taste**
¼   **cup red wine vinegar, or more to taste**
2   **tablespoons chopped fresh herbs, including basil, mint, parsley, oregano, and thyme**
     Kosher salt
     Freshly ground pepper
     Tabasco
1   **cup lump crabmeat, cleaned to remove shells**
2   **tablespoons chopped fresh chives or basil**
2   **limes, cut into wedges**
½   **cup alder wood chips, soaked in cold water for 30 minutes**

1. Preheat a charcoal or gas grill. On a gas grill, preheat with the smoker box or aluminum tray filled with wet wood chips. In a charcoal grill, place 2 handfuls of wet wood chips directly on ashed briquettes. Alternatively, you can smoke in the Cameron Stovetop Smoker.
2. Place the tomatoes, pepper, cucumbers, sweet onion, and green onions on the cooking grate over indirect medium heat. Cover and grill-smoke the vegetables until hot and beginning to soften, about 20 minutes. Remove the vegetables from the grill to a bowl that will collect any juices that escape from them.
3. Squeeze the garlic cloves from the skins. Combine them with the other smoked vegetables, Clamato, wine, oil, vinegar, herbs, salt, pepper, and Tabasco to taste in a blender or a food processor. Blend at high speed until smooth. Add more vinegar, salt, or Tabasco to taste. If the gazpacho seems too thick, thin it with a little vegetable stock or wine. The gazpacho should be highly seasoned. Chill it until serving.
4. Ladle the gazpacho into shallow bowls. Garnish each bowl with ¼ cup of lump crabmeat and a sprinkle of chopped fresh chives. Serve immediately with lime wedges.

Lobster Salad with Avocado Mayonnaise and Mango Chunks

One snowy night my friends, the Mose brothers (John, Doug, and Chris) and I were cooking an elaborate dinner that included grilled lobster, when I hit upon the idea to make a lobster salad with a rich avocado mayo and a tart tropical fruit. The succulent grilled lobster is tossed with the mayonnaise while warm and then chilled. A few hours before serving, fold in cool, sweet chunks of mango. If you can't find ripe mango, you can substitute orange sections. Don't try papaya or cantaloupe; neither has enough acid to balance the mayo. Serve in martini glasses garnished with slivers of basil or mint.

Makes 4 servings

4	grilled lobsters (pages 178–179), tail and claw meat only
½	cup mayonnaise, preferably Hellmann's
2	ripe avocados, roughly chopped
	Kosher salt
4	dashes Tabasco, or more to taste
½	lemon, juiced
1	ripe mango, cut in ½-inch chunks
	Fleur de sel
	Grains of paradise or freshly ground pepper
1	tablespoon chopped fresh mint or basil, optional

1. Cut the lobster meat into 1-inch pieces and set aside.
2. Mix the mayonnaise and avocado until completely smooth and light green in color. Season with salt, Tabasco, and lemon juice. Taste and adjust the seasonings. Mix in the lobster and stir to coat each piece evenly. Refrigerate for 1 to 2 hours or until completely chilled.
3. Carefully fold in the mango. Chill for 1 to 2 hours more to meld the flavors.
4. Spoon the salad into martini glasses and garnish, as desired, with fleur de sel, grains of paradise, and a sprinkle of mint or basil. Serve immediately.

Lobster Tail with Pastis Crème

Pastis is an aperitif native to the south of France. It is made with a secret recipe of herbs, spices, and spirits. The combination is reminiscent of tarragon and licorice, so it makes a perfect cooking partner—especially with shellfish and, oddly enough, green vegetables! The readily available Pernod is not a true pastis but has similar flavors. If you can't find the Ricard label, you can substitute Pernod in the recipe, but be aware that its slightly chartreuse yellow color will tint the cream. Serve this lobster with the Steakhouse Spinach (page 310).

Makes 4 servings

Grilling Method: Direct/Medium-High Heat

Lobster
4   lobster tails, 5 to 7 ounces each, defrosted and
      butterflied
    Olive oil
    Kosher salt
1   cup crème fraîche (page 325 or store-bought),
      plus more for serving
¼   cup pastis (Ricard or Pernod)
4   sprigs fresh tarragon or 1 teaspoon dried tarragon

1. Build a charcoal fire or preheat a gas grill.
2. Brush the lobster tails with oil, and season with
   kosher salt. Set aside. Make the sauce by combining the crème fraîche and pastis.
3. Place the lobster on the cooking grate, shell-side
   up, over direct medium-high heat, cover, and grill
   until the shells turn bright red and are just beginning to char, about 4 minutes. Turn the tails over
   and spoon the pastis crème generously into the
   butterflied tails. Continue grilling until the flesh
   is just cooked through, 2 to 3 minutes more.
4. Remove the lobsters from the grill and garnish
   with 1 tablespoon of crème fraîche and a sprig of
   tarragon, and serve at once.

Cape Porpoise Lobster Roll

*If you travel a little off the beaten track in Maine, you will
find the Cape Porpoise Lobster Company in Cape Porpoise.
Their main business is selling whole lobsters to restaurants
or consumers via overnight mail. However, they also make
the best lobster roll, bar none! Their secret is keeping the
number of ingredients to a minimum—heavy on the lobster
and a buttery grilled bun. One summer evening, I grilled a
half dozen chicken lobsters and made this rendition, which
is pretty close to the original! If you live near a lobstering
town, purchase the rolls made especially for this sandwich.*

Makes 4 servings

4   grilled lobsters (pages 178–179), claw and tail
      meat removed
½   cup mayonnaise, preferably Hellmann's

1   lemon, cut into wedges
½   cup (1 stick) unsalted butter, melted
4   lobster or hot dog rolls

1. Cut the lobster meat into large 1½- to 2-inch
   chunks. Fold the meat into the mayonnaise and
   season with a squirt or two of lemon juice. Add
   1 tablespoon of hot melted butter, mix to coat,
   and adjust the seasonings if necessary. Cover and
   refrigerate for 1 hour or up to 1 day.
2. If you have the grill on, just before serving, butter
   both the insides and outsides of the rolls. Grill the
   buttered surfaces until golden brown (like the top
   of a grilled cheese sandwich) over direct low heat.
   (Alternately, heat the buttered bread in an oven or
   toaster oven.)
3. Spoon the lobster mixture into the warm buns
   and serve immediately, with a wedge of lemon,
   if desired.

Smoked Oysters with Fresh Cranberry-Horseradish Relish

*I love oysters, and alder wood smoke accents their natural
briny flavor beautifully. This is a recipe that works exceptionally well in the Cameron Stovetop Smoker. If you don't
have a smoker, the oysters can be grilled, either on the half-
shell or whole over direct heat. The raw cranberries are
chopped and mixed with horseradish for a festive topping—
much more elegant than the traditional cocktail sauce. Try
substituting fresh cherries in the summertime—it makes a
delicious relish for any meaty fish as well as oysters.*

Makes 4 servings

Grilling Method: Indirect/Low Heat
Special Equipment: Cameron Stovetop Smoker, optional

Fresh Cranberry-Horseradish Relish
1   12-ounce bag fresh cranberries, coarsely chopped
1   large lemon, zested and juiced
1   large lime, zested and juiced

¼ cup Sugar in the Raw (castor sugar)
3 tablespoons refrigerated white horseradish (not cream), or more to taste
2 tablespoons vodka
Kosher salt
Tabasco

16 fresh shucked oysters, with their bottom shells
4 teaspoons unsalted butter
Pinch sea salt
Alder or hickory wood chips, soaked in water for 30 minutes

1. Make the relish: In a nonreactive bowl, mix the cranberries, lemon juice and zest, and lime juice and zest. Add the sugar, mix to combine, and let sit for 5 minutes. Mix in the horseradish and vodka, and let sit for 5 more minutes. Mix again and season with Tabasco and kosher salt. Let sit another 5 minutes and taste. Correct the seasonings and refrigerate until ready to use or up to 4 days in advance. Mix well before serving.

2. Arrange the oysters, with a little of their juice in each half shell, on a tray. Put about ¼ teaspoon butter and a pinch of sea salt in the center of each oyster. Refrigerate until ready to cook.

3. Meanwhile, preheat a charcoal or gas grill. On a gas grill preheat with the smoker box or aluminum tray filled with wet wood chips. In a charcoal grill, place 2 handfuls of wet wood chips directly on gray-ashed briquettes. Alternatively, you can smoke the oysters in the Cameron Stovetop Smoker.

4. When the chips begin to smoke, reduce the heat and place the oysters, shell-side down, in the center of the cooking grate over indirect low heat, cover, and smoke for 10 to 15 minutes or until the edges curl and the butter bubbles. Remove the oysters from the grill and serve immediately with a dollop of the Cranberry-Horseradish Relish.

NOTE: If smoking oysters on the half shell, buy them from a fish store that will shuck them and give you the oysters in their bottom shells.

Oysters and Shrimp with DIY Cocktail Sauce

When I lived in New Orleans, Felix restaurant was by far my favorite place to belly up to the bar and eat dozens of hand-shucked oysters. Part of the ritual was choosing from the tray of condiment ingredients and making my own cocktail concoction, which was slightly different every time. In this recipe, grilled oysters and shrimp are similarly set out on a platter next to a tray of sauce ingredients and individual bowls so everyone can make their own sauce.

Makes 4 servings

Grilling Method: Direct/Medium-High Heat

1 pound unshelled jumbo shrimp
12 oysters in the shell
Olive oil
Kosher salt
Freshly ground pepper, optional

Sauce ingredients
Tabasco
Louisiana hot sauce
Garlic hot sauce
Chili sauce
Ketchup
Prepared horseradish
Malt vinegar
Sherry vinegar
Chopped shallots
Cut lemons
Cut limes
Black pepper
Small bowls or plastic soufflé cups
Coffee stirrers

1. Build a charcoal fire or preheat a gas grill. If frozen, thaw shrimp in cold running water just before cooking. Pat the shrimp and oysters dry with paper towels. Toss them in a little olive oil to coat all surfaces. Season with salt and pepper, if desired.

2. Set up the sauce ingredients on a tray.

3. Using long-handled tongs, place the shrimp and oysters across the cooking grate to prevent them from falling through. Cover and grill over direct medium-high heat for 2 to 4 minutes, depending on size. Turn the shrimp once halfway through the cooking time. Do not overcook.

4. Remove the shellfish from the grill and put it on a clean platter. Serve immediately with the cocktail sauce ingredients and let your guests make their own sauces.

"Brick" Squid with Fried Garlic

I first made this dish with my friend, Culinary Institute of America Chef Bill Briwa. We were testing and developing recipes for a hands-on grilling and barbecue extravaganza at the CIA's beautiful Greystone campus in the Napa Valley. I wanted to replicate one of my favorite restaurant dishes, garlicky grilled squid, but I was having trouble charring the squid. As we started grilling, Bill had a brilliant idea: Use the foil-covered brick that we had prepared for our Tuscan brick chicken to flatten the squid and expose the maximum amount of the squid to the heat. It worked beautifully and "brick" squid was born! If you don't have a brick, use a cast-iron pan or a similar (clean) heavy object to flatten the squid as it grills.

Makes 4 servings

Grilling Method: Direct/Medium Heat
Special Equipment: Cast-iron skillet, grill press, or brick covered in foil

2	pounds medium squid, cleaned
2	cups buttermilk
	Olive oil
	Kosher salt
	Freshly ground pepper or grains of paradise

Fried Garlic Vinaigrette

1/2	cup extra-virgin olive oil
10	cloves garlic, minced or sliced paper thin
1/4	cup dry white wine
2	tablespoons minced fresh parsley
1	tablespoon minced fresh chives
2	teaspoons fresh lemon juice
4	shakes Tabasco, or more to taste
	Sea salt

1. If frozen, thaw the squid in cold running water. Place the squid in a glass or nonreactive bowl, making sure that all quills and insides are removed. Cover with the buttermilk. Cover the bowl with plastic wrap, and let it sit in the refrigerator for 2 to 12 hours.

2. Build a charcoal fire or preheat a gas grill.

3. Just before grilling, drain the buttermilk from the squid and pat lightly to remove excess liquid. Coat the squid lightly with oil and season with salt and pepper. Set aside.

4. Make the vinaigrette: Put the oil and garlic in a cold sauté pan. Slowly heat the oil until the garlic begins to turn brown. Be sure to watch carefully, as this process only takes a few minutes and the garlic can turn black and bitter very quickly. When the garlic is golden brown, turn off the heat, remove the garlic with a slotted spoon, and place it on a folded paper towel to cool. (When cool, put in a small airtight container until time to serve.)

5. Pour the oil out of the pan into a medium bowl and, while the pan is still hot, deglaze it by pouring the white wine in and stirring to incorporate all the browned bits into the liquid. Let the oil cool. When it is cool, in about 15 minutes, add the white wine deglazing liquid, parsley, chives, lemon juice, and Tabasco. Whisk to combine and adjust the seasoning as needed. Set aside.

6. Wrap a brick in aluminum foil just as you would wrap a gift.

7. Place the oiled and seasoned squid on the cooking grate over direct medium heat. Place the brick on top of the squid. (This will keep the squid flat as it cooks.) Cover and grill for 4 minutes, then turn the squid and replace the brick on top. Grill for 4 more minutes or until the squid is opaque and well marked.

8. Remove the squid from the grill, toss them with the vinaigrette immediately, and top them with the reserved fried garlic pieces. Serve warm or at room temperature.

TIP: Deglazing is a kitchen term for the process of adding liquid to a pan that has had food sautéed in it, to absorb the flavor left in the pan. Most of the time, this is done when the caramelization of the food renders brown bits of food (called fond) that have stuck to the bottom of the pan. The deglazing liquid can be as simple as stock or even water, but it is mostly wine, brandy, or a combination of the two. The liquid loosens and mixes with the browned bits of food to create a deeper flavored liquid that can be used as an ingredient or quick pan sauce. A cornstarch paste (1 teaspoon water mixed with 1 teaspoon cornstarch) will thicken the deglazed juices and turn it into a proper sauce if it is whisked into the liquid continually over medium heat for about 2 minutes.

Fire-Roasted Paella

My friend Nathanaël Teissier grew up in the South of France with a Spanish grandmother who made paella over glowing embers of wood for special family occasions. When he got married a few years ago, his grandmother's sons—the uncles—made paella for the rehearsal dinner. Well, it was a sight to behold, as three glowing fires were topped with shallow black-iron pans. The paella took all day to make, but no one minded since we snacked on dry sausage, cheese, orange wine, and whiskey while the paella cooked. It reminded me of the process and camaraderie of the American barbecue circuit. So if paella sounds too complicated, just think of it as Spanish barbecue!

Makes 8 to 10 servings

Grilling Method: Direct/Medium Heat
Special Equipment: Paella pan

- 1 pound chicken thighs, (Bone-In Chicken Pieces 101, page 34)
- 10 small chorizo sausage, (Hot Dogs and Sausage 101, pages 136–138)
- 5 cups chicken stock
- 1 cup white wine
- 1 cup diced tomatoes
- 1 tablespoon saffron threads
- ¼ cup olive oil
- 2 medium onions, diced
- 1 yellow bell pepper, diced
- 6 cloves garlic, chopped
- 3 cups short-grain Spanish or Arborio rice
- 15 to 20 mussels in the shell
- 1 pound calamari, cleaned
- 20 large shrimp (10 unshelled, 10 peeled)
- 1 cup frozen peas
- 1 cup green olives, such as picholine
- 2 red bell peppers, roasted, peeled, and sliced in strips (page 210)
- 2 lemons, cut in half

1. Build a charcoal fire or preheat a gas grill.

2. Grill the chicken thighs and sausage, and set aside until ready to use. Meanwhile, bring the chicken stock, wine, tomatoes, and saffron to a boil in a small stockpot. Reduce the heat and keep the stock simmering while making the rest of the paella. Scrub the seafood to remove any debris.

3. Place a paella pan or a large disposable aluminum roasting pan on the grill. Add the olive oil and sauté the onions, yellow peppers, and garlic over direct medium heat. Add the rice and stir to coat all of the grains. Add most of the stock and cover the grill. Cook for about 15 minutes or until the rice has softened and plumped up. Add the mussels, calamari, peeled shrimp, peas, grilled chorizo, and chicken, and olives to the rice. Bury these ingredients under the rice. Cover the grill and cook for 10 minutes.

4. Arrange the roasted red peppers and unpeeled shrimp in a sundial (starburst) design on top of the paella. Place ½ lemon in the center cut side up. Cover the grill and cook for an additional 10 to 15 minutes or until the shrimp is cooked and the rice is tender and slightly crunchy around the edges. Serve in the pan with the rest of the lemons cut into wedges.

TIP: There are two different types of chorizo sausage, Spanish and Mexican. Spanish chorizo looks like a small hard salami. Mexican chorizo is sold in plastic casing and needs to be cooked in a frying pan before being added to the rice. If you don't have saffron, you can substitute an equal quantity of paprika, which will give the paella a nice reddish color; but you won't get the distinctive saffron yellow color or flavor.

Vegetables and Fruit

Vegetables and Fruit 101

Rapid-Fire Checklist

✓ Preheat grill
✓ Choose whole or sliced produce
✓ Brush produce with oil or clarified butter
✓ Season produce with kosher salt and pepper or sugar, as applicable
✓ Reduce heat to medium, choose the right cooking method
✓ Place produce on cooking grate or cast-iron grill grate and cover
✓ Turn once halfway through cooking time or according to recipe

Tools of the Trade

• 12-inch locking chef tongs
• Silicone or natural-bristle brush
• Cast-iron grill grate
• Heavy-duty oven mitt

Common Problems

• Food sticking to the grate
• Food falling through the grate
• Burned or unevenly cooked food

While you may first think of succulent ribs or a nice juicy hamburger on the grill, the grilling process also intensifies the natural sugars that are inherent in vegetables and fruits, enhancing their flavor. This phenomenon is instantly apparent with a simple test using asparagus: Taste a piece of boiled asparagus versus a grilled spear, each of which has been seasoned with a little salt. I guarantee that 99.9 percent of you will choose the grilled spear.

Likewise the banana. People often complain that a banana is too starchy and has no flavor. Five minutes on the grill and it tastes like a banana should, because the Direct Heat intensifies the sugars, making the natural flavors more prominent and the texture less starchy. In fact, grilling brings out the best in produce so it tastes more like the garden-fresh, tree-ripe produce we remember. Now that you're ready to try your hand at veggies and fruits, you have to know two basic things: First, as with most grilling, you need a little oil. (I recommend olive oil for vegetables and vegetable oil, clarified butter, or nut oils for fruit. You can certainly use olive oil, but most people prefer a lighter tasting oil when grilling sweet foods.) Second, season lightly with salt for the veggies and sugar for the fruit and decide whether you want to grill whole or sliced produce. It's as easy as that. As a general rule, whole produce is grilled by Indirect Heat and sliced produce is grilled by Direct Heat or, as in the case of sliced potatoes and most root vegetables, a combination of the two—the Combo Method.

Fresh Versus Frozen

Although you can grill some frozen vegetables and fruit, like asparagus spears or peach halves, it is much better to grill produce when it is fresh and in season. Freezing changes the texture of produce and can be used to better effect in casseroles or cobblers where texture is less important. One exception is frozen artichoke hearts, which are often better frozen than fresh. Luckily, the three best fruits to grill—apples, pineapples, and bananas—are available year-round. But I urge you to vary your diet (and grilling repertoire) and experiment. You will discover that grilled whole squash in the fall are just as good as asparagus in the spring. (Note: I don't recommend grilling canned vegetables or fruit.)

Grill Placement

People are frustrated when they grill sliced or small pieces of vegetables because they often fall through the grates. Think about the size and shape of the fruit and vegetable you are grilling before you place it on the grill. For almost every sliced fruit or vegetable, it is best to put it on the grill horizontally or across the grates. This way it won't fall through the spaces in-between the grates and more surface area of the food will touch the grates, so you'll get better grill marks.

Vegetable Baskets and Other Grate Accessories

For years, I told people that vegetable baskets weren't necessary. Recently, however, a friend of mine who is a very accomplished cook and griller asked me to reconsider my position. She pointed out that it was still difficult to grill sliced veggies without losing half of them through the cooking grates. So, I decided to test a pallet of these baskets. I've found that the veggie baskets shaped like a wok work best, but the very best solution is to purchase a flat cast-iron grill grate from manufacturers such as Lodge and Le Creuset. Lodge is my number-one choice because they make an already seasoned (Lodge Logic) cast-iron grate that has holes to allow the juices to drip through and the smoke to flavor the food. The rectangular grate looks a little like cast-iron fishnet stockings, so the holes are small enough that the food—even cherry tomatoes—is guaranteed to remain on the cooking grate. All-Clad also makes an anodized aluminum grill that works well.

With the grill grates that don't have any holes, the vegetables will get appetizing marks from the hot ridges, and the juices will still run out but since there are no spaces between the ridges, you won't lose any of your sliced veggies or fruit. But be forewarned, you also won't get as much smoke flavor as with a grate or pan with holes.

Place the cast-iron grate directly on the cooking grate while you preheat the grill so it will get as hot as the grill's cooking grate. Not doing so is the biggest mistake that backyard cooks make when they use any kind of metal basket. If you don't preheat the basket or accessory grill grate, the cold food and the cold basket will heat up together and the food will take much longer to cook. It is almost impossible to get good grill marks this way. Think of the preheated grill accessory just like the preheated grill cooking grates or a preheated sauté pan on the stove. Preheating is essential, regardless of the food.

Follow the recipe, and turn once halfway through the cooking time so the produce cooks evenly on both sides. Remove the cooked produce with tongs. For sliced fruits, vegetables (and delicate fish), you can also use the silicone GrillMat (see page 150) that I designed. It is perforated to let the juices run out and create smoke flavor. Unlike metal, the silicone surface prevents any food from sticking. So, small pieces of fruit and vegetables won't fall through the grates or stick to the grates. Because it is made of silicone and not metal, the GrillMat doesn't need to be preheated (but cannot be placed over Direct Heat).

Approximate **VEGETABLE** *Cooking Times*

TYPE OF VEGETABLE	WHOLE OR SLICES	GRILLING METHOD	GRILLING TIME
Artichoke (precooked)	Whole	Direct Medium	Steam 20 to 25 minutes, cut in half, and grill 8 to 10 minutes
Asparagus	Whole	Direct Medium	6 to 8 minutes
Beet	Whole	Indirect Medium	1 to 1½ hours
Bell pepper	Whole	Direct Medium	10 to 12 minutes
Bell pepper	Half or Quarter	Direct Medium	6 to 8 minutes
Cabbage	Whole	Indirect Medium	2 to 2½ hours
Chile	Whole	Direct Medium	7 to 9 minutes
Corn	Shucked	Direct Medium	8 to 10 minutes
Corn	Unshucked	Direct Medium	10 to 15 minutes
Eggplant, large	Half-inch slices	Direct Medium	8 to 10 minutes
Eggplant, small (Japanese)	Cut in half lengthwise	Direct Medium	12 to 15 minutes
Fennel	Quarter-inch slices	Direct Medium	10 to 12 minutes
Garlic	Whole, unpeeled	Indirect Medium	45 minutes to 1 hour
Green bean	Whole	Direct Medium	8 to 10 minutes
Green onion	Whole	Direct Medium	3 to 4 minutes
Leek	Whole	Direct Medium	14 to 16 minutes
Mushroom, portobello	Whole	Direct Medium	8 to 10 minutes
Mushroom, shiitake or button	Whole	Direct Medium	8 to 10 minutes
Okra	Whole	Direct Medium	8 to 10 minutes
Onion	Whole, unpeeled	Indirect Medium	45 to 50 minutes
Onion	Cut in half crosswise	Indirect Medium	35 to 40 minutes
Onion	Half-inch slices	Direct Medium	8 to 12 minutes
Potato	Half-inch slices	Direct Medium	14 to 16 minutes
Potato, baking	Whole	Indirect Medium	45 minutes to 1 hour
Potato, red	Cut in half	Indirect Medium	20 to 25 minutes
Potato, small new	Whole	Indirect Medium	30 to 45 minutes (depending on size)
Pumpkin	3 pounds, cut in half lengthwise	Indirect Medium	1½ to 2 hours

TYPE OF VEGETABLE	WHOLE OR SLICES	GRILLING METHOD	GRILLING TIME
Squash, acorn	1 pound, cut in half lengthwise	Indirect Medium	40 to 45 minutes
Squash, butternut	2 pounds, cut in half lengthwise	Indirect Medium	50 to 55 minutes
Squash, pattypan	Whole	Direct Medium	10 to 12 minutes
Squash, spaghetti	3 pounds, cut in half lengthwise	Indirect Medium	$1\frac{1}{4}$ to $1\frac{1}{2}$ hours
Squash, yellow	Half-inch slices	Direct Medium	6 to 8 minutes
Squash, yellow	Cut in half lengthwise	Direct Medium	6 to 10 minutes
Sweet potato	Whole	Indirect Medium	50 minutes to 1 hour
Sweet potato	Half-inch slices	Indirect Medium	30 to 40 minutes
Tofu	2-inch cubes	Direct Medium	4 to 5 minutes/side
Tomatillo	Whole, unpeeled	Direct Medium	6 to 8 minutes
Tomato, cherry	Whole	Direct Medium	2 to 4 minutes
Tomato, globe	Cut in half lengthwise	Direct Medium	6 to 8 minutes
Tomato, green	Three-quarter–inch slices	Direct Medium	8 to 10 minutes
Tomato, plum	Whole	Direct Medium	8 to 10 minutes
Tomato, plum	Cut in half lengthwise	Direct Medium	6 to 8 minutes
Zucchini	Half-inch slices	Direct Medium	6 to 8 minutes
Zucchini	Cut in half lengthwise	Direct Medium	6 to 10 minutes

Times in the chart are guidelines. Specific recipes may call for variations.

Oil the Food, Not the Grates

This is paramount when grilling vegetables. The oil promotes caramelization—those tell-tale grill marks—and keeps the vegetables from drying out. If you don't oil the vegetables, especially sliced vegetables, they will dry out and resemble cardboard. But take heart, you won't have to spend a lot of time brushing each slice or piece if you use my plastic bag trick below. This makes oiling vegetables and other small foods so much easier that I travel with a box of heavy-duty resealable bags. The zipper bags are even easier to use.

Plastic Bag Trick: Place the sliced vegetables in a resealable plastic bag and drizzle just enough oil in the bag to coat all the pieces. Seal the bag and turn the pieces within the bag to coat them evenly. Sprinkle with salt, reseal the bag, and turn again to evenly distribute the salt. This is the easiest, fastest and cleanest way to insure that all the surfaces are coated with oil and evenly seasoned with salt, too.

Approximate *FRUIT* Cooking Times

TYPE OF FRUIT	WHOLE OR SLICES	GRILLING METHOD	GRILLING TIME
Apple	Whole	Indirect Medium	35 to 40 minutes
Apple	Slices	Direct Medium	4 to 6 minutes
Apricot	Cut in half crosswise	Direct Medium	6 to 8 minutes
Banana	Cut in half lengthwise	Direct Medium-Low	6 to 8 minutes
Cantaloupe	Wedges	Direct Medium-Low	6 to 8 minutes
Fig	Whole	Direct Medium-Low	5 to 7 minutes
Fig	Cut in half lengthwise	Direct Medium-Low	3 to 5 minutes
Nectarine	Cut in half crosswise	Direct Medium	8 to 10 minutes
Orange	Cut in half crosswise	Direct Medium	4 to 6 minutes
Peach	Cut in half crosswise	Direct Medium	8 to 10 minutes
Pear	Cut in half lengthwise	Direct Medium	10 to 12 minutes
Pear	Whole	Indirect Medium	35 to 40 minutes
Pineapple	Rings or Wedges	Direct Medium-Low	5 to 10 minutes
Plum	Cut in half crosswise	Direct Medium-Low	4 to 6 minutes
Strawberry	Whole	Direct Medium-Low	4 to 5 minutes

Times in the chart are guidelines. Specific recipes may call for variations.

Marinating

If you are buying best-quality produce in its natural season, then all you really need is the heat from the grill and a little seasoning to bring out the natural flavors. Think about it—it makes a lot of sense and makes meal preparation a whole lot easier!

If you still want to use a marinade, take the extra time to make one at home. I urge you not to use bottled salad dressing as a marinade because your food will taste more like the bottled salad dressing than the food itself. Homemade marinades can be as simple as lemon juice, garlic, and olive oil or as complex as your imagination.

MARINATING BASICS

Marinate in a nonreactive (glass or stainless steel) bowl or pan. I like using the Vacu Vin or Reveo vacuum marinating gadgets. They force the flavor of the marinades into the food in a short amount of time and I get much more flavor from my marinades. After marinating, blot excess marinade from the food before putting it on the grill to reduce flare-ups. For best flavor, use olive oil instead of vegetable oil in savory marinades.

Whole Versus Sliced

When you pick up produce at the grocery store or farmer's market, how do you decide whether to cook it whole or sliced? It all depends on how you want to eat it. The heavier and denser the produce, the longer it will take to cook. Some of these dense foods, like potatoes and onions, are delicious grilled whole or sliced. Others, like fall squashes and portobello mushrooms, are best grilled whole. Some vegetables, like asparagus, carrots, green beans, and okra, are naturally small and should always be left whole even though they may not take very long to cook. Pineapple, bananas, zucchini, and beefsteak tomatoes are best sliced and grilled. In the charts on pages 200–202, I've indicated whole or sliced for those foods that I think are great prepared either way. If it only has one notation, then I don't recommend the other option.

Salt Versus Sugar

Let your common sense be your guide. Most vegetables benefit from a sprinkling of salt while sweet fruits need the sugar. Salty ingredients like soy sauce, anchovies, and capers are good substitutes for salt. Maple syrup, honey, and brown sugar are good substitutes for white sugar. Sweet potatoes, some hard squashes, bananas, and plaintains can go either way—sweet or savory.

Testing for Doneness

If the vegetables and fruits are marked on the outside and tender to the touch, they are done. Because there are so many textures in produce, doneness is subject to personal taste. Use the recipe (or cooking times chart) as a guideline but develop a timetable based on your personal taste. For example, I like most of my produce crisp-tender, so I take it off when the colors are still bright. This might be too crunchy for some, so for a more tender texture I'd leave it on a little longer or until the produce relaxes and just becomes limp. As long as your produce isn't burned, it won't hurt to cook it longer. Since there are no food safety issues with raw produce that has been properly washed and cleaned, there is no minimum internal temperature to which it should be cooked.

Sliced Veggies 101

I hope that the 101 section will give you the confidence to buy whatever produce looks appealing or inspire your curiosity in the grocery store or better yet, at the curb stand, greenmarket or nearby farm. Knowing whether to use direct or indirect heat and the grilling trilogy of olive oil, salt, and pepper should free you up to cook anything without following a specific recipe. This improvising at the grill is my favorite way to cook in the summer.

Grilling Method: Direct/Medium Heat

> **Zucchini, eggplant, squash, asparagus, Belgian endive, etc., cut in quarters or into $\frac{1}{2}$-inch slices or rounds.**
> **Olive oil**
> **Kosher salt**
> **Freshly ground pepper**

1. Build a charcoal fire or preheat a gas grill.
2. Coat each vegetable slice with olive oil by placing clean, dry slices in a resealable plastic bag, pour in the oil, and massage to coat each vegetable piece with oil. Sprinkle with salt and pepper and massage again. Leave the veggies in the bag until ready to cook.
3. Place the vegetable slices on the cooking grate crosswise so they won't fall through the grates. Cover and grill over direct medium heat for 6 to 15 minutes, depending on the thickness and tenderness of each vegetable (see the chart on pages 200–201 for guidance). Turn once or twice during the grilling time to expose all sides to the heat. The vegetables should begin to brown in spots (indicating that their natural sugars are caramelizing) but should not be allowed to char.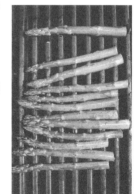
4. Remove each vegetable from the grill as it is finished, and serve hot or at room temperature.

Hard-Skinned or Root Vegetables 101

Grilling Method: Indirect/Medium Heat

> **Butternut, acorn, or delicata squash, or root vegetables such as whole potatoes, any variety**
> **Olive oil**
> **Kosher Salt**
> **Freshly ground pepper**

1. Build a charcoal fire or preheat a gas grill.
2. Cut squash in half and remove the seeds. Leave potatoes whole or cut them in half. You may need to cut a sliver off the bottom of a round squash so it will sit up straight. Coat the vegetables all over with olive oil, and season with salt and pepper.
3. Place the vegetables in the center of the cooking grate over indirect medium heat or on the warming rack, cover, and grill for 40 to 60 minutes, depending on the size of each vegetable. There is no need to turn large squash during grilling. Turn sliced potatoes once halfway through the cooking time to mark each side.
4. Remove each vegetable from the grill as it is finished and serve while still hot.

Sliced or Small Soft Fruit 101

Grilling Method: Direct/Medium-Low Heat

> **Bananas, strawberries, pineapple, melons, apples, plums, oranges, etc.**
> **Walnut or grapeseed oil or clarified butter**
> **Sugar, optional**

1. Build a charcoal fire or preheat a gas grill.
2. Cut each fruit in half, wedges, or rings ½ inch thick. Leave on any skin that can be eaten or easily peeled, such as for oranges, bananas, apples, and plums. It will be necessary to remove the skin from pineapple, mangos, etc. Brush the fruits lightly with oil or clarified butter. Sprinkle with sugar, if using.
3. Place the fruit, cut-side down, over direct medium-low heat, cover, and grill for 1 to 3 minutes or until they have grill marks. Turn the fruits over and continue cooking until warmed through. You can usually tell that the fruit is done when the skins starts to pull away.
4. Remove each fruit from the grill as it is finished. Serve warm, or let cool and refrigerate if desired.

Hard Whole Fruit 101

Grilling Method: Indirect/Medium Heat

> **Apples, pears, pineapple halves, or other very firm (hard) fruits**
> **Walnut or grapeseed oil or clarified butter**
> **Sugar, honey, or maple syrup, optional**
> **Spices, such as cinnamon, ground ginger, etc., optional**

1. Build a charcoal fire or preheat a gas grill.
2. Core the fruit. Wrap the bottom side of each piece or half with aluminum foil, but leave the top of the fruit exposed. Brush the cut surfaces with oil or clarified butter, and season with sugar, honey, maple syrup, and spice, if desired.
3. Place each piece in the center of the cooking grate over indirect medium heat, cover, and grill-bake until soft and fragrant, anywhere from 30 to 60 minutes, depending on how hard the fruit is.
4. Remove each fruit from the grill as it is finished. Serve hot, warm, or cold as a dessert or side dish.

Lip-Smackin' Asparagus Spears

Grilling asparagus miraculously transforms it from the kind of vegetable you hated as a kid to a sweet, meaty, lip-smackin' treat that you can't get enough of as an adult. Choose the thicker, shorter stalks instead of the pencil-thin asparagus because they cook much better on the grill. Deeply caramelized grilled asparagus amazes even my most jaded food friends. They can't believe that the recipe is as simple as high heat, olive oil, and salt—but it is!

Makes 4 servings

Grilling Method: Direct/Medium Heat

1 pound fresh asparagus (large stalks with firm
    deep green or purplish tips and moist ends)
    Olive oil
    Kosher salt, about 1 teaspoon

1. Build a charcoal fire or preheat a gas grill.
2. Rinse the asparagus and snap or cut off the bottom 1 inch of each spear. Place the asparagus in a resealable plastic bag and drizzle just enough oil in the bag to coat all the spears. Seal the bag and turn the spears to coat them evenly in the bag. Sprinkle with salt, reseal the bag, and turn again to evenly distribute the salt.
3. Place the asparagus on the cooking grate over direct medium heat, cover, and grill for 5 to 7 minutes or until marked and caramelized. As they brown, turn the spears to grill each side. The asparagus should begin to brown in spots (this indicates that the natural sugars are caramelizing) but should not char.
4. Remove the asparagus from the grill and serve immediately.

TIP: To trim the whole bunch of asparagus in seconds, leave the rubber bands on the asparagus. The lowest band is usually wrapped around the bunch about 1–inch from the bottom. Place the spears on the cutting service, and position your knife just above the rubber band; cut all the stalks at once. Remove the rubber bands and wash as usual. This is so much faster than washing and trimming each stalk individually.

Asparagus with "Truffle Lemonade"

I didn't think grilled asparagus could get any better until I created this "truffle lemonade" to dress up my favorite grilled veggie for a friend's birthday party. Try it, and use any leftover dressing on fresh salads or grilled fish. The little bit of cream in the recipe keeps the vinaigrette from separating and rounds out the sharp flavors of the lemon juice and the truffle oil.

Makes 4 servings

Grilling Method: Direct/Medium Heat

TO CLARIFY BUTTER

Melt butter, let cool in the refrigerator until the milk solids harden on top and can be removed easily. Underneath is the clarified butter. Clarified butter is good for most fruits, as well as for fish or any recipe that you prefer the taste of butter to olive oil.

Lemon-Truffle Vinaigrette
$1/3$ cup fresh lemon juice (about $2^1/2$ lemons)
1 teaspoon heavy whipping cream, at room
    temperature
$1/3$ cup olive oil or canola oil
$1/8$ to $1/4$ cup truffle oil
    Sea Salt
    Freshly ground pepper, optional
1 pound fresh asparagus (large stalks with firm
    deep green or purplish tips and moist ends)
    Olive oil
    Kosher salt, about 1 teaspoon

1. Build a charcoal fire or preheat a gas grill.
2. Make the vinaigrette: Whisk together the lemon juice and cream in a small bowl. Slowly add the olive oil a little at a time, whisking until well incorporated (emulsified). Continue, whisking in the truffle oil to taste. Season to taste with sea salt and pepper. Resist the urge to overseason since the grilled asparagus will be well seasoned. Set aside.
3. Rinse the asparagus and snap or cut off the bottom 1 inch of each spear. Place the asparagus in a resealable plastic bag and drizzle just enough oil in the bag to coat all the spears. Seal the bag and turn the spears to coat them evenly in the bag. Sprinkle with salt, reseal the bag, and turn it again to evenly distribute the salt. (This is the "plastic bag trick" and can be used for any food.)
4. Place the asparagus on the cooking grate over direct medium heat, cover, and grill for 5 to 7 minutes or until well marked and caramelized. Turn the spears during cooking to grill each side. The asparagus should begin to brown in spots (this indicates that the natural sugars are caramelizing) but should not char.
5. Remove the asparagus from the grill, drizzle with the vinaigrette, and serve immediately.

Grilled Corn in the Husk

The best part of grilling corn in the husk is that no one has to struggle with those stubborn pieces of silk that stick to the ears when you shuck raw corn. The husk protects the delicate corn and keeps it from charring, resulting in a sweet and slightly roasted flavor. It also makes a rustic and appealing presentation when you bring a platter of corn, still in the charred husk, to the table The cooking process makes the silk come off in one fell swoop and the husk can be bent back behind the corn and tied, acting as a handle and turning the corn into finger food.

Makes 6 servings

Grilling Method: Direct/Medium Heat

6 **ears corn, unshucked**
 Butter
 Kosher salt
 Freshly ground pepper
 Lime wedges, optional

1. Build a charcoal fire or preheat a gas grill.
2. Trim the silk ends of the corn with a pair of scissors. Fill the sink or a bucket with cold water and soak the corn, husk and all, for 30 minutes. Shake the excess water off of the corn.
3. Place the corn on the cooking grate over direct medium heat, cover, and grill for 10 to 15 minutes, turning occasionally, until the outside is slightly charred and the inside is steamed and tender. The fresher the corn, the less time it will take to cook. Field-fresh corn will only take 4 to 5 minutes to cook, and fresh grocery-store corn will take closer to 10 minutes.
4. Remove the corn from the grill, serve in the husk, and let everyone shuck their own corn. Serve with butter, salt, and pepper and lime wedges, if desired.

Fire-Roasted Corn with Smoked Paprika Butter

This recipe is inspired by the roasted corn-on-the cob that street vendors hawk in Mexico. The main spice is authentic wood-smoked red pepper that has been dried and ground to become "smoked paprika." If you can't find it in your town, log onto www.thespicehouse.com, where they sell it sweet or hot. This recipe is best made with summer corn that is husked and grilled to a blistery golden brown directly over the fire, bathed in the smoky butter, and finished with a squirt of lime. Serve the ears with a cool drink and forget about mañana!

Makes 6 servings

Grilling Method: Direct/Medium Heat

4 **tablespoons (½ stick) unsalted butter, at room temperature**
1½ **teaspoons smoked paprika**
½ **teaspoon garlic salt**
6 **ears corn, shucked**
 Olive oil
 Sea salt
 Lime wedges

1. Build a charcoal fire or preheat a gas grill.
2. In a small bowl, mash together the butter, paprika, and garlic salt. Set aside at room temperature.
3. Brush the corn lightly all over with olive oil. Place it on the cooking grate over direct medium heat. Cover and cook, turning occasionally, until the kernels are lightly browned and blistered all over, 8 to 10 minutes.
4. Spread the paprika butter evenly over the corn, and sprinkle it with salt and a squirt of lime just before eating.

Grilled Fennel Gratin

Fennel is one of the most underappreciated vegetables. I've found that even experienced and adventurous cooks don't know what to do with it. When I grill it with nothing more than the Grilling Trilogy (olive oil, salt, and pepper), it is always the first vegetable to disappear. When I grill it and then bake it with a touch of cream, nutmeg, and melted Gruyère cheese, dinner guests often fight over getting their share. Fennel is so sweet and delicious that it is hard to believe that it is good for you!

Makes 4 servings

Grilling Method: Direct/Medium Heat
Special Equipment: Shallow ovenproof casserole or pie plate

2 to 4 **bulbs fresh fennel, depending on size**
 Olive oil
 Kosher salt

½ cup heavy (whipping) cream
2 tablespoons water
Freshly grated nutmeg
½ cup grated Gruyère cheese

1. Build a charcoal fire or preheat a gas grill.
2. Clean and trim the fennel bulbs of their woody and furry stems. Leave the bottom intact as this will keep the fennel together as it grills. Cut the fennel in quarters so you have a total of 8 wedges. (If the fennel bulbs are really small, you may only get 2 wedges out of each.) Brush the fennel with oil and season with salt.
3. Place the fennel on the grill over direct medium heat, cover, and cook for 10 to 20 minutes, depending on the thickness of the wedges. Turn occasionally until brown on all sides and crisp-tender.
4. Remove the fennel from the grill, and put the wedges into a casserole or pie plate. Mix the cream and water and pour them over the fennel. Season with nutmeg to taste and sprinkle the cheese over the top. Return to the grill, covered, for another 20 minutes or until the cheese is bubbly and browned, and the liquid has reduced by half. Serve immediately.

Roasted Garlic

This is one of those pantry items that make almost any recipe better. And I use it in a lot of the recipes in this book. You can substitute roasted garlic for raw garlic for a more mellow flavor in most recipes. When you are roasting one head, go ahead and make a few more; roasted garlic keeps in the fridge for at least two weeks.

Grilling Method: Indirect/Medium heat

1 head garlic
2 teaspoons olive oil

1. Build a charcoal fire or preheat a gas grill.
2. Remove the first layer of papery skin from the garlic. Slice off the top ½ inch. Drizzle with olive oil. Wrap the garlic in foil and place it on the cooking grate over indirect medium heat. Cover and grill for 40 minutes or until the cloves are golden brown and soft.
3. Remove the garlic from the grill, and let it cool. (If making this for another recipe, follow those specific recipe instructions.) In almost all cases, remove the roasted cloves from their skins and place them in an airtight container until needed. Store in the refrigerator.

TIP: Having a few heads of roasted garlic in your refrigerator will allow you to "goose" a wide variety of dishes. In most recipes that call for garlic, you can substitute roasted garlic for a sweeter, deeper flavor.

Bello Portobello

Che bello! Stuffed mushroom caps may seem a little old-fashioned, but good taste never goes out of style. Every time I serve these portobellos, stuffed with spinach, garlic, and herbed goat cheese, someone inevitably asks for the recipe. It is one of those recipes that is so simple that people can't believe it. Feel free to add or subtract ingredients that you like. Sautéed chopped shallots and a drizzle of white truffle oil are great additions.

Makes 4 servings

Grilling Method: Indirect/Medium Heat

8 small portobello mushrooms
2 tablespoons olive oil
1 9-ounce package frozen chopped spinach, cooked and drained
1 5.3 ounce container goat cheese with garlic and herbs or Boursin cheese
½ teaspoon granulated garlic
Sea salt
Freshly ground pepper

1. Clean the mushrooms, and remove the gills by running a spoon around the inside of the mushrooms. Brush the mushrooms with olive oil and set aside.
2. Build a charcoal fire or preheat a gas grill. Meanwhile, make the filling by combining the spinach, goat cheese, garlic, and salt and pepper to taste.
3. When ready to grill, stuff each mushroom cap with a generous portion of the spinach mixture (this will vary depending on the size of your mushrooms).
4. Place the mushrooms on the grill, stuffed-side up, over indirect medium heat. Cover and grill until well seared and the topping is bubbling, about 20 minutes. Serve immediately.

Portobello Burgers

Portobello mushrooms are nature's meat substitute and perfectly suited for hearty sandwiches or burgers. This colorful medley of grilled portobello, peppers, fresh basil, prosciutto, and parmesan cheese is dressed with roasted garlic mayonnaise. Equally good hot or cold, the vegetables can be grilled ahead and the sandwiches assembled when needed—perfect picnic fare for summer concerts in the park.

Makes 6 servings

Grilling Method: Direct/Medium Heat

2	red or yellow peppers, or both
¼	cup olive oil, plus more as needed
½	cup balsamic vinegar
1	teaspoon dried rosemary
	Kosher salt
	Freshly ground pepper
2	fire-roasted red or yellow bell peppers (page 210), cut into strips
6	large portobello mushrooms, the same size as the rolls
6	kaiser or onion rolls
1	head garlic, roasted (page 207)
½	cup best-quality mayonnaise
1	bunch fresh basil, leaves only
8	ounces Parmigiano-Reggiano cheese, thinly sliced (slice with a vegetable peeler)
8	ounces thinly sliced prosciutto di Parma, optional

1. Build a charcoal fire or preheat a gas grill.
2. Place peppers on cooking grate and grill over direct medium heat until skin is charred. Remove peppers from grill with tongs and place in paper bag; let sit for 30 minutes. Take peppers out of bag; remove skin and seeds, and cut into strips.
3. Combine the balsamic vinegar, olive oil, rosemary, salt, and pepper. Add the peppers and let them marinate for up to 3 days in the refrigerator.
4. Clean the mushrooms with a damp paper towel, remove the stems, and set aside.
5. Just before grilling, pour the marinade off the peppers and onto the mushrooms. Let them sit for 5 minutes. Drain the mushrooms from the marinade. Place the mushrooms on the cooking grate, gill-side up, over direct medium heat, cover, and grill for 8 to 10 minutes. Turn them over for 1 minute more or until tender.
6. Split the kaiser rolls in half. Brush them lightly with oil. Place them, cut-side down, on the grill for 2 to 3 minutes or until lightly toasted. Meanwhile, mix the garlic and mayonnaise until smooth.
7. When the rolls are toasted, assemble the sandwiches by spreading the insides of the rolls with garlic mayonnaise and layering a mushroom, peppers, basil leaves, cheese (you may have some left over), and optional prosciutto on top. Season with salt and pepper, if desired. Place the top roll on each sandwich and cut in half before serving. Alternatively, you can plate the portobellos and other ingredients without bread for an elegant and delicious appetizer.

Portobello Pizza

I absolutely love repurposing things, and food is no exception. For me, it's one way of escaping a daily rut and creating unexpected pleasures! I am always looking for new things to do with the standard pantry items in my kitchen. Here, portobello mushrooms replace traditional bread crusts for a mini open-faced grilled pizza; great for those on a wheat-free diet. I've kept the toppings simple and mixed together a quick pizza sauce, which I find to be much fresher than prepared sauces. Feel free to individualize these pizzas with your choice of sauce and toppings. (Check the Pizza chapter for ideas, too.)

Makes 3 to 6 servings

Grilling Method: Direct/Medium Heat

6	large portobello mushrooms, stemmed
	Olive oil
½ to ¾	cup crushed canned tomatoes
¼	teaspoon dried oregano, or more to taste
1	clove garlic, grated
	Kosher salt
½	small red onion, thinly sliced
1	cup grated mozzarella
½	cup grated parmesan
2	tablespoons chopped fresh herbs, such as basil, parsley, thyme
	Freshly ground pepper

1. Build a charcoal fire or preheat a gas grill.
2. Wipe the mushroom caps clean with damp paper towels. Remove the gills, if desired.
3. Brush lightly with olive oil and sprinkle with salt. Mix 1 tablespoon olive oil with the crushed tomatoes. Add the oregano and garlic and stir to combine. Taste and adjust the seasonings if necessary.
4. Spread about 2 tablespoons of the tomato sauce on the gill side of each cap. Top with the sliced onions. Mix the 2 cheeses together and spoon them evenly onto the mushrooms.
5. Place the mushrooms on the cooking grate over direct medium heat, cover, and grill until the mushroom caps are tender and the cheese is melted, 8 to 10 minutes. Do not turn the mushrooms over.
6. Sprinkle the mushrooms with fresh herbs and pepper, if desired. Serve immediately.

Grill-"Fried" Okra

I love okra so much that many years ago, I was given a pair of okra-shaped earrings, which I wear proudly. My grandmother made the best fried okra I have ever eaten. It was so good that I couldn't wait until it got to the table to eat it—snitching all the crispy bits off the paper towels as it drained. Try as I might, I never perfected frying okra, so one day I tried to grill it. The high heat and a dusting of cornmeal give okra that "popcorn" flavor without the mess of frying. Be brave and try it; you'll like it.

Makes 4 servings

Grilling Method: Direct/Medium Heat

24 whole okra, cleaned
 8 bamboo skewers, soaked in water for 30 minutes
    Olive oil
    Kosher salt
    Fine yellow cornmeal, about ¹/₂ cup

1. Build a charcoal fire or preheat a gas grill.
2. If necessary, trim the stem ends off the okra, taking care not to cut into the inside. Lay the okra on a cutting board in 4 groups of 6. Line the vegetables up evenly. Thread both ends with a bamboo skewer, so the okra resembles a ladder (see page 28).
3. Brush the okra all over with olive oil. Sprinkle with salt. Spread the cornmeal out on a piece of

waxed paper or a flat plate. Dust both sides of each skewer with cornmeal. Shake off any excess.
4. Place the skewers on the cooking grate over direct medium heat, cover, and grill for 5 minutes per side, or until crisp and browned all over.
5. Remove the okra from the grill and serve immediately with a sprinkle of salt, if desired.

Forgotten Onion

Rose Levy Beranbaum is an award-winning author best known for her baking expertise. But in her free time, Rose really loves to grill. She discovered this method by forgetting an onion on the grill and waking up in the middle of the night to discover that instead of being ruined, it was the most savory caramelized onion she had ever eaten. For that reason, I dubbed the recipe Forgotten Onion. I changed the recipe so it is no longer a nocturnal process, but the flavor remains the same. Be sure to grill the onions until they ooze caramelized onion sugars.

Makes 4 servings

Grilling Method: Indirect/Medium Heat

4 medium, whole, unpeeled onions, preferably Vidalia
   Olive oil
   Fleur de sel or coarse sea salt

1. Build a charcoal fire or preheat a gas grill.
2. Leaving the skins on the onions, rub them lightly with olive oil.
3. Place the onions on the cooking grate over indirect medium heat, cover, and grill for 1 to 2 hours, depending on size. This can be done with any onion, including shallots. It is not necessary to turn them during the cooking time. Because all onions vary in size, check the onions periodically and use visual clues as the most important indicators of doneness. Remove them from the grill when you can see the dark onion juices bursting through the skin.
4. Remove the onions from the grill to cool. When cool enough to touch, peel off the skins and serve the onions as an accompaniment to grilled meat or fish. Rose says that onion layers also can be separated and then served as little vegetable cups to hold steamed peas, mashed potatoes, or other vegetables.

Fire-Roasted Pepper

This ingredient is also used in a multitude of recipes and is good to have on hand. Like the garlic, while you are fire-roasting one pepper, you should do several. They keep for at least two weeks in the refrigerator. Jarred red peppers from Spain are very expensive and a real delicacy—believe it or not, this is exactly how they are made!

Makes about ½ cup

Grilling Method: Direct/High Heat

> 1   bell pepper or poblano chile pepper
> 1   paper bag or resealable plastic container

1. Build a charcoal fire or preheat a gas grill.
2. Rinse and dry the pepper. Remove any produce stickers or labels. Place the pepper on the cooking grate over direct high heat and cover. Grill, turning occasionally, until the skin blackens and blisters all over.
3. Remove the pepper from the grill and immediately put it in a paper bag or sealed plastic container until cool to the touch. Skin and seed the pepper (the skin will slip off easily). Cut into strips. Refrigerate for up to 2 weeks in a sealed container.

Smashed Potatoes

There is nothing more comforting than warm, garlic-rich smashed potatoes. Grill-roasting the potatoes instead of boiling them makes the texture of the potatoes creamier and the skins crispy. I smash the potatoes in their skins with olive oil for a rustic texture and flavor that I find more satisfying than traditional mashed potatoes.

Makes 6 servings

Grilling Method: Indirect/Medium Heat

> 2   heads garlic, roasted (page 207)
> 24   new potatoes, cleaned (about 3 pounds)
> ¼   cup extra-virgin olive oil, or more to taste
>   Kosher salt
>   Freshly ground pepper

1. Build a charcoal fire or preheat a gas grill.
2. Squeeze the garlic from the individual cloves into a small bowl.
3. Toss the potatoes with some olive oil and sprinkle with salt. Place in the center of the cooking grate over indirect medium heat, cover, and roast for 25 to 30 minutes or until tender.
4. While still warm, put the potatoes in a large bowl and smash them with a large fork. Add the garlic to the potatoes and continue to smash, adding about ¼ cup of olive oil or more to taste. Season with salt and pepper and serve immediately.

Smashed Potatoes with Cheese: Before the final seasoning of the potatoes, add ½ cup grated parmesan and ½ cup grated white cheddar to the hot potatoes. Stir until the cheeses are well distributed and melted. Taste and adjust the seasonings. You probably won't need any salt, as the cheese is very salty, but you may need to add pepper.

Smashed Potatoes with Raw Garlic and Fresh Basil: Omit the roasted garlic. Before the final seasoning of the potatoes, add ½ cup of finely chopped basil and 4 cloves of minced garlic. The heat in the potatoes releases the natural flavors of the garlic and basil, making these the freshest tasting smashed potatoes ever—season to taste and serve immediately.

Sparkling Roasted New Potatoes

This is one of my ace-in-the-hole entertaining recipes. I make it at most dinner parties and many cooking classes. The long slow cooking process transforms the potatoes into puffy, tender morsels with a slightly chewy, caramelized skin. The kosher salt makes the potatoes sparkle, reminding me of pavé diamonds. The trick is in the timing, because the potatoes are best eaten within minutes of coming off the grill. As they sit, they deflate and lose some of their silky texture. When eaten hot-off-the-grill, they are so good you don't even want to add butter.

Makes 4 to 6 servings

Grilling Method: Indirect/Medium Heat

24 new potatoes about the size of a golf ball, cleaned
¼ cup olive oil
1 tablespoon kosher salt

1. Build a charcoal fire or preheat a gas grill.
2. Place the potatoes in a metal bowl. Pour in the oil and toss to coat. Sprinkle with the salt and toss again to coat evenly. Place the potatoes in the center of the cooking grate or on the warming rack over indirect medium heat and roast for 30 to 40 minutes until tender.
3. The potatoes are done when the skin puffs slightly and the potatoes are very soft in the center.
4. Serve immediately.

Cider-Glazed Sweet Potatoes

I created this recipe as an alternative to the traditional Thanksgiving candied yams. The tart-sweet-savory combination of apple cider, vinegar, and olive oil accents the natural flavors and contemporizes the sweet potatoes. They are a great vegetable to grill and serve any time of the year—I promise—no one will miss the marshmallows!

Makes 6 to 8 servings

Grilling Method: Indirect/Medium-High Heat
Special Equipment: Shallow roasting pan

6 medium sweet potatoes, preferably Garnet variety (about 5 pounds)
½ cup apple cider
2 tablespoons olive oil
1 tablespoon apple cider vinegar
1 tablespoon dark brown sugar
   Sea Salt

1. Build a charcoal fire or preheat a gas grill.
2. Peel and cut the sweet potatoes into 2-inch wedges or chunks. Whisk the cider, oil, vinegar, and sugar together and toss them with the sweet potatoes.
3. Place the potatoes and liquid in a large shallow roasting pan and place the pan in the center of the grill over indirect medium-high heat (or in an oven

preheated to 375°F) for 45 to 60 minutes. Stir occasionally or until browned on the edges, soft on the insides, and all of the liquid has evaporated.
4. While still hot, season to taste with sea salt. Serve warm.

Grilled Sweet Potato Chips

Sweet potato chips are roasty-toasty and reminiscent of hand-cut cottage fries without the deep frying. The deeply caramelized outside and soft-as-silk inside make them positively addictive! I often grill them at the beginning of my cooking classes to demonstrate how grilling and the caramelization process enhance even the simplest foods. Although they take a while to cook, resist the urge to precook the potatoes. They are so much better cooked entirely on the grill.

Makes 4 servings

Grilling Method: Combo/Medium Heat

2 medium sweet potatoes, preferably Garnet variety
   Olive oil
   Kosher salt

1. Build a charcoal fire or preheat a gas grill.
2. Peel the sweet potatoes and slice them into ½-inch-thick slices. Brush them lightly with olive oil. (If you are making these for a crowd—as I do a lot—put the potatoes in a resealable plastic bag, add the oil, and massage to coat all surfaces. This method works best and it the fastest and easiest.)
3. Just before putting the potatoes on the grill, season liberally with salt. Place the rounds on the cooking grate over direct medium heat, cover, and grill 2 to 3 minutes on each side or until well marked. They will still be raw and will need 20 to 30 more minutes to cook through. Move to indirect heat to finish cooking, and turn halfway through the cooking time.
4. When soft and tender, remove the "potato chips" from the grill, sprinkle with salt, if necessary, and serve immediately. They are best still hot, like french fries.

Acorn Squash with Fresh Sage and Olive Oil

This recipe is the perfect example of how less is more. Over the years, I've tested and retested the recipe, adding sugar and spices and even a sweet marinade, but I always come back to my original. The olive oil seals in the natural sugars while they slowly grill-roast until it tastes like candy. The fresh sage and the salt balance the flavors to make this a perfect fall and winter accompaniment for turkey or any other grilled meat.

Makes 2 to 4 servings

Grilling Method: Indirect/Medium Heat

2   acorn squash
8   fresh sage leaves
    Olive oil
    Kosher salt
    Freshly ground pepper

1. Build a charcoal fire or preheat a gas grill.
2. Cut the acorn squash in half lengthwise, seed it, and cut a slice off the rounded sides so it will stand straight. Bruise the sage leaves by crumpling them, and rub the inside of each squash half with sage. Coat the squash with olive oil, and season with salt and pepper. Place 2 sage leaves in each half.
3. Cover the bottom side of each squash half with aluminum foil, leaving the top exposed. Place the squash in the center of the cooking grate or on the warming rack over indirect medium heat, cover, and grill for 40 to 60 minutes, depending on the size. Cook until the squash is tender and browned on the edges.
4. Cut the squash into pieces and serve, or serve each person one half.

Grilled Butternut Squash Ravioli with Brown Butter

Who isn't nuts about butternut squash ravioli? A number of years ago, I sampled about a dozen versions during a week of extreme dining in New York. I was lamenting the fact that I couldn't make this dish at home, when I discovered that wonton wrappers make perfect "ravioli." It worked so well that I make it every fall. Cutting the squash in half and

roasting it on the grill is much easier than peeling and cubing it, as many recipes require. The roasting concentrates the flavor, whereas the traditional boiling technique reduces the flavor—and once again, the grill is win-win!

Makes 6 servings

Grilling Method: Indirect/Medium Heat

2   butternut squash or 4 sweet potatoes
    Kosher salt
    Freshly ground pepper
    Freshly ground nutmeg
1   egg
2   tablespoons water
1   10-ounce package round gyoza wrappers or wonton wrappers
1   cup (2 sticks) unsalted butter
4 to 6 fresh sage leaves
    Parmesan cheese curls
    Chopped fresh herbs, such as sage, chervil, parsley, etc.

1. Build a charcoal fire or preheat a gas grill.
2. Cut the squash in half lengthwise, remove the seeds, and coat it generously with oil and a sprinkle of salt. Place the squash in the center of the cooking grate, skin-side down, over indirect medium heat. Cover and cook until soft and the edges are browned, about 1 hour. If using sweet potatoes, prick them with a fork and grill the whole potatoes until soft and tender and the sugars are oozing from the skin, about 60 minutes.
3. Remove the squash from the grill. Set aside until cool enough to remove the flesh from the skin. Throw the skin away and mash the squash until soft and silky. Season with salt, pepper, and fresh nutmeg, and set aside. You can make the recipe up to this point the day before and refrigerate until ready to make the ravioli.
4. Make an egg wash by beating together the egg and water. Remove the wrappers from the package, and lay 2 on a piece of parchment paper or a silicone baking sheet. Paint 1 with the egg wash. On the other, place a dollop of squash mixture. Place the egg-washed wrapper on top of the filled wrapper, so that the edges match up. Seal the ends by pinching the edges and running your finger along the outline of the squash. Repeat the process until all the filling is used. Cover with plastic wrap until ready to cook.

5. Meanwhile, make a brown butter sauce by melting the butter and simmering it over low heat until the color changes to a light golden brown. Season to taste with salt, pepper, and fresh sage leaves. Set aside until ready to use.

6. When ready to serve, place the ravioli gently in boiling salted water until tender, 4 to 6 minutes. Remove with a slotted spoon. Serve immediately with brown butter, parmesan cheese, and herb garnish.

NOTE: To cut hard squash safely, use a serrated knife instead of a chef knife. A gentle sawing motion will slowly cut cleanly through the hard skin without any fear of the knife slipping.

Grilled Tomatoes with Parmesan Bread Crumbs

When I was 10 years old, I thought my mother's broiled tomatoes were the height of culinary sophistication. Since I love tomatoes prepared in any way, I still make these tomatoes but have added a few more ingredients—pesto and authentic parmesan cheese—and a lot more flavor by grilling them. The red and green colors and the crunchy bread crumbs make a pretty presentation and a tasty side dish for any grilled meat or fish.

Makes 4 servings

Grilling Method: Indirect/Medium Heat

| 4 | large red tomatoes, ripe but slightly firm
| | Olive oil
| ½ | cup best-quality pesto
| ¼ | cup freshly grated parmesan cheese
| ¼ | cup bread crumbs or panko
| | Freshly ground pepper

1. Build a charcoal fire or preheat a gas grill.

2. Wash the tomatoes and slice about ¼ inch off the top of each stem end—just enough to make the tomatoes flat on top. Using a melon baller or a grapefruit spoon, scoop out about ½ inch of the flesh from the top. (Leave the seeds.) Coat the tomatoes with olive oil. Cover the bottoms of the tomatoes with a piece of aluminum foil, leaving the tops exposed. Spoon about 2 tablespoons of pesto into each tomato. Mix the cheese and bread crumbs and spoon them onto the top of each tomato. Sprinkle evenly with pepper.

3. Place the tomatoes, cut-side up, on the cooking grate over indirect medium heat. Cover and grill without turning for 15 to 20 minutes, or until the tomatoes are warmed through and the bread crumbs are toasty.

4. Remove the tomatoes from the grill, discard the foil, and serve them as an accompaniment for grilled chicken, fish, or steak.

Smoke-Dried Tomatoes

This technique of drying tomatoes intensifies the natural sugars and makes grocery store tomatoes taste almost home grown! Moistened with a little olive oil and stored in the refrigerator, these are another pantry item to always have on hand. They brighten up everything from omelets and salads to cheese plates, sandwiches, pasta, and grilled meats and fish. Make a bunch—you'll finish them off in no time! These are particularly good on grilled bread with goat cheese and as an ingredient in the Grilled Zucchini Torte (pages 214–215).

Makes 40 tomato halves

Grilling Method: Indirect/Low Heat

| 20 | cherry tomatoes or plum tomatoes, cut in half
| | Kosher salt
| | Best-quality olive oil
| | Wood chips, optional, soaked for 30 minutes

1. Build a charcoal fire or preheat a gas grill. If using wood chips, put them in the grill during the pre-heat stage; for a charcoal grill, add to the prepared coals just before cooking.

2. Lightly coat the tomatoes with oil. Cover 1 large or 2 small cookie sheets lightly with kosher salt to form a salt bed. Place the tomatoes closely together, skin-side down, on the salt. Sprinkle the tomato tops lightly with salt.

3. Place the cookie sheet or sheets in the center of the cooking grate over indirect low heat, cover, and slowly roast for 1 to 3 hours or until most of the liquid has evaporated from the tomato halves. Alternatively, you can roast them in a 275°F oven.

4. Remove the sheets from the grill and let the tomatoes cool. When no heat remains, place the tomatoes in a clean jar and cover them with olive oil. Refrigerate until ready to use.

Grill-"Fried" Green Tomatoes

Any self-respecting southerner loves fried green tomatoes! Imagine my surprise when I discovered that grilling them is just as good. Green tomatoes are not quite ripe and much firmer than red tomatoes, making them easy to grill. I cut the tomatoes into thick slices and grill them slowly so the outsides are caramelized and the insides are tender. Serve them with your morning eggs, grilled ham steaks, as a bed for Shrimp Remoulade (page 187), or with any other food you can think of—they go with everything!

Makes 4 servings

Grilling Method: Direct/Medium Heat

2	green (unripe) tomatoes
	Olive oil
$\frac{1}{2}$	cup cornmeal
	Kosher salt
	Freshly ground pepper

1. Build a charcoal fire or preheat a gas grill.
2. Wash, but do not peel, the tomatoes. Cut the ends off, and slice the tomatoes into $\frac{3}{4}$-inch slices. Drain the slices on paper towels. Drizzle them with olive oil and set aside.
3. Mix the cornmeal with enough salt and pepper to season. Dip both sides of the sliced tomatoes in the seasoned cornmeal.
4. Place the tomatoes on the cooking grate over direct medium heat, cover, and grill for about 5 minutes on each side, turning only once halfway through the cooking time. Remove from the grill and serve immediately.

Grilled Zucchini Torte

This savory vegetable and cheese-rich torte is perfect for people who want the flavor and flexibility of a quiche but don't want to mess with a pastry crust—a great option for low-carb followers. The grilled zucchini and smoke-dried tomatoes add big bold flavors to the traditional egg tart. I bake it in a 10-inch silicone cake pan (Lekué brand makes a very good one), which makes unmolding it a breeze. The torte is great at all temperatures and keeps in the refrigerator for up to three days, which translates to dinner and at least two lunches or a great main course for a shower or book club.

Makes 6 to 8 servings

Grilling Method: Combo/Medium Heat
Special Equipment: 9- or 10-inch round cake pan, preferably silicone; cookie sheet

1	9-ounce package frozen chopped spinach
2	medium zucchini, sliced in $\frac{1}{2}$-inch rounds
	Olive oil
	Kosher salt
1	large shallot, peeled
4	cloves garlic
$1\frac{1}{2}$	heaping cups large-curd cottage cheese
	Freshly ground pepper
	Freshly ground nutmeg
2	tablespoons best quality extra-virgin olive oil
5	eggs
$\frac{1}{4}$	cup milk
1	2 x 3–inch chunk Parmigiano Reggiano cheese, grated
1	2 x 3–inch chunk Pecorino Romano cheese, grated
1	pint Smoked-Dried Tomatoes (page 213), washed and dried (If you don't want to grill-roast the tomatoes, substitute 10 oil-packed sun-dried tomatoes, roughly chopped)

1. Build a charcoal fire or preheat a gas grill.
2. Cook the spinach according to the package instructions and drain off all excess water; set aside. Slice the zucchini and place it in a resealable plastic bag with about 1 tablespoon of olive oil and a sprinkle of kosher salt. Massage to coat and set aside.
3. Place the zucchini on the cooking grate over direct medium heat, cover, and grill about 3 minutes on each side. Remove the zucchini when it is well marked and firm-tender.
4. Meanwhile, in a food processor fitted with a steel blade, process the shallot and garlic until chopped. Add the cottage cheese, $\frac{1}{2}$ cup at a time, and process until pureed. Season to taste with about 1 teaspoon pepper and $\frac{1}{2}$ teaspoon nutmeg and

pulse for about 10 seconds to incorporate. Add the olive oil and process until fully mixed, about 10 seconds. Set aside. If cooking in the oven, preheat it to 375°F. If cooking on the grill, it should already be preheated.

5. In a large metal bowl, mix the eggs and milk. Mix the cheeses together. Add 1 heaping cup of the cheese mixture to the egg mixture and mix again. Add the cottage cheese mixture and whisk until completely smooth. Add the reserved spinach and mix carefully to make sure there are no large clumps of spinach. Add the tomatoes and mix again.

6. Grease a 9-inch springform pan or a 9- or 10-inch silicone cake pan with olive oil. Dust the bottom and sides with about 1 tablespoon of the remaining grated cheese. Pour half of the egg and vegetable mixture into the pan, spreading it out to the sides. Place the zucchini rounds on top in a circle. Top with the remaining egg mixture and spread to make it even. Sprinkle the top with the rest of the cheese and place the torta on a sheet pan (I use a round pizza pan) to catch any drips or to support a silicone cake pan.

7. Bake in the oven for 35 to 45 minutes or grill over indirect medium heat until brown on the top and set in the center. If the torta is done, but the top is still not brown, broil it in the oven for 1 to 2 minutes before cooling.

8. Let the torte cool at room temperature for 30 minutes. Unmold it onto a flat plate by placing a plate on top of the torte and inverting it. Using another plate, invert again so the browned top is facing up. Cover with a kitchen towel and place in the refrigerator for a minimum of 3 hours or overnight before serving.

Raclette with Grilled Onions and Potatoes

Raclette is a traditional sheepherders' meal of melted raclette cheese over boiled potatoes, onions, tart little pickles, and dried beef. In the open fields, men would put the cheese on a stick, hold it towards the fire, and scrape the melted cheese onto their plate. When I was a student in

France, I had raclette dinner parties every week—it was easy, cheap, and fun.

Grilling the potatoes and onions in thick slabs makes this simple meal much tastier and, twenty years later, it is still a great meal for a party. Think of it as cheese fondue without the fancy pot and feel free to add other favorite grilled vegetables to the mix.

Makes 4 to 6 servings

Grilling Method: Indirect/Medium Heat
Special Equipment: 4 to 6 mini nonstick cake pans or small aluminum pan

2   pounds small potatoes, cleaned
     Olive oil
     Kosher salt
1   pound shallots, unpeeled
3 to 4 pounds raclette cheese, cut into 4 equal pieces
4   ounces bresaola (dried beef), such as Citterio brand
     Cornichon pickles
     Dijon mustard

1. Build a charcoal fire or preheat a gas grill.
2. Toss the potatoes and shallots with oil and season with salt. Place them in the center of the cooking grate or on the warming rack over indirect medium heat, cover, and grill-roast for 40 to 50 minutes, turning occasionally, until the potatoes are tender and the onions begin to ooze caramelized sugars from their skins. (A faster alternative is to cut slices from baking potatoes and onions and grill them until well marked on both sides.)
3. Divide the cheese equally among the mini cake pans or a small disposable aluminum pan. Place the pans in the center of the cooking grate during the final 10 minutes of the vegetable cooking time. You want the cheese to melt but not brown.
4. Remove the vegetables and cheese from the grill. To serve, place the potatoes, onions, bresaola, and cornichons on a platter. Let everyone serve themselves, topping the vegetables and meat with the cheese. Serve with the mustard.

TIP: Raclette cheese is imported from Europe as well as made in Wisconsin, so it is widely available; but if you can't find it, substitute fontina or muenster cheese.

Grilled Vegetable Antipasto Platter with Soprano Sauce

This antipasto plate is my favorite thing to offer guests at the beginning of a dinner party or cooking class. Since it is better made several hours before serving, I can take my time grilling and arranging the colorful vegetables before I need to socialize and supervise the fire. It never ceases to get a rousing reception, and everyone is amazed at how good the grilled seasoned veggies taste. The robust sauce is made up of classic Italian ingredients. Brushed onto warm grilled vegetables, it makes them "sing" with flavor, thus the name. If you have leftover veggies, save them to toss with hot pasta and the extra sauce to make Antipasto Pasta (page 312).

Makes 6 to 8 servings

Grilling Method: Direct/Medium Heat

Soprano Sauce
- 6 anchovy fillets, drained and finely minced
- 4 cloves garlic, finely minced
- 1 tablespoon capers, drained and coarsely chopped
- 2/3 cup extra-virgin olive oil, preferably Tuscan
  Grains of paradise or white pepper

Vegetable Antipasto
- 3 small sweet potatoes, peeled and cut into long 1/2-inch wedges
- 1 pound asparagus, trimmed
- 1 bulb fennel, cut in quarters
- 4 medium zucchini, each cut into 4 long slices
- 2 small radicchio, cut into quarters
- 1 large eggplant, cut into 1/2-inch rounds
- 4 small bunches green onions, trimmed
- 2 pints small, ripe, cherry tomatoes
  Olive oil
  Kosher salt

1. Make the sauce: Combine the anchovies, garlic, and capers in a small bowl. Slowly whisk in the olive oil and season with grains of paradise or pepper, if desired. Set aside.
2. Build a charcoal fire or preheat a gas grill. Lightly coat the vegetables with olive oil using the "plastic bag trick" (see page 201). Sprinkle lightly with salt.

3. Lay the vegetables one by one (except for the tomatoes) on the cooking grate over direct medium heat. (You may need to do this in batches so the grill is not crowded.) Cover and grill 5 to 9 minutes, turning once halfway through the grilling time.
4. As soon as each vegetable is done, remove it from the grill and transfer it to a platter. The zucchini, radicchio, and green onions should be done first; the eggplant will take a little longer, and the sweet potatoes and fennel will be the last to cook through.
5. While they are still hot, brush the vegetables liberally with the sauce so it is absorbed.
6. When all the other vegetables are done, place the tomatoes on the cooking grate to mark and warm them through, about 2 minutes. Place them on the platter with the other vegetables and brush with the soprano sauce. Serve at room temperature with extra sauce on the side.

Grilled Ratatouille

The first time I visited the South of France, I fell in love with this medley of eggplants, zucchini, tomatoes, and bell peppers. It is best in the late summer, when the vegetables are fresh-picked and at the height of their flavor. I've created a grilled version, which is even better the day after it is made. Serve it with grilled fish, chicken, or even tossed with hot pasta.

Makes 6 to 10 servings

Grilling Method: Combo/Medium Heat
Special Equipment: Aluminum drip pan or Dutch oven

- 2 large eggplants, cut in 3/4-inch rounds
- 3 zucchini, cut in half lengthwise
- 1 pound purple or red onions, quartered
- 3 large red bell peppers, sliced in 1-inch strips
  Olive oil
  Kosher salt
- 1 head garlic, roasted (page 207)
- 2 tablespoons herbes de Provence, divided
- 6 large tomatoes, cut in quarters
- 1 16-ounce can crushed tomatoes
  Freshly ground pepper
  Red wine vinegar

1. Build a charcoal fire or preheat a gas grill.
2. Brush the eggplants, zucchini, onions, and peppers with olive oil and sprinkle with salt. Set aside.
3. Place the vegetables on the cooking grate over direct medium heat, cover, and grill until crisp-tender, 15 to 20 minutes, turning once halfway through the cooking time, until soft and tender. Be careful not to overcook—you want the slices to maintain their shape. Remove each vegetable from the grill as it is finished.
4. In an aluminum drip pan or Dutch oven, coat the bottom with olive oil. Layer the drip pan with the grilled vegetables: first a layer of eggplant, then zucchini, then onion, then peppers, and then a layer of the garlic that has been squeezed from the skin. Sprinkle with half of the herbes de Provence. Repeat the layers until all of the vegetables have been used. To the top, add the fresh tomatoes, the crushed tomatoes and remaining herbes de Provence, season with salt and pepper to taste.
5. Place the pan on the grill over indirect medium heat, cover, and cook, stirring occasionally, until the juices have almost completely evaporated and the recipe looks like a vegetable stew, about 20 minutes. When done and still very hot, stir in several tablespoons of olive oil and red wine vinegar to finish the ratatouille. Let it cook for 5 more minutes, and remove from the grill. Serve hot, room temperature, or cold.

Fire-Roasted Succotash

Lima beans are like okra—there are people who love them and people who can't bear the sight of them! I love them, as well as okra. In the summer, I love combining them with charred corn and simmering them with cream in the traditional succotash style. When company is coming, I fancy it up a bit by adding a cup of cherry tomatoes cut in half and a chiffonade of basil. If you are phobic about lima beans, but like the idea of the recipe, substitute edamame (fresh soybeans) for a new-age succotash.

Makes 4 to 6 servings

Grilling Method: Direct/Medium Heat

- 8 ears fresh, white corn, shucked
  Olive oil
- 3 cups lima beans (fresh or frozen), cooked until tender

$\frac{1}{2}$ cup water
$\frac{1}{2}$ cup heavy (whipping) cream
4 tablespoons ($\frac{1}{2}$ stick) unsalted butter, optional
Pinch nutmeg
Kosher salt
Freshly ground pepper

1. Build a charcoal fire or preheat a gas grill.
2. Brush the corn all over with olive oil. Season it with kosher salt and place it on the cooking grate over direct medium heat. Cover and grill for 6 to 10 minutes, turning occasionally, until all sides are slightly charred.
3. Remove the corn from the grill and cut the kernels off the corn. Put the corn in a heavy-bottomed saucepan and add the lima beans, water, cream, and butter, if using. Bring to boil, reduce the heat, and simmer, uncovered, for 3 to 5 minutes. Season with nutmeg, salt, and pepper and simmer for about 5 more minutes. Serve immediately.

Tofu Kabobs with Summer Vegetables

These tofu kabobs are healthy and they taste great. I've used flavored tofu, which eliminates the need to marinate it. This recipe calls for Italian-flavored tofu, but feel free to choose whichever one suits your mood. If you prefer an Asian flavor to the Mediterranean one here, substitute soy sauce for the vinegar and add a touch of toasted sesame oil to the olive oil.

Makes 6 servings

Grilling Method: Direct/Medium Heat

- 1 pound Italian-flavored firm tofu, cut into 2-inch cubes
- 12 whole white mushrooms
- 1 large red bell pepper, cut into 2-inch squares
- 1 zucchini, cut into 1-inch rounds
- 1 yellow squash, cut into 1-inch rounds
- $\frac{1}{2}$ cup olive oil
  Kosher salt
  Freshly ground pepper
- $\frac{1}{4}$ cup balsamic vinegar
- 1 pint large cherry tomatoes
- 12 long bamboo skewers, soaked in water for 30 minutes

1. Build a charcoal fire or preheat a gas grill.
2. Place the tofu and all the vegetables except the tomatoes in a nonreactive bowl. Toss them with olive oil and season with salt and pepper. Add the vinegar and toss to coat well.
3. Thread the tofu and vegetables onto the soaked skewers, using the double skewer method (see page 28). End each skewer with a cherry tomato at the pointed end.
4. Place the skewers in the center of the cooking grate over direct medium heat. Cover and grill 4 to 5 minutes per side. Cook until the vegetables and tofu are browned, tender, and warmed through.
5. Serve with a drizzle of olive oil and a sprinkle of salt and pepper, if desired.

Grilled Baby Vegetables with Basil

The delicate taste and texture of baby vegetables is one of the true joys of garden-fresh produce. Look for these tender miniatures at roadside stands or any of the growing number of farmer's markets around the country. Once they are on the grill, watch these young veggies carefully—they cook much faster than their older, tougher siblings—something we can all understand!

Makes 4 to 6 servings

Grilling Method: Direct/Medium Heat

8	baby pattypan squash, whole
8	baby eggplant, halved lengthwise
8	baby summer squash or zucchini, halved
16	small mushrooms, cleaned and trimmed
1/2	cup extra-virgin olive oil, plus more for vegetables
	Kosher salt
4	cloves garlic, minced
1	tablespoon lemon zest (about 2 lemons)
	Freshly ground pepper
	Fleur de sel
1	bunch fresh basil, cut into chiffonade (see Tip, page 230)

1. Build a charcoal fire or preheat a gas grill.
2. In a large bowl, toss the vegetables with olive oil. Season lightly with kosher salt. Set aside.

3. Whisk together the olive oil, garlic, lemon zest, and pepper to taste. Set aside. Place the vegetables in the center of the cooking grate over direct medium heat, cover, and grill 6 to 8 minutes, turning once halfway through the grilling time. They are done when they are crisp-tender and well marked.
4. Transfer the warm grilled vegetables to a serving bowl and toss with seasoned olive oil. Sprinkle with fleur de sel and the basil. Serve warm or at room temperature.

Bananas for Grilled Bananas

I first grilled bananas at a barbecue contest when, looking for something besides pork to eat, I spied my forgotten breakfast banana. I was living in New Orleans and had a love-hate relationship with the butter and sugar-soaked, sautéed Bananas Foster. I loved the flavor but hated the mess and the absurd amounts of sugar and butter—aka calories—that are associated with the classic preparation. Well, hallelujah, grilled bananas to the rescue! Exploding with flavor, these cinnamon-spiced bananas taste every bit as good as the original, with all the sweetness coming from the fruit itself—slimmed down by the grill.

Makes 4 servings

Grilling Method: Direct/Medium-Low Heat

2	bananas (not too ripe)
2	tablespoons sugar
2	teaspoons ground cinnamon
2	tablespoons honey

1. Build a charcoal fire or preheat a gas grill.
2. Slice the bananas, in their skins, in half crosswise and then lengthwise so each banana yields 4 pieces. Set aside on a clean platter. In a small bowl, combine the sugar and cinnamon. Drizzle the honey on the cut sides of the bananas and sprinkle them with the cinnamon sugar. Let the bananas sit for 5 minutes.
3. Place the bananas, cut-side down, on the center of a clean cooking grate and cover. Grill for 2 minutes or until grill marks appear. Using a pair of long-handled tongs, turn them over and cook

5 more minutes, or until the skin pulls away from the bananas.

4. Remove the bananas from the grill and serve them immediately.

N'awlins Variation: Serve grilled bananas on top of vanilla ice cream and drizzle with bourbon or a liqueur such as Frangelico.

Cantaloupe with Prosciutto and Extra-Virgin Olive Oil

Melon and prosciutto is a classic combination. Unlike most classics, which shouldn't be tinkered with, grilling the melon improves the flavor of this dish immeasurably. The heat of the grill brings out the natural sugars of the fruit, and it is a great way to give less-than-perfect produce a burst of flavor. I first hit upon this idea when the melon I purchased for a dinner party turned out to be tasteless. Grilling the melon saved my appetizer and was so much better than cold melon that now I grill it even if my melon is vine ripe. Once again, the grill comes to the rescue!

Makes 6 servings

Grilling Method: Direct/Medium-Low

1   cantaloupe melon
    Olive oil
12 thinly sliced pieces prosciutto
    Extra-virgin olive oil
    Fleur de sel or coarse sea salt

1. Build a charcoal fire or preheat a gas grill.
2. Wash and dry the cantaloupe, cut it in half, and scoop out the seeds. Cut each half into thirds, leaving the rind on the melon. The wedges will look like half-moons and should be about 2 inches thick. Brush each piece lightly with olive oil.
3. Place the melon on the cooking grate over direct medium-low heat, cover, and grill for 6 to 10 minutes or until marked and warmed through. Turn once halfway through the cooking time.
4. Remove the melon from the grill and set aside on a clean platter. While the melon is still warm, wrap 2 slices of prosciutto around each wedge of melon. Drizzle with extra-virgin olive oil and sprinkle with fleur de sel. Serve immediately.

Grilled Figs with Candied Ginger, Lemon, and Honey

A few years ago, I was in Los Angeles with my friend and collaborator, John Lineweaver. Figs were at the height of their season—ripe to bursting, and I couldn't resist buying every variety I could find.

After we had our fill of them raw, I grilled the figs with a touch of crystallized ginger, honey, and lemon juice. The sharp-sweet flavors complement the delicate quality of the figs without overwhelming it. These grilled figs were the culinary highlight of the week and as pretty as a picture. If you live near a Trader Joe's store, you can buy a jar of pureed candied ginger, making this recipe even easier. These can also be served on top of slices of pound cake, grilled or not, or over best-quality vanilla ice cream.

Makes 4 servings

Grilling Method: Direct/Low Heat

8   large, ripe, fresh figs
¼   cup candied ginger (also called crystallized ginger)
¼   cup fresh lemon juice
¼   cup honey
¼   large lemon, zested
    Pinch sea salt
4   lemon wedges

1. Wash and dry the figs, and set aside. Meanwhile, heat the candied ginger, lemon juice, and honey in a saucepan over medium-low heat until soft and warm but not bubbling. While the mixture is still hot, puree it in a traditional blender or by using a hand immersion blender or food processor. Add the lemon zest and a pinch of sea salt. Adjust the seasonings to taste, adding more honey if the ginger is too sharp. Set aside to cool.
2. Build a charcoal fire or preheat a gas grill.
3. Cut the figs in half and squirt the cut sides with a lemon wedge. Using a teaspoon, dollop a small amount of the ginger puree on top of each fig. Place the figs, skin-side down, on the cooking grate over direct low heat, cover, and grill until warmed through and lightly marked, about 5 minute.
4. Serve warm with extra sauce on the side.

Prosciutto-Wrapped Figs with Walnuts and Saga Blue Cheese

This recipe was created during the late summer fig season for my fellow fig-crazy grill friend, Mary Burnham. We have spent many a night waxing poetic about the virtues of figs. Because it is sometimes hard to find fresh figs, I created this recipe to work equally well with dried figs, making it a great year-round grilled appetizer. If using fresh figs, make sure they are somewhat firm and not too ripe.

Makes 12 servings

Grilling Method: Direct/Medium Heat

12 round wooden toothpicks, not flat
12 large black Mission figs, fresh or dried
12 walnut halves (not pieces), toasted
4   ounces Saga blue cheese
6   thin slices prosciutto, cut in half lengthwise
1   bunch hearty fresh herbs, such as lemon verbena or rosemary, optional

1. Soak the toothpicks and the herbs (if using) in water for 30 minutes.
2. Build a charcoal fire or preheat a gas grill.
3. Discard the stems from the figs and cut an x through the top of each, almost to the base, so that you can see the center of the fruit. Set aside.
4. Place the walnuts on waxed paper and wrap a generous portion of Saga around each walnut. Place a walnut-cheese nugget gently in the center of each fig. Carefully push the figs back together and wrap each in a slice of prosciutto. Secure with a toothpick.
5. If using herbs, place them on the cooking grate. Position the figs on top of the herbs—or on the cooking grate—over direct medium heat, cover, and grill, turning occasionally, until the edges of the prosciutto begin to curl and the figs are hot throughout, 5 to 7 minutes. Serve the figs hot or warm.

TIP: In this recipe, I offer grilling on a bed of herbs as an option (see page 246). If using fresh figs, it is an ideal way to protect the delicate figs from the direct heat while infusing the food with a delicate herb flavor. I am particularly fond of rosemary and lemon verbena for this recipe—but any hearty herb that you like will do.

White Peaches Marinated in Balsamic Syrup

We associate balsamic vinegar with lettuce and salad dressing, but it has a natural affinity for fruit, especially stone fruit. I like making this recipe with peak-of-the-season white peaches or nectarines because the sweet balsamic marinade tints the fruit the prettiest shade of pink

Makes 4 servings

Grilling Method: Direct/Medium Heat

4   firm white peaches or nectarines, or other stone fruit
1   lemon, juiced
1   cup balsamic vinegar
1   cup water
½   cup sugar
1   navel orange, zested
     Pinch sea salt

1. Cut the fruit in half and remove the pits. Brush with the lemon juice and set aside.
2. Mix the vinegar, water, sugar, and orange zest in a small saucepan. Simmer over low heat, stirring occasionally, until the sugar is melted. Add a pinch of salt and take it off the heat. Let the mixture cool to room temperature.
3. Build a charcoal fire or preheat a gas grill.
4. Pour the vinegar-sugar liquid over the stone fruit and let it sit for 10 minutes, turning occasionally to submerge all cut sides in the marinade. Remove the fruit from the liquid. Reserve the marinade in a small saucepan. Simmer over medium-low heat until the liquid is reduced by half, about 20 minutes. Set aside.
5. Place the fruit, cut-side down, on the cooking grate over direct medium heat, cover, and grill for 2 to 3 minutes or until marked. Turn it over and grill for 5 to 7 more minutes or until warmed through and the skin begins to peel away from the fruit.
6. Remove the fruit from the grill and place it back into the marinade. Marinate it for at least 5 minutes. Serve warm or cold with a drizzle of the reduced marinade.

Grilled Pears with Stilton Cheese

When serving fresh pears, less is always more. A bit of the best English Stilton or other sharp blue cheese and a lightly toasted walnut half is all you need for a satisfying appetizer that truly excites the appetite instead of squelching it! This recipe also makes a great light dessert or cheese course. If your pear is not ripe, grill it for a few minutes to bring out the flavor; if it is perfectly ripe, skip the grilling and enjoy that rare experience!

Makes 4 to 6 servings

Grilling Method: Direct/Medium-Low Heat

- 4   firm but ripe pears, well washed
     Walnut oil
- 8   ounces best-quality Stilton or Saga blue cheese
- $^1/_2$ cup walnut halves, toasted

1. Build a charcoal fire or preheat a gas grill.
2. Using an apple corer or a knife, remove the seeds from the pears. Cut them in half and then again in $^1/_2$-inch slices. Coat each piece with walnut oil.
3. Place the pear slices on the cooking grate over direct medium-low heat, cover, and grill for about 3 minutes on each side, or until warmed through and marked.
4. Meanwhile, take the Stilton from the refrigerator and while it is still is very cold, cut thin slices with a vegetable peeler. If doing this in advance, cover and refrigerate the slices until time to serve.
5. Remove the pears from the grill. While they are still hot, put 1 to 2 slices of cheese on top of each pear. Garnish with a toasted walnut half and serve at room temperature.

Chinese New Year Pineapple Rings

Pineapple is one of those fruits that can fit into either a sweet or savory recipe, depending on the marinade or seasonings. This recipe's savory Asian flavors set off fireworks when served with grilled meat or fish. Because the marinade is so versatile, it can be doubled and used to marinate chicken, pork, and other fish at the same time as the pineapple. If you want to turn the marinade into a serving sauce, bring it to a gentle boil for three minutes while the meat and fruit are grilling.

Makes 4 servings

Grilling Method: Indirect/Medium Heat
Special equipment: Vacu Vin Pineapple Slicer and Instant Marinater, optional

- 1   fresh pineapple, sliced in rings
- 2   green onions, finely chopped
- $^1/_4$ cup toasted sesame oil
- 3   tablespoons low-sodium soy sauce
- 1   knob (1 to 2 inches) fresh ginger, grated
- 3   limes, 2 juiced, 1 cut into wedges
- 1   tablespoon maple syrup or brown sugar
     Pinch Chinese five-spice powder

1. Put the pineapple slices in a nonreactive bowl or the bottom of the instant marinater. Mix the onions, sesame oil, soy sauce, ginger, lime juice, maple syrup, and five-spice powder in a small bowl to make the marinade.
2. Pour the marinade over the pineapple, tossing gently to make sure all the surfaces are coated with marinade. Cover and refrigerate for 30 minutes.
3. When ready to grill, build a charcoal fire or preheat a gas grill.
4. Shake the excess marinade off the pineapple rings but do not dry them. You want as much marinade as possible to cling to the fruit. Place the rings on the cooking grate over indirect medium heat, cover, and grill for about 6 minutes on each side. The pineapple should be tender, well-marked, and warmed through. Serve or use as directed in a recipe.

Tropical Fruit Kabobs

Using tropical fruits and a dark rum, passion fruit, honey, and lime marinade evokes lazy days in the islands. I may only be going out my back door, but these grilled fruit kabobs take me a million miles away—at least in my mind! Feel free to substitute any fruit that is in season, providing it is big enough to fit on a skewer. Add a paper umbrella for good measure!

Makes 6 servings

Grilling Method: Direct/Low Heat

Kabobs
  2 mangos, slightly underripe and firm, cut into 2-inch cubes
  1 pineapple, ripe but firm, cut into 2-inch cubes
  2 pints firm strawberries
 12 bamboo skewers, soaked in water for 30 minutes
  1 teaspoon ground cinnamon
  1 teaspoon sugar
 $^1/_2$ teaspoon each ground nutmeg and cloves

Marinade
 $^1/_2$ cup dark rum
 $^1/_2$ cup fruit juice blend of orange, pineapple, and passion fruit
 $^1/_4$ cup honey
  2 tablespoons brown sugar
  1 lime, juiced

1. Make the kabobs. Thread the fruit onto the bamboo skewers, alternating fruits, using the ladder method of double skewering (see page 28). Combine the sugar and spices and sprinkle them over the kabobs.
2. Make the marinade: Combine all the ingredients and whisk until completely incorporated; reserve.
3. Build a charcoal fire or preheat a gas grill. Thirty minutes before serving, marinate the kabobs.
4. Remove the kabobs from the marinade and place them in the center of the cooking grate over direct low heat. Cover and grill, turning once halfway through the grilling time, until marked and the fruit is warmed through, no more than 5 minutes. Serve immediately.

Brandied Fruit Kabobs with French Cheese Plate

This dessert is almost as easy as putting together a plate of dried fruits, nuts, and cheese, but the flavor is ten times better! You can steep the fruit up to two days in advance, storing it in the steeping juices in the refrigerator. Assemble in advance and grill just before serving. Splurge and buy the best cheese possible, and remember to bring the cheese to room temperature before serving. This makes an elegant appetizer served with brandy, port, or ice-cold sparkling wine.

Makes 6 servings

Grilling Method: Direct/Medium Heat

 12 pitted dried plums (prunes)
 12 dried Mission figs
  6 large dried pears, cut in half
 12 pitted dried whole apricots
 $^1/_2$ cup brandy
 $^1/_2$ cup fresh orange juice
 $^1/_2$ cup water
 $^1/_2$ cup walnuts, toasted
  3 8-ounce pieces French cheese, such as Brie, Explorateur, Boursault, Chevre, Coulommiers, etc.
     Pinch salt
 12 bamboo skewers, soaked in water for 30 minutes

1. Place the fruits in a small, heavy-bottomed saucepan. Pour in the brandy, orange juice, and water. Simmer over low heat for about 20 minutes, or until the fruits are plump and rehydrated. Let them cool.
2. When cool, remove the fruits from the liquid and thread them on the bamboo skewers, using the ladder method of double skewering (see page 28).
3. Place the skewers on the cooking grate over direct medium heat, cover, and grill for 2 to 3 minutes, or until the fruits are marked and warmed through.
4. Serve immediately with the walnuts and cheese.

Pizza

Pizza 101

Rapid-Fire Checklist

✓ Preheat grill
✓ Roll or press out dough to ¼ inch uniform thickness (organic shapes are encouraged)
✓ Brush dough on both sides with olive oil
✓ Reduce heat to direct medium heat (325°F to 375°F)
✓ Place dough on cooking grate
✓ Grill first side of pizza
✓ Remove crust from grill with a pizza peel
✓ Switch to indirect medium heat
✓ Top cooked side of crust with sauce and toppings
✓ Place on grill and cook until cheese is melted, crust is crisp, and all toppings are hot
✓ Remove pizza from grill with tongs and a pizza peel
✓ Cut with pizza cutter, kitchen scissors, or chef's knife
✓ Serve immediately

Tools of the Trade

• Pizza peel (or flat cookie sheet)
• Small, shallow bowls
• Silicone or natural-bristle brush
• 12-inch locking chef tongs
• Tray or sheet pan
• Heavy-duty oven mitt
• Rolling pin (or a clean wine bottle), optional
• Pizza wheel or cutter, kitchen scissors, or a large knife

Common Problems

• Undercooked crust
• Burnt crust
• Fire is too hot
• Cheese won't melt
• Toppings are cold
• Uncooked toppings don't cook during grilling

Flatbreads are as old as fire itself. Mixing a grain that has been milled for flour, with water, salt, and yeast and then cooking it with the heat of a fire is an ancient and worldwide tradition. Adding cheese to that process, thus making the ancestor of pizza, was a transcendant development.

Pizza is at the top of the list of my favorite foods, and a great pizza would be my choice for a last meal. I have a weakness for pizzas with deeply caramelized, blistered bottoms that taste faintly of smoke. And you will be amazed at how easy it is to get this effect with grilled pizza.

Pizza is best when made with a super-hot oven, and the grill can simulate the heat and smokiness of a pizza oven better than an indoor oven. It may just be the best pizza you've ever eaten. Grilling pizza is easy and, with a little advance planning, can be done before Domino's can deliver—guaranteed.

Make Your Pizza Grill-Ready

Size Matters: Your ball of dough should resemble the size of a softball, about four inches in diameter but not much more; the larger the ball of dough, the harder it is to work with. This will yield one medium-size individual pizza (about a 12 x 8-inch rectangle or 12-inch circle)—enough for four people as an appetizer.

Room Temperature: Dough should be taken out of the refrigerator one hour before use and allowed to "relax" and come to room temperature. Bringing the dough to room temperature literally relaxes the dough, making it easier to work with. When it is cold, it resists being rolled out. Frozen dough needs two hours to thaw in the refrigerator in addition to the one hour needed to come to room temperature.

Rolling in Dough: Turn the dough out onto a clean work surface and flatten it with the palm of your hand. Sprinkle the work surface with either flour or cornmeal. This will prevent the dough from sticking. I prefer cornmeal because it will give a coarser, more "rustic" texture to the pizza. Roll out with a rolling pin, clean wine bottle (or other similarly shaped bottle), or use my preferred method of pulling and stretching the dough gently into either a rectangle or circle. It will have an irregular, organic shape, and that is the beauty of it. There is no need to try and make a perfect shape.

Thin Is in: Make the dough as thin as possible so you can ensure that the crust will cook all the way through and become crisp. The dough will rise and thicken when it cooks.

Keep It Soft and Supple: When not working with or cooking the dough, keep it covered or lightly coated with olive oil or the exterior will dry out and crack.

Get Saucy: If you are just starting out, stick with tomato sauce. Beyond that, anything spreadable is fair game for a sauce. I like to use pesto, tapenade, pureed vegetables such as mushrooms, artichokes, and peppers—or a combination of vegetables—in addition to traditional tomato sauce. Think of it as a hot open-face sandwich and that will make almost any condiment fair game, including barbecue and Thai peanut sauces.

Toppings: Precook any toppings that need to be cooked through before placing them on the cooked side of the dough. The high heat of the grill cooks the crust so quickly that there isn't enough time for raw toppings to cook. Per the grilling rule of thumb, use Direct Heat for any toppings that need to be pre-grilled and cook in under 20 minutes. For precooked toppings that take longer than 20 minutes, use Indirect Heat.

Breaking it Down

Grilled pizzas cook in less than 20 minutes. With any short cooking ti3me, you must be well organized and have everything prepared in advance. Keep your "mess in place" and remember what you need to do for the four key pizza components: dough, sauce, toppings, and cheese.

Dough Options

Homemade pizza dough is sure to impress, and it's as easy to make as, well, pie. But if you don't have time to make dough from scratch, there are other options that will yield a delicious pizza with a crisp, chewy crust. Choose the option that suits your taste and time requirements.

Homemade Dough: See the recipes (pages 227–229)

Fresh Dough: From a local pizza restaurant

Frozen Pizza Bread Dough: From a grocery store or Italian specialty shop

Refrigerated Pizza Dough: From the grocery store

Prebaked Pizza Crusts: From the grocery store; pita bread and flour tortillas will also work

Grill Ready

After you've preheated your grill, use the checklist below to make sure you have everything you need within arm's reach.

- Olive oil
- Basting brush
- 12-inch locking chef tongs
- Pizza peel with rolled out, oiled, and cornmeal-dusted dough on it
- Sauce, toppings, and cheese in individual bowls or on a plate, side by side
- Clean platter or pizza peel to serve on

Gas Versus Charcoal

Both charcoal and gas grills are well suited to making grilled pizza. The first time I ever ate the life-altering pizza from Al Forno in Providence, RI, it was at a special event, and they grilled the pizzas on huge charcoal grills. But given the option, I find that gas grills are easier to use because they provide a more consistent heat and better control of the temperature. Choose the grill that fits your lifestyle—if you are a die-hard charcoal fan, go ahead and grill your pizzas on charcoal. Don't forget that gas grills must be preheated for 10 to 15 minutes, and that it takes up to 30 minutes for charcoal briquettes to be covered with white-gray ash—the signal that the coals are ready for cooking.

On the Fire: Direct or Indirect Heat

The difference between direct and indirect cooking is that with direct, the food is cooked directly over the heat source. Indirect cooking means the food is cooked away from the heat source, the gas burner under the food is turned off, or the gray-ashed briquettes are pushed to either side of the food. In the case of grilled pizza, we combine both methods to get the best results.

Combo Method is the Key to Perfect Grilled Pizza

Use Direct Heat to cook the first side of your pizza crust. To finish the pizza, move it to Indirect Heat, which will allow the crust to brown and crisp and cook through slowly as the cheese melts.

For charcoal grillers, light your charcoal briquettes as usual. When they are covered with a white-gray ash, pile the charcoal on one side of the grill. This will let you cook the first side of the crust over direct heat and finish it off on the side of the grill with indirect heat. Pizza is the only food for which I recommend piling the briquettes on only one side of the grill. For all other foods, they will cook better if you make two equal piles on either side of the grill, separated by a drip pan.

If cooking on gas, it is as simple as turning one of the burners off to finish the pizza on Indirect Heat.

Cooking the Crust

This is probably the most important part of grilling pizza. Contrary to popular belief, the dough will not fall through the grates when you slip it onto hot cooking grates, but you must close the lid as soon as possible. The residual heat in the cooking box and the Direct Heat will make the crust rise, and the quicker you can put the crust on the grill and close the lid, the lighter and crisper your pizza will be.

Once you've grilled one side of your crust, you will take it off the grill, close the lid, and finish the pizza. Brush both sides with olive oil, and put the crust back on the cooking grate over indirect heat, with the grilled side face up. Add the toppings, cover, and grill until the cheese is melted and the bottom of the crust is brown and crisp. You should be able to tell if it is cooked through by looking at it—the crust will be golden brown and look a little dry, like a cracker. If the fire is too hot, the crust will burn on the outside and stay raw on the inside. If the heat is medium-low and the crust is still pale and white, then it is likely to be undercooked. Be patient: Finish the pizza over Indirect Heat and wait until it is golden brown and the cheese is melted and bubbly. See Grilled Pizza 101 (pages 228–229).

Slicing the Pie

Choose a pizza wheel that is sharp enough to make a quick, clean cut and that has a heavy and compact handle. The extra weight will help do the work for you, so you won't have to apply as much pressure when you cut the pizza. If you don't have a pizza wheel, a pair of sharp kitchen scissors does a great job, as does a large chef's knife held on both sides to "chop" the pizza in pieces, instead of cutting.

Pizza Dough 101, by Hand

To make the dough a little heartier, use a combination of whole wheat and white flour. The best ratio is 25 percent whole-grain flour and 75 percent all-purpose flour. If you use too much whole-grain flour, the crust will be leaden, not light and airy.

Makes 4 individual pizzas

- 1 cup lukewarm water (about 100°F)
- ¼ cup olive oil
- 1 teaspoon sugar or honey
- 1 envelope (2½ teaspoons) active dry yeast
- 3 cups unbleached all-purpose flour, plus extra as needed
- ¼ teaspoon kosher salt

1. Place the lukewarm water, oil, and sugar in a large mixing bowl, sprinkle the yeast on top, and let it sit until foamy, about 5 minutes.
2. Combine the flour and salt in a large bowl. Add it to the bowl with the water, ½ cup at a time, until well incorporated. If the dough is very sticky, add extra flour, 1 tablespoon at a time, and mix again, until the dough is soft and slightly sticky. Mix well until the dough feels elastic.
3. Turn the dough out onto a well-floured surface. Knead for 10 minutes, or until smooth and easy to work with, adding extra flour to your work surface as necessary to prevent the dough from sticking. Place the dough in a large, clean bowl that has been coated with olive oil. Cover tightly with plastic wrap, and let it rise in a warm spot until it more than doubles in volume, about 1 hour. Punch the dough down and knead it on a lightly floured surface for several minutes or until smooth.
4. Divide the dough into four 4-inch balls and proceed with pizza-making instructions. The dough may be made ahead, wrapped in plastic wrap, and placed inside a resealable plastic bag. Freeze until needed, up to 3 month, and thaw at room temperature.

Pizza Dough 101, by Machine

This recipe is so fast that you can whir it together as soon as you come in the door. By the time you listen to your phone messages or change your clothes, you'll be able to roll out the dough and eat your pizza in 30 minutes from start to finish. The rapid-rise yeast and the extra sugar in this method insure that the dough rises quickly. This method can also be done in a stand mixer with a dough hook attachment.

Makes 4 individual pizzas

1	cup lukewarm water (about 100°F)
¼	cup olive oil
1½	teaspoons sugar or honey
1	envelope (2½ teaspoons) rapid-rise yeast
3	cups bread flour or all-purpose flour, plus extra as needed
1½	teaspoons kosher salt

1. Preheat the oven to 150°F or the lowest setting. When it reaches temperature, turn off the oven. Pour the water into the work bowl of a large food processor. Sprinkle the oil, sugar, and yeast over the water and pulse several times until mixed. Add the flour and salt and process until the mixture comes together. The dough should be soft and slightly sticky. If it is very sticky, add flour 1 tablespoon at a time, and pulse briefly. If it is still too stiff, add 1 table-spoon of water and pulse briefly. Process another 30 seconds.

2. Turn the dough onto a lightly floured work sur-face; knead it by hand to form a smooth, round ball. Put the dough into a large, clean bowl that has been coated with olive oil and cover tightly with plastic wrap. Let it rise for 15 minutes in the oven before proceeding. Remove the dough from the oven, punch it down, and turn it out onto a lightly floured work surface.

3. Divide the dough into four 4-inch balls and proceed with pizza-making instructions. The dough may be made ahead, wrapped in plastic wrap, and placed inside a resealable plastic bag. Freeze until needed, up to 3 months, and thaw at room temperature.

Grilled Pizza 101

This recipe is really a detailed version of the Rapid-Fire Checklist at the beginning of this chapter. I add explanations here that should address your questions if you haven't grilled pizza before. In the other pizza recipes, I left out the extra details and focused on the flavors.

In these directions, I oil the crust a second time, which will makes a crispier crust. But it is not essential to making grilled pizza; it's good either way. After you make pizza once or twice, you'll master the technique, realize how easy it is, and want to make it all the time. Young children love to help make grilled pizza, and it makes a great theme for a birthday party!

Makes 2 to 4 servings

Grilling Method: Combo/Medium Heat

¼	cup cornmeal or all-purpose flour
1	4-inch ball prepared pizza dough, at room temperature
	Olive oil, about 3 tablespoons
½	cup tomato sauce or other sauce
	Toppings and cheese
	Sea salt
	Freshly ground pepper

1. Preheat the grill and set to medium direct heat. Make sure your grill is not too hot, or your dough will burn immediately. Foolproof method: Preheat all the burners on high and when the temperature reaches 550°F, reduce the temperature to medi-um and wait for about 5 minutes or lift the lid for a minute to quicken the process.

2. Brush both sides of the dough with olive oil.

3. Pick up the dough by the top 2 edges (like hanging a wet towel on the clothesline) and gently place it flat

on the grill by laying down the bottom edges first and ending with the top edges that you are holding.

4. Close the lid. Cook the dough over medium direct heat for 2 to 4 minutes, or until the bottom side is well marked and brown. The dough may bubble—a sign that it is cooking. If you don't like the bubbles, poke a hole in the top of the bubble with tongs to release the air and flatten the crust.

5. When the bottom is brown, slide the edge of a pizza peel under the bottom of the crust. Ease the whole peel under the pizza and remove it from the grill. Remember to close the lid on the grill.

6. Reset the grill to indirect medium heat. Keep the crust on the peel and brush the top, ungrilled side, with olive oil. Flip the dough over and brush that side with oil. Cover the grilled side with toppings and cheese.

7. Put the pizza back on the grill over indirect heat, close the lid, and cook for 5 to 10 minutes, or until the bottom is cooked through and browned. The cheese should be melted and the toppings warmed through.

8. Remove the pizza from the grill with the pizza peel. Slice and serve immediately.

TIP: If your gas grill has only one burner, grill the second side with toppings for 2 to 3 more minutes over direct heat, turn off the burner, and finish using residual heat. Do not lift the lid.

GREAT CHEESE=GREAT PIZZA

When purchasing cheese for pizza, look for the best quality. There are lots of great cheese producers in the United States who are making cheese in the European tradition. However, I find that Parmigiano-Reggiano imported from Italy is the best parmesan cheese. But almost any other cheese can be substituted. Just remember that you get what you pay for. And a great pizza is only the sum of great parts. For maximum flavor, grate cheese just before using. (Don't use pregrated cheeses, if you can help it. They are treated with preservatives to extend their shelf life and to prevent clumping, and they don't melt as well.)

Upside-Down Margherita

I love this pizza because it is delicious in its simplicity. The ingredients are the traditional tomato, cheese, and basil, but the technique is upside-down—thus the name. Putting the cheese on first and then topping with the tomatoes ensures that the cheese will be melted and bubbly since it is closest to the crust and thus closest to the heat. Top with lots of fresh basil just before serving.

Makes 2 to 4 servings

Grilling Method: Combo/Medium Heat

- ¼ cup cornmeal or all-purpose flour
- 1 4-inch ball prepared pizza dough, at room temperature
  Olive oil, about 3 tablespoons
- ½ cup tomato sauce or crushed canned tomatoes
- ½ cup grated Parmigiano-Reggiano cheese
- ½ cup grated mozzarella cheese
  Whole fresh basil leaves, cleaned and dried
  Sea salt
  Freshly ground pepper

1. Build a charcoal fire or preheat a gas grill.
2. Lightly sprinkle a work surface with cornmeal or flour. Place the dough in the middle of the work surface. Roll or stretch it gently into a 12-inch rectangle or circle, $\frac{1}{4}$ inch thick. Brush both sides with olive oil and set it aside until ready to grill.
3. Pick up the dough by the corners and lay it gently onto the center of the cooking grate over direct medium heat. Close the lid as quickly as possible. Grill for 2 to 4 minutes, until the bottom of the crust is well marked and browned.
4. Remove the dough from the grill and sprinkle it on the cooked side of the crust with parmesan and mozzarella cheeses. Top with dollops of tomato sauce or crushed tomatoes and spread with the back of a spoon.
5. Switch to indirect heat. Return the pizza to the center of the cooking grate and cook with the lid closed until the bottom is well browned, the toppings are warm, and the cheese is bubbly, 5 to 10 minutes.
6. Meanwhile, stack the basil leaves on top of each other and roll them up so they look like a cigar. Cut across the rolled leaves to create ribbon-like pieces (chiffonade). Do not do this in advance or the basil will turn black.
7. Remove the pizza from the grill, sprinkle it with basil chiffonade, and season with salt and pepper to taste. Slice and serve immediately.

TIP: Chiffonade refers to making strips, shreds—or ribbons, as I call them—of herbs or tender greens. You can do this with a knife or kitchen scissors: Roll the whole leaf—or a stack of leaves—lengthwise. It will resemble a hand-rolled cigar. Holding the "cigar" together, cut diagonally across the rolled leaves into very thin slices; then unroll them and use.

Whole Wheat Flatbread with Savory Toppings

Thin flatbreads are an elegant and refreshing change from cheese-stuffed crusts and pile-it-on "everything" pizzas. Fresh grilled flatbread will dress up any meal or cocktail hour. With whole wheat flour, brown sugar, and extra oil, the dough is more enriched and moist than the dough for pizza and can stand alone or with light toppings. The key to making the flatbread is to roll out the bread as thin as possible and make sure it cooks all the way through. Serve hot off the grill and, instead of neatly cutting the flatbreads, let your guests tear off pieces to dip into olive oil or spread with Don't Worry, Be Happy Baba Ghanoush (page 293). Embellish the grilled bread with one or more of the savory toppings I suggest here—or use your imagination. Serve with robust red wine such as Chianti Classico or Zinfandel.*

Makes 4 individual flatbreads

Grilling Method: Combo/Medium Heat

$1\frac{1}{2}$	cups lukewarm water (about 100°F)
1	tablespoon brown sugar
3	tablespoons olive oil, plus extra as needed
1	envelope ($2\frac{1}{4}$ teaspoons) active dry or rapid-rise yeast
$1\frac{1}{2}$	cups unbleached all-purpose flour, plus extra as needed.
$1\frac{1}{2}$	cups whole wheat flour
1	teaspoon kosher salt
$\frac{1}{4}$	cup cornmeal or flour
	Toppings, as desired (page 231)

1. Place the lukewarm water in a large mixing bowl. Sprinkle the sugar, oil, and yeast on top and let it sit until foamy, about 5 minutes.
2. Combine the salt and flours in a large bowl. Add 2 cups of the flour mixture to the water, 1 cup at a time, until well incorporated. Add more of the reserved flour, 1 tablespoon at a time, until soft and slightly sticky. Mix well until the dough feels elastic.
3. Dust a clean work surface with about half of the reserved flour. Turn the dough out onto the well-floured surface. Knead, adding extra reserved flour to your work surface as necessary to prevent the dough from sticking, for 10 minutes, or until smooth and easy to work with but not dry. Clean and oil the bowl and place the dough in it. Cover with plastic wrap and let rise in a warm spot or an oven that has been preheated to 150°F and turned off, until it more than doubles in volume, about 1 hour.
4. Punch the dough down and knead it on a lightly floured surface for several minutes or until smooth.

Divide the dough into four 4-inch balls. (The dough may be made ahead, frozen until needed, and thawed at room temperature.)

5. Build a charcoal fire or preheat a gas grill. Lightly sprinkle a work surface with cornmeal or flour. Place a ball of dough in the middle of the work surface. With a rolling pin or your hands, gently roll out the dough into either a 12-inch rectangle or circle about ⅛ inch thick. (Remember that flatbreads are thinner than pizzas.)

6. Brush both sides with olive oil, and set it aside until ready to grill. Pick up the dough by the corners and lay it gently onto the center of the cooking grate over direct medium heat. Close the lid as quickly as possible. Grill for 2 to 4 minutes, until the bottom of the crust is well marked and browned. Remove from the grill, brush with oil, and cover with one of the toppings below.

7. Switch to indirect heat. Return the flatbread to the center of the cooking grate and cook with the lid closed until the bottom is well browned and cooked through, 5 to 10 minutes.

8. Remove the flatbread from the grill, drizzle it with best-quality olive oil, and season with salt and pepper to taste. Slice (or tear apart) and serve immediately.

TIP: Season with more salt than you think you need, especially if serving plain. The saltiness is key to the flatbread's flavor.

Walnut Pesto Topping

Makes 1 cup

½ cup best-quality prepared pesto
½ cup grated fresh parmesan cheese
¼ cup walnut pieces, toasted
   Sea salt, optional

1. Spread the pesto over the entire surface of the crust once one side is grilled.

2. Sprinkle it with the cheese and walnuts and cook according to the instructions for grilling flatbread (page 230) or pizza (pages 228–229) until the bread is browned and crisp and the cheese is melted. Finish with a sprinkling of sea salt, if desired.

Sea Salt and Extra-Virgin Olive Oil

Tops 1 individual flatbread

2 tablespoons best-quality extra-virgin olive oil, plus more for dipping (Monini or McEvoy Ranch are good choices)
1 tablespoon coarse sea salt or Hawaiian pink sea salt
   Freshly ground pepper, optional

1. Brush the entire surface of the crust with oil once one side is grilled. Sprinkle liberally with pink salt. Cook according to the instructions for grilling flatbread (page 230) or pizza (pages 228–229) until well browned and crisp.

2. Drizzle generously with extra-virgin olive oil. Season with pepper, if desired and serve with extra oil for dipping.

TIP: If you can't find pink sea salt in your grocery store, contact Hawaii Specialty Salt Company at www.hawaiisalt.com.

Caramelized Garlic and Rosemary Topping

Tops 1 individual flatbread

2 heads roasted, caramelized garlic (page 207)
¼ cup olive oil
1 teaspoon kosher salt, plus more to taste
1 sprig fresh rosemary, leaves removed and chopped or 1 teaspoon dried rosemary
   Freshly ground pepper
   Coarse sea salt or fleur de sel

1. Squeeze the cloves of garlic from the skins. Mash the cloves in a medium bowl, until the garlic forms a paste. Add the oil and salt and mix until very smooth, adding more oil if necessary. Add the rosemary and pepper to taste. Use immediately or refrigerate for up to 1 week.

2. To use, spread the mixture over the entire surface of the crust once 1 side is grilled. Cook according to the instructions for grilling flatbread (page 230) or pizza (pages 228–229) until well browned and crisp. Remove from the grill, drizzle with additional olive oil, if desired, and sprinkle with coarse sea salt or fleur de sel. Serve immediately.

American Pie

Pepperoni is the classic American pizza pie topping. Luckily, it is also very easy to purchase good-quality, precut pepperoni in the grocery store. If you are a mushroom lover, feel free to add mushrooms before you artfully arrange the pepperoni slices on top of the pizza.

Makes 2 to 4 servings

Grilling Method: Combo/Medium Heat

- ¼ cup cornmeal or all-purpose flour
- 1 4-inch ball prepared pizza dough, at room temperature
  Olive oil, about 2 tablespoons
- ½ cup fresh tomato sauce or crushed canned tomatoes
- 4 ounces thinly sliced pepperoni
- 8 white mushrooms, sliced and sautéed, optional
- ½ cup grated mozzarella cheese
- ¼ cup grated parmesan cheese
- 1 teaspoon dried oregano
  Sea salt
  Freshly ground pepper

1. Build a charcoal fire or preheat a gas grill.
2. Lightly sprinkle a work surface with cornmeal or flour. Place the dough in the middle of the work surface. Roll it out gently into either a 12-inch rectangle or circle, ¼ inch thick. Brush both sides with olive oil and set aside until ready to grill.
3. Pick up the dough by the corners and lay it gently onto the center of the cooking grate over direct medium heat. Close the lid as quickly as possible. Grill for 2 to 4 minutes, until the bottom of the crust is well marked and browned.
4. Remove the crust from the grill and spread the tomatoes or tomato sauce, then the pepperoni and mushrooms, if using, on the cooked side of the crust. Top with the mozzarella, parmesan, and dried oregano.
5. Switch to indirect heat. Return the pizza to the center of the cooking grate. Cook with the lid closed until the bottom is well browned, the toppings are warm, and the cheese is bubbly, 5 to 10 minutes.
6. Remove the pizza from the grill and season with salt and pepper to taste. Slice and serve immediately.

Caprese Pizza

Who doesn't like a caprese salad? It's a perfect marriage of fresh mozzarella, tomato, pure olive oil, and basil. It is one of my favorite comfort foods, especially during the heirloom tomato season. For this pizza, I adapted the flavors of my favorite salad to make a light and refreshing pizza. Since the composition is so simple, use the best possible raw ingredients—even making your own pesto from fresh basil if you are so inclined! Use the upside-down layering technique, putting the cheese on first, adding slices of tomato, and then adding the pesto in small dollops to make sure every piece has a bite of cheese, tomato, and pesto.

Makes 2 to 4 servings

Grilling Method: Combo/Medium Heat

- ¼ cup cornmeal or all-purpose flour
- 1 4-inch ball prepared pizza dough, at room temperature
  Olive oil, about 2 tablespoons
- ½ cup best-quality pesto sauce
- 1 large heirloom or beefsteak tomato, cut into ¼-inch slices
- ¼ cup grated Parmigiano-Reggiano cheese
- 2 to 3 2-inch balls fresh mozzarella cheese, sliced
  Sprig fresh basil, cleaned and dried
  Kosher salt
  Freshly ground pepper

1. Build a charcoal fire or preheat a gas grill.
2. Lightly sprinkle a work surface with cornmeal or flour. Place the dough in the middle of the work surface. Roll it out gently into either a 12-inch rectangle or circle, ¼ inch thick. Brush both sides with olive oil and set it aside until ready to grill.
3. Pick up the dough by the corners, and lay it gently onto the center of the cooking grate over direct medium heat. Grill for 2 to 4 minutes, or until the bottom of the crust is well marked and browned.
4. Remove the crust from the grill and spread the pesto sauce on the cooked side of the crust. Top it with the mozzarella, parmesan, tomatoes, and dollop of pesto.
5. Switch to indirect heat. Return the pizza to the center of the cooking grate; cook with the lid closed until the bottom is well browned, the toppings are warm, and the cheese is bubbly, 5 to 10 minutes.

6. Remove the pizza from the grill, garnish it with the basil sprig, and season with salt and pepper to taste. Slice and serve immediately.

Smoked Salmon Pizza with Lemon Zest

This could be the perfect recipe for your maiden grilled pizza voyage. As only the crust is grilled, you can concentrate on the first step. The toppings are added while the crust is warm. It is eaten at room temperature. The finished pizza is deceptively fancy and luxurious since the flavorful toppings are a riff on the popular smoked salmon canapé. This is a recipe that I frequently teach in my grilling classes because it provides instant gratification! Not only is there something delicious to eat almost immediately, but after making it once, you hardly need to look at the recipe again.

Makes 2 to 4 servings

Grilling Method: Combo/Medium Heat

¼	cup cornmeal or all-purpose flour
1	4-inch ball prepared pizza dough, at room temperature
	Olive oil, about 2 tablespoons
½	cup spreadable garlic-herb cheese, such as Boursin
1	shallot, peeled and minced
4	pieces smoked salmon, cut into strips, about 4 ounces total
1	lemon, zested
	Freshly ground pepper

1. Build a charcoal fire or preheat a gas grill.
2. Lightly sprinkle a work surface with cornmeal or flour. Place the dough in the middle of the work surface. Roll it out gently into either a 12-inch rectangle or circle, ¼ inch thick. Brush both sides with olive oil and set it aside until ready to grill.
3. Pick up the dough by the corners, and lay it gently onto the center of the cooking grate over direct medium heat. Close the lid as quickly as possible. Grill for 2 to 4 minutes, until the bottom of the crust is well marked and browned.
4. Remove the crust from the grill and brush it with oil.
5. Return the pizza to the center of the cooking grate and cook with the lid closed until the bottom is well browned, 2 to 4 more minutes. (Since we are not melting cheese or warming any toppings, you do not need to switch to indirect heat in this recipe.)
6. Remove the crust from the grill and, while still warm, spread it evenly with the cheese and top it with the shallot and salmon. Sprinkle it with the lemon zest and pepper. Slice and serve immediately.

PIZZA: A LOVE STORY

And so the story goes … Italian immigrants brought pizza to America, and it gained in popularity when returning World War II GIs created a demand for the pizza they had eaten and loved in Italy. Pizza grew into the mainstream, and the regional varieties that we know and love flourished. New York became world famous for thin slices, similar to the traditional Neapolitan pizza, and Chicagoans created a deep-dish pie topped with pounds of mozzarella.

In the 1960s, home-delivery service and frozen varieties brought pizza out of restaurants and into the home. "Gourmet pizzas" evolved from the California restaurant scene in the 1980s, most famously at Wolfgang Puck's Los Angeles restaurant Spago, where wood-fired pizzas were topped with smoked salmon, Brie cheese, wild mushrooms, duck, and other nontraditional pizza ingredients. Meanwhile in Providence, RI, the proprietors of Al Forno began serving and popularizing grilled pizza following a trip to Italy.

Today, we eat more than three billion pizzas every year—an average of 46 slices for each man, woman, and child in the United States. When you think about crossing the most popular food with the most popular cooking technique, it only makes sense that grilled pizza would captivate our palate. And in another example of "everything that is old is new again," the crisp, slightly smoky flavor of grilled pizza echoes the traditional Italian versions that the WWII vets craved when they returned to the states—bringing 21st century pizza back to its roots, via the outdoor grill.

Eggplant Parmigiano Pizza

I love the delicate flavor of eggplant and think that it is often lost in eggplant parmesan dishes in which the eggplant is both fried and smothered with tomato sauce and cheese. Grilled pizza is the perfect foil for its delicate virtues. Here, baby or Japanese eggplant is grilled first and while still hot, dipped into freshly grated Parmigiano-Reggiano cheese on both sides. When the eggplant has cooled, it is time to grill the pizza. Resist the urge to add too much cheese or sauce; it will mask the beauty of the eggplant.

Serves 2 to 4

Grilling Method: Combo/Medium Heat

1 small (Japanese) eggplant, cut lengthwise into
 ¹/₂-inch slices
 Olive oil, about 3 tablespoons
¹/₄ cup cornmeal or all-purpose flour
1 4-inch ball prepared pizza dough, at room
 temperature
¹/₄ cup best-quality sun-dried tomato pesto
2 ounces mozzarella cheese, sliced or grated
1 small ripe tomato, sliced very thin
1 roasted yellow or red bell pepper (see page 210),
 sliced, or ¹/₂ cup jarred roasted peppers, drained
2 ounces Parmigiano-Reggiano cheese, sliced
 into strips the length of the cheese with a
 vegetable peeler and broken into pieces
1 tablespoon chopped fresh parsley
 Sea salt
 Freshly ground pepper

1. Build a charcoal fire or preheat a gas grill. Using about 1 tablespoon of olive oil, brush each eggplant slice on both sides with oil. Place the eggplant on the cooking grate over direct medium heat, cover, and grill for 5 minutes per side, or until the eggplant is well marked, browned, and tender. Take it off the grill and immediately dredge the hot slices of eggplant in the Parmigiano pieces. Set aside. Reserve the remaining cheese.

2. Lightly sprinkle a work surface with cornmeal or flour. Place the dough in the middle of the work surface. Roll it out gently into either a 12-inch rectangle or circle, ¹/₄ inch thick. Brush both sides with olive oil and set it aside until ready to grill.

3. Pick up the dough by the corners, and lay it gently directly onto the cooking grate over direct medium heat. Close the lid as quickly as possible. Grill for 2 to 4 minutes, until the bottom of the crust is well marked and browned.

4. Remove the crust from the grill and spread the sun-dried tomato pesto evenly on the cooked side of the crust. Sprinkle half the mozzarella cheese over that, evenly distribute the tomato slices on top, and sprinkle with half of the remaining parmesan cheese. Top with the grilled eggplant and roasted peppers and sprinkle the remaining cheese on top.

5. Switch to indirect heat. Return the pizza to the center of the cooking grate; cook with the lid closed until the bottom is well browned, the toppings are warm, and the cheese is bubbly, 5 to 10 minutes.

6. Remove the pizza from grill, sprinkle it with the parsley and season to taste with salt pepper. Slice and serve immediately.

Four Seasons Pizza

When I was a student in France, I fell in love with the Quatre Saisons (Four Seasons) pizza that cost a few francs at a pizza restaurant near where I lived in the Latin Quarter. The rustic, crisp, and chewy crust was fired in an old wood oven, and the toppings were sparse. The individual pie was perfect in its restraint. In my re-creation, each of the quadrants of the pizza is filled with a different topping: artichoke hearts, mushrooms, mozzarella, and French ham or prosciutto. The only cheese on the pizza is in the mozzarella quad. If you want to embellish this, you can add a few Niçoise olives and cook an egg in the center, leaving it runny to sauce the rest of the ingredients once you cut into it.

Makes 2 to 4 servings

Grilling Method: Combo/Medium Heat

¹/₄ cup cornmeal or all-purpose flour
1 4-inch ball prepared pizza dough, at room
 temperature
 Olive oil, about 3 tablespoons
¹/₄ cup Tuscan Red Sauce (page 132) or crushed
 canned tomatoes
¹/₂ cup grated Parmigiano-Reggiano cheese

¼ cup sautéed or raw sliced mushrooms
2 canned artichoke hearts, cut in quarters
2 large, thin slices prosciutto or French ham
1 small 2-inch ball fresh mozzarella cheese, sliced
　　Niçoise olives, optional
1 egg, optional
　　Sea salt
　　Freshly ground pepper

1. Build a charcoal fire or preheat a gas grill.
2. Lightly sprinkle a work surface with cornmeal or flour. Place the dough in the middle of the work surface. Roll or stretch it gently into either a 12-inch rectangle or circle, ¼ inch thick. Brush both sides with olive oil and set it aside until ready to grill.
3. Pick up the dough by the corners, and lay it gently onto the center of the cooking grate over direct medium heat. Close the lid as quickly as possible. Grill for 2 to 4 minutes, until the bottom of the crust is well marked and browned.
4. Remove the crust from the grill and spread a thin layer of the Tuscan Red Sauce evenly over the crust. "Draw" a cross with the grated parmesan cheese to make 4 sections. Working clockwise, spread the first section with the mushrooms. Fill the next section with the artichoke heart pieces, the third with the ham, and the fourth with the cheese. Place an olive in the center of each section. (If using the egg, crack it into the center of the 4 sections.)
5. Switch to indirect heat. Return the pizza to the center of the cooking grate; cook with the lid closed until the bottom is well browned, the toppings are warm, and the cheese is bubbly, 5 to10 minutes (if using the egg, cook for 20 minutes or until the white is opaque).
6. Remove the pizza from the grill, and season with salt and pepper to taste. Slice and serve immediately.

Caramelized Onion and Bacon Pizza

This caramelized onion and bacon pizza is a triple treat of grill-roasted Vidalia onion, raw minced shallots, and sautéed red onion. The grilled onion is pureed with caramelized garlic

for the base and topped with a tangle of darkly browned onion rings, crumbles of applewood-smoked bacon and fresh grated Gruyère. A crunchy sprinkle of shallots and parsley finish this pizza, which is slightly reminiscent of French onion soup.

Makes 2 to 4 servings

Grilling Method: Combo/Medium Heat

¼ cup cornmeal or all-purpose flour
1 4-inch ball prepared pizza dough, at room temperature
3 tablespoons olive oil
1 Vidalia onion, grill-roasted (Forgotten Onion, page 209)
1 head roasted garlic (page 207)
　　Olive oil
　　Sea salt
　　Freshly ground pepper
4 ounces Gruyère or other Swiss cheese, grated
2 red onions, sliced into rings and sautéed until deeply caramelized
4 slices center-cut bacon, cooked and crumbled
1 large shallot, minced
1 tablespoon chopped fresh parsley

1. Build a charcoal fire or preheat a gas grill.
2. Lightly sprinkle a work surface with cornmeal or flour. Place the dough in the middle of the work surface. Roll or stretch it gently into a 12-inch rectangle or circle, ¼ inch thick. Brush both sides with olive oil and set it aside until ready to grill.
3. Pick up the dough by the corners, and lay it gently onto the center of the cooking grate over direct medium heat. Close the lid as quickly as possible. Grill for 2 to 4 minutes, until the bottom of the crust is well marked and browned.
4. Remove the crust from the grill and spread a thick layer of the onion and garlic mixture evenly over the cooked side of the crust. Top with the cheese and the caramelized red onions. Sprinkle with the bacon and shallot.
5. Switch to indirect heat. Return the pizza to the center of the cooking grate; cook with the lid closed until the bottom is well browned, the toppings are warm, and the cheese is bubbly, 5 to 10 minutes.
6. Remove the pizza from the grill and sprinkle it with the parsley. Season with salt and pepper to taste. Slice and serve immediately.

Junior League Artichoke Pizza

This pizza has roots in every Junior League cookbook that was written in the seventies. It features the much-loved "cup a, cup a, can..." artichoke dip. The recipe goes: a cup a this, a cup a that, a can of artichokes. Regardless of the humble origins and the less than foodie-proud ingredients, it is delicious, and four out of five people that I polled applauded my tribute to the original dip with this new fangled pizza than eat any number of high falutin' appetizers.

Makes 2 to 4 servings

Grilling Method: Combo/Medium Heat

- 1 cup best-quality mayonnaise
- 2 14-ounce cans artichoke hearts in water or brine
- 1 cup grated parmesan cheese
- ½ cup grated Romano cheese
- 1 tablespoon Dijon mustard
- ½ teaspoon Worcestershire sauce
- ¼ cup cornmeal or all-purpose flour
- 1 4-inch ball prepared pizza dough, at room temperature
  Olive oil, about 3 tablespoons
- ½ cup grated mozzarella cheese
- 1 tablespoon fresh thyme leaves
  Freshly ground pepper

1. In a large bowl, mix the mayonnaise, artichokes, parmesan, Romano, mustard, and Worcestershire sauce with the back of a fork until completely incorporated. Put the mixture in an ovenproof dish and bake in the oven for 30 to 40 minutes, or until bubbly and golden on top. Alternatively, you can grill-bake over indirect medium heat in a preheated grill. This can be done up to 1 day in advance and refrigerated until ready to make pizza.
2. Build a charcoal fire or preheat a gas grill. Preheat the oven to 350°F.
3. Lightly sprinkle a work surface with cornmeal or flour. Place the dough in the middle of the work surface. Roll or stretch it gently into a 12-inch rectangle or circle, ¼ inch thick. Brush both sides with olive oil.
4. Pick up the dough by the corners, and lay it gently onto the center of the cooking grate over direct medium heat. Close the lid as quickly as possible.

Grill for 2 to 4 minutes, until the bottom of the crust is well marked and browned.

5. Remove the crust from the grill and spread a thick layer of the artichoke-cheese mixture evenly on the cooked side of the crust. Sprinkle with the mozzarella cheese.
6. Switch to indirect heat. Return the pizza to the center of the cooking grate; cook with the lid closed until the bottom is well browned, the toppings are warm, and the cheese is bubbly, 5 to 10 minutes.
7. Remove the pizza from the grill and sprinkle it with the thyme leaves. Season with freshly ground pepper to taste. Slice and serve immediately.

Greek Islands Pizza

When I lived in New Orleans, there was a little Italian restaurant that made the most delicious Greek pizza—go figure! About once a month, when I needed a break from the excesses of the French Quarter, I would go to this little restaurant in Uptown where the excesses were all their own, including a layer of butter spread on the crust before the tomato sauce. I've eliminated the butter for this pared down, grilled version but kept the crunchy white onions dripping with red-wine vinegar as well as the salty feta cheese, kalamata olives, and smoky shrimp. Finish the pizza with a squirt of lemon just before serving.

Makes 2 to 4 servings

Grilling Method: Combo/Medium Heat

- ¼ cup cornmeal or all-purpose flour
- 1 4-inch ball prepared pizza dough, at room temperature
  Olive oil
- ¼ cup tomato sauce or crushed canned tomatoes
- ¼ cup roasted red or green bell peppers (page 210)
  Sea salt
  Freshly ground pepper
- 1 small white onion, sliced in thin rings
- ⅔ cup red wine vinegar
- ½ cup crumbled feta cheese
- ½ cup grated mozzarella cheese
- 10 kalamata olives, pitted and cut in half
- ½ pound shrimp, peeled and grilled (page 178)
- 1 lemon, cut into wedges

1. Build a charcoal fire or preheat a gas grill.
2. Lightly sprinkle a work surface with cornmeal or flour. Place the dough in the middle of the work surface. Roll or stretch it gently into a 12-inch rectangle or circle, ¼ inch thick. Brush both sides with olive oil and set it aside until ready to grill.
3. In a heavy-bottomed saucepan, heat the tomatoes, peppers, and 2 tablespoons of olive oil. Puree them and season with salt and pepper. Set aside until ready to top the pizza. Put the onions in a nonreactive bowl and cover them with the red wine vinegar until ready to use.
4. Pick up the dough by the corners, and lay it gently onto the center of the cooking grate over direct medium heat. Close the lid as quickly as possible. Grill for 2 to 4 minutes or until the bottom of the crust is well marked and browned.
5. Remove the crust from the grill and spread the reserved sauce on the cooked side. Sprinkle it with both of the cheeses. Evenly distribute a layer of white onions with a little of the vinegar still clinging to the rings. Finally top with the olives and grilled shrimp.
6. Switch to indirect heat. Return the pizza to the center of the cooking grate; cook with the lid closed until the bottom is well browned, the toppings are warm, and the cheese is bubbly, 5 to 10 minutes.
7. Remove the pizza from the grill, and season with pepper and a squirt of fresh lemon to taste. Slice and serve immediately.

Windy City Sausage and Spinach Pizza

Chicago is famous for its overstuffed thick-crust pizza. Legend has it that they were the first to use spinach as a pizza topping. They bake their pizzas in 1-inch high pans that look like blackened cake pans. My grilled version was inspired by the classic version—it's just as delicious but a lot easier and faster to make.

Makes 2 to 4 servings

Grilling Method: Combo/Medium Heat

¼ cup cornmeal or all-purpose flour
1 4-inch ball prepared pizza dough, at room temperature
Olive oil, about 3 tablespoons
½ cup grated mozzarella cheese

½ cup grated parmesan cheese, divided
1 cup baby spinach leaves
1 clove garlic, minced
½ cup Tuscan Red Sauce (page 132) or crushed canned tomatoes
2 sweet or hot Italian sausages, grilled (see page 139) and cut into thin slices
Sea salt
Freshly ground pepper

1. Build a charcoal fire or preheat a gas grill.
2. Lightly sprinkle a work surface with cornmeal or flour. Place the dough in the middle of the work surface. Roll or stretch it gently into a 12-inch rectangle or circle, ¼ inch thick. Brush both sides with olive oil and set it aside until ready to grill.
3. Pick up the dough by the corners, and lay it gently onto the center of the cooking grate over direct medium heat. Close the lid as quickly as possible. Grill for 2 to 4 minutes, until the bottom of the crust is well marked and browned.
4. Remove the crust from the grill, and sprinkle it evenly with the mozzarella and half of the parmesan cheese on the cooked side. Top with a thin layer of the spinach leaves. Mix the garlic with the sauce and add dollops of the Sauce to the crust, spreading it with the back of a spoon. Finish with the pieces of grilled sausage and the rest of the parmesan cheese.
5. Switch to indirect heat. Return the pizza to the center of the cooking grate; cook with the lid closed until the bottom is well browned, the toppings are warm, and the cheese is bubbly, 5 to 10 minutes.
6. Remove the pizza from the grill, and season with salt and pepper to taste. Slice and serve immediately.

CHICAGO-STYLE PIZZA

To make an authentic Chicago pan pizza, place the crust in a shallow round cake pan that has been oiled then fit the dough into the bottom and up the sides, as you would a pie. Layer the toppings until you get to the top edge of the crust—the toppings will be about 1 inch deep. Cover the top of the pizza with crushed tomatoes or sauce and sprinkle with parmesan. Bake in the center of the cooking grate for 1 hour or until brown and the toppings are hot all the way through.

Truffled Wild Mushroom and Camembert Pizza

This is my idea of pizza nirvana. Mushrooms, some stinky cheese, a drizzle of truffle oil, and a great wine to wash it down with, such as a fruity Sauvignon Blanc, which is a perfect match for the truffle oil. The secret to this pizza is the mixture of cognac-scented, butter-sautéed mushrooms that is spread on the crust in place of the traditional sauce. Caramelized onions and morel mushrooms would be great additions if you were in a "more is more" mood.

Makes 2 to 4 servings

Grilling Method: Combo/Medium Heat

 1 cup dried or fresh wild mushrooms, such as oyster, morel, chanterelle, or porcini
 1 large shallot, chopped
 2 tablespoons butter
 2 tablespoons cognac
    Sea salt or fleur de sel
    Freshly ground pepper
 ¼ cup cornmeal or all-purpose flour
 1 4-inch ball prepared pizza dough, at room temperature
    Olive oil, about 3 tablespoons
 4 to 6 ounces ripe Camembert cheese, in ½-inch-thick slices
    White truffle oil

1. Build a charcoal fire or preheat a gas grill.
2. If using dried mushrooms, reconstitute by soaking them in warm water for 20 minutes. Strain, chop, and set aside. If using fresh, wipe any dirt from the mushrooms with a damp towel, slice, and set aside.
3. Sauté the shallot and mushrooms in butter until soft and slightly caramelized, about 10 minutes, adding olive oil if you need more fat for sautéing. Add the cognac during the final 1 to 2 minutes of cooking time. Season with salt and pepper and set aside.
4. Lightly sprinkle a work surface with cornmeal or flour. Place the dough in the middle of the work surface. Roll or stretch it gently into a 12-inch rectangle or circle, ¼ inch thick. Brush both sides with olive oil and set it aside until ready to grill.
5. Pick up the dough by the corners, and lay it gently onto the center of the cooking grate over direct medium heat. Close the lid as quickly as possible. Grill for 2 to 4 minutes, until the bottom of the crust is well marked and browned.
6. Remove the crust from the grill, and spread the sautéed shallots and mushrooms on the cooked side. Distribute the sliced Camembert on top.
7. Switch to indirect heat. Return the pizza to the center of the cooking grate; cook with the lid closed until the bottom is well browned, the toppings are warm, and the cheese is bubbly, about 5 to 10 minutes.
8. Remove the pizza from the grill, drizzle with truffle oil, and season to taste with salt and pepper. Slice and serve immediately.

TIP: For a more refined version, double the amount of mushrooms, shallots, butter, and cognac and puree the mixture before spreading it on the crust.

Fig, Walnut, and Roquefort Pizza with Port Reduction

This is the classic fruit and cheese course all in one bite. The crust of the pizza is glazed with clementine marmalade to anchor sweet dried figs that have been cut into bite-size slivers before being topped with crumbled blue cheese, and toasted walnuts. Even the accompanying glass of port has been incorporated into the pizza; it is reduced and drizzled over the fruit and cheese to add that "je ne sais quoi." Because you use dried instead of fresh figs, this is a dessert that can be made all year long.

Makes 2 to 4 servings

Grilling Method: Combo/Medium Heat

1/4 cup all-purpose flour (Don't use cornmeal for dessert pizzas)

1 4-inch ball prepared pizza dough, at room temperature
   Almond or other neutral nut oil, about 2 tablespoons

1/2 cup clementine or orange marmalade

2 ounces best-quality Roquefort or other blue cheese, crumbled

6 dried mission figs, cut in slices lengthwise

1/2 cup Port Reduction (at right)
   Sea salt
   Freshly ground grains of paradise

1. Build a charcoal fire or preheat a gas grill.
2. Lightly sprinkle a work surface with flour. Place the dough in the middle of the work surface. Roll or stretch it gently into a 12-inch rectangle or circle, 1/4 inch thick. Brush both sides with oil and set it aside until ready to grill.
3. Pick up the dough by the corners, and lay it gently onto the center of the cooking grate over direct medium heat. Close the lid as quickly as possible. Grill for 2 to 4 minutes, until the bottom of the crust is well marked and browned.
4. Remove the crust from the grill, and brush it with oil. Return the pizza to the center of the cooking grate over direct heat, and cook with the lid closed until the bottom begins to brown, about 3 minutes.
5. Remove the crust from the grill and, while still warm, spread it evenly with the marmalade. Sprinkle it with the cheese and top evenly with the fig pieces.
6. Switch to indirect heat. Return the pizza to the center of the cooking grate; cook with the lid closed until the toppings are heated through, 5 to 10 minutes.
7. Remove the pizza from the grill and, while still warm, drizzle it with the port reduction. Sprinkle with salt and grains of paradise to taste. Slice and serve immediately.

Port Reduction
Makes about 1 cup

1 350 ml bottle port wine

1. Pour the port into a 4-quart saucepan. Simmer over medium heat for about 1 hour, or until the port is reduced by about two-thirds and has a syrupy consistency. Let it cool.
2. Store indefinitely in the refrigerator in a plastic squeeze bottle (looks like a ketchup or mustard squeeze bottle and is available at large housewares or specialty cooking stores).

Raspberry–Chocolate–Hazelnut Pizza with Sweet Ricotta Cheese

My mother loves the classic combination of chocolate and raspberries, and I created this simple dessert pizza with her—and a couple of her grandsons—in mind. It is deceptively easy and is a great treat to make with young children. All the ingredients except the crust are purchased ready to use; think of it as a grown up open-face PB&J.

Makes 4 servings

Grilling Method: Combo/Medium Heat

1/4 cup all-purpose flour

1 4-inch ball prepared pizza dough, at room temperature
   Hazelnut or other neutral nut oil, about 3 tablespoons

3 to 4 tablespoons Nutella or other chocolate-hazelnut paste

1/2 cup seedless raspberry jam

2/3 cup fresh ricotta cheese
   Sugar in the raw or coarse white sugar

2 tablespoons hazelnuts (filberts), toasted and chopped

1/4 cup fresh raspberries

1. Build a charcoal fire or preheat a gas grill.
2. Lightly sprinkle a work surface with flour. Place the dough in the middle of the work surface. Roll or stretch it gently into a 12-inch rectangle or circle, ¼ inch thick. Brush both sides with oil and set it aside until ready to grill.
3. Pick up the dough by the corners, and lay it gently onto the center of the cooking grate over direct medium heat. Close the lid as quickly as possible. Grill for 2 to 4 minutes, until the bottom of the crust is well marked and browned.
4. Remove the crust from the grill and brush it with oil. Return the pizza to the center of the cooking grate over direct heat and grill with the lid closed until the bottom begins to brown, about 3 minutes.
5. Remove the crust from grill and, while still warm, spread it evenly with the Nutella, and spoon on dollops of jam and ricotta cheese so it looks like polka dots on a chocolate background. Sprinkle it with a light dusting of sugar.
6. Switch to indirect heat. Return the pizza to the center of the cooking grate; cook with the lid closed until the toppings are heated through, 5 to 10 minutes.
7. Remove from the grill and, while still warm, top with the nuts and raspberries. Slice and serve immediately.

Toffee Pizza

I can't decide what to call this dessert pizza. If I am entertaining food snobs, I choose the more formal title "Caramel au Fleur de Sel and Bittersweet Chocolate Pizza." If this pizza ends a down and dirty cook-out, I refer to it as my toffee pizza. No matter what you call it, it is a slice of heaven. Note: Don't skimp on the fleur de sel. It really does bring all the flavors together and intensify them, without making the pizza "salty."

Makes 2 to 4 servings

Grilling Method: Combo/Medium Heat

¼ cup all-purpose flour
1 4-inch ball prepared pizza dough, at room temperature
  Almond or other neutral nut oil, about 2 tablespoons
½ cup caramel sauce (Dulce de Leche, page 326)
½ cup chopped toasted almonds
½ cup chopped bittersweet chocolate, preferably 70 percent ScharffenBerger
  Fleur de sel
  Best-quality vanilla ice cream, optional

1. Build a charcoal fire or preheat a gas grill.
2. Lightly sprinkle a work surface with flour. Place the dough in the middle of the work surface. Roll or stretch it gently into a 12-inch rectangle or circle, ¼ inch thick. Brush both sides with oil and set it aside until ready to grill.
3. Pick up the dough by the corners and lay it gently onto the center of the cooking grate over direct medium heat. Close the lid as quickly as possible. Grill for 2 to 4 minutes, until the bottom of the crust is well marked and browned.
4. Remove the crust from the grill and brush it with oil. Return the pizza to the center of the cooking grate over direct heat, and grill until the bottom begins to brown, about 3 minutes.
5. Remove the crust from the grill and, while still warm, spread it evenly with the caramel sauce; then distribute the chopped almonds and chocolate evenly over the crust.
6. Switch to indirect heat. Return the pizza to the center of the cooking grate and cook with the lid closed until the toppings are heated through, about 5 minutes. Remove from the grill and, while still warm, sprinkle with fleur de sel.
7. Let it sit for 5 minutes to cool and serve in small pieces with vanilla ice cream, if desired.

Low-and-Slow Barbecue

Barbecue 101

Rapid-Fire Checklist

✓ Preheat grill
✓ Soak wood chips
✓ Brush meat with oil and season with kosher salt and pepper or barbecue rub
✓ Reduce heat to indirect medium-low heat
✓ Place meat on cooking grate and cover
✓ Cook to an internal temperature of 190°F to 200°F
✓ Remove meat from grill
✓ Let meat rest 15 to 20 minutes
✓ Shred, chop, or pull meat while still hot, as recipe requires

Tools of the Trade

• 12-inch locking chef tongs
• Instant-read thermometer
• Silicone or natural-bristle brush
• Squeeze bottle for mopping
• Heavy-duty oven mitt

Common Problems

• Meat is too lean
• Precooking
• Too much smoke
• Cooking temperature is too low
• Using sweet barbecue sauce too soon
• Mistaking a pink smoke ring for undercooked pork or poultry

America's love affair with barbecue grows stronger every year. Barbecue, originally known as *barbacoa* in the Caribbean, is a cooking method that is as old as fire and has inspired a one-word language—even a way of life. When referring to this slow-cooked meat, barbecue can be used as a noun, a verb, an adjective, and everything in-between. Barbecue as a noun is used the most, to mean various things: You cook on a barbecue (the cooking equipment on which food is slow cooked over low heat); you eat barbecue (meat cooked slowly with wood smoke); you have a barbecue (a gathering at which barbecued foods are featured); and many more colloquial uses. Where I come from in North Carolina, barbecue is a noun with an even more limited definition. It refers to one thing—pork that has been slowly cooked over a low heat and flavored by hickory smoke and the loving patience of time. When it is meltingly tender, the pork is pulled or chopped and doused with a thin vinegar-rich sauce—then and only then, is it barbecue!

Regardless, barbecue has such a positive connotation that it is used even when foods aren't cooked the barbecue way. Most people use the terms barbecue or BBQ interchangeably with grilling, even though, as I've said, grilling is mostly quick cooking over high heat. But as anyone who has done any grill-roasting knows, the Indirect Method of grilling is actually used more by experienced grillers than the Direct Method of open-flame grilling associated with cooking steaks, burgers, and kabobs. The technical differences between indirect grilling and barbecuing involve wood smoke and a lower heat. But what really sets barbecue a world apart is "feeling the love." That is the real secret to America's love affair with barbecue and the elusive ability to recreate it.

The word "barbecued" is in a lot of recipe titles on menus around the country, even if the food is not cooked in the barbecue style but simply served with a sauce that has some flavors of typical barbecue sauces from North Carolina, Texas, or Kansas City.

Even one of the most famous dishes out of New Orleans is called Barbecued Shrimp. Well, the shrimp isn't even grilled, much less barbecued—it is sautéed in butter and paprika, making it look like it was cooked with barbecue sauce and thus earning the label "barbecued"! What it comes down to is that people instantly link "barbecue" with "rich, lick-your-fingers flavor"—it casts a warm glow over whatever it is linked to.

Barbecue is thought to be a Southern tradition, which is mostly true except that Kansas City is firmly entrenched in the Midwest and it boasts more that 100 authentic barbecue restaurants and is the home of KC Masterpiece, America's baseline brand for barbecue sauce. Regardless of the region or the origins, barbecue unites, melting the prejudices of politics, race, heritage, social standing, and education for a few seconds in time. (See the sidebar on page 258 for some of my favorite authentic barbecue joints.)

When I teach "authentic barbecue" classes, I start by saying that I grill for a living and I barbecue for pleasure. I can hold my own against the barbecue circuit champs, and I have picked up more tips (because I ask and observe) along the barbecue trail than most barbecuers. But I call myself a hobbyist because on the circuit, unless you've won the Grand Champion trophy, you're no expert, you are still in training (see the baked bean recipe on pages 256–257 from the only four-time Memphis in May Grand Champion, Mike Mills). I would never insult the guys who seriously compete by calling myself a barbecue expert; if I did, they'd stop answering my questions, and I'd stop learning—and that would break my barbecue lovin' heart!

One thing I've learned along the way is that backyard barbecuers have a lot of misconceptions about what makes barbecue and how long it takes. Barbecued food is synonymous with low heat and slow cooking (more on this in the Telling Grilling Secrets chapter). It also usually involves flavoring the food with wood smoke.

NOTE: This chapter features recipes for more than just foods that can be barbecued. I also include a few extras: Brunswick Stew and sides (baked beans and cabbage among others) because they are so much a part of the barbecue table—they just go together. That doesn't mean you can't serve other sides or desserts with your pulled pork or barbecued brisket; just don't tell any barbecue folks that you're doing it!

Selecting Your Meat

Every champion pitmaster knows that the meat is the single most important part of making great barbecue. It's essential to choose cuts that have a generous fat to meat ratio. The next time you have a hankering for a Texas-style brisket, try barbecuing a lean, trimmed brisket, and you will understand my point completely. Here's why: During the long, slow cooking period, the meat needs its natural fat to baste it as it cooks. Choose meat that is both marbled on the inside and has a cap of fat on the outside. Don't worry—if cooked long enough over indirect heat, your barbecue will not be fatty or greasy—all the natural fat cooks out, leaving the flavor behind and creating melt-in-your-mouth barbecued meat.

Approximate **BARBECUE** *Cooking Times* (°F)

TYPE OF BARBECUE	WEIGHT	GRILLING METHOD	GRILLING TIME	INTERNAL TEMP.	REST TIME
Pork shoulder, with bone	5 to 7 pounds	Indirect Medium-Low	4 to 5 hours	190° to 200°	20 minutes
Boston butt	4 to 9 pounds	Indirect Medium-Low	3 to 5 hours	190° to 200°	20 minutes
Fresh ham	4 to 15 pounds	Indirect Medium-Low	2 to 6 hours	190° to 200°	20 minutes
Brisket, whole untrimmed	7 to 12 pounds	Indirect Medium-Low	4 to 9 hours	190° to 200°	20 minutes
Brisket, half untrimmed	4 to 5 pounds	Indirect Medium-Low	4 to 5 hours	190° to 200°	20 minutes
Pork ribs, 3 to 4 racks	2 to 3 pounds each	Indirect Medium-Low	1½ to 2 hours	190° to 200°	10 minutes
Beef ribs	1 rack, about 3 pounds; 7 bones	Indirect Medium-Low	30 to 40 minutes	190° to 200°	10 minutes
Lamb shoulder	5 to 7 pounds	Indirect Medium-Low	3 to 4 hours	190° to 200°	20 minutes
Chicken, wood smoked	3 to 5 pounds	Indirect Medium	1 to 1½ hours	180°	10 minutes
Turkey	12 to 16 pounds	Indirect Medium	11 to 13 minutes/ pound	180°	20 minutes
Salmon side	2 to 4 pounds	Indirect Medium	35 to 50 minutes	N/A	10 minutes

All internal temperatures are based on Barbecue Circuit recommended values, using an instant-read thermometer. Times and temperatures in the chart are guidelines. Specific recipes may call for variations.

On the Fire: Indirect Heat

The Indirect Method is the only grilling method you use for authentic slow-cooked barbecue. It is used primarily for large cuts of meat and other foods that require long cooking times at lower temperatures, such as the pulled pork, brisket, and smoking recipes featured here as well as whole turkey, chicken pieces, and ribs. The food cooks by reflected heat, as in a convection oven. And the signature smoked flavor comes from the addition of wood chips or chunks. This method provides a consistent cooking temperature and is similar to roasting or baking in your indoor oven. The result is food—mostly meat—that is both juicy and has a deeply caramelized crust. The food cooks evenly without turning during the entire cooking process. This method can only be used on a grill that is covered. In the Indirect Method, food is placed away from the heat source—*never* directly above lit gas burners or charcoal. Remember, Indirect Cooking is a no-peek cooking method—every time you lift the lid, heat escapes and that can increase cooking time.

Cooking Time and Temperatures

Most circuit barbecuers talk about super-low temperatures of 200°F to 225°F and very long cooking times. For backyard barbecue, I recommend using a temperature of 300°F to 350°F and less time for a number of reasons. Most of the proponents of such low temperatures are using huge barbecue rigs or pits with off-set fireboxes. In those monsters—the rigs, not the guys—it is very possible to keep the temperature that low, and you need a lot of time to barbecue a hundred racks of ribs or 50 Boston butts!

When you are making barbecue in your backyard, you are cooking much smaller quantities of meat and presumably you'd prefer that it didn't take so long. Most backyard grills cook at a higher temperature; but, more importantly, I believe that you need a slightly higher cooking temperature to properly render all the fat out of the meat, which results in falling-off-the-bone, succulent barbecue. In my experience, barbecue cooked at super-low (200°F and below) temperatures is often tough and still has pockets of white fat in the meat. I barbecue at a higher temperature, and I cook it to a higher end temperature. That is my technique and the way I like my barbecue. If you want to continue to barbecue at a lower temperature, go right ahead—that is the beauty of barbecue, everyone has her or his "secret." And when it comes to "barbecue," even the experts have agreed to disagree a long time ago!

A Note on Doneness

Compared to a lot of grilling and barbecue cookbooks, I specify a much higher end temperature. I recommend an end temperature of 190°F to 200°F. And most of

the time, my barbecue is at that 200°F mark, especially if it is a cut with a bone in it like a pork shoulder. Why? The more you barbecue, the more you use visual clues beyond temperature to tell whether or not the meat is done. For example, if you are testing doneness in a pork shoulder, you know that it is ready if the surface fat is completely rendered out and resembles pork cracklins, and the bone slips out of the meat, clean as a whistle with no meat sticking to it. When this happens, it is a beautiful thing, I promise you. I've been known to dance a jig or two every time I remove

Visual Clues *for* Doneness

MEAT	DONENESS CLUE
Pork shoulder, with bone	Bone slips out with no meat clinging to it
Boston butt (boneless pork shoulder)	The instant-read thermometer feels like it's going through soft butter—no resistance
Brisket, whole untrimmed	Charred blackened exterior, crispy burned ends (known as burnt ends), and soft on the inside like butter
Ribs	Meat recedes from bones, bones are blackened on the ends from the caramelized marrow, if the silverskin (membrane) is still on the ribs, it will pull away from the ribs like stiff, browned parchment paper
Poultry	185°F in the thigh, meat pulls away from the drumsticks, and the juices run clear
Salmon side	Color becomes opaque instead of translucent, and the white proteins between the orange flesh become cooked and solid

a clean bone, and I guarantee you will too after you experience this barbecue satisfaction for the first time. And if that doesn't convince you, follow the advice of one of my dearest barbecue buddies, Gary Pantlik, who contends, "If you have to cut it, it ain't fit to eat!" See his recipe for The Cook's Ribs (page 252–253).

Below are visual clues to guide you to perfect doneness—but to make sure your eyes are seeing the right clues, always use an instant-read thermometer as well, except for seafood because the fishery industry doesn't gauge end temperatures with internal temperatures.

A Note on Precooking (Parcooking)

I am very vocal about my distaste for parcooking in the rib chapter because so many recipes out there call for it. Parcooking is simply precooking—usually in boiling water—the meat before you put it on the grill to "barbecue." The boiling of the meat melts all the natural fats, and they stay in the pot of water instead of slowly basting and flavoring the meat during the slow barbecue process. Suffice it to say, it is not only going to rob your meat of precious flavor but it will make an awful ugly pot to wash.

Too Much of a Good Thing (Smoke) is a Bad Thing

There is nothing as good as smoke-kissed barbecued meat, but there is nothing as bad as smoke-smothered meat. I'll give you a sensory clue: It tastes like an old ashtray smells. Smoke is like salt: Just the right amount brings out the best in the meat and too much renders it inedible.

Smoke brings out salty flavors during the cooking process, so be careful with the amount of salt in your rub, sauce, and brine if you are using one. In most cases, if you are using a brine, you will only need a hint of salt to finish seasoning the meat. And remember, rubs and sauces are designed to taste good once the cooking is finished, not when you taste the sauce on the spoon before it has been added to the meat. It may taste too salty or not salty enough alone, but this will change during the barbecuing process.

Charcoal Grill Smoking

For smoke flavor, consider adding hardwood chips or chunks (soaked in water for at least 30 minutes and drained) or moistened fresh herbs such as rosemary, thyme, or lavender. Place the wet wood or herbs directly on the gray-ashed briquettes just before you begin cooking.

Gas Grill Smoking

For smoke flavor, use the smoker box if your grill has one, or place water-soaked wood chips in a small disposable foil pan in the upper left hand corner of the grill directly on the heat source (flavorizer bars or ceramic briquettes or lava rock). This must be done during the preheating stage when all burners are turned to high.

Hitting the Sauce...Too Soon

The most common barbecue blooper is putting sweet barbecue sauce on the meat too soon. The sugars in the

sauce will burn long before the meat is cooked. If using barbecue sauce, think of it as a finishing sauce and only put it on the meat, especially ribs, during the final 10 to 15 minutes of the cooking time. This is long enough for the sauce to caramelize and cook into the meat without burning.

Smoke Ring or My Pig's Pink!

The pink ring around the outside of a cut of pork is the barbecuer's pride and joy and called the smoke ring. The smoke ring is a natural chemical reaction between the meat and the smoke and does not mean that the pork is undercooked. On the contrary, it is the ultimate goal. In fact, you can get this same pink ring by cooking meat in a gas oven. Whole poultry and large pieces of beef, such as brisket, also get a smoke ring around the perimeter of the meat if cooked long enough.

Italian Grilled Cheese Skewers
(page 294)

Country Ham Steak with Cheddar Biscuits
(page 95)

Four Seasons Pizza
(page 234)

Build-Your-Own Burger Bar
(page 122)

Charred Onion Salad with Prosciutto and Parmigiano
(page 304)

Bacon and Cheddar Knockwurst Wrap-Arounds
(page 140)

Kenny's Wings of Fire with blue cheese dip,
cheddar cheese, and celery
(page 254)

North Carolina–Style Pulled Pork
(page 248)

NORTH CAROLINA BARBECUE: MY STORY

Growing up in North Carolina, I fell in love with North Carolina barbecue. But then the unthinkable happened...I moved out of state and a barbecue sandwich was only available when I made the trek home to visit. Being homesick for barbecue called for drastic measures so, one day, about 15 years ago, I decided that I was going to try making North Carolina barbecue at home. This doesn't sound so preposterous today, but when I was growing up, and even 10 years ago, no one made barbecue in his or her backyard—you bought barbecue at a pit or joint or restaurant.

For my barbecue experiment, I bought the biggest Boston butt I could find, and with no written guidance—just my memory—I generously seasoned it with salt and pepper and put it on my gas grill over indirect heat. Six hours later, I lifted the lid and saw the most beautiful piece of barbecued meat; all the fat had slowly rendered out, leaving a deeply caramelized, crisp, crunchy exterior with meltingly tender interior meat. The butt pulled apart "like butter." Once again, going from memory, I made the vinegar sauce, remembering notes of sour, sweet, salt, and a bit of heat. I concocted a sauce that was very close to the one I make today, after perfecting my recipe for all these years. I couldn't believe how good that first bite of homemade North Carolina barbecue was!

Since that fateful afternoon, I have made it my business to learn about every style of barbecue from pitmasters all over the South and parts of the Midwest. However, a nod to how simple it is to make meltingly tender pulled pork at home is that my extensively researched techniques are almost exactly the same as my first attempt.

The secret to my success is cooking slowly over low heat or "low and slow," as the saying goes—and that means indirect heat. And the trick that is never written into most recipes is to let the meat reach 190°F to 200°F. This internal temperature is higher than most books recommend; but trust me, I'm right! It is the temperature needed to be able to separate or pull the pork into perfect tender strands and melt all the connective tissue that is found on these traditionally tough cuts of meat. There is no other cooking method that has such a high flavor return for such a low investment of hands-on time. Slow-cooking with indirect heat couldn't be easier or more hands-off! Basically, you put it on the grill and forget about it for hours until the smoke, indirect heat, and the natural fat and flavors inherent in the meat work the magic.

Post-Smoking Tip

Sometimes the meat looks done—most of the fat has rendered out, leaving a dark richly carmelized crust—but the interior is not yet done (hasn't yet reached 190°F). To make sure your barbecue doesn't burn before it reaches the correct end temperature, wrap the meat in a double layer of heavy-duty aluminum foil, then put it back on the grill for 2 to 3 more hours or until the meat is meltingly tender.

Reheating Barbecue

Any type of barbecue is easy to reheat and, truth be told, most of it is better the second day after all the smoke and flavors from the rub and the sauce have had a chance to marry and infiltrate the meat. Just treat the meat gently.

Keep ribs wrapped in foil, two racks to a packet and reheat in a 275°F oven for about 30 minutes, depending on the quantity of meat. All other barbecue should be wrapped in foil and reheated in a 350°F oven for about 30 minutes, depending on size. A whole brisket should be reheated in a 250°F oven for closer to two hours. If you want a crispy top, expose the meat once it is warmed through for about 10 minutes.

NOTE: I do not recommend reheating barbecue in the microwave, as you run the risk of scorching the meat and drying it out. But if you must, use half power and add a little water or barbecue sauce to keep the meat tender and moist.

North Carolina–Style Pulled Pork

Barbecue in North Carolina is defined as pulled pork with a distinctive tangy vinegar sauce—no sweet tomato sauce allowed! The pork is either "pulled" into pieces or chopped with a meat clever and dressed with the sauce. It is served on a cheap, white flour hamburger bun topped with a simple slaw of chopped green cabbage dressed with the same vinegar sauce.

Makes 10 servings

Grilling Method: Indirect/Medium-Low Heat

1   Pork butt, Boston butt, or untrimmed
    end-cut pork shoulder roast, 7 to 9 pounds
    Olive oil
    Kosher salt
    Freshly ground pepper
    Hickory wood chips, soaked in water for
    30 minutes
    Lexington-Style Vinegar Sauce (page 249)
    or other Carolina Sauces (pages 249–250)
    North Carolina Coleslaw (see at right)
8   plain white hamburger buns, optional

1. Build a charcoal or gas grill for indirect cooking.
2. Do not trim any excess fat off the meat; this fat will naturally baste the meat and keep it moist during the long cooking time. Brush pork with a thin coating of olive oil. Season with salt and pepper. Set aside on a clean tray until ready to cook.
3. Before placing the meat on the grill, add the soaked wood chips. Place the chips directly on gray-ashed briquettes or in the smoking box of your gas grill. For more tips on smoking on a gas grill, see pages 13–15. If using a charcoal grill, you will need to add charcoal every hour to maintain the heat.
4. Place the pork in the center of the cooking grate, fat-side up, over indirect low heat. Cover and cook slowly for 4 to 5 hours at 325°F to 350°F, or until an instant-read thermometer inserted into the middle of the pork registers 190°F to 200°F. The meat should be very tender and falling apart. If there is a bone in the meat, it should come out smooth and clean with no meat clinging to it. (See the photo at right.) (This is the real test for doneness on the barbecue circuit.) Remember, there is no need to turn the meat during the entire cooking time.
5. Let the meat rest for 20 minutes or until cool enough to handle. Using rubber kitchen gloves (because it is so messy), pull the meat from the skin, bones, and fat. Set aside any crispy bits (fat) that have been completely rendered and look almost burned. Working quickly, shred the chunks of meat with 2 forks by crossing the forks and "pulling" the meat into small pieces from the butt. (See the photo at right.) Alternately, you can chop the meat with a cleaver. Chop the reserved crispy bits and mix into the pulled pork. While the meat is still warm, mix with enough Lexington-Style Vinegar Sauce to moisten and season the meat (about ¾ cup). The recipe can be made in advance up to this point and reheated with about ¼ cup additional sauce in a double boiler.

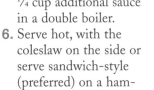

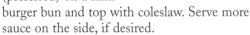

6. Serve hot, with the coleslaw on the side or serve sandwich-style (preferred) on a hamburger bun and top with coleslaw. Serve more sauce on the side, if desired.

North Carolina Coleslaw
Makes about 3 cups

1   recipe Lexington-Style Vinegar Sauce, (page 249)
1   medium head green cabbage, chopped

Toss the sauce and cabbage together until well mixed and not quite wet. You may have sauce leftover. Refrigerate. Let sit for at least 2 hours or overnight before serving.

Lexington-Style Vinegar Sauce

North Carolina barbecue (pulled pork) is distinctive and much revered because of the tangy vinegar sauce. The sauce enhances the smoky flavors of the meat without becoming the dominant flavor. The cider vinegar is mixed with two kinds of sugar, a touch of ketchup, salt, and three kinds of pepper, adding notes of sour, sweet, salt, and a bit of heat to the unctuous smoky slow-cooked pork. This is not a sauce to be tasted on its own but mixed in with the hot-off-the-grill meat since it literally makes the pork sparkle with flavor. The vinegar sauce cuts through the smoke and the natural fats to balance the dish and deliver a very clean pure pork flavor. It really proves the age-old adage that the sum of the parts is greater than the parts alone.

This sauce is a sweetened-up version of the Eastern Carolina-Style Sauce (below). It is traditionally used to dress pulled pork from Lexington, NC, and west to the mountains.

Makes about 3 cups

2	cups apple cider vinegar
1/2	cup ketchup
1/4	cup packed brown sugar
2	tablespoons sugar
1	tablespoon kosher salt
1	tablespoon ground white pepper
1/2 to 1	tablespoon red chile flakes (the more, the hotter)
1/2	teaspoon freshly ground black pepper

Mix all ingredients together in a large nonreactive bowl and let sit at least 10 minutes or almost indefinitely, covered in the refrigerator.

Eastern Carolina-Style Sauce

This eastern-style sauce is little more than vinegar and red pepper. It is the simplest of the Carolina sauces, and the most piquant, which is why it is sometimes diluted (like I did here) with water. This simple mixture is also referred to as "dip" because the pork gets dipped into the sauce to moisten and season it after it has been pulled or chopped.

Makes 4 cups

2	cups apple cider vinegar
1	cup white distilled vinegar
1	cup water
1	tablespoon kosher salt
1	tablespoon sugar
1/2	tablespoon red chile flakes (the more, the hotter—see Note below)
1	teaspoon ground white pepper
1	teaspoon freshly ground black pepper

Whisk all the ingredients together in a large non-reactive bowl and let sit at least 10 minutes. The sauce will keep almost indefinitely, covered in the refrigerator.

NOTE: The longer the sauce sits, the hotter it gets since the heat from the red pepper flakes is brought out by the vinegar. Start with 1/2 tablespoon red pepper flakes and then add more to taste.

Carolina Gold Sauce

In a few pockets of South Carolina, mostly around the state capital of Columbia, there is a tradition of a golden mustard sauce. If the sauce uses molasses as a sweetener like this one, the color is decidedly more brown than yellow, but it is still referred to as Carolina Gold. Some barbecue aficionados think it is fool's gold, but I think the mustard sauce has a natural affinity for the smoky slow-cooked pork shoulder. Besides the sauce, there is another significant difference in the way the pork is served. South Carolinians make their sandwiches minus the coleslaw on top and the bun is buttered and toasted before it's piled high with the mustard-dressed pulled pork!

Makes 2 cups

1	cup prepared yellow mustard
3/4	cup apple cider vinegar
1/2	cup molasses
1/4	cup honey
2	tablespoons peanut oil
2 1/2	teaspoons Worcestershire sauce
2	teaspoons fine-ground sea salt, optional
1/2	teaspoon ground white pepper
1/2	teaspoon freshly ground black pepper
3	dashes cayenne pepper

1. Pour the mustard, vinegar, molasses, honey, oil, and Worcestershire sauce into a stainless steel or nonreactive saucepan. Whisk to combine and bring to just under a boil, stirring well. Add the spices and whisk again.
2. Reduce to a simmer and let the sauce cook an additional 5 minutes, stirring occasionally. Let it cool before using. The sauce can be stored in a glass jar and kept for 2 weeks in the refrigerator.

TIP: The most popular Carolina mustard sauces do not include salt in their list of ingredients, because a very sweet sauce is preferred. I think that the pork tastes a little bland without the salt, so I add it, giving the sauce a little more complexity.

TIP: Most of the sauce recipes call for sticky or clinging ingredients like molasses, honey, and even ketchup. To make these ingredients literally "slip" out of the measuring cup, spray it first with a nonstick vegetable spray. It won't add any flavor to the sauce, and you'll be sure to get all the good stuff, down to the last drop.

Jack Hitt's South Carolina Mustard Sauce

Being a Piedmont, NC, girl, I didn't expect to like the controversial South Carolina mustard-sauced pork sandwich at all, but I thought—in the name of education—that I should at least try it. Passing through Columbia, SC, a few years ago, I ordered a junior barbecue sandwich with no trimmings at one of Maurice Bessinger's (a notorious Columbia barbecue figure) restaurants. Well, was I ever in for a surprise! It was absolutely delicious. As soon as I got back to Chicago, I called South Carolina native, Jack Hitt, to get his authentic take on Carolina Gold. I met Jack when he gave a rousing and expert account of the South Carolina Bessinger Brothers Barbecue Wars at the Southern Foodways Alliance Barbecue Symposium. The Carolina Gold Sauce (pages 249–250) is my version of what I tasted at Maurice's restaurant. This recipe is how Jack makes his hometown sauce. I've included his original spoken version and translated it into "recipe" writing for those who prefer a formula.

Jack's Description: "The simplest mustard sauce (though it doesn't taste anything like Maurice's) can be made by bringing a cup of white vinegar to a boil. Add a stick of margarine (you can try butter, but I find that it burns). Then add a few tablespoons of mustard. Turn it down to simmer very low for 20 minutes before using or permitting to cool.

My wife prefers Dijon. I like French's yellow mustard in the bright yellow plastic container. In fact, I find that the more processed the ingredients, the better the result. This is not a sauce known for its subtle shadings. It's a huge blast of mustard and vinegar—sharp and tart. So I can't say enough for White House vinegar, margarine, and French's. You can sweeten it from there with brown or white sugar or add weird stuff like day-old coffee. But that's the basic recipe.

Also, I always thought that if South Carolinians called it "mustard sauce" instead of barbecue sauce, we'd all have a lot less to fuss about."

The Recipe:

Makes about 1½ cups

1 cup white vinegar
½ cup (1 stick) margarine
3 tablespoons yellow (ballpark) mustard
1 to 2 tablespoons brown or white sugar or more to taste, optional

1. Bring the vinegar to boil in a medium nonreactive saucepan. Add the margarine and let it melt. Whisk in the mustard. Lower the heat and simmer for 20 minutes.
2. Remove the sauce from the heat, and let it cool before using. Store, covered in the refrigerator, for 2 weeks. Use it to moisten barbecued pork.

Texas Hill Country Market-Style Brisket

Ten years ago, my Houstonian friend Wycke Baker and I took a road trip through the Hill Country outside of Austin. Neither one of us had ever been there or eaten so much meat in so little time. We calculated that we ate 25 pounds of sausage and brisket in 48 hours, and the only vegetable was a couple of pickled jalapeños! The highlight of the trip was a private "lesson" on making smoky, melt-in-your-mouth brisket from the Elvis look-alike pitmaster at the old Kreuz Market in Lockhart, TX. His secret was starting with a whole, untrimmed brisket so the meat self-bastes during the long cooking time.

Serve with slices of white bread, sour pickles, pickled okra, and hot sauce. And, although "no sauce," is the Texas proclamation, it's pretty darn good with the Sweet K. C.–Style Dr. Pepper Barbecue Sauce (page 282).

Grilling Method: Indirect/Medium-Low Heat

Makes 8 to 10 servings

Brisket Rub

¼	cup smoked Spanish paprika (see Tip)
2	tablespoons kosher salt
1	tablespoon sea salt
2	tablespoons sugar
2	tablespoons brown sugar
1	tablespoon cumin
1½	tablespoons ground ancho chile powder (see Tip)
2	tablespoons freshly ground pepper
1	tablespoon onion powder
1	tablespoon garlic granules or granulated garlic
1	teaspoon cayenne pepper

1	whole beef brisket, untrimmed, 9 to 12 pounds
1	12-ounce bottle beer such as a Lone Star or Heineken
	Oak or mesquite wood chips, soaked in water for 30 minutes
	Texas Vinegar-Chile Hot Sauce (page 252)

1. Make the rub: In a medium bowl, combine the paprika, salts, sugars, cumin, ancho powder, pepper, onion powder, garlic granules, and cayenne; mix well. Store the rub in an airtight container or shaker-top jar.
2. Build a charcoal fire or preheat a gas grill.
3. Pat the brisket dry with paper towels. Do not trim any excess fat off the meat; this fat will naturally baste the meat and keep it moist during the long cooking time.
4. Using your hands or a shaker-top jar, sprinkle the brisket liberally with the brisket rub. Let it sit for about 5 minutes and pat the spices into the meat but do not rub—this mixture will form a dark savory crust on the meat, often referred to as the sought-after "burnt ends." Set aside on a clean tray until ready to cook.
5. If using a charcoal grill, place a drip pan between the 2 piles of white-gray ashed briquettes (on the charcoal grate). Pour the beer into the drip pan. Before placing the meat on the grill, place the soaked wood chips directly on the coals. You will need to add charcoal every hour to maintain the heat. If using a gas grill, place a drip pan with the beer in the upper left corner of the gas grill directly on top of the flavorizer bars or ceramic rock. Place the soaked wood chips in a smoker box. (For more tips on smoking, see pages 13–15.)
6. Place the brisket in the center of the cooking grate, fat-side up, over indirect medium-low heat. Cover and cook slowly for 4 to 5 hours at 325°F to 350°F, or until an instant-read thermometer inserted into the middle of the brisket registers 190°F to 200°F. The meat should be very tender and falling apart. It will feel like the consistency of butter when you insert it with the probe of the thermometer. Remember: Do not turn the meat during the entire cooking time.
7. Let the meat rest for 20 minutes or until cool enough to handle. The recipe can be made in advance up to this point and, once it is cool, wrapped in 3 layers of heavy-duty aluminum foil. To reheat the brisket, leave it in foil and heat for about 1 hour at 250°F. For a crispier crust, remove the foil at the end and put it back into the oven for another 15 minutes. Slice against the grain of the meat and serve with the Texas Vinegar-Chile Hot Sauce if desired.

TIP: Purchase smoked paprika in a Spanish food store or online at www.thespicehouse.com. If ground ancho chile powder is not available, buy dried ancho chiles and grind them in a food processor or spice grinder.

Texas Vinegar-Chile Hot Sauce

Here is how the Texas story goes. I'm not sure if it is true, or a Texas tall tale: Barbecue was first served to Mexican migrant farm workers in the Texas Hill Country out of small grocery and butcher stores. It was easy food-to-go, made for rough and tumble men—cheap, tasty, full of hot chiles, and filling. As it got more popular and the migrant farm workers were replaced by poor white residents, barbecue was served restaurant-style and many of the meat markets became barbecue restaurants. The women and children would come to join their husbands for a meal and thus were brought into the barbecue culture. Since they couldn't stomach the intense heat of the chiles, the spice was taken out of the meat—mostly sausages—and added to vinegar. That way, the men could still add all the heat they wanted to their barbecue and share a meal with the women and children.

Makes 1½ cups

1	cup white vinegar
½	cup apple cider vinegar
2	tablespoons cayenne pepper, or more to taste
1	tablespoon red chile flakes, or more to taste

Whisk all the ingredients together in a medium nonreactive bowl. Pour the sauce into a glass bottle with a top. It will keep indefinitely, covered in or out of the refrigerator.

TIP: In Texas Hill Country, a recycled Big Red soda bottle is used to hold the hot sauce. They put 1 or 2 holes in the top with an ice pick. That way, you can shake the heat on your barbecue by the bite.

Bacon-Wrapped Brisket

This is oh-so-good and adding the bacon is a great trick for reheating brisket. I created this variation on traditional brisket when I needed to make it for a party, three days in advance. You follow the brisket recipe, then wrap the brisket, mummy-style, in thick-cut smoked bacon. Mmmm good!

Makes 8 to 10 servings

1	whole beef brisket, untrimmed, 5 to 9 pounds, barbecued (pages 250–251)
2	pounds sliced hickory- or applewood-smoked bacon, at room temperature

1. After the brisket has rested for an hour, wrap it with the bacon, overlapping the slices a little so that all of the beef is completely covered. The room temperature bacon should be soft enough to adhere to itself, but if it doesn't, secure with solid wooden toothpicks.
2. Wrap the brisket twice with heavy-duty aluminum foil and store in the refrigerator until ready to reheat and serve, up to 3 days.
3. Preheat the oven to 250°F or a grill to indirect low heat and reheat the wrapped brisket for 3 hours. Remove the foil and heat it on a cookie sheet at a slightly higher heat, for an additional 30 minutes, to crisp the bacon.

The Cooks' Ribs

These smoky, tender, sweet pork ribs blew me away the first time I tasted them. Besides the meat melting off the bone, each rib had a deeply caramelized crust that reminded me

of the coveted burnt ends from pork shoulder or beef brisket. I had to find out what made them so special. My good friend Gary Pantlik created this recipe with fellow Swine and Dine barbecue team member James Prescott for a local Memphis rib competition and—no surprise—it won top honors.

Their secret is in the basting "bath" that the ribs are dipped in no fewer than five times during the barbecuing process. Since Swine and Dine only competes in the shoulder category, the boys have time to prepare some of these special ribs for the cooks—thus the name. It requires a grill with a lot of "real estate"—lots of space and some extra effort—but these ribs are worth it!

Makes 8 to 16 servings

Grilling Method: Indirect/Low Heat
Special Equipment: Rib racks, smoker box, large aluminum loaf pan, 13 x 5 x 3½ inches

8   racks back loin or baby back ribs, about
      3 pounds each
1   cup Willingham's WHAM dry rub or favorite
      rub, divided
      Hickory or oak chips or pellets, soaked in water
      for 30 minutes
2   quarts Wicker's (vinegar-based marinade)
      or Lexington-Style Vinegar Sauce
      (page 249)
4   cups Italian dressing, any brand
1   8-ounce jar clover honey

1. The night before you want to serve them, prepare
   the ribs: Remove the membrane on the back of
   each rack and generously rub them with about
   ½ cup of WHAM or your favorite barbecue rub.
   Once rubbed, cut each rack in half. Place ribs in
   a resealable plastic bag or wrap well with plastic
   wrap and refrigerate overnight.
2. When you are ready to cook, remove the ribs from
   the refrigerator and allow them to reach room
   temperature. Build a charcoal fire or preheat a gas
   grill and put on the wood chips. You want a consistent temperature of 250°F degrees.
3. This recipe replaces basting with "bathing." In a
   large disposable aluminum loaf pan, mix the
   Wicker's or Lexington-Style Vinegar Sauce and
   Italian dressing with about ¼ cup of rub. Place
   the pan on the grill to keep warm.
4. Once the grill has reached 250°F degrees, place all
   the ribs on the grill or on a rib rack over indirect
   low heat, cover, and let the smokin' begin. If the
   temperature drops a little bit, that's OK. Maintain
   a temperature between 250°F and 225°F as closely
   as possible.
5. After an hour has passed, the ribs will be ready for
   their first bath. Using a sturdy pair of locking chef
   tongs, submerge each slab in the bath pan. Give

them all a good dousing and return them to the
heat. Repeat this process each hour until the ribs
have been on the grill for 3 to 4 hours.

6. Finish the ribs: Take each half slab and give it
   one last "bath." Place it on aluminum foil for
   wrapping. Drizzle some honey on the slab and
   finish it off with one last dash of dry rub. Repeat
   the process for each slab. Stack 3 or 4 slabs on top
   of each other per foil package and wrap tightly.
   After all the ribs have been wrapped, place them
   back on the grill for 1½ more hours. Let them
   continue to slowly cook in the foil packages on
   indirect low heat. These ribs will take a total of
   4½ to 5½ hours to cook.
7. Remove the foil packages from the grill as needed
   and serve.

Ode to Owensboro Lamb Barbecue

*Owensboro, KY, is the only stop on the barbecue circuit
that I haven't had the good fortune to visit. For those who
don't know, Owensboro is famous for its barbecued mutton
or lamb. I had authentic barbecued lamb once at Gate's
in Kansas City, but never from the acclaimed source in
Kentucky. This recipe is patterned after my North Carolina
pork shoulder recipe—even if it isn't authentic, I can tell
you that it is mighty tasty!*

Makes 4 to 8 servings

Grilling Method: Combo/Medium-Low Heat

1   Lamb shoulder, 7 to 17 pounds
      Kosher salt
      Freshly ground pepper
      Olive oil
      Hickory wood chips, soaked in water for
      30 minutes
1   8-count package plain white hamburger buns
      Carolina Gold Sauce (pages 249–250) or
      Sweet K. C.–Style Dr. Pepper Barbecue
      Sauce (page 282)

1. Build a charcoal fire or preheat a gas grill.

2. Do not trim any excess fat off the meat; this fat will naturally baste the meat and keep it moist during the long cooking time. Brush the lamb with a thin coating of olive oil. Season with salt and pepper. Set aside on a clean tray until ready to cook.

3. Place the wood chips directly on the white-gray ashed briquettes or in the smoking box of your gas grill. For more tips on smoking on a gas grill, see page 14. If using a charcoal grill, you will need to add charcoal every hour to maintain the heat.

4. Place the lamb in the center of the cooking grate, fat-side up, over indirect medium-low heat. Cover and cook slowly for 4 to 8 hours, depending on size. A 7- to 9-pound leg will take 4 to 5 hours, and a 17 pound leg will take between 7 and 8 hours at 325°F to 350°F, or until an instant-read thermometer inserted into the middle of the lamb registers 190°F to 200°F. The meat should be very tender and falling apart. If there is a bone in the meat, it should come out smooth and clean with no meat clinging to it. (This is the real test for doneness on the barbecue circuit.) Remember: There is no need to turn the meat during the entire cooking time.

5. Let the meat rest for 20 minutes or until cool enough to handle. Using rubber food service gloves, pull the meat from the skin, bones, and fat. Working quickly, shred the chunks of meat with 2 forks by crossing the forks and "pulling" the meat into small pieces from the roast. Alternately, you can chop the meat.

6. Serve the lamb on buns with your favorite barbecue sauce. It is especially good with the Carolina Gold Sauce and the Sweet K. C.–Style Dr. Pepper Barbecue Sauce.

Kenny's Wings of Fire

My sister Mary Pat loves these spicy barbecued wings; they are Kenny Hay's championship recipe. Kenny is one of our Memphis in May buddies and the master of wings—among other delectable low and slow foods. His wife Lisa and daughter Erin tell him they'll fix the car, clean out the cat pan—do anything—if he'll make these wings! Once you try them, you might find yourself rich with the goods to trade for all kinds of household chores. Enjoy these with an ice cold beer and beware the heat!

Makes 4 to 6 servings

Grilling Method: Direct/Medium-Low Heat
Special Equipment: Disposable foil roasting pan

Wing Rub
2 teaspoons freshly ground black pepper
2 teaspoons ground white pepper
2 teaspoons garlic powder
2 teaspoons onion powder
2 teaspoons ground oregano
2 teaspoons sweet Spanish paprika
2 teaspoons dry mustard
2 teaspoons dried and ground sage
2 teaspoons dried and ground rosemary

4 to 5 pounds chicken wings or drumsticks, rinsed and dried

Wing Sauce
1/4 cup jalapeño hot sauce
1/4 cup Louisiana hot sauce
1/4 cup Tabasco sauce
1/4 cup barbecue sauce
3 tablespoons Worcestershire sauce
3 tablespoons cayenne pepper
3 tablespoons liquid from a jar of jalapeños
3 tablespoons red chile flakes

1. Make the rub: Combine all the spices until they are evenly distributed. Sprinkle the wings generously on all sides with the dry rub. Let the wings rest for at least 30 minutes.

2. Build a charcoal fire or preheat a gas grill.

3. Meanwhile, make the sauce: Mix together all of the sauce ingredients.

4. Place wings on the cooking grate over direct medium-low heat. Cover and cook for 10 to 15 minutes on each side. Kenny says, "the wings are done when they bounce after being dropped from 6 inches above the grill," or when the skin is brown and crisp and the meat has pulled away from the bone.

5. When thoroughly cooked, remove the wings and place them in a disposable aluminum pan. Pour the sauce into the pan of wings and stir thoroughly. Then cover the pan with foil and switch to indirect heat. Put the pan back on the grill for 15 minutes, stirring occasionally. Watch the wings vigilantly,

because the sauce will burn easily. Remove the pan from the heat and remove the foil. Stir, and then serve hot.

TIP: Every dried chile pepper or pepper hot sauce affects a different part of your tongue and throat. Decide what level of tickle is best for you and dial back the heat accordingly. This is Kenny's favorite "forehead glistening" combination.

Apple-Brined Turkey with Southern Comfort Glaze

During the years that I supervised the Butterball Turkey Talk Line, this is the turkey that I always made for those of us who had to work on Thanksgiving day. We would have a potluck dinner, and it only made sense that I would bring the turkey. This recipe is "the daddy" of turkey recipes.

The brine makes the turkey juicy, the smoke makes it taste better than a steak, and the sweet glaze makes the yummiest skin and gravy. This is not an authentic barbecue recipe, but I put it in this chapter because it's in the barbecue spirit— with wood smoking and the Southern Comfort glaze. Make it for Thanksgiving or any time you need to feed a crowd.

Makes 6 to 8 servings

Grilling Method: Indirect/Medium Heat
Special Equipment: V-rack roast holder, heavy-duty foil pan, cooler or 5-gallon bucket or stockpot or clean vegetable drawer

Brine
3	cups kosher salt
1	quart apple juice
1	cup packed brown sugar
1	cup Southern Comfort bourbon
2	oranges, quartered
1	apple, quartered
2	knobs of fresh ginger, about 4 inches total, thinly sliced
1	tablespoon whole cloves
6	bay leaves
6	large cloves garlic, cut in half
1	whole turkey, 12 to 14 pounds, defrosted

Applewood chips, soaked in water for 30 minutes
Olive oil
Kosher salt
Freshly ground pepper
2 cups Southern Comfort bourbon

1. In a large saucepan over high heat, bring the salt, apple juice, and brown sugar to a boil, stirring to dissolve the sugar and salt. Remove from the heat and add the Southern Comfort. Allow the mixture to cool to room temperature.

2. In a 5-gallon plastic bucket or other container large enough to easily hold the turkey, combine 3 quarts of water, the oranges, apple, ginger, cloves, bay leaves, and garlic. Add the apple juice–salt mixture and stir.

3. Remove the giblets from the turkey cavity. Rinse the turkey inside and out, if desired. Submerge it in the brine. Add just enough water to make sure the turkey is covered and stir to mix. If necessary, top with a resealable plastic bag filled with ice to weigh down the turkey so it is completely immersed. Refrigerate for 24 hours.

4. Remove the turkey from the brine and pat it dry. Build a charcoal fire or preheat a gas grill. On a gas grill add the wood chips to the grill during the preheat stage. Prepare the turkey as soon as you see and smell the smoke curling out of the grill.

5. Brush the turkey with oil and lightly sprinkle with salt and pepper. Place it, breast-side up, in a roasting rack set into an aluminum drip pan. Place the pan on the cooking grate over indirect medium heat. Grill-roast for 11 to 13 minutes per pound or until an instant-read thermometer inserted in the thickest part of the thigh (not touching the bone) registers 180°F and the juices run clear. During the cooking time, brush every 30 minutes with a generous amount of Southern Comfort.

6. About 30 minutes before the bird is done, remove the foil drip pan and place the bird in the center of the cooking grate. This allows the bottom of the bird to get some color and gives you the opportunity to make a gravy from the drippings that have accumulated in the foil drip pan. The Southern Comfort basting makes the most amazing gravy.

7. Transfer the turkey to a platter. Let the turkey rest for 20 minutes before carving.

The most frequent question that I get about brining is where to put the turkey while it is brining. In the winter, I put it in a cooler on my balcony. In Chicago, the winter nights are plenty cold to keep the turkey at the right temperature (below 40°F). In the summer, I opt for a smaller turkey and brine it in my vegetable drawer in the refrigerator. To do this, empty and clean out the vegetable drawer and line it with a couple of layers of plastic wrap. When the brine is cold, pour the brine into the drawer, gently add the turkey, slide the drawer closed, and brine the turkey overnight. When ready to grill, remove the turkey from the brine and follow the recipe above. Make sure you clean and rinse the vegetable drawer very well with hot water and lots of soap before and after brining.

Shortcut North Carolina Brunswick Stew

My favorite dinner as a child was my mother's slow-cooked Brunswick stew. We would have it early on Sunday nights served in deep bowls with fresh onion rolls. It is also sold as a side dish at many North Carolina barbecue restaurants, and the reason I've included it in this chapter. Brunswick stew has as many variations through the South as there are cooks. Most people start with a whole chicken, add a little pulled pork, and a few still add a squirrel or two. Since the traditional process takes so much time, I've created a shortcut version that uses boneless, skinless chicken breasts, chicken broth, and white wine or beer to replicate the depth of flavor that you get from starting with a whole chicken. The stew also freezes really well, for that homemade taste in microwave time, days after you make it.

Makes 6 to 8 servings

Olive oil
2   onions, chopped
4   celery sticks, chopped
2 to 3 15-ounce cans chicken broth
2   $14^{1}/_{2}$-ounce cans chopped or stewed tomatoes
2   11-ounce cans white corn, not creamed
1   24-ounce package lima beans, frozen or canned
4   red potatoes, unpeeled and cubed in
      $^{1}/_{2}$-inch pieces
4   carrots, sliced in $^{1}/_{2}$-circles
1   cup white wine or beer
3 to 4 pounds boneless skinless chicken breast
      halves, preferably Amish
$^{1}/_{2}$ cup chopped or pulled barbecue pork (page 248),
      optional
      Tabasco
      Kosher salt
      Freshly ground pepper

1. Heat a couple of tablespoons of olive oil in a stockpot and sauté the onions and celery until translucent, 15 to 20 minutes.
2. Add the remaining ingredients except one can of the chicken broth and the chicken. Stir to combine. Bring to a boil and add chicken.
3. Reduce heat and simmer, covered, for 2 hours. Stir occasionally. Watch to make sure that the liquid doesn't completely evaporate. Add chicken broth as needed. After 2 hours, turn the heat off and, with 2 forks, shred the chicken into small pieces. Stir so that the chicken is evenly distributed. Serve with warm onion rolls.

17th Street Bar & Grill's Tangy Baked Beans

I helped Mike Mills serve ribs and beans at the first Annual Big Apple Barbecue Block Party—hosted by Danny Meyer and his team of chefs and "pitmasters" from New York's Blue Smoke restaurant. Mike is the restaurant's barbecue partner, bringing an authentic barbecue experience to city slickers. During the weekend, I picked up some pointers from this very distinguished Murphysboro, IL, barbecue champ. He is the only four-time Memphis in May Grand Champion. I couldn't coax his prize-winning rib recipe from him, but he did give me this awesome recipe for five-bean baked beans that originated from his 17th Street Bar and Grill restaurant in Southern Illinois.

Special Equipment: Disposable aluminum container (10½ x 12½ x 2½), optional

2	15-ounce cans large butter beans, rinsed
2	10-ounce cans pork and beans, such as Campbell's
3	cups ketchup
1	15-ounce can large red kidney beans, rinsed
1	15-ounce can chili beans, such as Bush's Chili Starter
1	15-ounce can of a fifth bean of your choice, rinsed
1½	cups packed brown sugar
1	cup diced onion
1	small to medium green or red bell pepper, diced
½	cup sorghum molasses or honey
2	tablespoons yellow (ballpark) mustard
5 to 8	tablespoons Magic Dust (see Tip below) or Classic Barbecue Rub (page 280)
4 to 5	strips bacon

1. Preheat the oven to 350°F.
2. Mix together all the ingredients except the bacon in a large bowl. Put into a disposable aluminum pan (10½ x 12½ x 2½ inches) or a deep 9 x 13–inch pan. Lay the bacon strips across the top. Cover with aluminum foil and bake for 30 minutes. Remove the foil and bake for an additional 15 minutes, or until bubbly.
3. These beans reheat well. They will keep in the refrigerator for up to 1 week, well covered, and may also be frozen.

TIP: To order Mike Mills' Magic Dust, call 1-888-4-17TH-RIB or go to www.4-17TH-RIB.com

"Low and Slow" Cabbage

This is a favorite of the barbecue circuit, and it is one of those recipes that tastes much better than it sounds. The slow cooking process "melts" the cabbage, transforming it into a silky, sweet, smoky treat. Even the biggest naysaying cabbage-hater can't keep his hands off this cabbage once it is done. The real trick is to cook it until it is so tender that you can pluck a leaf from the center without any resistance.

Makes 4 servings

Grilling Method: Indirect/Medium Heat

1	medium-sized whole green cabbage
1	tablespoon barbecue spice rub, homemade (Classic Barbecue Rub, page 280) or store-bought, or kosher salt and freshly ground pepper
4	tablespoons (½ stick) unsalted butter, cut into small pieces

1. Build a charcoal fire or preheat a gas grill.
2. Remove the core of the cabbage with a sharp paring knife, leaving a hole about 3 inches deep. Gently loosen the cabbage leaves. If necessary, cut a small piece off the bottom to level the cabbage. Sprinkle the interior of the cabbage with the barbecue spice rub or salt and pepper, and spread pats of butter in the cavity and between leaves of the cabbage. Wrap the cabbage in heavy-duty aluminum foil so that all but the top is covered.
3. Place the cabbage in the center of the cooking grate over indirect medium heat. Cover and cook for 2 to 3 hours or until very tender and the leaves pluck from the core with little resistance. Baste occasionally with the butter in the cabbage core. Eat by pulling the leaves from the center or cut into wedges and serve.

Dressing the Cabbage: Everyone on the barbecue circuit has a version of this recipe. Because I truly believe that less is more, I like this simple pared-down version that I created, but that's me and might not be you. Some people I know add barbecue sauce during the last hour of cooking time, some add cream cheese to the butter, some sprinkle with grated cheese, and I even met a team whose secret ingredient was grape jelly! So, if you feel like adding your own personal touch, go right ahead; you are in good company!

HOT STOPS ON THE BARBECUE TRAIL

This list is not comprehensive or the only list to consider, but it includes my favorite places to visit when I'm in the area.

Alabama

Dreamland BBQ
1427 14th Avenue South
Birmingham, AL 35205
205-933-2133

Jim 'n Nick's Bar-B-Q
1660 Gadsden Highway
Birmingham, AL 35235
205-661-3100

Big Bob Gibson Bar-B-Q
1715 Sixth Avenue SE
Decatur, AL 35601
256-350-6969

Kansas City

Arthur Bryant's BBQ
1727 Brooklyn Avenue
Kansas City, MO 64127
816-231-1123

Fiorella's Jack Stack Barbecue
101 West 22nd Street No. 300
Kansas City, MO 64108
816-472-7427

Gates & Sons
4621 Paseo (Headquarters)
Kansas City, MO 64110
816-923-0900 or 800-662-7427

North Carolina

Allen & Son Pit-Cooked Bar-B-Q
6203 Millhouse Road
Chapel Hill, NC 27516
919-942-7576

Bar-B-Q Center
900 North Main Street
Lexington, NC 27292
336-248-4633

Lexington BBQ No. 1
10 U.S. 29/70 South
Lexington, NC 27295
336-249-9814

Stamey's BBQ
2206 High Point Road
Greensboro, NC 27403
336-299-9888

Mitchell's Barbecue
6228 South Ward Blvd.
Wilson, NC 27893
252-291-9189 or 252-291-3808

Wilber's Barbecue
4172 U.S. 70 East
Goldsboro, NC 27534
919-778-5218 or 888-778-0838

South Carolina

Bessinger's Barbecue (any of the brothers or cousins)
1602 Savannah Highway
Charleston, SC 29407
843-556-1354

Maurice's Gourmet Barbecue, original Piggie Park location
1600 Charleston Highway
West Columbia, SC 29171
803-791-0220 or 800-MAURICE

Bryan's The Pink Pig Bar-B-Que
Highway 170-A
3508 S. Okatie Hwy.
Hardeeville, SC 29927
843-784-3635

Mississippi

The Little Dooey
701 Highway 45 N
Columbus, MS 39701
662-327-0088

Tennessee

The Rendezvous Barbecue Restaurant
52 South Second Street
Memphis, TN 38103
901-523-2746

Memphis in May, international barbecue competition
Tom Lee Park
901-525-4686 (phone/fax)
(Every year, around the second week of May)

Texas

Black's BBQ
215 North Main Street
Lockhart, TX 78644
512-398-2712

Kreuz Market
619 North Colorado Street
Lockhart, TX 78644
512-398-2361

Louie Mueller BBQ
206 West Second Street
Taylor, TX 76574
512-352-6206

Meyer's Elgin Smokehouse
188 Highway 290
Elgin, TX 78621
512-281-3331

The Salt Lick
18300 FM 1826
Driftwood, TX 78619
512-894-3117

Sonny Bryan's
2202 Inwood Road
Dallas, TX 75235
214-357-7120

Angelo's
2533 White Settlement Road
Fort Worth, TX 76107
817-332-0357

Southern Illinois

17th Street Bar & Grill
32 North 17th Street
P.O. Box 382
Murphysboro, IL 62966
618-684-3722

BBQ Ribs, Rubs, and Sauces

Ribs 101

Rapid-Fire Checklist

✓ Preheat grill
✓ Soak wood chips
✓ Brush ribs with oil and season with kosher salt and pepper or barbecue rub
✓ Reduce heat to medium-low Indirect Heat
✓ Place ribs in a rib rack on cooking grate and cover
✓ Cook ribs until the meat recedes from the ends of bones and it pulls apart easily
✓ Sauce ribs only during the last 30 minutes of cooking time to prevent burning
✓ Remove ribs from grill
✓ Let ribs rest 5 to 10 minutes

Tools of the Trade

• Rubber (latex) kitchen gloves
• Heavy-duty aluminum foil
• Spice grinder (preferred) or mortar and pestle
• Spice shaker or small bowl
• Plastic tub or stainless steel hotel pan
• Immersion blender (preferred) or traditional blender
• Silicone or natural-bristle basting brush (Sources, 343–345) or long-handled natural-bristle brush
• Long-handled, locking chef tongs
• Rib rack (holder for ribs; looks like a shorter file-folder holder)
• Wood chips
• Heavy-duty oven mitt
• Plastic squeeze bottle

Common Problems

• Precooking (parcooking)
• Cooking over Direct Heat
• Saucing too soon
• Burned ribs

Who doesn't love ribs? If they are done correctly, I don't know anyone (short of a vegetarian) who can turn down a bone or two or three! Because barbecue in North Carolina, where I'm from, is all about pulled pork, I came to this conclusion about ribs late in my eating life. In 1986, when I moved to Chicago, "going out for ribs" was a very popular activity. Inevitably, all the "best" places steamed the meat, added a few drops of liquid smoke and drenched the ribs in sweet sauce. After wrestling with a half slab or two, I just thought I didn't like ribs.

Fast-forward a few years to the world's largest barbecue contest, aka Memphis in May. Talk about a rib awakening and a culinary epiphany. Not knowing what to expect, I wasn't all that excited about spending four days at a rib fest. All it took was that first bite of a grill-smoked rib for me to realize that real barbecued ribs very rarely come out of a restaurant kitchen. They are usually much better made and consumed in your own backyard. There is nothing like homemade ribs. They don't take nearly as long as the "old salts" would like you to think—they spin that yarn to give themselves more time to shoot the breeze and drink the brew!

I went on to spend many subsequent "spring breaks" on the banks of the Mississippi, experiencing, cooking, and playing at Memphis in May. I even formed my own team, Bubba Meets Bacchus (now defunct), and joined another, Swine and Dine, so I could continue my rib and pork education. In fact, in the last decade, I've only missed the contest one year. And in the name of continuing education, I make pilgrimages to all the best rib joints and barbecue shacks on and off the eaten path; it's a tough job, I know! I like to think of myself as a rib expert in perpetual training. And, in all the years since that first pivotal rib, I still contend that the best ribs are made at home, with one slight exception—Little Dooey's in Columbus, MS. Little Dooey's makes a deep-fried rib that I thought would be gilding the proverbial lily, but one bite proved me wrong. It was the best smoked rib that I have ever eaten, and I've included my version of this amazing rib so you can try it yourself.

As a certified Kansas City Barbecue Society judge, I've tasted a king's ransom of blue-ribbon ribs. In this chapter, I will share with you all the tips that I have learned from the barbecue circuit, rib masters (of their own backyards), the occasional restaurant pitmaster, and my own discoveries. So order up a few slabs from your favorite butcher, pop a beer, and let the backyard (or balcony) barbecue begin!

Common Types of Ribs

The first step to making any recipe is buying the raw ingredients. In this chapter, I focus on pork ribs and include a few recipes for beef and lamb in proportion to their availability. However, if you have ribs from another animal that you want to barbecue, you can follow these instructions and tips in this chapter.

PORK

Back Ribs: Cut from high up on the rib near the spinal column, back ribs are meaty, leaner than spareribs, and very flavorful—this is the area of the pig that produces the tenderloin. Back ribs are usually sold in either full slabs (13 bones) or half slabs (7 bones) and are the most expensive cut of rib. When they come from a pig that is less than a year old, they are referred to as baby back ribs; these generally offer more tender meat.

Spareribs: This type of rib is cut from the belly or side of the pig. Spareribs are longer and fatter than back ribs. While they have less meat, many parts of the country prefer them, and the St. Louis–style cut is gaining in popularity with restaurants, backyard barbecuers, and the barbecue circuit.

St. Louis–Style: The St. Louis cut is a sparerib trimmed to remove the flap of meat on the underside of the breast bone and squared off to more easily fit on the grill.

Country Ribs: Country ribs are not sold in slabs, but come in individual pieces. They look a little like a small pork chop and are very meaty. They are made by splitting the blade end of the loin, and the size varies greatly from one rib to the other. These are especially good if brined before cooking. (See page 98.)

BEEF

Back Ribs: Beef back ribs are often hard to find, but they are well worth the search. The (long) rib is the bone section of the standing rib roast (aka prime rib). Back ribs are the rib bones and the meat between the bones. Try to purchase them in a 7-bone rack; you can always cut them at home if you decide to grill them individually.

Short Ribs: These are much easier to find in your neighborhood grocery store. Beef short ribs are cut from the rib, chuck, or short plate sections. They are rectangular in shape, with alternating layers of lean meat and fat. Short ribs are most frequently prepared by braising, but they are perfect for barbecuing indirectly for an extended cooking time.

LAMB, VEAL, GAME

Lamb Ribs: These ribs are the easiest to find of the remaining types of popular ribs—and are some of the tastiest ribs around. Because of their small size, they make a great starter. They are so good that it's worth finding a good butcher who will order them for you.

Veal Ribs: These ribs can be found in specialty butcher shops or special ordered.

Game Ribs: Some game ribs, such as venison and elk, are very difficult to find unless you know a hunter or can order them through a game purveyor, but they are worth seeking out at least once because the meat is delicious.

Preparing the Ribs

WHAT IS THE SILVER SKIN OR BACK MEMBRANE?

Along the back (nonmeaty) side of a slab of ribs, there is a smooth covering or membrane that holds the ribs together that is sometimes referred to as the silver skin. Some people recommend removing it but it is purely optional whether you take it off or not. If you leave it on, it is a good indicator of when the ribs are done because it lifts away from the meat when the meat is cooked. It is very crispy when done and looks a little like cooked parchment paper and is slightly translucent.

Removing the Membrane

If you choose to remove the silver skin, roll up your sleeves and leave the gloves behind. In order to get a good grip on the skin, you need to use bare hands. Removing the membrane can be a little tricky; it is tightly connected to the ribs and slippery. However, if you start in the middle and wiggle your finger, an oyster knife, or the blunt end of a small stainless steel spoon underneath the thin covering, you can lift it up and pull it back toward the opposite end in a slow steady motion. Repeat the procedure for the other side

and discard the membrane. After removing the silver skin, brush a thin coat of oil along the back of the slab of ribs to seal the meat and proceed with the recipe as directed.

BUYING THE MEAT

There are a few things to remember when purchasing your meat. One: No matter what you are preparing, start with the best-quality, freshest product available. This goes for ribs and all other ingredients. Two: Find a butcher you trust. He'll give you tips on cooking, can cut meat to order, and can special order meat as well. If you don't have a local butcher, go to a grocery store that has high traffic and keeps the meat case rotated with fresh product every day. Three: Be sure to look at the expiration date on the label and give your purchases the old-fashioned smell test. If it smells "off" or a little funny, don't buy it!

Besides buying fresh meat, make sure that the ribs are meaty enough that you don't have any "bone shine" or exposed bones. Many butchers and commercial meat plants slice the fat off the ribs in one piece, leaving some of the bones exposed. This is not ideal as the meat will shrink away from the bone once it is cooked; and if the meat is already cut off, then the bones will fall out and the rack will fall apart. I also ask for ribs that still have the silver skin (back membrane), so I can decide whether to remove it.

RIB REFRESHER

If you buy ribs in the grocery store and they are not quite as pristine as you'd like them to be, try my "refresh" trick. Mix ¾ cup of apple cider vinegar with 3 cups of water and place the ribs in a large resealable plastic bag or nonreactive container with this mixture for about 20 minutes, turning frequently. Remove the ribs and proceed with the recipe as directed. Do not rinse the vinegar solution off. This trick is so good that I often do it even with really fresh ribs. The vinegar solution "cleanses" the meat and makes the flavors shine through without any "gamey" flavor.

Choosing Your Fire

Now that your ribs are waiting in the refrigerator and you're ready to start the cooking process, you have to decide what kind of fire to use. I've barbecued more ribs on gas than charcoal, and I promise you, no one can tell the difference once they are eating them. In fact, one year I barbecued a hundred slabs for 500 Memphis in May contestants all on gas grills—my guests raved about the ribs and not one of these experts could tell that they were cooked on gas.

You can smoke very effectively on both gas and charcoal grills—as long as they have a lid. You don't need a special smoker to turn out great smoked meats. However, once you barbecue ribs at home, you may discover that it's a hobby worth collecting toys for. The only kind of grill that you can't use to make ribs is a hibachi or open braiser; the grill must have a lid.

Can You Really Barbecue on a Gas Grill?

There is an age-old debate about gas versus charcoal cooking. And I will admit it is a fiery subject. But instead of getting into a heated discussion over which one is authentic or which one is better, just remember that the purpose of the heat is to cook the ribs slowly until they are meltingly tender and your mouth waters. Well, both systems do that. So the question and the answer is one of personal lifestyle preference. If you like playing with fire and stoking the coals, then charcoal is probably right for you. If you like to put the food on the grill, and forget about it until it's time to mop the ribs, or check for doneness, then gas makes sense. Gas grills also have the added benefit of keeping the temperature consistent during the whole cooking process.

The next question exploding on the tip of the debater's tongue is usually about the smoky flavor that charcoal imparts. Well, here's the truth: The "smoky" flavor that we all know and love comes from the fats and juices

dripping down and hitting a heat source (charcoal or flavorizer bars, lava rock or ceramic briquettes) and immediately vaporizing into smoke. When you cook ribs or any food "low and slow," you are cooking by indirect heat and, in a charcoal grill, that means that there is a drip pan, not a heat source underneath the food, so you actually get more of the vaporizing smoke from a gas grill. That said, wood chips *do* make a difference, and you can use them effectively on both a charcoal and a gas grill. For maximum smokiness, use a water or bullet smoker. This equipment also comes in gas, charcoal, and even electric units.

Precooking/Parboiling: Just Say No!

About now you may be thinking, "Many other books that I have tell me to precook or parboil; why shouldn't I?" The easy answer is because not a single contestant I have ever met on the barbecue circuit would let water get anywhere near their ribs.

Here's why it doesn't make sense: When you parboil, you lose all the precious fat and juices into the water. Sure, the meat starts cooking, but mostly you are losing the flavor of the meat. That is why barbecue sauce is usually so important to ribs. If ribs are cooked correctly, you really don't need much sauce. The spice and seasoning from the dry rub and the slow cooking should be enough to produce mouth-watering, complex-flavored ribs with a deeply caramelized crust and juicy tender meat that easily slips from the bone. If sauce is used, it should accentuate and complement the ribs, not overpower them.

Ribs need what little fat is on them to self-baste the meat while they slowly grill-roast or barbecue by the Indirect Method. And if the lost flavor isn't reason enough to stop this precooking madness, who wants to clean a large stockpot or roasting pan filled with cold pork fat? I can promise you that I have never, ever, precooked ribs before putting them on the grill, and I have barbecued hundreds and hundreds of slabs.

RIB TIPS

- Ribs don't take "days" to cook—just a few hours
- Anyone can master ribs with just a little information and practice
- Never precook or parboil them
- Only use the Indirect Method
- Add salt, but go easy
- Use a rib holder or rack

On the Fire: Indirect Heat

There is only one cooking method to use when barbecuing ribs and that is the Indirect Method. Because ribs are mostly bone and muscle, it takes slow cooking at a low temperature to cook the meat until it is tender and (almost) falls off the bone. This is where the colloquial barbecue term "low and slow" comes from. Ribs do require a little time and patience, but it's just enough time to make your side dishes and enjoy a nice cold libation. If you try to cook ribs by a direct heat, you will end up with burned, tough ribs—guaranteed!

Dry Versus Wet Ribs

Have you ever wondered what rib aficionados are talking about when they debate the merits of wet or dry ribs? Kansas City is famous for wet ribs and Memphis is known for dry rubbed ribs. Well, it's very simple. Dry ribs have been rubbed with a dry spice mixture known as a barbecue rub and cooked without any sauce. They are served "dry" with sauce on the side. Wet ribs are cooked with or without a rub on them and are brushed with sauce during the last 30 minutes of the cooking time. Wet ribs may also be "mopped" (see Sidebar, page 281) with a thin seasoned liquid during most of the cooking time.

Sauce on the Side

Barbecue refers to the process of cooking low and slow and should not conjure up memories of sweet tomatoey barbecue sauce. But most people associate the taste of barbecue with the taste of sauce. Once you cook ribs using these instructions, you might find that the meat tastes so good that there is no need to mask it with loads of barbecue sauce. For this reason, I almost always recommend serving the sauce on the side. But, just like everything else worth having, there are a few caveats. Some recipes need the sauce to complete them. This is particularly true with the Kansas City–Style Ribs (pages 267–268) and the Chinese Take-Out Baby Back Ribs (pages 272–273). These two recipes rely on the sauces being "barbecued" on the ribs and cannot be made to the same degree of success if served side saddle.

Testing for Doneness

How do you tell if the ribs are done? It's pretty difficult to use an instant-read thermometer on ribs, so here are some physical signs that make it easy to tell if they are done:

- The ends of the bones are exposed and dry (the meat has shrunk back from the ends of the bones).
- The meat pulls away easily from the bones. You could tear a rib from the rack without much resistance.
- The silver skin (if left on) is pulling away from the back of the rack.

If the ribs are as done as you like on the outside but the meat is still a little tough, take the ribs off the grill, wrap them in heavy-duty aluminum foil, and put them back on the grill over low indirect heat. If you have several racks, wrap them together or individually, stacked on top of each other. You can also reheat ribs this way. If you want to add a little barbecue sauce, take the ribs out of the foil when they are fully cooked and tender, brush with sauce, and put them on the grill grate, uncovered, until the sauce is warmed through, begins to bubble, and caramelizes.

Mix and Match Ribs or Ribs 101

This recipe is designed to help you find your own rib nirvana. Mix and match one rub and either a mop or a sauce from the selections in this chapter (pages 280–285). Since taste is subjective, I urge you to use these recipes as a point of departure—a road map to developing your own "secret recipe" for blue-ribbon ribs. You don't have to use both a mop and a sauce, but use at least one. You can also substitute good-quality commercial rubs and sauces if you prefer.

Makes 4 to 8 servings

Grilling Method: Indirect/Medium-Low Heat

> Wood chips, soaked in water for 30 minutes optional)
> 4   slabs ribs, about 3 pounds each
> 1/4   cup spice rub, such as Three-Chile Rub (page 278)
> 1   cup mop, such as Pineapple and Ginger Mop (page 282)
> 1   cup barbecue sauce, such as Smoky Chipotle Tequila Barbecue Sauce (page 284)

1. Build a charcoal fire or preheat a gas grill. Set up your grill for indirect heat and if using wood chips, place the soaked chips directly on the charcoal or in the smoking box of a gas grill.
2. Remove the silver skin from the back of the ribs, if desired. Pat the ribs dry with paper towels. Sprinkle the ribs liberally with spice rub and let them sit, covered, for 15 to 20 minutes.
3. Place the ribs, bone-side down, in the center of the cooking grate or in a rib holder or rack, over indirect medium-low heat. Grill, covered (at about 325°F, if your grill has a thermometer) for 1½ to 2 hours or until the meat is tender and has pulled back from the ends of the rib bones.

RIB GRILLED-OVERS

While the grill is hot, plan to barbecue a few extra racks of ribs to serve later in the week. They'll keep for up to 4 days in the refrigerator. Take the ribs off the grill and wrap them individually in heavy-duty aluminum foil. Refrigerate. When you are ready to serve them, preheat your oven to 300°F (or set your grill to Indirect/Medium-Low Heat). Place the foil wrapped ribs in the oven or grill for 15 minutes. Remove from oven and increase the oven temperature to 350°F (no need to increase the grill temperature). Unwrap the ribs and place them on a cookie sheet. Brush with sauce for "wet" ribs or brush with a thin coating of olive oil for "dry" ribs. Place the ribs back in the oven or on the grill to caramelize the sauce or "crisp" the crust, about 15 minutes. Remove them from oven, and let sit for 5 minutes before cutting and serving.

4. Leave ribs untended for the first 30 minutes— this means no peeking; especially important if you're using wood chips. After the first 30 minutes, if using a mop, baste the ribs with the mopping sauce every 20 minutes. If the ribs start to burn on the edges, stack them on top of one another in the very center of the grill and lower the heat slightly; 20 minutes before serving, unstack the ribs if necessary and brush with the "finishing" barbecue sauce.
5. Remove the ribs from the grill and place them on a clean platter. Let them rest for 10 minutes before cutting into individual or 2 to 3 rib portions.
6. While the ribs rest, warm any remaining sauce in a saucepan. Serve the ribs hot, with sauce on the side.

TIP: If you are using a rib rack or holder, place the rack of ribs with the larger end of the bone down. This way, the largest end of the bones will be closest to the heat and will protect the smaller ends from burning.

SOME OF MY ALL-TIME FAVORITE COMBINATIONS

> Classic Barbecue Rub (page 280) + Bloodshot Mop (page 281)
>
> Camera-Ready Rub (page 280) + Sassy Bourbon and Brown Sugar Barbecue Sauce (pages 284–285)
>
> Three-Chile Rub (pages 278–279) + Pineapple and Ginger Mop (page 282)

Salt and Pepper Ribs

Truth be told, I like my ribs seasoned with kosher salt, freshly ground pepper, and a light coating of olive oil as much as any of the other versions in this chapter. You have to prepare yourself for a milder taste, but it is the best choice when you want to let the natural goodness of really fresh pork (or beef) ribs shine. Make these with best-quality meat.

Makes 4 to 8 servings

Grilling Method: Indirect/Medium-Low Heat

  Applewood chips, soaked in water for
    30 minutes (optional)
4 racks baby back or beef ribs, about 3 pounds each
2 lemons, cut in half
2 tablespoons kosher salt
2 tablespoons freshly ground pepper
  Sassy Bourbon and Brown Sugar Barbecue
    Sauce (pages 284–285) (optional)

1. Build a charcoal fire or preheat a gas grill. Set up the grill for indirect heat; if using wood chips, place the soaked chips directly on the charcoal, or in the smoking box of a gas grill.
2. Remove the silver skin from the back of the ribs, if desired. Rub the cut lemons over the front and back of the ribs, squeezing to release as much juice as possible. Set aside for 5 minutes.
3. In a small bowl, mix the salt and pepper together and sprinkle the ribs liberally with the mixture.
4. Place the ribs, bone-side down, in the center of the cooking grate, or in a rib holder or rack, over indirect medium-low heat. Grill covered (at about 325°F, if your grill has a thermometer) for 1½ to 2 hours or until the meat is tender and has pulled back from the ends of the rib bones.
5. Leave the ribs untended for the first 30 minutes—this means no peeking; especially important if using wood chips. If the ribs start to burn on the edges, stack them on top of one another in the very center of the grill and lower the heat slightly. Twenty minutes before serving, unstack if necessary and brush the ribs with the barbecue sauce.
6. Remove the ribs from the grill; let them rest for 10 minutes before cutting into individual or 2 to 3 rib portions. Warm any remaining sauce in a saucepan and serve on the side.

Bubba's Bunch Barbecued Baby Back Ribs

This recipe is my version of ribs that won a Memphis in May Patio Porkers contest a few years back. The team Bubba's Bunch, took me under their wing and taught me everything they knew—or so they said—about ribs. Their secret was marinating the ribs in lemon juice before rubbing spices into the meat. Their spice rub of choice was WHAM (see Sources, pages 343–345), which they bought directly from barbecue circuit legend John Willingham in a brown paper bag before he started packaging it commercially. I've streamlined their process with cut lemons and a homemade rub. But if you have the opportunity, pick up a bottle of WHAM—it's truly one of the best barbecue spice rubs I've ever tasted.

Makes 4 to 8 servings

Grilling Method: Indirect/Medium-Low Heat

4 racks baby back ribs, about 3 pounds each
2 lemons, cut in half
¼ cup Classic Barbecue Rub (page 280) or
    Willingham's WHAM barbecue rub
  Wood chips, soaked in water for 30 minutes
    (optional)
1 cup favorite barbecue sauce

1. Build a charcoal fire or preheat a gas grill. Set up the grill for indirect heat and if using wood chips, place the soaked chips directly on the charcoal, or in the smoking box of a gas grill.
2. Remove the silver skin from the back of the ribs, if desired. Rub the cut lemons over the front and back of the ribs, squeezing to release as much juice as possible. Set aside for 5 minutes. Sprinkle the ribs liberally with spice rub and let them sit, covered, for 15 to 20 minutes.
3. Place the ribs, bone-side down, in the center of the cooking grate, or in a rib holder or rack, over indirect medium-low heat. Grill covered (at about 325°F, if your grill has a thermometer) for 1½ to 2 hours or until the meat is tender and has pulled back from the ends of the rib bones.
4. Leave the ribs untended for the first 30 minutes—this means no peeking; especially important if

using wood chips. If the ribs start to burn on the edges, stack them on top of one another in the very center of the grill and lower the heat slightly. Twenty minutes before serving, unstack the ribs if necessary, and brush them with barbecue sauce.

5. Remove the ribs from the grill and place them on a clean platter. Let them rest for 10 minutes before cutting into individual or 2 to 3 rib portions.

6. While the ribs rest, warm any remaining sauce in a saucepan. Serve the ribs hot, with sauce on the side, if desired.

Renaissance Ribs

I created these ribs quite by accident one year at Memphis in May. After barbecuing about 50 slabs of ribs for a party, I was tired of the traditional "barbecue" rub and tried a concoction of Italian herbs, red chile flakes, and sesame seeds. I had no idea what the result would be, but everyone loved them. So much so that I even featured them at a dinner that I did for the New York City–based culinary organization, The James Beard Foundation. These ribs are so popular in my house that I usually make a few slabs with this rub every time I make ribs. Serve them "dry,"—with only a light coating of olive oil. The oil will bring out the flavor of the pork and spices; barbecue sauce will mute the flavors. For the same reason, I do not recommend using wood chips to smoke the meat as it cooks.

Makes 4 to 8 servings

Grilling Method: Indirect/Medium-Low Heat

Italian Spice Rub
- 2   tablespoons sesame seeds
- 2   tablespoon granulated garlic
- 1   tablespoon dried Mediterranean oregano
- 1   tablespoon red chile flakes
- 2   teaspoons dried rosemary
- 2   teaspoons dried lemon peel

- 4   racks baby back ribs, about 3 pounds each (optional)
- 2   cups water
- 1/2   cup fresh lemon juice (about 2 lemons)
  Kosher salt
  Olive oil (preferred) or favorite barbecue sauce (optional)

1. Make the spice rub: Combine the sesame seeds and spices in a small bowl until well mixed.

2. Build a charcoal fire or preheat a gas grill, setting up the grill for indirect heat.

3. Remove the silver skin from the back of the ribs, if desired. Combine the lemon juice and water and set aside. Place the ribs in a plastic resealable bag or nonreactive container and cover them with the lemon juice mixture. Marinate for 20 to 30 minutes (no longer or the meat will get mushy).

4. Remove the ribs from the marinade and sprinkle them front and back with the spice rub. This can be done up to 1 day in advance, and they can be kept wrapped in aluminum foil in the refrigerator. Just before cooking, season with salt.

5. Place the ribs, bone-side down, in the center of the cooking grate or in a rib holder or rack over indirect medium-low heat. Grill covered (at about 325°F, if your grill has a thermometer) for 1½ to 2 hours or until the meat is tender and has pulled back from the ends of the rib bones.

6. Leave the ribs untended for the first 30 minutes— this means no peeking. If the ribs start to burn on the edges, stack them on top of one another in the very center of the grill and lower the heat slightly. Twenty minutes before serving, brush the ribs with a light coating of olive oil or the optional barbecue sauce.

7. Remove the ribs from the grill and let them rest 10 minutes before cutting into individual or 2 to 3 rib portions.

Kansas City–Style Ribs

In Kansas City, there's a saying that goes, "If it moves, we barbecue it!" That said, Kansas City is probably more famous for ribs than anything else. And in Kansas City, the sauce is as important as the meat. If you don't have time to make the sauce, opt for store-bought KC Masterpiece; it's the original Kansas City barbecue sauce, rich in the classic sweet and tangy flavors for which Kansas City is known.

Makes 4 to 8 servings

Grilling Method: Indirect/Medium-Low Heat

Sweet K. C. Barbecue Rub

- ½ cup packed brown sugar
- ½ cup freshly ground pepper
- ¼ cup sweet paprika
- ¼ cup kosher salt
- 1 tablespoon white pepper
- 1 tablespoon celery salt
- 1 tablespoon onion powder
- 1 tablespoon dry mustard
- 2 teaspoons good-quality chili powder or powdered ancho chiles
- 2 teaspoons ground cumin
- 1½ teaspoons ground thyme
- 1 teaspoon ground cinnamon
- ½ teaspoon ground cloves
- ½ teaspoon cayenne pepper, or more to taste

    Hickory or oak wood chips, soaked in water for 30 minutes
- 4 slabs pork back ribs, about 3 pounds each
- 1 cup favorite barbecue sauce or Sweet K. C.–Style Dr. Pepper Barbecue Sauce (page 282)

1. Make the rub: Mix together all the ingredients in a small bowl until well combined.
2. Build a charcoal fire or preheat a gas grill. Set up the grill for indirect heat; if using wood chips, place the soaked chips directly on the charcoal or in the smoking box of a gas grill.
3. Remove the silver skin from the back of the ribs, if desired. Sprinkle the ribs liberally with the spice rub and let them sit, covered, for 15 to 20 minutes.
4. Place the ribs, bone-side down, in the center of the cooking grate or in a rib holder or rack over indirect medium-low heat. Grill covered (at about 325°F, if your grill has a thermometer) for 1½ to 2 hours or until the meat is tender and has pulled back from the ends of the rib bones.
5. Leave ribs untended for the first 30 minutes—this means no peeking, especially important if using wood chips. If the ribs start to burn on the edges, stack them on top of one another in the very center of the grill and lower the heat slightly. Twenty minutes before serving, unstack them if necessary and brush with barbecue sauce.
6. Remove the ribs from the grill and let them rest for 10 minutes before cutting into individual or 2 to 3 rib portions. Warm any remaining sauce in a saucepan and serve on the side.

Memphis-Style "Dry" Ribs with Spicy "Drippings"

There's no question that Memphis, TN, is one of the best places in America to eat ribs. One of the distinguishing features of Memphis ribs is the style known as "dry" ribs. Popularized by Charlie Vergos' famous Rendezvous restaurant, dry ribs have no sauce, at least for the purists. Instead, the ribs are flavored with a spice rub and served with the "drippings"— the reserved juice from the barbecued ribs. I sat next to Charlie a few years ago year as we judged the Jack Daniel's World Championship Invitational Barbecue Contest and tried to charm him out of his recipe. While he was understandably reluctant to divulge his trade secrets, this recipe is my version of the ribs that put Memphis on the map. The combination of the rub and the mop makes a delicious crust for the ribs.

Makes 4 to 8 servings

Grilling Method: Indirect/Medium-Low Heat
Special Equipment: disposable aluminum turkey roasting pan

Rendezvous-Style Dry Rub

- ¼ cup kosher salt
- ¼ cup sugar
- 2 tablespoons black peppercorns, coarsely ground
- 1 tablespoon mustard seeds
- 1 tablespoon cumin seeds
- 1 tablespoon fennel seeds
- 1 tablespoon sweet paprika
- 2 teaspoons celery salt
- 2 teaspoons red chile flakes
- 2 teaspoons dried oregano
- 1 teaspoon dried thyme
- 1½ cups apple juice
- 1½ cups water
- ½ tablespoon fine sea salt

- 4 slabs back ribs, about 3 pounds each

1. Make the rub: Combine all the spices in a small bowl. Divide the mixture in half. Put half of the rub in a spice (coffee) grinder or mortar and pestle and grind the spices to a medium consistency. Mix that with the reserved spice rub.

(This will make a rub that is easily absorbed by the meat during "rubbing" and still has texture.) Set aside.

2. Make the mop: Mix 1 tablespoon of the dry rub with the apple juice, water, and salt until the salt is dissolved. Set aside.

3. Build a charcoal fire or preheat a gas grill, setting up the grill for indirect heat.

4. Remove the silver skin from the back of the ribs, if desired. Sprinkle the ribs liberally with the spice rub and let sit, covered, for 15 to 20 minutes. Place an aluminum pan on top of the cooking grate.

5. Using a rib rack, arrange the ribs on the rack. Place the ribs in the aluminum pan on the center of the cooking grate over indirect medium-low heat. Pour 1 cup of the apple juice mop into the drip pan.

6. Grill covered (at about 325°F, if your grill has a thermometer) for 1½ to 2 hours or until the meat is tender and has pulled back from the ends of the rib bones.

7. Leave ribs untended for the first 30 minutes—this means no peeking. Then using the apple juice mixture, baste or "mop" the ribs every 20 minutes, adding a little more apple juice mop (about ¼ cup) to the drip pan each time. You will do this twice. When the mop is gone and the juices have accumulated in the drip pan, baste the ribs with the drippings 1 more time. If the ribs start to burn on the edges, stack them on top of one another in the very center of the foil pan and lower the heat slightly.

8. About 10 minutes before the ribs are done, remove them from the pan and place them on the cooking grate over indirect heat to finish browning and crisp the surface crust. (If your ribs are already crispy and have a caramelized crust on the outside, this last step may not be necessary.)

9. Meanwhile, pour the pan drippings through a fine sieve or fine-mesh strainer into a saucepan and bring to a boil, adding any leftover apple juice mop. Taste and adjust the seasonings.

10. Remove the ribs from the grill and let them rest for 10 minutes before cutting into individual or 2 to 3 rib portions. Serve the ribs with warm drippings on the side.

Memphis in May World Championship Ribs

Memphis-style ribs are as dry as Kansas City–style ribs are wet! I created these very simple ribs after nosing around the rigs of many of the championship teams. The secret to these ribs is the thin mop that you baste the ribs with during the final hour of cooking time.

Makes 4 to 8 servings

Grilling Method: Indirect/Medium-Low Heat

Memphis in May Mop

1 **12-ounce beer, preferably Budweiser**
½ **cup Sassy Bourbon and Brown Sugar Barbecue Sauce (page 284) or favorite barbecue sauce**
1 **tablespoon Classic Barbecue Rub or favorite barbecue rub**

4 **slabs back ribs, about 3 pounds each**
 Hickory wood chips, soaked in water for 30 minutes (optional)
 Apple Cider Vinegar Marinade (page 278)
 Olive oil
 Classic Barbecue Rub (page 280)
 Favorite barbecue sauce, optional

1. Make the mop: Combine the ingredients in a bowl and mix well. Let them sit for 10 minutes, stirring occasionally to make sure all the carbonation is gone. Place the mop in a squeeze bottle or leave it in the bowl. Set aside until ready to use. The mop can be made in advance and refrigerated for up to 1 week.

2. Build a charcoal fire or preheat a gas grill. Set up the grill for indirect heat; if using wood chips, place the soaked chips directly on the charcoal or in the smoking box of a gas grill.

3. Remove the silver skin from the back of the ribs, if desired. Put the ribs in a resealable plastic bag or nonreactive container with the Apple Cider Vinegar Marinade for 15 minutes (no longer or the meat will become mushy), turning frequently to make sure all the surfaces are wet and marinating.

4. Remove the ribs and let them sit for 5 minutes. Discard the marinade. Brush the ribs with a light coating of olive oil and sprinkle liberally with the spice rub. Let them sit, covered, for 15 to 20 minutes.

5. Place the ribs, bone-side down, in the center of the cooking grate or in a rib holder or rack over indirect medium-low heat. Grill covered (at about 325°F, if your grill has a thermometer) for 1½ to 2 hours or until the meat is tender and has pulled back from the ends of the rib bones.

6. Leave the ribs untended for the first 30 minutes—this means no peeking, especially important if using wood chips. After the first 30 minutes, baste the ribs with the mopping sauce every 20 minutes. If the ribs start to burn on the edges, stack them on top of one another in the very center of the grill and lower the heat slightly. Ten minutes before the ribs are done, stop mopping them.

7. Remove the ribs from the grill and let them rest for 10 minutes before cutting into individual or 2 to 3 rib portions. Serve with warmed sauce on the side, if desired.

North Carolina Vinegar Sauce–Soaked Ribs

In North Carolina, pulled pork is king and "barbecue" means just that—pulled pork. You rarely see folks eating ribs unless they are at a franchised restaurant that specializes in ribs from Kansas City, Chicago, or Memphis. However, Ed Mitchell, from Mitchell's Barbecue in Wilson, NC, shared some ribs with me that he had made for himself. They were so good that I started making them at home. The trick is to barbecue the ribs as usual, and then soak and serve them in a North Carolina vinegar sauce. This is a taste near and dear to North Carolinian palates—although the sauce is well balanced by the sugar and other sweet ingredients, it is quite tart from all the vinegar and has a bit of a bite from the peppers.

Makes 4 to 8 servings

Grilling Method: Indirect/Medium-Low Heat

Wood chips, soaked in water for 30 minutes (optional)
4 racks baby back ribs, about 3 pounds each
Apple Cider Vinegar Marinade (page 278)
Olive oil
Kosher salt
Freshly ground pepper
Eastern Carolina–Style Sauce (page 249)

1. Build a charcoal fire or preheat a gas grill. Set up the grill for indirect heat; if using wood chips, place the soaked chips directly on the charcoal or in the smoking box of a gas grill.

2. Remove the silver skin from the back of the ribs, if desired. Place the ribs in a resealable plastic bag or nonreactive container and cover them with the marinade. Soak for 15 minutes (no longer or the meat will get mushy), turning frequently to make sure all the surfaces are wet and marinating.

3. Remove the ribs from the marinade and let them sit for 5 minutes. Discard the marinade. Brush the ribs with a light coating of olive oil and season with kosher salt and just a little pepper, because the sauce has a lot of pepper, in it

4. Place the ribs, bone-side down, in the center of the cooking grate or in a rib holder or rack over indirect medium-low heat. Grill covered (at about 325°F, if your grill has a thermometer) for 1½ to 2 hours or until the meat is tender and has pulled back from the ends of the rib bones.

5. Leave the ribs untended for the first 30 minutes—this means no peeking, especially important if using wood chips. If the ribs start to burn on the edges, stack them on top of one another in the very center of the grill and lower the heat slightly. Twenty minutes before serving, baste or "mop" the ribs with the Eastern Carolina–Style Sauce.

6. Remove the ribs from the grill, immediately place them in a shallow pan and pour the rest of the sauce over the ribs until they are soaking in the sauce. Let them rest for 10 minutes before cutting into individual or 2 to 3 rib portions.

7. Serve the ribs soaking in the sauce.

Applewood-Smoked, Cider-Steamed, Dry-Rubbed Ribs

The rib that was responsible for my "rib-awakening" was made by a team of graduated fraternity brothers from Georgia. Their secret was to steep the cooked ribs in just a little bit of apple cider—when they were hot off the grill—for added moisture. Here's my version of their sweet smoke-kissed ribs.

Makes 4 to 8 servings

Grilling Method: Indirect/Medium-Low Heat

	Applewood chips, soaked in water for 30 minutes
4	racks baby back ribs, about 3 pounds each
1/4	cup Three-Chile Rub (pages 278–279)
1	teaspoon ground cinnamon
1	cup apple cider or juice
	Favorite barbecue sauce, optional

1. Build a charcoal fire or preheat a gas grill. Set up the grill for indirect heat and place the soaked chips directly on the charcoal or in the smoking box of a gas grill.

2. Remove the silver skin from the back of the ribs, if desired. Mix the spice rub and cinnamon until well combined. Sprinkle the ribs liberally with the spice rub and let them sit, covered, for 15 to 20 minutes.

3. Place the ribs, bone-side down, in the center of the cooking grate or in a rib holder or rack over indirect medium-low heat. Grill covered (at about 325°F, if your grill has a thermometer) for 1½ to 2 hours or until the meat is tender and has pulled back from the ends of the rib bones.

4. Leave the ribs untended for the first 30 minutes— this means no peeking, especially important if using wood chips. If the ribs start to burn on the edges, stack them on top of one another in the very center of the grill and lower the heat slightly.

5. Twenty minutes before serving, remove the ribs from the grill and place each rack on a sheet of heavy-duty aluminum foil large enough to cover the ribs completely.

6. Pour 2 tablespoons of apple cider over each rack, and seal each packet tightly, making sure the liquid stays in the foil packets.

7. Place the foil-wrapped racks back on the covered grill for 20 to 30 minutes so the meat will absorb the apple cider. It is important that the foil-wrapped ribs are not over any direct heat and can be stacked one on top of another. Remove the foil packets from the grill and open them.

8. Let the meat rest for 10 minutes, uncovered, before transferring it to a carving board to cut the ribs into individual or 2 to 3 rib portions. If desired, warm your favorite barbecue sauce in a saucepan and serve it on the side.

A HINT OF GARLIC

Don't overlook granulated garlic, or dehydrated garlic, as it is sometimes labeled. It is a great pantry staple; it is all natural and gaining popularity among both restaurant chefs and home cooks. Here's how they make it: Fresh garlic is ground and dehydrated, resulting in a dried garlic that is ideally suited to dry spice rubs and sauces. The flavor releases and dissolves during the cooking process and is a great substitute for fresh garlic. The rule of thumb is that about 1/4 teaspoon granulated garlic equals 1 medium garlic clove. Granulated garlic does not contain salt and is not the same as "garlic salt" or "garlic powder." If you can't find this spice in your grocery store, you can purchase it at www.thespicehouse.com.

Chinese Take-Out Baby Back Ribs

These ribs remind me of early Sunday evenings waiting for take-out at my favorite Chinese restaurant. I usually snack on these ribs while I wait for the rest of the order to cook. The combination of the sweet and spicy marinade and sauce makes these Asian-flavored ribs explode with flavor. These ribs are truly ying and yang—with the sweet and spicy balancing each other—and rely on a fresh sprinkling of sea salt just before serving to bring out the sweetness of the ribs.

Makes 4 to 8 servings

Grilling Method: Indirect/Medium-Low Heat

Asian Marinade
- 1 cup sherry
- ³/₄ cup low-sodium soy sauce
- ¹/₂ cup chopped green onions, about 1 bunch
- ¹/₄ cup red wine vinegar
- ¹/₄ cup sugar
- ¹/₄ cup toasted sesame oil
- 2 small knobs (1 to 2 inches long) fresh ginger, peeled and grated, about 1 tablespoon
- 1 teaspoon granulated garlic
- 1 teaspoon red chile flakes
  Pinch freshly ground pepper

Hoisin-Style Barbecue Sauce
- 2 tablespoons peanut or olive oil
- 1 small onion, chopped
- 3 cloves garlic, chopped
- 1 cup plus 2 heaping tablespoons hoisin sauce (see Tip, page 273), divided
- ¹/₂ cup low-sodium soy sauce
- ¹/₂ heaping cup red currant or seedless raspberry jelly
- ¹/₃ cup red wine vinegar
- 2 small knobs (1 to 2 inches long) fresh ginger, peeled and grated, about 1 tablespoon
- 1 tablespoon garlic-chili sauce (*sriracha*), or more to taste
- 1 tablespoon brown sugar
- 1 tablespoon molasses
  Kosher salt
  Freshly ground pepper

- 4 slabs baby back ribs, about 3 pounds each
  Olive oil

Kosher salt
Freshly ground pepper
Fleur de sel or other sea salt (optional)

1. Make the marinade: Combine the ingredients in a medium bowl. Set aside until ready to use. If making up to 24 hours in advance, add all ingredients except the onions and store, covered, in the refrigerator. Add the onions just before marinating.
2. Make the barbecue sauce: Heat the oil in a heavy saucepan over medium heat for about 2 minutes. Sauté the onion and garlic until translucent, about 10 minutes. Add 1 cup of the hoisin sauce, the soy sauce, jelly, vinegar, ginger, chili sauce, sugar, and molasses. Simmer for 30 minutes or until slightly thickened. Whisk in the 2 tablespoons reserved hoisin sauce. Season to taste with salt and pepper. Let the sauce cool and set it aside.
3. Meanwhile, build a charcoal fire or preheat a gas grill. Set up the grill for indirect heat.
4. Remove the silver skin from the back of the ribs, if desired. Place the ribs in a resealable plastic bag or nonreactive container and cover them with the marinade. Soak for 20 minutes (no longer or the meat will get mushy), turning frequently to make sure all the surfaces are wet and marinating.
5. Remove the ribs from the marinade and let them sit for 5 minutes. Discard the marinade. Place the ribs, bone-side down, in the center of the cooking grate or in a rib holder or rack over indirect medium-low heat. Grill covered (at about 325°F, if your grill has a thermometer) for 1¹/₂ to 2 hours or until the meat is tender and has pulled back from the ends of the rib bones.
6. Leave the ribs untended for the first 30 minutes (no peeking). If the ribs start to burn on the edges, stack them on top of one another in the center of the grill and lower the heat slightly. Twenty minutes before the ribs are done, unstack them if necessary and brush them with barbecue sauce. (Don't sauce the ribs too soon; the high sugar content of the hoisin sauce causes it to burn easily.)
7. Remove the ribs from the grill and let them rest for 10 minutes before cutting into individual or 2 to 3 rib portions. Just before serving, sprinkle the ribs with sea salt or fleur de sel. This step is essential as the fresh salt brings out the sweetness of the sauce. Serve with warmed sauce on the side, if desired.

TIP: *Sriracha* and hoisin sauce are available in the Asian section of a large grocery store or at any Asian market.

TIP: Grating the ginger maximizes the flavor for the marinade and sauce, meaning more ginger flavor for the ribs. To get 2 tablespoons for the recipes, you will need a knob of fresh ginger that is 4 to 5 inches long. Peel the ginger with a vegetable peeler and use either my GrillFriends SuperGrater or a Microplane grater. Alternatively, you could puree the ginger in a food processor, but you will need to be careful not to pulverize it.

TIP: For an extra-pretty presentation of these Asian-flavored ribs, cut the ribs into 2-bone portions and tie a fresh chive or the green part of a green onion around the rib. Make a double knot and cut the ends, leaving 1-inch pieces on the rib bundles. Sprinkle toasted sesame seeds on the ribs and serve stacked up on a square or other geometric platter.

Backyard Version of Little Dooey's Fried Smoked Ribs

Admittedly unusual, I dubbed these ribs "pork popsicles." The idea to batter-up and deep-fry a smoked rib came from Little Dooey's restaurant in the Mississippi Delta. In my version, the twice-dipped batter coating seals the juicy tender meat and is a crunchy counterpoint to the smoky rib it encases. This is one recipe that you have to plan for, as it takes two days—one day to smoke the ribs, another to fry them. They rest in the refrigerator in between. Take the time at least once to make these ribs; I promise they are worth it, and it makes a great story to boot. This is also a great way to reheat any leftover ribs. This recipe will serve more people than a traditional recipe, as the fried coating makes the ribs richer and more filling.

Makes 8 to 10 servings

Grilling Method: Indirect/Medium-Low Heat
Special Equipment: Deep-fat fryer (optional), frying basket or pair of long-handled tongs

Simple Spice Rub
¼ cup kosher salt
¼ cup freshly ground pepper
¼ cup smoked paprika
¼ cup sugar
1 tablespoon garlic powder
1 tablespoon good-quality chili powder or powdered ancho chiles
2 teaspoons ground cumin
1 teaspoon cayenne pepper, or more to taste

Hickory or oak wood chips, soaked in water for 30 minutes
4 slabs St. Louis–style pork ribs (page 261), about 3 pounds each
2 lemons, cut in half

Seasoned Flour
1 tablespoon kosher salt
1 tablespoon black peppercorns, toasted
2 teaspoons cayenne
2 cups flour (not self-rising)

Egg Wash
1 egg
1 cup milk

1 24-ounce bottle peanut or other neutral oil
Gussied-Up Pennsylvania Black Vinegar Sauce (page 282–283) or favorite barbecue sauce

1. On day I, make the spice rub by mixing all the ingredients together in a small bowl until well combined.

2. Build a charcoal fire or preheat a gas grill. Set up the grill for indirect heat and place the soaked chips directly on the charcoal or in the smoking box of a gas grill.

3. Remove the silver skin from the back of the ribs, if desired. Rub the cut lemons over the front and back of the ribs, squeezing to release as much juice as possible. Set aside for 5 minutes. Then sprinkle the ribs liberally with the spice rub.

4. Make sure that the wood chips are smoking and place the ribs, bone-side down, in the center of the cooking grate or in a rib holder or rack over indirect medium-low heat. Grill covered (at about 325°F, if your grill has a thermometer) for 1½ to 2 hours or until the meat is tender and has pulled back from the ends of the rib bones.

5. Leave the ribs untended for the first 30 minutes—this means no peeking; this is especially important since this recipe hinges on getting a pronounced smoke flavor in the ribs. If necessary, add a few more handfuls of soaked chips. If the ribs start to burn on the edges, stack them on top of one another in the very center of the grill and lower the heat slightly.

6. When done, remove the ribs from the grill and let them cool before wrapping each rack individually and refrigerating them overnight.

7. On day II, start with making the seasoned flour: In a spice grinder or mortar and pestle, grind the salt and peppercorns to a fine consistency, add the cayenne pepper, and whisk in the flour. Set aside until ready to coat the ribs.

8. Make an egg wash by beating the egg and milk together in a large bowl until well combined. Refrigerate until ready to use.

9. Remove the ribs from the refrigerator and cut them into individual bones by placing the knife close to 1 bone and slicing. This will be very easy while the ribs are cold.

10. Place individual ribs on a cookie sheet fitted with a wire cooling rack. (The rack will help the coating set by letting air circulate around all sides of the ribs.) Before you start coating the ribs, turn on a deep fryer according to the manufacturer's instructions or start heating peanut oil in a heavy Dutch oven to 350°F–360°F on a candy thermometer.

11. To coat the ribs, one by one, place them in the egg wash until all surfaces are wet and then coat them in seasoned flour. Shake excess flour off and place each rib on the cooling rack. Repeat the process to double coat all the ribs. Let them sit for 10 minutes.

12. Fry the ribs about 4 at a time, depending on the size of your fryer. The ribs must be covered by the hot oil and are done when they turn brown and crispy. Remove them from the oil with the fryer basket or a pair of tongs and let them drain for several minutes on paper towels.

13. Serve hot with the barbecue sauce on the side.

Brontosaurus Bones

On a trip to Nassau, Bahamas, I asked a taxi driver to take me to his favorite restaurant. He took me to a barbecue shack way off the tourist path and introduced me to the finest plate of beef ribs that I have ever eaten. Not only were they the tastiest, but they were the biggest ribs I've ever seen! He aptly called them brontosaurus bones because of their dinosaur size, and it stuck with me. This recipe is best made with beef back ribs or "long bones," but they can be made with short ribs as well. I recommend serving these ribs sauceless with a sprinkling of fleur de sel if desired.

Makes 4 servings

Grilling Method: Indirect/Medium-Low Heat

Rosemary Rub
2 tablespoons black peppercorns
2 tablespoons dried rosemary
2 tablespoons sweet paprika
1½ tablespoons kosher salt
2½ teaspoons granulated garlic

8 long beef ribs or 1 rack beef ribs cut from the standing rib roast, about 3 pounds
4 cloves garlic, peeled and cut in half
   Olive oil
   Fleur de sel, optional

1. Make the rub: Mix the ingredients in a small bowl, making sure they are well combined. Puree the spice mixture to a medium-fine consistency (about 10 seconds) in a spice grinder or mortar and pestle.

2. Meanwhile, build a charcoal fire or preheat a gas grill, setting it up for indirect heat.

3. Rub the beef ribs all over with the cut sides of the garlic cloves and brush with a thin coating of oil. Set them aside for 20 minutes to come to room temperature. Then sprinkle the ribs liberally with the spice rub. Store any leftover rub in an airtight container. It will keep, covered, for 2 months.

4. Place the ribs, bone-side down, in the center of the cooking grate over indirect medium-low heat. Grill covered (at about 325°F, if your grill has a thermometer) for 1 to 1½ hours or until the meat has pulled back from the ends of the rib bones

and the ribs are well browned and slightly crusty. Individual beef ribs will be done before the full rack (connected rib bones) is done.

5. If grilling individual bones and the edges start to burn, stack them on top of one another in the very center of the grill and lower the heat slightly. About 30 minutes before the ribs are done, brush them lightly with olive oil.

6. Remove the ribs from the grill and let them rest 10 minutes. Transfer to a carving board to cut ribs and sprinkle them with fleur de sel, if desired. Serve hot.

TIP: If you love barbecue sauce, feel free to serve some warm on the side and try the Old Vines Zinfandel Barbecue Sauce (page 283), which is particularly well suited to beef.

Hug-Your-Momma Braised Short Ribs with Garlic-Cheese Grits

These ribs are so good, they make you want to hug your momma—or anyone else standing nearby. They are first barbecued with a dry rub and then braised until the meat literally slips from the bone. The hour-long grilling step caramelizes and browns the meat for a huge burst of added flavor. The reduced liquid and vegetables are pureed and spooned over the short ribs and the garlic-cheese grits are fabulously good. This is a winner dinner that will be welcomed for any occasion, from blue jeans to black tie.

Makes 4 to 8 servings

Grilling Method: Indirect/Medium-Low Heat

Dry Mustard Rub

$2^{1}/_{2}$	teaspoons dry mustard
$1^{1}/_{2}$	teaspoons granulated garlic
$1^{1}/_{2}$	teaspoons coarsely ground pepper
1	teaspoon sweet paprika
1	teaspoon dried thyme
$^{1}/_{2}$	teaspoon cayenne

6 to 8 pounds bone-in beef short ribs
    Olive oil
    Kosher salt
    Freshly ground pepper

2	large onions, roughly chopped
4	ribs celery, cut in $^{1}/_{2}$-inch pieces
6	large carrots, cut in $^{1}/_{2}$-inch pieces
1	head garlic, cloves peeled
1	750-milliliter bottle full-bodied red wine, such as a Cabernet Sauvignon or Shiraz
1	28-ounce can crushed tomatoes, juice reserved
$^{1}/_{3}$	cup Worcestershire sauce
4	bay leaves
1	teaspoon ground allspice
$^{1}/_{4}$	cup Dijon mustard
$^{1}/_{4}$	cup balsamic vinegar
	Fleur de sel or sea salt
	Garlic-Cheese Grits (page 276)

1. Make the rub: Combine all the ingredients in a small bowl and set aside until ready to use.

2. Build a charcoal fire or preheat a gas grill, setting up the grill for indirect heat.

3. Brush the ribs with a light coating of olive oil and sprinkle all over with the mustard rub. Sprinkle with kosher salt.

4. Place the ribs in the center of the cooking grate over indirect medium-low heat. Grill covered (at about 325°F, if your grill has a thermometer) for 45 to 60 minutes or until the meat is well browned, turning once halfway through the grilling time.

5. Leave the ribs untended for the first 30 minutes—this means no peeking. If the ribs start to burn on the edges, place them on a cookie sheet, return to the grill, and continue cooking them until browned all over. When browned, remove them from the grill, cover with foil, and set aside.

6. Meanwhile, heat 2 to 3 tablespoons of oil over medium heat in the bottom of a large Dutch oven or ovenproof pot with a lid—the oil should thinly cover the entire bottom of the pot. Add the onions, celery, and carrots and about 1 teaspoon of salt. Cook until the vegetables begin to brown, about 10 minutes. Add the garlic cloves and continue cooking until they begin to brown on the edges, 2 to 3 more minutes. Add the wine, tomatoes, and Worcestershire and simmer until the juices begin to bubble, about 5 minutes. Add the bay leaves and allspice and stir to mix. Add the short ribs and stir again.

7. Put the lid on the pot and return it to the grill to finish cooking by braising. Cook for another 2 to 2½ hours or until the meat is so tender that the bones slip out easily.

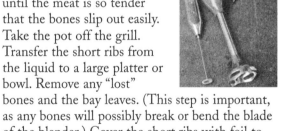

8. Take the pot off the grill. Transfer the short ribs from the liquid to a large platter or bowl. Remove any "lost" bones and the bay leaves. (This step is important, as any bones will possibly break or bend the blade of the blender.) Cover the short ribs with foil to keep warm.

9. Skim the fat off the top of the cooking liquid. Bring the pan juices to a boil. If the liquid needs to be reduced, simmer at a low boil for 10 to 15 minutes or until the liquid is reduced and begins to thicken. (If liquid is already thick, you can skip this step.)

10. Remove the pot from the heat and puree the liquid in the Dutch oven with an immersion blender. Return it to the heat and bring back to a boil. As the sauce boils, whisk in the mustard and vinegar and simmer for 3 to 5 more minutes. Taste and adjust the seasonings with about 1 teaspoon kosher salt and black pepper. Keep the sauce warm until you're ready to serve.

11. The sauce and short ribs can also be made in advance and reheated by adding the short ribs back into the sauce and simmering until warm. They are actually even better the second day!

12. Serve the ribs on a bed of the cheese grits with the pan juice sauce napped—or ladled—on top. Season individual portions with a sprinkling of fleur de sel or coarse sea salt and freshly ground black pepper.

TIP: The sweetness of the vegetables and wine-based braising liquid perfectly balances the savory, slightly smoky beef flavors and are best eaten together. Because all the vegetables are pureed in the sauce, it is a little sweet on its own.

TIP: Beef short ribs are usually braised, and with good reason—short ribs are a tough cut of meat that requires long slow cooking in liquid to break down the connective tissues. Braising transforms the connective tissue into gelatin, which give short ribs their delicious texture and tenderizes the meat. Grilling before braising caramelizes the meat and adds richness and depth to the flavor.

Garlic-Cheese Grits

These grits will make you forget that you have meat on your plate. Anson Mills grits are hand milled to a coarser grind than commercially distributed grits, and the corn is specially grown for maximum flavor. Even people who think they don't like grits, love these grits. Cooking them in a mixture of cream and water is my version of the South Carolina low-country tradition. Call Glenn Roberts at the Mill at 803-467-4122 to order them, or use any available stone-ground grits. This recipe cannot be made with instant or quick grits.

Makes 4 to 8 servings

5½	cups water
2	cups heavy whipping cream
3	cups Anson Mills grits or other coarse-ground grits
8	ounces white cheddar cheese, freshly grated (optional)
8	ounces Parmigiano-Reggiano cheese, freshly grated
4	tablespoons (½ stick) unsalted butter (optional)
2	teaspoons kosher salt, or to taste
1	teaspoon granulated garlic or garlic powder
½	teaspoon freshly ground pepper
	Tabasco

1. Bring the water and cream to a soft boil. Gradually add the grits, stirring occasionally. Simmer, continuing to stir, with the lid alternating on and off every 15 minutes for 1 hour or until the grits are soft but still al dente and have a little resistance (not mushy). The grits can be made with the lid off the whole time, but that will take twice as long. If the grits get too stiff, add milk or water.

2. Stir in the cheeses, butter, salt, granulated garlic, pepper, and Tabasco. Adjust the seasonings to taste—both cheeses have a lot of natural salt, so be careful when adding salt. Serve piping hot with short ribs and pan juice sauce on top.

GREAT GRITS

Grits are stone-ground corn and a coarser cousin to the more fashionable polenta. They can be cooked in either water, milk, or cream. The traditional cooking method calls for cooking with the lid off and stirring frequently for up to 2 hours. I've devised the method here to cut the cooking time in half. I alternate keeping the lid on and off the pot of grits. Cooking with the lid on the pot cuts the cooking time considerably. The steam makes the particles of corn expand and thus soften more quickly. Taking the lid off allows the excess liquid that accumulates when the lid is on (mostly steam) to evaporate. I've made grits using this technique many times to great success—in fact, I'll never do it the old-fashioned way again. I don't add salt at the beginning of the cooking time because it can result in oversalting when adding butter and cheese to the grits.

Lamb Riblets with Hickory House Barbecue Sauce

If you are ever in Chicago, call up Chef Susan Goss at West Town Tavern and request her lamb ribs—they aren't on the regular menu, but she makes them frequently as an appetizer since so many of her customers request them. She graciously shared her "secret" recipe with me, so now you can make them at home. Because of their size, I call them riblets.

Makes 4 servings

Grilling Method: Indirect/Medium-Low Heat

Dry Rub
1/2 cup paprika
1/4 cup kosher salt
1/4 cup sugar
1/4 cup packed brown sugar
1/4 cup pure ground red chile, such as New Mexico (not a blend)
1/4 cup ground cumin
1/4 cup freshly ground pepper

Hickory House Barbecue Sauce
1 tablespoon vegetable oil
1 large red onion, finely chopped
2 15-ounce cans diced tomatoes
1 1/2 cups packed dark brown sugar
1 1/2 cups chicken stock or one 15-ounce can low-sodium chicken broth
1/2 cup molasses
1/3 cup apple cider vinegar
2 tablespoons paprika
2 tablespoons Worcestershire sauce
1 tablespoon kosher salt
3/4 tablespoon New Mexico chile powder
1/2 tablespoon freshly ground pepper
1 1/4 teaspoons dried oregano
1/2 teaspoon dried thyme
1/4 teaspoon ground cumin
1 cup fresh orange juice

Hickory wood chips, soaked in water for 30 minutes (optional)
4 racks lamb ribs, about 1 1/2 pounds each (optional)

1. Make the dry Rub: Mix all the ingredients in a small bowl until well combined. Set aside until ready to use.
2. Make the sauce: Heat the oil in large heavy-bottomed pot for 2 minutes. Add the onions and sauté them until translucent, about 10 minutes. Add all the remaining ingredients except the orange juice and stir to combine. Bring to a boil. Lower the heat and simmer for 30 minutes or until slightly reduced and thickened. Let the sauce cool and then puree it using an immersion or traditional blender. Stir in the orange juice and set it aside until ready to use (it can be stored in a clean glass jar in the refrigerator for up to 2 weeks).
3. Meanwhile, build a charcoal fire or preheat a gas grill. Set up the grill for indirect heat; if using wood chips, place the soaked chips directly on the charcoal or in the smoking box of a gas grill.
4. Sprinkle the lamb ribs liberally with the rub. Make sure that the wood chips are smoking and place the ribs, bone-side down, in the center of the cooking grate over indirect medium-low heat. Grill covered (at about 325°F, if your grill has a thermometer) for 1 to 1 1/2 hours or until the meat is tender and has pulled back from the ends of the rib bones.

5. Leave the ribs untended for the first 30 minutes—this means no peeking. If the ribs start to burn on the edges, stack them on top of one another in the very center of the grill and lower the heat slightly.

6. When the ribs are done, remove them from the grill and let rest for 5 to 10 minutes before cutting them into individual bones. Serve immediately with warm Hickory House Barbecue Sauce on the side.

Apple Cider Vinegar Marinade

Makes 4 cups; enough for 4 racks of ribs

1 cup apple cider vinegar
3 cups water

Mix the vinegar and water. Use to marinate ribs or other cuts of pork and chicken. Soak meat no longer than 30 minutes.

Pineapple–Lemon Juice Marinade

Makes 4 cups; enough for 4 racks of ribs

1 cup canned pineapple juice
1/2 cup fresh lemon juice (about 2 lemons)
2 cups water
1/2 cup vegetable oil

Mix the juices, water, and oil. Use to marinate ribs or other cuts of pork, chicken, or salmon. Soak meat no longer than 30 minutes.

Hot-Hot-Hot Sauce Marinade

This is a trick I picked up when I lived in New Orleans. On the weekends, I would travel to the swampy bayous and go to cook-outs that featured this simple but stunning marinade. It took a lot of coercing and a few drinks to get this trick out of my host! If you use this marinade, skip the spice rub and use a sprinkling of

kosher salt and a coating of olive oil. The trick: The meat is marinated in a straight solution of Louisiana hot sauce.

Makes enough for 4 racks of ribs or 3 pounds of chicken wings

2 6-ounce bottles Louisiana brand hot sauce or Trappey's brand hot sauce (see Tip)

Use to marinate ribs or chicken wings. Soak meat no longer than 30 minutes. If you are "nervous" about the heat factor, dilute with 1/2 cup of water.

TIP: Louisiana brand hot sauce (much milder than Tabasco) is distributed nationally, but if you can't find it, use 1 small bottle of Tabasco, 1/2 cup white vinegar, and 3 cups of water or more to taste.

TIP: To get the maximum flavor out of pepper (and other dried spices), toast whole peppercorns in a dry skillet over medium-high heat until you can barely see a wisp of smoke and smell the spice, 3 to 5 minutes. The toasting process releases the spice's volatile oils and maximizes the flavor—and efficacy—of the spice. Toast peppercorns or whole spices before grinding and you'll find your spice rubs will explode with flavor.

Three-Chile Rub

Makes about 1/2 cup

This rub is especially good on beef and pork ribs. If you eliminate the salt, the rub can be used as a dry marinade and rubbed on ribs the night before you plan to barbecue. But don't forget to season with salt just before you put them on the grill.

1 tablespoon New Mexico chile powder (or any other pure chile powder)
1 tablespoon chipotle chile powder (if available, or 1 additional tablespoon New Mexican chile powder)
1/2 tablespoon smoked paprika
1/2 tablespoon white pepper
1 teaspoon freshly ground black pepper
1 tablespoon granulated sugar
1 tablespoon kosher salt

Combine chile powders, paprika, peppers, sugar, and salt in a medium-size bowl and mix well. Extra rub can be stored in an airtight container for up to six months.

The great thing about barbecue rubs is that they're so easy to adapt to your own taste. Everyone I know eventually makes their own adaptation of their favorite rub recipe and with practice, I am sure you will, too. If you don't "cotton" to a specific spice, leave it out; if you like it hotter, add more pepper or cayenne, and if you think something's lacking, add it. Just make sure to watch the salt content as you are mixing; many prepared spices include salt, and it adds up quickly.

TIP: When a recipe calls for "chile powder," this means pure chile pepper. The most popular peppers include ancho, chipotle, cayenne, New Mexico, jalapeño, and habanero. "Chili powder" refers to a mixture of spices that is often used to season classic ground-meat chili.

TIP: If the pure ground pepper spice is hard to find, it's easy to make your own. In every large grocery store, they sell dried chiles in the Mexican food aisle. Buy the dried chilies and cut them into ¼-inch pieces. Put these strips in an electric spice grinder (sold as coffee bean grinders) and grind until it is the texture of a powder. Not only are these homemade ground chiles much less expensive, they are also fresher and more flavorful. Alternately, they can be purchased at www.thespicehouse.com.

Make *Your Own* Barbecue Rub

This chart will help you make your own barbecue rub for ribs or any other food that you wish to season with a blended spice mixture. Follow the columns and mix and match to your heart's content. Be sure to taste along the way and remember that less is almost always more. If you add too many spices, you risk having them "fight" with each other, and the result will be a muddy, not a bright, flavor. Be especially careful not to add too much salt, sugar, or hot peppers. Remember this rule of thumb: The stronger the spice, the less you need to use. Start off with ½ tablespoon of the salt and peppers and add 1 tablespoon of everything else in equal parts. Taste and adjust per your palate.

SALT Choose 1	SUGAR Choose 1 to 2	PEPPERS Choose 1 to 3	SAVORY SPICES Choose 1 to 4	SWEET SPICES Choose 1 to 4	OTHER Choose 1 to 5
Kosher salt	Dark brown sugar	Ancho chile	Celery seed	Allspice	Dried chives
Fine sea salt	Light brown sugar	Black pepper	Coriander	Anise seed	Dried lemon peel
Coarse sea salt	Sugar in the Raw	Blended pure	Cumin	Cardamom	Lemonade powder
Celery salt	White sugar	Chile powder	Dill weed	Cinnamon	Dried lavender
		Chipotle chile	Dry mustard powder	Chinese five-spice powder	Dried parsley
		Cayenne pepper	Fennel	Cloves	Dried shallots
		Green peppercorns	Granulated garlic	Mace	Poppy seeds
		Red chili flakes	Hungarian paprika	Nutmeg	Sesame seeds
		Lemon pepper	Onion powder	Star anise	
		New Mexico chile	Oregano		
		Pink peppercorns	Sage		
		Szechuan peppercorns	Smoked (smoky) Spanish paprika		
		White pepper	Thyme		

All spices are dried and ground unless otherwise noted.

> To make any rub into a marinade, add ½ cup olive oil, 1 cup liquid such as water, fruit juice, wine or beer, and 1 tablespoon vinegar or lemon juice to each rub recipe. Marinate food covered, in the refrigerator, for 30 minutes, and season with salt just before grilling.

Camera-Ready Rub

One spring morning I got up before dawn to barbecue ribs for a rib-off that the Today show was hosting. My friend and barbecue buddy Steven Raichlen was one of the guests. After the show, he handed me a "dry-rubbed" no-sauce rib and said, "You've got to try this." One bite of the sweet, smoky rib and I was hooked. Here's my version of his very basic, but you can't beat it, barbecue rub.

Makes about ¾ cup

- ¼ cup packed brown sugar
- 1 tablespoon sweet paprika
- 1 tablespoon smoked paprika
- 1 tablespoon freshly ground pepper
- 1 tablespoon white pepper
- 1 tablespoon kosher salt
- 2 teaspoons garlic powder
- 2 teaspoons onion powder
- 2 teaspoons celery salt
- ½ teaspoon cayenne

Combine all the ingredients in a medium bowl and mix well. Use it to rub on meat before grilling. Extra rub can be stored in an airtight container for up to 6 months.

Classic Barbecue Rub

This rub has all the classic barbecue notes: salt, spice, sweet, and smoke. It is particularly great on ribs, but it works with pork chops and tenderloin, chicken, and even catfish for a beautifully authentic low 'n' slow barbecued flavor.

Makes about 1 cup

- 2 tablespoons smoked paprika
- 2 tablespoons kosher salt
- 3 tablespoons sugar
- 2 tablespoons brown sugar
- 1 tablespoon ground cumin
- 1 tablespoon chili powder
- 1 tablespoon freshly ground pepper
- ½ tablespoon cayenne
- 1 tablespoon onion powder
- 1 tablespoon garlic powder
- 1 tablespoon celery salt
- 1 teaspoon oregano, crushed

Combine all the ingredients in a medium bowl and mix well. For a smoother rub, process the ingredients in a spice grinder until well combined and all pieces are uniform (the rub will be very fine and tan in color). This step is important if making Sweet and Spicy Barbecue Glaze (page 285). Use it to rub on meat before grilling. Extra rub can be stored in an airtight container for up to 6 months.

Kansas City Rib Spice Rub

Makes just over 1 cup

- ¼ cup sea salt
- ¼ cup sweet paprika
- ¼ cup sugar
- 4 teaspoons good-quality chile powder or powdered ancho chiles
- 1 tablespoon garlic powder
- 1 tablespoon onion powder
- 1 tablespoon freshly ground pepper
- 1 tablespoon dry mustard
- 1½ teaspoons ground oregano
- 1 teaspoon cayenne
- 1 teaspoon ground cumin
- 1 teaspoon celery salt

Combine all the ingredients in a small bowl and mix well. Use it to rub on meat before grilling. Store in airtight container for up to six months.

TIP: If you don't like an individual spice, just omit it or substitute one of your favorites.

Bloodshot Mop

This recipe was created in honor of the bloodshot eyes that the barbecue pit masters have after a night of tending the 'que and the brew! This unusual mop is spicy and not sweet at all. It matches best with simple rib recipes such as the Salt and Pepper Ribs (page 266) or the Brontosaurus Bones (pages 274–275).

Makes about 2½ cups;

- 1 12-ounce beer, preferably Budweiser
- 1 cup spicy V-8 Juice
- 1 tablespoon Worcestershire sauce
- 2 tablespoons prepared horseradish
- 1 teaspoon finely ground pepper
- ¼ teaspoon sea salt
- 1 teaspoon granulated garlic
- 1 teaspoon Tabasco

Pour the beer into a medium bowl and whisk to remove the carbonation. Add the remaining ingredients and mix well. Funnel the mop into a squeeze bottle or put it in a clean glass jar until ready to use. It can be made ahead and refrigerated for up to 1 week.

Hot and Sweet Apple Cider Mop

Pork ribs and apples have a natural affinity for each other. I've used three different apple, ingredients in this recipe to intensify the apple flavor and imbue the sauce with sweet and sour notes. This mop is also good cooked down and pureed to make a sauce: Just double the ingredients and simmer for an additional 20 minutes.

Makes about 2 cups

- 2 cups apple cider
- 1 large shallot, minced
- 1 Granny Smith apple, peeled and grated
- 2 tablespoons hot pepper jelly
- 2 tablespoons apple cider vinegar
- 2 tablespoons tomato paste
- 2 tablespoons dark brown sugar
- 2 teaspoons ground ginger
- ⅛ teaspoon ground cloves
- ½ teaspoon kosher salt
- ¼ teaspoon freshly ground pepper

1. In a small saucepan, combine the apple cider, shallot, grated apple, and hot pepper jelly. Bring to a boil and simmer for 10 minutes.
2. Add the remaining mop ingredients, bring to a boil, and remove from the heat. When cool, strain the mop through a fine sieve and place it in a clean glass jar. Let it cool before using. It can be made ahead and refrigerated for up to 1 week until ready to use.

HOW TO APPLY A MOP

You can use a barbecue mop, which looks like a miniature cloth mop, for applying the "mop" basting sauce, but I think it is really much more of a novelty than a functional barbecue tool. I recommend mopping two ways: one traditional, and one all my own. The traditional way is to use a bowl and a brush, but be sure to use a brush with silicone or natural bristles—the synthetic bristles have a tendency to fall out and stick to the ribs. Try my new Super Silicone Angled BBQ Basting Brush (see Sources, pages 343–345) the next time you mop or sauce food on the grill. The other way is to use a plastic squeeze bottle (looks like a restaurant ketchup container). Funnel the mop into the squeeze bottle, screw the top on, and squeeze away, aiming the stream at the top of the ribs so it will flow down, covering all the surfaces equally. Be careful not to aim at the fire, as doing so will cause a serious flare-up. This way is faster than a brush—just don't leave it too close to the fire or the plastic container will melt.

Pineapple and Ginger Mop

Pineapple and ginger are both natural tenderizing agents, so you don't want to use this with ribs that you have soaked in an acid-rich marinade. I like using this mop with the Three-Chile Rub (pages 278–279) for a spicy sweet rib with tropical hints.

Makes about 2¼ cups

- 1 cup ginger beer or ginger ale
- 1 cup canned pineapple juice
- 1 tablespoon jalapeño hot sauce, such as Tabasco
- 1 small knob (1 to 2 inches) fresh ginger, peeled and grated
- 1 tablespoon honey
- ¼ cup garlic-chili sauce (*sriracha*)
  Sea salt
  White pepper

Pour the ginger beer into a medium bowl and whisk to remove the carbonation. Add the remaining ingredients and mix well. Let the mop sit for a minimum of 30 minutes or overnight, stirring occasionally. Season to taste. Strain the mop using a fine sieve and funnel into a squeeze bottle or put in a clean glass jar until ready to use. It can be made ahead and refrigerated for up to 1 week.

Sweet K. C.–Style Dr. Pepper Barbecue Sauce

Call it crazy, but there is a whole range of soft-drink–based barbecue sauces in the land of 'cue. I started adding this sauce to my rib repertoire after a trip to Kansas City, where I ate at 21 barbecue joints in two days—no kidding! On our last stop, almost overwhelmed by barbecued meat, we went into a fillin' station that had been retrofitted to include a barbecue restaurant and had the best sandwich of the day. When I inquired as to what made the sauce so good, the waiter replied, "Dr. Pepper." True or not, I tried it and it gives this sauce an edge over most basic, sweet barbecue sauces.

Makes 2 cups

- 4 tablespoons (½ stick) unsalted butter
- 1 large onion, chopped
- 4 cloves garlic, chopped
- 1 12-ounce can Dr. Pepper soft drink (about 1¾ cups)
- 1 cup ketchup
- ½ cup apple cider vinegar
- ½ cup packed brown sugar
- ⅓ cup Worcestershire sauce
- 3 tablespoons tomato paste
- 2 teaspoons ground ancho chile powder or New Mexican chile powder
- 1 teaspoon white pepper
- 1 teaspoon kosher salt
  Freshly ground pepper

1. Melt the butter in a heavy saucepan. Sauté the onion and garlic in the butter until translucent, about 10 minutes. Add the remaining ingredients and simmer for about 15 minutes, until the flavors have blended. Continue cooking until the sauce begins to thicken, 20 to 30 minutes. Taste and adjust the seasonings with salt and pepper. Remember, the ribs will have plenty of spice rub on them, so don't overseason the sauce.

2. Let the sauce cool for about 10 minutes or until it is warm but no longer "boiling" hot. Puree with an immersion or traditional blender. Let the mop cool and pour it into a clean glass jar for storing. The sauce can be made in advance and kept for 2 weeks in the refrigerator. To use: Brush it on meat 30 minutes before the cooking time is finished. If desired, serve extra on the side.

Gussied-Up Pennsylvania Black Vinegar Sauce

I first had this sauce in a restaurant, served with pot roast. I flipped over the sauce, which tasted like a savory, deeply caramelized version of hot toffee. I've added balsamic vinegar and molasses to the traditional recipe because I think it rounds out the flavor. Since the flavor is so concentrated, you only need a drizzle. To turn this into a dynamite finishing sauce, thin it out with one cup of apple cider and brush it on during the last 20 minutes of cooking time. This sauce is fantastic with the deep-fried ribs on pages 273–274.

MAKING YOUR OWN RIB RACK

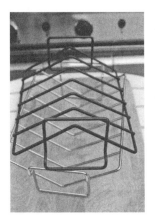

Nothing makes me happier than finding a second purpose for a tool that I already own. A few years ago, I was barbecuing a whole mess (24 racks) of ribs for a big party. I ran out of rib racks, and while I was trying to figure out what to do, I took my V-rack roast holder, turned it upside down … and old-new rib rack was invented. After that fateful rib roast, I've never used anything else to barbecue ribs. The V-rack must be the kind without metal "feet" on the bottom—it must have slots for the racks of ribs to go into. The best news is this repurposed cooking accessory holds the rack of ribs more securely and holds one more rack than most of the rib holders on the market.

Makes about 1½ cups

- 3 cups red wine vinegar
- 1 cup balsamic vinegar
- 1²⁄₃ cups packed brown sugar
- 2 tablespoons molasses
- 1 cup raisins

1. In heavy saucepan, combine the vinegars, sugar, and molasses and bring to a boil. Reduce the heat and simmer for 30 to 40 minutes, or until the liquid is reduced by half, to about 2½ cups. Add the raisins, reduce the heat, and simmer slowly, 5 to 10 more minutes. At this stage, watch that the sauce does not thicken too much or it will resemble toffee instead of a thick sauce.
2. Strain the sauce to remove the raisins. (The liquid should be black, syrupy, and not have a strong vinegar aroma.) Be careful not to overcook, as the sauce burns easily.
3. Let the sauce cool for about 10 minutes, or until it is warm but no longer "boiling" hot. Pour it into a clean glass jar for storing. The sauce can be made in advance and kept for 2 weeks in the refrigerator. To use as a finishing sauce, dilute with 1 cup of apple cider. Otherwise serve as a dipping sauce on the side.

TIP: Don't discard the raisins; the simmered raisins are particularly good in bran muffins or carrot cake.

Old Vines Zinfandel Barbecue Sauce

This deep, rich, barbecue sauce is so so good you'll be tempted to eat it on toast! The inspiration came one night when I was reducing a bottle of port into a syrup for a grilled pear and Stilton dessert pizza. By accident, I opened a bottle of Old Vines Zinfandel and started reducing it before I realized my mistake. Well, it was too hot to drink, so I decided to make a barbecue sauce instead. Here is the sweet reward.

Makes 2 cups

- 1 750-milliliter bottle Old Vines or other red Zinfandel wine
- ½ cup plus 2 heaping tablespoons seedless blackberry or raspberry jam
- 1 cup ketchup
- 3 tablespoons balsamic vinegar
- 2 tablespoons tomato paste
- 1 teaspoon smoked paprika
- ½ teaspoon ground cinnamon
- ½ teaspoon Tabasco
  Pinch ground cloves
  Kosher salt
  Freshly ground pepper

1. Bring the wine to a boil in a heavy saucepan, reduce the heat, and simmer until it is reduced to about half of its original volume, about 25 minutes. Add the jam and stir until combined. Simmer for 5 more minutes.
2. Add the ketchup, vinegar, tomato paste, and spices. Simmer for 15 minutes, stirring occasionally. Season to taste with about 1 teaspoon salt and ¼ teaspoon pepper and set aside.
3. Let the sauce cool and pour it into a clean glass jar for storing. The sauce can be made in advance and kept for 2 weeks in the refrigerator. To use: Brush it on meat 30 minutes before the cooking time is finished. If desired, serve extra on the side.

Smoky Chipotle Tequila Barbecue Sauce

Park Kerr, owner of the El Paso Chile Co. in El Paso, TX, is one of those larger-than-life personalities. We came up with this kickin' recipe one night while sampling his Nacionale brand of Tequila. Don't question the unusual array of ingredients—it might not be traditional, but it pleases the palate! The flavors of this barbecue sauce are as delightfully over-the-top as he is.

Makes about 4 cups

2 tablespoons vegetable oil
½ cup finely chopped yellow onion
2 cloves garlic, minced
6 canned chipotles with clinging adobo sauce, pureed
1 tablespoon dry mustard
1¼ teaspoons dried thyme
1¼ teaspoons ground ginger
1 teaspoon ground cumin, preferably from toasted seeds
1 teaspoon freshly ground pepper
2 bay leaves
1¾ cups ketchup
½ cup fresh orange juice
½ cup good-quality tequila
¼ cup orange marmalade
¼ cup unsulphured molasses
2 tablespoons soy sauce
1 tablespoon Worcestershire sauce

1. In a medium, heavy saucepan over low heat, warm the oil. Add the onion, garlic, chipotles, mustard, thyme, ginger, cumin, pepper, and bay leaves. Cover and cook, stirring occasionally, for 10 minutes.

2. Add the ketchup, orange juice, tequila, marmalade, molasses, soy sauce, and Worcestershire sauce and bring to a simmer. Cook, uncovered, stirring often as the sauce begins to thicken, for 20 minutes.

3. Remove the sauce from the heat. If desired, refrigerate for 24 hours to allow the flavors to mellow. Bring to room temperature and discard the bay leaves before using. This can be kept in the refrigerator for two weeks. To use: Brush it on meat 30 minutes before the cooking time is finished. If desired, serve extra on the side.

Sassy Bourbon and Brown Sugar Barbecue Sauce

The sweet pairing of brown sugar and bourbon is balanced by the savory vegetables, vinegar, and a touch of unsweetened cocoa powder for a sauce with a lot of sass! This is a very simple and versatile barbecue sauce.

Makes 4 cups

1 28-ounce can crushed tomatoes
1 cup packed brown sugar
½ cup bourbon
½ cup ketchup
¼ cup Heinz Chili Sauce
¼ cup apple cider vinegar
2 tablespoons red wine vinegar
¼ cup Worcestershire sauce
2 tablespoons molasses
2 teaspoons Classic Barbecue Rub (page 280)
  Kosher salt
  Freshly ground pepper
1 tablespoon unsweetened cocoa

1. In a large saucepan combine the tomatoes, sugar, bourbon, ketchup, chili sauce, vinegars, Worcestershire sauce, and molasses, stirring after each additional ingredient to combine. Add the rub and simmer until the flavors have blended and the sauce has thickened somewhat, about 30 minutes.

2. Let the sauce cool for about 10 minutes, or until it is warm but no longer "boiling" hot. Puree using an immersion or traditional blender. Taste and adjust the seasonings with about ½ teaspoon salt and pepper. Remember, the ribs already will have plenty of spice rub on them, so don't over-season the sauce. Add the cocoa powder and mix well to combine.

3. Let the sauce sit for 5 minutes and stir again to make sure the cocoa powder is well distributed. Let the sauce cool and pour it into a clean glass jar for storing. The sauce can be made in advance and kept for 2 weeks in the refrigerator. Brush it on meat 30 minutes before the cooking time is finished. If desired, serve extra on the side.

Sweet and Spicy Barbecue Glaze

Thinner than a traditional barbecue sauce, thicker and sweeter than a mop, this sauce will make your ribs, chicken, or pork chop picture-perfect and finger-lickin' good!

Makes about 1 cup

- ¼   cup apple cider vinegar
- 1   tablespoon ketchup
- 1   tablespoon honey
- 2   teaspoons favorite dry rub, such as Classic Barbecue Rub (page 280), finely ground

- 1¼   teaspoons prepared yellow mustard
- ¼ to ⅓ cup vegetable oil (not olive)

1. In a nonreactive bowl, whisk together the vinegar, honey, ketchup, rub, and mustard until well mixed. Slowly whisk in the oil until it is completely emulsified and balances the vinegar. Set aside.

2. If desired, let the sauce sit for 24 hours to allow the flavors to mellow. This sauce will keep for 1 month, covered in the refrigerator. To use: Brush it on meat 30 minutes before the cooking time is finished. If desired, serve extra on the side.

NOTE: This and most barbecue and grilling sauces contain sugar, which will burn if applied too early in the cooking process.

Pepper-Rum Hot Sauce

This homemade hot sauce is good for what ails ya—or any recipe that needs a little push. It is particularly good splashed on instead of Tabasco.

Makes 1 pint

- 1   pint dark rum
- 5 to 6 whole bird peppers or small Scotch bonnet chilies
- 6   whole cloves
- 3   whole peppercorns

Pour about 2 tablespoons of rum out of the pint bottle. Insert chilies, cloves, and peppercorns into the bottle. Replace cap on the bottle and let seasonings steep for one week before using. Store in the pint bottle and use sauce as a condiment, sprinkling it onto grilled or barbecued food. Keeps for about a year stored in a cool, dry cabinet.

So you've invited a crowd over for ribs and you know how to rub, mop, and sauce them. But how are you going to serve them? Here are simple suggestions for dressing up the ribs.

Finger Bowls

Place "finger bowls" of warm water with a slice of lemon or lime at everyone's place or, if serving in a buffet, on every tray. You can use small bowls, tea cups, or the very inexpensive glass Pyrex portion cups for the "bowls." This is also a gracious way to discourage finger-licking!

Napkins and Bibs

Since ribs are a little messy, I buy cloth tea towels (kitchen towels) to use at my rib fests. I usually buy them in red, black, and blue, but mix and match solids, plaids, and checks for a more colorful table. They are larger, more absorbent, and easier to wash than cloth napkin. They are also big enough to tie on children (and some adults) to keep clothes clean. They are readily found at most discount stores, and whenever I see a set I like, I buy them to have on hand for the next rib fest. When they get a little too ratty to use as napkins, I rotate them into my "rag bag" and break out the new cloths for napkins.

Speaking of bibs and napkins; when I decide to throw a western-themed barbecue, I rely on bandanas to dress up the party. I buy enough bandanas for everyone to have two. Half of them I fold in half like a triangle and the other half I reserve to use as napkins. As soon as the guests walk in, I tie a triangle-bandana around their necks (like in the old cowboy movies)—the guests are welcome and encouraged to keep their neck wear. These "props" double as bibs and put everyone in the mood. The reserved bandanas are rolled up and tied with a piece of raffia and used as the napkin. For a large crowd, I also roll the silverware in the bandana to streamline the buffet.

Sauce on the Side

I've talked a lot about serving the barbecue sauce on the side, but what to serve it in? It's nicer to give everyone their own sauce container so no one has to worry about "double dipping." If you have small sauce bowls, that's great, use them. If you are like most people, you don't have these little bowls. Use any small container that is wide enough at the top to dip a rib bone. I often use Japanese sake cups, espresso cups, or even souvenir shot glasses. If the shot glasses appeal to you, consider buying them new and letting everyone take one home as a memento of the party.

Perfect Plating

Sometimes white china, flowered pottery, or black stoneware, etc., just won't do for ribs. So before you break out the paper plates (great for portable rib eating), try serving the ribs on individual wooden cutting boards (the shape that can be hung on a wall, about 10 inches long). Cut each rack in half, and place it on a cutting board with a handle. Serve the half slabs with a heavy-duty steak knife and sauce in a souvenir shot glass. This way everyone can cut their own ribs on the cutting board, without scratching the china. But most importantly, it looks very rustic and quite clever.

Nibbles and Bits

It used to be that going out to a restaurant was a special treat; nowadays, it is often the reverse—entertaining at home is the more rare occasion. I, however, love to make the special effort and prepare tasty little bites for guests to enjoy while I finish the meal.

The cocktail hour sets the mood for the whole evening, and I always know the party will be a hit when there is nothing left for me to put away before dinner. The recipes in this chapter are my tried and true party staples. I usually choose two or three appetizers (including one very light and simple recipe like the Tumbled Tomatoes with Mediterranean Herbs (page 289) which appear at every one of my soirees), so my guests have a choice or can indulge in all three. When choosing appetizers to start the evening, make sure that you pair lighter fare with a heavier entrée and heavy hors d'oevres with a lighter entrée—that way your guests will be satisfied but not overstuffed. And, if you can't decide on just a few, try skipping the main course and throw a party of nibbles and bits!

I don't give serving amounts for these dishes because the amount per serving may vary greatly—you may have light nibblers or heavy nibblers at your gathering or the serving amount may change depending on how many nibbles you are serving.

Susie's Grilled Almonds

By day, Susie Middleton is the editor of Fine Cooking *magazine and, by night and on weekends, a consummate hostess. Not surprisingly, she always has the best food to snack on. I am including one of my favorites—her positively addictive seasoned almonds. Susie originally made them in the oven, but—no surprise—I've adapted them to the grill. They are so irresistible that I make them almost every week to snack on and serve with drinks.*

Makes about 4 cups

Grilling Method: Indirect/Medium Heat

1½ tablespoons unsalted butter
½ teaspoon Tabasco or other hot sauce
1 pound whole raw almonds, shelled and unsalted
1 teaspoon sea salt, divided
2 tablespoons extra-virgin olive oil

1. Build a charcoal fire or preheat a gas grill. In a small saucepan, melt the butter and add the hot sauce; stir to combine.
2. Put the almonds in a metal bowl and drizzle them with the spicy melted butter, stirring to thoroughly coat the almonds.
3. Spread the almonds in a single layer on a metal pan with sides or a disposable aluminum baking pan. Sprinkle with ½ teaspoon of salt, stirring once again to coat them evenly. Place the pan in the center of the cooking grate over indirect medium heat, cover, and grill for 15 to 20 minutes, or until darkly roasted and very fragrant. Stir the almonds occasionally while they are grilling to prevent burning.
4. Remove the almonds from the grill and drizzle them with the olive oil. Stir well and sprinkle liberally with another ½ teaspoon of salt. The almonds should glisten from the oil and the salt should be very visible on each almond. If necessary, add more salt to taste. Let them cool before eating. They will have a slightly chewy texture until they cool completely, then they will be very crisp. Store any uneaten nuts in an airtight container. I like to store (and give them away) in mason jars.

Spiced Pecans and Pumpkin Seeds

In the South, sweet spiced pecans signal the start of the fall holiday season. I've expanded my geography and mixed the sweet tastes of the South with the spicy tastes of the Southwest for the best "handful of nuts" I've had in a long time. They are good with a beer, but even better with a glass of champagne.

Makes about 5 cups

- 1 pound pecan halves
- 8 ounces pumpkin seeds, shelled
- 1 teaspoon chipotle chile powder or other chile powder
- 1 teaspoon ground cinnamon
- ¼ teaspoon ground cloves, optional
- 1 tablespoon superfine sugar
- 2 teaspoons fine sea salt
- 2 tablespoons olive oil

1. Preheat the oven to 300°F. Pick through the nuts and seeds to remove any shells. Set aside.
2. In a small bowl, mix all the spices with the sugar and salt until well combined.
3. In a large bowl, mix the nuts and seeds with the olive oil until all are coated evenly. Spread them on a cookie sheet and roast for 15 to 20 minutes, stirring occasionally.
4. Remove the cookie sheet from the oven, but leave the nuts on the sheet. Transfer the sheet to a cooling rack for 5 minutes.
5. While the nuts are still warm, sprinkle them evenly with the spice mixture, stirring to coat well. Adjust the seasonings to taste. Serve the mixture warm or at room temperature. Once they have cooled completely, store any extra nuts in an airtight container for up to 2 weeks.

Tumbled Tomatoes with Mediterranean Herbs

I think tomatoes are probably the best thing that comes from the earth! I created these "bet you can't eat just one" salt- and herb-crusted tomatoes as a quick cocktail snack. It is the simplest recipe, but it is a favorite of nearly everyone I know. I make these tomatoes at least twice a week to snack on or to have on hand when friends stop by for a drink. They are called tumbled tomatoes because you "tumble" them every so often to make sure all the water is evaporated, thus creating the flavorful crust.

Makes about 4 cups

- 1 tablespoon herbes de Provence
- 1 teaspoon coarse sea salt
- ½ teaspoon dehydrated or granulated garlic
- 2 pints cherry tomatoes

1. If you have a mortar and pestle or spice (coffee) grinder, mix the seasonings together and pulverize them slightly. If you don't have either, just skip this step.
2. Wash the tomatoes in cold water and drain all excess water, but do not dry them. Put the tomatoes in a bowl that is large enough to allow them to be tumbled. Toss the tomatoes with the herb mixture until they are evenly coated. Refrigerate, tossing and "tumbling" in the bowl occasionally, until all the water is evaporated. (The herb and salt mixture will form a crust on the tomatoes.) Serve chilled.

TIP: The tomatoes keep for 2 to 3 days, uncovered in the refrigerator—if they last that long—so make the full recipe and keep them on hand. The drier and crustier the salt and herb coating, the better they taste.
TIP: Because I make these so often, I mix up a big batch (recipe times five) of the seasoning and store it in a spice mill fitted with a ceramic grinder (salt will corrode the metal grinders over time). That way, I always have the seasoning on hand to make these tomatoes. A spice mill or grinder also grinds the herbs and spices to the perfect texture for crusting, eliminating another step. All you have to do is wash the tomatoes, grind the seasoning over them, tumble, and dry.

The World's Best Grilled Salsa

My barbecue buddy, Steven Raichlen, first introduced me to the concept of smoked vegetable gazpacho many years ago. Since then, I've made my own version and I make it every chance I get. I sometimes thin it out with Clamato juice and rosé wine to give it a soupy consistency and serve it as a starter (pages 189–190), but most of the time, I leave it chunky and thick and serve it with tortilla chips as the world's best grilled salsa! When I want a more pronounced smoke flavor, I use my stovetop smoker to smoke-cook the vegetables.

Makes about 4 cups

Grilling Method: Indirect/Medium Heat
Special Equipment: Cameron Stovetop Smoker, optional

    1   head garlic
  ½ to ¾ cup olive oil
        Kosher salt
    6   large ripe tomatoes, about 3 pounds
    1   yellow bell pepper
    1   red bell pepper
    2   cucumbers
    1   large sweet onion, cut in half
    2   bunches green onions
    2   tablespoons red wine vinegar
    2   tablespoons chopped fresh herbs, including
          basil, mint, parsley, oregano
    2   teaspoons hot smoked paprika
        Freshly ground pepper
        Tabasco
        Tortilla chips, optional

1. Build a charcoal fire or preheat a gas grill.
2. Prepare the head of garlic for roasting by cutting about ½ inch from the top. Brush the top with oil, sprinkle with salt, and place the garlic in a square of aluminum foil. Wrap the foil around the head of garlic. Place it on the warming rack of the grill or away from any direct heat to roast (this can be done in advance and will take about 45 minutes to roast and caramelize).
3. While the garlic roasts, stem the tomatoes. Clean the peppers but leave them whole for roasting. Peel, halve, and seed the cucumber. Peel the onion and cut the roots off the green onions. Brush all of the vegetables with oil and set aside.
4. Place all the vegetables but the peppers in the center of the cooking grate over indirect medium heat. Place the peppers over direct heat to blacken. (Alternatively, you can smoke the vegetables in a Cameron Stovetop Smoker.)
5. Cover and grill the tomatoes, cucumbers, onions, and green onions until well marked and soft but not mushy. The vegetables will take different lengths of time to cook: The tomatoes and green onions will only take about 5 minutes, and the rest of the vegetables will take closer to 20 minutes. As soon as each vegetable is done, transfer it to a platter or bowl to cool, reserving any juices.
6. When the peppers are blackened, place them in a closed container or paper bag until the steam loosens from the skin. Remove the skin and seeds and set aside. Check to make sure the garlic is done and remove it from the grill.
7. While they are still warm, puree the grilled vegetables, peppers, and garlic cloves squeezed from the skins in a food processor or blender at high speed. Slowly add ½ cup of oil, the vinegar, herbs, and paprika until smooth and still very thick. Adjust the oil, vinegar, salt, pepper, and Tabasco to taste. The salsa should be highly seasoned and thick. Chill at least 1 hour and up to 2 days until serving. Serve with tortilla chips, if desired.

Marti's at Midday Pimento Cheese

Marti Schimmel is one of those people who are impossible not to love at first meeting. She is the chef-owner of Marti's at Midday Café and Catering Company in Athens, GA. We always have a ball talking about, fixing, and eating food together! Marti's style is simple, sassy, and Southern—all of which add up to good, no, great, eating! Every time she sees me, she brings me a pint of her homemade pimento cheese, which is by far the best I have ever tasted. The only problem is that I can't stop eating it! Serve it at your next dinner party; I guarantee you'll be the talk of your grilling circle.

Makes about 3 cups

½   medium sweet white onion, such as Vidalia, grated
1   cup diced pimentos, with juice
1   teaspoon ground cayenne or more if you like it hotter
4   ounces cream cheese, softened
¾   cup best-quality, full-fat mayonnaise, preferably Hellmann's
6   cups (1 pound) freshly grated sharp white cheddar cheese
     Homemade Pita Points (page 292)

1. In a medium bowl, mix the onion, pimentos, and cayenne until well combined. Add the cream cheese and mayonnaise and stir until the mixture is smooth and all the ingredients are incorporated.
2. Add the cheddar and mix until just combined, keeping the texture a little chunky. The pimento cheese will keep in the fridge for 2 weeks (if it lasts that long).

Alan's Mustard Dip for Raw Vegetables

Alan Wagner is an old family friend who has lived in India for the past 25 years. When he swooped into Greensboro to teach drama, he brought his penchant for gourmet dinner parties and inspired quite a few good Southern cooks to up their kitchen ante. I was old enough to want to help with the meal, but too young to actually cook anything, so he taught me this simple dip. Making it became my family duty, which I still do to this day. Every time I make it for a party, at least one person asks for the recipe. It's so simple, I love to share it. But I generally pass along the recipe and tell a story or two about how Alan woke up a sleepy Southern town.

Makes 1¾ cups

1   cup mayonnaise, preferably Hellmann's
½   cup strong Dijon mustard, such as Grey Poupon, Maille, or Amora
1   heaping tablespoon whole-grain French mustard, such as Pommery or Maille
2½ teaspoons granulated garlic
     Freshly ground pepper
     Assortment of cut raw vegetables, such as carrots, celery, white mushrooms, red and yellow bell peppers, broccoli, cauliflower, blanched asparagus, and sugar snap peas, (about 2 pounds total)

1. In a small bowl, mix the mayonnaise and mustards until creamy and well combined. Add the garlic and pepper to taste (you will not need to add salt as the mayo and mustards are salty on their own).
2. Refrigerate, covered, until ready to use. Serve with raw veggies of your choice. The dip can be made up to 1 week in advance and kept covered in the refrigerator.

TIP: Alan's original recipe only called for mayo and Grey Poupon mustard (a very exotic ingredient for Greensboro, NC, in the 1970s). Over the years, I added a whole-grain French mustard—Moutarde de Meaux from Pommery is my favorite—to add texture and create a slightly more tangy and complex flavor. The dip is delicious either way—smooth or grainy.

TGIF Spinach-Artichoke Dip

This is a variation of the dip that everyone I know learned to make in high school or college. Even if you think you've "graduated" to fancier fare, give it a try—you'll remember why everyone made it all the time: Because it is simply delish!

Makes 3½ cups

1   14-ounce can artichoke hearts in water
1   9-ounce package frozen chopped spinach, cooked and drained of all excess water
1   cup mayonnaise
1   cup grated parmesan cheese
½   cup grated Romano cheese
1   tablespoon Dijon mustard
1   teaspoon Worcestershire sauce
½   teaspoon dehydrated garlic granules or powder
    Crackers, preferably Triscuits

1. Preheat the oven to 350°F.
2. In a medium bowl, mash the artichokes and spinach together with a fork. Add the other ingredients and stir until the vegetables are evenly distributed.
3. Put the mixture in a two-quart ovenproof dish and bake for 40 to 50 minutes, or until golden and bubbling. Serve immediately with crackers.

Portobello Mushroom Dip with Pita Points

This party dip is sure to become a staple in your entertaining repertoire. And once you make it a few times, you can substitute other grilled veggies for the portobellos. I often make this recipe substituting Fire-Roasted Peppers (page 210) for the mushrooms to make a smoky dip or Forgotten Onion (page 209) to make a delicious caramelized onion dip. Sometimes I serve all three on an appetizer platter. The trio is perfect for entertaining because the colors of the dips are warm and festive (brown, red, and cream). Not only can they be made in advance, but they are better made the day before serving. To make this dip really festive, serve it with blue, red, or green tortilla chips as well as the pita points.

Makes 3 cups or 4 to 8 servings

Grilling Method: Direct/Medium Heat

2   pounds whole portobello mushrooms, cleaned (about 10 large)
    Olive oil
4   shallots, roughly chopped
1   head garlic, roasted (page 207) and removed from skins or 2 cloves grated fresh garlic
8   ounces feta cheese
8   ounces cream cheese
3   tablespoons brandy, or more to taste
½   teaspoon dried thyme
    Kosher salt
    Freshly ground pepper

Homemade Pita Points
4   pieces pita bread

1. Build a charcoal fire or preheat a gas grill.
2. Remove the stems from the mushrooms and discard. Coat the mushrooms lightly with olive oil. Place them, gill-side up, in the center of the cooking grate over direct medium heat. Grill, covered, for 8 to 10 minutes or until marked and caramelized.
3. Remove the mushrooms from the grill with tongs, being careful not to lose the mushroom "liquor" (liquid) in the top of the mushrooms.
4. Puree the mushrooms and their "liquor" in a food processor or blender until smooth. Add the shallots and garlic and pulse to mix well. Add the feta and cream cheeses, brandy, and thyme and pulse again to puree and mix. Adjust the seasonings with salt and pepper. (Because the mushrooms and feta are naturally salty, you may not need to add more salt.)
5. Scrape the puree out of the processor with a spatula and into a bowl. Cover and refrigerate for at least 3 hours to chill and let all the flavors mellow. Keep in the refrigerator up to 1 week.
6. Preheat the oven to 300°F. Make the pita points by cutting each pita round in half and then each half into thirds to make 6 triangles.
7. Place the triangles on a cookie sheet and bake for 30 to 40 minutes, or until dried out and slightly brown. (You do not need to put oil or butter on the bread; it will toast beautifully in a low oven if you leave it there long enough.) The pita points can also be made in advance and kept in an airtight container for up to 1 week. Serve the chilled dip with the pita points.

Don't Worry, Be Happy Baba Ghanoush

This garlic and eggplant dip is my version of the Middle Eastern baba ghanoush. The dip and the homemade pita chips can be made way in advance—it keeps for a week in the refrigerator. I make it on the weekends when I am taking care of things around the house.— You basically put it on the grill and forget about it until it's cooked.

Makes 3 to 4 cups

Grilling Method: Indirect/Medium Heat

3	large eggplants
1½	heads garlic, about ½ head per eggplant
	Olive oil
	Kosher or sea salt
¼	cup minced fresh parsley, or a mixture of parsley and fresh mint
	Freshly ground pepper
	Homemade Pita Points (page 292)

1. Build a charcoal fire or preheat a gas grill.
2. Wash and dry the eggplants. Peel the garlic cloves and set them aside. If the cloves are very large, cut them in half lengthwise. Make multiple ½-inch slits in the eggplants and stud with garlic cloves or pieces. Push garlic towards the center of the eggplants so the garlic is not sticking out. When done, brush the eggplants with olive oil and sprinkle with salt.
3. Place the eggplants in the center of the cooking grate over indirect medium heat, cover, and grill until the eggplants have collapsed and are very soft. Using long-handled tongs, turn the eggplants occasionally for even cooking. This will take about 30 minutes, depending on the size of the eggplants.
4. When the eggplants have collapsed into themselves, remove them from the grill. Cut the eggplants in half and scrape the flesh and garlic from the skin. Mash the mixture with a fork or puree it in a food processor. Mix in enough olive oil to make the dip creamy. Season with the parsley, and salt and pepper to taste. Serve with the pita chips or flatbread.

Lisa's Famous Eggplant Rock and Roll-Ups

My college friend, Lisa Ryan, is not only an all-weather friend, but she is an all-weather griller. Once, in the frigid 3°F Chicago cold, she had a party that started with these grilled eggplant and red pepper appetizers. The veggies are stacked with fresh mozzarella and rolled-up with a paper-thin slice of prosciutto di Parma. The food was superb and everyone was thrilled that she did not let the elements scare her away from grilling. The roll-ups are gently heated to melt the cheese just before serving, so they can be made hours before your guests arrive. These veggie-packed starters also make a great light meal.

Makes 8 to 10 servings

Grilling Method: Direct/Medium Heat

2	large eggplants, peeled
	Olive oil
	Kosher salt
2	red bell peppers, cored, seeded, and cut into 1-inch strips
5	large balls fresh mozzarella cheese, sliced in ½-inch rounds
	1 to 2 pounds thinly sliced prosciutto di Parma, at room temperature

1. Build a charcoal fire or preheat a gas grill.
2. Slice the eggplants into ½-inch rounds. Brush them all over with olive oil and sprinkle with salt. Brush the pepper strips with oil and sprinkle with salt.
3. Place the vegetables on the cooking grate over direct medium heat, cover, and grill for 10 to 15 minutes, turning once halfway through the grilling time. The vegetables should be crisp-tender and well marked.
4. Remove the vegetables from the grill onto a clean platter and let them cool. When cool enough to handle, cut the larger pieces of eggplant in half and set aside. Begin assembling roll-ups by placing a piece of cheese on top of each eggplant slice. Add a piece of red pepper to each. Wrap each stack of veggies and cheese with a piece of prosciutto to

cover and hold the other ingredients together. If the prosciutto is at room temperature, it will adhere to itself, securing the eggplant roll-ups without toothpicks.

5. Place the roll-ups on a heat-resistant tray with the end of the prosciutto on the bottom and set aside until 10 minutes before you want to serve. If not cooking within 15 minutes, cover and keep in the fridge until ready to cook. You can prepare the roll-ups up to 24 hours in advance.

6. When ready to serve, heat the roll-ups in a pre-heated 350°F oven until the cheese melts, about 10 minutes. Serve immediately.

Blue Cheese Lovers' Blue Cheese Dip

I was tired of wimpy blue cheese dips, so I was thrilled when my friend John Mose shared his mother's recipe with me. It is pungent without being too strong, and the addition of garlic and shallots deepens the flavor of the blue cheese. I add a little more of the cheese and seasonings than the recipe calls for since I am at the top of the stinky cheese lover's scale. For best results use Societe Roquefort or another pungent blue cheese. Try the dip on a salad, veggies, chicken wings, or just about anything that needs a "dip" that rocks!

Makes 2 cups

1   cup mayonnaise
½   cup sour cream
4   ounces quality blue cheese or more to taste, crumbled
1½   tablespoons grated shallot or onion
1   tablespoon fresh lemon juice
2   cloves garlic, grated
     Fine-grain sea salt
     Freshly ground pepper

Combine all the ingredients except the salt and pepper in a large bowl, and refrigerate for at least 3 hours to let the flavors develop. Taste and adjust salt and pepper as needed. Serve chilled.

Italian Grilled Cheese Skewers

*These kabobs are inspired by a Roman specialty—*spiedini alla romana, *which is grilled skewers of stale bread and mozzarella cheese—and the flavors of the ever-popular caprese salad. In this version, the bread and cheese are threaded on skewers and grilled, topping a salad of cherry tomatoes and basil pesto. Alternatively, you can grill the tomatoes on separate skewers until warm, and toss everything in pesto for a warm and crunchy side dish. Either way, this unique kabob is equally at home as a colorful vegetarian entrée or hearty appetizer. Double as needed for a larger group.*

Makes 6 skewers

Grilling Method: Indirect/Medium-Low Heat

1   loaf country bread
8   ounces bocconcini (small fresh mozzarella balls) or regular fresh mozzarella balls, cut into quarters
     Olive oil
12   wooden skewers, soaked in water for 30 minutes
     Kosher salt
1   pint cherry tomatoes
¼   cup best-quality pesto, purchased or homemade
     Fleur de sel or coarse sea salt

1. Build a charcoal fire or preheat a gas grill. Slice the bread and cut it into 1½ x 1½–inch cubes. Coat the cubes with olive oil and set aside.

2. Using 2 skewers per kabob—1 on each side of the food like a ladder (see page 28)—thread the bread cubes and bocconcini balls, alternating ingredients. Sprinkle the skewers with salt and place them on the cooking grate over indirect medium-low heat. Cover and grill for 3 to 6 minutes, turning once halfway through to toast both sides of bread and warm the cheese.

3. Meanwhile, wash and dry the cherry tomatoes and cut them in half. Divide the tomatoes among 6 plates and drizzle them with the pesto sauce. Remove the skewers from the grill and place 1 kabob on each plate, directly on top of the tomato-pesto mixture. Sprinkle with fleur de sel to taste. Enjoy immediately.

Bacon-Wrapped Parmesan-Stuffed Dates

This appetizer was popular in the late sixties, along with white lipstick and go-go boots. Let's hope white lipstick will never return, but it is time to bring back this dish. I add a few toasted cumin seeds to the filling to balance the sweet and savory flavors. Alternatively, half of a walnut would work as well.

Makes 8 servings

Grilling Method: Direct/Medium-Low Heat

24 whole plump dried medjool or other dates, pitted
1 teaspoon cumin seeds or 24 walnut halves
8 ounces Parmigiano-Reggiano cheese, cut into twenty-four ½-inch pieces
12 pieces bacon, cut in half
24 round wooden toothpicks, soaked in water for 30 minutes

1. Build a charcoal fire or preheat a gas grill.
2. Cut an opening into the center of each date to make a pocket, but do not cut all the way through.
3. Place a few cumin seeds or 1 walnut half into the opening of each date, and push the seeds or the nut into the bottom of each date. Add a piece of cheese and push again to stuff each date. Wrap with half a slice of bacon and secure with a toothpick.
4. Place the stuffed dates on the cooking grate over direct medium-low heat, cover, and cook, turning occasionally with tongs, for 10 to 15 minutes, or until the bacon is crispy. (If your grill is prone to flare-ups, cook on indirect heat.) Serve the dates hot off the grill or at room temperature.

STORE-BOUGHT STARTERS

I love having people over, but I don't always have the time to make five or six recipes from scratch. For this reason, I often "cheat" with store-bought items and some of my own recipes (nuts, dips, etc.) that are left-over or made days in advance. I take everything that can possibly be used out of the fridge and "compose" them into a great array of appetizers. In fact, I have gotten so good at this that I can look into a fridge that I think has "no food" and with a little creativity put together a spread of little dishes that often becomes din-ner. I put everything in small mismatched ceramic bowls and plates and include an array of condiments so people can customize their own bites. Fleur de sel, strong Dijon mustard, artisanal honeys and jams, and compound butters are standard accompaniments. It's amazing how a few condiments in little plates and pretty bowls make a standard cheese tray come to (eclectic) life! Every time I do this (with a lick and a promise), I am amazed at how good the appetizers are, how easy it was, and how effusive the praise is. I urge you to do the same.

Here are some of my favorite out-of-the fridge starters:

- Mixed olives, plain or tossed with fennel, fresh garlic, chile flakes, or lemon zest
- Mixed dried fruit and nuts
- Sliced radishes with sweet butter and fleur de sel
- Selection of sliced meats, cheeses, olives, and marinated vegetables
- Selection of raw-milk cheeses and a warm baguette
- Manchego cheese served with fig jam, quince paste, salty almonds, and crusty bread
- Bocconcini (tiny fresh mozzarella balls) sea-soned with red chile flakes, olive oil, or pesto
- Black olive tapenade with toasts and a drizzle of Lulu's truffle honey
- A block of cream cheese topped with hot pep-per jelly, served with wheat crackers
- Hummus with carrots, celery, and warm pita bread
- Chilled foie gras with toasted brioche

Truffled White Bean and Caramelized Onion Toasts

At a recent impromptu cocktail party, my friends and I were looking for something to make out of the leftovers in my refrigerator. I had some white bean puree from a pork dish that I had made earlier in the week, slightly stale thick-crusted bread, and a bag of onions. While I caramelized the onions, a friend grilled the bread. Soon we were all standing in the kitchen, slathering the grilled toasts with the bean puree and topping them with warm onions and a drizzle of truffle oil. We couldn't believe our luck—they were divine! Try them once, and they just might become your standard starter.

Makes 8 toasts

Grilling Method: Direct/Medium-Low Heat

4   large yellow onion
8   1-inch slices country bread
    Olive oil
    White Bean Puree (pages 91–92)
    White truffle oil
    Minced fresh rosemary
    Freshly ground pepper

1. Build a charcoal fire or preheat a gas grill.
2. Slice the onions into thin rings. Heat about 2 tablespoons of oil in a large, heavy-bottomed sauté pan set over medium heat. When the oil is hot but not smoking, add the onions. Cook, stirring occasionally, until the rings are softened and caramelized, about 15 minutes.
3. Brush the bread with olive oil on both sides. Place the slices on the cooking grate over direct medium-low heat, cover, and grill for about 2 minutes per side, or until toasted. Remove the bread from the grill and let it cool on a rack for 5 minutes.
4. Spread each piece of toast with a generous layer of white bean puree, and top with a small mound of caramelized onions. Drizzle with a bit of truffle oil and sprinkle with minced rosemary. Serve immediately with a grind of pepper.

Grilled Country Ham Biscuits

Every self-respecting Southerner loves ham biscuits! When I go home to visit, I have my meals all planned out with the same precision that I do when I go to Paris or any other great food town. The main difference is that the places I frequent don't take reservations and often close before 8 p.m., since they start serving at the crack of dawn each day.

My father and I go to one of my favorites for breakfast— Alpat—every time I am home. It is one of those great restaurants that serves up old-fashioned Southern cooking.

But the real reason we've gone to Alpat (for breakfast) all these years is their country ham and biscuits. The last time I was there, I realized that grilling country ham would give it the coveted crust and caramelized spots more consistently than pan frying, so I tried it. The added bonus is that there is no messy pan to wash and no smell of fried food in the kitchen. Buy the packages of center-cut country ham for the best results. Serve this breakfast treat with strong coffee and blackstrap molasses, if desired. Drizzle the molasses over the ham, replace the biscuit top, and eat it like a sandwich.

Makes 10 servings

Grilling Method: Direct/Medium Heat
Special Equipment: Grill press, cast-iron skillet, or bricks wrapped in aluminum foil

4   pieces center-cut cured country ham
    Peanut or olive oil
    Karmel Family Biscuits (at right; do not
        make ahead)
    Blackstrap molasses, optional

1. Trim away any excess fat from the ham. Brush the ham lightly with oil, removing any excess with paper towels. (Do not add salt or pepper; the ham is already highly seasoned.)
2. Make the biscuits, and build a charcoal fire or preheat a gas grill. While the biscuits are in the

oven, place each piece of ham on the cooking grate over direct medium heat. Place something heavy like a grill press, cast-iron skillet, or bricks wrapped in foil directly on the ham—this will keep it flat. Cover and grill for 3 to 4 minutes, and turn the ham over, using heat-resistant mitts to remove the weight from the ham.

3. Replace the weight and grill for another 3 to 4 minutes, or until the second side is well marked. You may have to do this in batches if you do not have enough weights for all 4 pieces. Remove the ham from the grill, cut each piece into 3 equal pieces, and set aside.

4. Remove the biscuits from the oven to a cooling rack. While the biscuits are still warm, gently break them in half. Slip a piece of ham between the halves of each biscuit. Serve immediately with molasses, if desired.

Karmel Family Biscuits

Biscuits are as dear to me as barbecue. My grandmother made biscuits, my mother makes biscuits, and in the current family hierarchy, my sister Mary Pat is the new generation biscuit maker. We've even had "biscuit offs" with my mother, sister, and me baking biscuits with lard, butter, shortening, and combinations of the three to determine the perfect Karmel family biscuit. This recipe won by a crumb—the biscuit made with lard was mighty tasty but couldn't beat Mary Pat's everyday biscuit.

Makes 10 to 12 biscuits

2   cups all-purpose flour, plus extra as needed
1   tablespoon baking powder
½   teaspoon cream of tartar
¼   teaspoon fine- grain salt
½   cup plus 2 tablespoons Crisco shortening
½   cup plus 2 tablespoons milk
4   tablespoons (½ stick) unsalted butter, melted

1. Preheat the oven to 450°F.

2. In a large bowl, sift or whisk together the flour, baking powder, cream of tartar, and salt. Using a pastry blender or 2 knives, cut the Crisco into the flour until the mixture resembles coarse crumbs. Add the milk and, using a fork, stir until moistened and the dough holds together in a smooth ball. If the exterior is slightly sticky, don't worry; it will become smooth as you knead it on the floured board.

3. Turn the dough out on a floured surface. Knead it until it is smooth (about 6 strokes). Roll the dough with a rolling pin until it forms a circle about ½ inch thick. Brush it liberally with the melted butter and fold the dough in half to cover the butter. Pinch the edges to seal. Roll out again to form a circle about ½ inch thick. The thicker the dough at this stage, the higher the biscuits will be. (These biscuits will be about 1½ inches high and will open into 2 halves where the butter was brushed on and dough folded.)

4. Cut the dough with a 2½- to 3-inch biscuit cutter or round cookie cutter, as close together as possible, to avoid wasting the dough. The scraps can be rerolled to make more biscuits or baked in the irregular shapes as treats for the cook or your pet.

5. Place the biscuits on an ungreased cookie sheet, 1 inch apart. Brush the tops with melted butter, and bake for 10 to 12 minutes or until golden. Transfer them to a rack and serve immediately.

TIP: For those interested in the results of our informal family biscuit test, the lard biscuits had a great flavor, but were a little soft and fell apart when split and used to sandwich the grilled ham. The butter biscuit didn't rise as much as the other two and had a slightly dry and crumbly texture. The winning Crisco biscuit has a fluffier texture and holds together beautifully when split and stuffed with the grilled ham.

Straight-Up Deviled Eggs

I couldn't write an outdoor cooking book and not include a recipe for deviled eggs! Who doesn't love them? And good news! They are back in vogue and here to stay. This is a simple but powerful recipe. Every time I bring them to a party, I go home with an empty plate. If you are feeling a little ambitious, pipe the filling into the whites using a pastry bag and a decorative tip.

Makes 12 to 24 servings

1	dozen large eggs
1/3	cup mayonnaise, preferably Hellmann's
5	tablespoons unsalted butter, softened
1/4	cup strong Dijon mustard
1/2	lemon, zested
1	teaspoon fresh lemon juice
	Pinch garlic powder
2 to 4	shakes Tabasco
	Sea salt
	Smoked paprika or minced fresh chives

1. Place the eggs in a large stockpot and cover with cold water. Bring to a boil, cover, and turn off the heat. Let the eggs sit for 20 minutes. Drain and run them under cold water until they are cool to the touch. Let them sit another 10 minutes.
2. Peel the eggs carefully, keeping the whites intact. Cut in half lengthwise and remove the yolks. Set the whites aside on a platter or egg plate.
3. Put the yolks into a medium bowl and mash them with a fork, until all large pieces are broken up and smooth. Add the mayonnaise, butter, mustard, lemon zest and juice, garlic powder, and Tabasco to taste. Stir well. Taste and season with salt.
4. Place the mixture in a pastry bag and pipe it into the egg whites or use a small spoon to fill the egg white "boats" with yolk mixture. Sprinkle the eggs with smoked paprika for classic eggs, or chives for a fancier-looking version. Serve chilled.

COLD-WEATHER GRILLING

I love to grill in the winter—even Chicago winters! In fact, I grill more in the winter than the summer; it's when I crave big pieces of meat and heartier fare. Contrary to what most people think, grilling in the dead of winter doesn't really take any longer than fair-weather grilling. The only wild card is wind (which can be a problem in summer, too). Wind will add a lot of time to your cook-out regardless of the season. My grills are on an open balcony about five floors up and if it is really windy, it is almost impossible to keep the burners lit on my gas grills. On a charcoal grill, the wind can make the charcoal burn faster. Besides wind, the ambient temperature doesn't make that much difference. But like all grilling, keep in mind that you need to put a lid on it (the grill) as fast as possible. The longer the grill is uncovered, the more heat escapes and the longer it will take to get the inside of the grill back up to temperature, thus increasing the total time it takes to cook your food.

Salads and Sides

Salads have come a long way (and back) from the days of the iceberg wedge and "green goddess" dressing. In fact, on many days I crave a wedge with my Blue Cheese Lover's Blue Cheese Dip (page 294) and a crumble of smoky bacon. But the real reason I love that old throwback is that it is the perfect combination of cool, crunchy, creamy, and savory. Here, I include salads and sides that combine taste, texture, and, in some cases, grilled ingredients. They all are great accompaniments to simple grilled fish or meat, and many of them, including the Antipasto Pasta and the Grilled Mushroom Salad with "Rocket" and Comté cheese, make nice vegetarian entrees for meatless meals.

Sides or the "fixins," as they are colloquially called, round out the meal. In the world of barbecue and grilling, coleslaw and potato salad are the official side dishes. After that, baked beans, mac 'n' cheese, and even collards are often served. Fried foods are popular at restaurants and cold gelatin salads grace the family reunion picnic tables. Besides that, it's personal taste that determines what belongs on the side.

Because a cookout isn't a cookout for most people unless there is a big bowl of potato salad smack dab in the middle of the table, I've included my two favorites. And because coleslaw is equally important, I'm offering two of those, too—one plain and one fancy. After that, I've included an eclectic mix of side dishes that I serve over and over again. It is by no means exhaustive, just a few extra choices to get you started.

Luxurious Lettuce Salad

When I lived in France, I fell in love with the salade vert eaten at the end of the meal. When I returned to the States, I began my quest for the perfect salade vert recipe—and it took me 20 years to learn the secret. I mastered making a perfect vinaigrette, imported Dijon mustard, bought every tender lettuce I could find, yet nothing got close—until an accidental experiment.

When my favorite olive oil from Italy arrived in my local grocery store, I immediately bought a bottle and set to work making salad. I washed and dried Boston lettuce, sprinkled the leaves with fleur de sel, and drizzled it with olive oil. I tossed the salad, and came back a few minutes later ready to add some vinegar, but I greedily tasted it first. Oh, my! It was perfect. Fresh, clean, and luxurious. The only catch is that with so few ingredients, you have to use really fresh lettuce, premier quality fleur de sel (sea salt from Brittany), and first-press olive oil. (I like Monini Gran Frutto olive oil the best but Laudemino or Lucini are also good brands available nationwide.)

Makes 1 to 2 appetizer servings

1 head Boston or butter lettuce, washed and dried
   Fleur de sel or coarse sea salt
1 to 2 teaspoons best-quality olive oil
   Freshly ground pepper, optional

1. Place the lettuce leaves in a large bowl, sprinkle with about 2 pinches of fleur de sel or coarse sea salt, and toss. Drizzle the lettuce with 1 to 2 teaspoons (or more to taste) of olive oil; toss very well to coat all the leaves.
2. Let the salad sit for 5 minutes and toss it again. Add a little more oil if the leaves are not coated, but be careful not to use too much oil, otherwise the salad will be heavy and the lettuce will get soggy. Add freshly ground pepper, if desired.

Wilted Spinach Salad with Grilled Tomatoes

The traditional warm spinach and bacon salad is revitalized by the addition of fresh basil and grilled grape tomatoes tumbled in herbes de Provence. The heat from the tomatoes wilts the greens slightly and intensifies all of the flavors. I've added grilled bread and eliminated the traditional sliced egg, but feel free to include it.

Makes 4 appetizer servings

Grilling Method: Direct/Medium Heat

  8   ounces sliced center-cut bacon
  1   bunch fresh basil leaves (about 1½ cups), cleaned
 12   ounces baby spinach leaves, washed and dried
      Kosher salt
  1   pint grape or cherry tomatoes, washed and dried
      Olive oil
1½   teaspoons herbes de Provence
 ½   teaspoon granulated garlic
  2   1-inch slices country bread

Dressing
  1   tablespoon Dijon mustard
  2   tablespoons white wine vinegar
 ⅓   cup olive oil
  1   tablespoon bacon grease, warm
      Sea salt
      Freshly ground pepper
      Wooden skewers, soaked in water for
         30 minutes

1. Build a charcoal fire or preheat a gas grill.
2. Meanwhile, cut each slice of bacon into thirds. Cook the bacon in a medium skillet until crisp. Transfer it to paper towels to drain; reserve 1 tablespoon of the bacon grease from the pan.
3. In a large salad bowl, toss the spinach and basil with a pinch of salt. Crumble the bacon into pieces and toss it with the spinach. Set aside.
4. Toss the tomatoes with about 1 teaspoon of oil; add the herbs, garlic and salt to taste and toss together. Brush both sides of the bread lightly with oil and cut into 1-inch chunks.
5. Preheat the oven to 200°F. Make the dressing: Whisk together the mustard and vinegar in a small oven-safe bowl. Slowly incorporate the olive oil and reserved bacon grease until the dressing is emulsified. Season to taste with salt and pepper. Keep the dressing warm in the oven.
6. Just before serving, thread the tomatoes and bread chunks separately on 2 parallel skewers, ladder style (see page 28). Place the skewered tomatoes and bread on the cooking grates or on a cast-iron grill grate over direct medium heat. Cover and grill, turning occasionally, until the tomatoes are randomly blistered and warmed through, 4 to 5 minutes total, and the bread is toasted.
7. Toss the hot tomatoes into the warm salad dressing. Cut the grilled bread into bite-size cubes and set aside. Remove the tomatoes from the dressing and toss them lightly with the greens to coat. Add more dressing only if needed. (You do not want the salad to get soggy. Extra dressing can be stored in the refrigerator for several days.)
8. Divide the grilled bread cubes among 4 plates and serve a portion of the wilted salad over the grilled bread; this will allow the bread to soak up any extra dressing. Serve immediately.

TIP: To make it easier to grill the tiny grape tomatoes, use a cast-iron grill grate. Place the grill grate on the grill while you preheat it, and it will be ready to mark and warm the tiny tomatoes without having to skewer them—and you won't lose one!

Chicago Steakhouse Salad

In the steakhouses of Chicago, each chef has his or her version of a tomato and onion salad. For mine, I grill the tomatoes and serve them warm so the blue cheese melts into the tomatoes. When I eat the salad, I make a perfect bite with a bit of sweet onion, pungent cheese, crunchy pecan, and tart tomato. It just doesn't get any better—until the steak arrives.

Makes 4 servings

Grilling Method: Direct/Medium Heat

Classic Vinaigrette
- ¼ cup apple cider vinegar
- 1 heaping teaspoon Dijon mustard
  Kosher salt
  Freshly ground pepper
- ½ cup good-quality olive oil

- 2 large, ripe, beefsteak tomatoes
- 2 large Vidalia onions, trimmed
  Wooden skewers, soaked in water for 30 minutes
  Olive oil
  Kosher salt
  Freshly ground pepper
- 8 ounces crumbled blue cheese, preferably Societe Roquefort
- ⅔ cup whole pecans, toasted

1. Build a charcoal fire or preheat a gas grill.
2. Make the classic vinaigrette: In a small bowl, whisk together the vinegar, mustard, and salt and pepper to taste. Slowly whisk in the olive oil, making sure it is emulsified before adding more oil; continue until all the oil is incorporated.
3. Slice the tomatoes and onions into ½-inch slices. Thread a skewer through the edge of the onion rings to secure them—they will resemble lollipops. Coat them lightly with olive oil, and season with salt and pepper. Set aside.
4. Just before serving, place the onion rings on the cooking grate over direct medium heat, cover, and grill for 5 minutes on each side. Add the tomatoes and grill for 2 minutes on each side or until warmed through.
5. Place 2 slices of tomatoes and 2 slices of onion on each plate. While the vegetables are still warm, top them with blue cheese. Garnish with pecans and a drizzle of the vinaigrette. Serve at room temperature.

Asparagus and Arugula Salad with Shaved Parmesan

When you feel like having grilled asparagus with all the trimmings, try this recipe. It's simple but fancy enough to serve to your VIP guests. The sweetness of the grilled asparagus is perfectly balanced by the bitter arugula and rich Parmigiano-Reggiano cheese. I like it best served while the asparagus is still warm, warming the cheese and wilting the arugula.

Makes 4 appetizer servings

Grilling Method: Direct/Medium Heat

- 1 bunch asparagus, about 1 pound
  Olive oil as needed
  Sea salt
  Freshly ground pepper
- 1 bunch or 4 cups arugula
- 1 medium lemon, zested and juiced
  Parmesan cheese, cut into thin slices with a vegetable peeler

1. Build a charcoal fire or preheat a gas grill.
2. Clean and trim the asparagus, coat it lightly with olive oil, season with salt and pepper, and set aside.
3. Meanwhile, clean the arugula and remove any excess stems, dry, and set aside.
4. Place the asparagus crosswise on the cooking grate over direct medium heat, cover, and grill for 4 to 6 minutes, turning to expose all surfaces.
5. While the asparagus is on the grill, make the dressing by whisking together the lemon juice

with $\frac{1}{3}$ cup olive oil, half the lemon zest, and salt and pepper to taste in a small bowl.

6. While the asparagus is still warm (cut it into large pieces if desired), toss it in a large bowl with the arugula and dressing (this will wilt the arugula). Divide the salad among 4 plates and top with shaved parmesan cheese. Serve immediately.

TIP: This salad makes a mean entrée when tossed with cooked penne and chunks of grilled chicken.

Grilled Mushroom Salad with "Rocket" and Comté Cheese

I enjoyed a salad similar to this recipe during the cèpe mushroom season at L'Oustau de Baumaniere in Les Beaux de Provence. The warm mushrooms wilted the greens and softened the cheese, making a traditional dressing unnecessary. Only a drizzle of the local olive oil adorned the bitter "rocket" (arugula) and meaty mushroom salad. I'm not sure why, but I love the sound—and taste—of it.

Makes 4 appetizer servings

Grilling Method: Direct/Medium Heat

1 pound cèpe, chanterelle, or porcini mushrooms, cleaned
   Olive oil
   Kosher salt
4 cups arugula (rocket), cleaned
$\frac{1}{4}$ cup walnuts, toasted
1 ounce Comté or Gruyere cheese, sliced with a vegetable peeler
   Best-quality extra-virgin olive oil
   Fleur de sel or coarse sea salt
   Grains of paradise or white pepper

1. Build a charcoal fire or preheat a gas grill.
2. Brush the mushrooms with olive oil and season with salt. Place the mushroom caps on the cooking grate over direct medium heat, cover, and grill for

4 to 5 minutes on each side, or until tender and well marked.

3. Divide the arugula on 4 plates, and top it immediately with the hot mushrooms. Garnish with the walnuts and cheese and a drizzle of the olive oil. Sprinkle the salads with fleur de sel or other coarse sea salt and add a grind of grains of paradise or white pepper just before serving.

Crunchy Cucumber Salad

This cucumber salad is refreshing in the heat of the summer when cucumbers practically fall from the sky. I usually make a batch and keep it for a few days in the fridge, pairing it with all kinds of grilled fish and chicken. Try adding raw baby peas and tiny tomatoes if you can find them.

Makes 4 to 6 servings

2 large cucumbers
$\frac{1}{2}$ medium red or purple onion, thinly sliced
1 cup sour cream
1 tablespoon sherry vinegar or unsweetened rice wine vinegar
1 teaspoon sugar
   Fine-grain sea salt
   White pepper

1. Wash and dry the cucumbers and remove the ends. Using a vegetable peeler, peel alternate strips of the peel off the length of the cucumber so that there are $\frac{1}{2}$-inch strips of skin left on the cucumber. (The cucumber will have candy-cane stripes when finished.) Slice the cucumbers into discs about $\frac{1}{8}$ inch wide and put them in a bowl. Add the onion and set aside.
2. Combine the sour cream, vinegar, and sugar in a large bowl. Taste and adjust the seasonings by adding sea salt and white pepper.
3. Fold the cucumbers and onions into the dressing until well combined and all the vegetables are coated with the dressing. Refrigerate until ready to serve, up to 4 hours. Just before serving, stir and taste, adjusting salt and pepper if necessary.

Super Celery Salad

This crunchy celery salad is Super, with a capital "S." It is the most satisfying salad I know and elevates celery, the much maligned "rabbit food" to gourmet status. The secret is in slicing the celery paper-thin with a mandoline or the slicing blade of a food processor. The dish is enhanced by a lemon vinaigrette and ribbons of real Parmigiano-Reggiano. It is also a great foundation for add-ins—one of the reasons that I make it all the time. Depending on my mood or what I find at the market, I fancy it up with mushrooms, fennel, apples, pears, beets—all thinly sliced— or walnuts, pomegranate seeds, even mâche. Try any other ingredients that suit your fancy. Just keep the three main ingredients consistent.

Makes 4 servings

Special Equipment: Mandoline or vegetable slicer

8	ribs celery, cleaned, trimmed, and dried
2	ounce wedge Parmigiano-Reggiano
1/3	cup fresh lemon juice (1 to 2 lemons)
2/3	cup best-quality olive oil
	Kosher salt
	Freshly ground pepper or grains of paradise, optional
1	cup white mushrooms, fennel, fruits, nuts, or other foods that inspire you, optional

1. Using a very sharp knife, mandoline, vegetable slicer, or food processor, slice the celery very thinly. Transfer it to a large bowl. With a vegetable peeler, slice 18 to 24 curls of the parmesan cheese into a small bowl and set aside.
2. Whisking together the lemon juice and olive oil in a small bowl until emulsified. Season to taste with salt and pepper.
3. Toss the celery (and half of the cheese) with just enough dressing to coat. Top with the remaining cheese and any other optional ingredients. Add more dressing if needed. Serve immediately with more ground pepper at the table.

Charred Onion Salad with Prosciutto and Parmigiano

This charred onion salad is appealing on so many levels. First, it looks great on the plate. Second, I almost always have everything I need on hand or in the freezer to make it. And, finally, it is substantial, flavorful, and soulfully satisfying. If you do not have prosciutto, substitute bacon or thinly cut French ham.

Makes 4 to 8 servings

Grilling Method: Direct/Medium Heat

4	large red onions, peeled
	Olive oil
	Kosher salt
2	2-inch slices country bread
2	cloves garlic, cut in half
2	tablespoons balsamic vinegar, or more to taste
1/2	cup chopped fresh Italian (flat-leaf) parsley
4	pieces prosciutto, cut into strips
8	parmesan cheese curls or more to taste
	Wooden skewers, soaked in water for 30 minutes

1. Build a charcoal fire or preheat a gas grill.
2. Cut the rounded ends off the onions, and slice into rings 1 inch thick. Each onion should yield 2 to 3 onion rings. Reserve the ends for another use. Brush the onions with olive oil and spear them, parallel to the onion surface, straight through the centers with 1 of the wooden skewers to keep the rings intact. They will look like lollipops. Season with salt and set aside.
3. Brush the bread lightly with olive oil and sprinkle with salt. Place it on the cooking grate over direct medium heat, cover, and grill on both sides to toast, about 2 minutes on each side. Transfer the bread to a platter, then rub it on both sides with the cut sides of the garlic. Set aside.
4. Place the skewered onion rings on the cooking grate over direct medium heat, cover, and grill until charred on the edges and tender, about 10 minutes per side. Remove the onions from the grill and let them cool for 5 minutes.

5. Remove the wooden skewers and place all the onion rings in a bowl. Toss them with about 2 tablespoons of olive oil and the balsamic vinegar and season with salt and pepper.

6. To build the salad, put ½ piece of bread on each of 4 plates. Divide the onion rings equally among the plates. Top with the chopped parsley, prosciutto, and parmesan cheese curls. Season with freshly ground pepper and serve.

Family-Style Variation: Cut the bread into croutons, add them to the bowl of dressed charred onions, and top with parsley, prosciutto, and parmesan cheese curls.

TIP: To make parmesan cheese curls, use a vegetable peeler to shave slices of cheese off a wedge of solid Parmigiano-Reggiano.

Shout Hallelujah Potato Salad

A few years ago, I was appointed curator of the Southern Foodways Alliance First (and most likely only) Coleslaw and Potato Salad Invitational. I read through hundreds of submissions, made more coleslaw and potato salad than I care to remember, and after much debate, I selected the finalists. This recipe was created by Blair Hobbs, and it won the grand prize—not only does it taste great, but you can't help but love the name!

About mixing the salad, Hobbs said, "Don't stir. Dive in with your hands, mashing some of the potatoes to bond the intact golden chunks." And when you serve this salad, "Receive your kisses and happy praise."

Makes about 15 servings

5   pounds petite Yukon gold potatoes, scrubbed clean
4   stalks celery, chopped
6   eggs
1   cup plus 2 tablespoons mayonnaise, preferably Hellmann's
1   cup sweet (pickle) salad cubes (see Tip at right)
½   heaping cup chopped red onion
½   heaping cup chopped green bell pepper
1   4-ounce jar diced pimentos, drained
¼   cup prepared yellow mustard (don't go fancy with Creole or grainy mustard)
¼   cup seasoned rice wine vinegar
¼   cup chopped fresh parsley
1 to 2 jalapeño peppers, seeded and minced
1   tablespoon olive oil
2   teaspoons celery salt
4   fat drops Louisiana hot sauce
    Freshly ground pepper
    Kosher salt
    Smoked hot paprika

1. Put a large bowl in the refrigerator to chill.
2. Put the potatoes in a large stockpot filled with cold water and a generous sprinkle of kosher salt. Bring to a boil, and then simmer until the potatoes are tender. To test for doneness, slip a thin paring knife into the center of a potato; if the potato resists, it's not done. When to potatoes are done, dump them (gently) into the sink and, under cool running water, peel off the skins with your fingers (as if peeling a hard-boiled egg). Once they are cool, chop into ½-inch pieces.
3. While the potatoes are cooking, boil the eggs. Place the eggs in the bottom of a heavy 3-quart saucepan and fill it with cold water. Put the pan over high heat and bring to a boil, then turn off the heat. Let the eggs sit for 15 minutes, and then rinse under cold water to prevent discoloration. When the eggs are cool, peel and chop them and set aside.
4. In the chilled bowl, mix the cooled potatoes with the chopped eggs. Add all of the other ingredients except the paprika, and mix gently, with clean hands, until the ingredients are thoroughly blended. Salt to taste and shape into a mound with a spoon or spatula. Dust the top with paprika. Cover and chill.

TIP: This recipe works just as well divided in half if you want to make a smaller portion.
TIP: Sweet salad cubes (chopped sweet pickles) are labeled as such in parts of the South. If you cannot find them in your area, simply chop sweet pickles into cubes yourself.

Grandma Odom's Sitting Potato Salad

One bite of this potato salad brings me back to my childhood, where my Georgia-born grandmother would sit at the kitchen table peeling and dicing a steaming mountain of potatoes. Her secret was to make and mix the salad while the potatoes were still piping hot so they'd absorb more of the flavor of the dressing. She would usually drizzle in some of the juice from her (sweet) bread and butter pickles to season the dressing. Since I don't make homemade pickles, I use only apple cider vinegar. If you do make your own pickles, follow her lead and use half pickle juice, half vinegar. This recipe is best made the day before serving.

Makes 6 servings

3½ pounds red bliss potatoes (about 9 large
       potatoes), washed
     Kosher salt

Dressing

1½ cups mayonnaise, preferably Hellmann's
2   tablespoons plus 1 teaspoon apple cider vinegar
1   teaspoon sugar
1   teaspoon salt
2½ teaspoons dry mustard (Coleman's)
       or 1 tablespoon Dijon mustard

1   cup celery, chopped (about 2 large stalks)
1   bunch green onions, chopped, with only about
       2 inches of the green tops
½   cup bread and butter (sweet) pickles (about
       10 large slices)
⅓   cup sour gherkins or about 10 French-style
       gherkins (cornichons)
2   hard-boiled eggs, chopped, optional
     Sea salt
     Freshly ground pepper

1. Put the potatoes in a large stockpot filled with cold water and a generous sprinkle of kosher salt. Bring to a boil, and then simmer until the potatoes are tender. To test for doneness, slip a thin paring knife into the center of a potato; if the potato resists, it's not done. If it is done, drain the potatoes and let them cool just enough to handle them.

2. Meanwhile, make the dressing: Combine all the ingredients in a medium bowl, adding more vinegar if the mixture is too thick. Taste and adjust the seasonings. Set aside.

3. Peel the potatoes; the skin should literally slip right off. Dice them by cutting with a sharp knife in a side-to-side sawing motion. If you chop with an up-and-down motion, the potatoes will split and you won't have nice square pieces. As you dice the potatoes, put them in a large, nonreactive bowl and dress them each time with a little of the dressing.

4. Continue until all potatoes are cut and the salad has the right consistency—all the potatoes should be dressed without an excess of dressing.

5. Add the celery, green onions, pickles, gherkins, and eggs, if using, and mix to blend. If the salad is too dry, quickly blend a little more dressing together and add it to the salad. If it is too wet, drain the salad or add more potatoes. Mix well.

6. Put the salad in an airtight container and refrigerate overnight. Just before serving, adjust the seasonings to taste. Serve chilled.

Ice-Box Coleslaw

This coleslaw is as good as it is easy. My grandmother's "secret" was to peel the leaves off a very fresh cabbage and crisp them in ice water before grating them on a box grater. When I was growing up, my mother served this creamy version of coleslaw with corn sticks and fried fish, but I make it more often to accompany grilled meat or as a picnic side dish.

Makes 6 servings

1   fresh small green cabbage, about 1 pound
¾   cup mayonnaise, preferably Hellmann's
2   tablespoons apple cider vinegar
1   teaspoon sugar
½   teaspoon sea salt, or more to taste
¼   teaspoon white pepper, or more to taste

1. Fill a large bowl or 1 side of a clean double sink with ice water. Peel off the outer leaves of the cabbage and cut the remaining core in half. Soak the leaves in ice water for 15 minutes to crisp. Remove them from the water and drain on paper towels.

2. Meanwhile, make the dressing by combining all the remaining ingredients in a small bowl. The dressing should be fairly thick. Set aside.

3. Grate the cabbage on the coarsest side of a box grater into a large bowl or with a food processor. Pour the dressing into the bowl, mix well, and refrigerate for at least 2 hours or overnight before serving.

NOTE: Depending on the size of your cabbage, you may need to double the recipe for the dressing.

Black-Tie Blue Cheese Coleslaw

Blue cheese coleslaw is the brainchild of my friend Marti Schimmel from Athens, GA. This "black-tie" coleslaw is rich and creamy, with sharp blue cheese, sour cream, and sweet onion. It is much more at home served with slices of beef tenderloin or a charred New York strip steak than a deli sandwich. Since the amount of dressing and blue cheese varies based on the tenderness of your cabbage, use this recipe as a guideline and adjust it to suit your taste.

Makes 8 servings

1 medium green cabbage, about 1½ pounds, cored and shredded
2 carrots, peeled and shredded
¼ cup sweet onion or shallot, finely chopped
⅓ cup apple cider vinegar
3 tablespoons sugar
1 cup crumbled best-quality blue cheese, or more to taste
⅔ cup mayonnaise, preferably Hellman's
⅔ cup sour cream
   Kosher salt
   Freshly ground pepper

1. Combine the cabbage, carrot, and onion in a large bowl.

2. In a saucepan, heat the cider vinegar and sugar to a boil. Toss it with the vegetables and let them sit for 15 minutes. Drain the vegetables well.

3. In a medium bowl, combine the blue cheese, mayonnaise, and sour cream; mix until creamy. Add

that to the vegetables and season well with salt and pepper.

4. Let the coleslaw sit covered, in the refrigerator, at least 2 hours or overnight before serving. Adjust the seasonings and add more cheese, if necessary, before serving.

Cucumber Pickle

This recipe comes to me courtesy of a wonderful week that I spent at Ballymaloe Cookery School in County Cork, Ireland. The owner of the school, Darina Allen, invited me to teach a grilling class and since I had never been to Ireland, I couldn't possibly pass it up. The whole family promptly adopted me and, instead of traveling around the country, I stayed at Ballymaloe cooking, feeding the chickens, learning to butcher a pig, bake bread, smoke salmon, and even work the school's market stand. Almost every day, I ate lunch at the school, and my favorite item was a big bowl of cucumber pickle. When I got back to the states, I changed the recipe a bit and have made them a staple in my refrigerator. For a change of taste, try making the pickle with unsweetened rice vinegar.

Makes 4 servings

2 English seedless cucumbers
4 shallots
1 cup apple cider vinegar or rice vinegar
½ cup sugar
½ tablespoon kosher salt

1. Wash and dry the cucumbers. Peel off alternating strips of the green skin with a vegetable peeler. Slice the cucumbers very thinly with a mandoline slicer or a sharp chef's knife. Set aside.

2. Peel the shallots and slice them at the same thinness as the cucumber. Mix the cucumber and shallots. The shallot slices will unravel into small lilac-colored rings, which is what you want. Set aside.

3. In a medium bowl, whisk the vinegar, sugar, and salt together until completely dissolved. Pour it over the cucumber and shallot slices and mix well.

4. Put the pickle in a plastic or glass container with a tight lid and refrigerate, turning occasionally, for at least 3 hours before serving. Taste and adjust the seasoning if necessary. This keeps for up to 1 week in the refrigerator.

Southern Sausage Dressing

This very simple sausage dressing is based on the one that my mother makes for Thanksgiving. It is my family's favorite side dish, and the only recipe on the menu that absolutely can't be omitted or changed. It really does turn out better if you use the Pepperidge Farm herb (blue bag) stuffing mix, which is perfectly seasoned with just the right amount of herbs and spices, and Neese's sausage, made by a small family business just outside of Greensboro, NC.

You can stuff a turkey with the dressing just before cooking, but this will make it stuffing. "Dressing" is the preferred lingo in the South (where I'm from), and it is always cooked and served on the side! Also, don't limit this dressing to Thanksgiving; it's great with grill-roasted meats of all kinds—especially chicken and pork chops.

Makes 4 to 8 servings

1	16-ounce package herb-seasoned stuffing, preferably Pepperidge Farm
½	loaf (about 12 slices) favorite bread, grated on a box grater
1	pound bulk hot sausage, preferably Neese's
½	cup (1 stick) unsalted butter
1	bunch celery, chopped
2	yellow onions, chopped
1 to 2	cups low-salt, no-fat chicken broth or homemade stock
	Kosher salt
	Freshly ground pepper

1. Mix the stuffing mix and grated bread in a large bowl and set aside, tossing occasionally so all the bread pieces dry out.
2. Cook the sausage in a heavy-bottomed skillet over medium heat, breaking it into small pieces with a fork, until completely cooked through, about 20 minutes. Drain the sausage on paper towels, then transfer it to the bread crumb bowl.
3. Preheat the oven to 350°F. Drain off most of the grease from the pan, leaving about 1 tablespoon.

(Put the grease in a sealable plastic container to discard safely.) In the same skillet, melt the butter and sauté the celery and onions until soft and the onions begin to caramelize, about 15 minutes.

4. Mix the vegetables and butter in with the bread crumbs until well combined. Moisten with chicken broth, a little at a time, until the dressing holds together but is not too wet—you may not need all 2 cups of the stock.
5. Place the mixture in a buttered 9 x 13 casserole dish and bake for 35 to 40 minutes, or until the top is browned. Serve hot.

Creamed Corn Grilled Skillet Cornbread

There are two secrets in this recipe. The first is an actual ingredient: A can of creamed-style corn is added to the mix, making it wetter than most cornbread batters, resulting in a much moister, tender cornbread. The second is a technique: You melt butter in the pan, preferably cast-iron, before pouring the batter into it. The preheating makes the cornbread rise quickly and the melted butter assures a golden brown, crunchy crust that won't stick, regardless of the kind of pan you use.

Makes 4 to 8 servings

Grilling Method: Indirect/High Heat
Special Equipment: Cast-iron skillet or All-Clad petit braiser

1	cup all-purpose flour
1	cup yellow or white cornmeal
2	teaspoons baking powder
1	teaspoon sugar
1	teaspoon fine-grain sea salt salt
1	cup milk
1	large egg
2	tablespoons olive oil, melted butter, or bacon drippings
1	heaping cup canned creamed corn
6	pieces bacon, cooked crisp and cut into pieces, optional
2	tablespoons butter

1. Build a charcoal fire or preheat a gas grill.
2. Mix together the flour and cornmeal in a large bowl. Add the baking powder, sugar, and salt. Using a wire whisk, mix until well combined and set aside.
3. In a separate bowl, mix together the milk, egg, and oil. Add the wet ingredients to the bowl of dry ingredients and mix until just combined. Add the creamed corn and mix until just combined. If adding the bacon, stir it into the mixture. Do not overmix. Set aside.
4. Heat the butter in 10-inch cast-iron skillet or the braiser, if using. Once the butter is melted and the pan is hot, pour the batter into the warm skillet.
5. Immediately place the skillet in the center of the cooking grate over indirect high heat. Cover and cook for 35 to 40 minutes, or until a toothpick comes out clean when placed in the center. Cut and serve from the pan while still warm.

Couscous with Grilled Mediterranean Vegetables

Couscous is a snap to make, since all it takes is a little boiling water and five minutes. Added to chopped grilled veggies, it makes a tasty and filling vegetarian entrée, a great side dish, and a delicious way to use up leftover grilled vegetables. If the couscous seems a little dry, make a homemade vinaigrette and toss the couscous with just enough to moisten it.

Makes 8 servings

Grilling Method: Direct/Medium Heat

- 2 **small sweet potatoes, peeled and cut into 4 long slices**
- 4 **medium zucchini, each cut into 4 long slices**
- 1 **small radicchio, cut into quarters**
- 1 **medium eggplant, cut into 4 long slices**
- 1 **small bunch green onions, trimmed**
- 1 **pint small ripe grape tomatoes, tossed in a bowl with a little oil**
  Olive oil
  Kosher salt
- 1 **10-ounce package couscous or $1^{3}/_{4}$ cups uncooked couscous**
- 1 to 2 **tablespoons chopped fresh herbs, such as mint, basil, or parsley**
- 4 **lemons, cut into wedges**

1. Build a charcoal fire or preheat a gas grill.
2. Put the cut vegetables on a large platter and lightly coat them with oil. Sprinkle with salt.
3. One by one, lay the vegetables on the cooking grate over direct medium heat. (Do this in batches, if necessary, so the grill is not crowded.) Cover and cook for about 5 minutes. Turn the vegetables and cook 3 to 4 minutes more, or until well marked and tender.
4. Remove the vegetables from the grill as they are done and transfer them to a platter. The zucchini, radicchio, and green onions should be done first; the eggplant will take a little longer; and the sweet potatoes will be the last to cook through.
5. When all the vegetables are done, place the tomatoes on the cooking grate to mark and warm them through, about 2 minutes. Place the tomatoes on the platter with the other vegetables and set aside.
6. Meanwhile, bring 2 cups of water to a boil in a medium saucepan, and add $1/_2$ teaspoon salt and 1 tablespoon oil. Add the (uncooked) couscous. Stir well and remove the pan from the heat. Let it sit, covered, for 5 minutes.
7. While the couscous is cooking, chop all the grilled vegetables except the tomatoes. When the couscous is done, fluff it with a fork and transfer it to a large serving bowl. Add all the grilled veggies and chopped herbs and mix to distribute evenly. Serve warm or at room temperature with extra olive oil and lemon wedges.

Steakhouse Spinach

I could eat this spinach every night, all year long. It is my version of creamed spinach; unlike most versions, it is mostly spinach, with just a touch of half-and-half. If you prefer a looser dish, feel free to add cream. I add a touch of Pernod and a generous drizzling of white truffle oil to enhance this classic side dish. You can omit these ingredients, but I guarantee you won't want to. They are the secret to the best spinach dish you've ever eaten.

The other secret to this recipe is using frozen spinach that is sold in sealed bags, such as Green Giant. The sealed flash-freezing prevents the spinach from getting frostbite or picking up off flavors in the freezer. It tastes much better than fresh and makes the recipe easier to boot!

Makes 4 servings

Grilling Method: Indirect/Medium Heat

> 4   9-ounce packages frozen chopped spinach, cooked and drained
> 2   tablespoons butter
> 2   shallots, peeled and minced
> 1   tablespoon Pernod
> 1   tablespoon flour
> ½ to ⅔ cup half-and-half or cream
>   Freshly ground nutmeg
>   Freshly ground pepper
>   Drizzle white truffle oil (about 2 teaspoons)
>   Sea salt or fleur de sel, optional

1. Build a charcoal fire or preheat a gas grill. Or, preheat the oven to 375°F.
2. Make sure as much of the water as possible is removed from the spinach by pressing the cooled spinach tightly with the back of a spoon. Set aside.
3. Melt the butter in a skillet over medium heat, add the shallots, and cook until soft and slightly caramelized, about 10 minutes. Add the Pernod, stir, then add the flour. Whisk occasionally for 2 to 3 minutes, or until the flour is slightly browned (this eliminates the raw flour taste). Stir in the half-and-half until heated through. Add the spinach and mix until well combined and there are no clumps of spinach left. Season the mixture with a pinch of ground nutmeg, fresh pepper, the truffle oil, and salt. Mix well.
4. Spoon the mixture into a 3 or 4 quart ovenproof soufflé or casserole dish and place it on the cooking grate over indirect medium heat, cover, and grill (or put it in the oven) until hot and bubbly, about 30 minutes.

TIP: This can be made in advance and reheated just before serving.

Sweet Bourbon Mash

I've made a version of this for as long as I've been old enough to drink bourbon. But it wasn't until I was helping with dinner at the house of my college friend, Lisa Ryan, that I tasted the perfect sweet mash. Lisa gave me five flavoring ingredients and told me to make mashed sweet potatoes while she dressed. She had already roasted the sweet potatoes, so all I had to do was season them with the five ingredients—heavy cream, bourbon, brown sugar, blackstrap molasses, and salt. At first, I questioned the lack of butter and other spices, but I decided to follow her directions since it was her house. The result is a sweet potato dish that is silky in its consistency, rich from the cream, slightly bitter from the molasses, and full of deep vanilla from the bourbon. I added a few dashes of Tabasco and a touch of fresh nutmeg to balance the sweet and salty—scrumptious!

Makes 8 to 10 servings

> 8   large Garnet sweet potatoes
> 1   pint heavy whipping cream
> ½ to ¾ cup bourbon
> ½   cup packed dark brown sugar
> ½   cup molasses
> 1   teaspoon sea salt, or more to taste
> 3   dashes Tabasco
>   Freshly grated nutmeg, optional

1. Build a charcoal fire or preheat a gas grill. Or, preheat the oven to 350°F

2. Clean and dry the potatoes, cutting off any bad spots. If the potatoes have begun to sprout, do not use them. Prick them with a fork and place them in the center of the oven or on the cooking grate over indirect medium heat. Roast for 1 hour, or until tender in the center. To check for doneness, take a sharp knife and insert it in the potatoes; if it goes through with no resistance, it is done. Transfer the potatoes to a clean platter and let them cool.

3. When the potatoes are cool, peel them, and cut them into quarters. Put them in a large stockpot or Dutch oven. Add the cream, bourbon, sugar, molasses, and salt. Mash everything together with a large fork or potato masher. If the potatoes need more liquid, add a little water. Stir until smooth.

4. Simmer the mixture, covered, for 30 to 40 minutes, or until the potatoes are so soft that they resemble a puree. (This second cooking makes the potatoes foolproof since any hard pieces of sweet potato have a chance to cook down before serving.)

5. When the potatoes have cooked down, add the Tabasco and nutmeg, if using, then taste. Adjust the salt if necessary. Serve immediately. Refrigerate any leftovers. The mash reheats very well.

Homemade Mac 'n' Cheese

This recipe will make you throw all those boxes of macaroni and powdered cheese away. My friend Kirsten Newman Teissier's Grandmother Meme prepared this version of the American classic for her as a child. It's made with freshly grated cheese and topped with toasted, buttered bread crumbs. Kirsten makes it when she craves the comfort that only rich and cheesy from-scratch mac and cheese can give—especially during Chicago winters. I pass along Meme's advice: For best flavor and texture, grate the cheese just before mixing it with the hot pasta—and don't be tempted to use pregrated cheddar cheese.

Makes 6 to 8 servings

1 pound dried ziti or favorite dried pasta
1 pound extra-sharp cheddar cheese, preferably white
1 cup freshly grated parmesan cheese
Kosher or sea salt
Freshly ground pepper
2 cups whole milk
1/3 cup Homemade Bread Crumbs (below)
2 tablespoons butter

1. Preheat the oven to 400°F. Follow the instructions on the package and cook the pasta in a large pot of boiling water.

2. While the ziti is cooking, grate the cheddar cheese. When the ziti is al dente (tender yet firm to the bite), drain it in a colander; shake the colander until there is no excess water.

3. While the ziti is still hot, put it in a large bowl and mix it with both grated cheeses. Add salt and pepper to taste. Place the mixture in a 3-quart soufflé dish. Pour the milk over the mixture until the height of the milk is about a "pinky" finger from the top.

4. Sprinkle the bread crumbs on top. Cut the butter into thin slices and dab the butter on top of the bread crumbs. Bake the mac 'n' cheese for 45 to 60 minutes, or until the milk has evaporated and the bread crumbs are browned. Serve warm.

TIP: This recipe was written for the oven, but it can be "baked" on the grill. Set the grill for indirect/medium heat.

Homemade Bread Crumbs

1/4 loaf stale Italian or French bread
1/2 teaspoon salt
1/2 teaspoon freshly ground pepper
1/2 teaspoon minced dried garlic
1/2 teaspoon mixed Italian seasonings

In either a food processor with the steel blade or a chopper, break the stale bread into pieces and process it to crumbs. Add the seasonings. Blend until it is well combined and has a fine consistency.

Antipasto Pasta

Antipasto Pasta is a fresh take on pasta salad and a great "grilled-over" recipe for a side dish or next day entrée. Leftovers from the grill give a whole new meaning to the word. Follow the Grilled Vegetable Antipasto recipe on page 216 as a guideline, but add whatever fresh veggies you can find in your market. Vegetables prepared this way are so good that you might want to double the recipe and serve half for the antipasto platter at night and chop up the other half for your pasta the next day. The dish is versatile with a capital "V"; it can be served hot, cold, or at room temperature. Be sure to assemble it when the pasta is piping hot to pull the maximum flavor out of the grilled veggies and Soprano Sauce.

Makes 6 to 8 servings

Grilled Vegetable Antipasto Platter with Soprano Sauce (page 216)

1   **pound dried farfalle (bow-tie) or penne pasta, cooked al dente**

Best-quality olive oil
Sea salt
Freshly ground pepper
Grated Parmigiano-Reggiano cheese, to taste

¼   cup chopped fresh herbs, such as basil, mint, or Italian parsley

1. Prepare the grilled veggies according to the Vegetable Antipasto recipe, adding or substituting any favorite or market fresh vegetables.
2. Chop all the vegetables into bite-size pieces and toss them with extra Soprano Sauce and hot pasta. If you need a little extra dressing, drizzle with olive oil. Season to taste with sea salt, pepper, and grated parmesan cheese. Add salt with a very light hand since the sauce is naturally salty from the anchovies and capers.
3. Just before serving, toss the pasta with the fresh herbs. The pasta can be served hot, room temperature, or cold.

Libations

Wetting Your Whistle

When food manufacturers study preferences for preparing meals, outdoor cooking always turns out to be the favorite way to cook at home—at least for as long as I've been grilling for a living! And it is no wonder— grilling and barbecuing are considered fun activities, not a household chore. Although no research makes the correlation between cocktails and outdoor cooking, I have a hunch that outdoor cooking is perceived as a special occasion and thus, an excuse to relax with a cold one, a cocktail, or a glass of wine. No wonder it is so much fun!

So, I couldn't write a cookbook on grilling without including a nod to my favorite libations, including soft (nonalcoholic) drinks—like thirst-quenching lemonade and iced tea, hard cocktails, beer, and my beloved wine. After all, as an equal opportunity griller, it's important to be an equal opportunity imbiber!

As a rule of thumb, I reserve the hard cocktails for the premeal hour and serve any of the soft drinks, beer, or wine with the food. I usually decide among the latter three based on my guests (their taste and their age), my mood, and what I am serving. The nice thing about grilled food is that it can pair equally well with both beer and wine. Beer is commonly served at "barbecues" and cookouts, but more and more people are realizing that wine can be paired with great success with these same foods.

Beer, the Quintessential Barbecuer's Beverage

Don't limit your beer choices to the same beer you drank in college. There are so many great beers available, and they each have their own flavor profiles, just like different varieties of wine. Beer is categorized into four main styles:

1. Light-colored and lager beers
2. Dark-colored beers and stouts
3. Amber-colored beers and ales
4. Specialty and flavored beers

If you haven't experimented very much with beer, a simple way to explore your options is to try choosing a beer indigenous to the country that inspired the recipe. For example:

American: Any number of small and large breweries, including Brooklyn Brewery, New Belgium (home of Fat Tire), Sam Adams, etc.

Canadian: LaBatt's, Molsons

Central European: Heineken, Stella Artois, Pilsner Urquell

Great Britain and Ireland: Guinness, Newcastle, Killian's Red

Mexican: Corona, Negro Modelo

Carribbean: Red Stripe

Italian: Moretti

Thai: Singha

Wine Meets Swine

I am a dedicated wine hobbyist, and I love to serve wine with my grilled fare. It pairs with the food perfectly, enhances it and completes the dining experience.

When deciding what wine to serve with your meal, I suggest you drink what you like, but keep a few things in mind. I always did this, drinking big red wines with grilled fish—which flies in the face of conventional wine wisdom—because fish is my favorite food, and I prefer red wine. But I kept it to myself until seven years ago when the "preachings" of Tim Hanni, a very progressive Master of Wine and founder of WineQuest (www.winequest.com) gave me permission to drink what I like.

Tim conducted a seminar entitled, "Drink What You Like: You'll Never Look at Food and Wine Pairing the Same Way." Since that had been my "dirty little secret" for a long time, I attended the seminar to get outside validation for my wayward pairings. Well, he was right. The seminar was food-life changing and I "preached" his doctrine at every wine and food occasion for the next year—converting all who were within ear and taste range.

Libation *Legend*

DEGREE OF DIFFICULTY	OCTANE LEVEL
1 shaker = Child's Play	Unleaded = Thirst Quenching/No Alcohol
2 shakers = Easy	Premium = Refreshing/Low in Alcohol
3 shakers = Challenging	Regular = Relaxing/Medium in Alcohol
4 shakers = Difficult	Hi-Test = Knockout Punch/High in Alcohol

For those without a jigger or ounce measure, you can use standard tablespoons to mix your drinks:
1 ounce is equal to 2 tablespoons

Here is the gist of Tim's very smart, consumer-friendly doctrine: The taste of wine is affected by sweet, salty, and acidic properties. If you follow his theory, you can make any wine pair with any food by adjusting the seasoning of the food with a touch of a sweet ingredient, salty ingredient, or acidic ingredient. This is how it works: Sweet flavors, like those found in most barbecue sauces, intensify the taste of the wine, making it taste "stronger" and, to some people, bitter and not drinkable. For those who like the effect, they should continue to enjoy their "strong" wine. For everyone else, a squirt of lemon and a sprinkle of salt (in the sauce or on top of the food) will change the way the wine tastes—making it softer, rounder, and more pleasing to the palate. Likewise, if the wine is on the lighter side, add a little sweetness to the food you are eating with a pinch of sugar, honey, or sweet barbecue sauce. When you take your next sip of wine, it should taste bigger and more full-flavored.

Don't take my word for it; try it for yourself. The next time you are drinking wine that is too strong, bitter, or tannic, use my tequila technique—this is the trick I use to show my friends how this remarkable wine and food rule-of-thumb really works—lick your hand, sprinkle it with salt, and have a wedge of lemon or lime at the ready. Sip the wine to establish its level of tannic (mouth-puckering) qualities. Lick the salt, bite into the citrus wedge, and take another sip. It will be like magic—a new softer, rounder wine in your glass. That is what happens when you add a little acid and salt to your food—it changes the way the wine tastes.

If you are like most people, you will be amazed and you will welcome the world of wine with open arms.

You can, of course, work with traditional wine pairings if you like. Most simply put, think of red wines for richer, spicier meats and white wines for lighter-textured and lighter-flavored foods, such as vegetables and fish. Of course, since grilling adds a richer, smokier flavor to most foods, you can stick with the more fuller-bodied or more complexly flavored wines.

Party Planning

When you are planning a party for a crowd and don't know everyone's wine preference, play it safe and buy both red and white wine. I usually buy more red than white, since I've found that most people switch to red after the cocktail hour.

Serious Drinking

Everyone who knows me, knows that I think that bourbon makes everything taste better—even ice cubes! It is no secret that (for me) a drink or two is as much a part of an enjoyable evening as a great meal; and I often design my menus around what wine I want to drink. That said, I am emphatic about responsible drinking. There is no excuse for drinking and driving. Take a cab, go out with a friend who isn't drinking, call your mother, better yet, stay at home. All the more reason to be the one doing the grilling and hosting the gathering—you can enjoy your libations and not worry; it doesn't get better than that!

Simple Syrup

Sugar does not dissolve well in cold drinks, but Simple Syrup does and can be used to sweeten any cold cocktail or thirst quencher. It is the basis of homemade lemonade and many cocktail recipes. It is a "lost art" in many homes today, but very simple to make and great to have on hand.

Makes 2 cups

Degree of Difficulty: 1 shaker
Octane Level: Unleaded

- 2 cups water
- 1 cup sugar

1. Mix the water and sugar together in a small, heavy-bottomed saucepan. Heat over low heat until the sugar is completely dissolved and the syrup is clear.
2. Simmer for 5 minutes and remove from the heat. Let the syrup cool. Store it, covered in the refrigerator, for up to 4 weeks.

Rockin' Chair Lemonade

Nothing quenches summertime thirst like homemade lemonade. It is just as easy as using frozen concentrate and, to my way of drinking, so much better! I like to make a pitcher full and float thin slices of lemon in it, because it looks refreshing and pretty. For a rustic presentation, serve in mismatched canning jars and dream of a wrap-around porch with well-worn rocking chairs.

Makes 4 servings

Degree of Difficulty: 2 shakers
Octane Level: Unleaded

- 2 cups Simple Syrup (above)
- 1 cup fresh lemon juice (about 6 lemons)
- 2 cups water
- 1 lemon, thinly sliced
  Fresh mint leaves, optional

1. If you don't have simple syrup, add 3/4 cup superfine sugar to the lemon juice and increase the water to 4 cups.
2. Mix the syrup and lemon juice in a 2-quart pitcher, add the water, and stir. Garnish with lemon slices and fresh mint.
3. To serve, fill 4 glasses with crushed ice. Pour the lemonade over the ice and serve immediately.

Berry-Infused Pink Lemonade

This pleasing pink lemonade was inspired by the delicious pink lemonade from the Chick-Fil-A chain. (Among Southerners, Chick-Fil-A is as famous for their lemonade as for their sandwiches.) I've made it even better by adding macerated berries that lend both a pink hue and a berry sweetness to the lemonade. Try it in the summer with blueberries for an even darker color.

Makes 6 servings

Degree of difficulty: 1 shaker
Octane Level: Unleaded

- 2 quarts cold water
- 1/2 cup plus 1 teaspoon sugar
- 3/4 cup fresh lemon juice (about 3 large lemons), or more to taste
- 1/4 cup fresh or frozen raspberries or chopped strawberries

1. Combine the water and 1/2 cup of the sugar in a 3-quart saucepan set over low heat, until the sugar melts. Remove it from the heat and stir in the lemon juice; set aside.
2. Mash the berries with the remaining 1 teaspoon of sugar until they are liquefied. Use a blender if necessary. Add the mashed berries to the lemonade. Chill for at least 2 hours before serving.
3. Just before serving, stir and strain the lemonade to remove seeds or chunks of fruit and serve on crushed ice.

Sweet Southern Iced Tea

This country-club classic is easy to make and easy to drink. It's not too sweet and is just the thing to help a harried cook cope with the heat coming off the grill grate. It's also non-alcoholic, but I won't tell if you decide to spike it up with a little extra "ooompf."

Degree of Difficulty: 1 shaker
Octane Level: Unleaded

Unsweetened iced tea (home-brewed or plain ice tea mix)
Lemonade, preferably freshly made (pages 316–317)

1. Fill a highball glass with ice cubes, then pour in equal parts iced tea and lemonade. Garnish with a lemon wedge.

Honeydew Lemonade

My friend Gretchen Belmonti and I made this lemonade for one of our dinner parties. It was so delicious that it has become the star of my summer drink repertoire. The recipe was originally developed by John Ash for Fine Cooking *magazine. I've changed it to include a couple of shots of iced vodka, and I use the lemon syrup as a base for all sorts of summer fruit. Add the vodka as you pour the drink so it remains "pure" for the nondrinkers in your group.*

Makes 6 servings

Degree of difficulty: 4 shakers
Octane Level: Premium

- 1 cup fresh lemon juice
- 3/4 cup sugar
- 2 lemons, zested
- 1 small honeydew melon (about 3 pounds) peeled, seeded, and cut into 1-inch cubes to yield 6 cups
- 2 cups cold still water (no bubbles)
- 1½ cups best-quality iced vodka, optional
  Thin lemon slices

1. Combine the lemon juice, sugar, and zest in a small saucepan and bring it to a boil. Simmer until the sugar dissolves, about 5 minutes. Strain and cool.
2. Puree the melon in a blender. In a pitcher, combine the melon puree and the cooled syrup and mix well. Chill, covered in the refrigerator, for at least 1 hour or until ready to use.
3. Just before serving, add the water and vodka, if using, and serve over crushed ice. Garnish with lemon slices. Serve in highball or iced-tea glasses.

NOTE: If you are adding the vodka on a per drink basis, add 2 shots or 4 tablespoons per glass of melon lemonade.

Bloody Mary

Bloodies aren't just for breakfast anymore. I love drinking a bloody Mary while I am chopping away in the kitchen or tending the grill outside. And I can't think of a better way to eat your veggies—besides grilling them of course!

Makes 1 serving

Degree of Difficulty: 2 shakers
Octane Level: Premium

- 1/4 cup best-quality vodka
- 1 cup tomato or V-8 juice
- 1/4 lemon, juiced
- 2 shakes Worcestershire sauce
- 2 shakes Tabasco
- 1/2 tablespoon prepared horseradish
- 1 lime wedge
- 1 celery stalk with leaves
  Celery salt, optional

1. In a tall glass, combine the vodka and juice; stir to combine. Add the lemon juice, Worcestershire, Tabasco, and horseradish. Stir together.
2. Add ice cubes, garnish with the lime wedge and celery, and sprinkle with celery salt.

Bloody Matthew

This is the stiff counterpart to Mary's bloody drink. It is made with gin instead of vodka and is guaranteed to put hair on your chest or back on the dog that bit you!

Makes 1 serving

Degree of Difficulty: 2 shakers
Octane Level: Premium

- 1/4 cup gin
- 1/2 cup tomato juice
- 1/4 lemon, juiced
- 1 teaspoon Worcestershire sauce
  Dash Tabasco
  Celery salt
- 1 lime wedge

1. In a tall glass, combine the gin and juice; stir to combine. Add the lemon juice, Worcestershire sauce, Tabasco, and celery salt to taste and stir together.
2. Add ice cubes, and garnish with the lime wedge. Serve immediately.

Pomegranate Margarita

This drink recipe is inspired by the pomegranate margaritas at Layla restaurant in Manhattan. Years ago, my friends and I would travel the length of the island just to go to Layla for "the drink." Then we went to out-of-the way ethnic markets so we could buy pomegranate juice and make them at home. Thankfully, pomegranate juice is now available in the average grocery store, making this drink an easy way to wind down the day—anytime!

Makes 2 servings

Degree of Difficulty: 2 shakers
Octane Level: Hi-Test

- ¼ cup silver tequila
- ¼ cup orange liqueur, such as Grand Marnier
- ⅓ cup pomegranate juice, such as POM Wonderful or Torani pomegranate syrup
- ¼ cup fresh lemon juice
- 2 lime wedges

1. In a cocktail shaker half filled with ice, combine the tequila, orange liqueur, pomegranate juice, and lemon juice.
2. Shake, strain, and pour over crushed ice in an old-fashioned glass or straight up in a martini glass.
3. Squeeze the lime wedge into the margarita and serve immediately.

Blue Agave Margarita

There is nothing like a blue agave margarita, straight up in a martini glass. Blue agave tequila is made from 100 percent blue agave, not a blend like some of the harsher and less expensive tequilas. It is my preferred cocktail and a great way to use all of those martini glasses that are collecting dust. If you don't already own a cocktail shaker, buy one and start shaking your way to the best margarita you have ever tasted!

Makes 2 servings

Degree of Difficulty: 2 shakers
Octane Level: Premium

- 2 lime wedges
  Kosher salt on a small plate
- ⅓ cup premium silver tequila, preferably 100 percent blue agave
- ¼ cup orange liqueur, such as Grand Marnier
- ¼ cup fresh lime juice

1. Run the lime wedges around the rims of 2 martini glasses. Dip the moistened rims in the salt. Set the lime wedges on the edge of the glasses.
2. In a cocktail shaker half filled with ice cubes, combine the tequila, orange liqueur, and lime juice. Shake well. Strain the cocktail into the glasses. Serve immediately.

Bahama Mama

If it weren't so tasty, I'd have to include the Bahama Mama just because, like the Quirky Turkey, it is so much fun to say! Don't skimp on the quality of the ingredients—it's the difference between a hot mama and a haute mama!

Makes 1 serving

Degree of Difficulty: 2 shakers
Octane Level: Premium

- 3 tablespoons dark rum
- 1 tablespoon Triple Sec
- 2 tablespoons coconut rum or liqueur, such as Malibu
- ¼ cup fresh orange juice
- ¼ cup pineapple juice
  Dash grenadine
- 1 orange slice, optional
- 1 pineapple wedge, optional
- 1 maraschino cherry, optional
- 1 paper umbrella, optional

1. Combine all the ingredients in a cocktail shaker filled with ice. Shake and strain, pouring it into a high-ball glass filled with crushed ice.
2. Garnish with the orange slice, pineapple wedge, cherry, and paper umbrella, if desired.

Cosmopolitan

This is a party drink destined to stay in fashion! Girls of all ages love the pretty pink hue of a Cosmo and the festive feeling that drinking out of a martini glass gives to any occasion.

Makes 2 servings

Degree of Difficulty: 4 shakers
Octane Level: Hi-Test

- 2 teaspoons sugar
- 1 teaspoon finely grated lime zest (try a Microplane grater)
- 1 lime wedge
- ¼ cup best-quality vodka
- 2 tablespoons Cointreau (orange liqueur)
- 2 tablespoons fresh lime juice
- 1 teaspoon superfine sugar
  Splash cranberry juice

1. On a small plate, mix together the sugar and lime zest. Moisten the rims of 2 martini glasses with a lime wedge and roll the rims of the glasses in the sugar and lime zest.

2. Fill a cocktail shaker with ice. Add the vodka, Cointreau, lime juice, superfine sugar, and just enough cranberry juice to color the drink a pale pink. Shake until frothy. Strain into the glasses and serve.

Kir Royale

The official drink of the Queen of the Grill! This is a great way to make your budget stretch if you're giving a celebration party where champagne is a must. Buy an inexpensive champagne or sparkling wine, and let the Chambord transform the drink into an expensive-tasting cocktail—kind of like kissing the frog and having it turn into a prince!

Degree of Difficulty: 1 shaker
Octane Level: Regular

Chambord (raspberry liqueur)
Sparkling wine or champagne

1. Just before serving, pour ¹/₂ tablespoon of Chambord in the bottom of a champagne flute or wine glass.

2. Add sparkling wine or champagne until the glass is filled. Do not stir. (If you stir, you'll get rid of some of the bubbles.) The 2 liquids will mix naturally.

Quirky Turkey

Even if the combo of bourbon and bog (cranberry) juice didn't taste so good, I'd still have to offer it to my guests because it is so much fun to say—and cocktails are all about the fun! The Quirky Turkey is an obvious natural to serve at holiday gatherings.

Makes 1 serving

Degree of Difficulty: 1 shaker
Octane Level: Hi-Test

¹/₄   **cup Wild Turkey bourbon (or any other bourbon you like)**
¹/₃   **cup cranberry juice**
1   **lime wedge**

Fill an old-fashioned glass with ice, and pour in the bourbon and cranberry juice. Stir, and garnish with the lime.

Lemon Drop

Beware the Lemon Drop. It's sweet surface disguises a powerful kick, as at least a certain someone discovered—much to her chagrin—a few years back at the Memphis in May barbecue contest. Still, it's a great drink and tastes so good while you are outside grilling up a storm. I must caution, don't drink more than one, or I have to say, I told you so!

Makes 1 serving

Degree of Difficulty: 4 shakers
Octane Level: Hi-Test

2   **teaspoons sugar**
1   **lemon, zested (try a Microplane grater)**
1   **lemon wheel or wedge**
¹/₃   **cup lemon-flavored vodka**
2   **tablespoons fresh lemon juice**
1   **tablespoon Simple Syrup (page 316) or 2 teaspoons superfine sugar**

1. On a small plate, mix together the sugar and lemon zest. Moisten the rim of a martini glass with the lemon wedge and roll the rim in the mixed sugar and lemon zest.

2. Fill a cocktail shaker with ice. Pour in the vodka, lemon juice, and simple syrup. Shake well and strain into the glass. Garnish with the lemon wedge and stand back.

Caipirinha

Brazil's national drink, the Caipirinha, packs a punch. But it's also a delicious and refreshing way to whet the appetite before a meal of grilled steak and chimichurri sauce or a Brazilian-style mixed grill.

Makes 1 serving

Degree of Difficulty: 3 shakers
Octane Level: Hi-Test

1   **lime, cut into wedges**
2   **teaspoons sugar**
¹/₄   **cup *cachaca* (Brazilian sugarcane liquor) or white rum**

1. Put the lime wedges in a very sturdy double old-fashioned glass. Sprinkle the sugar over them.
2. Using a strong wooden spoon or a pestle, muddle (mash together) the limes and the sugar until the sugar is dissolved and the limes have released their juice.
3. Top off the glass with crushed ice and pour in the *cachaca*. Stir and serve.

Front Porch Mint Julep

Famous throughout the South, and absolutely synonymous with the Kentucky Derby, the julep has passed the test of time for good reason—bourbon and mint are natural partners. This drink is traditionally served in a julep cup—silver or pewter. It is just the thing to keep a southern belle from wilting as the ice inside the drink causes the metal cup to frost. This version involves making a simple syrup infused with fresh mint and is slightly more delicate than the Back Porch version (at right).

Makes 1 serving

Degree of Difficulty: 4 shakers
Octane Level: Premium

Mint syrup
2   cups water
2   cups sugar
1   large bunch fresh mint leaves, cleaned

1/4   cup Kentucky bourbon (such as Woodford Reserve)
1   mint sprig

1. Make the mint syrup: Mix the water and sugar together in a heavy-bottomed saucepan. Heat over low heat until the sugar is completely dissolved. Bring to a roaring simmer for 1 to 2 minutes.

Bruise (crush) the mint leaves in a bowl to release their flavor, then add them to the syrup. Remove the pan from the heat. Let the syrup cool.

2. Using cheesecloth or a very fine sieve, strain the syrup and put it in a nonreactive container. The syrup can be made in advance and stored in the refrigerator for up to 2 weeks.

3. Fill a julep cup, preferably silver or pewter, or other old-fashioned glass, with ice. When it is cold on the outside, pour 2 teaspoons of the mint syrup through the ice. Add the bourbon, stir gently, and serve garnished with a sprig of mint.

Back Porch Mint Julep

Slightly rougher than it's refined front porch cousin, but it tastes just as good. This version is so easy that you can make it on the back porch or in a parking lot—for tailgates, that is.

Makes 1 serving

Degree of Difficulty: 2 shakers
Octane Level: Premium

1   teaspoon sugar
1   teaspoon water
6 to 7 large fresh mint leaves, cleaned
1/4   cup Kentucky bourbon (such as Woodford Reserve)

1. Put the sugar, water, and mint leaves in the bottom of a sturdy glass, silver cup, or pint-size mason jar. Mash the mint with a spoon to "muddle" the ingredients until the sugar is dissolved. Fill the glass with ice.

2. When it is cold on the outside, pour the bourbon through the ice. Stir gently and serve.

Sweet Endings

Everyone loves dessert or a sweet bite of something to end a meal—and if they don't, I'm suspicious! Perhaps it's my southern upbringing, where it was common to have more than one dessert to end the meal, or simply the idiosyncrasies of my family. After all, my mother often ate homemade cake and pie for breakfast, saying life was too short to eat dessert last!

I've included my favorite dessert recipes for entertaining, because it is as important to the meal as the appetizers and side dishes. Some of the recipes call for using the stove and the oven and some are grilled.

I have a certain fondness for the grilled recipes—a simple dinner of beer-can chicken makes me crave grilled bananas—but after eating pulled pork, for example, nothing beats a lemon bar or homemade ice cream sandwich—and nothing—and I mean nothing—beats my mother's fresh grated coconut cake!

Theoretically, you can grill-bake on your outdoor grill anything you bake in your oven using the Indirect Method (see page 7). I encourage you to experiment on your own to use your grill for grill-baking, or even for grilling elements of your favorite desserts. For example, fruit is especially well suited to the grill; my guests are always amazed at how the grill intensifies the flavor of fruit and makes it taste so much better! (See the Vegetables and Fruit chapter for more recipes.) The main thing is that you make a meal that you and everyone else enjoys!

Baked Apples with Caramel Sauce and Cinnamon Toast

Baked apples are a comforting, healthy, and familiar dessert. They are also usually a little boring. To turn ho-hum into humdigger, I've added a drizzle of delicious caramely dulce de leche *and a piece of grilled cinnamon toast. The combination of the fragrant soft apples with the rich sauce and the crunchy, slightly smoky cinnamon toast is anything but boring! The method for the cinnamon toast may be a little different than you are used to; I cook the butter and sugar on the stovetop before spreading it on grilled bread to cut that final step of re-baking it in the oven.*

Makes 8 servings

Grilling Method: Indirect/Medium Heat

 8   Granny Smith or other cooking apples, cored
       and rubbed with lemon juice
 1/2 to 3/4 cup apple cider or undiluted
       apple juice concentrate
 2   cinnamon sticks, broken into large pieces
 2   tablespoons sugar
 2   tablespoons Sugar in the Raw
 2   tablespoons ground cinnamon
 1/2 teaspoon ground cloves
       Pinch salt

Cinnamon Toast

 8   1-inch slices sweet yeast bread, such as challah
       or brioche
 1/2 cup (1 stick) unsalted butter
 1/2 cup sugar
 2   teaspoons ground cinnamon

 1   tablespoon Grand Marnier, optional
 2   pints vanilla ice cream
       Homemade Dulce de Leche (Mexican caramel
       sauce; see under Grilled Bananas with Dulce
       de Leche, page 326)

1. Build a charcoal fire or preheat a gas grill. Or preheat the oven to 375°F.
2. Put the apples in a nonreactive glass or heavy stainless steel pan, making sure all apples touch.
3. If an apple will not stand up, slice a piece off the bottom to level it. Pour the cider over the apples, making sure a little goes inside each of the cored

apples. The liquid should come up to about ½ inch from the bottom of the pan; if it doesn't, add more cider. Distribute the cinnamon sticks evenly in the bottom of the pan.

4. Mix the sugar, Sugar in the Raw, cinnamon, cloves, and salt in a medium bowl, then divide them equally among the apples, filling the cores.

5. Place pan in the center of the cooking grate (or in the preheated oven) over indirect medium-heat, cover, and cook for 45 minutes, or until the liquid has reduced and the apples are tender. Transfer the pan to a cooling rack.

6. Just before the apples are ready, make the cinnamon toast: Place the slices of bread directly on a very clean cooking grate over direct medium-low heat, cover, and toast for 1 to 2 minutes on each side. Place them on a cookie sheet and set aside.

7. On the side burner of your grill or inside on the stove, melt the butter in a sauté pan over medium heat. Remove it from the heat and stir in the sugar, cinnamon and Grand Marnier, if using. Put the pan over the heat again and cook until the sugar begins to bubble and caramelize. Remove it from the heat and immediately spread a thin layer on each piece of bread with a small spoon or spreading knife. Let the toasts cool to room temperature.

8. Serve the apples at room temperature with a scoop of vanilla ice cream, a generous drizzle of the caramel sauce, and the cinnamon toast.

The Best Apple Pie (You've Ever Eaten)

My Grandmother Odom was an excellent southern cook and famous for her masterful pies. She often said that if she couldn't eat dessert then life wasn't worth living. My sister, Mary Pat, took those words to heart as she spent many an afternoon in our sun-drenched kitchen watching our grandmother make pies of all kinds. Consequently, Mary Pat became the new generation family baker and her apple pie is the best I've ever had. This star-spangled version of the classic American apple pie is perked up with dried cherries and crust cut-outs in the patriotic shape of stars. Using cream instead of water makes the crust even flakier and more delicious. Mary Pat says you can use store-bought pie dough if pressed for time; but, of course, her homemade version is always better. Serve warm with vanilla ice cream, if you like.

Makes 6 to 8 servings

Pastry

3 ½   cups all-purpose flour
½   cup sugar
½   teaspoon salt
1   cup (2 sticks) cold unsalted butter (or ½ cup butter and ½ cup Crisco), cut into ½-inch pieces
¾   cup cold heavy whipping cream, plus extra as needed
½   cup dried beans or pastry weights

Filling

6   to 8 apples, peeled, cored, and thinly sliced (Granny Smith is good for pies)
½ to 1 cup dried cherries, as desired
⅓   cup plus 2 tablespoons sugar, divided
2   teaspoons ground cinnamon
½   teaspoon ground cardamom, optional

Raw (turbinado) sugar or granulated sugar

1. Make the pastry: Mix the flour, sugar, and salt in a large bowl. Using a pastry cutter or 2 knives, cut the butter into the flour until the butter and flour are combined and resemble small, pea-shaped balls. (You can use a food processor, but don't overmix; 3 to 5 pulses should be enough.)

2. Using a blending fork or a large dinner fork, mix in the cream until the pastry is smooth and will form a ball. Add more cream if the mixture is dry. Divide the pastry in half and pat into 2 flat discs. Wrap the dough in waxed paper or plastic wrap and refrigerate for 30 minutes.

3. Meanwhile, make the apple filling: Place all the ingredients in a large bowl and mix to blend. Cover the bowl or transfer the mixture to a large resealable plastic bag. Set it aside at room temperature for at least 15 minutes but no more than 30.

4. Preheat the oven to 400°F. Use half the crust and place the dough in the center of a lightly floured surface. Using a rolling pin, roll the dough into a circle that is uniformly ¼ inch thick.

5. Place the dough circle evenly into a 9-inch glass or metal pie pan, cover it with waxed paper, and place it in the freezer for at least 30 minutes.

6. While the crust is chilling in the freezer, roll the remaining dough in a circle that is uniformly $1/4$ inch thick. Using a 2-inch star cookie cutter, cut out as many stars as the crust will yield. Set aside in the refrigerator until ready to assemble.

7. When the pie dough is frozen, prick the bottom 4 or 5 times with the tines of a fork, line it with parchment paper or aluminum foil, and weigh it down with $1/2$ cup dried beans or pie weights.

8. Bake the pie for 15 minutes, then remove the pan from the oven and take the aluminum foil and weights off. (This is called blind baking. It crisps up the bottom crust, which keeps it from getting soggy when a moist filling is added.) Lower the oven temperature to 350°F.

9. When the oven temperature has decreased, return the pie to the oven and bake it for 10 more minutes. The crust should be dry and lightly browned at this point.

10. Remove the crust from the oven, and let it cool for 15 minutes. Gently spoon the apple filling inside the crust. It should come to about $1/2$ inch above the crust since the apples will settle and shrink during cooking. Beginning at the edge of the pie plate, place the pastry stars on top of the apples, slightly overlapping them around the edges. Keep placing the stars, working in a circle, until all the stars are used. There will be gaps between the stars where you will see the apple filling. Brush the top with cream and sprinkle the entire top of the pie lightly with raw (turbinado) sugar or white sugar.

11. Bake the pie for 45 to 50 minutes or until the apples are crisp-tender and the stars are browned on top. Let cool for at least 1 hour before serving. Serve warm.

TIP: Pie pastry is very forgiving. If the raw pastry splits after placing it in the pie shell, simply push it together and rub water on either side of the fissure. Then take a knife and cut across the tear and rub more water on top. This is effectively performing surgery on the pastry and repairs the tear without even leaving a scar.

Grilled Apple Upside-Down Cake with Crème Fraîche

This upside-down apple cake is a cross between my grand-mother's apple black walnut cake and a French tarte tartin. I like to bake it just before my guests arrive so the intoxicating smells of butter, apples, and cinnamon waft through my apartment, whetting everyone's appetite for the evening to come. The added bonus is that it is still warm from the oven when we are ready for dessert. If you don't devour it all at dinner, finish it off for breakfast—you'll be in for a treat. My favorite pan for this cake is a 10-inch Lékué silicone cake pan, which bakes and releases the cake more easily than any other that I have tested.

Makes 8 servings

Grilling Method: Indirect/Medium Heat

$1/2$	cup (1 stick) unsalted butter
$2^1/4$	cups sugar, divided
4	small Granny Smith apples, peeled, cored, and cut into quarters
2	cups Granny Smith apples (about 3 large), roughly chopped
2	large eggs
$1/2$	cup vegetable oil
2	teaspoons pure vanilla extract
3	cups all-purpose flour
$1^1/2$	teaspoons ground cinnamon
$1^1/2$	teaspoon baking soda
$1/2$	teaspoon sea salt, plus a pinch for sautéed apples
1	cup black walnuts, lightly toasted Homemade Crème Fraîche (page 325) or store-bought, for serving

1. Build a charcoal fire or preheat a gas grill. Or, preheat the oven to 350°F.
2. Heat a 10-inch cast-iron skillet, small braiser, or other ovenproof pan over medium heat. Add the butter to the pan and melt it. Add $1/4$ cup of the sugar and stir until it starts to turn brown, 3 to 5 minutes. Be careful not to burn the sugar; it will

continue to cook even after you add the apples. (Lower the heat if necessary.) Add a pinch of sea salt. Stir to combine. Lower the heat and add the quartered apples. Sauté for about 5 minutes or until caramelized and slightly soft.

3. Arrange the sautéed apples neatly in the bottom of the skillet or in a 10-inch cake pan (preferably silicone). Let them cool to room temperature.

4. Mix the roughly chopped apples with the remaining 2 cups of sugar; set aside for 15 minutes. Meanwhile, whisk the eggs and oil just to combine. Add the vanilla.

5. In a large bowl, sift together the flour, cinnamon, baking soda, and salt. Mix the flour mixture into the egg mixture with a fork or wooden spoon, a little at a time, until all the flour is incorporated and there are no lumps.

6. Add the apple-sugar mixture and the juice to the batter. Mix well to evenly distribute the apples, sugar, and batter. Add the walnuts. If the batter still seems dry, let it sit for 5 to 15 more minutes to extract the juices from the apples. Mix again to incorporate any apple juices. The batter will be very thick, almost like cookie dough.

7. Spoon the batter on top of the sautéed apples in the pan, only to ¾ of the way up the pan. Do not fill to the top. If you have any batter left over, bake it in muffin cups.

8. Place the cake pan on a cookie sheet and put it in the center of the oven or the cooking grate of your grill over indirect medium heat. Bake for 1½ hours or until a toothpick inserted in the center comes out clean and the cake pulls away from the sides of the pan. (Start testing for doneness after 1 hour.)

9. Let the cake cool in the pan on a cooling rack for 15 minutes. Invert it onto a cake plate. Serve warm with a healthy dollop of crème fraîche.

TIP: All ovens and grills are a little different, so keep in mind that baking times are only a general guide for this cake and for other baking recipes in this book. For example, this cake takes a full 1½ hours in my oven, but it takes just over an hour in my mother's oven.

Homemade Crème Fraîche

I love making my own crème fraîche and like the taste better than store-bought. I urge you to make it, but plan ahead: It takes a couple of days to thicken before you can use it.

Makes 2 cups

2   pints heavy whipping cream
2   tablespoons buttermilk

1. Pour heavy whipping cream in a clean glass jar with a lid. Add the buttermilk, close the lid, and shake gently. Place the jar in the warmest part of your house (for example, on top of the refrigerator) and let it sit for 2 to 3 days, until thickened (cultured); keep a close watch.

2. When the cream has cultured, put it in the refrigerator to chill for at least 2 hours before using. Use or refrigerate for up to 1 week.

Dirty Bananas

This dessert is the perfect compromise for a chocolate lover and a fruit lover. The banana and chocolate are wrapped in puff pastry with a touch of cinnamon-sugar for a quick and easy dessert that tastes much more impressive than it would seem based on the the time it takes to make. As it bakes, the chocolate melts, making the banana appear dirty, thus the name.

Makes 4 servings

1   8-ounce package frozen puff pastry (found in the freezer case)
2   bananas, not too ripe
4   teaspoons cinnamon-sugar
2   ounces bittersweet chocolate, preferably 70 percent ScharffenBerger, broken into pieces
1   pint vanilla ice cream

1. Thaw the puff pastry in the refrigerator overnight or at least 3 hours before making the dessert. Preheat the oven to 350°F.

2. Meanwhile, peel and cut the bananas in half crosswise and then lengthwise, so each banana yields 4 pieces. Set them aside. Set the cinnamon-sugar and chocolate in bowls so all of the ingredients are at your fingertips when you assemble the puff pastry packets.

3. On a lightly floured board, cut the pastry into 4 equal pieces about 8 inches square.

4. When ready to assemble, sprinkle each piece of puff pastry with cinnamon-sugar, place 2 bananas pieces in the center and top with some of the chocolate pieces. Fold the edges of the pastry over the filling as if wrapping a present. Pinch the sides and edges of the pastry together to make sure they are securely wrapped.

5. Place the puff pastry packets, seam-sides down, on parchment paper and a cookie sheet and bake for 30 minutes, or until browned. Serve immediately, with vanilla ice cream.

Grilled Bananas with Dulce de Leche

Dulce de leche is one of the best-selling ice cream flavors in the United States, and it is no mystery why. The luscious caramel sauce swirled with vanilla ice cream translates to delicious in any language! It gets even better in this recipe. You start out by making the rich caramely dulce de leche at home—much easier than it sounds! Serve it with warm grilled bananas and real vanilla ice cream. Everyone raves and raves about this dessert, and the true beauty of it is that it is a cinch to make. One can of sweetened condensed milk will make enough caramel sauce for about 10 servings—if you don't eat it up directly from the can with a spoon!

Makes 4 servings

Grilling Method: Direct/Medium-Low Heat

1   14-ounce can sweetened condensed milk
1   recipe Bananas for Grilled Bananas
      (pages 218–219)
1   pint best-quality vanilla ice cream

1. Remove the label from the can. Place the can in a 4-quart heavy-duty saucepan and cover it with water. Bring it to a boil and then reduce the heat to a simmer. Continue simmering for 2½ to 3 hours, making sure the can is covered by water the entire time. You will need to add water several times during the cooking process. The milk will slowly caramelize inside the can.

2. Remove the can from the water with tongs and a mitt—it will be very hot—and let it cool on a heat-proof surface for about 15 minutes. Shake the can and open it with a can opener. Transfer the contents to a glass or plastic container. The dulce de leche will keep, covered in the refrigerator, for several weeks.

3. Serve the grilled bananas immediately on top of scoops of vanilla ice cream. Drizzle with the dulce de leche.

NOTE: Making caramel (dulce de leche) in the can is a great and virtually foolproof method. However, if you boil the can instead of simmering it or neglect to keep the can covered by water, there is a chance that it will explode. I have made dulce de leche in the can dozens of times and have never had any problems. But, if you are uncomfortable with this method, pour the condensed milk into a heavy-duty saucepan and cook very slowly over low heat, stirring constantly until the milk is reduced and caramelized—about 40 minutes.

Queen of the Grill Banana Split Sundae

One sure-fire way to become the king or queen of your grilling universe is to make a "better" banana split by grilling the bananas. Grilling makes the fruit sweeter by caramelizing its natural sugars. But most importantly, the warm fruit is a much better match for the cold ice cream and hot fudge sauce. I recommend making your own chocolate sauce with the Ganache recipe (page 328) or, at least, buying the best-quality sauce you can find.

Makes 4 servings

Grilling Method: Direct/Medium-Low Heat

4   firm but ripe bananas, unpeeled
1   tablespoon honey, or more if needed
8   small scoops best-quality vanilla ice cream
1   cup jarred chocolate fudge sauce or Chocolate
      Ganache (page 328), heated
½   cup coarsely chopped pecans or walnuts, toasted
      Whipped cream, optional
      Maraschino cherries, optional

1. Build a charcoal fire or preheat a gas grill.
2. Slice the bananas, in their skins, in half crosswise and then lengthwise, so each banana yields 4 pieces. Place the bananas on a platter. Drizzle the honey on the cut sides of the bananas. Let them sit for 5 minutes.
3. Place the bananas, cut-sides down, on the center of a very clean cooking grate over direct medium-low heat, and cover. Cook for 2 minutes, or until grill marks appear. Using a pair of long-handled tongs, turn the banana pieces over and let them cook for 5 more minutes, or until the skin pulls away from the bananas.
4. Let the bananas cool slightly, then remove the skins. Arrange 2 banana halves on each serving plate or bowl. Top each serving with 2 scoops of ice cream. Ladle ¼ cup of hot fudge over each sundae. Sprinkle each with 1 tablespoon of chopped nuts, and if desired add whipped cream and a cherry on top. Serve immediately.

Maple-Rum Pineapple with Toasted Coconut Ice Cream

Make this once and the next time you won't need to consult the recipe. It is a great dessert for a crowd because it looks and sounds fancy; but it takes only a few ingredients and little time to make. You can use dried unsweetened coconut or the more common dried sweetened coconut. If you do opt for the sweetened grocery-store variety, I've found that the best brand is Mounds.

Makes 4 servings

Grilling Method: Direct/Medium-Low Heat
Special Equipment: Vacu Vin pineapple slicer, optional

1½ cups dried coconut, toasted
1 pint best-quality vanilla ice cream, softened
1 golden pineapple
½ cup dark rum
¼ cup (½ stick) unsalted butter, melted
¼ cup maple syrup

1. Put 1 cup of the toasted coconut in a metal or glass bowl. Add the softened ice cream and mix until incorporated. Put the ice cream back into the pint container to refreeze.
2. Build a charcoal fire or preheat a gas grill. Meanwhile, cut the top off the pineapple and, using a pineapple slicer or a knife, peel and cut the pineapple into half-rings and set aside.
3. Mix the rum, butter, and maple syrup in a small bowl. Brush both sides of the pineapple rings with the sweet glaze.
4. Place the pineapple rings on a very clean cooking grate over direct medium-low heat, cover, and grill for 2 to 3 minutes per side, or until marked and warmed through. Be careful not to leave them on much longer, as the pineapple burns easily. Transfer the pineapple to a platter.
5. Divide the ice cream among 4 bowls. Top each bowl with grilled pineapple and a sprinkle of the remaining coconut.

Grilled Fruit Fondue with Dark Chocolate and Ginger

At a small country inn in the South of France, just as fall was turning into winter, I was served an after-dinner drink with a small skewer of fruit and a warm chocolate dipping sauce. I thought at the time that it was a really nice change from chocolate truffles and cookies. When I got home, I decided the idea was too clever to leave in France. I decided to warm the fruit by grilling it, thus intensifying the natural flavors of the fruit and making the temperature of the fruit more appealing. That experiment morphed into this full-blown grilled fruit fondue recipe with a sharp ginger cream to balance out the sweet chocolate. Grill the fruit in large slices or chunks and then cut it into bite-size pieces for dipping.

Makes 4 to 6 servings

Grilling Method: Direct/Medium-Low Heat
Special Equipment: Fondue forks

Chocolate Ganache (below)
Ginger Cream (at right)
2 cups seasonal fruit, such as pineapple, apples,
 pears, strawberries, melon, peaches, etc.,
 cut into 1-inch cubes
 Bamboo skewers, soaked in water for 30 minutes

1. Bring the Chocolate Ganache and Ginger Cream
 to room temperature. Put them in serving bowls,
 cover, and set aside.
2. Build a charcoal fire or preheat a gas grill. Thread
 the fruit ladder style on skewers. Grill the fruit
 over direct medium-low heat until marked and
 warmed through (see page 202). Cut into smaller
 bite-size pieces if desired.
3. Place the grilled fruit on small plates or a platter
 with fondue forks. Serve them with the dipping
 sauces on the side—if you own a fondue pot, keep
 the chocolate warm in the pot while serving.

Chocolate Ganache

6 ounces 70 percent bittersweet chocolate,
 preferably ScharffenBerger
1/3 cup heavy whipping cream
2 tablespoons sugar
2 tablespoons liqueur (either Kahlua,
 Frangelico, or bourbon), optional
1/2 teaspoon pure vanilla extract

1. Make the ganache up to 2 days in advance.
 Chop the chocolate into bite-size pieces and
 put it in a heatproof bowl. Heat the cream in
 a heavy-bottomed saucepan to almost boiling,
 add the sugar, and stir to combine. Remove
 the cream from the heat and pour it over the
 chocolate pieces. Whisk vigorously until
 the chocolate is melted and the cream is
 completely incorporated. Add the liqueur,
 if using, and vanilla, stirring constantly until
 the mixture is cool the touch.
2. Cover the ganache with plastic wrap and set
 aside or refrigerate. (If refrigerated, it will need
 to be brought to room temperature and
 rewarmed before serving.)

Ginger Cream

8 ounces cream cheese, softened
2 tablespoons packed brown sugar
2 tablespoons fresh lemon juice
2 tablespoons minced crystallized ginger,
 or more to taste
 Pinch salt
2 tablespoons Grand Marnier or Canton
 Ginger liqueur, optional, or half-and-half

1. In a small bowl, beat together the cream
 cheese, brown sugar, lemon juice, ginger, and
 salt on the medium speed of electric mixer or
 by hand, until well blended. Add the liqueur, if
 using. If not using liqueur, thin the sauce with
 half-and-half or milk. Cover and chill until
 serving time.
2. Bring to room temperature before serving,
 rewhipping if necessary.

Give Me S'more
S'mores Bar

*If there is one thing that will get adults to act like kids
again, it is s'mores. I use this interactive recipe in my cooking classes as the sweet ending to a hard night of grilling!
You can make these around a bonfire, in a fireplace, on a
gas grill, over glowing embers of charcoal, or even over the
flame on your gas stove. Boy- and Girl-Scout s'mores are
good, but this do-it-yourself candy bar adds a bit of adventure to the campfire classic. Give me s'more!*

Makes 8 servings

Grilling Method: Direct/High Heat

8 graham crackers, each one split in half to make
 16 pieces
8 1-ounce squares premium (bittersweet
 or semisweet) chocolate, such as
 ScharffenBerger
16 large marshmallows
 Toppings, optional (see Variations, page 329)
8 extra-long wooden skewers, soaked in water for
 30 minutes

CLASSIC S'MORES

When my grill friend, Lisa Taylor, made these s'mores, she couldn't wait to show me her take on the camping classic. Use the classic Hershey chocolate bar, generic marshmallows—which aren't quite as sweet as the name-brand version—and plain graham crackers. Roast the marshmallows over the burners, turning to brown all sides. Meanwhile, warm the graham crackers and 6 squares of the Hershey bar over indirect heat. Place 2 roasted marshmallows on top of the melted chocolate and press down with the top half of the graham cracker. This way, the chocolate is melted and the graham crackers are warm, which makes the cold chocolate, burned marshmallow s'mores of Girl Scout fame pale in comparison. Each wrapped package of graham crackers will actually make 9 s'mores ... that's an extra one for the griller!

1. Place the graham cracker halves on a baking sheet. Set a square of chocolate on top of half of them. If desired, add 1 or 2 pieces of fruit or other s'more topping to each half.
2. Thread 2 marshmallows onto the end of each skewer: Hold the marshmallows just above the cooking grate over direct high heat and turn them slowly until they're lightly browned, 2 to 3 minutes.
3. Gently slide 2 warm marshmallows off the skewers onto each graham cracker and candy half. Place the remaining graham cracker halves on top. Gently press together and enjoy immediately.

S'mores Variations: To set up your own s'mores bar, give each guest 4 marshmallows, a skewer, and a plate, and let them use their imagination to build a candy-land fantasy s'more. Here are some possibilities to dress up the white fluff.

- Instead of the regular graham crackers, try: cinnamon sugar or chocolate covered, or try chocolate chip cookies.

- Instead of the plain chocolate, try: dark chocolate, peanut butter cups, caramels, white chocolate with almonds, chocolate-covered mints, peppermint bark, any favorite candy.

- For additional toppings, try: crystallized ginger, dried cherries, chopped nuts, lemon or orange peel.

All My Heart Brownies

I created this recipe for my nephew, August "Monkey" Wachter, who has captured my heart. By the time he was a year old, he wanted to help in the kitchen. When he was two-and-a-half, he took a kids' cooking course and really fell in love with cooking. Since this is an interest that I happily encourage, I immediately gave him a real wooden spoon with a short, kid-friendly handle and a heart-shaped silicone muffin pan. From then on, "heart brownies with Aunt EAK" was on our agenda no matter what. The recipe is full of adult-friendly ingredients like 70 percent bittersweet chocolate, but the method has been simplified so that it is easy enough for a toddler to make with adult supervision.

Makes 6 servings

½	cup (1 stick) unsalted butter, plus more for greasing pan
6	ounces bittersweet chocolate, preferably 70 percent ScharffenBerger percent
2	large eggs
1 ⅔	cups sugar
2	teaspoons pure vanilla extract
½	teaspoon sea salt
1	cup all-purpose flour
⅔	cup coarsely chopped toasted pecans or walnuts

1. Preheat the oven or grill to 350°F. Grease a square (8 x 8– or 9 x 9–inch) brownie pan or mini-heart muffin pan.
2. Melt the butter and chocolate in the top of a double boiler or in a metal bowl set over a saucepan of simmering water. Put the eggs, sugar, vanilla, and salt in a large bowl and beat them by hand with a large fork or wooden spoon until combined.

3. Slowly add the melted butter and chocolate. Mix until incorporated. Add the flour a little at a time until fully incorporated. Add the nuts and stir with a spatula until the batter is evenly mixed.

4. Pour the batter into the prepared pan. (If using the muffin tin, fill each cup ³/₄ of the way up the sides.)

5. Bake the brownies for 40 minutes, or until they pull away from the sides of the pan and a little chocolate clings to a toothpick when it is inserted in the center. (The center should be moist but not runny.) If you use a heart-shaped muffin tin, it may take less time; check at 25 minutes.

6. Let the brownies cool in the pan on a rack for several hours before cutting (or if using the muffin tins, before turning them out of the pan).

Chocolate Cherry Variation: Add ¹/₂ cup dried cherries and 2 ounces chopped bittersweet chocolate to the batter when you add the nuts, or instead of the nuts.

Zesty Lemon Bars

Nothing finishes off a meal of ribs, pulled pork, or even a grilled chicken Caesar salad like a lemon bar. I created this recipe for all those fellow lemonheads out there. It is a lot more tart than most lemon bars and is just the thing for summertime entertaining.

Makes 12 servings

Shortbread Crust

1	cup (2 sticks) unsalted butter, cold
2	cups all-purpose flour
¹/₄	cup sugar
¹/₄	cup packed light brown sugar
¹/₂	teaspoon sea salt
1	lemon, zested

Lemon Filling

4	extra-large eggs
1¹/₂	cups sugar

³/₄	cup fresh lemon juice (about 3 large lemons)
¹/₃	cup all-purpose flour
1	lemon, zested
	Confectioners' sugar

1. Preheat the oven to 350°F.

2. Make the crust: Cut the butter into ¹/₂-inch pieces. In a food processor or using a handheld pastry cutter, process all the shortbread ingredients until the mixture begins to form small pea-shaped lumps.

3. Sprinkle the dough into a rectangular 13 x 9 x 2–inch baking pan. (The bars can also be made in a square 8- or 9-inch baking pan—they will be thicker and take about 15 more minutes to bake.) Using your fingers or a metal spatula, press the dough firmly and evenly onto the bottom and ¹/₂ inch up the sides of the pan to form a ¹/₂-inch layer of shortbread. Prick all over with a fork.

4. Bake the shortbread in the middle of the oven until golden, about 25 minutes. Remove it to a cooling rack. (Cover with foil to keep warm if necessary.)

5. While the crust is baking, make the filling: In a large metal bowl, whisk the eggs and sugar together until well combined and a light yellow color. Stir in the lemon juice, flour, and zest.

6. When the shortbread crust is ready and still hot, pour the lemon mixture evenly over it. Lower the oven temperature to 300°F. When it has reached the lower temperature, bake the bars in the middle of the oven until set, about 30 minutes. The top should be light brown and look a little bubbly and crusty.

7. Let the bars cool completely in the pan on a cooling rack, then cut them into 3-inch squares with a nonserrated knife.

8. Lightly sift confectioners' sugar over the cool bars before serving. If making these the night before a party, refrigerate them and reapply the confectioners' sugar just before serving. The sugar is absorbed as the lemon bars sit.

Greensboro Ice Cream Pie with Hot Fudge

This recipe was inspired by the famous ice-cream pies of my North Carolina childhood. It is still so popular in Greensboro that my best friend ordered a dozen of them from the Greensboro Country Club to serve at her wedding rehearsal dinner. The only real cooking is in making the meringue and the chocolate sauce. I use my fail-proof Chocolate Ganache (page 328) for the hot fudge sauce, but feel free to use any good-quality sauce. And if push comes to shove, you can substitute real whipped cream for the meringue.

Makes 6 servings

- 1 graham cracker pie crust in a foil pan
- 2 pints best-quality French vanilla ice cream, softened

Meringue
- 4 egg whites, at room temperature
- 1 teaspoon pure vanilla extract
- 1/2 teaspoon cream of tartar
- 1/2 cup sugar

- 1 cup prepared hot fudge sauce or Chocolate Ganache (page 328), warmed for serving

1. Make the pie at least 1 day before you want to serve it. Fill the crust with the softened ice cream. Smooth the ice cream out so that it is even and goes all the way to the edge of the crust. Cover it with plastic wrap or aluminum foil and put it in the coldest part of the freezer for 24 hours.

2. A few hours before serving, preheat the oven to 475°F and make the meringue: Combine the egg whites, vanilla, and cream of tartar in a large metal (preferably copper) mixing bowl.

3. Beat the mixture with an electric mixer on high for about 4 minutes, or until soft peaks form. (When you pick up a beater, a thickened peak will flop over.) Gradually add the sugar, beating on high speed until the egg whites form stiff glossy peaks (the peak will hold its shape) and all the sugar is dissolved.

4. Immediately spread the meringue over the frozen pie, carefully sealing the edges of the pie all the way around. Bake for 5 minutes, or until the meringue is set. It will not be very brown. If you like your meringue browned, turn on the broiler and leave the pie in the oven with the door open for 2 to 3 more minutes, watching the whole time so the top won't burn. Let it cool briefly, then place it back in the freezer for 3 hours or overnight.

5. When you're ready to serve, cut the pie into slices and serve them with hot fudge sauce. The pie will keep, covered in the freezer, for almost 1 week.

HOMEMADE ICE CREAM SANDWICHES

My fondest childhood food memory is of summer days during peach season when my grandmother would make homemade peach ice cream. For hours, she would peel peaches with a well-worn paring knife that was like a sixth finger, putting up most of the fruit but reserving enough for a gallon or so of her coveted ice cream. My sisters, cousins, and I would take turns sitting on the old wooden-cased ice cream maker, churning it until the ice cream was creamy and frozen.

I no longer use rock salt and a hand-cranked ice-cream maker, but I love to make all kinds of homemade ice cream. And, as good as the ice cream is, I think it is infinitely better between homemade cookies served as an ice-cream sandwich. The good news is that they can be made and assembled up to one day in advance and kept wrapped in wax paper in the freezer until serving time. If you are pressed for time, make the cookies and substitute a premium ice cream for the homemade, but no surprise here—homemade is always better!

Tri-Berry Crisp with Pecan Topping

What's a summer without a crisp? A lost summer—or at least a lost opportunity—in my book! Crisps are a great way to make the most out of ripe seasonal fruit. I usually prepare this light and fruity dessert in advance and put it on the grill to bake when I take off the main dish. That way, when everyone starts looking around for dessert, a bubbling, hot-off-the-grill crisp is ready for its grand entrance. Top with real vanilla ice cream and you'll get a standing ovation.

Makes 6 to 8

Grilling Method: Indirect/Medium Heat

Streusel Topping

1½	cups packed light brown sugar
1½	cups all-purpose flour
1½	cups regular or quick-cooking oatmeal (not instant)
⅓	cup coarsely chopped pecans
1	teaspoon ground cinnamon
½	teaspoon kosher salt
¾	cup (1½ sticks) unsalted butter, softened, cut into small pieces

Berry Filling

2	pints strawberries, halved
2	pints blueberries
2	pints blackberries or raspberries
1	orange, zested and juiced
1	lemon, zested and juiced
½ to ⅔	cup sugar, depending on sweetness of fruit
¼	cup cornstarch
1	teaspoon ground cinnamon
2 to 3 tablespoons Grand Marnier, optional	

1. Build a charcoal fire or preheat a gas grill.
2. Make the streusel: In a large bowl, combine all the topping ingredients except the butter. Work in the butter with a pastry blender or fork until the mixture resembles large, coarse bread crumbs. Set aside.
3. Make the filling: In another large bowl, mix the berries together. Add the orange juice, lemon juice, orange and lemon zests, sugar, cornstarch, and cinnamon; mix lightly. Add the Grand Marnier, if using. Set aside for 5 minutes.
4. Place the berry mixture in an ovenproof, 4-quart, round casserole or soufflé dish. Top it evenly with the streusel mixture. Place the dish in the center of the cooking grate over indirect medium heat, cover, and bake for 35 to 45 minutes, or until bubbly and the top is browned. Transfer the baking dish to a cooling rack. Serve warm with ice cream, if desired.

Sunday Brunch Sour Cream Coffee Cake

In Greensboro, NC, we southern girls learned to entertain from a young age. This coffee cake was my specialty in high school, served often when I had my girlfriends, the Luasions, over for brunch. Once I graduated from high school, I forgot about the coffee cake as new food experiences passed my palate. Recently, fellow North Carolinian and food friend Lisa Callaghan and I reminisced about the legendary sour cream coffee cake—apparently it was a North Carolina phenomenon. I dug the recipe out from my dusty recipe relics and baked it with low expectations since the memory of something is almost always better than revisiting it. This time that wasn't the case; it more than lived up to the memory! I tweaked it to include pecans and both a filling and a topping.

The moist, soft, butter cake is perfectly balanced by the crunchy cinnamon-pecan concoction that doubles as a filling and a topping. Real sour cream keeps the cake moist, so don't substitute the light stuff! The cake can be made up to two days in advance if kept tightly covered; but believe me, it won't last that long.

Makes 6 to 12 servings

1	cup (2 sticks) unsalted butter
1½	cups sugar
1¼	cups whole milk sour cream (not light or nonfat)
2	large eggs
1	teaspoon pure vanilla extract
2	cups all-purpose flour
1	teaspoon baking powder
½	teaspoon baking soda
½	teaspoon sea salt

Cinnamon Pecan Filling

1 cup chopped pecans
¾ cup packed brown sugar
¼ cup sugar
1 tablespoon ground cinnamon

1. Preheat the oven to 325°F. Grease a 9 x 13–inch cake pan.
2. Put the butter and sugar in the bowl of a stand mixer or in a large bowl. Beat them with electric beaters until light and creamy. Add the sour cream, eggs, and vanilla and mix again until well incorporated.
3. Measure and sift the flour, baking powder, baking soda, and salt. Add the flour mixture to the butter-sugar mixture a little at a time, until well mixed. Scrape down the sides of the bowl periodically. Set aside.
4. Make the filling: Combine the pecans, brown sugar, sugar, and cinnamon in a large bowl. Mix well.
5. Pour half the batter into the pan. Sprinkle two-thirds of the filling evenly to cover all of the batter. Cover with the rest of the batter. Smooth the top with a spatula. Sprinkle the remaining filling on the top of the cake.
6. Bake for 50 to 60 minutes, or until the cake pulls away from the sides of the pan and a toothpick inserted in the center comes out clean. Start testing for doneness after the cake has baked for 40 minutes, since ovens and pans vary in the way they bake. Transfer the cake to a cooling rack.
7. Let the cake cool before slicing. Slice it directly from the pan and transfer to a serving platter.

Gretchen's Cinnamon-Chocolate Sheet Cake

This irresistible cake was inspired by my friend Gretchen Belmonti's holiday trips to Mexico, where chocolate is often seasoned with a pinch of cinnamon to intensify the flavor. This chocolatey creation is baked in a jelly roll pan (cookie sheet with 1-inch sides) and frosted while still hot, so it is unbelievably moist and flavorful. It is as easy to make as it is to eat, and it is great for large crowds since it makes a good number of slices. If you are making this cake for a party, you can also use a deep metal cookie cutter to cut out special shapes.

Makes 12 to 16 servings

1 cup (2 sticks) unsalted butter
1 cup sour milk (fresh whole milk plus 1 teaspoon white vinegar)
5 tablespoons unsweetened cocoa powder
1½ teaspoon ground cinnamon
2 large eggs
½ cup water
1 teaspoon pure vanilla extract
1 teaspoon baking soda
2 cups all-purpose flour
2 cups sugar
½ teaspoon salt

Icing

½ cup (1 stick) unsalted butter
6 tablespoons milk
¼ cup unsweetened cocoa powder
1 pound confectioners' sugar
1 teaspoon pure vanilla extract
½ teaspoon ground cinnamon

1. Preheat the oven to 375°F. Grease an 11 x 18–inch jelly roll pan.
2. Heat the butter, sour milk, cocoa, and cinnamon to just under a roaring boil in a small heavy-bottomed saucepan.
3. In a small bowl, beat the eggs with the water, vanilla, and baking soda. In a large bowl, sift together the flour, sugar, and salt. Add the butter and egg mixtures to the flour, mixing gently.
4. Pour the batter into the prepared pan. Bake for 20 minutes, or until the cake pulls away from the sides and a toothpick or thin-bladed knife inserted into the center comes out clean.
5. Meanwhile, make the icing: Heat the butter, milk, and cocoa to just under a boil in a small heavy-bottomed saucepan. In a separate bowl, combine the confectioners' sugar, cinnamon, and vanilla. Add the butter mixture to the sugar and blend thoroughly with a wooden spoon or fork. Scrape down the sides with a rubber spatula.
6. Spread the icing on the hot cake when it comes out of the oven. Let it cool on a cooling rack for 2 hours. Cut the pieces directly from the pan and place them on a platter for serving. Serve the cake at room temperature. It will keep for 3 days if kept covered.

Hot Peach Shortcake

There are a few barbecue joints known almost as much for their dessert as for their barbecue. Big Bob Gibson's in Alabama is famous for mile-high pies, and Stamey's Barbecue in my hometown of Greensboro, NC, is famous for their peach cobbler. Stamey's make theirs with pie crust on top, but my recipe calls for a trick I picked up from my Midwestern farm-family friends—topping. Top fruit cobblers with old-fashioned cream biscuits and a generous sprinkling of sugar. This change of topping turns cobbler into shortcake, and I guarantee it will be the best hot peach shortcake you have ever eaten. When fresh blackberries are in season, add them to the mix for an even better shortcake.

Makes 6 to 8 servings

4 pints of fresh peaches, peeled and sliced or
    6 cups frozen sliced peaches
1 to 2 pints fresh blackberries, optional
1 lemon, juiced
1/4 lemon, zested
1/2 cup sugar
5 tablespoons cornstarch
1 lemon, zest removed and juiced
1 teaspoons ground cinnamon

Biscuits
2 cups all-purpose flour, plus more as needed
3 tablespoons white sugar, plus more for topping
2 teaspoons baking powder
1/2 teaspoon sea salt
1 1/2 cups heavy whipping cream, plus more for
    brushing tops

1. Preheat the oven to 375°F.
2. In a large bowl, combine the peaches and blackberries, if using. Add lemon juice, lemon zest, the sugar, cornstarch, lemon juice, 1/4 of the zest, and the cinnamon; mix lightly. Let the mixture sit for 5 minutes. Place the fruit mixture into a 4-quart soufflé dish or 9 x 13–inch rectangular baking dish.
3. Meanwhile, make the biscuits: Combine all of the dry ingredients in a large bowl and whisk until completely incorporated. Stir with a fork until well mixed. Add about 1 cup of the cream, and stir with the fork until the dough comes together. If the dough is still very dry, add the rest of the cream. If it is forming into a ball, add half the

remaining cream (1/4 cup) and stir with fork. You don't want the dough to be too wet. When the dough forms a ball, turn it out onto a floured surface and knead until smooth.
4. Roll the dough out with a rolling pin until the dough is 3/4 inch thick. Cut with a floured biscuit cutter and place on top of the fruit mixture.
5. Brush the tops with the reserved cream and sprinkle with a generous coating of sugar. Place the pan in the oven and bake.
6. Cook for 30 to 40 minutes, or until the top is golden brown and the fruit is bubbly.

Gingerbread Stout Cake with Bittersweet Marmalade Glaze

Make this recipe in the fall when you crave a toothsome dessert. The stout gives this gingerbread a more complex sweet and savory flavor than traditional gingerbread. If you can't find cream stout, you can substitute Guinness. I like topping the gingerbread as soon as it comes off the grill with bittersweet orange marmalade so it melts into the cake as it cools. If you don't already have a favorite marmalade, try one of the organic fruit combinations, including a delectable Meyer lemon, made by California jam artisan June Taylor (www.junetaylorjams.com).

Makes 12 servings

Grilling Method: Indirect/Medium Heat

2 1/2 cups all-purpose flour
2 tablespoons plus 1 teaspoon baking soda
2 tablespoons ground ginger
2 teaspoons ground cinnamon
1/2 teaspoon ground cloves
1/2 teaspoon salt
1 cup (2 sticks) unsalted butter, at room temperature
1 1/4 cups packed light brown sugar
2 large eggs, at room temperature
1 cup molasses
3/4 cup cream stout, such as Samuel Adams
    or Guinness, flat, at room temperature
1 cup orange, lemon, lime, or clementine
    marmalade, warmed
    Whipped cream, optional

1. Build a charcoal fire or preheat a gas grill. Or, preheat the oven to 350°F. Butter and flour a 9 x 13–inch Pyrex or metal baking pan.
2. Sift together all of the dry ingredients and set them aside.
3. Using an electric mixer set on high speed, cream the butter and sugar in a large bowl until light in color and fluffy in texture. Beat in the eggs 1 at a time. Beat in the molasses (the batter may look like it is curdling at this point; don't worry, that is what it is supposed to look like). Lower the mixer speed to medium. Beat in the flour mixture, $1/3$ at a time, alternating with the flat cream stout.
4. Scrape the batter into the prepared pan and smooth the top. Bake for 50 to 60 minutes. If baking on the grill, place the pan in the center of the cooking grate over indirect medium heat, cover, and bake for 25 minutes without looking. If your grill or oven has uneven heat and the cake looks more done on one side than the other, rotate the cake and continue baking for 25 to 35 more minutes, or until a toothpick inserted in the center of the cake comes out clean.
5. Cool the cake in the pan on a rack for 10 minutes. Glaze the top of the cake with the marmalade, covering it evenly. Serve warm or let it cool completely. Serve with a dollop of whipped cream, if desired. This cake is so moist that it stays fresh for 4 to 5 days if kept covered.

My Mother's Fresh Grated Coconut Cake

I am crazy for coconut! This cake is my all-time favorite dessert, although my grandmother's coconut cream pie runs a close second. I request it every time I go home to North Carolina. The secret is making it the night before you serve it so the coconut milk in the fresh coconut has a chance to seep into the cake, resulting in the most flavorful and moist cake I have ever tasted.

I never made it myself until about five years ago, when friends of mine, known collectively as the brothers Mose, asked me to bring it to their annual Easter feast. I must have called my mother fifty times to walk me through the process. In reality, the only thing that is hard about making the cake is cracking and grating the fresh coconut. I solved that by

purchasing frozen fresh grated coconut and coconut milk in an Asian market. They both keep indefinitely, so buy them even before you think you need them—you never know when a coconut cake craving will hit, and you will want to be prepared.

Makes 8 to 12 servings

Cake

1	cup (2 sticks) unsalted butter, softened
2	cups sugar
3	cups sifted cake flour
4	teaspoons baking powder
1	teaspoon sea salt
$1^1/3$	cups canned lite coconut milk (not cream of coconut)
2	full teaspoons pure vanilla extract
6	large egg whites, stiffly beaten

Icing

$2^1/2$	cups sugar
1	cup bottled water
1	tablespoon white corn syrup, preferably Karo
3	large egg whites
1	overflowing teaspoon pure vanilla extract
2	cups grated unsweetened coconut (thoroughly thawed, if frozen)

1. Preheat the oven to 350°F. Grease and flour two 9-inch cake pans (or use Baker's Joy).
2. Make the cake: In a large bowl, cream the butter and sugar together with an electric mixer until fluffy.
3. In a large bowl, sift the dry ingredients together. Mix the coconut milk and vanilla together. Add the dry ingredients to the butter-sugar mixture in 3 equal batches, alternating with the coconut-vanilla milk, until the batter is smooth and all the flour is incorporated. Set aside.
4. In another bowl, beat the egg whites with an electric mixer set on high until they hold a stiff peak. (When you hold up the beater, the whites will keep their shape.) Add the egg whites to the batter in batches, gently folding them in until just incorporated.
5. Pour the batter into the prepared pans. Bake the layers for 30 to 35 minutes, or until the cakes pull away from the sides of the pans, the tops are golden brown, and a toothpick inserted in the center come out clean.

6. Transfer the cakes in the pans to cooling racks. Let them cool for 10 minutes. (To make it easier to remove the cakes from the pan, gently slide a thin sharp knife along the inside rim of the pan, being careful not to cut into the cake.) Turn each cake out of the pan onto a plate, then flip it back over to cool for at least 2 hours on cooling racks.

7. Meanwhile, make the icing: Mix the sugar, water, and corn syrup in a heavy-bottomed saucepan. Cover the pan for the first 3 minutes to prevent crystallization on the sides. Boil without stirring until an 8-inch thread of the sugar syrup spins from a spoon when you hold it up. (It will register 242°F on a candy thermometer.)

8. While syrup is cooking, beat the egg whites in a large bowl with an electric mixer on high until they hold a stiff peak. (When you hold up the beater, the whites will keep their shape.)

9. Pour the hot syrup slowly over the egg whites, beating constantly with the electric mixer. Add the vanilla and beat until the icing is fluffy and holds its shape. Divide the icing into 2 equal parts.

10. Add 1½ cups of the coconut to 1 part of the icing and mix it with a spatula to incorporate. (Make sure the coconut is thawed and drained of any excess moisture or the icing will become too runny.)

11. Spread the top of the cooled cake layers with the coconut icing. Place 1 layer on top of the other. Ice the sides and top of the cake with the plain icing. Once this is done, spread any remaining coconut icing on top of the cake. Sprinkle the top and sides of the cake with the reserved ½ cup of grated coconut. Serve it immediately or wait a day for the best flavor. Store the cake covered in a cake carrier or lightly covered with waxed paper.

Menus

My Favorite Menu
Tumbled Tomatoes with Mediterranean Herbs
   (page 289)
The Original Beer-Can Chicken (page 47)
Lip-Smackin' Asparagus Spears (pages 204–205)
Grilled Sweet Potato Chips (page 211)
Homemade or store-bought ice cream sandwiches
   (Sidebar, page 331)

Ready, Set, Grill, No. 1
Chicken Paillard with Greek Farmer's Salad and
   Tzatziki (pages 37–38)

Ready, Set, Grill, No. 2
Portobello Pizza (pages 208–209)
Rock-Star Skirt Steak with Jicama-Orange Salad
   (pages 65–66)

Ready, Set, Grill, No. 3
Double-Cut Veal Chops with Garlic Butter
   (pages 77–78)
Acorn Squash with Fresh Sage and Olive Oil
   (page 212)
Grilled Bananas with Dulce de Leche (page 326)

Spur of the Moment Menu
Store-bought hummus, pita bread, and veggies
Bone-In Chicken Pieces 101 (page 34)
Ruffled potato chips
Fire-Roasted Corn with Smokey Paprika Butter
   (page 206)

First Backyard BBQ
Buffalo-Style Chicken Wings (pages 36–37)
Pork Chop 101 (page 84)
Cucumber Pickle (page 307)
Creamed Corn Grilled Skillet Cornbread
   (pages 308–309)
Tri-Berry Crisp with Pecan Topping (page 332)

Burger Night
Don't Worry, Be Happy Baba Ghanoush
   (page 293)
Build-Your-Own Burger Bar (pages 122–123)
Wilted Spinach Salad with Grilled Tomatoes (page 301)
Smashed Potatoes (page 210)
All My Heart Brownies (page 329)

Steak Night
Shrimp Scampi with Artichokes and Black Olives
   (pages 182–183)
Chicago Steakhouse Salad (page 302)
Steak 101 (page 60)
Steakhouse Spinach (page 310)
Dirty Bananas (page 325)

Veggie Night Out
Truffled White Bean and Carmelized Onion Toasts
   (page 296)
Portobello Burgers (page 208)
Grilled Corn in the Husk (page 206)
Grilled Figs with Candied Ginger, Lemon, and
   Honey (page 219)

Summer Seafood Supper (Uptown)
Smoked Gazpacho with Lump Crabmeat
   (pages 189–190)
Lobster Tail with Pastis Crème (pages 190–191)
Nantucket Swordfish with Browned Butter and
   Sautéed Pecans (pages 163–164)
White Peaches Marinated in Balsamic Syrup
   (page 220)

Summer Seafood Supper (Down Home)
Beer-Brined Smoked Catfish Pate (pages 167–168)
Grilled Shrimp and Grits (pages 183–184)
Hickory-Smoked Bacon-Wrapped Rainbow Trout
   (page 168)
Zesty Lemon Bars (page 330)

Mom's Day Off

Alan's Mustard Dip for Raw Vegetables (page 201)

Rubbed and Sauced Barbecued Half Chickens
(pages 43–44)

Grilled Corn in the Husk (page 206)

Crunchy Cucumber Salad (page 303)

Bananas for Grilled Bananas (pages 218–219) and
vanilla ice cream

Stars and Stripes

Straight-Up Deviled Eggs (page 298)

Country Club Bacon Cheeseburgers (page 126)

Smoked Sausages with Apple-Fennel "Sauerkraut"
(pages 141–142)

Shout Hallelujah Potato Salad (page 305)

17th Street Bar & Grill's Tangy Baked Beans
(pages 256–257)

Give Me S'more S'mores Bar (pages 328–329)

Winter Holiday

Grilled Vegetable Antipasto Platter with Soprano
Sauce (page 216)

Bacon-Wrapped Sea Scallops (page 188)

Christmas Prime Rib with Decadent Horseradish
Cream (page 75)

Sparkling Roasted New Potatoes (pages 210–211)

My Mother's Fresh Grated Coconut Cake
(pages 335–336)

Or replace prime rib with:

Orange-Brined Maple-Glazed Turkey (pages 48–49)

Southern Sausage Dressing (page 308)

North Carolina BBQ

Marti's at Midday Pimento Cheese (page 291)

North Carolina-Style Pulled Pork (page 248)

Taylor Grocery Hush Puppies (page 349)

Memphis BBQ

Hot Peach Shortcake (page 334)

Kenny's Wings of Fire (page 254)

Bubba's Bunch Barbecued Baby Back Ribs (page 266)

Memphis-Style "Dry" Ribs with Spicy "Drippings"
(page 268)

Texas BBQ

Texas Hill Country Market-Style Brisket (page 250)

Texas Vinegar-Chile Hot Sauce (page 252)

Longhorn cheddar cheese

Sliced white bread

Pickled okra

Kansas City BBQ

Kansas City Style Ribs (page 267)

Icebox Cole Slaw (page 306)

Grandma Odom's Sitting Potato Salad (page 306)

Barbecue: 1. Noun: A specific and traditional style of grilled food. Originally native to the southern United States, barbecue is characterized by the slow cooking of meat (usually pork or beef) over a low (heat) fire, using wood smoke. Strictly speaking, grilling a hamburger or hot dog is not barbecue. However, the two terms are commonly used interchangeably. 2. Noun: Outdoor cooking appliance: grill. 3. Noun: Food (especially pork) cooked by a low (heat), slow fire. 4. Verb: To cook food using the indirect cooking method on outdoor cooking equipment.

Basting: Also referred to as "mopping" on the barbecue circuit. Brushing or squirting a thin seasoned liquid onto barbecue or other slow-cooked food during the cooking process.

Bathing: Term coined by Gary Pantlick, avid barbecuer and co-developer of the Cooks' Ribs (pages 252–253). Instead of basting his ribs, he submerges them into a warm "bath" of seasoned liquid. Bathing replaces basting as a means for keeping the meat moistened and seasoned.

Briquettes: Compressed charcoal and (sometimes) fillers. Invented by Henry Ford, briquettes are the most common fuel in grills used in the United States. The better briquettes have few, if any, additives and provide a clean, long-burning fire with even heat. Briquettes that have been impregnated with lighter fluid are not recommended.

BTUs: British Thermal Units is the measurement used by the grilling industry for heat output on gas grills. Generally, 35,000 BTUs is sufficient for a backyard grill.

Caramelization: The concentration of natural sugars in foods during grilling and other quick, direct heat cooking methods, such as sautéing, or during prolonged indirect roasting, such as barbecuing. Deep brown grill marks and crispy meat skin are the result of caramelization.

Ceramic Briquettes: One of three materials that cover the internal gas burners and distribute heat evenly in a gas grill (a grill will only feature one). Ceramic briquettes are pressed and shaped in the form of a charcoal briquette.

Charcoal: Natural charcoal is the byproduct of wood burned in the absence of oxygen. It is the traditional grill fuel that is sold as briquettes or lump charcoal.

Chimney Starter: A metal cylinder used to start a charcoal fire. Charcoal is placed in top of the chimney and kindling (newspaper or starter cubes) is placed in the bottom. The walls of the chimney starter focus the flames and heat of the kindling onto the charcoal, thereby rapidly decreasing the amount of time it takes for the coals to light and ash over.

Combo Cooking: A combination of Direct and Indirect Heat cooking Methods. The Combo Method sears foods over high heat and finishes the cooking process slowly over Indirect Heat. Place food directly over the heat source until well seared, generally only a few minutes. Then move it to the area of the grill that is set up for Indirect Heat, generally the center of the cooking grate (with the heat on either side), and complete cooking. The method for double-cut chops, steaks, whole tenderloins, and bone-in chicken pieces that benefit from a seared, caramelized exterior and a juicy, tender interior. (See detailed explanation on page 7.)

Covered Grill: Any grill with a lid or cover and top and bottom vents, which allows the grill to function as a convection oven.

Direct Method: Method of grilling used primarily for searing foods and for cooking foods that take less than 20 minutes to cook, such as shrimp, steaks, hamburgers, and most vegetables. Food is placed directly above the heat source and must be turned at least once halfway through the cooking time to expose both sides of the food to the heat. The Direct Method can be done on any grill and works best with the grill lid closed during cooking. This method is similar to broiling in an indoor oven. (See detailed explanation on page 7.)

Drip Pan: 1. A disposable aluminum pan used to catch fat and juices produced while grilling, especially while using the indirect method of cooking. 2. A grill's system for channeling grease away from the fire.

Flavorizer Bars: One of three materials that cover the internal gas burners and distribute heat evenly in the grill (a grill will only feature one). Flavorizer bars are a trademark of Weber gas grills; they are pyramid-shaped metal bars that conduct the heat and facilitate the vaporization of fats and juices into smoke. Anything that does not instantly vaporize flows off the sloped sides to the drip pan, reducing flare-ups.

Grate, Charcoal: The metal framework on which the burning charcoal fire is placed.

Grate, Cooking: The metal framework that is placed over the heat source. Also called the grill. Food is placed directly on the cooking grate.

Grill: 1. Noun: An outdoor cooking appliance with a framework of metal bars (cooking grate) set over a charcoal or gas flame for the purpose of cooking. The spaces between the metal bars allow the fat and juices from the food to drip onto the fire, producing a distinctive scent and taste. Not to be confused with the flat griddle frequently used in both corner diners and fast-food restaurants to fry hamburgers, eggs, and cheese sandwiches. 2. Verb: To cook using one of three methods (Direct, Indirect, or Combo) on outdoor cooking equipment.

Grill, Charcoal: A grill fueled by a charcoal fire. The charcoal may be either lump hardwood or processed briquettes. Charcoal grills are the original and traditional American outdoor cooking appliance.

Grill, Gas: Any grill fueled by either natural gas or liquid propane (LP) gas. More convenient than charcoal grills, gas grills are the fastest growing segment of the grill market.

Grill-Roast: Grill-roasting temperatures can be as low as 350°F and as high as 400°F. Beer-can chicken is perfect grill-roasted at 350°F, whereas a whole prime rib needs the higher temperature of 400°F.

Grill-Bake: The grill-baking temperature is generally 350°F; but for foods like cornbread, it is as high as 400°F.

Indirect Method: This is the only grilling method used for authentic slow-cooked barbecue. It is used primarily for large cuts of meat and other foods that require long cooking times at lower temperatures, such as the pulled pork and brisket recipes featured here as well as whole turkey, chicken pieces, and ribs. Foods are cooked by reflected heat and circulated hot air, as in a convection oven. This method provides a consistent cooking temperature and is similar to roasting or baking in your indoor oven. The result is food—mostly meat—that is both juicy and has a deeply caramelized crust. The food cooks evenly without the need to turn during the entire cooking process. This method can only be used on a grill that is covered. In the Indirect Method, food is placed between two heat sources— *never* directly above lit gas burners or charcoal. (See detailed explanation on page 7.)

Lava Rock: One of three materials that cover the internal gas burners and distribute heat evenly in a gas grill (a grill will only feature one). It is irregularly shaped and more porous than ceramics briquettes or flavorizer bars and can cause more flare-ups if not regularly cleaned of the excess fats and juices that can collect in the crevices of the lava rock.

Marinade: A liquid mixture usually containing at least one type of acid ingredient (vinegar, lemon juice, wine, etc.), herbs, spices, oil, and other flavoring ingredients. Marinades are used to tenderize meat and add flavor.

Mop: A basting sauce used to flavor food and add moisture during cooking. Unlike barbecue sauce, a mop is traditionally very thin and does not contain much, if any, sugar.

Rub: Also known as spice rub or dry rub. Rub is a mixture of spices, herbs, and sometimes sugar that is used to season food before grilling. A rub should be thought of as a dry marinade that adds flavor to food.

Sauce, Barbecue: Any sauce used to flavor a dish cooked in a barbecue. Traditionally these sauces are based on tomato (frequently ketchup) and flavored with tamarind (from Worcestershire sauce), vinegar, sugar, and spices. Less frequently (but no less traditionally) sauces are based on cider vinegar and may include mustard. Barbecue sauces that contain sugar of some sort (which is almost all of them) should never be used to baste the food until the last 15 to 20 minutes of cooking time.

Smoking: Flavoring food cooked on a grill with wood smoke. Can be done using either a charcoal or a gas grill and adding presoaked wood chips or chunks. This method of smoking cooks the food with heat and accents the flavor with smoke. It does not preserve the food, as does cold smoking.

Smoke Ring: The coveted pink ring around the exterior of food that has been slow cooked (barbecued) with wood smoke. This is one of the signs of well-cooked, authentic barbecue.

Sources

Ingredients

Anson Mills: *stoneground grits*
Web site: www.ansonmills.com
Telephone: 803-467-4122

Coastal Goods: *specialty salt blends and spices*
Web site: www.coastalgoods.com
Telephone: 508-375-1050

Culver Duck: *whole duck, duck breasts*
Web site: www.culverduck.com
Telephone: 574-825-9537

Frontera Kitchens: *tomatillo salsa, chips*
Web site: www.fronterakitchens.com
Telephone: 800-509-4441 ext. 120

French Feast: *Amora dijon mustard*
Web site: www.frenchfeast.com
Telephone: 212-860-7716

Huy Fong Foods: *sriracha garlic-chili sauce*
Web site: www.huyfong.com
Telephone: 626-286-8328

Mike Mill's Magic Dust: *barbecue rub*
Web site: www.4-17th-rib.com
Telephone: 888-417-8474 or 618-684-3722

Monini: *olive oil*
Web site: www.monini.com
Telephone: 203-750-0531

Nantucket Offshore Seasonings: *grill rubs*
Web site: www.nantucketoffshore.com
Telephone: 888-742-7837

Nielsen-Massey: *vanilla extract*
Web site: www.nielsenmassey.com
Telephone: 800-525-7873

Niman Ranch: *premium beef, lamb, and pork*
Web site: www.nimanranch.com
Telephone: 510-808-0340

Saltworks: *fine-grain and coarse sea salt, fleur de sel, pink Hawaiian salt*
Web site: www.saltworks.us
Telephone: 425-885-7258

ScharffenBerger Chocolate: *70 percent bittersweet chocolate and cocoa*
Web site: www.scharffenberger.com
Telephone: 800-930-4528

The Spice House: *salts, ground and whole spices—such as pepper and grains of paradise*
Web site: www.thespicehouse.com
Telephone: 312-274-0378

Virginia Gentleman: *barbecue sauce*
Web site: ashmanco.com
Telephone: 800-641-9924

WHAM Original: *barbecue rub*
Web site: www.willinghams.com
Telephone: 800-641-9924, or 800-737-WHAM, or 901-767-6759

Equipment

All-Clad: *pots, pans, baking sheets, paella pan, fondue pot*
Web site: www.allclad.com
Telephone: 800-255-2523

Basketville: *woven baskets, wine coolers, entertaining accessories*
Web site: www.basketville.com
Telephone: 802-387-5509

Camerons Professional Cookware: *stovetop smoker*
Web site: www.cameronssmoker.com
Telephone: 888-563-0227

Charcoal Companion: *smoker box, grill accessories*
Web site: www.companion-group.com
Telephone: 800-521-0505

Chef Revival: *fish lifter*
Web site: www.chefrival.com
Telephone: 800-352-2433

Cuisinart: *food processor, electric skillet, ice cream maker*
Web site: www.cuisinart.com
Telephone: 203-975-4600

DeMarle: *Silpat silicone and fiberglass baking liner*
Web site: www.bedbathandbeyond.com
Telephone: 800-462-3966

Duncan's: *Bar-B-Que Grips, heat resistant mitts*
Web site: www.kitchengrip.com
Telephone: 800-785-4449

European Sources Direct: *Love plates and platters*
Web site: www.loveplates.com
Telephone: 877-354-7263

Grill Friends Tools and Ceramics: *GrillMat silicone grilling mat*
Web site: www.laprimashops.com or
    www.legourmetchef.com
Telephone: 312-951-8394 or 800-530-4546

SuperGrater
Web site: www.laprimashops.com or
    bakercatalogue.com
Telephone: 312-951-8394 or 1-800-827-6836

Grill Friends: *Super Silicone BBQ Basting Brush*
Web site: www.laprimashops.com or
    www.gourmetcatalog.com
Telephone: 312-951-8394 or 214-855-0005

Grill Friends Ceramics: *Grilling Trilogy set, corn platter*
Web site: www.laprimashops.com or
    www.gourmetcatalog.com
Telephone: 312-951-8394 or 214-855-0005

John Boos: *wooden cutting boards*
Web site: www.johnboos.com
Telephone: 217-347-7701

KitchenAid: *immersion blender, stand mixer, meat grinder attachment, gas grills*
Web site: www.kitchenaid.com
Telephone: 888-222-8608

Le Creuset: *enamel cast-iron pots and grill grate*
Web site: www.lecreuset.com
Telephone: 877-273-8738

Leifheit USA: *meat tenderizer and pounder, mandoline slicer*
Web site: www.leifheit.com
Telephone: 866-695-3434

Lékué: *platinum-silicone cake pans, grill mitt*
Web site: www.fantes.com
Telephone: 800-443-2683

Lodge Manufacturing Company: *cast-iron barbecue grill grate, grill press, Wedge cornbread pan, preseasoned Lodge Logic pans*
Web site: www.lodgemfg.com
Telephone: 423-837-7181

Microplane: *graters*
Web site: www.chefrevival.com
Telephone: 800-352-2433

OXO: *tongs, veggie peeler, bidirectional grater, mandoline, instant-read thermometer*
Web site: www.oxo.com
Telephone: 800-545-4411

Revéo: *MariVac Food Tumbler*
Web site: www.freethemeat.com
Telephone: 877-738-3648

Rhubarb USA: *vases, Zara shopping trolley, plates, ceramics*
Web site: www.rhubarbusa.com
Telephone: 201-460-1020

Staub USA: *covered dutch ovens, cast-iron enamel pots, serving pieces*
Web site: www.staubusa.com
Telephone: 866-782-8287

Summit Views, LLC: *goodwood mesquite charcoal (in the easy-light burlap bag)*
Web site: www.goodwoodproducts.com
Telephone: 877-872-8341

Turkey Sitter: *vertical roaster for beer-can turkey*
Web site: www.Grillfriends.com
Telephone: 312-951-8394

VitaMix: *high-speed blender*
Web site: www.vitamix.com
Telephone: 800-848-2649

Vacu Vin: *Instant Marinater, pineapple slicer, wine saver*
Web site: www.vacuvin.com
Telephone: 415-382-1241

Waring Pro: *blenders, deep-fryer*
Web site: www.waringproducts.com
Telephone: 800-492-7464

Western Linen: *tea towels, table cloths, napkins*
Web site: www.westernlinen.com
Telephone: 877-335-2900

Wüsthof: *Asian Santuko-style knife, steak knives, chef's knife, tomato knife*
Web site: www.wusthof.com
Telephone: 800-289-9878

Grills

Big Green Egg: *ceramic charcoal grills*
Web site: www.biggreenegg.com
Telephone: 404-320-2066

Broilmaster: *gas grills with smoker shutter attachment*
Web site: www.broilmasters.com
Telephone: 800-851-3153

Coleman: *charcoal and gas grills*
Web site: www.coleman.com
Telephone: 800-835-3278

Dynasty: *gas grills manufactured by Jade Products*
Web site: www.jadeappliances.com (go to the "outdoor" link) or www.universalakb.com/dynoutgasgri.html
Telephone: 800-884-5233 or 818-380-9999

Frontgate: *gas grills and accessories*
Web site: www.frontgate.com
Telephone: 888-263-9850

Hasty-Bake: *charcoal grills*
Web site: www.hastybake.com
Telephone: 800-426-6836

Primo: *Oval Primo, Oval primo in Cypress Cart charcoal grills*
Web site: www.primogrill.com
Telephone: 770-729-1110

Viking: *gas grills*
Web site: www.vikingrange.com
Telephone: 888-845-4641

WeberGrills.com: Company: *charcoal and gas grills, grill brush, chimney starter, firestarters, accessories*
Web site: www.webergrills.com
Telephone: 888-469-3237

Weber-Stephens Products: *charcoal and gas grills and accessories*
Web site: www.weber.com
Telephone: 800-446-1071

Acknowledgments

I've always been fortunate to have a family of cheerleaders behind me, starting with my immediate family and then gaining momentum and friends as the years passed. I am truly blessed with a sea of positive, supportive, and cheering people. Thanks past, present, and future go to the following:

My sister, Mary Pat, pushed me to get out and do my own grill thing for nearly a decade. Without her constant nudging and thoughtful cooking questions, I wouldn't have followed my dream. She is my best friend, my daily adviser, my cooking buddy and the mother of my beloved nephews—most of all, she keeps me *real*. Her husband, Karl, is truly a brother, and as the wisest sage I've ever met, he functions as my general counsel and partner in Cabernet Franc crimes. My mother, Marylin Odom Karmel, was a huge influence as she instilled culinary courage and confidence in me by teaching by example. She always could and still can do anything. I must thank her for unflinchingly reading, editing, and proofing the manuscript during the entire process. My father, Louis J. Karmel, is the head cheerleader! He encouraged my interest in food by taking our family to the best restaurants in the United States and Europe and by enthusiastically eating anything I prepared for him (except one inedible tuna noodle casserole when I was 19).

Kirsten "Cookie" Teissier is my daily rock. She plodded along with me on every step of this long and sometimes arduous process. I quite literally couldn't have written this book or coordinated the photography without her. Extra thanks to her husband, Nat, for his support and his parents, Jean-Louis and Christine, for the care packages from Provence.

Great thanks go to Rose White for coming out of retirement to help me get the tail end of this book and many other projects in order.

My friends and fellow Chicagoans, Rick and Deann Bayless, gave me the gift of shooting in their heavenly garden at the peak of the season and encouraged me to ask Christopher Hirsheimer to photograph my book.

Their setting and her photography made my recipes explode with life. I was a huge fan of Christopher's work since the early *Saveur* days, and it was a dream come true to have her photograph my book. Equally important to the photography was my crackerjack team, headed up by Kirsten West, who made the food look good while keeping it real.

Gretchen Belmonti is my Girls at the Grill cohort and as close to me as a sister. She and her husband, Jeff—and his whole family, especially Peggy and Jimmy Belmonti—have adopted me and 13 of the grills that I used in testing and preparing this book. I can't thank them enough for everything that they have done, and continue to do, to support me in my life. Gretchen's and Jeff's adorable and cheerful daughter, Hannah, is officially the littlest Girl at the Grill, and I'm proud to say that she loves anything grilled and barbecued!

A sloppy kiss goes to John Lineweaver, who keeps me warm and fuzzy—and laughing—on a daily basis. Years ago, we formed a creative partnership that grew way beyond our Greensboro childhood friendship, and everything I do is better because of it. The gorgeous bold look and feel of the book is evidence of his expert design skill.

Extra big thanks go to Brother Tough Love Bob Blumer, my culinary compatriot, adventure companion, and "chopsickle" wordsmith. I am eternally grateful for the time he spent in Chicago at the end of the writing process helping me fine-tune and edit my thoughts.

Rose Levy Beranbaum has been beyond generous with her deep well of experience and unfailing support for more than a baker's dozen of years! She is such an effusive fan that it would be embarrassing if I didn't know that it came straight from her heart. But more important, Rose is a treasured friend way beyond our mutual love of food and wine.

Richard Ruben has helped in more ways than I can count. Besides his unconditional friendship and being a great culinary resource, he gave me the key to his apartment in New York and carte blanche to stay there.

Marian Temesvary is my Chicago sounding board, dear friend, and a great griller in her own right. I am indebted to all the hours she listened, gave advice, and reviewed my manuscript.

Mary Burnham is cheerleader personified. She is enthusiastically supportive and has kept me excited about this book—and all my other ventures—through all its stages.

More thanks go to my agent, Amy Cook, who believed in me from the start and stood by me all the way.

To my editor, Linda Ingroia, who is one of the most thoughtful and conscientious people I have ever worked with. She took my passion for detail to a whole new expert level. And she wasn't alone. Extra big thanks to publisher Natalie Chapman, who supported this book from the beginning. And it wouldn't have come together without the hard work and dedication of the Wiley team, including eagle-eyed production editor Ava Wilder and production manager Paul Sobel, creative cover art director Jeffrey Faust, assistant editor Adam Kowit, and the enthusiastic publicity, marketing, and events team of Gypsy Lovett, Todd Fries, Michael Friedberg, P. J. Campbell, and Anna Christensen.

Thanks to Sara Moulton who forced me in front of the camera when I thought my job was only behind the scenes. And to Al Roker shared his love of barbecue and invited me to cook with him on *Today*. My barbecue buddy, Steven Raichlen, and his wife, Barbara, have been in my corner for years; and, in Steven's words, it is a great way to make a living! I'm proud to keep company with him. We probably wouldn't have met so early on the barbecue trail if it hadn't been for his editor, and my friend, Suzanne Rafer. I've known Suzanne twice as long as Steven, and it was she who introduced us while Steven was researching *The Barbecue Bible*. Suzanne encouraged me to get out and do my own thing, and since she is one of the smartest people in the business, it meant more to me than she could know.

Justin Freidman and his lovely wife, Skylar, helped me launch Grill Friends Ceramics and Tools and introduced me to the amazing Robert Laub, who is my Grill Friends distributor and friend.

A cookout isn't a cookout without libations, and so thanks go to my favorite bartender, John Mose, for help mixing the cocktails. Additional hugs go to his wife, Stacy, mother, Sue, and the rest of the brothers Mose for adopting me into their farm-raised family. Kudos for perseverance to Michael Krusch, who has come up with hundreds of book ideas in the past 26 years in an effort to get me to write one—and one apology for not including his favorite recipe, Viula's Oatmeal Cookies.

Merci Beaucoup to Wycke Baker, who has driven and eaten with me 24/7 in locations all over the world, from the Hill Country of Texas to St. Barts, St. Maarten, and all over France—indulging my every food curiosity even when his stomach cried "uncle."

A heap of gratitude to John T. Edge and the wonderful folks of the Southern Foodways Alliance for helping me reconnect with my southern roots.

Crescent Dragonwagon and her late husband, Ned Shank, who helped me find my voice.

Alix Salyers, who gave me my first spokesperson gig and encouraged me to tell my stories.

Nancy Newton, who gave me her ear and rarely disagreed with me.

Lisa Taylor, who expertly tested recipes for eight weeks straight and worked double duty to make sure all my days were good hair days! Reggie Drahnak, who among other things, cheerfully spent 24 hours checking USDA temperatures. Mildred Amico and the James Beard Foundation, who have hosted me on more than one occasion and are amenable to anything that I ask! Heartfelt thanks to Alfred Geller, Laura Sher, and the whole crew at Geller Media Management, especially Yvonne for keeping my best interests in mind at all times. Brian O'Donnell, owner of www.webergrills.com, and Ron, who keep my grills in great shape all year long! David Joss, who inherited me from his father and still gives me the family treatment, and Elizabeth Terry, who is unflappable, no matter what!

I pop open a cold one in honor of my first-rate barbecue buddies: Lynne and Gary Wilkinson and Gary and Mary Pantlik, for great friendship, expert hosting, and helping me become a member of Swine and Dine; Jimbo Billy Bob, who embodies all that I love about Memphis in May (MIM); fast friends and fellow chroniclers of the trail, Amy Mills Tunnicliffe and her father, Mike Mills—the only four-time MIM World Champion; my home-state champion, Ed Mitchell, from Wilson, NC; and finally, the first barbecue team to take me under their wing, Bubba's Bunch.

I would like to thank the following people, corporations, associations, and groups for their unbelievable generosity and support—many of you have become treasured friends in the process; Gretchen Holt and Stephanie Karlis from OXO, manufacturers of my beloved tongs; fellow North Carolinian Lisa Callaghan from All-Clad, who worked with me to create a "system" that lets me teach outdoor grilling indoors; Brian Maynard from KitchenAid; Rick Smilow, Sarah Abrams, and the staff at the Institute of Culinary Education (ICE), where I am a guest teacher; and Lynette Cayson for making beautiful chef coats and supporting me from the very beginning. Sarah Powers and St. Francis Winery, Susan and Drew Goss and the whole crew at West Town Tavern; Frankie Whitman from Niman Ranch—my absolute favorite meat purveyor; Linda Funk from the Iowa Soybean Council for being as excited about my website as I am; ditto Lorena Rull from Cargill Turkey and her Associated partners, Mike Snyder and Sarah Coleman; George Samaras from Primo Grill; Tom Hoefitz and Jeff Cleveland from Broilmaster; Ann Walden from Coleman Grills; Eric Aigen, John Chitwood, and Yvonne Bedoy from Jade Products/Dynasty Grills; Lou West and Steve Benson from Big Green Egg; Bob Kellerman from Lodge (Cast-Iron) Manufacturing; John Mulligan, Megan, Pamela, Dan, and Jason at Harold Import Company; Julia Stanbulis, representing Staub, Wüsthof, and Lefheit Housewares; Brian Blake from Rhubarb; Susan McRae from Basketville; Rena Somerville from European Sources Direct, distributors of LOVE plates; Harvey Maslin from Western Linen; Bobbi Pauline from Charcoal Companion, Rachel Litner representing Cuisinart and Waring, Brenda McDowell and the Beef Council; Quito McKenna, Sal Merlo and Maxine; Lawrence Smith, Mike Kempster, Sr., for fanning my love affair with grilling and barbecue; Mark Lapine, and his always helpful team and the entire membership of the GATG LadyBug Club.

Thanks to those who kept the home front in order during the writing, testing, editing, and every other day: Teresa, Eva, Murray, Gabriel, Benny, and Perkins. Treats to my canine mascots, Rosie the Dog, Sam, and Tokaj, too.

More thanks go to the following people who encouraged, supported, and urged me on through my career: Margaret Corwin and my late Uncle Bobby, Don and Magda; Tim Warmath, Ned Walley, Gwen Connelly, Kendra Chaplin, Harvey Ginsberg, Pete Savely, Barbara Molotsky, Mary Mathews, Jamie Purviance, Susie Middleton, Martha Holmberg and the Gang at FC, Jerry DiVecchio, Sharon Franke, Bonnie Tandy LeBlang, Suzanne Hamlin, Martha Johnson, and so many others at Southern Progress; Lou Ekus, Nancy Hopkins, Carolyn Wells, Sarah Leah Chase, Nigel Dyche, Elliott Beranbaum, Jen Fite, the Rucker family, all The Luasions, Jim Millican; the Hollins contingent, especially Lisa and Bill Ryan, Temple and Sean Lapp, Cindy Wilson, and Kathryn Hallahan. And finally, the late Alex Gant, who for twenty years supported me, encouraged me, laughed with me unconditionally in all parts of my life and gave me my first magazine food writing assignment. She was a dear friend and is sorely missed by me and all others who ever knew her.

For me, talking about cooking, sharing, and eating food is all about connecting with other people. I believe that that is what makes food so compelling and that is why I tried very hard to make the collection of recipes in this book reflect many of these times. I think of it as culinary snapshots and hope you will too.

A final thanks to my editor, Linda Ingroia, who let me add one last recipe that didn't really fit anywhere else, just because I love it so. For all my friends, students and barbecue fans out there, here is a little lagniappe (something extra) for you and for me!

TAYLOR GROCERY FRIED CATFISH AND HUSHPUPPIES

Does a fried catfish recipe belong in a grilling book? Absolutely! Heck, everyone knows that the one thing besides beer and whiskey that goes with barbecue is anything deep fried! And especially when it's the catfish and hushpuppies recipe from Taylor Grocery.

I met Lynne Hewitt on my first trip to Oxford, MS, when John T. Edge took me to eat the world's best catfish at Lynne's eating establishment, Taylor Grocery. Indeed it was, and still is, the best fried catfish and hushpuppies I've ever eaten—but Lynne and I didn't stop there; we really bonded over barbecue, trading stories from Memphis in May (barbecue contest). He took me out back to show off his big-as-a-boat cooker, which barbecue buddies are known to do. With drinks in hand, we compared notes and started a friendship based on barbecue, fried catfish, and whiskey.

Serve the catfish and hushpuppies hot out of the fryer with tartar sauce and butter, respectively...and a few french fries never hurt either!

Makes 4 to 8 servings

Hushpuppies
- 2 cups yellow cornmeal
- 1 cup White Lily self-rising flour
- 4 green onions, chopped (stem and all)
- 1 egg
- 1 tablespoon sugar
- 1 teaspoon salt
- 1²/₃ cups buttermilk

Fried Catfish
- 2 cups yellow cornmeal
- ¼ cup all-purpose flour
- 2 tablespoons coarsely ground pepper
- 1 tablespoon lemon pepper
- 1 teaspoon paprika
- 1 teaspoon granulated garlic
- Kosher salt

- 4 to 8 catfish fillets, about 8 ounces each, preferably Mississippi pond-raised
- 2 cups whole milk
- 4 dashes Louisiana hot sauce
- Peanut oil

1. Make the hushpuppies batter: Mix the cornmeal, flour, onions, egg, sugar, and salt in a medium bowl. Add the buttermilk until the batter reaches a thick, mashed potato-like consistency (1²/₃ cups should be perfect, but add a little more if the batter is still too dry). Refrigerate the batter for 45 minutes to 1 hour before using.

2. Meanwhile, make the catfish batter: Pour about 4 inches of peanut oil into a large, deep pot and heat it to about 350°F on a deep-frying thermometer. Put the cornmeal, flour, peppers, paprika, garlic and salt into a large brown paper bag. Roll the ends of the bag down to seal it, then shake the bag until the ingredients are well mixed.

3. Fry the catfish: Cut each catfish fillet in half lengthwise. Pat it dry with paper towels. Mix the milk and hot sauce. Dip each fillet in the milk bath, put it in the paper bag, and shake until covered. Place the catfish in the pot without crowding and cook until brown and firm, 6 to 7 minutes. As each fillet is done, remove it to a plate lined with paper towels. Cover to keep warm.

4. Fry the hushpuppies: Reheat the oil to 350°F. Using 2 teaspoons, dip the first teaspoon into water and then fill it with hushpuppy batter. Use the other teaspoon to push the batter into the oil. Cook for about 4 minutes or until golden brown. The hushpuppies should roll over in the oil by themselves. If they do not, you may have to turn them. As they are finished, remove them to another plate lined with paper towels.

5. Serve the catfish and hushpuppies immediately.

Index